Uncle John's

GIGANTIC

BATHROOM READER®

Uncle John's GIGANTIC BATHROOM READER®

Including

*Uncle John's Giant 10th Anniversary
Bathroom Reader*

and

*Uncle John's Absolutely Absorbing
Bathroom Reader*

by the Bathroom Readers' Institute

Uncle John's Gigantic Bathroom Reader
is a compilation of the following two previously
published Bathroom Reader titles:

Uncle John's Giant 10th Anniversary
Bathroom Reader
ISBN: 1–879682–68–0
(first printing 1997)
and
Uncle John's Absolutely Absorbing
Bathroom Reader
ISBN 1–879682–73–7
(first printing 1999)

For information, write: The Bathroom Readers' Hysterical Society
Portable Press, 5880 Oberlin Drive, San Diego, CA 92121
E-mail: unclejohn@advmkt.com

Cover design by Michael Brunsfeld
BRI Technician on back cover: Larry Kelp

ISBN 10: 1–59223–606–5
ISBN 13: 978–1–59223–606–0

Printed and bound in Canada

First printing: February 2006
06 07 08 09 10   10 9 8 7 6 5 4 3 2 1

THE TEAM

This compilation of great Uncle John titles
was put together by:

Allen Orso, Publisher, Portable Press
JoAnn Padgett, Director, Editorial & Production
Jennifer Browning, Production Editor
Jennifer Thornton, Managing Editor
Connie Vazquez, Product Manager
Eva Hoffman, Editorial Intern

As for the many writers, editors, and other contributors
from the Bathroom Readers' Institute who provided
the material for this book, we'd like to thank
them, too. So we gave them the next page.

THANK YOU!

The Bathroom Readers' Institute sincerely thanks the people
whose advice and assistance made this book possible.

Jeff Altemus
Antares Multimedia
Ask Janis Editorial
Claudia Bauer
Bloomsbury Books
Casey Bourgeois
Shelley Brigman
Steve Brummett
Michael Brunsfeld
Jeff Cheek
Lisa Cooper
Faye Courtenay
Bill Crawford
Scott Dalgarno
John Darling
John Dollison
Kathy Dratch
Bill Eriksen
Andrea Freewater
Debra Gates
Abby Granach
Janet Harris
Tim Harrower
Valerie Hendel
Sharilyn Hovind
Jay Ingram
Gordon Javna
John Javna
Jesse & Sophie, B.R.I.T.
Mary Kaufman
Bela, Erin, and
Stephanie Keenan
Douglas Keeslar

Lonnie Kirk
Lenna Lebovich
Paula Leith
Eric Linden
Jennifer Massey
Jim McCluskey
Jim McCluskey
Peter McCracken
Jack Mingo
Richard Moeschl
Mustard Press
Jay Newman
Jeff Painter
Sherry Powell
Barb Porshe
Marley & Catie Pratt
Paul Protter
Julie Roeming
Chris Rose-Merkle
Melissa Schwarz
Lorien Sekora
Douglas Sigler
Bennie Slomski
Dee Smith
Mike Schuster
Andy Sohn
Rich Stim
David Sugar
Tessa Vanderkop
Uncle Edgester
Dale Vidmar
David Wallechinsky
Peter Workman

CONTENTS

INTRODUCTION

If you're a longtime Bathroom Reader fan, you've probably already said to yourself, "Now, that's a darn big Bathroom Reader," and you'd be right. That's because we took two of our favorite vintage volumes: *Uncle John's Giant 10th Anniversary Bathroom Reader* and *Uncle John's Absolutely Absorbing Bathroom Reader* and combined them to create this leg-numbering, shelf-crashing volume called *Uncle John's Gigantic Bathroom Reader*. We've put together the very best content from the two vintage volumes to create a book that will keep you company through many nights, days, weekends, and sit-down sessions.

We at the BRI often feel we have the most satisfying job in the world. We get to find great information and off-the-wall subjects to write about . . . and then we get to "field test" the material.

Surprisingly, after 18 years and producing over 10,000 pages of Bathroom Readers, it's still easy to find new things to write about.

Keep the cards, letters, and e-mails coming. Let us know what you want to read about and send us suggestions on what you'd like to see in our Readers. We're always looking for new ideas.

Happy reading—and remember to always go with the flow.

—Uncle Al

P.S. Visit us at www.bathroomreader.com

YOU'RE MY INSPIRATION

It's always fascinating to find out who, or what, inspired cultural milestones like these.

OSCAR THE GROUCH. "At a restaurant called Oscar's Tavern in Manhattan, Jim Henson and *Sesame Street* director Jon Stone were waited on by a man so rude and grouchy that . . . going to Oscar's became a sort of masochistic form of lunchtime entertainment for them. They immortalized him as the world's most famous grouch." (*Sesame Street Unpaved*)

FREDDY KRUEGER. Writer/director Wes Craven reportedly named the evil character of his *Nightmare on Elm Street* film after a kid at high school who harassed and bullied him.

MEN ARE FROM MARS . . . In the early 1980s, "John Gray was looking for a playful way to talk [to an audience] about the differences between men and women." He borrowed the inter-planetary theme from Steven Spielberg. "Men, he said, were like the alien E.T.—and from Mars to boot, the planet of the warriors. The audience loved it, [so he added that] women . . . were from Venus, the planet of love and affection." (*USA Today*)

BMW SYMBOL. The Bavarian Motor Works once manufac-tured airplanes. Their logo represents a plane's propeller.

LAVERNE & SHIRLEY. In 1959 Gary Marshall was eating at a Brooklyn restaurant with his date when "another woman approached the table and began arguing with Marshall's compan-ion. Before he knew what was happening, his quiet, demure date was shucking her coat and wrestling in the aisle." The incident made such an impression on Marshall that in 1975 he wrote it into an episode of his TV show *Happy Days*. He named the two brawling women Laverne and Shirley. Audiences loved the pair, and the following year they had their own sitcom. (*New York Daily News*)

What food are you most likely to be allergic to? Nuts.

COURT TRANSQUIPS

We're back, with one of our regular features. Do court transcripts make good bathroom reading? Check out these quotes. They're things people actually said in court, recorded word for word.

Q: "James shot Tommy Lee?"
A: "Yes."
Q: "Then Tommy Lee pulled out his gun and shot James in the fracas?"
A: "No sir, just above it."

Q: "Doctor, did you say he was shot in the woods?"
A: "No, I said he was shot in the lumbar region."

Q: "Have you lived in this town all your life?"
A: "Not yet."

Q: "The hospital is to the right?"
A: "It was on this side."
Q: "When you say this side, can you say right or left?"
A: "Sure. Right or left."

Judge (to jury): "If that be your verdict, so say you all."
Two Jurors: "You all."

Q: "Doctor, will you take a look at those X-rays and tell us something about the injury?"
A: "Let's see, which side am I testifying for?"

Q: "How would you expect somebody to react, being stabbed six times in this fashion?"
A: "Well, it might slow him down a little."

Q: "How was your first marriage terminated?"
A: "By death."
Q: "And by whose death was it terminated?"

Q: "And what did he do then?"
A: "He came home, and next morning he was dead."
Q: "So when he woke up the next morning he was dead?"

Q: "Can you describe the individual?"
A: "He was about medium height and had a beard."
Q: "Was this a male or a female?"

The Court: "You've been charged with armed robbery. Do you want the court to appoint a lawyer to represent you?"
Defendant: "You don't have to appoint a very good lawyer. I'm going to plead guilty."

Q: "What happened then?"
A: "He says, 'I have to kill you because you can identify me.'"
Q: "Did he kill you?"
A: "No."

Judge: "Well, gentlemen of the jury, are you unanimous?"
Foreman: "Yes, your Honor, we're all alike—temporarily insane."

Leaf-cutter ants can build anthills 16 feet deep and an acre square.

MADE IN THE USA

*You've heard of inventors Thomas Edison and Alexander
Graham Bell. But what about Chester Greenwood
and Frank Rose? Let's give them their due, too.*

THE EAR-MUFF. When he was 15 years old, Chester
Greenwood went ice skating on a pond near his home in
Farmington, Maine. He nearly froze his ears off. The next
day he covered his ears with a thick woolen scarf . . . but it was
too heavy and itchy. So the next day, he bent some wire into ear-
shaped loops and asked his grandmother to sew fur around them.
That worked perfectly. So many neighbors asked Chester for a pair
of "muffs for ears" that he patented his design and founded the
Greenwood Ear Protector Factory in 1877. He became extremely
wealthy supplying them to U.S. soldiers during World War I.

THE OUTBOARD MOTOR. According to company lore, Ole
Evinrude, a Norwegian immigrant, got the idea for an outboard
motor while on a picnic with his sweetheart Bessie. They were on
a small island in Lake Michigan, when Bessie decided she wanted
some ice cream. Ole obligingly rowed to shore to get some, but by
the time he made it back the ice cream had melted. So Ole built a
motor that could be attached to his rowboat, and founded the
Evinrude company in 1909.

THE FLY SWATTER. Dr. Samuel J. Crumbine of the Kansas
State Board of Health was watching a baseball game in Topeka in
1905. It was the bottom of the eighth inning, the score was tied,
and Topeka had a man on third. Fans were screaming "Sacrifice
fly! Sacrifice fly" to the batter, or "Swat the ball! Swat the ball!"
Crumbine, who'd spent much of the game mulling over how to
reduce the spread of typhoid fever by flies during hot Kansas sum-
mers, suddenly got his inspiration: "Swat the fly!" Crumbine didn't
actually invent the fly swatter; he just popularized the idea in a
front-page article titled "Swat the Fly," in the next issue of *Fly
Bulletin*. A schoolteacher named Frank Rose read the article and
made the first fly swatter out of a yardstick and some wire screen.

More babies are born in the month of September than in any other month.

FOREIGN FUNDS

Ever wonder why different kinds of money are called what they are? Why is a franc called a franc, for example? We did. So, we put together a list of various currencies and how they got their names.

POUND. (*English*) Named for its weight in *Sterlings*—the unit of currency in Medieval England. The first *pound* coin was issued in 1642.

LIRA. (*Italy*) From the Latin word *libra*, or "pound."

DRACHMA. (*Greece*) Means "handful."

RUPEE. (*India*) Comes from the Sanskrit *rupa*, which means "beauty" or "shape."

KORUNA. (*Czechoslovakia*) Means "crown."

GUILDER. (*Netherlands*) From the same root as "gilded," the guilder was originally a gold coin. It was first introduced from Florence in the 13th century.

ROUBLE. (*Russia*) Means "cut-off," a term that dates back to the days when portions of silver bars were literally "cut off" the bars and used as coins. The rouble was first issued as a silver piece in 1704.

PESO. (*Mexico*) Means "weight." It was introduced by Spain in 1497, then adopted by Mexico and other Latin American countries in the late 19th century.

PESETA. (*Spain*) Means "little peso," and was created in the 18th century as a "companion" coin to the Spanish peso (no longer in circulation).

FRANC. (*France*) First issued in 1360, as a gold coin. Gets its name from its original Latin inscription, *Francorum Rex*, which means "King of the Franks," the title given to kings of France in the 1300s.

RIYAL. (*Saudi Arabia*) Borrows its name from the Spanish *real*, meaning "royal."

ESCUDO. (*Portugal*) Means "shield," referring to the coat of arms on the original coin.

YEN. (*Japan*) Borrowed from the Chinese *yuan*, which means "round," and describes the coin. First issued in 1870.

Take a guess: How many muscles are there in your ear? Nine.

OOPS!

Everyone's amused by tales of outrageous blunders—probably because it's comforting to know that someone's screwing up even worse than we are. So go ahead and feel superior for a few minutes.

HAPPY BIRTHDAY!

"Matt Brooks of Cheshire, England, a furnaceman, thought he was 63 years old in 1981. When he applied for early retirement, he learned that he was really 79 and should have retired 14 years earlier."

—Encyclopedia Brown's Book of Facts

BLIND JUSTICE

"Judge Claudia Jordan caused panic in her court in Denver when she passed a note to her clerk that read: 'Blind on the right side. May be falling. Please call someone.' The clerk rang for help. Informed that paramedics were on the way, the judge pointed to the sagging Venetian blinds on the right side of the room. 'I wanted someone from maintenance,' she said."

—The Fortean Times

HIGH WIRE ACT

"During a parade through Ventura, California, a drum major twirled his baton and threw it high into the air.

"It hit a power cable and melted. It also blacked out ten blocks, put a radio station off the air and started a grass fire."

—The World's Greatest Mistakes

AMEN

"Warren Austin, U.S. ambassador to the United Nations in 1948, expressed the wish that Arabs and Jews would settle their differences 'like good Christians.'"

—Not a Good Word About Anybody

FLOUR POWER

"After great expense and preparation, British climber Alan Hinkes attempted to scale the 26,000-foot-high Nanga Parbot mountain in

---

First TV show to win an Emmy for Outstanding Drama: *Pulitzer Prize Playhouse* (1950).

Pakistan. He got about halfway up and was eating a Pakistani bread called *chapati*, which is topped with flour, when the wind blew the flour in his face, causing him to sneeze. It resulted in a pulled back muscle that made further climbing impossible."
—*News of the Weird*, Nov. 28, 1998

THAT'S B-U-R-T, RIGHT?
"Scrawling his way into immortality in the concrete in front of Mann's (formerly Grauman's) Chinese Theater in Hollywood, Burt Reynolds misspelled his own name."
—*Hollywood Confidential*

LETTER BOMB
NORWALK, CT—"The Caldor department store chain apologized this week after 11 million copies of an advertising circular showed two smiling boys playing Scrabble around a board with the word 'rape' spelled out. Caldor said it does not know who did it or how it got past the proofreaders. 'Obviously, it's a mistake,' said Caldor spokeswoman Jennifer Belodeau."
—*The Progressive*, February 1999

FORGET ABOUT THAT RAISE
LONDON—"A trader cost his employers an estimated $16 million when he pressed the wrong key on his computer during training, launching the largest single trade in German futures.

"The *Daily Telegraph* did not name the trader of the firm, but described him as a junior trader working out of London for a German finance house.

"Apparently, while training on what he thought was software *simulating* financial transactions, he posted an offering of 130,000 German bond futures contracts, worth $19 billion. But he had pressed the wrong button, entering the system for actual dealing."
—*Medford Mail Tribune*, Nov. 20, 1998

AND EYES LIKE BONZO?
"During a high-level meeting with Arab leaders, Reagan off-handedly remarked to the Lebanese foreign minister, 'You know, your nose looks just like Danny Thomas's.'"
—*Hollywood Confidential*

Surprising poll result: 53% of Americans think they're paid "the right amount."

LET ME WRITE SIGN— I GOOD SPEAK ENLISH

When signs in a foreign country are in English, any combination of words is possible. Here are some real-life examples.

At a Tokyo bar: "Special cocktails for the ladies with nuts."

At a Budapest zoo: "Please do not feed the animals. If you have any suitable food, give it to the guard on duty."

At a Budapest hotel: "All rooms not denounced by twelve o'clock will be paid for twicely."

In a Hong Kong supermarket: "For your convenience, we recommend courteous, efficient self-service."

At a Norwegian cocktail lounge: "Ladies are requested not to have children in the bar."

In a tailor shop in Rhodes: "Order your summer suit. Because is big rush we will execute customers in strict order."

A laundry in Rome: "Ladies, leave your clothes here and spend the afternoon having a good time."

In a Czech tourist agency: "Take one of our horse-driven city tours—we guarantee no miscarriages."

On a Viennese restaurant menu: "Fried milk, children sandwiches, roast cattle, and boiled sheep."

In a Swiss mountain inn: "Special today—no ice cream."

A doctor's office in Rome: "Specialist in women and other diseases."

In a Moscow hotel room: "If this is your first visit to the USSR, you are welcome to it."

At a Vienna hotel: "In case of fire, do your utmost to alarm the hotel porter."

At a Hong Kong dentist: "Teeth extracted by the latest Methodists."

At a Swedish furrier: "Fur coats made for ladies from their own skin."

Vitamin rule of thumb: The darker green a vegetable is, the more vitamin C it contains.

FAMILIAR PHRASES

Here are the origins to some common phrases.

STUMP SOMEONE
Meaning: Ask someone a question they can't answer
Origin: Actually refers to tree stumps. "Pioneers built their houses and barns out of log . . . and they frequently swapped work with one another in clearing new ground. Some frontiersmen would brag about their ability to pull up big stumps, but it wasn't unusual for the boaster to suffer defeat with a stubborn stump." (From *I've Got Goose Pimples*, by Marvin Vanoni)

PAINT THE TOWN RED
Meaning: Spend a wild night out, usually involving drinking
Origin: "This colorful term . . . probably originated on the frontier. In the nineteenth century the section of town where brothels and saloons were located was known as the 'red light district.' So a group of lusty cowhands out for a night on the town might very well take it into their heads to make the whole town red." (From *Dictionary of Word and Phrase Origins Vol. 3*, by William and Mary Morris)

STAVE OFF
Meaning: Keep something away, albeit temporarily
Origin: "A *stave* is a stick of wood, from the plural of staff, *staves*. In the early seventeenth century *staves* were used in the 'sport' of bull-baiting, where dogs were set against bulls. [If] the dogs got a bull down, the bull's owner often tried to save him for another fight by driving the dogs off with a *stave*." (From *Animal Crackers*, by Robert Hendrickson)

WING IT
Meaning: Do something with little or no preparation
Origin: "Originally comes from the theater. The *Oxford English Dictionary* suggests that it refers to the hurried study of the role in the wings of the theater." (From *The Whole Ball of Wax*, by Laurence Urdang)

First announcer to say, "He shoots, he scores!" during a hockey game: Foster Hewitt (1933).

FAMOUS FOR 15 MINUTES

Here it is again—out feature based on Andy Warhol's prophetic remark that "in the future, everyone will be famous for 15 minutes." Here's how a few folks have used up their allotted quarter-hour.

THE STAR: Jeff Maier, a kid from Old Tappan, New Jersey
THE HEADLINE: *Most Valuable Player? 12-year-old Cinches Playoff Game for Yankees*
WHAT HAPPENED? On October 9, 1996, Jeff Maier was sitting in the front row of Yankee Stadium's right-field stands, watching a critical playoff game between the Yankees and the Baltimore Orioles. In the eighth inning New York's Derek Jeter hit a long fly to right field. The Orioles's outfielder probably would have caught it, but Maier stuck out his hand . . . and deflected it into the stands for a game-tying home run. The Yankees went on to win 5–4 in 11 innings.
THE AFTERMATH: The home run was replayed on TV so many times that by the end of the game Maier was famous. The next day he made appearances on *Good Morning America*, *Live with Regis and Kathie Lee*, and *Hard Copy*. But he turned down a chance to appear on the *Late Show with David Letterman*, *The Larry King Show*, and *Geraldo* so that he could take a limo (provided by the *New York Daily News*) to see the next playoff game from front-row seats behind the Yankee dugout.

THE STAR: John Albert Krohn, an ex-newspaperman
THE HEADLINE: *Circular Logic: Man Pushes Wheelbarrow Around the Country—Literally*
WHAT HAPPENED: In 1908 Krohn decided to become the first person to push a wheelbarrow around the perimeter of the United States. He did it for the money—Krohn figured he could sell aluminum souvenir medals along the way, and then sell the rights to his story when he made it home. "Sure, money is the root of all evil," he admitted, but "most of us need the 'root.'"

Ketchup was once sold as a medicine.

Krohn left Portland, Maine, on June 1, 1908, and wheel-barrowed his way west to Washington State, then south to the Mexican border, then east to the Atlantic and north back to Maine. He covered 9,024 miles in 357 days, wearing out 11 pairs of shoes, 121 pairs of socks, and 3 rubber tires. TV and radio didn't exist, but he received plenty of news coverage and an enthusiastic response nearly everywhere he went; in some communities he was even "arrested" and sentenced to a meal and a bed at the best hotel in town.

THE AFTERMATH: Krohn did write a book—no word on how well it sold—and then spent the rest of his life working in his garden.

THE STAR: Fawn Hall, a 27-year-old, $20,000-a-year government secretary assigned to the U.S. National Security Council in 1987. Her boss: Lt. Col. Oliver North.

THE HEADLINE: *Fawn Stood by Her Man . . . And He Fed'er Into the Shredder*

WHAT HAPPENED: Oliver North was the mastermind behind the Iran-Contra scandal, a plan to sell arms to Iran in exchange for the release of U.S. hostages, then divert the profits to the Contras in Nicaragua—a direct violation of U.S. law.

As word of the scheme began leaking to the press in mid-1986, North, assisted by loyal secretary Fawn Hall, began altering and destroying incriminating documents. After North was fired from his post, Hall continued the shredding on her own. When she testified about her role in the cover-up before a nationally televised congressional hearing, she became a celebrity overnight.

THE AFTERMATH: Hall kept a low profile, turning down several lucrative endorsement offers (including one from Revlon to become part of the "America's Most Unforgettable Women" campaign). "I was so out of my league," she says. "One day you're a normal girl walking down the street; the next, they want to put you in movies."

Hall worshiped North as "a hero," and at the end of her congressional testimony let his friends know she "wanted to hear from him" . . . but North never spoke to her again, not even to thank her for the risks she'd taken on his behalf.

When mating, a hummingbird's wings beat 200 times per second.

Hall later transferred to a job at the Pentagon, but she attracted so much attention that she eventually had to quit. "People would come in and stare at me," she says.

She moved to Los Angeles to write a book and married Danny Sugerman, former manager of the rock group The Doors, and an ex-heroin addict. He introduced his new wife to crack cocaine. "I took one hit on the crack pipe, and I was addicted, instantly," she told *Redbook* magazine.

Hall surfaced again in mid-1994, when the *National Enquirer* revealed she was being treated for crack addiction at a Florida halfway house. By late 1995, both Hall and Sugerman had kicked their habits. Still no word from North, not even a postcard or a phone call. "Ollie used me," she says. "I was like a piece of Kleenex to him."

THE STAR: Lenny Skutnick, 28, a clerk in the Congressional Office Building in Washington, D.C., in 1982

THE HEADLINE: *Just Plane Brave: Man Saves Woman from Icy Grave*

WHAT HAPPENED: Skutnick was driving home from work one winter day in 1982 when Air Florida's Flight 90 crashed into the Potomac River. Skutnick parked his car and went down to the river, where a crowd was gathering.

A rescue helicopter managed to pluck four passengers from the icy water, but by the time it got to 23-year-old Priscilla Tirado, she was too cold to grab the dangling life ring, and the helicopter propeller wash kept pushing it out of reach. "Won't somebody please come out here and save me?" she screamed.

Skutnick jumped into the Potomac, swam to Tirado, and dragged her back to shore. "She was going to drown if no one moved," he explained later. Meanwhile, a television crew recorded the entire rescue and broadcast it live to 50 million viewers.

THE AFTERMATH: One of the people watching was President Reagan. He was so impressed that he invited Skutnick to the White House and publicly thanked him during the State of the Union Address.

The navel divides the body of a newborn baby into two equal parts.

"IT'S NOT A WORD...
IT'S A SENTENCE"

A page by people who know the true meaning of "wedded bliss."

"Bigamy is having one husband too many. Monogamy is the same."
—**Erica Jong**

"Marriage is the triumph of imagination over intelligence. Second marriage is the triumph of hope over experience."
—**Anonymous**

"Marriage is really tough because you have to deal with feelings and lawyers."
—**Richard Pryor**

"Marriage is a three-ring circus: engagement ring, wedding ring, and suffer-ring."
—**Anonymous**

"A man in love is incomplete until he has married. Then he's finished."
—**Zsa Zsa Gabor**

"Love is blind, but marriage restores the sight."
—**Georg Lichtenberg**

"Politics doesn't make strange bedfellows—marriage does."
—**Groucho Marx**

"Before marriage, a man yearns for the woman he loves. After marriage, the 'Y' becomes silent."
—**Anonymous**

"The poor wish to be rich, the rich wish to be happy, the single wish to be married, and the married wish to be dead."
—**Ann Landers**

"Marriage teaches you loyalty, forbearance, self-restraint, meekness, and a great many other things you wouldn't need if you had stayed single."
—**Jimmy Townsend**

"Love is an ideal thing, marriage a real thing; a confusion of the real with the ideal never goes unpunished."
—**Johann von Goethe**

"It's a bit dangerous out there, and I guess men have to choose between marriage and death. I guess they figure that with marriage at least they get meals. But then they get married and find out we don't cook anymore."
—**Rita Rudner**

Two dogs were hanged for witchcraft during the Salem witch trails.

FLUBBED HEADLINES

These are 100% honest-to-goodness headlines.
Can you figure out what they were trying to say?

British Left Waffles on
Falkland Islands

Shot Off Woman's Leg Helps
Nicklaus to 66

Plane Too Close to Ground,
Crash Probe Told

Juvenile Court to Try
Shooting Defendant

Stolen Painting Found by Tree

BOMB HIT BY LIBRARY

After Detour to California
Shuttle Returns to Earth

Boy Declared Dead, Revives
as Family Protests

Dead Coyote Found in Bronx
Launches Search for Its Mate

CHILDBIRTH IS BIG STEP
TO PARENTHOOD

42 Percent of All Murdered
Women Are Killed by the
Same Man

National Hunting Group
Targeting Women

Fire Officials Grilled Over
Kerosene Heaters

POLICE CAN'T STOP
GAMBLING

Ability to Swim May Save
Children from Drowning

LOW WAGES SAID KEY
TO POVERTY

Youth Hit by Car Riding
Bicycle

Hostage-Taker Kills Self;
Police Shoot Each Other

TESTICLE CARGO SEIZED

Check with Doctors Before
Getting Sick

Police Kill Youth in Effort to
Stop His Suicide Attempt

INTERN GETS TASTE OF
GOVERNMENT

Convicted S&L Chief
Donated to University

Study: Dead Patients
Usually Not Saved

PARKING LOT FLOODS
WHEN MAN BURSTS

U.S. Ships Head to Somalia

U.S. Advice: Keep Drinking
Water from Sewage

SUICIDES ASKED TO
RECONSIDER

Cold Wave Linked to
Temperatures

MOVIE STAR FOR A DAY

Every actor hopes for that Big Break. But what if it comes . . . and nothing happens? Here are four examples of Hollywood's version of one-hit wonders, from Douglas Brode's book, Once Was Enough.

KATHERINE HOUGHTON

You're a Star! At age 21, shortly after graduating from college, Houghton won a lead role in the film *Guess Who's Coming to Dinner*, starring Spencer Tracy and Katherine Hepburn. Incredibly, she only had one year of acting under her belt . . . and didn't even have to take a screen test.

Just Kidding. Was she a prodigy? Nope—she was Hepburn's niece. And in the months leading up to the film's premiere, the movie studio and media hyped her as "another Hepburn." They built such high expectations that it was impossible for her to meet them. *Guess Who's Coming to Dinner* won an Oscar for best picture, but Houghton's performance was dismissed as "silly, shrill, and unsubstantial." It was the only blemish in an otherwise classic movie. There were no more film roles forthcoming, so Houghton retreated to regional theater.

NEIL CONNERY

You're a Star! In 1966 Italian film producer Dario Salsotello wanted someone who resembled Sean Connery to play the lead in a cheapo James Bond takeoff he was planning. A friend happened to mention that Connery had a younger brother who was working for $10 a day as a construction worker in Edinburgh. Astonished, Salsotello decided to hire Neil and make him the second big star in the Connery family.

Just Kidding. The movie, about "the younger brother of the world's greatest secret agent," was entitled *Operation Kid Brother.* Salsotello spared no expense to make it seem like an authentic part of the Bond series. He raided the casts of past 007 films, hiring Bond girls Daniela Bianchi (*From Russia with Love*) and Yashiko Yam (*You Only Live Twice*), and Bond villain Adolfo Celi (*Thunderball*) to reprise their roles. He even managed to hire Bernard Lee (M) and Lois Maxwell (Miss Moneypenny), although

---

If the average male never shaved, his beard would be 13 feet long on the day he died.

their characters' names weren't used, for fear of a lawsuit. All that was missing was big brother Sean. Brode writes:

Neil was asked if his big brother might help out by making a cameo appearance; Neil admitted he and Sean were not particularly close. Sean had given him a Jaguar sports car that the superstar was ready to discard, but, Neil sighed, "I soon discovered the motor was shot." Sean Connery scoffed that the producers should "let Neil go back to plastering."

The movie, considered "the most expensive B-movie ever made" ($1.2 million) bombed . . . and Neil did go back to plastering.

GEORGE LAZENBY

You're a Star! Lazenby, a male model and onetime Marlboro Man, was handpicked by producer Albert "Cubby" Broccoli to play James Bond in the film On Her Majesty's Secret Service after Sean Connery quit the series in 1967.

Just Kidding. Broccoli offered Lazenby a second Bond film, but the actor turned it down and went sailing for 15 months, figuring he'd still be famous when he got back. Bad idea—while he was at sea, Connery returned to the Bond series and made Diamonds Are Forever. "When Lazenby returned home," Brode writes, "he was a forgotten has-been." Afterwards, he bounced from one bit part to another in bad kung fu movies and TV shows like Hawaii Five-0. His advice to Pierce Brosnan when Brosnan finished his first Bond film, Goldeneye: "Do two."

NICK APOLLO FORTE

You're a Star! Forte was an overweight, over-the-hill lounge singer in 1983 when a casting agent for Woody Allen saw his picture on an album in a record store bargain bin. The agent happened to be looking for an "overweight, over-the-hill lounge singer" to play a lead role in Broadway Danny Rose.

Just Kidding. Forte had never seen a Woody Allen film or acted in a movie, but he took the part. Allen even made Forte's song "Agita" (Italian for "indigestion") the movie's theme song . . . but the role had almost no real impact on Forte's life—though his lounge-singing rate went up from $100 to $150 per night. He never acted again.

Experts tell us that the human body has about 60,000 miles of blood vessels.

RESCUED FROM THE TRASH

In the last few Bathroom Readers, we've included a section called "Lucky Finds" (see page 276), about the amazing things people have picked up at flea markets and garage sales. Here's a variation on the theme: the unexpected treasures in this section were literally rescued from the trash, as they were about to be lost forever.

CARRIE, Stephen King's first novel

Trash: King, 24, was making $9,500 a year teaching high-school English and living in a trailer—a rented trailer—with his wife and two kids when he began work on *Carrie*. At the time, he was selling short stories to magazines just to make ends meet. "Carrie" started out as a short story, but the author couldn't finish it because it was "too realistic" and too focused on the "world of girls," which he didn't understand. "After six or eight pages," he says,

> I found myself in a high-school locker room with a bunch of screaming girls who were all throwing sanitary napkins and screaming "Plug it up!" at a poor, lost girl named Carrie White who had never heard of menstruation and thought she was bleeding to death.

Appalled by what he'd written, he threw the pages away.

Rescue: That night, as King's wife was emptying the wastebasket, she noticed the crumpled papers. "[She] got curious about what I'd been writing, I guess," he says. She thought it was great, and insisted that he finish it.

> I told her it was too long for the markets I'd been selling to, that it might turn out to be a short novel, even. She said, "Then write it." I protested that I knew almost nothing about girls. She said, "I do. I'll help you." She did, and for the last 28 years, she has.

Doubleday paid a meager $2,500 advance for the book, thinking it might be a sleeper. It wasn't—it was a blockbuster. *Carrie* became a nationwide bestseller, and was later made into a hit film. "The book's reception floored everyone, I think," King says, "except my wife."

Jackrabbits got their name because their ears look like a donkey's (jackass).

EMILY DICKINSON'S POEMS

Trash: Dickinson was a homebody and virtual recluse. She hid her writings from everyone, including family, and was so private that she asked her sister Lavinia to burn her letters, unopened packages, and manuscripts after she died. So when Emily passed away in 1886 at age 56, Lavinia respected her wishes.

After destroying hundreds of manuscripts and letters without reading them, Lavinia opened a bureau drawer and found more than 600 poems in one box, and hundreds more "totally unordered and in various stages of completion." Surprised by the discovery, she stopped to read some before burning them . . . and was astonished by the quality of the writing.

Rescue: Years later editor Mabel Loomis Todd recounted what happened next:

> Soon after Emily's death, Lavinia came to me, in late evening, actually trembling with excitement. She told me she had discovered a veritable treasure—quantities of Emily's poems which she had no instructions to destroy. She had already burned without examination hundreds of manuscripts, and letters . . . carrying out her sister's expressed wishes but without intelligent discrimination. Later she bitterly regretted such inordinate haste. But these poems, she told me, must be printed at once.

Todd spent the next four years sorting and editing Dickinson's surviving letters and poems. The first volume of poems was published in November 1890, and sold out six printings in the first five months. Today, she is considered one of America's greatest poets.

JACKSON BROWNE'S CAREER

Trash: Browne was still an unknown singer in the late 1960s, when David Crosby, of Crosby, Stills, and Nash, urged him to send a demo tape to manager David Geffen. Browne did . . . and as Fred Goodman writes in *Mansion on the Hill*, "Geffen did exactly what most people in the entertainment industry do with unsolicited material from unknown performers—he threw it away without a listen."

Rescue: "As luck would have it, Geffen's secretary happened to notice the 8 x 10 glossy" that Browne had sent and thought he was attractive. Curious about how he sounded, she fished the recording out of the trash. Goodman writes:

Odds of being injured by a toilet seat in your lifetime: 1 in 6,500.

"You know that record and that picture you threw out?" she asked Geffen the next day.

"You go through my garbage?" asked her boss.

"Well, he was so cute that I took it home. And he's very good. Listen to the record."

Geffen did . . . and took Browne on as a client. When he couldn't get anyone to sign Browne to a record contract, he started his own label, Asylum—and Browne became its first star. Browne then helped fill out the label's roster, turning it into a monster success by bringing Geffen acts like the Eagles and Linda Ronstadt. The "rescue" made Geffen a billionaire.

YOU BET YOUR LIFE, *a quiz show starring Groucho Marx*

Trash: "You Bet Your Life"—featuring hours of Groucho's comedy—was one of America's top 10 shows in the 1950s. But by 1973, it was off the air and long forgotten. In August of that year, the program's producer/creator, John Guedel, got a call from NBC:

They asked me, "Would you like to have a set of films for your garage as mementos of the show?" I said, "What do you mean?" They said, "We're destroying them to make room in our warehouse in New Jersey." I said, "You're kidding. How many have you destroyed so far?" They said 15 of the 250 negatives. I said, "Stop! Right now! Let me talk to New York."

Rescue: Guedel immediately called NBC's top brass and made a deal to syndicate "You Bet Your Life" rather than destroy it. He approached several TV stations . . . but no one bought it. Finally he went to KTLA, Channel 5 in Los Angeles, and asked them to run the show as a favor to Groucho—so he wouldn't have to drag out his projector every time he wanted to watch it. They agreed and, to everyone's surprise, it was a hit. In fact, it was so popular that other stations signed up, sparking a Groucho fad. "The boom in Groucho-related merchandise exceeds the Davy Crockett craze of twenty years ago," a surprised Groucho told a reporter in the 1970s. "So now, they tell me, I'm a cult," Groucho remained a pop icon until his death in 1977.

"Hollywood is the place where they shoot too many pictures and not enough actors."

—Walter Winchell

If you lined up all the Slinkys ever made in a row . . .

"I SPY" . . . AT THE MOVIES

You probably know the kids' game "I spy, with my little eye" . . . that was turned into a popular series of books called I Spy. Well, movie-makers have been playing that game with each other (and their actors) for years. Here are some in-jokes and gags you can look for the next time you watch these films (from Reel Gags, by Bill Givens and Television In-Jokes, by Bill van Heerden).

SCREAM (1996)
I Spy . . . Wes Craven, the film's director
Where to Find Him: He's the school janitor, wearing a
Freddy Krueger sweater from his *Nightmare on Elm Street* movie.

E.T.—THE EXTRA-TERRESTRIAL (1982)
I Spy . . . Harrison Ford
Where to Find Him: He's the biology teacher who explains that "the frogs won't feel a thing." Screenwriter Melissa Mathison wrote this bit part for her husband. You won't see his face, because his back is to the camera.

CLOSE ENCOUNTERS OF THE THIRD KIND (1977)
I Spy . . . The Grateful Dead's Jerry Garcia
Where to Find Him: Among the masses in the Indian crowd scene.

BEETLEJUICE (1988)
I Spy . . . Elwood (Dan Aykroyd) and Jake (John Belushi) Blues from *The Blues Brothers*
Where to Find Them: The scene in which Barbara (Geena Davis) and Adam (Alec Baldwin) go to their caseworker's office. Elwood and Jake are peeking through the blinds.

THE ADDAMS FAMILY (1991)
I Spy . . . Barry Sonnenfeld, the film's director
Where to Find Him: The scene in which Gomez (Raul Julia) is

playing with his train set. When he looks into the window of a train car, a tiny commuter looks back up at him. That's Sonnenfeld.

THE LOST WORLD: JURASSIC PARK (1997)

I Spy . . . Ads for some improbable new movies: *King Lear*, starring Arnold Schwarzenegger; *Jach and the Behnstacks*, starring Robin Williams; and *Tsunami Surprise*, with Tom Hanks's head attached to a surfer's body
Where to Find Them: In the window of a video store.

THE ROCKY HORROR PICTURE SHOW (1975)

I Spy . . . Easter eggs
Where to Find Them: Various places during the movie. For example, one is under Frank's throne, one is in a light fixture in the main room, and you can see one when the group goes into an elevator to the lab. What are they doing there? The film crew had an Easter egg hunt on the set, but didn't find all the eggs . . . so they show up in the film.

TRUE ROMANCE (1993), PULP FICTION (1994), FOUR ROOMS (1995), FROM DUSK TILL DAWN (1996)

I Spy . . . Big Kahuna burgers and Red Apple cigarettes
Where to Find Them: They're writer/director Quentin Tarantino's special signature on his work. They first showed up in *True Romance.* "In *Pulp Fiction*," says Bill Givens in his book, *Reel Gags*, "Samuel L. Jackson recommends Big Kahuna burgers and both Bruce Willis and Uma Thurman smoke Red Apple cigarettes. In *From Dusk Till Dawn*, George Clooney carries a Big Kahuna burger bag, and you can spot a pack of Red Apples in his car. In *Four Rooms*, Red Apple smokes are near the switchboard."

HALLOWEEN (1978)

I Spy . . . William Shatner
Where to Find Him: On the psycho's face. The film's budget was so small, they couldn't afford a custom-made mask. So they bought a William Shatner mask, painted it white, and teased out the hair.

Which part of a map is the ideo locator? The part that says "You Are Here."

CLASSIC (B)AD CAMPAIGNS

Companies are always trying to come up with new ways to make their products look attractive. These efforts are notable for achieving the opposite result.

CASHING IN YOUR CHIPS

Brilliant Marketing Idea: In 1998 the Bangkok subsidiary of the American ad agency Leo Burnett came up with a novel way to sell Thailand's "X" brand potato chips: show that they're so much fun, even "the sourest man in history" can't help turning into a fun guy.

Oops: The historical figure they used was Adolf Hitler. In the commercial, Hitler eats some chips, then strips off his Nazi uniform and dances merrily as a Nazi swastika morphs into the brand's "X" logo. The ad generated so many complaints—especially from the Israeli Embassy in Bangkok—that they had to pull it and issue apologies. "The campaign was never intended to cause ill feelings," an agency spokesperson told reporters.

MYSTERY OF THE EAST

Brilliant Marketing Idea: In England, Smirnoff Vodka's ad agency created a campaign using the slogan "I thought the Kama Sutra was an Indian restaurant . . . until I discovered Smirnoff."

Oops: They were forced to cancel it, a company spokesperson admitted, "when we conducted a survey and discovered that 60% of people *did* think it was an Indian restaurant."

HIGH FLYER

Brilliant Marketing Idea: In 1967 Pacific Airlines, a commuter airline on the West Coast, hired award-winning adman/comedian Stan Freberg to design an unorthodox new campaign. As Bruce Nash and Allan Zullo write in *The Misfortune 500*, Freberg "suggested PAL poke fun at the one thing airlines never mention—fear of flying."

Oops: Pacific Airlines, at Freberg's direction, placed full-page ads in newspapers that read:

Hey there! You with the sweat in your palms. It's about time an airline faced up to something: Most people are scared witless of flying. Deep down inside, every time that big plane lifts off that runway, you wonder if this is it, right? You want to know something, fella? So does the pilot deep down inside.

Freberg also arranged for flight attendants to hand out survival kits containing rabbits' feet and the book *The Power of Positive Thinking*, and instructed that when the plane touched down on the runway, flight attendants were supposed to exclaim, "We made it! How about that!" The airline went under two months after the campaign started.

AH-NOLD GO BOOM!

Brilliant Marketing Idea: In 1993 Arnold Schwarzenegger was America's #1 box-office attraction. Columbia Pictures decided to promote his latest movie, *The Last Action Hero*, with a 75-foot-tall balloon of Schwarzenegger's character in New York's Times Square. Instead of holding a gun, like he does in the movie, Ah-nold had a fistful of dynamite in his hand. "We thought a gun was too violent an image," a Columbia spokesperson explained.

Oops: After months of planning, Columbia Pictures finally launched the balloon. Unfortunately, it was just days after the terrorist bombing of the World Trade Center. The studio tried replacing the dynamite with a police badge, but ended up just taking the balloon down. *The Last Action Hero* was one of the biggest flops of the decade.

LOVELY RING, MRS . . . UH . . .

Brilliant Marketing Idea: Executives in the jewelry department of Neiman-Marcus, an upscale department store, thought it would be good business to send a personal note of thanks to each of their biggest customers.

Oops: According to *The Business Disaster Book of Days:* "Most of the notes were addressed to the men, the people who had paid for the expensive baubles. But most of the envelopes were opened by women. Unfortunately for Neiman-Marcus, many of these women—wives of the purchasers, mostly—had not been the recipients of the costly purchases."

What do rabbits and horses have in common? They can't vomit.

THE RIGHT STUFF

Thoughts from a conservative with a sense of humor—P. J. O'Rourke.

"Remember the battle between the generations twenty-some years ago? Remember all the screaming at the dinner table about haircuts and getting jobs and the American dream? Well, our parents won. They're out there living the American dream on some damned golf course, and we're stuck with the jobs and haircuts."

"Seriousness is stupidity sent to college."

"Every government is a parliament of whores. The trouble is, in a democracy the whores are us."

"A number of . . . remarkable things show up in holiday dinners, such as . . . pies made out of something called 'mince,' although if anyone has ever seen a mince in its natural state he did not live to tell about it."

"There's one . . . terrifying fact about old people: I'm going to be one soon."

"Everybody knows how to raise children, except the people who have them."

"You can't shame or humiliate modern celebrities. What used to be called shame and humiliation is now called publicity."

"A fruit is a vegetable with looks and money. Plus, if you let fruit rot, it turns into wine, something Brussels sprouts never do."

"Feminism is the result of a few ignorant and literal-minded women letting the cat out of the bag about which is the superior sex."

"The sport of skiing consists of wearing three thousand dollars' worth of clothes and equiment and driving two hundred miles in the snow in order to stand around at a bar and get drunk."

"Politicians *are* interested in people. Not that this is always a virtue. Dogs are interested in fleas."

"I like to do my principal research in bars, where people are more likely to tell the truth or, at least, lie less convincingly than they do in briefings and books."

Bestselling posthumous hit of all time: *(Just Like) Starting Over*, by John Lennon.

"SHE'LL ALWAYS BE DAD TO ME!"

What would you do if your gender prevented you from pursuing the career of your choice? Many women faced this problem in the past. For a rare few the solution was "If you can't beat 'em, join 'em." They lived their lives as men.

DR. JAMES BARRY, *British army surgeon and pioneer of sanitary reforms in medicine in the 19th century*
Background: Barry entered Edinburgh University's medical school in 1808 when he was just 15 (only men were admitted to medical school then). He rose to become one of the most skilled doctors in England. As Carl Posey writes in *Hoaxes and Deceptions*, the "tiny, beardless doctor" was no shrinking violet:

> Far from keeping a low profile, the medic courted attention, picked quarrels, fought a duel, flirted outrageously with the ladies, and once horsewhipped a colonel in public. Adored by patients, but despised by colleagues, Barry was finally forced into early retirement in 1859.

Surprise! Shortly after Barry died in 1865, at the age of 73, acquaintances discovered why, despite his having spent 57 years in the army, no one had ever seen him naked: he was a woman.

Note: Apparently, not everyone had been fooled. "Many people seem to have known her secret all along," Posey writes, "and simply—perhaps because of Barry's powerful patrons—declined to mention it."

CHARLIE PARKHURST, *"one of the toughest stagecoach drivers of the Old West"*
Background: Parkhurst worked for the California Stage Company at the height of the Gold Rush in the 1850s. He was 5'7" tall, had broad shoulders, gambled, and chewed tobacco. "Once," Carl Sifakis writes in *Hoaxes and Scams*, "this legendary master of the whip raced a team across an unstable bridge, reaching the other site just before it collapsed. Another time, stopped by highwaymen, Charlie shot the leader and escaped with passengers and goods intact."

Parkhurst, who claimed to be an orphan, never grew any facial hair, something that friends attributed to a "fetish" for shaving every day. Unlike his rowdy friends, he also avoided prostitutes, and preferred to sleep apart from other men. Other than that, for all appearances he was one of the guys.

Surprise! In the late 1860s, an illness forced Parkhurst into retirement, and on December 31, 1879, he died alone in his cabin near Watsonville, California. A doctor called in to investigate the death found not only that he had died of cancer, but also that he was a woman who had given birth at some point in her life. Who was this mystery woman? Nobody knows—that was one secret she did manage to take to the grave.

BILLY TIPTON, *jazz musician and leader of the Tipton Trio*
Background: Tipton was a popular jazz musician in Washington from the 1930s to the late 1980s. He married three times and his last marriage, to Kitty Oakes, lasted 19 years. He had three children, all adopted, a fact he attributed to an "injury" that he claimed made "normal" sexual relations impossible. Early in his jazz career his baby face and high-pitched voice caused some listeners to joke that he was too feminine to be a man. But that was about as close as anyone came to suspecting the truth.

Surprise! After years of refusing to see a doctor despite his failing health, Tipton died in 1989 of a bleeding ulcer at his mobile home in Spokane, Washington. He was 74. The paramedics who responded to the call quickly discovered that Tipton was a female, something that apparently only Kitty Oakes had known.

It turns out that at the age of 18, Tipton had borrowed her brother's name and began dressing as a man so she could work as a jazz musician. In those days, most women in jazz were "girl singers," whose careers were short and of limited range.

Tipton's children were shocked. "I'm just lost," her son Jon Clark told reporters after learning his father was a woman. "The guy at the funeral home showed me a little yellow piece of paper where it was marked 'female" under sex. I said, 'What?' and he said it was true. Even so, she'll always be Dad to me."

The tomato comes in over 4,000 varieties.

VEGETABLE TRIVIA

*Did you eat your vegetables today? BRI member Jeff Cheek,
a former CIA man (no kidding) loves to write about food.
He sent us this potpourri of vegetable facts.*

CORN. The most versatile of all food plants, it can be eaten at every stage of development. You can find it in more than 3,000 grocery items. In fact, according to *The Great Food Almanac*, "the average American eats the equivalent of three pounds of corn each day in the form of meat, poultry, and dairy products."

GARLIC. One of the first foods ever cultivated. First written reference: 5,000 years ago, in Sanskrit. At banquets, ancient Greeks served each guest a bowl of parsley, believing it would mask "garlic breath." A vestige of this custom survives. Many restaurants still drop a sprig of parsley on every plate.

LETTUCE. The name comes from the Latin *lactuca* (milk) because of the white liquid that oozes from broken stalks. The Romans prized it so highly that any slave caught eating lettuce was given 30 lashes.

EGGPLANT. Originated in China, where it was grown as a decoration. The Chinese called eggplants "mad apples," believing they caused insanity. It was accepted as a food only after it was brought to the Mediterranean.

LEEKS. These members of the onion family originated in Egypt, then spread to Rome. (Emperor Nero drank a quart of leek soup every day, thinking it improved his singing voice.) The Romans introduced the leek to Wales and it became the Welsh national symbol in 640, when Saxons invaded from England. With no uniforms, it was hard to tell friend from foe in the battle, so each Welsh soldier pinned a leek on his cap to identify himself. They won, and every March 1, St. David's Day, the Welsh pin a leek to their hats or lapels to commemorate the victory.

RADISHES. Since they're ready to harvest after only 42 days, the Greeks named them *Raphanos*, meaning "easy to grow." The Romans changed this to *Radix*, meaning "root."

Is the tongue the only muscle attached at just one end? Our sources say yes.

THE ORIGIN OF BASKETBALL, PART I

Unlike baseball and football, which trace their roots to games that have been played for centuries, basketball was invented by one man— a Canadian named James Naismith—in a couple of days in 1891. It is the only major sport considered native to the U.S. Here's its history.

SOMETHING NEW

Today the YMCA is synonymous with sports, but that hasn't always been the case. In the mid-1880s, it was primarily a missionary group. "In fact," Ted Vincent writes in *The Rise and Fall of American Sport*, "the Young Men's Christian Association condemned almost all sports, along with dancing, card playing, and vaudeville shows, on the grounds that these activities were 'distinctly worldly in their associations, and unspiritual in their influence,' and therefore 'utterly inconsistent with our professions as disciples of Christ.'"

Good Sport

Then, at the YMCA's national convention in 1889, 24-year-old Dr. Luther Gulick started a revolution when he suggested that "good bodies and good morals" might actually go together. He insisted that keeping physically fit could make someone a better person, rather than inevitably leading them down the path of sin . . . And he proposed that the YMCA use organized athletics to reach out to youngsters who might otherwise not be interested in the Y's traditional emphasis on religion.

His proposal met with heavy opposition from conservatives, who argued that a "Christian gymnasium teacher" was a contradiction in terms. But when Gulick's idea was put to a vote, he won. Gulick was put in charge of a brand-new athletics teaching program at the YMCA School for Christian Workers in Springfield, Massachusetts.

CHANGING TIMES

Gulick's ideas were actually part of a larger social movement. For decades, America had been making the transition from a largely rural, farm-based society to an industrialized economy, in which

---

About 8,000 Americans are injured by musical instruments each year.

much of the population lived and worked in cities. Americans who had once labored in fields from sunup to sundown were now spending much of their working lives cooped up inside a factory, or behind a desk or sales counter.

"Middle-class Americans in particular reacted to the growing bureaucracy and confinement of their work lives, and to the remarkable crowding of their cities, by rushing to the outdoors, on foot and on bicycles," Elliot Gorn writes in *A Brief History of American Sports*. "Hiking, bird-watching, camping, rock-climbing, or simply walking in the new national parks—participation in all of these activities soared in the years around the turn of the century."

MASS APPEAL

Middle-class Americans who embraced physical activity as the answer to their own yearnings also began to see it as an answer to some of society's ills. The repeal of child labor laws and high levels of immigration meant that the tenement districts in America's major cities were full of immigrant youths who had little or nothing to do. Leaders of the "recreation movement," like Dr. Gulick, felt that building public playgrounds and bringing organized play programs into the slums would help the kids stay out of trouble and make it easier for them to assimilate into American life.

"Reformers thought of themselves as being on an exciting new mission, Americanizing children by helping them to have fun," Gorn says. "Playground reformers sought to clean up American streets, confine play to designated recreational spaces, and use their professional expertise to teach 'respectable' athletics." In an era in which public playgrounds were virtually unheard of, the facilities and athletic programs that organizations like the YMCA were beginning to offer often provided the only positive outlet for urban kids' energies.

BACK TO SCHOOL

As Gulick set up his program to train YMCA physical education instructors, he also decided to require men training to be "general secretaries" (the official title for men who ran local YMCA chapters) to take phys ed classes.

These students were older and more conservative than other

students. They hadn't been sold on Gulick's newfangled sports ideas and, left to their own devices, would avoid physical education classes entirely. Gulick feared that if he didn't bring these future YMCA leaders around to his point of view while they were in Springfield, they wouldn't implement his programs when they got back home . . . and his efforts would be fruitless.

Cold Shoulder
Working with the general secretaries was a snap at first: in the early fall they just went outside and played football or soccer. But when the weather turned cold and they were forced indoors, things got difficult. The best recreation Gulick could come up with was a schedule of military drills . . . followed by German, French, and Swedish gymnastics. Day after day, the routine was the same, and the students became thoroughly bored.

THE INCORRIGIBLES
Within weeks, the class was in open rebellion, and two successive physical education instructors resigned rather than put up with their abuse. They told Gulick that he might as well give up on "The Incorrigibles," as the class had become known.

Gulick wasn't ready to quit yet. For weeks, an instructor named James Naismith had been arguing that The Incorrigibles weren't to blame for the situation. "The trouble is not with the men," he said, "but with the system we are using. The kind of work for this class should be of a recreative nature, something that would appeal to their play instincts." At one faculty meeting, he even proposed inventing a new indoor game. So when Gulick put Naismith in charge of the class, he commented pointedly: "Now would be a good time for you to work on that new game that you said could be invented."

For Part II, turn to page 152.

* * *

"I cannot imagine any condition which could cause this ship to founder. I cannot conceive of any vital disaster happening to the vessel. Modern shipbuilding has gone beyond that."
　　　　　　　　　　　—E.J. Smith, captain of the *Titanic*

Fetuses can hiccup.

THE UNFINISHED MASTERPIECE

Even if you're not an art lover, you've probably seen the best and most famous picture of the first U.S. president, George Washington, painted by Gilbert Stuart—it's the one on the dollar bill. But did you know that it was never finished? Here's the story.

PRESIDENTIAL PORTRAITURE

Before photography, sitting for a portrait was a long, tedious process. George Washington never liked it, and by the time he retired from the presidency, he'd vowed never to do it again. He routinely refused requests from artists who wanted to capture his likeness one more time for posterity. But in 1796, he got a request he couldn't refuse: his wife Martha wanted them both to pose for portraits to be hung together in a central place in their home.

The painter Martha had in mind was Gilbert Stuart—a celebrated artist in both Britain and America and the portraitist of choice for hundreds of politicians and dignitaries. George agreed with her decision; he'd already posed for two other paintings with Stuart and found him relatively easy to sit for.

STUART'S STORY

Stuart didn't feel the same way about Washington. He thought the ex-president was too stiff, and complained to friends about his stony countenance, his foul teeth, and the dead look in his eyes.

But Stuart still took Mrs. Washington's assignment gladly. Alcoholism and exorbitant spending had put him in debt, and he needed cash. Besides, he'd made quite a bit of money from his first two Washington portraits:

- He sold the first one to a wealthy merchant for a tidy sum . . . but before delivering it, quickly painted and sold at least 15 copies. (One was later used for the image on U.S. quarters.)

- The second painting—a full-length portrait this time—was so well received that Stuart was able to sell dozens of copies before delivering it to the banker who originally commissioned it.

In medieval Japan, dentists extracted teeth with their hands.

Aware of Stuart's past duplicities and not wanting to spend months waiting while the artist copied her paintings, Martha Washington made a careful deal: she insisted that Stuart agree to deliver the portraits the moment they were finished.

WORKING WITH GEORGE

The sitting with Washington began much like the previous efforts. Stuart was relieved to see that the president was wearing a new set of false teeth that made his face look more natural. But he was exasperated when, once again, Washington's face turned to stoniness the minute he sat down.

Stuart told jokes and anecdotes trying to capture an engaging, interested look. It didn't work . . . but in the middle of the sitting, Washington's face momentarily lit up with a pleasant expression. Stuart began drilling him to find out what had happened . . . and discovered that Washington had seen a horse go by outside.

Stuart began talking horses—anything and everything he could think of. Then he talked about farming, and anything to do with rural life. Washington's entire demeanor changed: he became more natural, more lighthearted; his face became brighter.

CREEP OR GENIUS?

The result was the best portrait of the first president ever painted. In fact, Stuart was so pleased that he immediately began trying to figure out a way to keep it. If he could just get out of his deal with Mrs. Washington, he could make more than just a dozen hurried copies—he could do *hundreds* at his leisure and finally get out of debt. But how could he pull it off?

Then he hit on a plan. He stopped a few brushstrokes short of completing the painting, leaving a little canvas peeking through where Washington's collar should have been. Then he told messenger after messenger from the impatient ex-First Lady, "Sorry, it's not finished yet."

SECOND-RATE ART

Even a visit from the former president couldn't shake the painting loose. Instead Stuart sent along one of his copies of the original. Mrs. Washington hung it up, but told her friends: "It is not a good likeness at all."

Do you alphabetize your spice rack? Only one in twelve Americans does.

In fact, not many of the copies *were*. Stuart was interested in speed, not quality. According to one of his daughters, on a "good day" he could pump out a copy every two hours. Many had little or no resemblance to Washington at all. An acquaintance of Stuart's wrote, "Mr. Stuart told me one day when we were before this original portrait that he could never make a copy of it to satisfy himself, and that at last, having made so many, he worked mechanically and with little interest."

Regardless, the portrait became a wildly popular commodity and Stuart dashed off more than 200 copies, calling them his "hundred dollar bills." But he still couldn't completely rid himself of debt. Ironically, in the end there were so many inferior copies of the Unfinished Portrait (by other artists as well) that they actually did significant damage to Stuart's reputation. When he died in 1828, he still owed considerable money, and his youngest daughter, Jane—also a portrait painter—had become the breadwinner for the family.

BY THE WAY

The original paintings, still technically "unfinished," never were delivered to the Washington family. The Boston Athenaeum wound up owning them, and today they're shared part of the year with the Boston Museum of Fine Arts and the National Portrait Gallery in Washington.

* * *

LAST LAUGH

"On Nixon's death in 1994 President Clinton declared an official day of mourning and closed the federal government for a day, as had been done upon the deaths of former Presidents Truman, Eisenhower, and Johnson. The cost of closing the federal government for one day in 1994? More than $400 million. Of that total, $23 million was extra premium pay for 'essential' workers who had to go to work anyway to keep the government functioning. They received time and a half for that day."

—*Stupid Government Tricks,* by John Kohut

In 1797 James Hetherington invented the top hat and . . .

IT'S A WEIRD, WEIRD WORLD

Proof that truth really is stranger than fiction.

STRANGE BE-LEAF

"A Swiss woman has left over a half-million dollars to a houseplant. The millionairess, from Geneva, once described her newly rich jade plant as her 'best and only friend.' She is believed to have conversed with the plant for the last five years."

—*The Edge,* **April 19, 1999**

LOOK AT THOSE MELONS!

"Britain's biggest supermarket chain has asked growers to supply smaller melons after research showed women shoppers subconsciously compared them to the size of their breasts.

"The *Daily Telegraph* said buyers working for Tesco were told by researchers that a current preference for smaller busts was the reason why traditional big, fleshy melons were remaining unsold.

"'We were surprised,' said a Tesco spokesman. 'But it's certainly produced results. Since we introduced smaller melons two months ago we have sold more than a million.'"

—**Reuters, May 3, 1999**

A SILLY SUPERSTITION?

"Gerald Steindam, 24, of Miami, Florida, vowed never to fly Eastern Airlines' flight 401 (New York–Miami) after luckily missing a flight 401 in 1972 that went down in the Everglades.

"In 1980 he overcame his superstitious fear and took the flight. The plane was hijacked to Cuba."

—*Encyclopedia Brown's Book of Strange Facts*

A REAL CONDOM-NATION

"Police in Sri Lanka recently arrested a man after finding a condom in his wallet. 'Why would anyone want to carry a condom in his wallet, unless of course he was up to some mischief,' a police officer was quoted as saying. The man was released after questioning."

—*San Francisco Chronicle,* **1993**

... wore it in public. He was arrested for disturbing the peace.

Q & A:
ASK THE EXPERTS

Everyone's got a question or two they'd like answered—basic stuff, like "Why is the sky blue?" Here are a few of those questions, with answers from books by some of the nation's top trivia experts.

KNUCKLE UNDER
Q: *Why do our knuckles crack?*
A: "The bones in our fingers are separated by small pads of cartilage, and in between are small pockets of a thick liquid. When you bend your fingers, the bones pull away from the pads of cartilage and a vacuum forms. As the bending continues . . . the vacuum bubble bursts, making the cracking sound you hear. The process is very similar to what happens when you pull a rubber suction cup off a smooth surface." (From *Ever Wonder Why?*, by Douglas B. Smith)

SEEING THINGS
Q: *What are those little squiggles you see floating on your eyes when you look at the sky?*
A: "They're called 'floaters.' To some people they look like spots; to others, like tiny threads. They're not on your eyes, though; they're in your eyes. That's why blinking doesn't make them go away. Floaters are all that's left of the hyaloid artery. The hyaloid artery carried blood to your eye and helped it grow . . . when you were still inside your mother's womb.

"When your eyes were finished growing, the hyaloid artery withered and broke into pieces. But since these pieces were sealed up inside your eye, they had no place to go. You'll see them floating around the rest of your life." (From *Know It All!*, by Ed Zotti)

STOP, POP, AND ROLL
Q: *How does quicksand work?*
A: "Not by pulling you down. Quicksand is nearly always found above a spring, which creates a supersaturated condition that makes the sand frictionless and unable to support weight. In addition, quicksand is airless, which creates suction as you struggle to

---

The United States has never lost a war in which mules were used.

get free. The most effective way to escape quicksand is to position yourself on top of it and 'roll' out." (From *The Book of Answers*, by Barbara Berliner)

LONG-DISTANCE RUNAROUND

Q: *Why does the alphabet on a phone start on the #2 button rather than on the #1?*
A: Back when dial phones were used, a pulse or clicking sound was made whenever you dialed. The pulses corresponded to the number dialed, so "when you dialed the number 1, it sent out one click . . . 2, sent two clicks, and so on. Sometimes a random clicking caused equipment to think someone was dialing a number beginning with 1, when they actually weren't. Thus a rule was made: No phone number can start with 1. This rule is still observed, though solely for the sake of tradition." (From *Why Things Are, Volume II: The Big Picture*, by Joel Achenbach)

I CAN SEE CLEARLY NOW

Q: *How does an X-ray photograph your bones but not your flesh?*
A: "An X-ray camera fires electrons at a plate covered with silver halide crystals, which are sensitive to light. Your leg is put in the way of the penetrating stream of particles. When an electron reaches the plate unimpeded, it turns a halide crystal black. The crystals that receive no electrons fall away when the plate is developed and leave that area white under the light. X-ray particles are so highly energized that most of them pass right through flesh. Bones, on the other hand, are very densely packed and contain large amounts of calcium. They stop the X-rays by absorbing them—the crack in your tibia shows up black on the plate because that's where bone isn't." (From *How Do They Do That?*, by Caroline Sutton)

* * *

SLIPPERY WHEN WET

Ice isn't slippery. What makes people and things slip on ice is water. A thin layer of ice melts when pressure is applied to it and it is this wet layer on top of the ice that is slippery.

During the 1980s, the average speed of traffic in New York City was less than 10 mph.

POLITICALLY INCORRECT

Observations from Bill Maher, host of TV's late-night political talk show.

"I believe Dr. Kevorkian is onto something. I think he's great. Because suicide is our way of saying to God, 'You can't fire me. I quit.'"

"The economy is incredibly good. It's too good. It's happy, excited. The GNP is up, the Dow Jones is up. Inflation is at its lowest level since 1963. I went to the ATM today, and I inserted my card—it moaned."

"We survived the 1980s. Back then, the economic program was called 'trickle down.' That actually meant they were pissing on you. How the whole theory goes was this: 'We have all the money. If we drop some, it's yours. Go for it.'"

"My mother is Jewish, my father Catholic. When I went to confession, I'd pray, 'Bless me, father, for I have sinned. And I think you know my lawyer, Mr. Cohen.'"

"Kids, they're not easy, but there has to be some penalty for sex."

"I saw a product in the market, Mr. Salty pretzels. Isn't that nerve? Everything nowadays is low salt or salt-free. Here's a guy who says, 'The hell with you, I'm Mr. Salty pretzels.' Like Mr. Tar and Nicotine cigarettes, or Mr. Gristle and Hard Artery beefsteak."

"This country loves guns; we even have salad shooters. This country thinks that salad is too peaceable, you have to find some way to shoot it."

"Remember, kids, guns aren't for fun. Guns are for killing things like songbirds, and deer, and intruders, and Spice Girls, and busybodies who just won't leave your cult alone, and women who don't understand you're the best man for them. That may sound crazy, but when you're holding a gun, you decide who's crazy."

"They added up all the people in this country who consider themselves a minority and it added up to more than the population of the country."

Your brain uses 40% of the oxygen that enters your bloodstream.

WEIRD THEME
RESTAURANTS

*For a while, it looked as though restaurants modeled after
the Hard Rock Cafe were going to sweep the world. Guess
which of the following is Uncle John's personal favorite.*

THE ROADKILL CAFE, Greenville, Maine
Theme: Animals squashed on the highway
Details: The menu features only "critters that don't move
fast enough" to get out of traffic. Sample items: "The Chicken That
Didn't Make It Across the Road," and "Bye Bye Bambi Burgers." It's
actually just a little black humor, but the staff gets into the act: "A
cook named Freddy is fond of yelling 'down boy, down boy' as he
pounds on chicken breasts before grilling them. When he's done, he
might throw handfuls of feathers out the door."

THE OUTHOUSE, Winnipeg, Manitoba
Theme: Bathrooms
Details: The entire restaurant was decorated to look like a public
restroom—"toilet bowls alternate with tables in the main dining
room. And their logo, a toilet seat, was on all the menus." Shortly
after the Grand Opening in the mid-1970s, health officials shut it
down. The reason: "Not enough working bathrooms."

ALACATRAZ BC, Tokyo
Theme: Maximum-security prison
Details: "Diners are handcuffed, eat in cells, and must beg permis-
sion from the guards to be allowed out to visit the restroom."

CRASH CAFE, Baltimore
Theme: Disasters and human carnage (just what we like to con-
template over dinner)
Details: The smoking fuselage of what appears to be a crashed DC3
juts from the exterior of the flagship restaurant. "The roof is askew,
windows are cracked and the outer wall is shattered in spots. In the
drive, a car looks as if it has just smashed into a fire hydrant, which
is spewing water." Inside, diners are "entertained" by film clips of

What's a *suriphobe*? Someone who's afraid of mice.

train wrecks and collapsing bridges and buildings. "Some may say that it teeters on the verge of unacceptable," says founder Patrick Turner, "but that is precisely its strength. Crash Cafe seduces us to look closer, to indulge our undeniable fascination with the destructive, erotic nature of crashing."

DIVE!, Los Angeles and Las Vegas
Theme: Submarines
Details: "A submarine-shaped restaurant that specialized in gourmet submarine sandwiches." Partners included Hollywood moguls Steven Spielberg and Jeffrey Katzenberg. It had "millions of dollars in special effects," including "computer-controlled flashing light, steam blasts, deep-sea scenes on video screens, and a surging water wall to recreate the experience of 'an actual submarine dive.'" Singer Thomas Dolby provided interactive sound effects that were just a little too real: "Apparently, the virtual aquatic experience was so convincing that it prompted an upsurge in customers visiting the toilet." The L.A. restaurant closed in 1999.

HOUSE OF MAO, Singapore
Theme: Chairman Mao Tse-tung—who ruled China from 1950 until his death in 1976—as a pop icon
Details: "Scores of Mao pictures, poems, and sculptures peer down from the walls. The staff wear uniforms similar to those of China's People's Liberation Army (though waitresses are miniskirted)."

"Chairman Mao was one of the most feared individuals in the world," the founder says, "but when you come to the restaurant, you see the human side of him, swimming, playing poker." On the menu: Mao burgers, Mao pizza, Mao fajitas, and Mao pasta. "Mao would probably turn in his grave," one Singapore journalist wrote following the restaurant's grand opening.

* * *

TRUTH OR URBAN LEGEND?

On an American one-dollar bill, there's supposedly an owl in the upper left-hand corner of the "1" encased in the "shield" and a spider hidden in the front upper right-hand corner.

There are an estimated 171 billion U.S. pennies in circulation.

STRANGE LAWSUITS

These days, it seems that people will sue each other over practically anything. Here are a few real-life examples of unusual legal battles.

THE PLAINTIFF: A Chinese restaurant in Stansted, England
THE DEFENDANT: Kevin Clifford, a customer
THE LAWSUIT: In 1996 Clifford walked into the restaurant and ordered a large meal. While he was waiting for it, he explained later, the smells from the kitchen made him so hungry that he lost control. He began ripping the leaves off potted plants, eating them. "By the time his order was ready," according to one report, "he had eaten the leaves off every plant in the place." The restaurant owner sued him for the cost of the plants.
THE VERDICT: Guilty. Clifford's unusual salad cost him $700.

THE PLAINTIFF: Donald Drusky
THE DEFENDANT: "God, the sovereign ruler of the universe"
THE LAWSUIT: In 1999 the 63-year-old Drusky filed suit against God for "taking no corrective action" against an ex-employer who'd fired him 30 years before. His demands: God must grant him guitar-playing skills and resurrect either his pet pigeon or his mother.
THE VERDICT: Drusky claimed that since God didn't show up in court, he won by default. The judge declared the suit "frivolous."

THE PLAINTIFF: Nellie Mitchell, a 98-year-old Arkansas woman
THE DEFENDANT: Globe International, publishers of the super-market tabloid the *Sun*
THE LAWSUIT: In 1990 the *Sun* ran a "report" about a 101-year-old newspaper carrier in Australia "who'd quit her route because she'd become pregnant by a millionaire customer." They picked a photo of Mitchell to illustrate it. Why? They assumed she was dead. She wasn't, and sued for invasion of privacy.
THE VERDICT: The jury awarded her $1.5 million (later reduced

Bird rule of thumb: If they could sweat, they wouldn't be able to fly.

to $850,000). A judge compared her experience to being "dragged slowly through a pile of untreated sewage."

THE PLAINTIFF: Dave Feuerstein
THE DEFENDANT: Tesco supermarkets, an English chain
THE LAWSUIT: Enthusiastic about Tesco's low prices during a special promotion, Feuerstein kept going back to buy more. In three days, he redeemed over 300 coupons . . . then claimed he'd hurt his back carrying all the cheap merchandise, and sued. "Offers like this are too good to refuse," he told a reporter. "Tesco should have been more considerate and made it impossible to do what I did. If Tesco hadn't had this offer, I wouldn't have hurt my back."
THE VERDICT: Unknown.

THE PLAINTIFF: Kenneth Bruckner of Gering, Nebraska
THE DEFENDANT: Presbyterian/St. Luke's Medical Center in Denver
THE LAWSUIT: In the spring of 1993, Bruckner sued the hospital, claiming the "highly toxic" cleanser they used to disinfect toilet seats had caused him "permanent burns, neurological injuries, and urologic and sexual dysfunction." Said Bruckner's attorney: "What's the world coming to if it's not safe to sit on the toilet and read the paper?"
THE VERDICT: Unknown . . . but you know how *we'd* rule.

THE PLAINTIFFS: Two college students
THE DEFENDANT: Pace University, New York
THE LAWSUIT: The students took an introductory computer-programming course at Pace. One day the teacher required them, as homework, to calculate the cost of an aluminum atom. The answer is $6.22054463335 x 10^{-26}—less than a *trillionth* of a penny. Outraged that such a high level of work was required in an introductory course, the pair sued.
THE VERDICT: Believe it or not, the judge found their instructor guilty of "educational malpractice."

Queen termites can lay an egg every second, or 86,000 eggs a day.

NO GOOD DEED GOES UNPUNISHED

Some Good Samaritans, like Lenny Skutnick (see p. 11),
wind up honored by the president of the United States.
Others get their cars stolen. Life isn't fair.

LATE FEE
"In 1994, New York City's Metropolitan Transit Authority docked Michael Durant, a 31-year-old bus driver, a day's pay for being twelve minutes late for work. His excuse: He had stopped to pull a man out of a burning car on the highway."
—*Esquire,* **January 1995**

THANKS, YOU ##*!#@!
"New York Jets quarterback Boomer Esiason . . . was driving home after a 28–24 loss to the Miami Dolphins when he had to stop his car because of an accident . . . He got out and asked a woman in the car in front of him whether she was all right. Her window was broken and she was crying. Esiason recalls: 'She looked at me and said, 'Boomer?' I said, 'Yes.' She said, 'You guys really (stink). How'd you lose that game today?'"
—*San Francisco Chronicle,* **December 7, 1995**

ALL WET
"In 1981 Peter Stankiewicz of Rockville, Maryland, stopped his car and dove into the Potomac River to rescue a driver whose lumber truck had crashed through a bridge railing and plunged 60 feet into the icy water. After hauling the driver to shore, Stankiewicz was informed that his car had been towed to the pound because it was blocking traffic."
—*Encyclopedia Brown's Book of Strange Facts*

THAT'S WHAT YOU GET
"When Lorne Murdock saw a delivery truck collide with a car in L.A., he pulled over his own car and rushed out to calm the bleeding motorist until help arrived. For his trouble, somebody stole Murdock's 1980 AMC Spirit.

Food for thought: Peanut butter sandwiches weren't popular until the 1920s.

"'It's incredible, you try and save someone's life, do the right thing, help somebody out, and this happens,' said the 29-year-old Murdock.

"'That's what you get for being a Good Samaritan,' said officer Kirk Hunter."

—*Santa Rosa Press-Democrat*, May 2, 1993

METER-FEEDING GRANNY

"Sylvia Slayton was just trying to spare a stranger a ticket in Cincinnati, when she plunked a dime and a nickel into two expired parking meters. Instead she got handcuffed and arrested, and Thursday was convicted of a misdemeanor for interfering with an officer trying to ticket overdue cars.

"'I tried to do what I thought was the right thing,' the 63-year-old grandmother of 10 said. She faces as many as 90 days in jail and a $750 fine when she is sentenced later this month."

—Burlington, Vermont, *Free Press*, February 7, 1997

REWARD FOR VALOR

"In 1982 Timothy George, a part-time busboy at a family restaurant in Vallejo, California, chased and captured a mugger who had robbed a customer in the men's room. Timothy was promptly fired for 'leaving work' and 'fighting.'"

—*Encyclopedia Brown's Book of Strange Facts*

GULL OF MY DREAMS

"In June 1994, Don Weston found a young seagull squawking on the ground in his driveway in Gloucester, England, and put the bird on top of his garage to keep it safe from cats. A few hours later it flew off. Mr. Weston thought he'd done a good deed, but every June and July for the last three years he has been pursued by a vengeful seagull—the very one, he believes, whose life he saved.

"'Its evil squawking is so distinctive,' he said. 'It sounds like a banshee wailing. I've had nightmares about it.' The bird pecks his head, bombs him with droppings . . . and stalks him through the city by air. 'At the sight of me, it goes crazy,' said Weston."

—*The Fortean Times*

Estimated cost of maintaining a chimpanzee in captivity for 60 years: $300,000.

WHO'S ON FIRST?

America's national pastime is more than just a game—it's a tradition. The component parts are traditions, too. We got curious about where they come from.

B ASEBALL GLOVES
Introduced by: Charles Waite, first-baseman for the Boston team of the National Association (forerunner of the National League), in 1875
History: Until Waite started wearing a thin, unpadded, flesh-color glove, everyone played barehanded. In fact, when he showed up on the field with it, rivals jeered that he was a softy. One contemporary wrote: "Waite confessed that he was a bit ashamed to wear it, but had to save his hand. He also admitted he'd chosen a color as inconspicuous as possible, because he didn't want to attract attention."
Note: Though a few players copied Waite, it took a superstar to popularize the use of gloves. In 1883 the shortstop for the Providence, Rhode Island, team broke a finger on his left hand. To protect it, he wore an oversized, padded buckskin glove. One of baseball's biggest heroes, John Montgomery Ward, decided to wear one too . . . which inspired manufacturers to begin mass-producing them. (From *The Baseball Catalog*, by Dan Schlossberg)

SHIN GUARDS
Introduced by: "One of two black second-basemen, Binghamton [New York]'s Bud Fowler or Buffalo's Frank Grant, who played minor league ball in the 1880s in the International League." (*From Only the Ball Was White*, by Robert Peterson)
History: In the 1880s, white ballplayers openly tried to injure black players. Grant and Fowler "knew that about every player that came down to second base on a steal . . . would, if possible, throw their spikes into them." So one of them came up with the idea of wrapping wooden slats around their shins.
Note: It only worked for a while . . . and then the bigots got more vicious. As one player recalled in 1891: "[When] Grant put wooden armor on his legs for protection, the opposition just proceeded to file their spikes to a sharp point and split the shin guards."

Marriage makes a woman more likely to become depressed; a man, less likely.

Gruesome trivia: According to *Only the Ball Was White*, that's what first made the feet-first slide popular among white players. Grant ultimately moved to the outfield.

The first catcher to wear shin guards was Roger Bresnahan in 1907. He fashioned them after the leg guards used in the English game of cricket.

SEVENTH-INNING STRETCH

Introduced by: No one's sure
History: According to legend, the stretch began in 1910 when President William Howard Taft got up to leave during the seventh inning of a game between Washington and Philadelphia. "His entourage followed," the story goes, "and fans, seeing a crowd of people standing, stood up also."

That may have happened, but according to *Baseball's Book of Firsts*, the seventh-inning stretch was already part of baseball tradition: "In reality, fans had been standing and stretching at about the seventh inning since the early 1870s." The book says it started in Boston, where the local team tended to score most of its runs near the end of the game. Around the seventh inning, fans would stand and "cheer on the hometown boys."
Note: There's one other claimant—Manhattan College. According to one sports historian: "In 1882 during a baseball game at New York's Manhattan College, the athletic director, a man named Brother Jasper, called a time out during the seventh inning so that the fidgeting students in the stands would have a moment to stretch." True? Who knows?

UNIFORM NUMBERS

Introduced by: The New York Yankees
History: Around 1915, teams experimented with small numbers on uniform sleeves, but they made no difference to fans. In 1929, however, the Yankees—realizing they were attracting lots of new fans who didn't know the players by sight—put big numbers on the backs of uniforms. The original numbers followed the batting order. For example: Babe Ruth, who batted third, got number 3; Lou Gehrig, who batted fourth, was number 4. Later, numbers were assigned at random. It took another 31 years before teams

The first movie shown in a drive-in theater was *Wife Beware*, in 1933.

started putting names on the uniforms. Why so long? Apparently, clubs were afraid they'd lose the profits they made from selling scorecards.

CATCHER'S MASKS

Introduced by: Fred Thayer, coach of Harvard University, in 1875 or 1877, depending on the source

History: Catchers originally wore no protection—they stood off to one side of the plate so they wouldn't get hit. In 1877 Thayer decided his catcher would have an advantage if he stood right behind the plate. But the student, James Tyng, refused. Thayer explained: "He had been hit by foul tips and had become timid . . . I [had] to find a way to bring back his confidence."

Thayer's solution: armor. He took a fencer's mask to a tinsmith, who cut eyeholes in the wire mesh. "Tyng placed the contraption over his head for a game against the Lynn Live Oaks Baseball Club," writes Lloyd Johnson in *Baseball's Book of Firsts*.

Note: Thayer later changed the mesh to wide-spaced iron bars, and added forehead and chin rests. He patented the mask in 1878, and it immediately became popular. Chest protectors were added in 1885.

BATTING HELMETS

Introduced by: Willie Wells, in 1939

History: In 1905 a "pneumatic batting helmet" that looked like a leather football helmet was introduced, but it was too cumbersome and no one used it. Even after Ray Chapman died when he was hit in the head by a pitch in 1920, there was no interest in helmets. Once again, one player trying to protect himself changed baseball tradition. Wells, a good-hitting shortstop in the Negro Leagues, hung his head over the plate when he batted—which made him especially vulnerable. He finally got sick of being hit in the head, and showed up at a game wearing a miner's helmet. (No word on whether it had the light in front.) In 1942 he switched to a construction hardhat . . . which eventually led to helmets made especially for the Major Leagues in 1952.

President Grover Cleveland's nickname was "Uncle Jumbo."

UNCLE JOHN'S "STALL OF FAME"

You'd be amazed at the number of newspaper articles BRI members send in about the creative ways people get involved with bathrooms, toilets, toilet paper, etc. So we're creating Uncle John's "Stall of Fame."

Honoree: Will Simmons, a freshman at Duke University
Notable Achievement: Turning toilet paper into a political issue
True Story: In his first year at Duke, Simmons discovered that the toilets in his dorm were outfitted with single-ply toilet paper. Outraged, he decided to run for a seat in the student government. His single campaign platform: a promise that students would get two-ply paper in dorm bathrooms.

Simmons won, of course—students know what's important. After the election, university housing officials pledged to cooperate.

Honoree: Donna Summer, pop singer
Notable Achievement: Writing a Top 10 song in the bathroom
True Story: At a posh hotel, Summer was washing her hands in the ladies' room. She mused to herself that the washroom attendant there had to work awfully hard for her money. It suddenly hit Summer that she had a song title. So she rushed into a stall and wrote lyrics for it. "She Works Hard for the Money" was an international hit that went to #3 on the *Billboard* charts.

Honoree: Jacob Feinzilberg, a San Jose, California, inventor
Notable Achievement: Inventing the ultimate port-a-potty
True Story: In 1993 Feinzilberg came up with the Inflate-a-Potty, a toilet so portable it can actually fit in a purse. It can be inflated in seconds and is used with an ordinary eight-gallon kitchen bag as a disposable liner. He came up with the idea for it at a picnic when his young daughter suddenly "heard nature's call and found no place to answer it."

What company holds the most U.S. patents? IBM.

Honorees: Philip Middleton and Richard Wooton of Chantilly, Virginia
Notable Achievement: Creating a "commode for dogs"
True Story: According to a 1993 news report, it's called the Walk-Me-Not. The dog walks up stairs at the side of the bathroom toilet, steps onto a platform over the toilet bowl, and squats down to use.

Honorees: Chiu Chiu-kuei and Lee Wong-tsong, a Taiwanese couple
Notable Achievement: Creating a public bathroom nice enough for a wedding . . . and then getting married in it
True Story: In the mid-1990s, Chiu Chiu-kuei designed, and her fiancé Lee Wong-tsong built, a bathroom for a public park in the city of Taichung. According to news reports: "The couple said the lavatory, complete with elaborate decoration, had cost about $1 million to build." Chiu explained: "Since the bathroom is the creation of me and my husband it is very meaningful to us and therefore we decided to have our ceremony in here." Not explained: Why seven other couples joined them, making it the largest group wedding ever performed in a lavatory.

Honoree: Bryan J. Patrie, a Stanford graduate student
Notable Achievement: Inventing the *Watercolor Intelligent Nightlight*, which informs bleary-eyed midnight bathroom-goers whether the toilet seat is up or down . . . without turning on a blinding light.
True Story: Patrie introduced the device in the early 1990s. He explained: "When you get within five feet of the dark commode, it will sense your motion. It looks to see if the room is dark. Then it looks upward by sending out an infrared beam. If it gets a reflection, it knows the seat is up. If it is, the red light comes on."

* * *

. . . **And some vital "Stall-of-Fame" info:** According to the *Philadelphia Inquirer* Toilet Paper Report, women's #1 bathroom complaint is men leaving the toilet seat up. Men's #1 complaint is having to wait to get into the bathroom.

Proper English: Technically speaking, a female "dude" is known as a "dudine."

MR. TOAD'S
WILD RIDE, PART I

The Wind in the Willows is one of the best-loved books in the English language, and a milestone in children's literature. But it took some very unusual circumstances to get it written and published. And then it took the intervention of the president of the United States to make it a success. Here's the story.

BACKGROUND

By the 1890s, Kenneth Grahame was already a celebrated author. His two books, *The Golden Age* and *Dream Days*—tales of childhood written for adults—had established him as an authority on children's literature. Editors were constantly asking him to review new books and to edit collections of poems and stories.

But Grahame didn't want to write for a living. He was solidly middle-class, and the English middle-class ideal at the time was to be a "gentleman author"—someone who wrote part-time, for love, not money. In his professional life, Grahame was a successful banker—in 1898 he landed the prestigious job of Secretary of the Bank of England.

Wedded Miss

In 1899 Grahame married Elspeth Thompson. It was an unmitigated disaster. Elspeth wound up writing despondent letters and poems to her friends; Grahame developed a severe case of writer's block. He became so distracted that, less than a decade later, he was asked to retire from the bank.

The only good thing to come from the marriage was their son, Alastair. But he had problems, too—he was born "blind in one eye and squinting out of the other." His parents called him Mouse.

MAN OF LETTERS

Writing was difficult for Grahame, but he could still tell stories. Every evening he invented one for Mouse, letting the little boy choose the subject.

One night, Mouse asked his father to make up something about a rat, a mole, and a giraffe. (The giraffe was soon replaced with

Why did Thomas Henry Huxley invent the word *agnostic* in 1869?

Toad—a loose caricature of Alastair.) The trio's ongoing experiences became such a favorite that in 1907, when Mouse was supposed to leave on a vacation with his governess, he refused to go—he didn't want to miss his father's bedtime stories.

Grahame promised to write down a new adventure every day and send it to his son . . . luckily, he kept his word. According to Elspeth, the child's governess was so impressed by the unusual stories that she saved the 15 letters and brought them back to her. These later became the basis for *The Wind in the Willows*.

A SAMPLE LETTER
[*Ed. note: Toad was sent to prison for stealing a newfangled motorcar (it was 1907, remember) but escaped dressed as a washerwoman. Now, as he nears home, he looks up and sees the same car he stole headed toward him, and assumes it's pursuing him.*]

16 Durham Villas
Campden Hill, W.
7th August, 1907

Dear Mouse:
When the Toad saw that his enemies were close upon him . . . he sank down in a shabby miserable heap in the road, murmuring to himself . . . "It's all over now! Prison again! Dry bread and water again! . . . O what a fool I have been! What did I want to go strutting around the country for, singing conceited songs? . . . O unhappy toad! O miserable animal!" And his head sank down in the dust.

The terrible motor-car drew nearer and nearer . . . Then it stopped. Some gentlemen got out. They walked round the trembling heap of misery lying in the road, & one of them said—"O dear! Here is a poor washerwoman who has fainted in the road . . . Let us lift her into the motor-car and take her to the nearest village."

When the Toad heard them talk that way, & knew he was not recognized, his courage began to revive, & he opened one of his eyes. Then one of the gentlemen said: "See, she is feeling better already! The fresh air is doing her good! How do you feel now, washerwoman?"

The toad answered in a feeble voice, "Thank you kindly, Sir, I'm feeling rather better. I think if I might sit on the front

He got tired of being called an atheist.

seat, beside the chauffeur, where I could get more air, I should soon be quite right again."

"That's a very sensible woman," said the gentleman. So they helped ~~her~~ him into the front seat . . . The Toad began to sit up & look about & presently he said to the chauffeur, "Please Mr. Chauffeur, I wish you would let me try to drive the car for a little; it looks so easy; I'm sure I could do it quite well!"

The chauffeur laughed, heartily. But one of the gentlemen said, "Bravo, washerwoman! I like your spirit! Let her try. She won't do any harm."

So the chauffeur gave up his seat to the toad, & he took the steering wheel in his hands, and set the car going, & off they went, very slowly and carefully at first, for the toad was prudent. The gentlemen clapped their hands & cried, "Bravo, washerwoman! How well she does it! Fancy a washerwoman driving a motor-car! Bravo!"

Then the Toad went a little faster. The gentlemen applauded . . . The Toad began to lose his head. He went faster and faster still. The gentlemen called out warningly, "Be careful, washerwoman!" Then the Toad lost his head entirely. He stood up in his seat and shouted "Ho, ho! Who are you calling washerwoman! I am the Toad! The famous Mr. Toad! The motor-car driver, the toad who always escapes, who baffles his enemies, who dodges policemen, who breaks out of prison, the always victorious, the triumphant Toad!"

Grahame had already written much of the story, but he had no intention of turning it into a commercial work. Nothing could have been further from his mind.

For Part II of Mr. Toad's Wild Ride, turn to page 333.

* * *

"All women become like their mothers. That is their tragedy. No man does. That's his."

—*Oscar Wilde*

If you visit, bring sunblock: Neptune's summer is 40 years long.

THEY WENT THATAWAY

Malcolm Forbes wrote a fascinating book about the deaths of famous people. Here are a few of the stories he found.

POCAHONTAS
Claim to Fame: Daughter of Native American chief Powhatan and friend of the Jamestown, Virginia, settlers in the early 17th century
How She Died: "Old World" fever
Postmortem: In 1616 Pocahontas, her husband John Rolfe, their infant son Thomas, and 12 Native Americans sailed to England. Their purpose: to expose Pocahontas and her entourage to the charms of the Old World. Instead, they were exposed to Old World diseases . . . for which they had no natural immunity. By the time they set sail for Virginia in March 1617, Pocahontas was suffering from tuberculosis and possibly pneumonia. The party made it only about 20 miles downriver from London when Pocahontas fell so ill that they had to pull into port and take her ashore. Pocahontas, 22, died there three weeks later.

CLARK GABLE
Claim to Fame: One of the biggest film stars in Hollywood history
How He Died: Heart attack, probably caused by the strain of working with Marilyn Monroe
Postmortem: In 1960 Gable was offered the lead role in *The Misfits*, which co-starred Marilyn Monroe. His salary: $750,000 plus a percentage of the film's profits—the largest film deal ever (at the time). Friends warned Gable not to make a film with Monroe, who had a reputation for being extremely difficult to work with. But he liked the script and couldn't resist the money, so he took the deal. Filming began on location in the desert outside of Reno, Nevada, in the summer of 1960.

Working with Marilyn turned out to be even worse than Gable's friends had warned. Her marriage to playwright Arthur Miller was disintegrating and she was in the early stages of the mental break-down that would eventually lead to her suicide. She threw tantrums, arrived for scenes hours late—when she showed up at all—and rarely knew her lines. Gable was so frustrated and bored that

Sloths even sneeze slowly. And they give birth upside down. Slowly.

he dismissed his stuntmen and began doing his own stunts, hoping that it would help him blow off some steam. At 59, he wasn't in the best shape, and the stunts—including lassoing horses and being dragged by ropes behind a truck across the desert—left him battered, bruised, and sometimes even bloodied. "Christ, I'm glad this picture's finished," he told a friend when filming ended. "Marilyn damn near gave me a heart attack."

Two days later, Gable was changing the tire on his Jeep when he felt chest pains. He didn't think much of it, but that night he complained of a headache and "indigestion." By the next morning he was doubled over in pain. His wife took him to the hospital, where doctors diagnosed a mild heart attack. He seemed to be making a quick recovery, but 10 days later suffered a second, massive heart attack and died.

NERO

Claim to Fame: Ruthless Roman emperor who killed his mother, wife, half-brother, and countless others. Was emperor during the fire that destroyed half of Rome in 64 A.D.

How He Died: Committed suicide to avoid an even worse fate

Postmortem: Contrary to popular belief, he never "fiddled while Rome burned." In fact, as one historian says, "Nero didn't even own a fiddle—he owned a lyre—and he was 50 miles away when the fire began." And he responded to the emergency admirably, "opening shelters for the homeless, reducing the price of corn, and bringing in food from the provinces."

Nevertheless, the fire sealed his fate. In its aftermath, he imposed heavy taxes to rebuild Rome. The huge construction project was never finished—he spent much of the money on himself while ordinary Romans starved and the military went unpaid. Finally, Rome revolted against his tyranny. Nero tried to flee to Egypt, but never made it out of the city: when the Senate learned he was hiding in his mansion, they sent a messenger to tell him he'd been declared a public enemy and would be punished in the "ancient style"—"stripped naked and, with his head thrust into a wooden fork, flogged to death with rods." Just as the cavalry arrived to take him away, Nero cheated fate by stabbing himself in the throat.

In 1947 Marilyn Monroe was crowned the first Queen of Artichokes.

AMERICAN TRADITIONS

There are some things Americans do because . . . well, it's just what we do. How many of you know how these three traditions started?

THE PLEDGE OF ALLEGIANCE

Tradition: At the beginning of events or meetings, Americans face the U.S. flag with hand on heart and recite:

I pledge allegiance to the flag of the United States of America. And to the Republic for which it stands, one Nation under God, indivisible, with liberty and justice for all.

Is it an old patriotic verse dating back to the American Revolution? Was it written by the Founding Fathers? Nope. It was created as a promotional gimmick by a magazine in 1892.

Origin: As the 400th anniversary of Columbus's voyage to the New World approached in 1892, the U.S. made plans to celebrate the event with a huge World's Fair in Chicago (the Columbian Exposition). Editors at *The Youth's Companion*—the *Reader's Digest* of its day—jumped on the bandwagon and became sponsors of the National Public School Celebration for Columbus Day, 1892. Their goal: To get every public school in the U.S. to honor the occasion by raising a U.S. flag and reciting a flag salute. This meant, of course, that they needed an official flag salute.

The man assigned to write it was an editor named Francis Bellamy, a former Baptist minister who had been forced out of his Boston church for delivering socialist sermons. The pledge he wrote—which was recited by an estimated 10 million school-children on that day in 1892—is slightly different than the one we know now. It was:

I pledge allegiance to my Flag and the Republic for which it stands, one nation, indivisible, with liberty and justice for all.

According to scholar John W. Baer, Bellamy "considered placing the word 'equality' in his Pledge, but knew that the state superintendents of education . . . were against equality for women and African Americans." The pledge Bellamy wrote quickly became part of

---

Actor with the most leading roles ever in Hollywood films: John Wayne, at 141.

America's culture. But people couldn't leave it alone. Baer adds:

> In 1923 and 1924 the National Flag Conference, under the "leadership of the American Legion and the Daughters of the American Revolution, changed the Pledge's words "my Flag," to "the Flag of the United States of America." Bellamy disliked this change, but his protest was ignored.
>
> In 1954 Congress, after a campaign by the Knights of Columbus, added the words "under God," to the Pledge. The Pledge was now both a patriotic oath and a public prayer.
>
> Bellamy's granddaughter said he also would have resented this second change . . . In his retirement in Florida, he [had] stopped attending church.

HAIL TO THE CHIEF

Tradition: When a U.S. president enters a room on a formal occasion, the song "Hail to the Chief" is played.

Origin: The 11th president, James K. Polk (1845–49), was so "physically undistinguished" that visitors to the White House often didn't notice when he'd entered a room. To make sure they knew Polk was there, his wife, Sarah, arranged for the Marine band to play this old Scottish anthem whenever he walked through the door. It was immediately adopted as a tradition, and all presidents have honored it since.

THE PURPLE HEART MEDAL

Tradition: U.S. soldiers who are wounded in combat are awarded the Purple Heart.

Origin: At the time of the American Revolution, European military tradition dictated that only officers could receive medals; it was unheard of to honor a common soldier for bravery. George Washington changed this practice. On August 7, 1782, he ordered the creation of the Badge of Military Merit, in the "figure of a heart in purple cloth or silk." (Purple was traditionally the color reserved for royalty.) The medal was awarded for "any singularly meritorious action," not necessarily for being wounded in action.

The medal fell into disuse for more than 150 years, but in 1932, to commemorate the 200th anniversary of Washington's birth, Gen. Douglas MacArthur revived it and gave it its current meaning.

In the old days, freckles were called "moth-patches" and were considered an affliction.

THE NOSE KNOWS

Smell is an amazing and complex function carried out in
a tiny chamber, half the size of an egg, situated just behind our
nose. With it, we are able to smell thousands of different odors.

THE SCIENCE OF SMELL

How do we smell things? The mystery is still unfolding, but it starts with "odor molecules." Scientists tell us the air is filled with them. They enter your nasal cavity every time you breathe, 23,000 times a day.

• Just behind your nose, these molecules are absorbed by mucous-covered tissue.

• This tissue is covered with "receptor" cells. (You may have millions of them.) Each one is mounted on a microscopic hair.

• The receptor cells stick out and wave in the air currents we inhale. Forty of them must detect odor molecules before a smell is registered.

• When a new smell is detected, the tiny olfactory bulb, located just above the nasal cavity, flashes data directly to the most ancient and mysterious part of your brain—the limbic system—which "handles feelings, lust, instincts, and invention." The limbic system reacts immediately, without intervention of reason or language, and may provoke powerful emotions, images, or nostalgia.

THE DARK AGES OF SMELLING

A keen sense of smell is now accepted as part of the good life—coffees, wines, cheeses, and gourmet foods would all be lost on us if we lacked our immense range of smell. However, this faculty wasn't always appreciated.

• The ancient philosopher Plato looked down on smell as a lowly instinct that might lead to gluttony and lust, while vision and hearing opened one to geometry and music, and were therefore "closer to the soul."

• During the 18th and 19th centuries, it was commonly believed that many diseases were caused by smells. Odors from corpses, feces, urine, swamps, and Earth fissures were called "miasmas"

Full of life: There's an estimated one trillion bacteria on each of your feet.

and were thought to have the power to kill you. To ward off these smells, people carried and inhaled "antimephitics," such as garlic, amber, sulfur, and incense. When exposed to miasmic odors, people did not swallow their saliva, but spit it out. The Viennese physician Semmelweis was ostracized by colleagues when he declared that washing one's hands, not breathing antimephitics, would stop most disease from spreading.

- According to some sources, the stethoscope was invented not to hear the heartbeat better, but to give doctors some distance from a patient's bodily odors.

TASTE AND SMELL

- We taste only four things: sweet, sour, salt, and bitter. It's the smells that make things really taste. For example, wine's smell, not its taste, is what makes it delicious. With a head cold, drinking wine is an entirely different experience.

- Scientists have categorized smells into seven groups: minty like peppermint, floral like roses, ethereal like pears, musky like— well—musk, resinous like camphor, foul like rotten eggs, and acrid like vinegar.

- Talking with your mouth full expels taste molecules and diminishes the taste of food.

SMELL FACTS

- Women have a keener sense of smell than men.

- By simply smelling a piece of clothing, most people can tell if it was worn by a woman or man.

- Each of us has an odor that is, like our fingerprints, unique. One result, researchers say: Much of the thrill of kissing comes from smelling the unique odors of another's face.

- Smells stimulate learning. Students given olfactory stimulation along with a word list retain much more information and remember it longer.

- Many smells are heavier than air and can be smelled only at ground level.

- We smell best if we take several short sniffs rather than a long one.

Cool fact: The average American eats 5 gallons of frozen desserts a year.

NEVER SAY NEVER

A *few pearls of wisdom from* 599 Things You
Should Never Do, *edited by Ed Morrow.*

"Never lend your car to anyone to whom you have given
birth."
—**Erma Bombeck**

"Never test the depth of a
river with both feet."
—**African adage**

"Never stand between a dog
and the hydrant."
—**John Peers**

"Never raise your hand to
your children—it leaves your
midsection unprotected."
—**Robert Orben**

"Never teach your children to
be cunning, you'll be one of
their very first victims."
—**Josh Billings**

"Never say 'oops' in the operating room."
—**Dr. Leo Troy**

"Never try to pick up a
woman who's wearing a Super
Bowl ring."
—**Garry Shandling**

"Never interrupt an enemy
while he's making a mistake."
—**Napoleon Bonaparte**

"Never ask what goes into a
hot dog."
—**American adage**

"Never call a man a fool; borrow from him."
—**Addison Mizner**

"Never be afraid of the deaf-
eningly obvious. It is always
news to somebody."
—**P. J. Kavanagh**

"Never marry for money. You
can borrow it a lot cheaper."
—**Ann Landers**

"Never feel remorse for what
you have thought about your
wife; she has thought much
worse things about you."
—**Jean Rostand**

"Never tell a woman she
doesn't look good in some
article of clothing she has just
purchased."
—**Lewis Grizzard**

"Never start a project until
you've picked someone to
blame."
—**Johnny Hart and
Brent Parker**

Russians celebrate the October Revolution in November (on the 7th).

JUST PLANE WEIRD

If you bought this book in an airport, you might want to skip reading this chapter until your flight is over and you're safely back on the ground.

NOTHING TO SNOOZE AT
In May 1995 the pilot of Delta Airlines Flight 198, approaching Palm Beach International Airport, was unable to make contact with the control tower. The pilot landed the plane without any assistance, then alerted the Federal Aviation Administration. According to news reports, "Palm Beach sheriff's deputies entered the control tower and found the lone air traffic controller shoeless and apparently just waking up." The deputies also found a pistol, ammunition, and a gun-cleaning kit nearby (it's against federal law to have a gun in a control tower), and speculate he was cleaning the gun and fell asleep. FAA officials launched an investigation. "Meanwhile," the Associated Press reported, he "remains on the job."

UNLUCKY BREAK
In June 1999 a plane approaching Benbecula Airport in Western Scotland was forced to circle for half an hour while the air traffic controller stopped working to eat lunch. According to wire service reports, "Officials at the airport said there was just one controller at Benbecula, and she had to take a break at the time she did because national air traffic rules forbid any controller from working more than two hours without one . . . There was an uproar in the terminal building as families watched the plane from Glasgow linger in a holding pattern, 'tantalizingly within view.'"

UNLUCKIER BREAK
In 1999 the air traffic controller in Bournemouth Airport in southern England stepped away from his post for a few minutes to get some coffee . . . but was gone a lot longer than he'd planned. Greg Fanos, 39, fell down a flight of stairs and broke his ankle. "Crawling back to the tower was only two or three yards," Fanos says, "but it took forever." By the time he made it back to his desk and called an ambulance, several planes, unable to reach the

---

Tiniest snowflakes ever recorded: 1/500th of an inch in diameter . . .

tower on the radio, had gone into a holding pattern over the airport. Two other planes landed safely without assistance.

CLOSE ENCOUNTER

In April 1998 an air traffic supervisor at New York's LaGuardia Airport spilled some coffee in the control tower. One of the controllers turned from his position to help clean it up, and the momentary distraction caused what may be the closest near miss in U.S. aviation history. A landing U.S. Airways plane came within 20 feet of colliding with an Air Canada plane that was taking off from an intersecting runway. According to news reports, "experts were unable to immediately cite another incident in which two airborne passenger jets came so close without colliding." When the National Transportation Safety Board investigated the incident and began taking statements from people in the control tower, "neither the supervisor nor the controller mentioned the spilled coffee in their statements."

RATS!

In August 1999 a woman on an Air New Zealand flight from Los Angeles to Auckland felt something on her leg. She lifted her blanket and saw a rat sitting on her knee. The rat had been spotted earlier, but according to an airline spokesperson, "attempts by the crew to catch it failed." According to wire service reports, "Quarantine officials met the plane when it landed in Auckland and conducted a search of the plane including passengers' hand baggage. The rat wasn't found, so the plane was quarantined and fumigated."

SUFFICIENT GROUNDS

In 1999 guards manning security checkpoints at more than 300 U.S. airports began ordering travelers carrying cups of coffee to sip their coffee to prove it really *was* coffee. "That's policy," says security spokesman Jeff Sledge. "It's so we'd be able to make sure that what's supposed to be in the cup is in the cup—not a weapon of some sort." The policy was reportedly put into place following an FAA test in which an FAA employee made it past security with a "simulated device in a coffee cup." But the FAA denies that it's behind the "clearing of liquids," or "sip test." "It's not an FAA requirement at all," a spokesperson told the *Wall Street Journal*. If the airlines are doing it, she said, "they're doing it on their own."

Largest: 15 inches in diameter and eight inches thick. They fell in Montana in 1887.

HIS NAME IS MY NAME, TOO!

Remember the tune that goes, "John Jacob Jingleheimer Smith, his name is my name too . . ."? If you do, you probably won't be able to get it out of your head for the rest of the day. Sorry. Anyway, we've come across some stories about people with the same names as other folks (and one Supreme Being). Here they are.

NOT THE DICTTATTOR

"Adolf Hittler is alive and well. But probably not the guy you're thinking about. Unlike the Nazi leader, this gentleman spells his last name with two T's, disdains fascism, and never aspired to take over the world. He's a 61-year-old retired school bus driver from Landeck, Austria, and he doesn't like to be teased. 'My whole life this has been a problem,' he says. 'Just try checking into a hotel with my name . . . But it is in part my choice. I decided not to change my name. I thought it would be an insult to my parents.'

"Hittler's problem is rare. Only about 2% of German men before World War II were named Adolf, and during his reign, Hitler forbade Germans to name children after him."

—The Wolf Files, October 1, 1998

GOD AMONG MEN

"A man who legally changed his name to Ubiquitous Perpetuity God began serving a nine-month sentence for indecent exposure in Marin County, California, on Wednesday. God, 68, has been convicted 18 times for similar offenses since 1968. His latest arrest came in October, when he exposed himself to a woman waiting in line at a coffee shop. He did it so that women 'could have some type of awareness of God,' according to police reports . . . God will be released to a residential mental health facility, if one agrees to admit him."

—Ashland, Oregon, Daily Tidings, 1996

FRANK STATEMENT

"Say hello to Frank J. Manibusan and his brother, Frank, both of Alameda, California. And their brother, Frank. And their other

---

Less is more: 95% of the creatures on Earth are smaller than a chicken egg.

brother, Frank. And his brother, Frank, and one other brother: Frank. Then, of course, there are children: Frank, Frank, Frank, Frank, Frank, and Frank. Frankly speaking, there are 12 Franks in all, at the moment—13 if you count the patriarch, 58-year-old Francisco . . . The sons and grandsons all have middle initials: J., J., J., J., J., J., J., J., J., J., J., and J.

"Of course, the advantages definitely outweigh the detriments, they explain. Can't do jury duty? Not to worry. Which Frank are the authorities going to chastise? And if one brother is out of cash, who cares? He need only tear out a check from the wallet of one of his siblings. 'We don't leave no checks lying around,' explained Frank Joe, No. 2 son, while his brothers and father nodded in agreement."

—San Jose Mercury News

A FAN AMONG FANS
"A fanatical British pop fan has changed his name to include the titles of his favorite group's records. And for good measure, Anthony Hicks, 23, added the names of the original line-up of the group, Level 42.

"Hicks this week signed legal papers changing his name to: 'Ant Level Forty Two The Pursuit Of Accidents The Early Tapes Standing In The Light True Colors A Physical Presence World Machine Running In The Family Platinum Edition Staring At The Sun Level Best Guaranteed The Remixes Forever Now Influences Changes Mark King Mike Landup Phil Gould Boon Gould Wally Badarou Lindup-Badarou.'

"'If they release any album or single, I will alter my name to have the new title incorporated into it,' Hicks told reporters."

—Reuters, July 30, 1994

SPLIT DECISION
"When Denise Mason of Glasgow, Scotland, gave birth to a son six weeks ago, picking a name created a stir. Clark Kearny, the child's father and a big fan of the Glasgow Rangers soccer team, wanted to name the boy after his favorite Ranger but couldn't make a decision. So, he didn't. The lad is named Cairo Lionel Sergio Lorenzo Colin Giovanni Barry Ian Jorge Gabriel Stephane Rod Mason Kearney—after 11 Rangers."

—USA Today, February 3, 1999

The first open-heart surgery was performed in 1893.

FAMILIAR PHRASES

Here are some more origins to everyday phrases.

PUT ON YOUR THINKING CAP

Meaning: Carefully and thoughtfully consider something
Origin: In previous centuries, it was customary for judges to put a cap on before sentencing criminals. Because judges were respected thinkers, it was referred to as a "thinking cap." (From *Gordon's Book of Familiar Phrases*)

PLAY FAST AND LOOSE

Meaning: Stretch the truth or meaning of words or rules, deceive or trifle with someone
Origin: This term dates from the 16th century. It comes from a game called "fast and loose," which was played at fairs. Operators rolled up a strap and left a loop hanging over the edge of a table. To win, a player had to catch the loop with a stick before the strap was unrolled. But they never won. Cheating operators rolled it up in such a way that the feat was impossible. (From *Have a Nice Day—No Problem!*, by Christine Ammer)

BOTCH A JOB

Meaning: Repair badly
Origin: "In old England, bodgers were peasant chairmakers . . . They produced, by traditional handicraft methods, simple and serviceable objects. When chairmaking was transformed into high art, the bodger was correspondingly downgraded to 'bodge' or '*botch*,'" which came to mean an item or service of poor quality. (From *To Coin a Phrase*, by Edwin Radford and Alan Smith)

IN HOCK

Meaning: Broke; have all of your belongings in a pawn shop
Origin: Comes from the Old West. In a common gambling card game called "faro," "the last card [to be played] was called the *hocketty card*. It was said to be *in hocketty* or *in hock*. When a player bet on a card that ended up *in hock*, he was himself *in hock*, at risk of losing his bets." (From *The Whole Ball of Wax*, by Laurence Urdang)

Q: What's an *erythrophobe?* A: Someone who blushes easily.

TAKE ANOTHER TACK
Meaning: Try a different strategy
Origin: "Sailing ships could not move directly into the wind but had to tack—zigzag back and forth with the wind first on one side, then on the other. If a skipper approaching harbor found that his vessel couldn't make the harbor mouth on the starboard tack, he was obviously on the *wrong tack*, and would have to take the other (port) tack." (From *Loose Cannons and Red Herrings*, by Robert Claiborne)

GET OFF (OR GO) "SCOT-FREE"
Meaning: Escape punishment
Origin: "In the thirteenth century, *scot* was the word for money you would pay at a tavern for food and drink, or when they passed the hat to pay the entertainer. Later it came to mean a local tax that paid the sheriff's expenses. To go *scot-free* literally meant to be exempted from paying this tax." (From *How Does Olive Oil Lose Its Virginity?*, by Bruce Tindall and Mark Watson)

SLUSH FUND
Meaning: A hidden cache of money used for illegal or corrupt political purposes
Origin: "Derived from Scandinavian words meaning 'slops,' this phrase is derived from the nineteenth-century shipboard practice of boiling up large pots of pork and other fatty meats. The fat that rose to the top of the kettles was stored in vats and then sold to soap and candle makers. The money received from the sale of the 'slush' was used for the crew's comfort and entertainment." (From *Eatioms*, by John D. Jacobson)

TAKE SOMEONE DOWN A PEG
Meaning: Humble someone who is self-important and conceited
Origin: "The expression probably originally referred to a ship's flags. These were raised or lowered by pegs—the higher the position of the flags, the greater the honor. So to take someone down a peg came to mean to lower the esteem in which that person is held." (From *Get to the Roots*, by Martin Manser)

Poll results: 57% of women would rather go on a shopping spree than have sex.

COURT TRANSQUIPS

Here's more 100% real-life courtroom dialogue.

Q: "Could you see him from where you were standing?"
A: "I could see his head."
Q: "And where was his head?"
A: "Just above his shoulders?"

Q: "Do you drink when you're on duty?"
A: "I don't drink when I'm on duty . . . unless I come on duty drunk."

Q: "When he went, had you gone and had she, if she wanted to and were able, for the time being excluding all the restraints on her not to go, gone also, would he have brought you, meaning you and she, with him to the station?"
D.A.: "Objection. That question should be taken out and shot."

Q: "What is your relationship with the plaintiff?"
A: "She is my daughter."
Q: "Was she your daughter on February 13, 1979?"

Q: "How did you happen to go to Dr. Cherney?"
A: "Well, a gal down the road had had several of her children by Dr. Cherney, and said he was really good."

Q: "Was that the same nose you broke as a child?"
A: "I have only one, you know."

Q: "How long have you been a French Canadian?"

Q: "What can you tell us about the truthfulness and veracity of this defendant?"
A: "Oh, she will tell the truth. She said she'd kill that son of a bitch—and she did!"

Q: "Were you alone or by yourself?"

Q: I understand you're Dean Roberts' mother.
A: Yes.
Q: How long have you known him?

Q (to opposing attorney): "Why don't you let her ask a question?"
Witness: "I thought you did."
Opposing Attorney: "I thought I did, too."
Q: "Well, I don't know what it is."
Opposing Attorney: "Well, the witness does, and I do."
Witness: "What's your question?"

Q: "What is the meaning of sperm being present?"
A: "It indicates intercourse."
Q: "Male sperm?"
A: "That is the only kind I know."

Q: "You say you're innocent, yet five people swore they saw you steal a watch."
A: "Your Honor, I can produce 500 people who didn't see me steal it."

Food for thought: Twinkie inventor Jimmy Dewar ate 40,177 Twinkies in his lifetime.

POLI-TALKS

*Politicians aren't getting much respect these days—but
then, it sounds like they don't deserve much, either.*

"I have the most reliable
friend you can have in
American politics and that is
ready money."
　　　　　—Sen. Phil Gramm

"Do you come here often?"
　　　　　—Ted Kennedy,
　　　　to a patron of a
　　Brooklyn soup kitchen

"There's nothing wrong with
this country that we couldn't
cure by turning it over to the
police for a couple of weeks."
　　　　　—George Wallace,
　　　　　　　　in 1967

"We've never had a president
named Bob. And I think it's
time."
　　　　　—Bob Dole

"There's no ethical problem
there. I used to teach ethics—
trust me."
　　　　　—William Bennett,
　　　Bush's antidrug czar,
　　championing the idea of
　decapitating drug dealers

"Too bad ninety percent of
the politicians give the other
ten percent a bad reputation."
　　　　　—Henry Kissinger

"I've got a lot to learn about
Washington. Why, yesterday I
accidentally spent some of my
own money."
　　　　　—Sen. Fred Thompson

"Liberals feel unworthy of their
possessions. Conservatives feel
they deserve everything
they've stolen."
　　　　　—Mort Sahl

"I never use the words 'Democrats' and 'Republicans.' It's
'liberals' and 'Americans.'"
　　　　　—James Watt, interior
　　secretary in the Reagan
　　　　　administration

"Washington is a city of
southern efficiency and northern charm."
　　　　　—John F. Kennedy

"You can lead a man to
Congress, but you can't make
him think."
　　　　　—Milton Berle

"You might be interested to
know that the Scriptures are
on our side on this."
　　　　　—Ronald Reagan,
　　defending his arms-
　　buildup program

According to *Guinness*, the longest recorded bout of hiccups lasted for 65 years.

THE SHAPE OF
THE EARTH

What shape is Earth? You'd say round, right? But scientists would hem and haw about it . . . and then answer "oblate spheroid." Read on . . .

YOU ARE HERE

In the age of space travel, we all know the world is "round." But ancient civilizations had no way to measure the size or shape of the Earth. So they came up with their own imaginative explanations. For example:

- In the Cherokee nation, people believed that mud rose from under the waters and formed an island with four corners—the Earth. The sun went underneath the island at night, and rose again the next day.

- Ancient Babylonians thought the Earth was inside a hollow mountain, floating on a sea. Everything—the sun, moon, sky, stars, water—was inside this mountain.

- Ancient Egyptians believed the whole Earth was part of their god, Keb. The stars were the jewels of a goddess in the sky and their god of air held her aloft.

- Ancient Hindus thought the Earth was in an upside-down bowl, being carried by elephants. The elephants stood on the back of a turtle that was standing on top of a snake. What the snake stood on, they hadn't quite worked out.

- Polynesian creation stories set the Earth in a basket with a lid. A hole cut in the top by a god lets in light. The woven grass at night lets light peek through in the form of stars.

THE GREEKS KNEW

Many people believe that Columbus was the first to realize that the world is round. Actually, the round-Earth concept has been with us since ancient Greece.

The very early Greeks thought Earth was a flat disc floating on water. But in about 540 B.C., the renowned mathematician

---

Gezundheit! The longest recorded sneezing fit was 978 consecutive days.

Pythagoras proposed the theory that the world was a sphere. The concept had many supporters, including Aristotle.

ALL'S WELL . . .

In about 250 B.C., Eratosthenes, librarian at the Library of Alexandria, even came up with a calculation of the Earth's spherical size.

He'd heard that in midsummer in the town of Syene, Egypt, the noonday sun shone directly into a deep well. He measured and discovered that in Alexandria, 787 kilometers north, the angle of the sun was about 7.2 degrees on the same date. With these measurements, he computed the circumference of the Earth.

Amazingly enough, considering how he came up with the numbers and how little he had to prove them, Eratosthenes's estimates were very close.

Another scholar, Posidonius (135–151 B.C.) did something similar over a century later, using the bright star Canopus. He measured the angles of the star from the horizon in two locations to get a fairly accurate estimate of the Earth's circumference.

IN FOURTEEN HUNDRED AND NINETY-TWO . . .

Fifteen hundred years later, Christopher Columbus came along, trying to make his now-famous voyage to Asia by going west. The decision of whether to fund his trip came down to analyzing the accumulation of estimates that had been gathered over the centuries.

Based on Eratosthenes' numbers, King Ferdinand believed that Columbus's fleet could never make it all the way to Asia: it was simply too far. He didn't see any reason to supply ships and crews only to have them die halfway from their goal.

Columbus used a ploy common in modern-day politics, marketing, and engineering: If the numbers don't support your conclusion, find some numbers that do. He found another estimate by Ptolemy dating from about A.D. 150. It was completely erroneous, but estimated that the Earth was about half its true size . . . so Queen Isabella agreed to support the voyage.

Luckily for Columbus, America got in his way, or he never would've reached India or anywhere else. Crossing both the Atlantic and the Pacific combined would've been an impossible feat with the ships and supplies he had.

Roll over, Rover: 63% of pet owners sleep with their pets.

FLAT AND FAT

It wasn't until 1958 that the Vanguard I satellite took the first photographs of earth from space and scientists were able to determine the planet's exact shape. The photographs proved the world is round . . . right?

Well, not exactly. Scientists reported that the Earth is an *oblate spheroid*—i.e., it's not *quite* round.

Since the Earth spins, it gets a slight bulge near the equator. Near yes, but not (as you might suspect) exactly *on* the equator.

Because of this bulge, the Earth is flattened very slightly on either end. Its circumference at the equator is 24,902 miles, and the circumference around the poles is 27 miles less than that: 24,875 miles. Not a big deal, really—if the world were the size of a basketball, it would be more perfectly round than a real basketball is. But still, after guessing for so long, scientists can't resist the opportunity to get it exactly right.

* * *

THE WORLD IS PEAR-SHAPED

Ironically, toward the end of his life, Columbus came to believe the Earth was shaped like a pear. He developed this theory during his third voyage to the New World: When he was sailing west near the equator, he noticed that the North Star made a wider circle around the Pole than it did when he was sailing in more temperate latitudes.

From this he deduced that he had been sailing gradually uphill and therefore closer to the sun, which explained why the weather was getting warmer. "I have come to the conclusion," he wrote in a letter to Queen Isabella, " . . . that the Earth is not round, but of the form of a pear . . . Where the stalk grows being the highest and nearest the sky."

Columbus believed that if he sailed far enough, he would eventually reach the Garden of Eden, which was located in the pear's stalk. (*Ripley's Believe It or Not*)

Belgians once tried to deliver mail using cats. (It didn't work.)

THE EARTH IS FLAT!

For centuries, scientists have been able to prove that the Earth is round, but that hasn't stopped people from developing their own unique—and entertaining—theories about its shape.

THE EARTH IS FLAT

Who Says So: The International Flat Earth Research Society
What They Believe: The world is a big flat disc, with the North Pole at the center. What is mistakenly believed to be the South Pole is actually a 150-foot-high mass of ice that forms a big square around the Earth-disc (the way an album cover makes a square around a record). People who *think* they're sailing around the world are actually sailing in a circle on the surface of the disc.

Flat-Earthers believe the Bible must be interpreted literally. Passages like Revelation 7:1 and 20:8, which refer to "the four corners of the earth," are all the proof they need.

History: In 1849 an English "itinerant lecturer" named Samuel Birley Rowbotham resurrected the flat-Earth theory (which had been widely discredited by the eighth century). The flat-Earth movement grew sporadically over the next 70 years, finally peaking in the 1920s when Wilbur Glen Voliva organized a flat-Earth religious community with several thousand followers in Zion, Illinois. Voliva owned one of the country's first 100,000-watt radio stations, and used it to preach the flat-Earth gospel to folks in the American Midwest.

Today the movement lives on in Charles Johnson's Flat Earth Society, which published *Flat Earth News* . . . until Johnson's house burned down in 1995, incinerating the 3,500-person mailing list. No word on what he's doing now.

THE EARTH IS HOLLOW

Who Said So: Captain John Cleves Symmes, a hero of the War of 1812
What He Believed: The Earth has four layers, like a big onion. Each is a "warm and rich land, stocked with vegetables and animals, if not men . . . " What we perceive as the surface of the Earth is actually the fifth and outer layer. And the North and South poles aren't just poles, they're also *holes* leading to the four interior worlds.

Fred Astaire's dancing shoes were size 8 and a half.

History: In 1823 Symmes managed to get a bill introduced in the U.S. Congress to finance a steamship voyage to the "North Hole" and to the inner worlds beyond. When the bill received only 25 votes, Senator Johnson of Kentucky talked President Adams's secretaries of the Navy and the Treasury into outfitting three ships for a voyage to the middle of the Earth. But before it got underway, Andrew Jackson became president and scuttled the trip. Symmes died in 1829, unfulfilled, but his theory remained popular with unconventional thinkers until 1909, when Robert Peary set foot on the North Pole (or at least came close) . . . and found no hole.

Even after 1909 the hollow-Earth theory had its admirers—including Adolf Hitler. Today a few diehard hollow-Earthers believe that Hitler survived World War II, escaped to an interior world under the South Pole, and may still be hiding there, mingling with "a race of advanced hollow-Earth beings who are responsible for the UFO sightings throughout history."

THE EARTH IS SHAPED LIKE THE INSIDE OF AN EGG
Who Said So: Cyrus Reed Teed, in the late 1860s.
What He Believed: Instead of living on the outside of a solid round ball, we're on the inside surface of a hollow one. The rest of the universe—sun, stars, etc.—is where the yolk would be.
Background: For years, Teed grappled with the notion of an infinite universe . . . but just couldn't accept it. Then one night in 1869, he had a dream in which a beautiful woman explained everything:

> The entire cosmos . . . is like an egg. We live on the inner surface of the shell, and inside the hollow are the sun, moon, stars, planets, and comets. What is outside? Absolutely nothing! The inside is all there is. You can't see across it because the atmosphere is too dense. The shell is 100 miles thick . . .

The woman in Teed's dream also said he would be the new Messiah, and he took it to heart. In the 1890s he bought land outside Fort Meyers, Florida, and founded a community called The New Jerusalem that he preached would one day be the capital of the world. He expected 8 million residents, but only got 200. In 1908 Teed died from injuries suffered during a run-in with the local marshal; his dwindling community held on until the late 1940s, when the last of his followers disbanded following a property dispute.

The average American receives their first romantic kiss at age 13.

THE WHO?

Ever wonder how rock bands get their names? So did we.
After some digging around, we found these "origin" stories.

THE GIN BLOSSOMS. A gin blossom is slang for the capillaries in your nose and face that burst because of excessive drinking.

PROCUL HARUM. Named after a friend's cat. It's Latin for "Beyond All Things."

THE BOOMTOWN RATS. Named after a gang in Woody Guthrie's autobiography, *Bound for Glory*.

GENERATION X. Named after a book that singer Billy Idol found in his mother's bookcase. It was a mid-1960s sociological essay by Charles Hamblett and Jane Deverson that featured interviews with U.K. teenagers in competing gangs called the Mods and Rockers.

10,000 MANIACS. Came from the cult horror film *2,000 Maniacs*. One of the band members misunderstood the film's name.

FOO FIGHTERS. World War II fighter pilot slang for UFOs.

RAGE AGAINST THE MACHINE. Name refers to a (hoped-for) reaction of ordinary people against corporations, governments, and other invasive institutions that control our society.

HOT TUNA. Originally Hot S**t. The band's record label made them change the second word to Tuna.

DIRE STRAITS. Suggested by a friend who was concerned about the state of the band's finances.

MOTHERS OF INVENTION. Frank Zappa's group was originally just The Mothers. But their record company was concerned it would be interpreted as an Oedipal reference and insisted they change it. The band chose the name from the old saying, "Necessity is the mother of invention."

PEARL JAM. Singer Eddie Vedder suggested the name in honor of his Aunt Pearl's homemade jam, supposedly a natural aphrodisiac containing peyote. "Pearl Jam" is also slang for semen.

BEASTIE BOYS. Beastie supposedly stands for Boys Entering Anarchistic States Towards Inner Excellence.

SQUIRREL NUT ZIPPERS. From a brand of old-time peanut-flavored candy containing caramel and nuts.

BLIND MELON. According to bassist Brad Smith, the name was slang for unemployed hippies in his Mississippi town. Also sounds suspiciously like an anagram of blues singer Blind Lemon.

BLUE ÖYSTER CULT. An anagram of "Cully Stout Beer." It was chosen by a band member one night as he was mindlessly doodling while at a bar with the band's manager.

DEVO. An abbreviation of *de-evolution*, something that the members of the group believe is happening to the human race.

REM. An acronym for rapid eye movement. REM sleep is the state of sleep in which dreams occur.

MATCHBOX 20. Took its name from the combination of a softball jersey bearing the number 20 and a patch that read "matchbox." The name is meaningless. "The two parts aren't even related," singer Rob Thomas has said.

311. The police code for indecent exposure in California.

ZZ TOP. Said to be have been inspired by a poster of Texas bluesman Z. Z. Hill, and rolling-paper brands "Zig Zag" and "Top."

COUNTING CROWS. A reference to an old British poem that said life is as meaningless as counting crows.

L7. Fifties slang for someone who is "square," or uncool.

THE WHO. According to legend, the group, first called The High Numbers, was looking for a new name. Every time someone came up with an idea, they jokingly asked, "The *who?*" Finally, a friend said "Why not just call yourselves 'The Who'?"

Crocodiles can't move their tongues.

THE LAST LAUGH: EPITAPHS

Some unusual epitaphs and tombstone rhymes from the U.S. and Europe, sent in by our crew of wandering BRI tombstone-ologists.

In New York:
Harry Edsel Smith
Born 1903–
Died 1942
Looked up the
elevator shaft
To see
If the car was on
the way down.
It was.

In Massachusetts:
Matthew Mudd
Here lies Matthew
Mudd,
Death did him no
hurt;
When alive he was
only Mudd,
But now he's only
dirt.

In England:
Sir John Strange
Here lies an honest
lawyer,
And that is Strange.

In Scotland:
Stranger, tread
This ground with
gravity:
Dentist Brown is
filling
His last cavity.

In England:
My wife is dead

And here she lies:
Nobody laughs
And nobody cries:
Where she is gone
to
And how she fares
Nobody knows
And nobody cares.

In New York:
He angled in the
babbling brook
With all his angler's
skill.
He lied about the
fish he took
And here he's lying
still.

In Ireland:
Tears cannot
Restore her:
Therefore I weep.

In England:
Beneath this stone
Lie Humphrey and
Joan,
Who rest together
in peace,
Living indeed,
They disagreed,
But now all quarrels
cease.

In Belgrave:
John Racket
Here lies John

Racket
In his wooden
jacket:
Kept neither horses
nor mules
Lived a hog
Died a dog
And left all his
money to fools.

In Massachusetts:
Here lies Ann
Mann.
She lived an old
maid
But died an old
Mann.

In England:
Mrs. Nott
Nott born, Nott
dead . . . Here lies a
woman who was,
And who was Nott.

In England:
Dr. I. Lettsom
When people's ill,
they comes to I,
I physics, bleeds,
and sweats 'em;
Sometimes they
live, sometimes
they die; What's
that to I? I.
Lettsom.

The annual odds of dying by falling from your bed: 2 in 1 million.

BIRTH OF A GIANT, PART I

Ever wonder why Uncle John drives an old Buick? Part of the reason is because he likes old Buicks . . . and part is because David Buick was more than a car manufacturer—he was a bathroom hero. Here's the story of Mr. Buick . . . and the giant auto company that grew out of his work.

A BATHROOM HERO

In 1882 the Alex Manufacturing Company of Detroit, a maker of iron toilet bowls and wooden water-closet tanks, went bankrupt. The company's plant foreman, David Dunbar Buick, and a partner, William Sherwood, took over the company, renamed it Buick and Sherwood, and nursed it back to health.

Buick was an ingenious man; he received 13 patents on various plumbing fixtures between 1881 and 1889, including valves, flushing devices, and even a lawn sprinkler. But his most significant patent was for an improved method of fixing white porcelain onto an iron surface, such as a bathtub.

In other words, Buick is the father of the modern bathtub.

QUIT WHEN YOU'RE A HEAD

If there was ever a time to be in the plumbing business, the early 1890s was it. "With the rapid growth of urban areas and the great increase in the adoption of indoor plumbing facilities, David Buick's fortune would seem to have been assured," George S. May writes in *A Most Unique Machine.* "Instead, he threw this away in favor of another interest—gasoline engines and automobiles."

In 1899 Buick and Sherwood sold their company for $100,000. Buick used his share of the money to found the Buick Auto-Vim and Power Company, which manufactured gasoline motors for use in industry, in farming, and on riverboats. In 1902 Buick changed the name to the Buick Manufacturing Company and began making automobiles. Buick's automobile engine was one of the most advanced of its day, but Buick himself was apparently a terrible businessman.

Odds that you'll be killed by a plane falling from the sky:

DOWN THE DRAIN

By the fall of 1903, Buick had used up all the money he'd made selling his plumbing business . . . and still owed so much money to Briscoe Brothers (his sheet metal supplier) that he signed over ownership of nearly the entire company to Benjamin and Frank Briscoe—on the condition that he'd get it back when he repaid them. But Buick never did repay them, so in September 1903 the Briscoes sold their stake in the company to Flint Wagon Works, a carriage maker in Flint, Michigan.

Buick, still in debt, stayed on to manage the company for the new owners.

ENTER WILLIAM DURANT

The owners of the Flint Wagon Works quickly came to realize that running an automobile company was going to cost a lot more than they were willing to spend. Furthermore, for all his talent as an inventor, David Buick was a terrible manager; the auto company would probably never make any money as long as he was in charge. So in 1904, Flint Wagon Works shoved David Buick aside and turned the reins of the company over to William "Billy" Crapo Durant, owner of a competing carriage company in Flint. Their plan: Flint Wagon Works would continue to own a stake in Buick, but Durant would run it and would raise new money by selling stock to outside investors.

If anyone could turn Buick around, Billy Durant could. In 1884 Durant, then a young insurance salesman, had seen a horse-drawn road cart while on a selling trip in Michigan. He was so impressed with the design that he abandoned insurance, bought the patent rights to the cart, and, together with a hardware clerk named Dallas Dort, formed a company to manufacture and sell the cart.

TYCOON

By the time Durant joined Buick in November 1904, he'd built Durant-Dort into the largest carriage company in the nation, with 14 factories across the U.S. and Canada and a nationwide network of dealerships that sold more than 75,000 carriages a year. It was an awesome achievement, and the owners of the Flint Wagon Works hoped that Durant would be able to work the same magic at Buick.

one in 25 million. Odds that it will happen today: 1 in 7 trillion.

BOO-ICK

As for David Buick: He retained the title of company secretary and still had a seat on the board of directors, but his days of running the firm that bore his name were over. In fact, the Flint Wagon Works considered changing the name to the Durant Motor Company to capitalize on Durant's business fame.

Durant, however, insisted that the car retain the name of its inventor, even though he was worried that the public might mispronounce it "Boo-ick."

For Part II, turn to page 312.

* * *

CONSUMER REPORTS

BRI member Diana Wynn sent us this list, which originated in England, along with the comment: "In case you needed further proof that the human race is doomed through stupidity, here are some actual label instructions on consumer goods."

On a Sears hairdryer: *Do not use while sleeping.*

On a bag of Fritos: *You could be a winner! No purchase necessary. Details inside.*

On a bar of Dial soap: *Directions: Use like regular soap.*

On some Swanson frozen dinners: *Serving suggestion: Defrost.*

On packaging for a Rowenta iron: *Do not iron clothes on body.*

On Boot's Children's Cough Medicine: *Do not drive car or operate machinery.*

On Tesco's Tiramisu dessert (printed on bottom of box): *Do not turn upside down.*

On Marks & Spencer Bread Pudding: *Product will be hot after heating.*

On Nytol sleep aid: *Warning: may cause drowsiness.*

On a Korean kitchen knife: *Warning keep out of children.*

On a string of Chinese-made Christmas lights: *For indoor or outdoor use only.*

On Sainsbury's peanuts: *Warning: contains nuts.*

Goldfish have a memory span of three seconds.

SILENCE IS GOLDEN

The old adage may be true, but would you buy a "recording" with absolutely nothing on it? Apparently, some people would. Here are a few examples of silent "music" . . . proof that you can sell anything.

U N-CAGED. "The highly eccentric American composer, John Cage, is responsible for composing the sheet music for his extremely quiet opus '4 minutes 33 seconds,' which is exactly that much silence. The sheet music is blank and just tells you how long *not* to play."

—The Worst Entertainment

YOURS AND MIME. "In the 1970s a record company in Los Angeles issued a record entitled, 'The Best of Marcel Marceau.' It contained forty minutes of silence followed by a burst of applause. Strangely enough, it sold very well. The company also issued a recording especially for children—it was exactly the same pressing, but had a redesigned cover."

—The Mammoth Book of Oddities

STOP THE MUSIC! In 1953 jukeboxes were so popular that there was no way to get a moment of quiet in some places . . . until Columbia Records issued a disc called "Three Minutes of Silence." According to jukebox operators, it was a big hit.

—The Worst Entertainment

SILENCE THERAPY. "In the 1960s a Staten Island, New York, speech pathologist named Jerry Cammarata did a brisk business with a 52-minute LP designed to 'conjure up previously learned musical experiences, and provide a welcome relief from noise pollutions . . . ' It had no sound on it."

—Oops

SOUND FREE EUROPE. "The Netherlands' Foundation of the Museum of Silence opened an exhibition featuring 75 years of great silences from Dutch radio and television. The silent moments, on loan from the Museum of Broadcasting in Hiversum, are played to visitors over loudspeakers in the museum. Curator Bob Vrakking said he started the foundation in 1990 to promote silence "because it is so scarce."

—Dumb, Dumber, Dumbest

Siberia contains more than 25% of the world's forests.

TRICK SHOTS: FAMOUS FAKED PHOTOS

If there's a lesson to be learned from these historic phonies, it's that people believe what they want to believe. In the face of overwhelming logic—or even solid contrary evidence—people have clung to the notion that the real truth was revealed in these photographs.

FAIRY TALE

Famous Photo: English fairies

Trick Shot: In 1917 Sir Arthur Conan Doyle, "an ardent believer in the occult," announced that, just as he'd always believed, sprites, gnomes, and other types of fairies really did exist. His proof: photographs of fairies taken by 16-year-old Elsie Wright and her 10-year-old cousin Frances Griffiths. "The pictures showed the girls by a wooded stream, with winged sprites and gnomes who danced and pranced and tooted on pipes," Michael Farquhar writes in the *Washington Post*. "Several of the photography experts who examined the pictures declared them free of superimposition or retouching," and the photos, backed by Conan Doyle's testament to their authenticity, launched a national fairy craze.

The Real Picture: "In 1983, the girls, by then old women, admitted that they had posed with paper cutouts supported by hatpins."

SECOND TIME AROUND

Famous Photo: American troops raising the flag on Iwo Jima

Trick Shot: The bloody battle of Iwo Jima (an island 650 miles from Tokyo) began on February 23, 1945. The Japanese were nearly wiped out, and the Americans lost over one-third of their troops. When the U.S. Marines finally took Iwo Jima's highest point, Mt. Suribachi, on February 23, they raised an American flag at the summit. AP photographer Joe Rosenthal was on hand to catch it on film; his dramatic picture is one of the most famous images of the 20th century. It won the Pulitzer Prize, was commemorated with a postage stamp, and was the inspiration for the Marines Memorial in Arlington National Cemetery.

The Real Picture: Rosenthal's photograph was so good that *Life*

No wonder they're gone: In ancient Egypt, pillows were made of stones.

magazine editor Daniel Longwell wondered if it was too good. He asked a *Life* correspondent on Iwo Jima to investigate. Stephen Bates writes in *If No News, Send Rumors*:

> The correspondent reported, that as Longwell suspected, the photo had been staged. The marines had raised a small flag [on their first run up the mountain, which was caught by] a photographer from *Leatherneck*, the Marine Corps magazine. Rosenthal had arrived four hours later . . . [When] the marines reenacted the event with a larger flag.

Longwell refused to use a staged photograph in *Life*, but other publications ran it, and it caught on with the public. "The country believed in that picture," Longwell recounted later, "and I just had to pipe down."

UN-LOCH-ING THE TRUTH
Famous Photo: Loch Ness monster
Trick Shot: On April 19, 1934, Robert Wilson and a companion were walking along the shore of Loch Ness when the friend suddenly shouted, "My God, it's the monster!" Wilson grabbed his camera and snapped a quick photograph of what appears to be "a sea beast with a humpback and a long neck"—the legendary Loch Ness monster, an elusive creature with sightings dating as far back as A.D. 565 The *Daily Mail* ran the photograph, and news of the find spread around the world. Based largely on the strength of Wilson's photograph, it remains one of the most widely believed monster legends to this day. Nearly one million tourists visit Loch Ness each year, hoping to spot "Nessie," and they pump $37 million into the local economy while they're there.
The Real Picture: In 1995 a friend of Wilson's, Christian Spurling, made a deathbed confession that the photograph was a hoax and the "monster" was actually "a toy submarine fitted with a fake sea-serpent head" that Spurling had made himself. "Wilson," the Associated Press reported, "was part of a hoax hatched by his friend Marmaduke Wetherell, a film maker and self-styled big game hunter hired by London's *Daily Mail* newspaper in 1933 to look for Nessie."
Note: Hard-core believers are unimpressed by the revelation. "Eyewitness accounts still suggest that there is something powerful in the loch," says Adrian Shine, founder of a group called The Loch Ness Project.

Oldest form of surgery on Earth: trepanning—drilling holes into the skull.

WEIRD TOYS

Looking for a gift for a special young friend or relative? Want to surprise them with something out of the ordinary? Well, if you don't mind being thrown out of the house, you might want to pick up one of these 100% real (we guarantee it) playthings.

The Tamahonam. Sold in Hong Kong, the Tamahonam is a Tamagotchi toy with Mob connections. Instead of feeding Tamahonam like you would other virtual pets, you "care" for Tamahonam by plying him with cigarettes and booze; instead of playing with him, you give him a knife "to let him wage turf battles."

Feral Cheryl. "A doll that has unshaved legs, dreadlocks, tattoos, pubic hair, and pierced nipples." Made in Australia.

The Grossinator. Made by SRM, the company that brought you the Insultinator. "A minicomputer with a sound chip and programmable buttons with phrases you can mix and match." This one says things like, "I'm going to make a horrible, gross fart" and "How about a foul, smelly barf?"

Brian Jones Pool Toy. "An inflatable, life-size pool toy of Brian Jones, deceased member of the Rolling Stones, that floats face-down in the water, simulating the guitarist's death by drowning in his pool."

Gooey Looey. Exciting action! "Children use their fingers to relieve Louie's congested proboscis before the top of his head flies off."

Savage Mondo Blitzers. "A line of 48 characters named Bad Fart, Snot Shot, Projectile Vomit, Puke Shooters, Loaded Diaper, Eye Pus, and the like."

Letter Bomb. The manufacturer urges kids to "have fun and become a terrorist." Looks like an airmail envelope—"kids write the target's name on it, clap on it heavily, and then give it to the victim within seven seconds so it 'explodes' in his hand." Sold in the Philippines.

A spider's blood is transparent.

OLDER & WISER

Here are some observations about aging from folks who should know. They're from the book Older & Wiser, *by Gretchen B. Dianda and Betty J. Hofmayer.*

"I will never be an old man. To me, old age is always 15 years older than I am."
—**Bernard Baruch, at age 85**

"I don't deserve this award, but I have arthritis and I don't deserve that either."
—**Jack Benny**

"You know you're getting old when you stoop to tie your shoes and wonder what else you can do when you're down there."
—**George Burns**

"If you continue to work and to absorb the beauty in the world around you, you will find that age does not necessarily mean getting old."
—**Pablo Casals, at age 93**

"Old age isn't so bad when you consider the alternative."
—**Maurice Chevalier, at age 64**

"We don't grow older, we grow riper."
—**Pablo Picasso**

"An archaeologist is the best husband any woman can have; the older she gets, the more interested he is in her."
—**Agatha Christie, at age 64**

"We are happier in many ways when we are old than when we were young. The young sow wild oats. The old grow sage."
—**Winston Churchill**

"To be 70 years young is sometimes far more cheerful and hopeful than to be 40 years old."
—**Oliver Wendell Holmes, Sr., at age 80**

"Since I came to the White House I got two hearing aids, a colon operation, skin cancer, a prostate operation, and I was shot. The damn thing is, I've never felt better in my life."
—**Ronald Reagan, at age 69**

"What a wonderful life I've had! I only wish I'd realized it sooner."
—**Colette**

Mmm-mmm good: In the Middle Ages, chicken soup was considered an aphrodisiac.

FOUNDING FATHERS

You already know the names. Here's who they belonged to.

William Colgate. In the early 1800s, making soap at home was a matter of pride with American housewives: 75% of U.S. soap was made at home (although it smelled terrible). In 1806 Colgate opened a soap business and succeeded by offering home delivery, and by adding perfume to his soap.

Gerhard Mennen. While recovering from malaria in the 1870s, he learned so much about the pharmaceutical trade that he opened his own drug store. He made his own remedies, including Mennen's Borated Talcum Infant Powder—America's first talcum powder.

Dr. William Erastus Upjohn. Until he invented a process for manufacturing soft pills, prescription pills were literally hard as a rock—you couldn't smash them with a hammer, and they often passed through a person's system without being absorbed by the body. Upjohn's invention changed all that.

John Michael Kohler. A Wisconsin foundry owner in the 1880s. One of his big sellers was an enameled iron water trough for farm animals. In 1883, convinced that demand for household plumbing fixtures was growing, he made four cast-iron feet, welded them to the animal trough, and began selling it as a bathtub.

William Boeing. When he wasn't working for his father, a timber and iron baron, Boeing and a friend named Conrad Westervelt built seaplanes as a hobby. In 1916 the pair founded Pacific Aero Products. When the U.S. entered World War I in 1917, the Navy bought 50 of his planes. He never worked for his father again.

William Rand and Andrew McNally. Rand and McNally printed railroad tickets and timetables. In 1872 they added maps to their line. Other companies used wood or metal engravings for their maps; Rand McNally used wax engravings, allowing them to update and correct maps at a fraction of the cost. By the early 1900s Rand McNally was one of the largest mapmakers in the country.

The Gold rush of 2075? Scientists think there's gold on Mars, Venus, and Mercury.

ROCK GOSSIP

*Honorary BRI member and Texas author Bill Crawford
submitted these outrageous tales of rock heroes. For more of the
same, check out Margaret Moser and Bill Crawford's
book* Rock Stars Do the Dumbest Things.

BATTLE OF THE STARS

- Neil Diamond collaborated for many years with guitarist
  Robbie Robertson of The Band. In 1976 Robertson invited
  Diamond and Bob Dylan to perform at The Last Waltz, The
  Band's final concert, which was documented by Martin
  Scorsese. Diamond sang first, went backstage, and smugly said
  to Dylan, "You'll have to be pretty good to follow me." Dylan
  snapped back, "What do I have to do, go onstage and fall
  asleep?"

- Though many musicians put them down, former Beatle George
  Harrison appreciated the true talent of the Spice Girls. "The
  good thing about them," Harrison said, "is that you can look at
  them with the sound turned down."

BEATLEMANIAC

In 1967 John Lennon decided that a TV repairman named John
Alexis Mardas was his guru. Lennon called him Magic Alex and
gave him a bunch of money to build a flying saucer, an artificial
sun, and "loudpaper"—wallpaper that was really a speaker system.
None of the inventions worked.

HELL ON EARTH

Kurt Cobain of Nirvana was not a housekeeper. There was old
garbage and rotting food all over his Seattle digs. When the
Cobains tried to hire some help, the maid walked into their house,
then ran out screaming, "Satan lives here!"

WHAT CHILD IS THIS?

For a while, Mick Jagger introduced Bebe Buell as "the mother of
one of my illegitimate children." Jagger got a bit jealous, though,

---

Your stomach has 35 million digestive glands.

when Buell informed him that Steven Tyler of Aerosmith was actually the father of her daughter, who grew up to be actress Liv Tyler.

GROUPIE PROBLEMS
When Linda McCartney died, Paul revealed that he and his wife had spent almost every day together since marrying. That wasn't always how he felt. When she came to visit him in London in 1968, Paul complained to a friend that "an American groupie" was "flying in. I've thrown her out once," explained Paul, "had to throw her suitcase over the wall, but it's no good, she keeps coming back."

VIOLENT OUTBURSTS
In 1988, after allegedly shooting at the walls of his bedroom, the Godfather of Soul, James Brown, pulled out a shotgun at an insurance seminar in Augusta, Georgia, and threatened people because someone had used the bathroom in his trailer. Brown then jumped into his truck and led police on a high-speed chase through two states. Brown finally stopped when police blasted the tires out from under his bullet-riddled vehicle. He was arrested and served two years in a penitentiary.

DOG DAYS
Madonna's pet chihuahua Ciquita was reportedly depressed over the attention lavished on Madonna's new baby, Lourdes. So Madonna sent the pooch to a canine shrink.

PETER PAN
Michael Jackson spent a lot of time with one young friend, trying to fly. Jackson and the boy would close their eyes, hold hands, stand in the middle of his room, and concentrate on floating to the ceiling. "I'd get bored after half an hour or so," recalled the youngster years later, "but Jackson just kept standing there with his eyes closed, wishing he could fly. Once he asked Tinkerbell to sprinkle him with pixie dust. No, I'm sure he wasn't kidding."

POOR TABLE MANNERS
In 1971 brothers Ray and Dave Davies of the Kinks were dining in Manhattan. Dave tried to steal one of Ray's french fries. Ray responded by stabbing his brother in the chest with a fork.

Half of all forest fires are started by lightning.

HOW WE GOT
THE DOLLAR

*Ever wondered why we call our money the "dollar"? At the BRI, we've
been trying to find a good explanation for years. Finally, courtesy of
BRI member Erin Keenan, we've got the answer.*

BACKGROUND

In 1519 Stephan Schlick, a Czech nobleman, discovered a
rich vein of silver on his estate in the Joachimsthal Valley.
He began minting his own coins, which were accepted as *groschen*,
the official currency of the Holy Roman Empire, in 1520.

Schlick's coins were first referred to as *Joachimsthalergroschen*,
after the valley in which they originated. But that was too hard to
pronounce; people began shortening it. The coins became known
as *thalergroschen* . . . and eventually *talers* or *thalers*.

Schlick and his neighbors produced millions of thalers. By 1600
there were 12 million of the coins (an enormous amount for the
time) circulating around Europe. One result was that the *thaler*—
which started out as the equivalent of three German marks—lost
its specific value. It was considered local currency wherever it was
used, and its value changed from region to region.

After a while, the term *thaler* didn't even refer to Schlick's
money anymore. It became generic—synonymous with "any large
silver coin." Eventually, many cultures came up with their own version of the word. In Italy, for example, a large silver coin became
known as a "*tallero*"; in Holland, it was a "*daalder*"; Denmark and
Sweden had "*dalers*"; in Hawaii, silver coins were "*dalas*"; Ethio-
pians exchanged "*talari*"; and in English-speaking countries, a silver
coin was called a "*dollar*."

COMING TO AMERICA

The term dollar was particularly popular in Scotland. As Jack
Weatherford writes in *The History of Money:*

> The Scots used the name dollar to distinguish their currency,
> and thereby their country and themselves, more clearly from
> their domineering English neighbors to the south [who used

Side by side, 2,000 cells of the human body would cover about one square inch.

pounds, shillings, pence, etc]. Thus from very early usage, the word "dollar" carried with it a certain anti-English or anti-authoritarian bias that many Scottish settlers took with them to their new homes in the Americas and other British colonies. The emigration of Scots accounts for much of the subsequent popularity of the word "dollar" in British colonies around the world.

THE AMERICAN WAY
That explains how the term dollar got here . . . but not why it became the official currency of the U.S. After all, American colonists were still mostly loyal British subjects, and would have preferred to trade in pounds, shillings, and other English currency.

The problem was that the colonists suffered from a constant shortage of all coins—especially English ones. Starting in 1695, laws aimed at keeping gold and silver inside Britain's borders were passed by Parliament. "Britain forbade exporting gold and silver to anywhere in the world," Weatherford writes, "including its own colonies."

For a while, colonies minted their own money. But in the mid-1700s, Parliament prohibited that, too. As a result, the only coins available to the American colonists in adequate supplies were Spanish silver *reales* (pronounced ray-ahl-ehs; "royals" in Spanish), which were minted in Mexico, Bolivia, and Peru. The colonists didn't call them *reales*; they preferred the already familiar term *dollar*.

By the time the colonists declared independence in 1776, the "Spanish dollar" was the *de facto* currency of the United States.

WHAT NOW?
In 1782 Thomas Jefferson began to address the issue of a new national currency. It was logical to call it a dollar, as he wrote in his *Notes of a Money Unit for the U.S.*, "The unit or dollar is a known coin and the most familiar of all to the mind of the people. It is already adopted from south to north."

So on July 6, 1785, Congress declared that "the money unit of the United States of America be the dollar." Interesting note: Neither Jefferson nor Alexander Hamilton, the first secretary of the treasury, liked the term. Though they wrote laws that used the term "dollar" or "unit," they did it, Weatherford says, "with the idea that they would think of a better name later."

Americans consume an average 736 million pounds of peanut butter each year.

The U.S. allowed the Spanish dollar to continue as unofficial U.S. currency until the Mint was finally constructed nine years later. The Mint was the first public building, and the dollars it turned out were silver coins—not paper. It wasn't until many years later that the dollar bill came into existence.

* * *

WHERE DID PENNIES, DIMES, AND QUARTERS COME FROM?

- In the 1700s, the relationship of values between coins was arbitrary and confusing. In England, for example, 4 farthings were worth 1 pence, 12 pence were worth 1 shilling, and 20 shillings were worth 1 pound. Plus, the guinea—a slightly larger coin than the pound—was worth 1 pound and 1 shilling. Prices had to be written out explicitly for each coin (12 pounds, 13 shillings, and 4 pence, abbreviated to £12 s.13 p.4). Making change or converting prices from one coin to another was complex and time-consuming.

- In 1535 the Russians realized it would be easier to use a decimal system, and experimented by splitting the ruble into 100 coins, called *denga* (later *kopeks*). But as Jack Weatherford writes, "No matter how rational the new Russian system might have appeared to be, no other monarch wanted to copy Russia, which they regarded as a backward country."

- After the American Revolution, the U.S. was "eager to break with all things royal." In 1782 the "U.S. superintendent of finance sent a report to Congress recommending that the U.S. adopt a decimal system of currency." The goal: To divide the dollar into 100 equal parts. "Jefferson suggested that the smallest part, 1/100 of a dollar, be called a *cent*, from the latin word for 'hundred,' and that a tenth of a dollar be a *dime*, from the latin for 'tenth.' . . . In 1792 America became the first country with a completely decimalized money system." *Note:* England didn't adopt a decimal system of currency until 1971.

The earliest form of electric shock treatment involved the use of electric eels.

UNCLE JOHN'S TOP 12 "CURES" FOR BALDNESS

Now we've got Rogaine and other assorted chemicals to grow hair. But in the past, desperate baldies (like Uncle John) had to resort to everything from shock treatment to "hair-popping." These are 100 percent real, from the book Baldness: A Social History, *by Kerry Seagrave.*

12. BEAR GREASE. In the Old Testament, the second book of *Kings*, Chapter 2, the prophet Elisha tried to cure baldness by applying bear grease to his head. Bad news for bears: It was a popular remedy until the 16th century.

11. SNAKE "SOUP." A popular remedy prescribed by first-century physicians: "boil snakes and rub the broth into the bald areas."

10. ESTROGEN. In the 1980s doctors found that the female hormone estrogen rubbed on a man's scalp could restore hair. Downside: It could also turn a man's voice from bass to soprano, reduce his libido, enlarge his breasts, and produce other female secondary-sex characteristics.

9. DOG PEE. From a pharmaceutical text in 17th-century Scotland came this recipe: "Wash the Head with a Dog's urine, and you shall not be bald."

8. HAIR IN A CAN. Invented in the early 1990s, GLH Formula #9 was an aerosol-based dye with some polymers to frizz up the hair and thicken it. With the scalp dyed the same color as the hair, it gave the appearance of making balding men hair-bearing . . . at least on television. (By the way—it was created by Veg-o-Matic's Ron Popeil . . . and GLH stood for Great-Looking Hair.)

7. THE "ZOO" TECHNIQUE. The Ebers Papyrus, the first known medical record, was written around 1500 B.C., and recommended applying a mixture containing "the fat of a lion, a hippopotamus, a crocodile, a cat, and a serpent to the bald area."

The single most ordered item in American restaurants: French fries.

Alternate suggestion: apply the "burned prickles of a hedgehog, fingernail scrapings, and a mixture of honey, alabaster, and red ocher."

6. FILING IT. A "remedy" used in the 1980s, "head-filing" was a treatment that involved slitting open the scalp and filing the tissue between the skull and hair follicles to thin membranes over the skull. This was supposed to "wake up the follicles."

5. "LOVE" POTION. In the 1880s and 1890s, French physician M. Vidal used cantharides (crushed insects better known as the so-called aphrodisiac Spanish fly) applied to the scalp. His formula combined the crushed bugs with acetic acid in a solution of 90% alcohol.

4. RUBBING IT RAW. A popular baldness treatment during the late 19th century was blistering (vesication) of the scalp. Irritating the area in this manner was thought to produce pooling of blood in the scalp (hyperemia), which provided more nourishment for the hair follicles there.

3. POP CURE. Cosmetologist Rita Hartinger was the foremost practitioner of the "hair popping" technique of hair preservation and regrowth in the 1980s. "When you lift up the scalp from the bone structure by popping," she says, "it stimulates circulation and nourishes the tissue." A journalist described the sound: "as if a kernel of popcorn had exploded on [the] head."

2. SHOCK THERAPY. In the 1890s a German doctor named Seeger recommended the application of frictional electricity to the scalp by means of a special plate. This was rubbed over a dry cloth or piece of soft leather and then over the bald areas several times a day.

And the top baldness cure of all time . . .

1. THE COW LICK. In 1983 John Coombs of Wiltshire, England, was feeding his cow, Primrose, when dust from the feed settled on his bald head. As he bent to fill the trough, Primrose licked his scalp. Eight weeks later, Coombs's wife noticed his hair returning. Coombs went public with his story, and people were soon lining up to get their heads licked by cows.

UNCLE JOHN'S PAGE OF LISTS

For years, the BRI has had a file full of lists. We've never been sure what to do with them . . . until now.

TITLES OF 4 HOLLYWOOD FILMS RE-DUBBED IN HONG KONG:

1. **Fargo:** "Mysterious Murder in Snowy Cream."
2. **The English Patient:** "Don't Ask Me Who I Am."
3. **Boogie Nights:** "His Powerful Device Makes Him Famous."
4. **Nixon:** "The Big Liar."

4 NAMES FOR THINGS YOU DIDN'T KNOW HAD NAMES

1. **Aglet:** "The covering on the end of a shoelace."
2. **Phosphenes:** "The lights you see when you close your eyes hard."
3. **Kick or Punt:** "The indentation at the bottom of wine bottles."
4. **Harp:** "The metal hoop that supports a lampshade."

2 PRESIDENTIAL SUPERSTITIONS

1. Franklin Roosevelt (1933–1945) refused to sit at a table set for thirteen guests.
2. Woodrow Wilson (1913–1921) believed 13 was his lucky number. He once ordered a ship to slow down so he would arrive in Europe on the 13th instead of the 12th.

9 BEANS THAT CAUSE THE MOST GAS

1. Soybeans
2. Pink beans
3. Black beans
4. Pinto beans
5. California small white beans
6. Great northern beans
7. Lima beans
8. Garbanzos
9. Blackeyes
—U.S. Department of Agriculture

5 THINGS YOU SHOULDN'T SAY WHEN A COP PULLS YOU OVER

1. "Aren't you the guy from the Village People?"
2. "That's great. The last guy only gave me a warning also."
3. "You're not gonna check the trunk, are you?"
4. "Hey, you must've been doing 100 just to keep up with me."
5. "I thought you had to be in good physical condition to be a cop."

In Antarctica, sunsets can be green.

JUST THE FAX, PLEASE

Here are a few things to think about the next time you find yourself standing at a fax machine.

ONE WORLD

Fax machines are so common today that it's easy to forget how rare they once were. In 1977 fax machines cost more than $20,000 each . . . and transmitted one blurry, hard-to-read page every six minutes.

By 1989 fax machines began changing not just the way the world did business, but perhaps even the course of history. For example:

- When Lithuania seceded from the USSR, the secessionist government bypassed Soviet censors and communicated directly with the outside world using fax machines.

- Pro-democracy demonstrators on China's Tiananmen Square used fax machines to communicate with supporters within the country and around the world.

- When Nelson Mandela, still a political prisoner in South Africa, began negotiating the terms of his release from prison, the end of apartheid, and South Africa's transition to a full democracy, he did it using a fax machine.

The fax machine revolution "makes totalitarianism impossible," says Max Kampelman, the head of Freedom House, a human rights organization. "Totalitarianism requires the total control of information. That isn't possible anymore."

FAX HISTORY

The fax machine isn't a new idea. Believe it or not, the first one—called a *pantelegraph* because it was supposed to transmit messages over telegraph lines—was patented in 1843, 33 years before Alexander Graham Bell patented the telephone. It was created by Alexander Bain, a Scottish clockmaker who envisioned using

Nothing's new: Ancient Rome had rent-a-chariot businesses.

pendulums at each end of the telegraph to transmit messages, (we won't get into exactly how it worked—it's too confusing). Unfortunately, Bain never figured out how to synchronize the pendulums, and he eventually gave up.

However, in 1864 a Catholic priest named Giovanni Caselli and his partner, Gustav Froment, finally got all the bugs out of Bain's invention. Their version not only worked, it sent messages written on ordinary paper, and could send several of them simultaneously over a single wire.

The duo demonstrated their machine to Emperor Napoleon III of France . . . and he loved it. Under his direction, the French legislature passed a law establishing the world's first fax service between Paris and Lyons—a distance of more than 200 miles. It was inaugurated on May 16, 1865, and by 1868 it was capable of sending more than 110 telegrams an hour. But it never really had a chance to catch on with the public. The system was disrupted by war and the siege of Paris in 1870, and was never resumed.

PHOTO AGE
Over the next four or five decades, scientists worked at perfecting the technique of sending not only messages, but pictures. In 1902 a German physicist named Arthur Korn figured out how to send photo-quality images using special wires. And in 1913 Edouard Belin invented what he called a "Belinograph" (Belino for short), a portable machine, smaller than a typewriter, that could transmit photographic images over standard telephone lines.

This invention revolutionized news reporting. For the first time in history, a newspaper could send someone to any corner of the globe (or at least any corner that had telephones) and, with the portable Belino machine, get photographic images in a matter of minutes—not weeks or months as had been the case before. Invented just in time for the outbreak of World War I, the Belino had an immediate impact on wartime news coverage. By the early 1920s, it was even possible to send "wirephotos" using radio waves, eliminating the need for telephones.

MODERN FAXES
For the next 50 years, these early machines were used almost exclusively to send news pictures around the world and to transmit weather maps by radio to ships at sea. The system was too expen-

sive and too slow to be of much interest to other types of businesses. Besides, AT&T had a monopoly on telephone service in the United States—and because they didn't manufacture fax machines, they fought to prevent customers from using telephone lines for anything other than voice. However, by the late 1960s, the FCC and the courts abolished most AT&T restrictions, opening the way for big companies like Xerox, IBM, and others to create the technology that resulted in the modern fax.

MADE IN JAPAN

- Still, fax machines might never have come into widespread use were it not for the fact that the Japanese language uses thousands of characters (too many to fit on a typewriter keyboard). Typing and telexing is thus much more difficult in Japanese than it is in English.

- Japanese businessmen needed a way to send handwritten communications quickly and accurately over the telephone, so companies like Matsushita, Ricoh, Canon, and NEC spent tens of millions of dollars figuring out how to make fax machines cheaper, faster, and easier to use. They succeeded.

- Sales of fax machines boomed in Japan in the early 1980s, and by the late 1980s the fever had spread to the rest of the world. The steady decline of the price of the machines fueled the boom: by 1983 fax machines that had cost $21,000 in 1977 were selling for $2,600; by 1988 the price slipped under $1,000 for the first time, enabling millions of small business to afford them. By the mid-1990s, the price was as low as $130 and most companies—even small ones—couldn't afford not to have a fax machine. Of course, now everyone needs computers and e-mail . . . but that's another story.

* * *

FAX LINGO

Fax Potato: Someone who faxes materials from one floor of a building to another, because they're too lazy to use the elevator.

Lubberwort is another word for junk food.

ZORRO

*"Out of the night, when the full moon is bright, comes a
horseman known as Zorro." Here's the story of how
the masked man known as Zorro was created.*

PULP FICTION

In 1919 a hack fiction writer named Johnston McCulley published a story called "The Curse of Capistrano" in *All-Story Weekly*, the country's premier serial fiction magazine.

The story was set in Los Angeles during the Spanish Mission period of the late 18th and early 19th centuries. The hero was Don Diego de la Vega, son of a wealthy hacienda owner—a foppish dilettante who detested violence as much as he loved poetry, intellectual pursuits, and finely tailored clothing. By night, however, Don Diego was El Zorro—"the Fox"—a sword-fighting, masked man in black who protected the helpless peasants from the territory's corrupt and greedy land barons.

THE END . . . AND A NEW BEGINNING

"The Curse of Capistrano" ran for five installments. In the end, Zorro defeats his enemy and reveals his true identity to the assembled crowd, saying, "It was difficult to fool you all . . . and now Señor Zorro shall ride no more."

The story was over . . . or so McCulley thought.

Using pen names, McCulley had written hundreds of stories, featuring such characters as Captain Fly-By-Night, Señor Vulture, Señor Devil-May-Care, and Don Peon. None of these survive today, and the same fate might have befallen El Zorro if actor Douglas Fairbanks hadn't picked up a copy of *All-Story Weekly* while he was on his honeymoon in March 1920.

Fairbanks, the "King of Hollywood," was famous for his action-comedy films. They were hits at the box office, but appealed mostly to men . . . and in the early 1920s, afternoon matinee audiences were made up mostly of females, who preferred romances. Theater owners complained that although Fairbanks's films packed the house in the evening, they played to empty theaters during the day.

Snow skiing rule of thumb: Most men fall on their faces, most women on their behinds.

When he read "The Curse of the Capistrano," Fairbanks knew he'd found the role that would allow him to combine the athletics for which he was famous with romantic subplots that would bring women into the theater. He was right.

OPENING NIGHT

The Mark of Zorro, which opened in the Capital Theater in New York—then the world's largest movie theater—made more money on opening day than any previous film had. The theater was so full that the police had to be called after the 9 o'clock show to disperse the crowds.

The film propelled Fairbanks's career to even greater heights: by the end of 1920, he ranked higher in film popularity polls than his wife, Mary Pickford, and higher even than Charlie Chaplin. But it also made Zorro a star. Over the next 80 years, the masked avenger would make hundreds of appearances on film and TV, becoming one of the best-known and most influential icons of pop culture.

For the "Return of Zorro," turn to page 279.

* * *

THE TRUTH ABOUT TAROT CARDS?

Apparently, Tarot cards weren't always used to tell people's fortunes—they originally made up a game called *tarocchi* that was popular with the Italian nobility in the 15th century. Tarocchi was played much like bridge or whist, except that there was a fifth suit of cards which trumped all the other suits. The earliest recorded use of tarot cards in fortune telling is in Venice, Italy, in 1527, but the fad didn't take off until 1781, when a French scholar proposed that cards in the deck contained the knowledge of the Egyptian hieroglyphic *Book of Thoth*, which he claimed had been saved from the ruins of sacked and burned Egyptian temples centuries earlier.

Ropesville, Lariat, and Loop are all towns in Texas.

MADONNA: TEST-MOUSE OR HUSSY-WOMAN?

Many thanks to BRI member Pete McCracken for sending this article to us. It was found in the Edge section of the Portland Oregonian.

GROUND RULES

According to the Edge, when Madonna was in Hungary filming *Evita*, she granted an interview to *BLIKK*, a Budapest magazine.

First, the magazine would ask a question in Hungarian. The question was then translated into English for Madonna. Then, Madonna's answer was translated into Hungarian for the magazine. Finally, Madonna's words were translated again into English at *USA Today's* behest. The resulting chat was, like most events on Planet Madonna, freakishly entertaining. A sampling:

BLIKK: "Madonna, Budapest says hello with arms that are spread-eagled. Did you have a visit here that was agreeable?"

MADONNA: "Thank you for saying these compliments. [Holds up hands.] Please stop with taking sensationalist photographs until I have removed my garments for all to see [laughs]. This is a joke I have made."

BLIKK: "Madonna, let's cut toward the hunt: Are you a bold hussy-woman that feasts on men who are tops?"

MADONNA: "Yes, yes, this is certainly something that brings to the surface my longings. In America, it is not considered to be mentally ill when a woman advances on her prey in a discotheque setting with hardy cocktails present."

BLIKK: "Is this how you met Carlos, your love-servant who is reputed? Were you dating many other people in your bed at the same time?"

There are twice as many billionaires in the U.S. today as there were 10 years ago.

MADONNA: "No, he was the only one I was dating in my bed then, so it is a scientific fact that the baby was made in my womb using him. But as regards these questions, enough! I am a woman and not a test-mouse!"

BLIKK: "OK, here's a question from left space: What was your book *Slut* about?"

MADONNA: "It was called *Sex*, my book."

BLIKK: "Not in Hungary. Here it was called *Slut*."

Note: We called Uncle Edgester, and he says this may be an urban legend. Oh well, it's still great.

* * *

"I'M HERE FOR THE PAYCHECK. ISN'T EVERYBODY?"

Office Team, a temporary employment agency in Menlo Park, California, asked clients to describe the strangest things they've seen in job interviews. Here are some of the answers they received:

- A candidate waiting in the lobby opened a large bag of cheese curls and began eating them. When the interviewer greeted him, the applicant extended a hand covered with orange dust.

- An interviewer walked into the lobby to meet a nervous candidate, whose mouth displayed a ring of antacid from the bottle he was holding.

- When asked why she wanted the job, a recent graduate replied, "I'm here for a paycheck—isn't everybody?"

- When asked where she saw herself in five years, the candidate replied, "How am I supposed to know—isn't that your job?"

- A candidate who was chewing gum noticed the interviewer staring at her mouth. The candidate said: "Oh, I'm sorry. Did you want a piece?"

- A candidate with long fingernails, when asked to take a typing test, reached over the interviewer's desk, grabbed his scissors, and snipped off the nails, one by one. She then said, "That just doubled my number of words per minute."

Big shoes to fill: George Washington's feet were size 13.

RUDNER'S RULES

*Have you heard Rita Rudner yet? At the BRI, we think
she's pretty funny. Here are some of her lines.*

"Blondes have more fun, don't they? They must. How many brunettes do you see walking down the street with blond roots?"

"When I want to end relationships I just say, 'I want to marry you so we can live together forever.' Sometimes they leave skidmarks."

"Waiters and waitresses are becoming much nicer and more caring. I used to pay my check, they'd say, 'Thank you.' That graduated into 'Have a nice day.' That's now escalated into 'You take care of yourself, now.' The other day I paid my check—the waiter said, 'Don't put off that mammogram.'"

"I have to talk to my girlfriend every day on the phone. My husband says, 'Why do you have to talk to her again today? You just talked to her yesterday. What could you possibly have to tell her?' 'Well, for one thing, I have to tell her you just said that.'"

"My husband is English and I'm American. I wonder what our children would be like. They'd probably be rude, but disgusted by their own behavior."

"I'm afraid of planes—I don't trust the oxygen mask. The little orange cup—attached to that bag that's full of nothing."

"Maybe I'm cynical. I don't even think that it's an oxygen mask. I think it's more to just muffle the screams."

"We've begun to long for the pitter-patter of little feet—so we bought a dog. Well, it's cheaper, and you get more feet."

"I think men who have a pierced ear are better prepared for marriage. They've experienced pain, and bought jewelry."

"I have a friend who's so into recycling she'll only marry a man who's been married before."

The average cat has 24 whiskers—12 on each side of its nose.

REEL DUMB

From Stupid Movie Lines by Ross and Kathryn Petrus.

"I am not here for your cold roast chicken. I am here for your love."
— **Vanna White,**
Goddess of Love

"I've had it with cheap sex. It leaves me feeling cheap."
— **John Travolta,**
Moment by Moment

"She was in great pain. We cut off her head and drove a stake through her heart and burned her, and then she was at peace."
— **Anthony Hopkins,**
Bram Stoker's Dracula

"Is it just me or does the jungle make you really, really horny?"
— **Owen Wilson,**
Anaconda

"You goddamned chauvinistic pig ape! . . . You want to eat me? Then go ahead!"
— **Jessica Lange,**
King Kong

"You may know about corpses, fella, but you've got a lot to learn about women."
— **Policeman to morgue worker,** ***Autopsy***

"Your puritan upbringing holds you back from my mon-sters, but it certainly hasn't hurt your art of kissing."
— **Horror writer to woman,**
Orgy of the Dead

"There's a lot of space out there to get lost in."
— **William Hurt,**
Lost in Space

"The dead look so terribly dead when they're dead."
— **Tyrone Power,**
The Razor's Edge

Man: "I'd like to take you out in a monster-free world."
Woman: "I'd like that."
— ***Gamera: Guardian of the Universe***

"I don't want to be killed! I just want to teach English."
— **Panicking teacher,**
Echoes in the Darkness

"War! War! That's all you think of, Dick Plantagenet! You burner! You pillager!"
— **Virginia Mayo,**
King Richard and the Crusaders

The king of hearts is the only king without a mustache.

RANDOM ORIGINS

*Once again, the BRI asks—and answers—the
question: where did this stuff come from?*

GOLD RECORDS

In 1941 RCA Victor released Glenn Miller's "Chattanooga Choo Choo" after he performed it in the movie *Sun Valley Serenade*. It was a huge hit: 1.2 million records were sold in less than three months. So RCA came up with a great publicity gimmick to promote it: They sprayed one of the "master records" with gold paint and on February 10, 1942, presented it to Miller during a radio broadcast in honor of his selling a million copies.

Eventually the Record Industry Association of America (RIAA) copied the idea and started honoring million-selling records with an official Gold Record Award.

Nobody knows for sure what the first million-selling record was. One likely candidate: "Ragging the Baby to Sleep," recorded by Al Jolson on April 17, 1912. (*Yankee Ingenuity*)

CIRCUS TIGHTS

"Tights are believed to have been introduced in 1828 by Nelson Hower, a bareback rider in the Buckley and Wicks Show, as the result of a mishap. The performers wore short jackets, knee breeches, and stockings, but Hower's costume failed to arrive and he appeared for the show in his long knit underwear." (*The People's Almanac*)

KITTY LITTER

In January 1948 in Cassopolis, Michigan, a woman named Kay Draper ran into trouble: the sandpile she used to fill her cat's litter box was frozen solid. She tried ashes, but wound up with paw prints all over the house. Sawdust didn't work, either.

As it happened, her neighbors, the Lowes, sold a product called Fuller's Earth, a kiln-dried clay that was used to soak up oil and grease spills in factories. Ed Lowe, their 27-year-old son, had been looking for a new market for the stuff—he'd tried unsuccessfully to sell it to local farmers as nesting material for chickens.

Average surface temperature of Venus: 864°F, the hottest planet in the solar system.

On the spur of the moment, he convinced Draper that this stuff would make great cat litter. He really had no idea if it would . . . but it did! He sensed the sales potential, put some Fuller's Earth in paper bags and labeled it "Kitty Litter" with a grease pen. Then he drove around, trying to sell it. (Actually, he gave it away at first to get people to try it.) Once people tried it, they invariably came back for more.

"The success of kitty litter enabled pet owners to keep cats inside their homes with little muss or fuss (let's not discuss smell). As a result, an entire industry consisting of cat foods, toys, grooming products, and the like was launched." (*Useless Information* Web site)

RUGBY
William Webb Ellis was playing soccer at the Rugby School in Warwickshire, England, in 1823. His team was losing so badly that he grabbed the ball (a foul—in soccer, you're not allowed to touch the ball with your hands) and started running for the opposing goal. When he got close he drop-kicked the ball into the goal. The score didn't count, of course, and the captain of Ellis's team was so embarrassed that after apologizing to the officials, he suspended Ellis from the team.

The tale of "that play at Rugby" circulated for years afterward, and in 1839 Arthur Pell, the star forward of the Cambridge soccer team, drew up some rules for a new game—named after the Rugby School—that legalized holding, throwing, and running with the ball. The new sport was also the direct forerunner of American football. (*Fenton & Fowler's Best, Worst and Most Unusual*)

AEROSOL CANS
In 1943 the U.S. Agriculture Department came up with an aerosol bug bomb. It used liquid gas inside steel cans to help World War II soldiers fight malaria-causing insects (malaria was taking a heavy toll on the troops). By 1947 civilians could buy bug bombs, too, but they were heavy "grenadelike" things. Two years later, Robert H. Abplanalp developed a special "seven-part leak-proof" valve that allowed him to use lightweight aluminum instead of heavy steel, creating the modern spray can.

Two most dangerous jobs in the U.S.: commercial fishing and logging.

IT FITS YOU TO A "T"

A brief history of the most popular shirt in the world.

YOU BE THE JUDGE

T-shirts have been around so long that nobody knows for sure where they originated or how they got their name. One theory: They were first worn by longshoremen who unloaded tea from merchant ships in Annapolis Maryland during the 17th century. They became known as "tea shirts" and eventually "T-shirts."

Another theory: They were invented by the British Royal Family for use by sailors in the Royal Navy. According to that version, "the monarchy ordered sailors to sew sleeves on their undershirts to spare royalty the unseemly experience of witnessing an armada of armpits. Ergo, the shirt shaped like the letter T."

UNDERSHIRTS ARE SUNK

T-shirts were part of American life as early as 1913, when the U.S. Navy added crew-necked cotton undershirts to its uniform. But they were generally limited to military use. To most American men, the only real undershirt was the sleeveless variety, "with over-the-shoulder straps, a deep neck, and totally exposed armpits."

These, however, were dealt a serious blow in 1934 by actor Clark Gable. In the Oscar-winning film *It Happened One Night*, Gable took off his shirt . . . and wasn't wearing anything underneath.

"Hardly a young man from coast to coast would be caught wearing one after that," Jim Murray wrote in the *Los Angeles Times*. "It almost wrecked an industry, put people out of work."

By then, the T-shirt's transition from underwear to outerwear was already underway, and in the early 1930s, some sports shops began selling shirts with university insignias on them. But they were still primarily considered undershirts. In 1938 Sears, Roebuck & Co. added the "gob-style" short-sleeved undershirts (U.S. Navy sailors were known as "gobs") to its catalog. Price: 24¢ apiece. They sold poorly—it was still too soon after the Gable fiasco.

Q: What golf club did Alan Shepard use on the moon? A: A six iron.

T-SHIRT FASHION

It wasn't until World War II that T-shirts really began to take hold in American culture. Each branch of the military issued millions of "skivvies" in its own color, and in the Pacific islands it was so hot that they were virtually the only shirts that most soldiers wore. When the fighting boys returned home from the war, they brought their taste for T-shirts with them.

"For a while," says J. D. Reed in *Smithsonian* magazine, "the T-shirt suggested the kind of crew-cut cleanliness and neatness indigenous to the new, postwar suburbs." Then, in 1951, the movies struck again: Marlon Brando electrified audiences by wearing a skin-tight T-shirt in Tennessee Williams's *A Street Car Named Desire*. The actor's rippling muscles "gave the garment a sexual *je ne sais quoi* from which America has never recovered," writes one critic. "Elvis Presley cheered it on, sneering in a T-shirt and leather jacket. And James Dean perpetuated the Attitude-with-a-T look in *Rebel Without a Cause* in 1955."

By the end of the 1950s, the T-shirt was no longer just a piece of underwear—it was a fashion statement. Today the American T-shirt industry sells over a billion T-shirts a year. The average American owns 25 of them.

* * *

NEXT TIME YOU USE DUCT TAPE . . .

Think about this: "Duct tape was invented in 1930 by Johnson & Johnson—the Band-Aid people—as a white waterproof cloth tape for use in hospitals. They called it Drybak. It didn't acquire its modern name and distinctive gray color until after World War II, when air-conditioning took off and sealing air-conditioning ducts became an occupation . . .

"Americans use 250 million square yards of duct tape a year. How much is that? Well, if it takes a foot or so to reattach a floppy shoe sole, you could fix 13.5 billion shoes a year, a pair for everyone on the planet, and still have enough left over to repair a La-Z-Boy recliner."

—**Vince Staten,** *Did Monkeys Invent the Monkey Wrench?*

A whale's heart beats about once every 6 1/2 seconds.

STRANGE CELEBRITY LAWSUITS

*Uncle John noticed that a number of the cases in
our "Strange Lawsuits" file involve celebrities
of one sort or another. Here's a sampling.*

THE PLAINTIFF: Mark Twain
THE DEFENDANT: Estes and Lauriat Publishing Co.
THE LAWSUIT: In 1876 the Canadian publishers pirated the text of Twain's book *Tom Sawyer* and put out a low-priced edition. It cut into legitimate U.S. sales and deprived Twain of royalties. When he wrote *The Adventures of Huckleberry Finn* in 1884, he was determined to prevent a recurrence. He decided to publish *Huck Finn* himself . . . but hold off printing it until he had orders for 40,000 copies. That way, the book pirates wouldn't have a chance to undercut him.

Yet somehow, Estes and Lauriat got hold of a manuscript and started selling a pirated edition two months before Twain's authorized edition was available. Livid, Twain sued them.
THE VERDICT: Believe it or not, Twain lost the case. He issued this statement: "[The judge has allowed the publisher] to sell property which does not belong to him but me—property which he has not bought and I have not sold. Under this same ruling, I am now advertising the judge's homestead for sale; and if I make as good a sum out of it as I expect, I shall go on and sell the rest of his property."

THE PLAINTIFFS: Ten people named Jeff Stone, including the mayor of Temecula, California, a guy who works for NASA, and Paul Peterson—who isn't actually a Jeff Stone, but played a character with that name on TV's *Donna Reed Show* from 1958 to 1966
THE DEFENDANT: Jeff Gillooly, Tonya Harding's infamous ex-husband, who had served seven months in jail for plotting the 1994 attack on her skating rival, Nancy Kerrigan

THE LAWSUIT: In 1995 Gillooly filed to change his name to Jeff Stone (so he could have some anonymity). Other Jeff Stones announced that they were outraged. Mayor Stone said his "hard-earned good name would be sullied"; Peterson insisted Gillooly was mocking his sitcom; NASA's Stone spread the word that he simply didn't want to share his name with Gillooly. And then they sued to prevent it.

THE VERDICT: In a ten-minute hearing, the judge ruled there was no basis for stopping Gillooly from becoming a Jeff Stone.

THE PLAINTIFF: Saddam Hussein
THE DEFENDANT: Le Nouvel Observateur, a French magazine
THE LAWSUIT: In an article about Hussein, the magazine described him as a "monster," an "executioner," "a complete cretin," and a "noodle." Saddam sued for libel.
THE VERDICT: Case dismissed.

THE PLAINTIFF: A dentist
THE DEFENDANTS: Johnny Carson and NBC
THE LAWSUIT: In the early 1980s, during a broadcast of the *Tonight Show*, Carson mentioned he'd seen a report saying that dentists were closing their offices due to lack of business. "News like this," he quipped, "hasn't made me so happy since I heard the Gestapo disbanded." An angry dentist immediately sued Carson and the station for $1 million for libel.
THE VERDICT: Case dismissed.

THE PLAINTIFF: Dustin Hoffman
THE DEFENDANT: Los Angeles magazine
THE LAWSUIT: In its March 1997 issue, the magazine superimposed a picture of Hoffman's face—from the film *Tootsie*, in which he dressed as a woman—on the body of a model "wearing a smashing gown and smart high heels." The caption: "Dustin Hoffman isn't a drag in a butter-colored silk gown by Richard Tyler and Ralph Lauren heels." Hoffman sued for $5 million, saying they had turned him into "an unpaid fashion model."
THE VERDICT: Calling Hoffman "one of our greatest living treasures," the judge ordered the magazine to pay the actor $3 million.

Pharmacist rule of thumb: If it's a drug, it has a side effect.

HOW TO MAKE A
MONSTER, PART I

Godzilla is one of the most popular movie monsters in film history.
We told you the story of King Kong in the Giant Bathroom
Reader. *Now here's the story behind Japan's largest export.*

NUCLEAR AGE

On March 1, 1954, at the Bikini atoll in the South
Pacific, the United States tested the world's first hydrogen
bomb. It was 1,000 times more powerful than the A-bombs that
had been dropped on Hiroshima nine years earlier.

American ships were warned to stay out of the test area . . . but
because the project was top-secret, the U.S. government provided
little advance warning to other countries. U.S. officials were certain that the resulting nuclear fallout would land in an empty
expanse of the Pacific Ocean and no one would be in jeopardy.

Unfortunately, they were wrong. The fallout didn't travel in the
direction they expected, and a small Japanese fishing boat named
the *Daigo Fukuryo Maru* ("Lucky Dragon") was in the area where
the nuclear cloud came to earth. Within hours of the blast, the
boat's entire crew became violently ill from radiation poisoning.

On September 23, 1954, after more than six months of agony, a
radioman named Aikichi Huboyama died.

The fate of the crew of the *Daigo Fukuryo Maru* made interna-
tional news. In Japan, headlines like "The Second Atomic
Bombing of Mankind" compared the incident to the bombing of
Hiroshima and Nagasaki in 1945.

ART IMITATES LIFE

While all of this was going on, Japanese movie producer
Tomoyuki Tanaka arrived in Indonesia to oversee a film called
Beyond the Glory. It was scheduled to be the main release for
Japan's Toho Studios the following year, but it never got off the
ground; the Indonesian government refused to issue work visas
to the film's two stars.

Suddenly, Tanaka found himself with time, money, and actors—

but no film to make. In addition, Toho Studios had a big hole in their release schedule. The producer had to come up with a new movie concept . . . fast.

On his flight back to Tokyo, Tanaka stared out the window at the ocean below, desperately trying to think of something. His mind wandered to the H-Bomb tests in the South Pacific and the crew of the *Daigo Fukuryo Maru* . . . and then it hit him: He would combine an American-style monster movie with a serious message about the threat of radiation and nuclear weapons tests.

PROJECT G

Commercially, it made sense. For obvious reasons, the Japanese public was very concerned about nuclear testing. And in theaters, monster movies were hot. The 1933 classic *King Kong* had been re-released in 1952 and made more than $3 million in international ticket sales—four times what it had earned the first time around. *Time* magazine even named the giant ape "Monster of the Year." Its huge success inspired a "monster-on-the-loose" film craze.

One of the first to cash in on the fad was *The Beast from 20,000 Fathoms*, which featured a dinosaur attacking New York City after nuclear tests awakened it from a million-year sleep. The film cost $400,000 to make and was a critical flop—but with $5 million in box office receipts, it was one of the top-grossing movies of the year.

Tanaka got approval from his studio to do a Japanese version. He hired a prominent Japanese science fiction writer to write a knock-off screenplay tentatively titled *Big Monster from 200,000 Miles Beneath the Sea*, but he still wasn't sure what kind of monster to use, or what to call it. So to start out, the film was referred to simply as "Project G" (for Giant).

A PAIR OF EXPERTS

Meanwhile, he began assembling a crew. For director, Tanaka picked Ishiro Honda, a documentary filmmaker who had been Akira Kurosawa's assistant on *The Seven Samurai* (considered the best Japanese film ever made by most critics). Like many of the Toho Studios crew, Honda was a veteran of the Imperial Army. He had visited Hiroshima several months after the atomic bomb was dropped. "When I returned from the war and passed through Hiroshima," he told an interviewer years later, "there was a heavy

On average, 25% of the fish you eat are raised on fish farms.

atmosphere—a fear that the Earth was already coming to an end. That became my basis. Believe it or not, we naively hoped that Godzilla's death in the film was going to coincide with the end of nuclear testing."

Special effects were handled by Eiji Tsuburaya. During the war, he had made unusual propaganda films for the Imperial Army—he recreated battles in miniature, so Japanese movie audiences could follow the progress of the war. His work was so skillful that when the American occupation forces got hold of his reenactment of the bombing of Pearl Harbor, they were convinced they were watching actual combat footage. Since childhood, Eiji had dreamed of making monster movies with his miniature sets. Now he would have his opportunity.

FAT CHANCE

As it turned out, finding a name for the monster was easy. "At the time there was a big—I mean huge—fellow working in Toho's publicity department," director Ishiro Honda recalled. "Employees would argue, that guy is as big as a gorilla.' 'No, he's almost as big as a *kujira* (whale).' Over time, the two mixed and he was nicknamed Gojira' (pronounced GO-dzee-la). So when we were stuck for a name, Tanaka said, 'Hey, you know that guy over in publicity?'"

The name *Gojira* would turn out to be a great choice, but in the beginning it was very confusing. "Very few people, even the cast, knew what *Gojira* would be," says actor Yoshio Tsuchiya. "Since the name was derived from *kujira* [whale] and gorilla, I imagined some kind of giant aquatic gorilla."

GETTING STARTED

Since the scenes using human actors were filmed separately from the special-effects monster footage, Honda didn't have to wait for Tanaka to work out the monster details before beginning to film.

And he didn't: "Honda would direct me to act surprised that Gojira was coming," recalled actor Yu Fujiki, who played a sailor in the film. "But since I didn't know what Gojira would look like, it was kind of weird. So I asked Honda what Gojira would be like, and he said, 'I don't know, but anyway, the monster is coming!'"

For Part II of "How to Make a Monster," turn to page 233.

Virus means "poison" in Latin.

DUMB CROOKS

With crooks like these, we hardly need cops.
Here's proof that crime doesn't pay.

GIVE ME ALL YOUR COUPONS

OSWEGO, NY—"His name may be Jesse James, but that's where any similarity ends. Jesse Clyde James IV was arrested last week after he used his shopper's bonus card to get a discount . . . just before allegedly robbing a grocery store.

"Police said James asked a market clerk if three pies would be cheaper if he used his card, police said. The clerk scanned the card. Then James and two accomplices pulled out a pellet gun and demanded money, police said. They made off with $600. James was arrested soon after."

—**Medford, Oregon, *Mail Tribune*, June 8, 1999**

MUG SHOT

"There are dumb criminals, and then there's the fellow who was found guilty of stealing Matthew Holden's car in London. In the glove compartment, the thief found a camera, which his girlfriend used to photograph him posing with the car in front of his own house. The vehicle was later recovered—with the camera and film still inside. Holden had it developed and brought the prints to the cops on the case . . . who recognized the crook, and arrested him."

—***Christian Science Monitor*, July 26, 1999**

CAUGHT WITH HIS PANTS DOWN

"Knife-wielding James Boulder was caught in September 1993 when his [pants] fell down as he fled from a store in New Jersey that he'd just robbed. He then tripped over a fire hydrant and knocked himself out."

—*The Fortean Times Book of Inept Crime*

DUMB AND UNLUCKY

CARDIFF, WALES—"Mark Cason, 29, decided to rob a local post office. He purchased gloves and a mask but forgot to put them on . . .

"Mark took more than $15,000 worth of British pounds, but his

Sleeping around: Louis XIV owned 413 beds.

arms were so full he could not open the post office door to leave. So he asked two children to hold the door for him. They did, and jotted down his car license number as he pulled into traffic.

"Mark promptly got stuck in a traffic jam, so he ran to a train station, where he caught a train to a nearby town. He checked into a hotel using a fake name and said to the clerk, 'If the police ask for me, I'm not here.' He asked if he could put 'a large amount of money' in the hotel safe.

"When police arrived, Mark told them his occupation was 'armed robber.' He was sentenced to five years in prison."

—*The Portland Oregonian*

NO ANCHOVIES, PLEASE

"Christopher Kennedy, 36, and Johnny Poston, 26, allegedly ordered a couple of pizzas using their real names, phone number, and home address. When the delivery man had trouble finding their house, he called and arranged to meet the two men nearby.

"The delivery person got out carrying the pizzas and they put a gun to his face,' Lt. Julius Lee said. 'So the delivery person threw the pizzas at them, got back in his car and drove off.' He called the police, who had no problem finding the correct house. The pair was charged with armed robbery."

—*Dumb Crooks* Web site

HOW 'BOUT A BREAKFAST BURRITO?

YPSILANTI, MI—"The *Ann Arbor News* reported that a man failed to rob a Burger King because the clerk told him he couldn't open the cash register without a food order. So the man ordered onion rings, but the clerk informed him that they weren't available for breakfast. The frustrated robber left."

—*A Treasury of Police Humor*

RIGHTEOUSLY INDIGNANT

"A robbery suspect in a Los Angeles police lineup apparently just couldn't control himself. When detectives asked each man in the lineup to repeat the words, 'Give me all your money or I'll shoot,' the man shouted, 'That's not what I said!'"

—*The Edge*, April 12, 1999

What's a *melcryptovestimentaphiliac?* Someone who compulsively steals ladies underwear.

THE REAL POP ARTISTS

*The works of pop artists like Andy Warhol and Roy Lichtenstein
sell for millions of dollars . . . but what about the artists
who created images that are really part of popular
culture—do they make millions, too? Not quite.*

HARVEY BALL
Famous Work of Art: The smiley face
Compensation: $45
Inspiration: In 1963 the Massachusetts-based State Mutual Life
Insurance Company took over a small Ohio insurance company.
The transition was so rocky that State Mutual launched an inter-
nal "friendship" campaign to improve staff morale. They hired
Ball, a freelance artist, to come up with a friendly graphic for a
lapel button employees could wear. He came up with the smiley
face.

State Mutual made up about 100 buttons and used the graphic in
a consumer ad showing President John Adams wearing one. That
was about it . . . until tens of thousands of people who saw the ad
wrote to the company asking for buttons. State Mutual Life took
advantage of the PR opportunity and distributed them until the
late 1960s. Then the symbol took on a life of its own and was used
on everything from clocks to underwear.

Note: Ball never filed for a copyright or a trademark, and never
made any more money off his creation. But he's angry now: In 1998
he learned that a Frenchman named Franklin Loufrani had trademarked the design in France . . . and owns the symbol in 79 other
countries. Loufrani, who's made millions from the smiley face,
claims he invented it in 1968 "to illustrate positive stories" after
student riots rocked France that year. However, there are photographs taken in 1964 that disprove this.

Ball says he's less concerned about the money than he is about
receiving credit for inventing the design. "Never in the history of
mankind or art," he says, "has any single piece of art gotten such
widespread favor, pleasure, enjoyment, and nothing has ever been
so simply done and so easily understood in art."

PHIL KRACZKOWSKI
Famous Work of Art: The original GI Joe head
Compensation: $600
Inspiration: In 1963 Hasbro was planning the first boy's doll ever.
They spent most of their time creating a fully articulated body . . .
then realized they still needed a head. So they contacted
Kraczkowski.

"I asked them exactly what they wanted," Kraczkowski recalls,
"and they said they would like a young, good-looking American
man . . . It wasn't a big deal because I was used to doing faces . . . I
did the Kennedy-Johnson inaugural medal, the Johnson-Humphrey
inaugural medal. I had three sittings with J. Edgar Hoover for a
life-size bust."

The executives didn't tell Kraczkowski the young man was going
to be a soldier—that was top secret. "They said the head had to fit
a certain doll," Kraczkowski says. "I said okay."

Ten days later, he turned in the head. "Apparently it was perfect,"
Kraczkowski says. "Does GI Joe look like John Kennedy? I'd done . . .
full busts of him preceding the GI Joe project, so maybe the resemblance got in there subconsciously . . . I made six hundred dollars on
the project—pretty good money. My first and last toy job."

CAROLYN DAVIDSON
Famous Work of Art: The Nike Swoosh
Compensation: $35
Inspiration: In 1972 the Portland, Oregon-based Blue Ribbon
Shoe Company was looking for a new name and logo. They
couldn't afford a big-time graphics firm, so the company's founder,
Phil Knight, asked an art student from nearby Portland State
University to design something. It was Carolyn Davidson's first
"real job." Knight wanted to imitate the Adidas logo—a stripe
that was "functional" because it provided support, but looked
"distinctive."

"Try to make it reflect movement and speed," he told Davidson.

But, as J. B. Strasser and Laurie Becklund write in their book
Swoosh, that wasn't so easy. "Davidson fretted for hours over her
designs, coming up with, among other ideas, a thick stripe with a
hole in the middle. After hours of frustration, she informed Knight
that support and movement were hard to reconcile, graphically
speaking. Support was static, movement was the opposite. She rec-

ommended he incorporate the support system into the shoe itself, and that he use the stripe to convey movement."

None of the shoe execs were particularly enthusiastic about Davidson's designs. But they flipped through her drawings and finally settled on "a fat, fleshy checkmark."

"I don't love it," Knight told Davidson, "but I think it'll grow on me." She named her own price for the work.

Note: The company's new name, Nike (the goddess of victory in Greek mythology), was selected a few days later. The term "swoosh" had been coined to describe the fabric of an early shoe; today no one remembers why or when it became associated with the logo.

GARY ANDERSON
Famous Work of Art: The recycling symbol
Compensation: $2,500
Inspiration: In 1970 Anderson, a 23-year-old college senior at the University of Southern California, entered an Earth Day contest to produce a universal symbol of recycling. It was sponsored by the Container Corporation of America (CCA), one of America's largest producers of recycled paper.

Anderson based his symbol on the Möbius strip, which is created by twisting a piece of paper once over and connecting the tips to create a continuous, single-edged, one-sided surface. CCA allowed Anderson's design to become public domain, and now it belongs to everyone. Anderson works at an "engineering, architectural, and planning firm" in Baltimore, and remains "environmentally concerned."

*　*　*

"Ever wonder if illiterate people get the full effect of alphabet soup?"

—*John Mendoza*

The Statue of Liberty is patented.

VIDEO TREASURES

Ever found yourself at a video store staring at thousands of films you've never heard of, wondering which ones are worth watching? It happens to us all the time—so we decided to offer a few recommendations.

CHAN IS MISSING (1982) *Comedy* (B&W)
Review: "Two cab drivers try to find the man who stole their life savings. Wry, low-budget comedy filmed in San Francisco's Chinatown was an art-house smash. The first full-length American film produced exclusively by an Asian-American crew." (*VideoHound's Golden Movie Retriever*) Director: Wayne Wang.

THE YEAR OF LIVING DANGEROUSLY (1983) *Drama*
Review: "Indonesia, 1965: In the middle of revolutionary fervor, a wet-behind-the-ears reporter and a member of the British Embassy find steamy romance. This politically charged, mega-atmospheric winner has the romance and intrigue of a modern *Casablanca*." (*Seen That, Now What?*) Stars: Sigourney Weaver, Mel Gibson, Linda Hunt (won an Oscar for the role). Director: Peter Weir.

THE BIG SLEEP (1946) *Mystery*
Review: "One of the most stylish and satisfying film noir mysteries of the '40s. Lauren Bacall is at her sexiest and Humphrey Bogart is at his peak. The plot is exquisitely intricate, so don't blink—and don't miss this movie. The atmosphere and dialogue are impeccable." (*Mark Satern's Illustrated Guide to Video's Best*)

EUROPA, EUROPA (1991) *French-German/Drama*
Review: "Based on the death-defying autobiography of Solomon Perel, this stunning film traces the author's real-life adventures during World War II. A Jewish teenager accepted into the Nazi Youth Party, Perel sees the war from all sides in this ironic, spine-tingling story." (*Video Movie Guide*) Director: Agnieszka Holland

CHASING AMY (1997) *Romantic Comedy*
Review: "Winning, original comedy-drama about a comic book artist who lives with his dour work partner—until he meets an attractive up-and-coming female artist with a dynamic personality. He's seriously smitten—and stays that way even after learning that she's gay."

The Oval Office in the White House is only 22 feet long.

Writer-director Kevin Smith hits all the right notes in this honest and appealing film, which refuses to take the easy way out (just like his lead character) right to the end." (*Leonard Maltin's 1998 Movie and Video Guide*) Stars: Ben Affleck, Joey Lauren Adams.

THE MAN WHO SHOT LIBERTY VALANCE (1962) *Western*
Review: "One of the greatest of director John Ford's westerns, a moving, bitter meditation of immortality and survival. Jimmy Stewart is cast as an idealistic lawyer who becomes famous for killing a notorious badman, played by Lee Marvin. John Wayne incarnates his own with subtle melancholy." (*Movies on TV*)

TAMPOPO (1986) *Japanese/Social comedy*
Review: "The tale of a Japanese widow who perfects the art of making noodles under the instruction of an urban cowboy truck driver is cleverly interspersed with amusing vignettes about food and social pretension. Funny, enjoyable, and you'll find yourself craving a bowl of hot ramen." (*Seen That, Now What?*) Director: Juzo Itami.

THE EMERALD FOREST (1985) *Adventure*
Review: "Captivating adventure about a young boy who is kid-napped by a primitive tribe of Amazons while his family is traveling through the Brazilian jungle. Boothe is the father who searches 10 years for him. An engrossing look at tribal life in the vanishing jungle. Beautifully photographed and based upon a true story." (*VideoHound's Golden Movie Retriever*) Director: John Boorman.

A GREAT WALL (1986) *Comedy*
Review: "A warm comedy about the clash of cultures that results when a Chinese-American family returns to its homeland. It is the first American movie to be made in the People's Republic of China. As such, it gives some fascinating insights into Chinese culture and often does so in a marvelously entertaining way." (*Video Movie Guide*) Director/Star: Peter Wang.

THE NASTY GIRL (1990) *German/Drama*
Review: "A teenage girl innocently decides to write about 'My Town in the Third Reich' . . . and her research reveals the truth behind the good citizens' official story. Based on a true story." (*Seen That, Now What?*) Director: Michael Verhoeven.

Researchers say 1 in 4 people admit to snooping in their host's medicine cabinet.

MYTH-SPOKEN

We hate to say it (well actually, we like to say it), but some of the best-known quotes in history weren't said by the people they're attributed to . . . and some weren't even said at all!

L INE: "Go west, young man, go west."
SUPPOSEDLY SAID BY: Horace Greeley, publisher of the *New York Tribune*, in 1851
ACTUALLY: Even in 1851, big-city media had all the influence. Greeley merely reprinted an article from the Terre Haute, Indiana, *Express*, but ever since, people have identified it with him. The line was really written by a "now forgotten and never very famous" newspaperman named John Soule.

LINE: "Taxation without representation is tyranny!"
SUPPOSEDLY SAID BY: James Otis, a lawyer arguing in a Boston court against British search warrants, in 1761
ACTUALLY: For years, schoolchildren were taught that this was "the rallying cry of the American Revolution." But no one in Otis's time ever mentioned him saying it. It wasn't until 1820, almost 60 years later, that John Adams referred to the phrase for the first time.

LINE: "This is a great wall!"
SUPPOSEDLY SAID BY: President Richard Nixon
ACTUALLY: It's one of the lines used to denigrate Nixon . . . and he did say it to Chinese officials in 1972 when he saw the Great Wall for the first time. But it's a bum rap. As Paul Boller and John George write in *They Never Said It*:

> This was not his complete sentence, and out of context it sounds silly. It is only fair to put it back into its setting: "When one stands here," Nixon declared, "and sees the wall going to the peak of this mountain and realizes it runs for hundreds of miles—as a matter of fact, thousands of miles—over the mountains and through the valleys of this country and that it was built over 2,000 years ago, I think you would have to conclude that this is a great wall and that it had to be built by a great people."

Top speed of a chicken at full gallop: 9 mph.

LINE: "Let them eat cake."
SUPPOSEDLY SAID BY: Marie Antoinette, Queen of France, when she was told that conditions were so bad that the peasants had no bread to eat
ACTUALLY: She was alleged to have said it just before the French Revolution. But the phrase had already been used by then. It has been cited as an old parable by philosopher Henri Rousseau in 1778—a decade or so before Marie Antoinette supposedly said it. Chances are, it was a rumor spread by her political enemies.

LINE: "There are three kinds of lies: lies, damn lies, and statistics."
SUPPOSEDLY SAID BY: Mark Twain
ACTUALLY: Twain, one of America's most quotable writers, was quoting someone else: Prime Minister Benjamin Disraeli of England.

LINE: "Keep the government poor and remain free."
SUPPOSEDLY SAID BY: Justice Oliver Wendell Holmes
ACTUALLY: Ronald Reagan said it in a speech. But it wasn't written by a speechwriter. Reagan's "speechwriting office" told a reporter, "He came up with that one himself."

* * *

CRÈME DE LA CRUD

The Portsmouth Symphonia was unique in that fully two-thirds of its members did not know how to play a musical instrument.
Result: Their music (if you could call it that) was appallingly bad . . . but also "refreshingly original," one reviewer wrote. "Unhampered by preordained melody, the orchestra tackled the great compositions, agreeing only on when they should start and finish. The cacophony which resulted was naturally an immense hit."

Conductor Leonard Bernstein credited the Symphonia with "changing his attitude to *The William Tell Overture* forever." The Symphonia recorded two records, both of which "became very popular, demonstrating yet again the public's great appreciation of incompetence."

When astronomer Tycho Brahe lost the tip of his nose in a duel, he replaced it with a gold one.

"SPEAK FOR YOURSELF, JOHN!"

Ever let someone speak for you? Sometimes it works, sometimes it doesn't. The other day Uncle John was in the . . . uh . . . reading room with nothing but a book of poetry. He opened it to Longfellow's "The Courtship of Myles Standish," and emerged wondering out loud how often "that sort of thing" happened. We took the hint and began looking for examples. Here's what we found.

MARRIAGE PROPOSAL

Who Said It: John Alden

Speaking For: Myles Standish

What Happened: As military leader of the pilgrims, Capt. Myles Standish was fearless. With ladies, however, he was the opposite. Standish was so afraid of expressing his love to Priscilla Mullens that he asked his young friend Alden to do it for him. The only problem: Alden was also in love with Mullens. Nonetheless, he went off to proclaim Standish's love to the woman, keeping his own a secret.

As it happened, Mullens harbored her own secret feelings for Alden. When Alden delivered Standish's proposal instead, legend has it she replied, "Why don't you speak for yourself, John?" Note: Mullens married Alden. Standish supposedly went into the woods for a few days and sulked. He eventually got over it.

HISTORIC SPEECH

Who Said It: Norman Shelley

Speaking For: Winston Churchill

What Happened: A week after the demoralizing defeat of British and French troops by Germany at Dunkirk in 1940, Prime Minister Winston Churchill made one of the most stirring radio addresses in history. Speaking to the English public, he declared, in no uncertain terms, that the British would not fold.

> We shall fight on the beaches, we shall fight on the landing grounds, we shall fight in the fields and in the streets, we shall fight in the hills; we shall never surrender.

First president to shake hands in greeting: Thomas Jefferson. Earlier presidents bowed.

Historians say that this specific speech provided the morale boost that helped England summon the strength to continue the war effort . . . and ultimately win.

But Churchill didn't make the speech. He was "too busy to appear on the radio," so he asked Shelley to fill in—an actor who had perfected the Churchillian delivery to such a degree that few people could pick which voice was Shelley's and which was Churchill's.

PRESIDENTIAL QUOTE
Who Said It: Larry Speakes
Speaking For: President Ronald Reagan
What Happened: In 1985 President Reagan and Soviet premier Mikhail Gorbachev met for a summit in Reykjavik, Iceland. Afterward, Speakes told the press that Reagan had declared to the Russian: "There is much that divides us, but I believe the world breathes easier because we are talking together."

In truth, Reagan hadn't said it—or anything Speakes considered worth quoting that day. So the press secretary made it up. No one at the White House objected at the time. But when Speakes later admitted it in his 1988 book *Speaking Out*, all hell broke loose. The press was "outraged," and Reagan (who had to have at least implicitly condoned it at the time) strongly condemned the quotes as "fiction." Speakes paid for it: he was pressured to resign his job as senior public relations officer at Merrill Lynch, which had hired him after he left the White House. Speakes later apologized publicly for his "mistake."

PHILOSOPHICAL RAMBLINGS
Who Said It: Yoda
Speaking For: Obi-Wan-Kenobi (Alec Guinness)
What Happened: On the set of *The Empire Strikes Back*, Alec Guinness had an easy way of avoiding dialogue he didn't feel comfortable saying. Yoda was in nearly all of his scenes, so "if he didn't want to deliver one of his philosophical speeches," Dale Pollock writes in *Skywalking*, "he'd say to the director, 'Why doesn't the little green thing do this one?'" And Lucas would accommodate him.

At the moment of conception, you spent about half an hour as a single cell.

THE ULTIMATE
GOLDEN TURKEY

*There are bad movies . . . and then there are BAD movies. Years ago
the Medved brothers reintroduced stinkers like Plan 9 From Outer
Space to the public in their groundbreaking books, The 50 Worst
Films of All Time and The Golden Turkey Awards. Then Mystery
Science Theater 3000 gave us a chance to watch the best of the worst
on TV. Today there are millions of bad movie buffs . . . and
Uncle John is one of them. Here's one of his favorite stinkers.*

R OBOT MONSTER (1953)
Starring George Nader, Claudia Barrett, Selena Royle, John
Mylong, George Barrows
BACKGROUND: Director Phil Tucker made this opus for less
than $20,000. He couldn't afford to rent a real robot costume, but
(fortunately for bad movie lovers) he knew a guy named George
Barrows, who owned his own gorilla suit. "When [moviemakers]
needed a gorilla in a picture," Tucker explained to the Medveds in
The Golden Turkey Awards, "they called George. [He] got like forty
bucks a day . . . [but] I thought, 'George will work for me for nothing. I'll get a diving helmet, put it on him, and it will work!'"

It did work. Years later, Tucker's robot even won an award.
Okay, it was a Golden Turkey Award for "The Most Ridiculous
Monster in Screen History." But it was well-deserved. "Unlike
many other cinematic robots," Ken Begg writes in *Jabootu's Bad
Movie Universe,* "[this one] has the appearance of a morbidly obese
man in a shaggy gorilla costume, adorned with a deep-sea diving
helmet over his nylon-stocking-bedecked noggin"—and the helmet
was topped with a rabbit-ears TV antenna. You have to see it to
believe it.

Note: Strange anomaly for such a seat-of-its-pants production:
Robot Monster was filmed in 3-D, and the music recorded in
stereo. Even more surprising: the score was written by Elmer
Bernstein, later one of Hollywood's most accomplished composers
(he wrote the music, for example, for *The Magnificent Seven* and
The Great Escape).

Fast food: A bat can eat as many as 1,000 insects an hour.

THE PLOT: Ro-Man, from the planet Ro-Man, arrives on Earth. His mission: wipe out all human life with his deadly Calcinator Ray. He unleashes a barrage of cheesy-looking death rays, then reports to his master—the "Great One"—via a bubble machine, that the entire human population is dead.

Wrong. Ro-man's boss—who looks suspiciously like Ro-Man (with a different diving helmet)—informs him that there are still eight people left alive . . . and six happen to be hiding behind a force field right near Ro-Man's cave. Who are they? The Professor, Mary Anne, Ginger . . . oops, wrong castaways. A German professor, his hunky helper (Roy), a mom (Mom), her two little kids (Johnny and Carla), and her grown daughter (Alice).

Ro-Man's job is to wander around the desert and find them, then figure out why they're not dead—and then kill them. But the shaggy robot runs into a little problem: he falls for Alice. The Great One is pretty ticked off about that.

Meanwhile, Alice and Roy are inspired by the apocalypse, and fall in love. (Lucky for Alice, since he's "the only male alive not related to her.") They kiss, Roy takes his shirt off, then they get married. The Great One gets a bit upset with Ro-Man and vaporizes him . . . along with the Earth.

The end? Not exactly—turns out Johnny has hit his head and dreamed the whole thing. Ha-ha-ha! Now *The End.*

WATCH FOR . . .

- Ro-Man (Barrows) walking . . . and walking . . . and walking in the desert. It must have been 120° in that suit—it's amazing Barrows survived. You gotta feel for the guy—and he was doing it for nothing!

- The Cave. Why is Ro-Man, who has wiped out everyone on Earth and can have his pick of locations, hanging out in a cave with a bubble machine?

- George Nader gratuitously taking his shirt off. Nader was apparently on his way to being a star in the late 1940s when he got caught doing something he . . . umm . . . wasn't supposed to be doing. He was relegated to tripe like this, but he still had the bod.

Mayonnaise is an excellent skin moisturizer.

- Ro-Man kills the little girl. This was actually pretty strange and out of place. At least one reviewer speculates it was unplanned—the girl who played her was just so annoying that the rest of the crew insisted on getting her off the set any way they could.

- Ro-man's moment of indecision: "I need guidance Great One, for the first time in my life I am not sure." What's confusing him? He's hot for Alice, and it doesn't compute.

- The "surprise" ending.

MEMORABLE DIALOGUE:
Ro-Man: (informing his master that he has wiped out the human race): "All are gone now. The way is clear for our people."
Great One: "I want facts, not words!"
Ro-Man: "Fact A! My pulse has been reduced to plus zero zero."
Great One: "Reject! Error!"
Ro-Man: "Error? But Great Guidance, I have proved it! My energizer has scan-checked by square feet! No life above lepidopteron level exists!"
Great One: "My calculator is more accurate! In the twenty-second category there is an error of sixteen-billionths!"
Ro-Man: "The Great One is never wrong. Then there are perhaps eight people left on Earth?"
Great One: "Not perhaps! Precisely! Find and destroy them!"

Roy (Arguing with Alice, who accuses him of being bossy): "I'm bossy? You're so bossy you should be milked before you come home at night!"

Ro-Man: "Calculate your chances! Negative, negative, negative . . . is there a choice between a painless surrender death and the horror of resistance death? Show yourselves!"

(Uncle John's favorite)
Johnny: "I think you're just a big bully, picking on people smaller than you are!"
Ro-Man: "Now I will kill you."

Most-mentioned woman in the Bible: Sarah, 56 times.

CARLINISMS

Irreverent thoughts from comedian George Carlin.

"The other night I ate at a real nice family restaurant. Every table had an argument going."

"If the shoe fits, get another one just like it."

"McDonald's 'breakfast for under a dollar' actually costs much more than that. You have to factor in the cost of coronary bypass surgery."

"Recently, in a public bathroom, I used the handicapped stall. As I emerged, a man in a wheelchair asked me indignantly, 'Are you handicapped?' Gathering all my aplomb, I looked him in the eye and said, 'Not now. But I was before I went in there.'"

"There is something refreshingly ironic about people lying on the beach contracting skin cancer in an attempt to acquire a purely illusory appearance of good health, while germ-laden medical waste washes up on the sand all around them."

"I think we should attack Russia now. They'd never expect it."

"Honesty may be the best policy, but it's important to remember that apparently, by elimination, dishonesty is the second-best policy."

"Some people see things that are and ask, Why? Some people dream of things that never were and ask, Why not? Some people have to go to work and don't have time for all that s***."

"Who says life is sacred—God? Hey, if you read your history, God is one of the leading causes of death."

"A lot of times when they catch a guy who killed twenty-seven people, they say, 'He was a loner.' Well, of course he was a loner; he killed everyone he came in contact with."

"Whenever I hear about a 'peacekeeping force,' I wonder: If they're so interested in peace, why do they use force?"

"Most people work just hard enough not to get fired and get paid just enough money not to quit."

The Mayan Empire lasted six times as long as the Roman Empire.

LET'S PLAY BALLBUSTER!

Millions of dollars were spent trying to make these toys work. But the only amusement they'll ever bring is a few bathroom laughs. Here are six classic toy flops.

BALLBUSTER
Product: No joke—the Mego Toy Co. introduced it in 1976 as "a family game that's loads of fun." It consisted of wire stalks attached to a gridlike base. Each was topped with a hinged red plastic ball. The object, according to Mego, was to "use your balls to bust your opponent's, if you can. Break 'em all and you're a winner!"

Problem: Somehow, Mego thought it could get away with the name. But the first preview of the Ballbuster TV commercial—shown to buyers from major toy and department stores—ended that illusion. The ad showed a family playing the game, after which the husband turned to his wife and said, "Honey, you're a real ball buster!" "The stunned silence that followed," Kirchner writes, "triggered the first suspicions that Ballbuster was not destined to displace Parcheesi in the pantheon of classic games."

FLUBBER
Product: Hasbro's Flubber was tied to Walt Disney's 1962 hit film, *Son of Flubber* (sequel to *The Absent Minded Professor*). It was similar to Silly Putty: "Flubber is a new parent-approved material that is non-toxic and will not stain," the company proclaimed. "Flubber acts amazing. It bounces so high. It floats like a boat. It flows and moves." Flubber was made out of synthetic rubber and mineral oil, so it was cheap to produce . . . but it was sold for a high profit. Hasbro, still a relatively small company at the time, was expecting a good year.

Problem: Flubber had one significant difference from Silly Putty—it made people sick. More than 1,600 kids and their parents came down with sore throats, full body rashes, and other reactions from handling the stuff. Hasbro had to recall Flubber . . . and then had

An anemophobic person is someone who's afraid of high winds.

to find a way to get rid of several tons of it. Flubber floated, so they couldn't dump it in the ocean; they couldn't incinerate it, because it gave off "noxious black smoke" . . . so they buried it behind a new warehouse and put a parking lot over it. According to company legend, "on the hot summer days, Flubber oozed through cracks in the pavement—a primordial reminder of the vagaries of the toy business." Hasbro had been profitable in 1961, but Flubber almost put them out of business in 1963.

THE OOBIE

Product: It's the world's first—and so far, the last—hitchhiking toy, introduced by Parker Brothers at a time when hippies were bumming rides around the country and hitchhiking was still considered reasonably safe. Oobie was a clam-shaped plastic container with an address label and cartoon eyeballs painted on the lid. The idea was this: kids would write a note to a friend and put it inside, then put the friend's address on the outside and leave Oobie someplace where strangers would find it. If the stranger was headed in the direction of the address of the intended recipient, they could "help Oobie on his journey, hitchhiker style, across the street or across the country." With enough help, Oobie would eventually be delivered.

Problem: "Most parents," Paul Kirchner writes in *Forgotten Fads and Fabulous Flops*, "even in that more innocent age, did not like the idea that some pervert finding the Oobie would not only get their child's address, but be equipped with a splendid excuse to drop by. Parker Brothers quickly got the message—and Oobie was a dead letter."

ANGEL BABIES

Product: In the late 1970s, the Ideal Toy Corp. bought a product called "Fairies" from another toy company. They were tiny dolls with mechanical fluttering wings, and might have sold quite well . . . if an executive at Ideal hadn't insisted on changing the name to Angel Babies. They had to change the doll, too. "Now," says one toy industry insider, "they were these chunky little toddlers with halos and wings. They lived on clouds, played harps, very cute." Ideal introduced the toy at the annual New York Toy Fair in February, and waited for Christmas orders to pour in. They never came.

At least 8,000 human-made objects are orbiting the Earth.

Problem: Ideal forgot something important. "The buyers said, 'OK, Angel Babies,'" recalls the toy industry insider. "'They're dead babies, right? Babies that died and now they're in heaven.' So of course, nobody would touch it." The product died an instant death (and went to . . . ?).

THE ELVIS DOLL
Product: Hasbro made a fortune with New Kids on the Block dolls, so in 1994 they came up with another rock 'n' roll "sure thing"—a high-priced collector's doll of Elvis Presley. The Elvis stamp was a smash, and surveys showed that, 16 years after his death, the King was bigger than ever. Hasbro envisioned offering a new series of Elvis dolls every year, "enticing middle-aged women with memories and money to burn." Hasbro hired a top-notch sculptor to design the dolls, paid $1.5 million as an advance to Presley's estate, and put out the first three in the series.

At the end of December 1994, the company tried a limited sale of 16,000 dolls at Wal-Mart. With no advertising, they sold out in two weeks. It looked good for the big rollout in January, the anniversary of the King's birth.

Problem: It turned out that Elvis fanatics were the only ones seriously interested in the dolls—and once they finished snapping up their dolls in the first weeks, sales went into a freefall. Within a couple of months retailers had slashed prices from $40 to $19.99. Some retailers actually experienced negative sales, as angry shoppers who'd paid full price a week or two earlier returned to stores demanding a $20 refund. The Elvis doll, launched with one of the largest promotional campaigns in the history of the toy industry, ended up as one of Hasbro's biggest duds.

WORLD OF LOVE DOLLS
Product: Another Hasbro loser. World of Love Dolls were the company's response to the twin challenges of the astonishing success of Mattel's Barbie doll and the emerging hippie subculture. There were five dolls: Love, Peace, Flower, Adam, and Soul (an African American). Love, a longhaired blonde, was the doll that looked most like Barbie. "Love is today's teenager," the company's sales catalog read. "Love is what's happening."

Problem: Kids didn't want a World of Love—they wanted Barbie.

The fishing reel was invented around the year 300 A.D.

CLASSIC HOAXES

*The BRI library has a whole section of books on hoaxes and
frauds. We've noticed that there are a few dozen hoaxes that
appear in almost every book that set the standard for all
hoaxers to come. Here are two of our favorites.*

THE MANHATTAN ISLAND HOAX

Background: In 1824 a well-known retired carpenter and
charismatic speaker named Lozier stood on a soapbox in
Manhattan's busy Centre Market and announced to the crowd that
because of all the buildings recently constructed, the southern tip
of Manhattan Island had become too heavy and was in danger of
sinking. The solution, he said, was to saw the island off at the
northern end, tow it out to sea, turn it 180 degrees around, and
reattach it.

Lozier claimed that sawing Manhattan Island in half would be one
of the biggest public works projects New York had ever seen, and
that Mayor Stephen Allen had put him in charge of the project.

The idea sounded preposterous to most of Lozier's listeners; but
then again, so had the Erie Canal, and that wonder of the world
was nearly finished, wasn't it? Besides, if it wasn't true, why would
he publicly declare that the mayor had authorized him to handle
the project?

What Happened: Lozier began signing up hundreds of laborers for
the task, offering triple wages to anyone willing to saw underwater.
He directed blacksmiths and carpenters to begin designing the 100-
foot saws and 250-foot oars needed to saw the island and row it out
to sea. He also arranged for the construction of barracks and a mess
halls for his laborers, and the delivery of 500 cattle, 500 hogs, and
3,000 chickens, so his workers would have plenty to eat.

After two months of planning, the date arrived for construction
to begin. Scores of laborers, carpenters, blacksmiths, butchers, and
animals—as well as a marching band and hundreds of onlookers—
arrived at Spring Street and Bowery to see the historic project get
underway. About the only people who didn't show up were Lozier
and his accomplices, who'd suddenly left town "on account of their
health."

Fully grown, Argentina's falabella horses are only 16 inches tall.

They were actually holed up in Brooklyn, and although there was talk of having them arrested, Alexander Klein writes in *Grand Deception*, "no one seemed willing to make a complaint to the authorities or admit that he had been duped, and Lozier went scot-free."

THE WILD ANIMAL HOAX

Background: On November 9, 1874, subscribers to the *New York Herald* opened their morning papers to read an eyewitness account of the "escape" the night before of every wild animal from the Central Park Zoo. According to the *Herald* article, 49 people had been killed by the rampaging beasts, 200 more had been injured, and a Who's Who of New York notables, including future president Chester A. Arthur, were hunting the animals up and down Broadway and Fifth Avenue. At least a dozen of the animals were still at large, the story reported, the mayor had declared a "state of siege," and "all citizens, except members of the National Guard, are enjoined to keep within their houses or residences until the wild animals at large are captured and killed."

What Happened: "Much of the life of the city came to an abrupt halt," Carl Sifakis writes in *Hoaxes and Scams*, "and few ventured out, most cowering behind furniture that barricaded home doors and windows." Even James Gordon Bennett, owner of the *New York Herald*, collapsed in bed upon reading his own newspaper's story, and stayed there for the rest of the day. The *Herald*'s war correspondent, George Hosmer, showed up in the newsroom with two large Navy revolvers shouting, "Well, here I am."

What Bennett, Hosmer, and tens of thousands of other *Herald* subscribers failed to do that morning was read the story to the very end—where, in the last paragraph, managing editor Thomas Connery revealed that the story was "a huge hoax, a wild romance, or whatever epithet of utter untrustworthiness our readers may care to apply to it." Connery's motive for publishing the story: to "direct attention to the zoo's shortcomings," so that such escapes might never happen in the future. (So far, they haven't.)

More hoaxes on page 340.

World's highest city: Lhasa, Tibet, at 12,087 feet above sea level.

A BRIEF HISTORY OF BUGS BUNNY

Who's your favorite cartoon character? Ear's ours.

I MPRESSIVE STATS
Bugs Bunny is the world's most popular rabbit:

- Since 1939, he has starred in more than 175 films.

- He's been nominated for three Oscars, and won one—in 1958, for "Knighty Knight, Bugs" (with Yosemite Sam).

- Every year from 1945 to 1961, he was voted "top animated character" by movie theater owners (when they still showed cartoons in theaters).

- In 1985 he became only the second cartoon character to be given a star on the Hollywood Walk of Fame (Mickey Mouse was the first).

- For almost 30 years, starting in 1960, he had one of the top-rated shows on Saturday-morning TV.

- In 1976, when researchers polled Americans on their favorite characters, real and imaginary, Bugs came in second . . . behind Abraham Lincoln.

THE INSPIRATIONS
Bugs was born in the 1930s, but cartoon historians say his ancestry goes further back. A few direct descendents:

Zomo. You may not have heard of this African folk-rabbit, but he's world-famous. Joe Adamson writes in *Bugs Bunny: Fifty Years and Only One Grey Hare:*

> Like jazz and rock 'n' roll, Bugs has at least some of his roots in black culture. Zomo is the trickster rabbit from Central and Eastern Africa who gained audience sympathy by being smaller than his oppressors and turning the tables on them through cleverness—thousands of years before Eastman invented film.

Highest-grossing sports movie in history: *Jerry McGuire.*

A con artist, a masquerader, ruthless, and suave, in control of
the situation. Specialized in impersonating women.

Br'er Rabbit. Slaves brought Zomo to America and in the New
World, he became Br'er Rabbit, whose stories were retold by Joel
Chandler Harris in *Tales of Uncle Remus* (1880). Typical plot: Br'er
Fox catches Br'er Rabbit, who begs not to be thrown in the briar-
patch (which is exactly where he wants to go). Br'er Fox falls for
it, tosses him in, and the rabbit laughs all the way home.
Occasionally, you'll see Bugs pull the same trick.

Closer to home, a few comedic geniuses helped mold Bugs:

Charlie Chaplin. "It was Chaplin who established that 'gestures
and actions expressing attitude' give a screen character life,"
Adamson writes. The Looney Tunes directors, all fans of Chaplin,
even stole many of his gags. For example:

> The abrupt and shocking kiss Charlie plants [on] someone
> who's getting too close for comfort in *The Floorwalker* went
> on to become one of Bugs' favorite ways to upset his adver-
> saries. [And] the walking broomstick in "Bewitched Bunny"
> does Chaplin's trademark turn, with one foot in the air, at
> every corner.

There are dozens of other Chaplin rip-offs. Bugs also lifted bits
from silent comedians Harold Lloyd and Buster Keaton.

Groucho Marx. "Bugs uses his carrot as a prop, just as Groucho
used his cigar," points out Stefan Kanfer in *Serious Business.*
"Eventually Bugs even stole Marx's response to an insult: 'Of
course you know, this means war!'"

TIMELINE
1937: Warner Bros. animation director Tex Avery makes "Porky's
Duck Hunt." Porky Pig hunted a screwball duck named Daffy—
"who didn't get scared and run away when somebody pointed a gun
at him, but leapt and hopped all over the place like a maniac."
"When it hit the theaters," recalls another director, "it was like an
explosion."

1938: Warner Bros. director Ben "Bugs" Hardaway remakes the
cartoon with a rabbit instead of a duck, as "Porky's Hare Hunt."
Says one of Bugs's creators: "That rabbit was just Daffy Duck in a
rabbit suit."

127 people ran the first New York City Marathon in 1970; 32,000 ran in 1998.

1939: Bugs Hardaway decides to remake "Porky's Hare Hunt" with a new rabbit (as "Hare-um Scare-um"). Cartoonist Charlie Thorson comes up with a gray and white rabbit with large buck teeth. He labels his sketches "Bugs' Bunny."

1940: Director Tex Avery becomes the real father of Bugs Bunny with "A Wild Hare." Bugs is changed from a Daffyesque lunatic to a streetsmart wiseass. "We decided he was going to be a smart-aleck rabbit, but casual about it," Avery recalled. "His opening line was 'What's up, Doc?' . . . It floored 'em! . . . Here's a guy with a gun in his face! . . . They expected the rabbit to scream, or anything but make a casual remark . . . It got such a laugh that we said, 'Let's use that every chance we get.' It became a series of 'What's Up, Docs?' That set his entire character. He was always in command, in the face of all types of dangers."

Bugs also gets his voice in "A Wild Hare." Mel Blanc, who did most Looney Tunes voices, had been having a hard time finding one for the rabbit . . . until Bugs Hardaway showed him the latest sketch for "A Wild Hare." Blanc wrote:

> He'd obviously had some work done. His posture had improved, he'd shed some weight, and his protruding front teeth weren't as pronounced. The most significant change, however, was in his facial expression. No longer just goofy, he was a sly looking rascal.

"A tough little stinker, ain't he?" Hardaway commented . . . and the light went on in Blanc's brain.

> A tough little stinker . . . In my mind I heard a Brooklyn accent . . . To anyone living west of the Hudson River at that time, Brooklynites were associated with con artists and crooks . . . Consequently, the new, improved Bugs Bunny wouldn't say "jerk," he'd say "joik."

The rabbit is now so popular that he needs a name. According to some sources, he is about to be dubbed "Happy Rabbit." Tex Avery wants "Jack E. Rabbit." But when Thorson's year-old drawing labeled "Bugs' Bunny" is turned up, producer Leon Schlessinger chooses that. Avery hates it. "That's sissy," he complains. "Mine's a rabbit. A tall, lanky, mean rabbit. He isn't a fuzzy little bunny!" But the name sticks.

1941: Bugs Bunny becomes competitive. Four extremely talented directors—Avery, Friz Freleng, Bob Clampett, and Chuck Jones—try to top each other with new gags and aspects of Bugs's personality. It's the key to the character's success—he's constantly growing. "As each director added new levels to this character," Adamson explains, "it was picked up by the others and became a part of the mix."

1943: Animator Robert McKimson (later a director himself), working for Bob Clampett, refines Bugs's features into what they are today. "We made him cuter, brought his head and cheeks out a little more and gave him just a little nose," McKimson says. He looks more "elfin" and less "ratlike" now.

1945: During World War II, Bugs has become a "sort of national mascot." Critic Richard Schickel writes: "In the war years, when he flourished most gloriously, Bugs Bunny embodied the cocky humor of a nation that had survived its economic crisis [in surprisingly good shape], and was facing a terrible war with grace, gallantry, humor, and solidarity that was equally surprising." By the end of the war, Bugs isn't just a cartoon character, but an American icon.

BUGS FACTS

Saved by a Hare. The inspiration for the original rabbit came from Walt Disney. In 1935 Disney put out a cartoon featuring a character called Max Hare. Hardaway's rabbit looks suspiciously like Max.

Trademarks. Where did Bugs's carrot-crunching and "What's up, Doc?" come from? No one's sure, but experts have suggested they might have been inspired by a couple of popular films:

- In Frank Capra's 1934 Oscar-winning comedy, *It Happened One Night*, Clark Gable nervously munches on carrots.

- In the classic 1939 screwball comedy *My Man Godfrey*, William Powell uses the line "What's up, Duke?" repeatedly.

On the other hand, Tex Avery had a habit of calling everyone Doc—so he may have inspired the phrase. (Mel Blanc also claims in his autobiography that he ad-libbed the line, but he seems to take credit for everything—so we don't believe him.)

Tough Act. Blanc, Bugs's voice, says that recording the "What's up, Doc?" line turned out to be the most physically challenging part of doing the voice:

> "What's up, Doc?" was incomplete without the sound of the rabbit nibbling on the carrot, which presented problems. First

---

An *ergasiophobe* is someone who's afraid of work.

of all, I don't especially like carrots, at least not raw. [Ed note: In another BR, we erroneously reported that he was allergic to carrots. Oops.] And second, I found it impossible to chew, swallow, and be ready to say my next line. We tried substituting other vegetables, including apples and celery, but with unsatisfactory results. The solution was to stop recording so that I could spit out the carrot into the wastebasket and then proceed with the script. In the course of a recording session I usually went through enough carrots to fill several wastebaskets. Bugs Bunny did for carrots what Popeye the Sailor did for spinach. How many . . . children were coerced into eating their carrots by mothers cooing . . . "but Bugs Bunny eats *his* carrots." If only they had known.

Eat Your Veggies. Actually, there were pressures to switch from carrots. "The Utah Celery Company of Salt Lake City offered to keep all the studio's staffers well supplied with their product if Bugs would only switch from carrots to celery," Adamson reports. "[And] later, the Broccoli Institute of America strongly urged The Bunny to sample their product once in a while . . . Mel Blanc would have been happy to switch . . . but carrots were Bugs's trademark."

Surprise Hit. To his creators, Bugs Bunny was just another character that would probably run in a few cartoons and fade unnoticed into obscurity. "We didn't feel that we had anything," Avery recounted years later, "until we got it on the screen and it got a few laughs. After we ran it and previewed it and so forth, Warners liked it, the exhibitors liked it, and so of course [the producer] ran down and said, 'Boy, give us as many of those as you can!' Which we did."

Bugs Bunny became so popular with the public that he got laughs even when he didn't deserve them. "He could do no wrong," remembers dialogue writer Michael Maltese. "We had quite a few lousy Bugs Bunnies. We'd say, 'Well, we haven't got time. Let's do it.' And we'd do it, and the audience would laugh. They loved that rabbit."

* * *

- The name "Looney Tunes" is a takeoff on Walt Disney's popular 1930s cartoon series "Silly Symphonies."

- The real name of the Looney Tunes theme song is "The Merry-Go-Round Broke Down." It's a pop tune from the 1930s.

Average cost of a movie ticket in 1940: 24¢.

RABBIT BRINGS FIRE TO THE PEOPLE

In honor of Bugs Bunny (see page 129), we've included this Native American folklore from the Creek tribe, explaining how they acquired fire. This adaptation was contributed by BRI mythologist Jeff Altemus.

In the beginning there was no fire and the earth was cold. Then the Thunderbirds sent their lightning to a sycamore tree on an island where the Weasels lived. The Weasels were the only ones who had fire and they would not give any of it away.

The people knew that there was fire on the island because they could see smoke coming from the sycamore, but the water was too deep for anyone to cross. When winter came the people suffered so much from the cold that they called a council to find some way of obtaining fire from the Weasels. They invited all the animals who could swim.

"How shall we obtain fire?" the people asked.

Most of the animals were afraid of the Weasels because they were bloodthirsty and ate mice and moles and fish and birds. Rabbit was the only one who was brave enough to try to steal fire from them. "I can run and swim faster than the Weasels," he said. "I am also a good dancer."

"Every night the Weasels build a big fire and dance around it. Tonight I will swim across and join in the dancing. I will run away with some fire."

He considered the matter for a while and then decided how he would do it. Before the sun set he rubbed his head with pine tar so as to make his hair stand up. Then, as darkness was falling, he swam across to the island.

The Weasels received Rabbit gladly because they had heard of his fame as a dancer. Soon they had a big fire blazing and all began dancing around it. As the Weasels danced, they approached nearer and nearer the fire in the center of the circle. They would bow to the fire and then dance backwards away from it.

When Rabbit entered the dancing circle, the Weasels shouted to him: "Lead us,

---

Attention windsurfers: Wind speeds on Neptune can reach 1,500 mph.

Rabbit!" He danced ahead of them, coming closer and closer to the fire. He bowed to the fire, bringing his head lower and lower as if he were going to take hold of it. While the Weasels were dancing faster and faster, trying to keep up with him, Rabbit suddenly bowed very low so that the pine tar in his hair caught fire in a flash of flame.

He ran off with his head ablaze, and the angry Weasels pursued him, crying, "Catch him! Catch him! He has stolen our sacred fire! Catch him, and throw him down!"

But Rabbit outran them and plunged into the water, leaving the Weasels on the shore. He swam across the water with the flames still blazing from his hair.

The Weasels now called on the Thunderbirds to make it rain so as to extinguish the fire stolen by Rabbit. For three days rain poured down upon the earth, and the Weasels were sure that no fire was left burning except in their sycamore tree.

Rabbit, however, had built a fire in a hollow tree, and when the rain stopped and the sun shone, he came out and gave fire to all the people. After that, whenever it rained, they kept fires in their shelters, and that is how Rabbit brought fire to the people.

*   *   *

LESSON IN STRESS MANAGEMENT

This arrived by Internet one day—we don't know who sent it, but it's become a favorite at the BRI offices, so we pass it on to you. Take a deep, gentle breath, relax . . . read this slowly and thoughtfully.

Picture yourself near a stream. Birds are softly chirping in the crisp, cool mountain air. Nothing can bother you here. No one knows this secret place. You are in total seclusion from that place called "the world." The soothing sound of a gentle waterfall fills the air with a cascade of serenity. The water is clear. You can easily make out the face of the person whose head you're holding under the water.

48% of men think balding has a negative effect on business and social relationships.

LOONEY LAWS

Believe it or not, these laws are real!

It's illegal to ride an ugly horse down the street in Wilbur, Washington.

It's against the law to step out of an airplane while it's in the air over Maine.

If you don't like a statue in Star, Mississippi, hold your tongue—it's illegal to ridicule public architecture.

Ninth-grade boys can't grow moustaches in Binghamton, New York.

It's against the law to drink milk on a train passing through North Carolina.

Virginia law prohibits "corrupt practices or bribery by any person other than candidates."

You can't carry an ice cream cone in your pocket in Lexington, Kentucky.

It's illegal to spit against the wind in Sault Sainte Marie, Michigan.

Goats can't legally wear trousers in Massachusetts.

It's illegal to swim on dry land in Santa Ana, California.

In Lawrence, Kansas, it's against the law to carry bees around in your hat on city streets.

In Washington, D.C., you're breaking the law if you paint lemons all over your car to let people know you were taken advantage of by a specific car dealer.

If you complain about the condition of the street in Baton Rouge, Louisiana, you can be forced to fix it yourself.

Oregon prohibits citizens from wiping their dishes. You must let them drip-dry.

If you mispronounce "Arkansas" when you're in that state, you're breaking the law.

In Hartford, Connecticut, it's illegal to educate your dog.

You can't go barefoot in Austin, Texas, without a $5 permit.

On an average day, the president of the United States receives 20,000 letters.

LIFE AFTER DEATH

What do Sherlock Holmes, Davy Crockett, and Superman have in common? They were all popular characters whose creators killed them off . . . and then had to bring them back from the dead.

SHERLOCK HOLMES

Born: 1887 — **Died:** 1893 — **Resurrected:** 1903
Background: Sherlock Holmes first appeared in 1887 but didn't become famous until 1891, when "A Scandal in Bohemia" was published in London's *Strand* magazine. Overnight, Holmes and his creator, Arthur Conan Doyle, became national celebrities.
Over the next two years, Doyle turned out an average of one new story per month. But the more popular Holmes became, the less Doyle liked him. Doyle considered his historical novels to be his real work and felt that Holmes kept people from appreciating them. By 1893 Doyle loathed the detective.

Untimely Death: In 1893, at the end of *Strand*'s 24th Holmes story, Doyle placed Holmes on top of Switzerland's Reichenbach Falls, grappling with his arch-enemy, Professor Moriarty. Then he had both characters plunge to their deaths.

The author gleefully wrote to his mother: "The gentleman vanishes, never to return!" But others weren't so happy. Twenty thousand *Strand* readers (an enormous number for the time) cancelled their subscriptions; businessmen in London wore black bands to mourn Holmes's death; Doyle was inundated with letters.
But he was unmoved, and snapped: "Holmes is at the bottom of Reichenbach Falls, and there he stays."

Resurrection: What could change Doyle's mind? Money. In 1903 *McClure's* (a U.S. magazine) offered him the astronomical sum of $5,000 dollars per story if he would resurrect the character . . . and *Strand* offered more than half that for the British publication rights. Doyle decided to "accept as much money as slightly deranged editors were willing to pay." Soon after, excited readers learned that Holmes hadn't died after all; he had merely gone into hiding.

The publisher couldn't print copies of the new Holmes stories fast enough. People waited in huge lines and mobbed bookstalls to

The average American dog will cost its owner $14,600 over its lifetime.

get them. Doyle continued writing about Sherlock Holmes until 1927, then retired the detective for good.

DAVY CROCKETT

Born: December 15, 1954 — **Died:** February 23, 1955 — **Resurrected:** November 16, 1955

Background: Walt Disney's first TV program, *Disneyland*, debuted in October 1954. A few months later, it featured TV's first miniseries—a three-part adventure about a real-life Tennessee politician and frontiersman named Davy Crockett (see page 401 for more about him). The Disney version was mostly fiction, but America took it to heart. One critic recalls, "Disney's Crockett instantly became the most popular hero television had ever seen. Just about every boy in the country owned a coonskin cap like Davy's." Coonskin caps sold so quickly that raccoons actually became hard to find . . . forcing hat makers to use foxes and rabbits instead. All Crockett items—coloring books, play sets, bubblegum cards, etc.—sold like wildfire. It was TV's first huge, merchandising fad, and it was making Disney a fortune.

Untimely Death: There was just one problem—when the three episodes had been filmed months earlier, no one at Disney had a clue the public would respond so enthusiastically. So they followed Crockett's standard biography, and killed him off at the end of the third episode (while defending the Alamo). Uncle Walt couldn't believe the blunder. "We had one of the biggest hits in television history," he moaned, "and there we were with a dead hero."

Resurrection: "This was the first time that a major hero had died in a television series," writes Jeff Rovin in *The Great TV Heroes*, "and many youngsters went into mourning for the noble warrior. More important, however, is the way in which television and the profit incentive were able to conquer death! Disney was not so foolish as to let a financial giant stay long expired."

The company went to work on new episodes, which they set before the Alamo. But it took too long to produce them. "We tried to come back with two more called *The Legend of Davy Crockett*," Walt Disney told a reporter, "but by that time the fever had run its course." The King of the Wild Frontier returned on November 16, 1955, in *Davy Crockett's Keelboat Race* and December 14, 1955, in *Davy Crockett and the River Pirates*.

If you're standing on a mountaintop and the conditions are just right . . .

"Those two never did catch on the way the original three did," Disney sighed. After that, Crockett stayed dead.

SUPERMAN

Born: 1938 — **Died:** November 18, 1992 — **Resurrected:** 1993

Background: DC Comics' Superman was the nation's first superhero. He was introduced in 1938, took the nation by storm, and over the next three decades, became the most successful comic-book character in history.

Untimely Death: By the 1990s, comics had changed. They featured complex heroes who were tormented by angst and who killed their foes in vengeful bloodbaths. Comic fans delighted in "the smart-aleck snarl of Wolverine," and "the devilish depravity of Spawn." But Superman never killed his enemies; he preferred to turn them over to the proper authorities. Fans found his patriotism and politeness . . . boring. Superman's comic sales "plummeted faster than a speeding bullet," so DC Comics made plans to kill him.

The impending death was nationwide news. Social commentators lamented a society that could no longer find interest in a "decent" hero. Comic stores played up the hype, flying flags with the Superman "S" dripping blood, displaying Superman art, and having the "Death" issue delivered in hearses. Sales of Superman skyrocketed, but after a few issues that explored the world without Superman, DC stopped publishing the title.

Resurrection: But not for long. It turned out that Superman's death was a publicity stunt. Only four months later, the Superhero was back in a new form. It turned out his dead body had been taken to a space-age "regeneration center," which brought him back to life. Buyers of the "Death" issue who thought they were getting a collector's item were outraged, and loyal fans resented DC's toying with them. But the publicity did increase sales, at least temporarily—leading DC's executive editor Mike Carlin to happily proclaim death "good for Superman."

JEFF'S BRAINTEASERS

BRI member Jeff Altemus collected these puzzles and sent them to us via the BRI Web site (www.bathroomreader.com) . . . daring us to solve them. Naturally, Uncle John immediately took them to our "research lab." When he emerged, he pronounced them bona fide bathroom reading. Now, we "pass" them on to you.

1. A train enters a tunnel at 7 o'clock. Another train enters the exact same tunnel, also at 7 o'clock, on the same day. The tunnel has only one track, no passing places, and no other means for the trains to pass, around, under, or over. However, both trains make it to the other end of the tunnel, untouched. How did they do it?

2. You have two hourglasses—a 4-minute glass and a 7-minute glass. You want to measure 9 minutes. How do you do it?

3. If 2 hours ago it was as long after 1 o'clock in the afternoon as it was before 1 o'clock in the morning, what time is it now?

4. A donkey is tied to a rope 10 feet long. Twenty feet away is a field of carrots. How does the donkey get to the carrots?

5. If you were to put a coin into an empty bottle and then insert a cork into the neck, how could you remove the coin without taking out the cork or breaking the bottle?

6. You threw away the outside and cooked the inside. Then you ate the outside and threw away the inside. What did you eat?

7. What is the easiest way to throw a ball, and have it stop and completely reverse direction after traveling a short distance without hitting anything?

8. Two boxers are in a boxing match (regular boxing, not kick boxing). The fight is scheduled for 12 rounds but ends after 6 rounds, after one boxer knocks out the other boxer. Yet no man throws a punch. How is this possible?

9. In 1990 a person is 15 years old. In 1995 that same person is 10 years old. How is this possible?

10. A man is lying dead in a field. Next to him there is an unopened package. There is

no other creature in the field. How did he die?

11. Uncle John was driving to the plumbing supply house the other day and saw a car with a license plate that read: 1 DIV 0. What kind of car was it?

12. A man lies dead in an alley with a tape recorder next to him and a gun in his hand. A police officer saw him and picked up the tape recorder in hopes of determining the cause of his death. He pushes play on the tape recorder and hears the man's voice say "I'm ending my life because I went bankrupt," followed by a gunshot. The policeman filed a homicide report instead of suicide. Why?

13. A girl is running home. She sees a person with a mask and then runs back to where she started. Why?

14. Captain Russo was out for a walk when it started to rain. He did not have an umbrella and he wasn't wearing a hat. His clothes were soaked, yet not a hair on his head got wet. How could this happen?

15. A man takes his car to a hotel. As soon as he reaches the hotel, he is declared bankrupt. Why?

For answers, turn to page 749.

* * *

KIDS ON MUSIC
From *Fractured English* by Richard Lederer.

- "Rock Mananoff was a famous post-Romantic composer of piano concerti."

- "Bach was the most famous composer in the world and so was Handel. Handel was half German, half Italian, and half English. He was very large."

- "Henry Purcell was a well-known composer few people have ever heard of."

First baseball team to pay its players: Cincinnati Redstockings.

UNFINISHED MASTERPIECES

Uncle John was chatting by e-mail with BRI stalwart Jack Mingo, and this topic came up. "How many are there, do you think?" Uncle John asked . . . and Mingo sent back a list that was so long, he probably still hasn't finished it. Here are our favorites—so far.

THE UNFINISHED SYMPHONY. Composed by Franz Schubert, this is perhaps the most famous unfinished modern masterpiece. Ironically, no one is sure if it really is unfinished.

Background: Schubert grew up in early 19th-century Vienna. He was a prodigy who could dash off brilliant songs on the back of envelopes, but his genius was unrecognized. He was never able to attract the patronage that would have enabled him to concentrate exclusively on music . . . so he never heard many of his own works performed by a full orchestra (or even by professional musicians). He died of venereal disease in 1828, at age 31.

Unfinished Masterpiece: By 1865 Schubert was recognized as a master. A group of his ardent fans (The Schubert Society) heard a rumor that an old lawyer acquaintance of Schubert's had a copy of a lost symphony . . . and it turned out to be true. The piece was Schubert's Eighth Symphony, written in 1822. He had submitted it to an orchestra called the Gesellschaft der Musikfreunde, asking them to perform it. When it was rejected, he sent it to the lawyer . . . who held onto it for over 40 years. At the fans' request, he dug out the symphony . . . "but it was soon clear that the two last movements were missing. Only the first three bars of the third movement were found." What makes this particularly frustrating for music lovers is that the symphony is generally considered Schubert's best work.

Update: The Schubert Society begged the lawyer to find the rest, but he insisted he'd only received two movements. True? Maybe. There are three theories:

1.   Schubert wrote the first two movements as a sampler to see if any

---

When it was introduced in 1848, the modern golf ball was called a "gutta-percha" ball.

orchestras would be interested, then never bothered to finish it.

2. The last movement was incorporated into one of Schubert's later works.

3. The second half had to have been lost. Potential proof: The last page of the second movement was not blank— three bars of the third movement were at the bottom of the page, "strongly implying that it continued . . . somewhere," explains one Schubert expert. "Since then, a sketchbook apparently containing 250 bars of the third movement has been discovered. Fans hope that the rest of the papers are in an attic somewhere, waiting to be found."

KUBLA KHAN. By Samuel Taylor Coleridge. One of the best-known poems in the English language, notorious as an unfinished piece because of the explanation Coleridge gave for not completing it.

Background: Coleridge was sedated with opium and recovering from an illness one summer day in 1797 when he nodded off reading a book called *Purchas's Pilgrimage.* The last sentence he read before falling asleep was "Here the Khan Kubla commanded a palace to be built, and a stately garden thereunto. And thus ten miles of fertile ground were enclosed with a wall."

Coleridge said that he slept deeply for about three hours, during which he dreamed a complete 200- to 300-line poem about Khan.

Unfinished Masterpiece: When he awoke, Coleridge immediately started putting the words on paper. He had written the first 40 lines or so when a knock came at the door. But instead of sending his visitor away (some accounts say it was a salesman)—or refusing to answer the door altogether—Coleridge chatted for over an hour.

On his return to his room, Coleridge wrote, he found, to his "surprise and mortification, that though [I] still retained some vague and dim recollection of the general purport of the vision, with the exception of some eight or ten scattered lines and images, all the rest had passed away!" He managed to put a total of 54 lines to paper, but that was it—the rest of his 300-line poem was lost forever.

Update: Today scholars question whether Coleridge was being honest about his unfinished work. It's possible he simply wasn't sure what to write next, and never got around to working it out.

Oldest American college sport still in existence: rowing.

SPECIAL UNDERWEAR

At the BRI, we don't believe in keeping underwear innovations under cover. Here are three to take us into the next millennium.

SAFETY FIRST

"A Vermont inventor has figured out a way to prevent senior citizens from breaking bones when they take a spill: underwear air bags. Carl Clark, who also devised the first air bags for Lockheed Martin in the 1960s, says his emergency underwear has a sensor that automatically inflates two cushions around the wearer's hips when it detects the person starting to fall."

—Los Angeles Times

LARGER THAN LIEE

"A Tokyo man made international news recently when his inflatable underpants accidentally went off in the subway. He had invented the special underwear to allay his phobia of drowning. The good news is, they worked, inflating to 30 times their normal size. They had to be stabbed with a pencil to stop them from crushing other passengers."

—The Edge

THE ARMAGEDDON BRA

"Every Japanese has heard of Nostradamus, and millions lend credence to his prophecy that a terrible calamity will strike in July this year (1999)—a war destroying a third of the world's population.

"Now the lingerie firm, Triumph International Japan, is cashing in on the nation's doomsday boom with a hi-tech 'Armageddon Bra' that alerts its wearer to incoming missiles.

"Presented at a fashion show yesterday, the 'Armageddon Bra' includes a sensor on the shoulder strap, and a control box to warn of objects falling from the skies.

"Ideally the Armageddon Bra should be worn without outer garments to work efficiently."

—The Times of London

The average car in Japan is driven 4,400 miles a year. In the U.S., it's 9,500 miles.

MY BODY LIES OVER THE OCEAN . . .

This section was inspired by an article in Harper's *about the fact that Albert Einstein's brain was removed when he died. We at the BRI wondered if other famous people "lost" a body part or two when they died. We did a little research . . . and were surprised by what we found.*

GALILEO'S MIDDLE FINGER
Where It's Located: Museum of the History of Science, Florence, Italy
How It Got There: In 1737, when Galileo's body was being moved from a storage closet to its final resting place in a mausoleum in the church of Santa Croce, a nobleman named Anton Francesco Gori cut off three fingers from Galileo's right hand for a souvenir. The middle finger was eventually acquired by the Museum of the History of Science; the other two surviving fingers "are in a private collection."

NAPOLEON'S "NOBLE ORGAN"
Where It's Located: Columbia University's College of Physicians and Surgeons
How It Got There: In 1828 Abbé Ange Paul Vignali, the priest who administered last rites to Napoléon in 1821, was murdered. Among the many Napoleonic souvenirs found in Abbé Vignali's personal effects was the most personal effect of all—a tiny, "unpleasant looking piece of desiccated tissue" alleged to be Napoleon's private part—which was supposedly removed from the deposed emperor's corpse following his autopsy.

The artifact remained in the Vignali family until 1916, when it was sold to a London dealer of rare books. In 1924 it was sold to Dr. Abraham Rosenbach, who placed the withered item "inside a glass casket, in a tasteful case of blue morocco leather and velvet bearing Napoleon's crest," where it was displayed to friends, family, and just about anyone else who asked to see it. "Few so intimate portions of a man's anatomy," Rosenbach's biographer writes, "have ever been displayed to so many."

In November 1944 the "shriveled short arm,"—which by now

The Pentagon spent $50 million on Viagra for American troops and retirees in 1999.

was said to look like "a maltreated strip of buckskin shoelace, or a shriveled eel"—was sold to a Philadelphia autograph dealer named Bruce Gimelson. He tried to auction it at Christie's, but withdrew it when it "failed to attract a $40,000 minimum bid." Seven years later, he sold it to a urologist named John K. Lattimer for a mere $3,000. Dr. Lattimer owns it to this day, and it's only one of the many odd but historically significant items in his collection. As Harvey Rachlin reports in *Lucy's Bones, Sacred Stones, and Einstein's Brain*, Dr. Lattimer also owns "Hermann Goering's suicide capsule container, a lock of Hitler's hair, and the nooses used to hang two of the conspirators for the murder of President Lincoln, Mary Surratt and Lewis Powell."

EINSTEIN'S BRAIN
Where It's Located: Lawrence, Kansas
How It Got There: When Einstein died in April 1955, he left a request that his friend and colleague Dr. Harry Zimmerman examine his brain. So Dr. Thomas Harvey, the pathologist who performed the autopsy on Einstein, removed the brain and had it cut into 200 pieces, some of which he gave to Zimmerman. The rest (representing about 75% of Einstein's brain) he took home and stored in formaldehyde-filled jars that he kept under his sink for nearly 40 years—occasionally doling out specimens to brain researchers upon request. (One such researcher keeps his section in his refrigerator, in a jar marked "Big Al's Brain.")

At last report, Harvey, who'd lost his medical license and was working in a plastics factory, was looking for a research lab or some other institution to take possession of Einstein's brain and preserve it for posterity.

OTHER CELEBRITY BODY PARTS

- Walt Whitman's brain. Donated to the Wistar Institute at the University of Pennsylvania, where it "was dropped on the floor by a lab technician and was discarded long ago." The Wistar Institute is no longer accepting new brains.

- Lord Byron's lungs. "Kept in a jar, somewhere in Greece."

More on page 241.

AMAZING LUCK

*Sometimes we're blessed with it, sometimes we're cursed with
it—dumb luck. Here are some examples of people who've
lucked out . . . for better and for worse.*

CELLULAR MEMORY

"In the Dent de Crolles region in France, shepherd
Christian Raymond, 23, was rescued from a cliff from which
he had been hanging by his fingers. He had called the emergency
rescue operator on his cell phone earlier in the day and managed to
make another call from the cliff by pressing "redial' with his nose
against the phone, which had fallen down the mountain with him
but had landed right beside him."
— *The Edge,* **March 25, 1999**

TRAIN KEPT A-ROLLIN'

"Participants in this tale of survival still can't believe it really
happened. Thrown through the steel roof of his car in a head-on
collision, a Denver man landed a hundred feet away—on railroad
tracks, directly in the path of a speeding train. Too late to brake
before passing over the body, the engineer stopped as fast as he
could and rushed back to the spot, certain he had killed the man.
What he found was a guy limping, shaken, but very much alive.
His only injury was the broken leg he suffered in the car collision."
— *Oops*

LUCK BE A LADY

"A mistake on a national Pick 7 ticket was worth $1.6 million to a
bettor who selected the wrong number on Breeders' Cup Day.

"The 51-year-old engineer who bought the winning ticket said
he punched 11 instead of 1 for his selection in the seventh race.

"'I liked the one and 11 horses in the sixth race, and I liked the
No. 1 in the seventh,' the bettor said. 'But when I punched out my
ticket for the seventh, I hit one and 11—the same numbers I had
in the sixth—by mistake.'

"The 11 turned out to be Arcangues, the unknown French horse
who won the Classic at odds of 133 to 1. It was the largest in
Breeders' Cup history.

General Dwight Eisenhower owned a pair of pajamas with five stars on the lapels.

"He had three other tickets with six winners, too, and collected a total of $1,152,317 after taxes."
—*San Francisco Chronicle,* November 11, 1993

BLESS THE TORPEDOES!

"A charmed life. That describes the experience of seaman Roy Dikkers during World War II. Sealed in a compartment when a German torpedo struck his tanker, he was freed by a second torpedo explosion. Racing on deck he found the sea around the floundering vessel ablaze with oil fires. He never had to make the fateful decision whether to stay with the sinking ship or risk the fiery sea. A third torpedo blew him far from the scene, beyond the oil slick. Landing near a floating raft, he crawled aboard and was found by a Norwegian freighter three days later."

—*Oops*

MY FORTUNE FOR A KISS

"Hauled before a Melbourne court in 1907 for hugging and kissing spinster Hazel Moore when she entered his shop, young Michael O'Connor defended himself by claiming it had been a lovely spring day and he was in high spirits. O'Connor had to serve a few months for breach of peace. So imagine his amazement ten years later when an attorney representing Miss Moore's estate gave him her bequest of 20,000 pounds! She left the fortune in memory of the only kiss she had received from a man in her adult life."

—*Oops*

AMAZING LOTTERY WINNERS

- "Randy Halvorson was one of 14 employees to share a $3.4 million jackpot in 1988. The Iowa resident then won $7.2 million with his brother in 1990."

- "In Wisconsin, Donald Smith of Amherst has won the state's SuperCash game three times: On May 25, 1993, June 17, 1994, and July 30, 1995. He won $250,000 each time. The odds of winning the SuperCash game just once are nearly one in a million."

- "Joseph P. Crowley won $3 million in the Ohio lottery in 1987. Six years later, he retired to Boca Raton, Florida, and played the Florida Lotto on Christmas Day of 1993. He won $20 million."

—**The Good Luck Book**

Q: What is a *gnomon?* A: The thing that casts a shadow on a sundial.

"BUT IT SAYS ON THE LABEL..."

You might assume that with all the regulations on labeling,
you can always tell what's in that product you just bought.
Well, guess again. Here are five examples that prove it's
still "buyer beware" in the marketplace.

FRESH IS FROZEN
The Label Says: "This Turkey Never Frozen"
You Assume: It's fresh.
Actually: Until 1998 any turkey that was stored at temperatures above 0°F could be called "fresh." Then, says the *Wall Street Journal*, the FDA changed the rules. Nowadays, to be called fresh, a turkey has to be stored at above 26°F—the freezing point for poultry. But the label still doesn't have to say frozen unless it was stored at 0°F or less. So a company can legally say it was never frozen, even if it was stored at 1° F.

YOUR LAWN OR YOUR LIFE?
The Label Says: "Pesticide Ingredients" and then lists them
You Assume: All the ingredients—particularly the toxic ones—are in the list.
Actually: According to a recent study, "more than 600 toxic chemicals included in pesticides aren't disclosed on the brand labels." Why not? "Under federal pesticide regulations, these chemicals don't have to be disclosed when they are inert ingredients, chemicals that assist in killing bugs and weeds, but aren't the active agent of destruction." And why aren't they listed? Pesticide companies say they need to protect trade secrets.

SOUNDS OFF
The CD Label Says: *Cape Cod . . . Enchanting Sounds of the Surf*
You Assume: This "sounds of nature" CD was recorded off Cape Cod.
Actually: According to a report in the *Wall Street Journal*, the CD was recorded in Naples, Florida. So was *Cocoa Beach . . . The*

Makes sense: The giraffe has the highest blood pressure of any animal.

Enchanting Sounds of the Surf and the rest of the 200-title series. "I'd be an idiot to do separate recordings [for each title]," the producer told a reporter. "It's all surf."

Apparently, many (but not all) of the popular "sounds of nature" recordings are fakes. One "burbling stream" is really a toilet: "I wound up using a stereo recording of my toilet bowl filling up," a producer admitted. "It sounded more like a stream than the streams did." Another producer says he once "turned an 87-second roll of thunder into a 30-minute storm." Other tricks include "hosing down backyard pine trees to tape the drip of rain, or crouching in elevator shafts to catch the howl of wind."

DO IT AGAIN
The Label Says: "Recycled Paper"
You Assume: It's been used by a consumer, sent to a recycling center, and turned back into paper.
Actually: The only time you can be sure that's true is if the label includes the words "post-consumer." Otherwise, it could be something else. The government allows manufacturers to gather paper cuttings from the mill floor, dump them back into the paper pulp, and call the paper "recycled." The mills would do that anyway because it's cost-effective to save the scraps, so there's no savings of resources. But it sounds good . . . and it's legal.

DEM BONES
The Label Says: "Chicken Nuggets"
You Assume: It's chicken meat.
Actually: According to the National Consumer League, when "convenience foods such as chicken frankfurters, chicken nuggets, turkey salami, and turkey bologna" are mechanically deboned, there's no telling what's in them. "The problem is that mechanically deboned poultry may contain bone fragments, marrow, skin, kidneys, sex glands, and lungs as by-products of the mechanical process. However, these by-products are not listed on the ingredients panel, so consumers do not know that they are both paying for, and eating, this extraneous material . . . Labeling requirements allow the poultry industry to hide behind a vague designation of product either as 'chicken' or 'chicken meat.'"

ANIMAL MYTHS

*Here are a few examples of things that some people
believe about animals . . . but just aren't true.*

MYTH: Bats are blind.
FACT: Bats aren't blind. But they have evolved as nocturnal
hunters, and can see better in half-light than in daylight.

MYTH: Monkeys remove fleas in each other's fur during grooming.
FACT: Monkeys don't have fleas. They're removing dead skin—
which they eat.

MYTH: Male seahorses can become pregnant and give birth.
FACT: What actually happens is this: The female seahorse expels
eggs into the male's brood pouch, where they are fertilized. And
while the male does carry the gestating embryos until they are born
10 days later, he doesn't feed them through a placenta or similar
organ (as had previously been thought). Instead, the embryos feed
off of nourishment in the egg itself—food provided by the female.
Basically, the male acts as an incubator.

MYTH: Porcupines can shoot their quills when provoked.
FACT: A frightened porcupine tends to run from danger. If a hunter
catches it, though, a porcupine will tighten its skin to make the
quills stand up . . . ready to lodge in anything that touches them.

MYTH: Whales spout water.
FACT: Whales actually exhale air through their blowholes. This
creates a mist or fog that looks like a water spout.

MYTH: Moths eat clothes.
FACT: Not exactly. Moths lay their eggs on your clothes, which
eventually develop into larvae. It's the larvae that eat tiny parts of
your clothes; adult moths do not eat cloth.

MYTH: Bumblebee flight violates the laws of aerodynamics.
FACT: Nothing that flies violates the laws of aerodynamics.

Ratio of people to TVs in the world: 6 to 1.

THE ORIGIN OF BASKETBALL, PART II

Here's more on how the game of basketball
was invented. Part I starts on page 27.

PROMISES, PROMISES . . .
As James Naismith admitted years later in his memoirs, the
new game he had in mind was an indoor version of an existing sport, like baseball or rugby. And when Dr. Gulick put him in charge of The Incorrigibles' physical education classes, he set out to find one he could adapt.

Naismith spent two weeks experimenting with different games, but something always seemed to get lost in the translation: Indoor soccer, for example, was fun—but too many windows were broken. And rugby turned out to be too dangerous on the gymnasium's hardwood floors. Other sports were safer . . . but they were so boring, The Incorrigibles refused to play them.

Outdoor games were meant to be played outdoors, Naismith concluded, and that was that.

BACK TO THE DRAWING BOARD
Time was running out. With only 24 hours left till his deadline for reporting to the faculty on the success of his efforts, Naismith decided to try a different approach: he would analyze a number of different games systematically, and figure out what made them challenging and fun. Then he would incorporate many of those elements into a new game that would be, as he put it, "interesting, easy to learn, and easy to play in the winter and by artificial light."

DO UNTO OTHERS
Naismith's new game would also have to walk a political tightrope: it had to be physically challenging enough to sustain the interest of The Incorrigibles, but not so rough or violent that it would offend conservatives within the YMCA movement. They had opposed getting involved with sports in the first place . . . and Naismith didn't want to give them any excuse to declare the experiment a failure.

Insect rule of thumb: Drunk ants always fall over on their right side.

HE GOT GAME

Amazingly, Naismith then sat down and, step-by-step, invented one of the most popular games in sports history.

Step 1. He figured that since nearly all popular sports have balls, his game should have one, too. But should it be small or large? Small balls like baseballs and lacrosse balls required bats, sticks, and racquets. Naismith was afraid players might use them to hit each other. He chose a big ball.

Step 2. Naismith felt that running with a ball would invariably lead to tackling the person carrying it—and tackling was too violent for the YMCA (not to mention too dangerous on a wood floor). So in the new game, the person who had the ball wouldn't be allowed to run with it; they wouldn't even be allowed to move. Instead, the player with the ball would have to stand in one place and pass it to the other players. That was the key to the game. "I can still recall how I snapped my fingers and shouted, 'I've got it!'" Naismith recalled years later.

Step 3. And what about the shape of the ball? It would either have to be round or shaped like a rugby ball (the predecessor of the football). Rugby balls were easier to carry under the arm, but that would encourage tackling. Round balls were easier to throw, which made them perfect for a passing game. Naismith decided to use a soccer ball.

Step 4. Naismith figured that there should be a goal at each end of the gymnasium . . . but what kind of goal? A huge one, like a soccer goal, would make scoring too easy—so the goal would have to be smaller. But a tiny goal would be easy to block . . . and blocking the goal would lead to pushing and shoving. So he decided to put the goal high over people's heads, where it would be impossible to block.

Step 5. This led to another consideration: if the goal was vertical, like the goalposts in football, players would throw the ball at it as hard and as fast as they could—which would be dangerous indoors. It would also reward force over skill, which was the antithesis of what Naismith wanted.

Naismith suddenly remembered a game he'd played as a child, called Duck on the Rock. The object was to knock a "duck" off of a

The islands of Antigua and Barbuda issued Elle Macpherson postage stamps in 1999.

rock by throwing stones at it. The best players always threw their rocks in an arc rather than directly at the duck, so that if they missed, they wouldn't have to run as far to retrieve the rock.

That inspired Naismith to use a horizontal goal, parallel to the ground. That way, players wouldn't be able to score just by throwing the ball as hard as they could: they'd have to throw it in an arc to get it in.

SERENDIPITY STRIKES
Naismith figured a wooden box nailed to the balcony that ran around the gym would work pretty well as a goal, and asked the janitor if he had any boxes lying around.

"No," the janitor told him, "but I have two old peach baskets down in the store room, if they will do you any good." "Thus," Robert Peterson writes in *Cages to Jump Shots*, "did the game miss being called box ball."

Naismith nailed one peach basket to the balcony at one end of the gym, and one at the other end. The balcony of the YMCA in Springfield just happened to be 10 feet off the floor—which is why, today, a regulation basket is 10 feet high.

THE FIRST GAME
Naismith typed up a list of 13 rules and posted them on the gym's bulletin board. The following morning, he read The Incorrigibles the rules; then he divided the 18-man class into two teams of 9 and taught them to play the game.

He promised to change any rules that didn't work out. "It was the start of the first basketball game," he recounted in his memoirs years later, "and the finish of the trouble with that class." Basketball still had a long way to go.

Turn to page 270 for the last part of our story.

Turn to page 270 for the last part of our story.

* * *

"Women want mediocre men, and men are working hard to be as mediocre as possible."

—Margaret Mead

Each year Americans use enough foam peanuts to fill ten 85-story skyscrapers.

HOW EN-LIGHTNING

*Zap! BRI member Kurt Stark requested
these facts about lightning.*

Every second, there are 100 to 125 flashes of lightning somewhere on Earth.

A lightning bolt can be anywhere between 200 feet and 20 miles long, but the average length, cloud-to-ground, is 2 to 10 miles.

Lightning speeds toward the Earth at an average of 200,000 miles per hour.

The average flash of lightning contains 125 million volts of electricity—enough to light a 100-watt bulb for more than three months.

The chances of being hit by lightning in your lifetime are about 1 in 600,000. Still, anywhere from 500 to 1,000 people are struck by lightning every year in the U.S.

The temperature of a lightning stroke can reach 50,000°F—hotter than the sun's surface.

Lightning bolts actually flicker—a flash is a series of strokes that follow the exact same path as the first one. The record number of strokes ever recorded in a single flash is 47.

When you see a lightning flash, count the seconds until you hear the bang of thunder. Divide by five—sound travels about one mile every five seconds—and this will give you an approximation of the storm's distance from you.

About one-quarter of all lightning strikes occur in open fields; 30 percent happen in July; 22 percent in August.

You can get struck by lightning while you're on the phone. It happens to about 2.5 percent of all lightning-strike victims.

Trees are lightning bolts' favorite targets—lightning is the largest cause of forest fires in the western U.S.

Estimated diameter of a lightning channel: 0.5 to 1 inch.

A charge of 100 million to 1 billion volts of electricity needs to be generated in a cloud to start a cloud-to-ground lightning strike.

For the last decade, an average of 20 million cloud-to-ground flashes have been counted over the continental U.S. each year.

The Tour de France bicycle race is 2,300 miles long.

THE DUSTBIN
OF HISTORY

Think your heroes will go down in history for something they've done?
Don't count on it. These folks were VIPs in their time . . . but they're
forgotten now. They've been swept into the Dustbin of History.

FORGOTTEN FIGURE: John "Bet-a-Million" Gates, a com-
pulsive gambler in the late 1800s, who once tried to bet $1
million on a horse at Saratoga Race Track, "causing book-
makers to run for cover"
CLAIM TO FAME: Gates started out as a $30-a-month barbed-
wire salesman, but after a few years of skilled gambling, built a $50
million fortune. He was notorious for parting robber barons from
their money, taking millions from Andrew Carnegie and relieving
financier J. P. Morgan of $15 million on a single bet. Beating capi-
talists at their own game—making money—made him a hero with
the public.

Gates's luck eventually ran out and he lost everything in a bet
with J. P. Morgan . . . or almost everything. Gates reportedly got
down on his knees and begged Morgan not to bankrupt him;
Morgan relented—on the condition that Gates leave New York
forever.

Gates had to accept. He moved to Texas and invested what little money he had left in drilling for oil. Most of the wells he dug
were dry holes, but the few that weren't produced so much oil that
John D. Rockefeller offered to buy him out for $25 million. Gates
refused, returned to New York triumphantly, and by the time he
died in 1911 once again had a fortune valued at between $50 and
$100 million.
INTO THE DUSTBIN: Gates was buried in an opulent mausoleum near Wall Street. Still, hardly anyone remembers him today.

FORGOTTEN FIGURE: Anthony Comstock, an anti-vice crusader at the turn-of-the century
CLAIM TO FAME: Known as "The Great American Bluenose,"
he was, for a time, one of the most powerful men in public life. In

---

Poll result: 58% of schoolkids say pizza is their favorite cafeteria food.

1873, at age 29, he founded an organization called the New York Society for the Suppression of Vice. A few years later he became the U.S. Post Office's special agent to enforce a federal anti-obscenity law . . . which he had created. Congress didn't even bother to define "obscenity"—they left that up to Comstock.

The problem was, Comstock seemed to think just about everything was obscene: He had Walt Whitman fired from the Department of the Interior for writing *Leaves of Grass* and had the George Bernard Shaw play *Mrs. Warren's Profession* banned after one showing because he found it "reeking" with sin. He even arrested a woman for calling her husband a spitbub (rascal) on a postcard. He was also notorious for personally dragging to jail any art dealer who refused to remove paintings with nudes in them from public display.

Comstock eventually developed a reputation as a kook: In 1915 he hauled some department-store window dressers into court for dressing their naked mannequins in full view of the shopping public—prompting the judge to exclaim partway through the trial, "Mr. Comstock, I think you're nuts." Comstock never lived the humiliation down, and died shortly afterward.

INTO THE DUSTBIN: About all that remains of Comstock today is the word *Comstockery*, which the *American College Dictionary* describes as "overzealous censorship of the fine arts and literature, often mistaking outspokenly honest works for salacious productions." The term was coined by a thankful George Bernard Shaw after Comstock's efforts to shut down *Mrs. Warren's Profession* turned it into a smash hit.

FORGOTTEN FIGURES: Daisy and Violet Hilton, two sisters who played jazz on the vaudeville circuit in the 1920s
CLAIM TO FAME: Daisy was an excellent alto saxophone player; Violet was an excellent pianist. But that isn't what attracted crowds to their performances wherever they went: Daisy and Violet were Siamese twins, joined at the hip. They made a fortune performing up and down the East Coast.
INTO THE DUSTBIN: By the late 1950s, the sisters had spent all of their performance money and were working at a supermarket in Charlotte, North Carolina. They died within hours of each other from influenza in 1960.

New data: 32% of singles polled said they think they'll meet their future mate online.

WE AIN'T LION: THE MODERN ZOO IS BORN

It wasn't that long ago that seeing an elephant at the London Zoo was about as shocking to the average person as meeting a Martian would be today. Here's the story of how zoos got their start.

O LD-TIME MENAGERIES
People have "collected" exotic animals for more than 5,000 years. Priests in ancient Egypt raised lions, tigers, and other sacred animals in and around temples, and as early as 1100 B.C., China's Zhou Dynasty established what was called the "Garden of Intelligence," a 900-acre preserve filled with deer, antelope, birds, fish, and other animals that were studied as well as hunted.

Exotic animals were also popular in ancient Rome, where they were collected by wealthy families and used in gladiator games.

Sometimes the lions, tigers, bulls, bears, and other creatures fought each other to a bloody death for public amusement; other times they were pitted against Christians, heretics, or condemned criminals (or, if none were available, ordinary criminals). Sometimes the Romans even filled their coliseums with water, so gladiators in boats could hunt water animals like hippos and crocodiles.

These games were so popular—and killed so many animals— that by the time they finally came to an end in the 6th century A.D., numerous species in the Roman empire, including the elephants of North Africa, the hippopotami of Nubia, the lions of Mesopotamia, and the tigers of Hycrania, had all been driven to extinction.

THE DARK AGES

When Rome fell in the 5th century A.D., interest in animals declined, and it wasn't until the 13th century that nobles and other wealthy Europeans began collecting animals on a large scale again. They even exchanged them like trading cards.

When it was invented in India, badminton was known as *poona*.

King Frederick II of Sicily was a typical collector of the era: his menagerie included hyenas, elephants, camels, lions, monkeys, cheetahs, and a giraffe . . . and when he got tired of the giraffe, he traded it to the sultan of Egypt for a polar bear.

THE LONDON ZOO

In 1235 King Henry III of England moved his grandfather's animal collection to the Tower of London. The collection included camels, lions, leopards, and lynx . . . and King Louis IX of France contributed an elephant—the first one ever seen in Great Britain. The animals were put on display for the royal family and its guests, but were also occasionally pitted against one another—tigers vs. lions, bears vs. dogs—to entertain royal visitors. However, the novelty eventually wore off, and the animals became neglected.

Then, in 1445, Margaret of Anjoy, wife of Henry VI, received a lion as a wedding gift . . . which inspired her to have the entire Royal Menagerie—what was left of it—restored. But when the royal family moved out of the Tower in the early 1700s, they left their animals behind. That created a problem: if the royal family wasn't going to support the menagerie, who was? Finally, someone came up with the idea of opening the collection to the public, and charging them admission. Price: three half-pence, or if you preferred, a dog or cat to feed to the lions.

CHANGING TIMES

As the British Empire expanded to the far corners of the globe in the early 1800s, interest in exotic animals grew beyond mere curiosity. In 1826 an explorer named Sir Stamford Raffles founded the London Zoological Society, which took its name from the ancient Greek word *zoion*, which means "living being."

Two years later, the Society moved the royal family's animal collection from the Tower of London to a new site in Regent's Park. It was a big hit with members of the royal family, many of whom contributed animals.

But unlike the Tower of London, the Zoological Park was closed to the public—the animals were "objects of scientific research," Raffles explained, "not of vulgar admiration." Only members of the Zoological society and their guests were allowed to visit. (A written voucher would allow a nonmember to enter, and these became very common and were even traded in pubs.)

On average, the Statue of Liberty's fingernails weigh 100 pounds each.

The public was officially excluded from the "zoo," as it had become known, until 1846, by which time the novelty had worn off and attendance had fallen dramatically. So the Zoological Society opened its doors to anyone with a penny, and hundreds of thousands of new visitors streamed into the park. "For the city dweller," Linda Koebler writes in *Zoo*, "[it] provided a place of greenery that was a relief from the ugly, dirty cities of this period."

The term "zoo" entered mainstream culture a year after the London Zoological Garden opened to the public, thanks to the popularity of one particular song: "Walking in the Zoo Is an Okay Thing to Do."

ZOOS IN EUROPE

In the early 1800s, having a public zoo became a status symbol for any European city that considered itself modern and sophisticated. If they still had royal collections of animals available, they quickly converted them to zoological parks. If they didn't, they created new zoos. Zoos in Dublin, Berlin, Frankfurt, Antwerp, and Rotterdam were among the best known.

LE ZOO

In France, however, the development of public zoos was slowed by the Revolution of 1789. Common people saw private collections of captive animals as a way for the rich to flaunt their wealth.

According to one account, when a mob of revolutionaries arrived at the Ménagerie du Parc to free the animals, "The crowd wanted the animals set free so that others could catch them and eat them, outraged that these animals grew fat while the people starved. But once the zoo director explained that some of the creatures would eat the crowd rather than vice versa, the du Parc revolutionaries decided to liberate only the more edible captives."

Cat got your tongue? Did someone call you a cheetah? Don't monkey around, turn to page 349 for more wild facts about zoos.

ODD JOBS

Looking for an exciting new job? Here's a list of the most unusual-sounding occupations we could find.

Killer Bee Hunter. Your mission: Track down Africanized "killer" bees, which are migrating north from Central America, and destroy them before they can take up residence in North America.

Chicken Shooter. Fire dead chickens out of a cannon at aircraft to see what kind of damage occurs.

Mother Repairer. It's not what you think. It actually entails repairing metal phonograph record "mothers" (the master from which records are pressed) by removing dirt and nickel particles from the grooves.

Anthem Man. A unique profession: King Alfonso of Spain was tone deaf . . . he employed one man whose job was to alert him when the Spanish national anthem was playing (so he would know when to salute).

Worm Collector. Get ready to crawl through grass at night with a flashlight, to catch the best worms for fishing. Tip: Grab them in the middle to avoid bruising.

Weed Farmer. If you like gardening, here's a change of pace: grow weeds . . . then sell them to chemical companies for herbicide research.

Pig Manure Sniffer. Workers try to recognize chemical markers in manure so researchers can determine which foods make pig manure so foul smelling. Women only, because estrogen increases sensitivity to smell.

Sewage Diver. Put on a diving suit and plunge into a sewage-containment vat.

Animal Chauffeur. We've only heard of one—a guy named Stephen May. His "limousine" is equipped with, among other things: a blanketed floor, eight-inch color television, stereo speakers, and silk flowers.

Flush Tester. A gold star from Uncle John to the gallant professionals who test toilet-bowl standards by trying to flush rags down various toilets.

Armpit Sniffer. Enough said.

ARE YOU DYING TO WATCH TV?

Numerous scientific studies suggest that you may live longer—and be happier—if you trade in your TV Guide for an exercise bike and a copy of Uncle John's Bathroom Reader *(it's a great way to pass the time while you're working out, too).*

TV CAN GIVE YOU: High cholesterol
Evidence: In a study at the University of California, Irvine, scientists found that children who watch more than two hours of TV or video games each day have twice the blood cholesterol levels of those watching less than two hours.
Why Is This True? Three things happen when kids sit in front of the TV: they snack more, they exercise less, and their metabolic rate drops even lower than if they were laying in bed doing nothing.
More Evidence: Advertisers know it too. According to Dr. Thomas Starc of Columbia University, ads for high-fat foods (such as pizza and fast-food burgers) during children's cartoon shows rose from 16% of the total in 1989 to 41% in 1993.

TV CAN MAKE YOU: Violent
Evidence: A team led by Prof. Ronald Huesmann, University of Michigan, studied 1,300 children in the United States, Europe, and Israel from the early 1970s on. Did the children who watched TV violence get in more fights, bully others, commit crimes, or get more traffic tickets? Yes—especially right after seeing violence on TV. There were exceptions, of course, but Prof. Huesmann insists that the correlation was statistically as strong as that between smoking and lung cancer. This outcome was enhanced if the TV perpetrator was attractive, if the violence was socially sanctioned, or if guns were used. The violent outcome was reduced if the resulting pain and suffering were shown, if the children talked with adults about TV violence being unrealistic, or if there were strong social sanctions against imitating the violence.

Estimated value of a single pair of Elvis' underpants: $1,300.

TV CAN MAKE YOU: Paranoid

Evidence: Prof. Barbara Wilson of the University of California-Santa Barbara, found that children who watch the news have an unrealistically fearful picture of crime, war, and natural disasters in today's world. In a survey of parents of kids in third through sixth grades, she found that 37 percent of the parents thought their children had reacted with fear to a TV news story within the past year. But when she asked the kids directly, 51 percent could describe a TV news clip that scared them. Her conclusion: Kids under eight years old aren't ready for news programs.

TV CAN MAKE YOU: Depressed

Evidence: In a study of 4,280 people conducted by Dr. Stephen Sidney at Kaiser Permanente Hospital, people watching more than four hours of TV daily were 54 percent more likely to score high on a test measuring depression. Sidney cautioned that the study does not prove TV causes depression, but insisted that there is a correlation.

TV CAN MAKE YOU: A poor reader

Evidence: According to a study by the National Assessment of Educational Progress, a large majority of heavy-TV-watching students fall in the "basic" reading level, just able to get the meaning of what they read. Around a quarter to a third of students, depending on age, are "proficient,"—which means reading at their grade level, and only 2 percent to 4 percent fall in "advanced," or able to make complex analyses from what they read.

TV CAN MAKE YOU: An addict

Evidence: As part of a scientific study in 1971, 184 German TV watchers agreed to quit TV cold turkey. According to the Society for Rational Psychology, the group showed a sudden increase in moodiness, child spanking, wife beating, extramarital affairs, and less interest in sex. Several of the subjects had to go back to TV after only a few days. Although they were being paid, no one lasted more than five months. However, once back at the tube, all of their behavior returned to normal.

* * *

Random Household Hint: For perfectly round pancakes every time, use a turkey baster to "squirt" the batter onto the griddle.

Until 1937, the referee tossed a jump ball after every basket in basketball.

UNEXPECTED HAZARDS OF TV

And then there are risks in watching TV that no scientist can predict.

WATCH OUT FOR: Angry relatives
Detectives in Boynton Beach, Florida, called it "the couch potato murder." The wife and daughter of Joe Grieco, 52, and the daughter's boyfriend conspired to shoot Grieco because he was "depressed and cranky all the time and all he wanted to do was lay on the couch and watch TV." They tried to give Grieco a heart attack by putting LSD in his chicken dinner and cocaine in his wine, but it didn't work. Finally Mrs. Grieco shot him while he snored in bed.

WATCH OUT FOR: Burnout! (Not you, the set)
Charlotte Gardener, 86, of London, England, kept her TV on 24 hours a day. After two years a component burned out. The fumes killed her.

WATCH OUT FOR: Falling objects
In 1995 a 30-ton boulder fell 500 feet off a cliff, crashed through a mobile home roof and killed Jackie Johnson, 19, of Adams Beach, Kentucky, while he was watching TV on the couch. The man's grandmother, who had been watching TV beside him, had just gotten up to let her dog in. His grandfather, who was also sitting on the couch, was thrown up in the air and got a broken shoulder.

WATCH OUT FOR: Just dropping dead and no one notices

- The fully-dressed skeleton of a man who died 10 months earlier while watching TV was discovered in Roubaix, France. The TV was still on. Neighbors thought the man, 55, was in the hospital.

- In Bonn, Germany, a landlord entered the apartment of Wolfgang Dircks when he fell behind on rent. He was found dead with the TV on . . . and a TV guide on his lap dated December 5, 1993. It was then November 1998. Police ruled he died around the date of the TV guide.

In 1948, 2.3% of American households had a television; today 99% do.

THE GREAT "MARY" DEBATE

In Uncle John's Great Big Bathroom Reader, we mentioned the inspiration for the poem "Mary Had a Little Lamb." Little did we know that we were opening a Pandora's box of controversy and intrigue. Here are details about a little-known fight between two New England towns that each claim to be the birthplace of the legendary ditty.

WHODUNNIT . . . AND WHERE?

Theory #1: A schoolboy named John Roulstone in Sterling, Massachusetts. He happened to be visiting a classroom in Sterling one day in 1815, when a pet lamb followed its owner, a girl named Mary Sawyer, to school. When the teacher called Mary to the front of the class to recite a lesson, the lamb followed her up the classroom aisle. The teacher "turned it out," as the poem relates, and Roulstone was so amused by the spectacle that he jotted down the first three stanzas of "Mary Had a Little Lamb."

Evidence: In an 1879 letter, Mary Sawyer herself describes the schoolroom incident and credits Roulstone with writing the poem. This version of the story has been widely accepted for more than a century; in 1927, Henry Ford even bought the framework of the original schoolhouse and moved it to Sudbury, Massachusetts, where it still stands.

Theory #2: A nationally prominent writer and editor named Sarah Josepha Hale wrote the poem in Newport, New Hampshire (70 miles north of Sterling), in 1830. Hale, editor of the popular *Godey's Ladies Book* (a women's magazine) for nearly 40 years, was the author of more than 20 books and hundreds of poems.

Evidence: Hale, who is also credited with mounting the successful lobbying effort that helped make Thanksgiving a national holiday, published "Mary Had a Little Lamb" under her own name in 1830 in a publication called "Poems for Our Children." Then in 1889, shortly before she died, she signed a statement claiming authorship.

Hop to it: In the 13th century, Europeans baptized children with beer.

Supporters assert that she was simply too distinguished a person to falsely claim ownership of a poem she had not written. "She was shaping public opinion. Why would she stoop to plagiarize a lousy children's poem?" says Hale enthusiast Andrea Thorpe.

BUT REALLY, WHO CARES?

Aside from idle curiosity, why make a big deal out of authorship of the poem? Apparently it's the primary claim to fame of both Newport (New Hampshire) and Sterling (Massachusetts). So residents have a lot at stake. According to Linda Matchan, who wrote about them in the *Boston Globe* in 1998, they're trying to preserve . . .

Tourist Dollars

Sterling: The town "promotes itself as the home of Mary and her lamb. A small bronze lamb statue stands in tribute on the town common. The Sterling Historical Society sells Mary's lamb T-shirts and notecards and fuzzy lamb statuettes."

• In 1999 a dozen people in Sterling formed the Mary's Little Lamb Association, hoping "to parlay the Mary's lamb connection into a major fund-raising campaign." Their dream: attract $250,000 in donations to restore Mary Sawyer's original farmhouse (or at least the one that was supposedly hers) and turn it into a historical monument.

Newport: "Like Sterling, Newport proudly displays its link to the lamb. A memorial plaque to Hale states that 'she composed the poem now called "Mary Had a Little Lamb."'" Tour guides talk about it, and it's a subject of the Newport information guide produced by the Chamber of Commerce."

A Native Daughter's Reputation . . .

Sterling: If Hale really did write the poem, then Mary Sawyer—Sterling's pride and joy—was a liar. Mary's sixth-generation relative (and current Sterling resident), Diane Melone, won't have any of that. But she is willing to allow that Hale may have written the last three verses.

Newport: However, that would mean Mrs. Hale didn't write the whole thing . . . so she'd be a liar. That's completely unacceptable to Hale-ites in Newport. "Like she needs to be given the last three

verses," says Andrea Thorpe. "We have no doubt that Sarah wrote it. Absolutely none . . . Everyone except Sterling agrees with me."
Sterling: Mary's defenders then gleefully point to Henry Ford. "If there is such credibility to the New Hampshire story," Melone says, "Henry Ford would have gone to Newport to obtain a school-house."
Newport: But Thorpe, who is also the administrator of a New England writer's prize called (surprise) "The Sarah Josepha Hale Award," is unmoved. "Let's face it," she said. "Henry Ford . . . made good cars. I don't think he is a good historian."

Local Pride . . .
Sterling: "Everybody, including both sets of my grandparents, knew [the poem is part of Sterling history]," says Melone. Denying it is "like living in Gettysburg and saying the Battle of Gettysburg didn't happen there."
Newport: From her battle-station in New Hampshire, Thorpe monitors the national scene. Whenever she discovers that some-one has taken Sterling's side, she sends "a standard indignant let-ter": "Your article about the authorship of the poem 'Mary's Lamb' shows a complete disregard for literary history . . . and an igno-rance of the contributions made by one of the most famous people to come from Newport."

UPDATE
Meanwhile, two scholars—Lee Swanson and B. G. Thurston—are involved in a research project that could undermine both claims.

They're trying to trace the history of "Mary Had a Little Lamb" back before Roulstone or Hale—and they say they've succeeded. Matchan reports that "their research has led them to a nearly iden-tical British version of the poem published earlier than Hale's, about a 'Lucy' and her little lamb. They are in the process of veri-fying the information.

"Where would this leave Sterling and Newport?" Matchan asks. "A little sheepish perhaps?"

"I don't know," says Thurston. "I truly believe neither side is correct, though I don't have the full research to support it. It might be one of those mysteries that will never be solved."

What do grape juice and the blesbok antelope have in common? Same color.

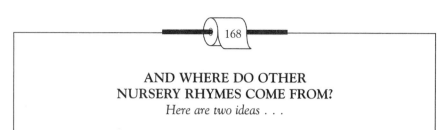

AND WHERE DO OTHER NURSERY RHYMES COME FROM?
Here are two ideas . . .

"London Bridge is falling down . . ."
Inspiration: Human sacrifice. Experts say the poem ("Take the key and lock her up . . .") reflects an ancient superstition that the only way to keep a bridge from collapsing was to offer up a human sacrifice, usually a child, to the gods. The child would actually be imprisoned in the bridge as it was built.
Details: "All over the world," reports the *Oxford Dictionary of Nursery Rhymes*, "stories of human sacrifice are associated with bridges, to the erection of which the rivers are supposed to have a special antipathy."

- For example: "When the Bridge Gate at Bremen was demolished in the last century the skeleton of a child was found embedded in the foundations."

- "London Bridge itself is not without a tainted reputation, for there is in the capital a tradition that the stones of this great bridge, too, were once bespattered with the blood of children."

"Jack be nimble, Jack be quick, Jack jump over the candlestick."
Inspiration: An ancient fortune-telling superstition
Details: For centuries, it was a common practice in England for people to tell their fortunes by jumping over lit candles. St. Catherine's Day festivities, for example, were traditionally brought to a close by "jumping the candlestick for luck." When someone jumped over the candlestick without extinguishing the flame, they were said to have good luck in the coming year.

* * *

A BAA-A-A-AD JOKE

Q: Where do sheep get their hair cut?
A: At the baaa-baaa shop.

Female cigar store Indians once outnumbered male ones by four to one.

YEAH, WRIGHT

*BRI members have been asking for more Steven
Wright quotes—so here they are.*

"For my birthday I got a humidifier and a dehumidifier . . . I put them in the same room and let them fight it out."

"I hate it when my foot falls asleep during the day because that means it's going to be up all night."

"I bought a dog the other day . . . I named him Stay. It's fun to call him . . . 'Come here, Stay! Come here, Stay!' He went insane. Now he just ignores me and keeps typing."

"I stayed up all night playing poker with tarot cards. I got a full house and four people died."

"It doesn't matter what temperature the room is, it's always room temperature."

"A lot of people are afraid of heights. Not me—I'm afraid of widths."

"I just bought a microwave fireplace . . . You can spend an entire evening in front of it in only eight minutes."

"Last year I went fishing with Salvador Dali. He was using a dotted line. He caught every other fish."

"When I turned two I was really anxious, because I'd doubled my age in a year. I thought, if this keeps up, by the time I'm six I'll be ninety."

"I bought some land. It was kind of cheap. It was on somebody else's property."

"The guy who lives across the street from me has a circular driveway, and he can't get out."

"I bought some batteries, but they weren't included, so I had to buy them again."

"Babies don't need a vacation. But I still see them at the beach. It pisses me off. When no one's looking I'll go over to a baby and ask, 'What are you doing here? You haven't worked a day in your life.'"

"I went to a general store, but they wouldn't let me buy anything specific."

How did "venereal disease" get its name? From Venus, the Roman goddess of love.

THE BEST BUSINESS DEAL IN U.S. HISTORY, PART I

The early days of the auto industry were like today's Internet boom—people could make huge fortunes by investing in the right car company. But no high-tech rags-to-riches story quite matched the return on investment that the Dodge brothers got for their $7,000 in auto parts and $3,000 in cash. It's a great, little-known business tale.

RAGS TO ROADSTERS

In 1901, the early days of the automobile, Ransom Eli Olds was looking for subcontractors who could manufacture parts for his Curved Dash Oldsmobile. The best machine shop in the Detroit area was a company called Leland and Faulconer, but they were already committed to supplying parts for the new Cadillac Automobile Company (see page 410). So Olds turned to the second-best machine shop in town, owned and operated by John and Horace Dodge.

Experience Counts

The brothers Dodge were only in their mid-30s, but they already had more than 20 years' experience working with internal combustion engines. Their father owned a machine shop on the river that connected Lake Huron with Lake Erie, and the brothers spent much of their childhood helping him repair and rebuild ship engines.

By the time John and Horace were in their 20s, both were working as machinists in Detroit. They spent the next several years perfecting their skills at various companies, and in 1897 opened a bicycle company to manufacture an "improved" bicycle they'd designed themselves. Two years later, they sold the company and used the money—$7,500 in cash and $10,000 worth of machine tools—to open the Dodge Brothers Machine Shop in Detroit.

What's the common name for the animal *anobium pertinax*? Bookworm.

SHIFTING GEARS

Dodge Brothers started out manufacturing parts for a types of products, including firearms, bicycles, autom steam engines. But they got so much business from C dropped everything else and began manufacturing auto parts exclusively. Olds sold 2,000 cars in 1902, more than any other carmaker in the country, and every one of them had a Dodge transmission. As production continued to climb, Dodge Brothers moved to a newer, larger shop and spent tens of thousands of dollars on new machine tools to keep up with the demand.

Then in 1903, the Dodge brothers took a huge risk: they dumped the Olds Motor Works account and agreed to begin manufacturing engines, transmissions, and chassis for the Ford & Malcomson Company—which, unlike Olds, had only recently opened for business and had yet to manufacture a single car.

HARD BARGAIN

Why would the Dodge brothers abandon Olds for Ford-Malcomson? Part of the reason was that Henry Ford, the company's co-founder, had showed them the plans for his Model A "Fordmobile," and the Dodges were impressed. They thought it had a good chance of succeeding.

But there was an even bigger incentive: Ironically, Henry Ford's track record of failure (he had already run two companies into the ground) actually made doing business with him more lucrative for the Dodge brothers than if he had been a success. His credit rating was so bad that he had to offer the brothers a sweeter business deal than they could have gotten anywhere else in town.

Normally, in the machine parts industry, an auto company like Ford-Malcomson would have 60 days to pay for auto parts after delivery. But since the Dodges weren't sure if Ford would still be in business in 60 days, they demanded cash up front on the first shipment of parts, and payment within 15 days on each subsequent delivery. If Ford couldn't pay, ownership of all unsold parts automatically reverted to the Dodge brothers. The terms were tough, but Ford had to agree.

HOWDY, PARDNER

There was one more perk. When Henry Ford and Alex Malcomson, Detroit's leading coal merchant, set out to found an auto com-

How do you know when you're playing with an Italian deck of cards? No queens.

pany together, they had hoped to finance the entire venture with their own savings. But they soon realized they didn't have enough money: Malcomson's credit was so overstretched that he took his name off of Ford-Malcomson (renaming it the Ford Motor Company) so his bankers wouldn't find out he had money tied up in the business. (Plus, if the company went under, as Malcomson feared it might, he worried his name would become associated with failure.)

Henry Ford's financial position wasn't much better: he had very little money of his own, and had already alienated Detroit's business community with his two earlier business failures. Nobody wanted to invest in a company run by a two-time loser like Ford.

With so few people willing to invest in Ford, Malcomson pushed the company's stock onto friends and colleagues who owed him favors. He also pitched the shares to people who had a direct financial stake in the company's survival, two of whom were John and Horace Dodge. Malcomson offered them a 10% stake in the Ford Motor Company, in exchange for $7,000 worth of auto parts and $3,000 in cash.

Now you know what the deal is. Turn to page 255 for the rest of the story.

* * *

HOLY BAT FACTS!

- Most species of bats live 12 to 15 years, but some live as long as 30 years. Some species can fly as fast as 60 miles per hour and as high as 10,000 feet.

- Bats are social animals and live in colonies in caves. The colonies can get huge: Bracken Cave in Texas contains an estimated 20 million Mexican free-tailed bats.

- Vampire bats drink blood through a "drinking straw" that the bat makes with its tongue and its lower lip. The bats' saliva contains an anticoagulant that keeps blood flowing by impeding the formation of blood clots.

- It's not uncommon for a vampire bat to return to the same animal night after night, weakening and eventually killing its prey.

Theodore Roosevelt's boyhood friends called him Teedie, not Teddy.

AESOP:
FACT OR FABLE?

Chances are, you've heard of Aesop's fables—people have been repeating them for thousands of years. But did you know there was a real person named Aesop?

BACKGROUND
If you were asked to name to the most influential writers in Western history, you might include Aristotle . . . or Shakespeare . . . or even Dr. Spock. But you probably wouldn't think of Aesop.

Yet his works have been around for over 2,000 years, and he's had an impact on everything from ancient Greek philosophy to 20th-century American culture. Adages such as "Don't cry over spilled milk" and expressions like "sour grapes," for example, come directly from his fables.

On the other hand, Aesop wasn't technically a writer. Nothing was written down during his lifetime; it was oral tradition that kept both his legend and his fables alive. Still, scholars are reasonably certain he existed—and that he was a revered storyteller. "The best evidence we have of Aesop's life comes from remarks about him in early ancient sources like Herodotus, Aristotle, Aristophanes, and Plato," writes Leo Groarke Wilfrid of Laurier University. In fact, Socrates, considered the greatest philosopher of ancient Greece, "is said to have passed the time awaiting execution by putting Aesop's fables into verse."

A BRIEF BIOGRAPHY
Scholars have established a few facts about Aesop's life:

- He was born a Greek slave in the 6th century B.C.

- He had a natural gift for fables and became famous in ancient Greece because of it. Eventually his "learning and wit" earned him his freedom.

- As a freed man he traveled widely until Croesus, the rich and powerful king of ancient Lydia, invited him to become an ambassador. Aesop accepted and was sent to various republics of Greece, trying to establish peace "by telling his wise fables."

Write this one down: The typewriter was invented before the fountain pen.

- Aesop's last diplomatic mission was to Delphi. Croesus gave him gold to distribute to the citizens. However, Aesop was so offended by the Delphians' greed that he just sent the loot back to Croesus. Proving his point, the Delphians became so enraged that they accused Aesop of "impiety"—a major crime—and executed him as a public criminal. According to legend, they pushed him off a cliff.

- Following the execution of Aesop, a myth grew up around the incident. It was said that a series of calamities befell the citizens of Delphi. The disasters got worse and worse until, finally, the people confessed their crime and made reparations. After that, "the blood of Aesop" became a common reference to the fact that evil deeds will not go unpunished.

HOW THE FABLES CAME TO US

After his death, Aesop became a sort of mythical figure (like Mother Goose) to whom fables were automatically attributed, no matter who invented them. For a thousand years after his death, he was more famous than ever. But with the coming of the Dark Ages, he was forgotten.

Then in the 1300s, a Turkish monk named Planudes assembled a collection of about 150 of Aesop's fables. When Italian scholars of the mid-1400s became interested in antiquity, Planudes' book was one of the first works they translated and printed, along with works by Homer and Aristotle.

Aesop's tales spread from Italy to Germany, where his popularity grew. The "great fathers of the Reformation" used his fables to inveigh against the Catholic Church; Martin Luther himself translated 20 of Aesop's fables and said that next to the Bible, he valued *Aesop's Fables* above all other books.

Finally, in 1610, a Swiss scholar named Isaac Nicholas Nevelet printed a version of Aesop's fables called *Mythologica Aesopica*. It was popular all over Europe and made Aesop a permanent part of Western civilization. "No book," wrote the compiler of a 19th-century collection, "with the exception of the Holy Scriptures, has had a wider circulation than *Aesop's Fables*. They have been translated into the greater number of the languages both of Europe and of the East, and have been read, and will be read, for generations by the inhabitants of all countries."

Before Prohibition, the most common method of drinking beer at home was . . .

AESOP'S FABLES

Aesop's fables (see page 173) have been told and retold for thousands of years. Here are some of our favorites.

THE FOX & THE CRANE

A fox once invited a crane to dinner and served soup in a very shallow dish. He thought it was funny that the crane, with his long beak, couldn't drink any of the soup.

Then he said, "My dear crane, I'm so sorry to see that you're not eating anything. Didn't you like the soup?"

"Oh, everything is just fine," the crane answered. "And now you must do me the honor of paying me a visit."

When the fox came to the crane's house and sat down to dinner, a very tall jar was placed in front of him. It was so tall and narrow that the fox couldn't get his snout into it.

"I'm so glad to be able to return your courtesy," said the crane as he reached his long beak into the jar. "I hope you enjoy your dinner every bit as much as I did mine when I visited you."

Moral: What goes around, comes around. You get what you deserve.

THE FIR TREE & THE BRAMBLE

A fir tree boasted to a bramble, "You're useful for nothing at all; while I am used for roofs and houses and all kinds of things." The bramble answered: "You poor creature, if you would only call to mind the axes and saws which are about to cut you down, you would wish you'd grown up a bramble, not a fir tree."

Moral: Better poverty without care, than riches with a worried life.

BELLING THE CAT

Long ago, a group of mice had a general council to consider what measures they could take to outwit their common enemy, the cat. Some said this, and some said that; but at last a young mouse got up and said he had a proposal to make, which he thought would meet the case. "You will all agree," said he, "that our chief danger consists in the sly and treacherous manner in which the enemy approaches us. Now, if we could receive some signal of her approach, we could easily escape from her. I venture, therefore, to propose that a small bell be procured, and attached by a ribbon round the neck of the cat. By this means we should always know when she was about, and could easily retire while she was in the neighborhood."

This proposal met with general applause, until an old mouse got up and said: "That is all very well, but who is to bell the cat?" The mice looked at one another and nobody spoke. Then the old mouse said: "It is easy to propose impossible remedies."

Moral: Talk is cheap.

THE BUFFOON & THE COUNTRYMAN

At a country fair there was a Buffoon who made all the people laugh by imitating the cries of various animals. He finished off by squeaking so like a pig that the spectators thought that he had a porker concealed about him. But a Countryman who stood by said: "Call that a pig's squeak! Nothing like it. You give me till tomorrow and I will show you what it's like." The audience laughed, but next day, sure enough, the Countryman appeared on the stage, and putting his head down squealed so hideously that the spectators hissed and threw stones at him to make him stop. "You fools!" he cried, "see what you have been hissing," and held up a little pig whose ear he had been pinching to make him utter the squeals.

Moral: Men often applaud an imitation and hiss the real thing.

THE DOG'S REFLECTION

Once there was a dog who was given a fine, meaty bone. With the bone firmly between his teeth, the dog trotted homeward, thinking of what a fine meal he was going to enjoy.

On the way, he had to cross a narrow bridge over a brook. As he looked over the side of the bridge, he caught sight of his own reflection in the water. Thinking it was another dog carrying a bone between his teeth, the foolish animal made up his mind that he would have that bone, too. He leaned over and snapped at the dog beneath him. As he did, the bone fell into the water and was lost.

Moral: Be careful that you don't lose what you have by trying to get more.

What do people and lobsters have in common? Both like to eat lobster.

COINED BY SHAKESPEARE

Sure, Shakespeare is considered the best writer in the history of the English language. But did you know that he also helped create it? Uncle John didn't . . . until he found a book called Coined by Shakespeare, *written by Jeffrey McQuain and Stanley Malles.*

ALLIGATOR: Before the Bard, it was known in English as a lagarto or an aligarto (from the Spanish *el lagarto*). **First Use:** *Romeo and Juliet* (V.i.42-43)—"in his needy shop a tortoise hung, / An *alligator* stuff'd, and other skins."

DAWN: The verb *dawning*, for "daybreak," already existed; Shakespeare turned it into a noun.
First Use: Henry V (IV.i.274–275)—"next day after *dawn*, /Doth rise and help Hyperion to his horse."

LONELY: Shakespeare added the *-ly*.
First Use: *Coriolanus* (IV.i.29–30)—"I go alone, / Like to a *lonely* dragon."

DRUG: He changed it into a verb, and gave it the negative connotation it has today.
First Use: *Macbeth* (II.ii.6)—"I have *drugg'd* their possets."

EYEBALL: The words *eye* and *ball* already existed; Shakespeare was the first to put them together.
First Use: *A Midsummer Night's Dream* (III.ii.369)—"make his *eyeballs* roll with wonted sight."

UNDRESS: Shakespeare added the *un-*.
First Use: *The Taming of the Shrew* (Induction.ii.117)—"*undress* you, and come now to bed."

PUKE: The Bard spewed this one out all by himself.
First Use: *As You Like It* (II.vii.144)—"Mewling and *puking* in the nurse's arms."

The Platinum American Eagle has the highest denomination of any U.S. coin. Value: $100.

DOMINEERING: Shakespeare adapted this word into English from the Dutch verb *domineren*.
First Use: *Love's Labor Lost* (III.i.177)—"A *domineering* pedant o'er the boy."

INAUDIBLE: Shakespeare added the *in-*.
First Use: *All's Well That Ends Well* (V.iii.40–42)—"We are old, and on our quick'st decrees / Th' *inaudible* and noiseless foot of time / Steals ere we can effect them."

PANDER: From Pandarus, a character in Homer's Iliad. The Bard trimmed the name and added the *-er*.
First Use: *Hamlet* (III.iv.88)—"reason *panders* will."

AMAZEMENT: Shakespeare added the *-ment*, changing the word to a noun.
First Use: *King John* (V.i.35–36)—"Wild *amazement* hurries up and down / The little number of you doubtful friends."

LEAPFROG: Though the game was familiar to his audience, Shakespeare gave it its name.
First Use: *Henry V* (V.ii. 136–39)—"If I could win a lady at *leapfrog* . . . I should quickly leap into a wife."

BEDROOM: Shakespeare invented this word to mean "room or space *within* a bed."
First Use: *A Midsummer Night's Dream* (II.ii.51)—"Then by your side no *bed-room* me deny."

HINT: Shakespeare took the Middle English verb *hent*, and used it as a noun.
First Use: *Othello* (I.iii.165–66)—"I should but teach him how to tell my story, / And that would woo her. Upon this *hint* I spake."

SUBMERGE: The Bard combined the Latin prefix *sub-* ("under") with the Latin word *mergere* ("to plunge") to create this verb.
First Use: *Antony and Cleopatra* (II.v.94–95)—"Half my Egypt were *submerg'd* and made / A cestern for scal'd snakes."

The top 3 products for coupon redemption are cold cereal, soap, and deodorant.

CULTURE SHOCK

Do you take it for granted that our culture is the "real" one . . .
and that other peoples' traditions are just sort of quaint?
Some Americans do and we wind up accidentally offending
people in other parts of the world. A few cases in point:

PURELY COMMERCIAL

"Hindus are up in arms about Madonna's performance at the MTV Video Music Awards. Madonna wore 'Vaishnava tilak,' holy facial markings representing purity. But, says the World Vaishnava Association, 'wearing this sacred marking while wearing clothing through which her nipples were clearly visible and gyrating in a sexually suggestive manner with her guitar player . . . offended Hindus . . . throughout the world.' The WVA seeks apologies."
—USA Today, September 14, 1998

DEJA VU

"Following weeks of protest from Hindu groups, Renaissance Pictures has agreed to pull out of worldwide circulation an entire episode of *Xena: Warrior Princess.* The storyline involved the Hindu deities Lord Krishna and Hanuman aiding Xena in her escape from a demon king . . . 'Not only does this make the viewing audience think that Lord Krishna and other Hindu deities are fictional,' said one protester, 'it makes Hindus themselves look foolish. After all, nobody but a superstitious fool would worship a fictional god.'"
—The Nation, June 7, 1999

IT'S GREEK TO ME

"Disney's animated film *Hercules* has spurred a wrath in Greece worthy of the mighty Zeus . . . Critics have lashed out at the Mickey Mouse empire, accusing its creators of messing with ancient Greek lore to a ludicrous degree . . . In the Hollywood film, the mighty hero is born on Mount Olympus, the son of a happily wed Zeus and Hera. He's kidnapped by wicked Uncle Hades, and on Earth takes on more than a dozen tasks, including thrashing the Minotaur and defeating the Medusa.

"One need not be a classics scholar to know that the Minotaur was killed by Theseus, the Medusa by Perseus. Hades was not the

One in three dog owners say they've talked to their pets on the phone.

personification of evil. And Hercules's household practiced promiscuity, not family values. The muscle-bound hero was loathed by Hera because he was proof of her husband's notorious infidelity . . .

"To avoid further controversy, Greek distributors changed the film's title to *Beyond the Myth of Heracles*."

—*USA Today*, October 2, 1997

LOCAL HERO

"Nike Inc. agreed to scrap a billboard of an inner city Los Angeles basketball player nicknamed 'Allah' after an Islamic American group complained that the ads were offensive . . . The ad featured an L.A. Crenshaw High School graduate named John Williams, who was pictured hanging from the rim of a basket with the caption,' . . . and they called him Allah' and a Nike logo. "The creative team that researched the ad found that, 'Whenever Williams stepped on the court, the crowd would chant "Allah,"' said Nike spokesperson Erin Patton. But he conceded Nike made a mistake in 'overlooking the spiritual relevance of the word.'"

—**Reuters, 1995**

IN THE TRASH

"McDonald's inadvertently offended thousands of Muslims by printing a Koran scripture on throwaway Happy Meal bags, then staged a retreat after Islamic leaders complained. The stir . . . began with a World Cup promotion that featured flags of the 24 competitors in this summer's soccer championship. The green and white Saudi flag contains an Arabic passage translated as 'There is no God but Allah, and Mohammed is his Prophet,' sacred words that Muslims say should not be crumpled up and thrown in the trash."

—*Fresno Bee*, June 8, 1994

FASHION STATEMENT

"In 1994 a dress that Karl Lagerfeld designed for Chanel was pulled from the season's line. The Arab world was up in arms after the sexy black item with Arabic words embroidered across it was modeled on the runway. The objectors complained that the words were from the Koran. Lagerfeld apologized, explaining that he was under the impression that the words were from a love poem. The dress was destroyed, along with all film and pictures of it."

—*The Business Disaster Book of Days*

Experts say: 46% of all violence on TV occurs in cartoons.

ANIMALS FAMOUS FOR 15 MINUTES

When Andy Warhol said, "In the future, everyone will be famous for 15 minutes," he obviously didn't have animals in mind. Yet even they haven't been able to escape the relentless publicity machine that keeps cranking out instant celebrities.

THE HEADLINE: Vote for a Chimp, Not a Chump
THE STAR: Tiao, a chimpanzee in Rio de Janeiro
WHAT HAPPENED: Before he entered political life, Tiao ("Big Uncle") was one of the main attractions at the Rio zoo, where he'd developed a reputation for "losing his temper, spitting, and throwing excrement at visiting dignitaries." Then in 1988, anti-establishment activists decided he was the perfect candidate to clean up the mess at Rio's city hall. They formed the Brazilian Banana Party and ran Tiao for mayor. He came in third, with more than 400,000 votes.
AFTERMATH: Tiao never ran for office again, but when he died in 1996, Rio's mayor declared a week-long mourning period and ordered that all flags at the zoo be flown at half-mast. "It is a great loss," the mayor said. "He demonstrated the joyfulness of Rio."

THE HEADLINE: Dog Panics, Pig Stays Calm, Woman Is Saved
THE STAR: Lulu, a 150-pound Vietnamese pot-bellied pig in Beaver Falls, Pennsylvania
WHAT HAPPENED: In August 1998, JoAnne Altsman was vacationing in a trailer with her dog, Bear, and her pig, Lulu, when she had a heart attack and collapsed. "I was yelling, 'Somebody help me . . . Call an ambulance,'" Altsman says. Bear could sense that something was wrong, but all he did was bark. Lulu, on the other hand, squeezed through the trailer's doggy door, pushed open a gate she'd never opened before, and ran into the street, where she lay on her back in front of passing cars.

The first driver who stopped was too frightened to get out of his car, but the second followed Lulu back to the trailer, found Altsman and called 9-1-1. At the hospital, doctors said that with-

Honeybees can fly as fast as 30 mph.

out help, in another 15 minutes she probably would have died.
AFTERMATH: Altsman underwent open-heart surgery and is recovering; Lulu, who received a cut on her belly trying to squeeze through the too-small doggy door, was treated by a veterinarian and released. For her bravery, Lulu was awarded a jelly donut.

THE HEADLINE: Dog Emigrates to U.S., Master Doesn't
THE STAR: Diana, a dog owned by Cuban refugees
WHAT HAPPENED: In the mid-1990s, a U.S. Coast Guard ship rescued 11 Cubans and one dog they found floating on a raft near Florida. It was U.S. policy to take Cubans rescued on the high seas to the U.S. Naval Station at Guantánamo Bay (instead of Florida), but dogs aren't allowed there. Normally that would have meant Diana would be shot . . . but on this day a *CBS News* crew was on board the Coast Guard ship. CBS producer Larry Doyle volunteered to take responsibility for the dog.
AFTERMATH: When *CBS News* broadcast the story of the rescue, it was deluged with calls from viewers (and even the Florida Humane Society) asking if Diana was okay. "She's better than okay," Doyle reported. "It turns out she's pregnant and will give birth to puppies soon." He placed the dog with friends living in Key West, Florida. Unfortunately, Diana's Cuban master wasn't so lucky—he was shipped back to Cuba.

THE HEADLINE: Choking Kitten Calls 9-1-1, Saves Self
THE STAR: Tipper, a cat in Tampa, Florida
WHAT HAPPENED: Tipper was home alone, chewing on her flea collar one afternoon in August 1996 when she began choking on it. As she struggled to free the collar from her mouth, the cat somehow hit the speed dial on the phone, which her owner, Gail Curtis, had programmed to dial 9-1-1. The emergency dispatcher, hearing only meows, sent paramedics . . . who arrived several minutes later. They found Tipper, removed the flea collar, and saved her life.
AFTERMATH: The story was featured on news programs all over the country. Tipper hasn't used the phone since.

"RUMORS OF MY DEATH . . . "

While he was visiting England in 1897, Mark Twain received an inquiry from the U.S. about a report that he had died. "Rumors of my death," he cabled back, "are greatly exaggerated." He's not the only celebrity whose death has been erroneously reported. Here are three of our favorite "false death" stories, and their impact.

A PRIZE MISTAKE

WHO "DIED": Alfred Nobel, Swedish inventor of dynamite, blasting caps, smokeless gunpowder, and hundreds of other explosion-related items

CAUSE OF "DEATH": Mistaken identity. On April 13, 1888, Nobel awoke in Paris, opened a newspaper, and was astonished to read his own obituary. But it was actually his brother Ludwig who'd died; the newspaper had goofed.

WHAT HAPPENED: As a result of this mistake, Nobel was given a rare gift—a chance to see how he would be remembered . . . and he didn't like what he saw. As David Zacks writes in *An Underground Education:*

Alfred was shocked to see himself portrayed as the Merchant of Death, the man responsible for escalating the arms race . . . [Even though] he had made high-powered explosives much easier to use and was proud of how this power had been unleashed to mine precious minerals and to build roads, railways, and canals.

The obituary painted him as a "bellicose monster" whose discoveries "had boosted the bloody art of war from bullets and bayonets to long-range explosives in less than 24 years."

Determined to change his image and redeem the family name, Nobel hatched a shrewd plan. He used his wealth to create prizes in several areas—including peace. (Sort of like "the Exxon award for environmental safety . . . [or] the John F. Kennedy award for marital fidelity," Zacks says.) It was successful spin control. Today, the Nobel Prizes are the most prestigious in the world . . . and few of us connect their creator to "the art of killing."

. . . 26 of them have been tested to see if they cause cancer in laboratory rats; 13 do.

JUST A RUMOR

WHO "DIED": Vice President Thomas Jefferson

CAUSE OF "DEATH": Dirty politics. America's first really nasty presidential campaign was underway in 1800 when, on June 30, the *Baltimore American* reported that Jefferson (running against incumbent president John Adams) had died suddenly at his Virginia home. The story was confirmed the next day by the *Philadelphia True American.*

WHAT HAPPENED: According to Bruce Felton and Mark Fowler in their book *The Best, Worst and Most Unusual:*

Reports of the death of the vice president elicited no statements of sympathy, no words of grief from President Adams, vice presidential candidate Charles Cotesworth Pinckney, or any other prominent Federalist politician, which is a measure of the bitterness of the campaign. On the other hand, Jefferson's friends spent July 4 in somber mourning. News traveled slowly in that era, and reports of Jefferson's death did not reach some outlying areas until the middle of July. And the truth followed about one week behind.

The Gazette of the United States finally explained: "An old Negro slave called Thomas Jefferson, being dead at Monticello, gave rise to the report of the demise of the Vice-President—the slave having borne the name of his master."

But the whole episode "was no innocent misunderstanding," write Felton and Fowler. "The rumors and reports were cleverly calculated to underscore Jefferson's slave-owning status, and the gossip about his affairs with black women. Had the timing been better, it might have influenced the election."

WRITTEN IN THE STARS

WHO "DIED": John Partridge, best-known English astrologer of the early 1700s and publisher of the annual astrology almanac *Merlinus Liberatus*

CAUSE OF "DEATH": A practical joke. Satirist Jonathan Swift, author of *Gulliver's Travels,* hated astrologers (he thought astrology was nonsense) but loved April Fools' Day jokes. In 1708 he pulled one on Partridge. Taking the pen name Isaac Bickerstaff and posing as a "true astrologer" who wanted to expose the "gross abuses . . . nonsense, lies and folly" put out by "false astrologers" like Partridge, Swift published a penny pamphlet of bogus prophesies,

titled *Predictions for the Year 1708*. He wrote:
> [My first prediction] relates to Partridge the almanac-maker; I have consulted the star of his nativity by my own rules, and find he will infallibly die upon the 29th of March next, about eleven at night, of a raging fever.

WHAT HAPPENED: On March 30, Swift—using a different pen name this time—published a second pamphlet: *The Accomplishment of the First of Mr. Bickerstaff's Predictions*. It supplied a graphic description of Partridge's supposed final moments, including a scene in which the anguished, repentant astrologer admitted in a deathbed confession that he was a fake. "All pretences of foretelling by astrology are deceits," Partridge supposedly said, "and none but the poor ignorant vulgar give it any credit." As historian Rowse writes,

> Swift's plan succeeded beyond his wildest expectations. His own penny pamphlet sold in multitudes and pirate publishers were soon offering halfpenny reprints, replies, and imitations . . .What had begun as a simple practical joke grew into a full-blown fantasy until more people knew of Partridge's death than had ever heard of him alive.

> In the next issue of his almanac, Partridge protested that he wasn't really dead, and attacked Bickerstaff as an "impudent, lying fellow." Swift anonymously shot back with another pamphlet: *Vindication of Isaac Bickerstaff*, in which he provided several "proofs" that Partridge really was dead. He even accused Partridge of being an impostor of himself.

RESULT: People really came to believe that Partridge was dead and that the person claiming to be him—Partridge—was an interloper trying to take over the business. Because of this, sales of Partridge's almanacs plummeted, forcing him out of business. He never found out who was behind the hoax.

* * *

DOES "ONE BAD APPLE" SPOIL THE BARREL?

According to apple experts, it does: When an apple starts to rot, it releases a chemical called ethylene that causes it to decay. The other apples in a barrel can sense this chemical reaction, and when they do, they start producing their own ethylene, causing all the apples in the barrel to spoil.

"We hang the petty thieves, but appoint the great ones to public office"—Aesop

OOPS!

*More tales of outrageous blunders to let us know that
someone's screwing up even worse than we are. So
go ahead and feel superior for a few minutes.*

JUST DO IT
TICONDEROGA, New York—"A company is trying to erase
an embarrassing mistake it made on pencils bearing an antidrug message. The pencils carry the slogan: 'Too Cool To Do
Drugs.'

"But a sharp-eyed fourth-grader in northern New York noticed
when the pencils are sharpened, the message turns into 'Cool To
Do Drugs' then simply 'Do Drugs.'

"'We're actually a little embarrassed that we didn't notice that
sooner,' spokeswoman Darlene Clair told today's *Press-Republican of
Plattsburgh*."

—**Associated Press, December 11, 1998**

WELL, NEVER MIND THEN
"We shall never know the identity of the man who in 1976 made
the most unsuccessful hijack attempt ever. On a flight across
America, he rose from his seat, drew a gun and took the stewardess
hostage.

"'Take me to Detroit,' he said.

"'We're already going to Detroit,' she replied.

"'Oh . . . good,' he said, and sat down again."

—**Book of Heroic Failures**

STAMPS OF APPROVAL
WASHINGTON—"The Grand Canyon has been misplaced by
the post office.

"A newly printed batch of 100 million 6-cent international
stamps carry a picture of the canyon and, on the bottom of each
stamp, the words 'Grand Canyon, Colorado.'

"The Grand Canyon is actually located in the state of Arizona."

—**Associated Press, May 17, 1999**

Q: Why was the shark model in *Jaws* called Bruce?

BEASTLY MISTAKE

"After Cody Johnston, 22, of Bozeman, Montana, was fined $195 for a traffic violation, a court computer error turned it into a conviction for deviate sexual conduct. That's the way it appeared in a crime report in the *High Country Independent Press*, where Johnston's parents read it. When he told them it wasn't true, his wife and his sister accused him of being in denial and urged him to seek counseling. Even though the *Independent Press* printed a correction, Johnston filed a libel suit against the paper and the court system, noting, 'I've heard every sheep joke you can imagine.'"

—Weird News

IF YOU DON'T COUGH, YOU MIGHT GET OFF

CARDIFF, Wales—"When a juror coughed, defendant Alan Rashid had a right to feel sick.

"The cough came just as the jury foreman announced a verdict of 'not guilty' in Rashid's trial on a charge of threatening homicide.

"The cough coincided with 'not,' Judge Michael Gibbon only heard 'guilty' and Rashid was sentenced to two years in prison.

"As the jury left the court Thursday, one inquisitive member of the panel asked an usher why Rashid was going to jail after being found innocent. So the jurors were herded back into court.

"Rashid was brought back to court, the jury confirmed its 'not guilty' verdict and Gibbon told the defendant he was free to go.

" 'I am very relieved, as you would imagine,' Rashid said."

—Associated Press, April 16, 1999

HAPPINESS IS A WARM GUN

"Madison, Wisconsin, police chief Richard Williams turned on his oven to roast some turkey but forgot that was one of his favorite hiding places for his gun. "Shortly thereafter: boom!" police spokesperson Jeanna Kerr said, adding that Williams was given a one-day, unpaid suspension for violating his department's firearms policy."

—News of the Weird, November 1998

A: Steven Spielberg named it after his lawyer.

CRÈME de la CRUD

*Most celebrities are famous because they're good
at what they do . . . but a rare few are remembered as
the absolute worst. We at the BRI salute them.*

THE CHERRY SISTERS: World's worst variety act
BACKGROUND: In the mid-1890s, Broadway impresario Oscar
Hammerstein promoted a number of spectacular stage shows, only
to see them lose money due to lack of public interest. So he
decided to change gears. "I've been putting on the best talent and
it hasn't gone over," he groused to reporters. "Now I'm trying the
worst." He was referring to the Cherry Sisters.
CAREER NOTES: The four Cherry Sisters were from Cedar
Rapids, Iowa. Tall, thin Addie, Effie, and Lizzie were the singers in
the group; short fat Jessie "kept time," thumping intermittently on
a bass drum.

- The sisters started by touring vaudeville houses in the Midwest
  and were so awful—even to small-town audiences starved for
  entertainment—that wire screens had to be erected across the
  front of the stages where they performed, to protect them from
  rotten vegetables and other garbage that audiences routinely
  threw at them.

- Hammerstein signed them to a $1,000-a-week contract to play
  at his Olympia Theater. Their debut on November 16, 1896,
  marked a turning point in their career: instead of being pelted
  with garbage, they were met with a shower of bad reviews. In
  an article titled "Four Freaks From Iowa," a *New York Times*
  reviewer described the sisters as "genuine products of the barn-
  yard," and speculated that their performance might be due to
  poor diet. "It is sincerely hoped," he wrote, "that nothing like
  them will ever be seen again."

- Just as motorists slow down to look at traffic accidents, more
  and more people went to see the Cherry Sisters perform. Their
  reputation for being the world's worst variety act grew, and
  soon they were playing to sold-out crowds. Hammerstein made
  a small fortune off the act, and the Cherry Sisters became "the
  best-known, if not the best-loved stage performers in America."

In *Gone With the Wind*, Clark Gable worked 71 days and made $120,000.

FLORENCE FOSTER JENKINS: World's worst opera singer
BACKGROUND: There may have been worse opera singers, but none who achieved fame for it. "She clucked and squawked, trumpeted and quavered," said one observer. Another noted that she was "undaunted by . . . the composer's intent." And in *The Book of Heroic Failures,* Howard Pyle writes: "No one, before or since, has succeeded in liberating themselves quite so completely from the shackles of musical notation."
CAREER NOTES: Singing opera was Jenkins's lifelong dream. But she was unable to pursue it until 1909, at age 40, when her father died and left her a fortune. Since no one in their right mind would finance Jenkins's recitals, she paid for them herself, and developed an enthusiastic following.

- "Different audiences reacted in various ways," writes Carl Sifakis in *Great American Eccentrics.* "Some roared with laughter until tears rolled down their cheeks; others sat in utter silence, according her unique voice an attention befitting the world's greatest singers."

- Critics were at a loss as to how to describe her. Some called her "The First Lady of the Sliding Scale." When she released a record, *Newsweek* commented: "In high notes, Mrs. Jenkins sounds as if she was afflicted with a low, nagging backache."

- Jenkins's trademark was outrageous costumes. Pyle writes: "One minute she would appear sporting an immense pair of wings to render 'Ave Maria.' The next she would emerge [as] a señorita, with a rose between her teeth and a basket full of flowers." She often threw roses into the audience . . . then sent her accompanist to gather them up so she could throw them out again. Once she became so excited that she threw the basket, too.

- On October 25, 1944, the beloved 75-year-old diva rented out Carnegie Hall . . . and performed to a sold-out crowd. "So great was the demand for tickets," writes Sifakis, "that they were scalped at the then-outrageous price of $20 apiece. More than 2,000 lovers of music had to be turned away." La Jenkins took it in stride, as she had over her 30-year career. "Some may say I couldn't sing," she quipped, "but no one can say that I didn't sing." A month later, she died.

Vivien Leigh worked 125 days and made $25,000.

THE BIRTH OF THE AMERICAN FLAG, PART I

*How much do you know about the history of the American flag?
Much of Old Glory's history—who made it, what inspired it, or
when it first flew in battle—is shrouded in mystery. Here's
a look at what little we do know about the flag.*

A SIGHT TO SEE

On January 1, 1776, George Washington announced the formal existence of the Continental Army. A huge ceremony was staged to mark the occasion on Prospect Hill in Somerville, Massachusetts, and Washington ordered a flag hoisted to the top of a 76-foot flagpole.

The flag that flew that day consisted of 13 alternating red and white stripes, with the British Union Jack as its canton (the design in the top left corner). The stripes represented the colonies, united in their struggle against tyranny. The Union Jack signified their loyalty to the ideals of the British constitution and the colonists' hope for reconciliation with England. The flag was known as the Grand Union flag and would serve as the official flag of the Continental Army until the signing of the Declaration of Independence that summer.

NEW GLORY

The Declaration of Independence, signed in July 1776, officially severed all ties with England, so the Grand Union had to go. But no one bothered to replace it for nearly a year. It wasn't until June 1777, when the Continental Congress met to plan defenses for an expected attack on Philadelphia and decide other pressing issues, that they got around to passing a resolution on the design of a new flag—which, it turns out, was very similar to the old one. They wrote:

Resolved, That the flag of the thirteen United States be thirteen stripes alternate red and white; that the union

Only U.S. president to head a labor union: Ronald Reagan.

be thirteen stars, white in a blue field, representing a new constellation.

Who introduced the resolution? What was the inspiration for the details of the flag? Was there a ceremony for the unfurling of the first stars and stripes? All of this has been forgotten. Apparently no one at the time thought it was important enough to record. However . . .

- Historians guess red, white, and blue were chosen for practical, not patriotic, reasons: Fabric-making and dying techniques were limited, and there were few other colors to choose from.

- The stripes were also practical. "There aren't many ways to incorporate the number thirteen into a flag," one historian writes, "at least not ways that are easy to sew by hand, as all flags were in the 1770s. Long, straight strips of cloth were as simple as it got, so a number of colonial flags had them."

LEFT UNSAID

The first flag resolution, important as it was, left out details of size, shape, and layout, so flag makers were free to interpret it any way they wanted. As a result, at least 18 different versions of the American flag came into use over the next few years. Stars on some flags had as few as four points; others had as many as eight. Some flags had the stars arranged in squares; others had them arranged in circles, rectangles, in an X shape, in an arch, or sometimes just in one long row.

HEAVENS TO BETSY

For all their variety, one thing that these early American flags had in common is that none of them were invented or first sewn by Betsy Ross—contrary to common belief. That story didn't even surface until 1870, when Ross's grandson, William J. Canby, delivered a paper before the Historical Society of Pennsylvania claiming that she was the first person to sew an American flag.

According to Canby (who claimed he'd heard the story from Ross herself): In early June 1776, George Washington and two representatives from the Colonial Congress paid a visit to Ross at her home in Philadelphia. Washington brought with him a crude sketch of the flag he wanted: 13 red and white stripes, and 13 six-pointed stars arranged in a circle on a field of blue. Ross suggested that five-pointed stars would be easier to cut out and sew, and Washington agreed. Ross made the flag, and it was taken to the

Why don't wolves bark like dogs? One theory: They don't want to.

Pennsylvania State House, where the Congress adopted it.

Although this story immediately found a place in American mythology, there is no contemporary reference to the incident any-where—not in the record of Congressional business transactions or in George Washington's diary. The record of the Committees of Congress from that time doesn't even mention a flag committee. In fact, the date of the "visit" was a month before the Declaration of Independence—before there even was a United States.

SETTING THE RECORD STRAIGHT

The Betsy Ross fable clearly filled a need in the late 1800s to turn the creation of Old Glory into a dramatic moment. But the truth is, it wasn't a top priority for many of the Founding Fathers.

For example:

- When Benjamin Franklin and John Adams were asked to describe the new flag during a diplomatic trip to Paris in 1778, they got it wrong, describing it as consisting of "thirteen stripes, alternately red, white, and blue."

- And despite his numerous requests for flags for his troops, George Washington did not receive his first flag from the Continental Congress until 1783, after the Revolutionary War had ended. Historians aren't even sure the flag he received that year really did have stars and stripes: it might have been a blue banner with an eagle on it, similar to the presidential seal today. So it's likely that the American flag, born of revolution, never flew in a single battle during the Revolutionary War.

The Birth of the American Flag, Part II is on page 375.

The Birth of the American Flag, Part II is on page 375.

* * *

BIRTH OF A NICKNAME

"I had a dog named Duke. Every fireman in town knew that hound, because he chased all the firewagons. They knew the dog's name, but not mine, so the next thing I knew, I was Duke, too. I was named for a damn dog!"

—John Wayne

Experts say: If you're typical, your body contains about four ounces of salt.

THE DISAPPEARANCE OF JUDGE CRATER

*Every once in a while, somebody famous or controversial disappears
and is never found, despite intense searches. How can a
recognizable person vanish without a trace? It's probably
more fun to speculate than to know. Here is one of the most
talked-about unsolved disappearances in American history.*

JUDGE JOSEPH CRATER

Claim to Fame: Newly appointed justice of the New York Supreme
Court—a shoo-in to win reelection in November, and a potential
appointee to the U.S. Supreme Court

Disappearance: Crater and his wife were vacationing in Maine on
August 3, 1930, when he received a phone call from New York
City. Clearly disturbed, he announced to her that he had to go
"straighten those fellows out." Then he left for New York.

Crater was apparently taking a break from business when, on the
evening of August 6, he bought a ticket for a show and arranged to
pick it up at the box office. Then he went to Billy Haas's restaurant, where he ran into friends and joined them for dinner. Later,
he took a cab to the theater, waving from the taxi as it disappeared. Someone did pick up the theater ticket . . . but no one
knows if it was Crater—he was never seen again. Nine days later,
his wife notified the police, and a massive manhunt began.

What Happened: Police searched Crater's apartment and found
nothing suspicious. They offered rewards for information . . . but
not even the taxi driver came forward. Even after interviewing 300
people—resulting in 2,000 pages of testimony—they still had no
clues to his whereabouts.

But as the investigation continued, police—and the public—
were astonished to see Crater's carefully constructed facade
unravel. It turned out, for example, that he'd kept a number of
mistresses and had often been seen on the town with showgirls.
More surprising however, was his involvement in graft, fraud, and
political payoffs. Crater was a player in two major scandals, which
came to light after he vanished. It also seemed as though he'd be
implicated in the Ewald Scandal, which involved paying for a city

Naturalists tell us: An adult crocodile can go two years without eating.

appointment; there was even evidence that Crater had paid for his own appointment to the bench.

Crater's fate was hotly debated by the public. Some were sure he was murdered by gangster associates. Others—noting that the judge had removed files containing potentially incriminating evidence from his office just before he disappeared—speculated that political cronies had killed him to shut him up. Or maybe a mistress who'd been blackmailing him had done it. Then again, perhaps the judge had committed suicide rather than watch his career crumble because of scandal. Whoever was responsible, and whatever happened to the body, it was assumed Crater was dead.

Postmortem: Crater's wife suffered a nervous breakdown and didn't return to their New York apartment until January 1931. There, she found an envelope in the top drawer of her dresser. It contained $6,690 in cash, the judge's will, written five years before (leaving his entire estate to her), and a three-page penciled note that listed everyone who owed the judge money. It closed with the words, "Am very weary. Love, Joe." The police department had searched the apartment thoroughly, and had kept a 24-hour guard on it since the disappearance—so no one could imagine how or when the envelope had gotten there. But it gave rise to another possibility: Crater had intentionally disappeared.

Nothing more came of it. In July 1937 Judge Joseph Force Crater was declared legally dead, and his wife collected on his life insurance. By then, New York's police commissioner believed that "Crater's disappearance was premeditated." The famous file 13595 remains open to this day—no trace of Crater or his body have ever been found.

* * *

UGH!

"The Hotel Odeon in Paris is allegedly offering tourists the 'Diana Tour'—a personal reenactment of Princess Diana's last night alive. You dine at the Ritz, ride a black Mercedes along the route where she was chased by paparazzi to the tunnel where she crashed, and wind up at the hospital where she was pronounced dead." (*AM News Abuse*)

AMAZING ANAGRAMS

*We were thinking about doing a page of anagrams (a word or
phrase that's made by rearranging the letters of another word or
phrase), when this list arrived from BRI member Ryan Kulkarni:
"It's my Anagram Hall of Fame," he wrote. "These anagrams
are freaky because when the letters are reordered, the basic
meaning remains the same. Check them out for yourself!"*

DORMITORY
becomes . . . DIRTY ROOM

CLINT EASTWOOD
becomes . . . OLD WEST
ACTION

MOTHER-IN-LAW becomes
. . . WOMAN HITLER

ELEVEN PLUS TWO
becomes . . . TWELVE PLUS
ONE

DAVID LETTERMAN
becomes . . . NERD AMID
LATE TV

WESTERN UNION
becomes . . . NO WIRE
UNSENT

THE COUNTRYSIDE
becomes . . . NO CITY DUST
HERE

EVANGELIST
becomes . . . EVIL'S AGENT

ASTRONOMERS becomes . . .
NO MORE STARS

DEBIT CARD
becomes . . . BAD CREDIT

THE MORSE CODE
becomes . . . HERE COME
DOTS

SLOT MACHINES
becomes . . . CASH LOST IN
'EM

CONVERSATION
becomes . . . VOICES RANT
ON

STATUE OF LIBERTY
becomes . . . BUILT TO STAY
FREE

CONTRADICTION becomes
. . . ACCORD NOT IN IT

TOM CRUISE
becomes . . . SO I'M CUTER

ANIMOSITY
becomes . . . IS NO AMITY

THE RAILROAD TRAIN
becomes . . . HI! I RATTLE
AND ROAR

THE HILTON
becomes . . . HINT: HOTEL

SNOOZE ALARMS
becomes . . . ALAS! NO
MORE Z'S

THE DETECTIVES becomes
. . . DETECT THIEVES

A GENTLEMAN becomes . . .
ELEGANT MAN

How do you know when a roadrunner is content? It purrs.

BRI'S FLATULENCE HALL OF FAME

It used to be that no one talked about farts . . . now, it's no big deal. You can't get away from it. Which is fine by us. Here is the very first section honoring people and institutions that have made an art out of passing gas.(By the way—if this is your favorite part of the book, we recommend a tome called Who Cut the Cheese?, *by Jim Dawson.)*

HONOREE: Caryn Johnson, a.k.a. Whoopi Goldberg
NOLTABLE ACHIEVEMENT: First Hollywood star named after frequent farting
TRUE STORY: In her autobiography, Goldberg says she came up with the stage name Whoopi because she "frequently passed gas and sounded like a walking whoopee cushion."

HONOREE: Taoism
NOLTABLE ACHIEVEMENT: Most interesting philosophy about farts
TRUE STORY: A 1996 BBC-TV program about the first Chinese emperor, reported that "Chinese Taoists believe everyone is allotted a certain amount of air at birth which it is important to conserve. Belching and farting are considered to shorten one's life. Taoists therefore carefully control their diet, avoiding foods which lead to flatulence."

HONOREE: King Ahmose of Egypt
NOLTABLE ACHIEVEMENT: Most effective use of a fart as a political statement
TRUE STORY: In 568 B.C., King Apries of Egypt sent a trusted general named Amasis to put down a mutiny among his troops. But when Amasis got there, the troops offered to make him their leader instead . . . and he accepted.
   King Apries couldn't believe it. He sent a respected advisor named Patarbemis to bring Amasis back. Amasis responded to the king's entreaties by raising himself from his saddle and farting. Then he told Patarbemis to "carry that back to Apries."

Unfortunately, the king was so enraged by the message that he had Patarbemis's nose and ears hacked off. Committing such a barbarous act against such a respectable man was the last straw for many Egyptians—they turned pro-Amasis. With their support, Amasis's troops attacked and defeated Apries's army.

NOTE: Amasis became King Ahmose and reigned for 44 years, from 569 to 525 B.C., which modern historians call one of Egypt's most prosperous periods.

HONOREE: Richard Magpiong, a career criminal
NOLTABLE ACHIEVEMENT: The ultimate self-incriminating fart
TRUE STORY: In 1995 the residents of a home on Fire Island (near New York City) were awakened by a noise. They got up and looked around, but couldn't find anyone. They were about to go back to bed when, according to the *New York Daily News*, "they heard the sound of a muffled fart." Magpiong was discovered hiding in a closet and was held until the police arrived.

HONOREE: Edward De Vere, the seventh earl of Oxford and a courtier in Queen Elizabeth's court
NOLTABLE ACHIEVEMENT: Craziest overreaction to a fart
TRUE STORY: De Vere accidentally farted while bowing to the queen. He was so embarrassed that he left England and did not return for seven years. When he got back, the queen pooh-poohed the whole affair. "My Lord," she reportedly said, welcoming him back, "I had forgot the Fart."

HONOREE: Spike Jones and His City Slickers
NOLTABLE ACHIEVEMENT: Bestselling fart record
TRUE STORY: According to *Who Cut the Cheese?*: "During World War II, Bluebird Records released a disc called 'Der Fuehrer's Face' by Spike Jones and His City Slickers (an orchestra noted for parodying pop tunes), only a few months after the U.S. joined the war. Jones's band, armed with rubber razzers to create flabby farting noises, [created] a zany gas attack on Adolf Hitler: "And we'll Heil! [fart!] Heil! [fart!] right in der Fuehrer's face!" It sold a million and a half copies in the United States and Great Britain.

Besides human sacrifices, what did Aztecs offer the gods? Tamales.

LIBERAL JUSTICE

William O. Douglas was one of the most respected but controversial justices in the history of the Supreme Court. He was also one of the most liberal. Here are some of the thoughts that made him so well-known.

"We must realize that today's Establishment is the new George III. Whether it will continue to adhere to his tactics, we do not know. If it does, the redress, honored in tradition, is also revolution."

"If Nixon is not forced to turn over tapes of his conversations with the ring of men who were conversing on their violations of the law, then liberty will soon be dead in this nation."

"At the constitutional level where we work, 90 percent of any decision is emotional. The rational part of us supplies the reasons for supporting our predilections."

"I do not know of any salvation for society except through eccentrics, misfits, dissenters, people who protest."

"There is more to the right to vote than the right to mark a piece of paper and drop it in a box or the right to pull a lever in a voting booth . . . It also includes the right to have the vote counted at full value without dilution or discount."

"Political or religious dissenters are the plague of every totalitarian regime."

"Communism has been so thoroughly exposed in this country that it has been crippled as a political force. Free speech has destroyed it as an effective political party."

"It is better, the Fourth Amendment teaches us, that the guilty sometimes go free than that the citizens be subject to easy arrest."

"Advocacy and belief go hand in hand. For there can be no true freedom of mind if thoughts are secure only when they are pent up."

"The great postulate of our democracy is confidence in the common sense of the people and in their maturity of judgment, even on great issues—once they know the facts."

"I have the same confidence in the ability of our people to reject noxious literature as I have in their capacity to sort out the true from the false in theology, economics, or any other field."

The jaws of a decapitated snapping turtle can keep snapping for about a day.

MR. CONSERVATIVE

Arizona Senator Barry Goldwater was defeated in a landslide when he ran as the Republican candidate for president in 1964. But at the same time, he started the modern conservative movement. Often outrageously blunt, he was widely respected as a man of honesty and principle.

"The income tax created more criminals than any other single act of government."

"Sometimes I think this country could be better off if we would just saw off the Eastern seaboard and let it float off to sea."

"The Democrats want to save more on defense so they can spend more money to buy votes through the welfare state."

"We cannot allow the American flag to be shot at anywhere on earth if we are to retain our respect and prestige."

"We are not far from the kind of moral decay that has brought on the fall of other nations and peoples."

"We should get back to the...doctrine of brinksmanship, where everybody knows we have the power and will use it."

"If they chased every man or woman out of this town who has shacked up with somebody else or got drunk, there wouldn't be any government left in Washington."

"I don't necessarily vote a straight ticket in my own state because there are sometimes Democrats out there who are better than Republicans. It's hard to believe but it's true."

"War is but an instrument of international policy."

"We can be lied to only so many times. The best thing that he [President Nixon] can do for the country is to get the hell out of the White House, and get out this afternoon."

"No matter what you do, be honest. That sticks out in Washington."

"I don't want to see this country run by big business and big labor."

The London Zoo reportedly employs an "entertainment director" for the animals.

SIT ON A POTATO PAN, OTIS

Palindromes are phrases or sentences that are spelled the same way backward or forward. Some people spend their whole lives making new ones up. Here are some of Uncle John's favorites.

So, Ida, adios!

Rats live on no evil star.

Go deliver a dare, vile dog.

Vanna, wanna V?

Man, Oprah's sharp on A.M.

(. . . Yawn.) Madonna fan? No damn way!

Too bad, I hid a boot.

Cain: A maniac!

Plan no damn Madonna LP.

Sex-aware era waxes.

Solo gigolos.

Sit on a potato pan, Otis!

Ah, Satan sees Natasha.

Cigar? Toss it in a can, it is so tragic.

A Toyota! Race fast, safe car. A Toyota

U.F.O. tofu.

Golf? No sir, prefer prison-flog.

Draw, O coward!

Egad! No bondage!

Lepers repel.

Flee to me, remote elf.

Sh . . . Tom sees moths.

Kay, a red nude, peeped under yak.

Egad, an adage!

Must sell at tallest sum.

"Reviled did I live," said I, "as evil I did deliver."

No lemons, no melon.

Doc, note, I dissent. A fast never prevents a fatness. I diet on cod.

Gnu dung.

Lager, Sir, is regal.

Poor Dan is in a droop.

Sex at noon taxes.

Evil olive.

Flesh! Saw I Mimi wash self!

Sniff'um muffins.

Tuna nut.

Never odd or even.

SECRETS OF
THE LAVA LAMP

It oozes, it undulates, it never stops . . . and it never goes away.
Most people thought Lava Lamps had died and joined Nehru
jackets in pop culture heaven. But no—they're still
around. Here's a quick course in lava lampology.

EGG-STRAORDINARY HISTORY

Not long after he left the Royal Air Force at the end of World War II, an Englishman named Edward Craven-Walker walked into a pub in Hampshire, England, and noticed an odd item sitting on the counter behind the bar. It was a glass cocktail shaker that contained some kind of mucouslike blob floating in liquid.

Craven-Walker asked what it was, and the bartender told him it was an egg-timer. The "blob" was actually a clump of solid wax in a clear liquid. You put the cocktail shaker in the boiling water with your egg, the bartender explained, and as the boiling water cooked the egg, it also melted the wax, turning it into an amorphous blob of goo. When the wax floated to the top of the jar, your egg was done.

LIGHT DUTY

Craven-Walker saw a money-making opportunity floating in front of him—he could turn the egg timer into a lamp and sell it to the public. He set about tracking down its inventor—a man known today only by his last name, Dunnet—and found out he was dead. The good news was that Dunnet had died without patenting the invention, so Craven-Walker could patent it himself.

Craven-Walker spent the next 15 years perfecting Dunnet's invention so that it could be mass-produced. In the meantime, he supported himself by making "art-house" films about his other passion: nudity. (In those days, pornography was illegal in many places, and the only way around the law was by making "documentaries" about nudism. Whether Craven-Walker was a genuine nudist or just a pornographer in disguise is open to interpretation.)

. . . but women are more likely to switch lanes without signaling.

COMING TO AMERICA

In 1964 Craven-Walker finished work on his lamp—a cylindrical vase he called the Astrolight—and introduced it at a novelty convention in Hamburg, West Germany, in 1965. Two Americans named Adolph Wertheimer and Hy Spector saw it and bought the American rights to the lamp. They renamed it the Lava Lite and introduced it in the U.S., just in time for the psychedelic 1960s. "Lava Lite sales peaked in the late sixties," Jane and Michael Stern write in *The Encyclopedia of Bad Taste*, "when the slow-swirling colored wax happened to coincide perfectly with the undulating aesthetics of psychedelia . . . They were advertised as head trips that offered 'a motion for every emotion.'"

FLOATING UP, AND DOWN, AND UP . . .

At their peak, more than 7 million Lava Lites (the English version was called a Lava Lamp) were sold around the world each year, but by the early 1970s the fad had run its course and sales fell dramatically. By 1976 sales were down to 200 lamps a week, a fraction of what they had been a few years before.

By the late 1980s, however, sales began to rebound. "As style makers began to ransack the sixties for inspiration, Lava Lites came back," Jane and Michael Stern write. "Formerly dollar-apiece flea-market pickings, original Lava Lites—particularly those with paisley, op art, or homemade trippy motifs on their bases—became real collectibles in the late eighties, selling in chic boutiques for more than a brand-new one." Not that brand-new ones were hurting for business—by 1998 manufacturers in England and the U.S. were selling more than 2 million a year.

LAVA LIGHT SCIENCE

Only the companies that make lava lights know precisely what chemicals are in the lamp, and in what combination—the recipe is a trade secret. But the principles at work are pretty easy to understand:

- When the lamp is turned off and at room temperature, the waxy "lava" substance is slightly heavier than the liquid it's in. That's why the wax is slumped in a heap at the bottom.

- When you switch on the bulb and it begins to heat the fluid, the wax melts and expands to the point where it is slightly lighter than the fluid. That's what causes the "lava" to rise.

Blue neckties sell best. Red ties are second.

- As the wax rises, it moves further away from the bulb, and cools just enough to make it heavier than the fluid again. This causes the lava to fall back toward the bulb, where it starts to heat up again, and the process repeats itself.

- The lava also contains chemicals called "surfactants" that make it easier for the wax to break into blobs and squish back together.

- It is this precise chemical balancing act that makes manufacturing the lamps such a challenge. "Every batch has to be individually matched and tested," says company chemist John Mundy. "Then we have to balance it so the wax won't stick. Otherwise, it just runs up the side or disperses into tiny bubbles."

TROUBLESHOOTING
What if you have a vintage lava lamp, but can't get it to work right? No problem. The Internet is full of lava light lovers. Here are sample queries we found on the Web site www.OozingGoo.com:

Q: I have an older style lamp that I bought in the late 1970s. It was in storage, but I came across it last year, and I've been using it from time to time. It was working fine, until it was knocked over (darned cats). Nothing broke, but now, the liquid has gone cloudy. Is there anything I can do? I don't want to get rid of it, but it's not as enjoyable any more.
A: Sorry. I'm afraid you can't fix it, but you can buy a replacement bottle in a range of colors. (Order through the Web site.)

Q: My son went to college, and his lava lamp was turned off for a year. Now it won't work. The red lava is lying at the base like a can of worms, and there seems to be some metallic substance/rings in the lava. There is also one-half inch of fluid missing from the lamp. Can this lamp be fixed?
A: STOP! DON'T MESS WITH IT! You may not even have a problem. The liquid is supposed to be about one-half inch down—gives room for expansion due to heat. Are you sure you have the right bulb? 40 watt frosted appliance. Leave the lamp on for long periods—4 hours each day for a week—sometimes they come back. Good luck!

A typical redwood tree's roots are only 5 to 6 feet deep and spread out over an acre.

MYTH-CONCEPTIONS

*Common knowledge is frequently wrong. Here are a few examples
of things that people believe . . . but that just aren't true.*

MYTH: The captain of a ship at sea can perform weddings.
FACT: U.S. Navy regulations—and those of the navies of many
other nations—actually prohibit ships' commanders from joining
couples in marriage.

MYTH: Your hair and nails continue to grow after you die.
FACT: They don't. Your tissue recedes from your hair and nails,
making them appear longer.

MYTH: Bananas spoil faster when you put them in a refrigerator.
FACT: This belief comes from an old ad jingle. The purpose of the
jingle was to tell people to keep bananas out of the refrigerator . . .
but only until they had ripened. Once ripened, bananas will last
longer in the refrigerator.

MYTH: You should never wake a sleepwalker.
FACT: There's no reason not to wake a sleepwalker. This superstition comes from the old belief that a sleepwalker's spirit leaves the
body and might not make it back if the person is wakened.

MYTH: Shaving your hair makes it grow in faster and thicker.
FACT: The rate of your hair's growth is determined by hereditary
factors. Shaving will have no effect on the rate of its growth.

MYTH: During a flight, you'll sometimes hit an "air pocket."
FACT: What's often called an "air pocket" is actually a downdraft.

MYTH: It's darkest just before the dawn.
FACT: Actually, it's darkest at about 2 a.m.

Queen bees only sting other queen bees.

FAT CHANCE: THE WAR BETWEEN BUTTER AND MARGARINE

These days, you expect to find both butter and margarine on grocery shelves . . . but did you know that margarine companies had to fight to get there? This article was written by Jack Mingo.

MARGINAL USE

"Oleomargarine" was a word coined in the late 1860s by a French chemist, Hippolyte Mège-Mouriès. The price of butter had soared, so Napoleon III, expecting shortages because of an anticipated war with Prussia, offered a prize at the Paris World Exhibition in 1866 to anyone who could come up with a cheap, plentiful butter substitute.

Mège-Mouriès did some research and discovered that even starving cows give milk containing milkfat. Since this fat isn't coming from their food, he reasoned that it must be coming from the cows themselves. Deciding that it must be possible to do the same thing mechanically, he invented a process to render oil from beef fat and combined the oil with milk to form a butterlike spread. He won Napoleon's prize, but lost the first marketplace skirmish—his margarine factory opened in 1873 near Paris, then had to close when peace unexpectedly broke out and ruined the expected butter shortages.

ACROSS THE OCEAN

Mège-Mouriès's process, however, found a home in the United States. The U.S. Dairy Company bought the rights to it in 1874 and licensed the process to 15 factories around the country. By 1882, it was making 50,000 pounds of the imitation spread every day. Soon, Armour and other meat-packing houses began producing margarine of their own, using fatty by-products left over from meat processing.

According to sleep researchers, only about 5% of people dream in color.

Farmers and butter manufacturers were beginning to get worried by this new product, especially those who made cheaper, lower-grade butter. Margarine was roughly comparable in price, but it was often of better quality.

In 1877 the dairy industry engineered the passage of laws in New York and Maryland requiring that oleomargarine "be marked, stamped, and branded as such, under penalty of $100 and imprisonment for thirty days." Even the margarine manufacturers agreed that these laws were reasonable, and didn't object when other states followed suit. In the words of a spokesman in 1880, "Of course, this had for a time its effect upon the sale of the product; but as oleomargarine is a pure and wholesome article of food, possessing all the qualities of good dairy butter, the people have overlooked the name and have decided to eat it."

GOING FOR THE JUGULAR

But that wasn't enough for the dairy interests. Ironically—since farmers of the time were notorious for extending and whitening milk and cream with water, chalk, magnesia, and even plaster of Paris—the dairy concerns created new organizations like the National Association for the Prevention of Adulteration of Butter, to combat the "adulteration and risk to health" supposedly posed by margarine. In lurid anti-margarine propaganda, the dairy interests featured slanderous tales of the repulsive ingredients used to make "bogus-butter."

"The slag of the butcher shop," they called margarine, "a compound of diseased hogs and dead dogs" that contained "the germs of cancer and insanity." They paid one Professor Piper, a mysterious researcher with dubious credentials, to do an imaginative "study" in which he found in samples of margarine "many kinds of living organisms, dead mould, bits of cellulose, shreds of hair, bristles, etc., doubtful worms, corpuscles from a cockroach, small bits of claws, corpuscles of sheep, the egg of a tapeworm, a dead hydravirus . . ."

The margarine companies tried to defend themselves. But while the president of the New York Board of Health spoke of margarine's purity at their behest, dairy lobbyists in Maine, Michigan, Minnesota, New York, Ohio, Pennsylvania, and Wisconsin rammed through legislation that banned "any article designed to take the place of butter." By 1885 two-thirds of all margarine manufacturers in those states had gone out of business.

After court challenges in New York and Maine, courts ruled that the laws were too broad. The New York ban was ruled unconstitutional on the grounds that the unwholesomeness of margarine was not demonstrated and, "without persuasive evidence, the government could not prohibit the whole industry just to protect another." The Supreme Court struck down the rest of the bans in 1894, while suggesting an alternative: since it was the color of margarine that led to fraud, states could ban colored margarine, while letting uncolored margarine be sold freely.

SLIPPERY MANEUVERS
Once again, dairy concerns rammed through laws—this time convincing 30 states, by the turn of the century, to ban colored margarine. (Ironically, the butter makers themselves routinely added annatto to their butter to make it more yellow.) Pallid off-white was an unappetizing color, and margarine sales went down again. But not down far enough for the butter lobby. They pushed harder, getting laws passed in five states that required margarine producers to dye their product pink. Not surprisingly, margarine sales in those states plummeted.

In 1902 the butter industry persuaded the federal government to get into the act as well, slapping a 10¢ tax on artificially colored margarine. This effectively increased the price to the consumer by 50%, making it more expensive than most grades of butter. In response, the margarine manufacturers began using vegetable oils for margarine—especially those with a natural yellow hue. It gave the margarine some color without incurring the tax. By World War I, vegetable-based margarine dominated the market.

In 1931 the government closed the loophole of allowing naturally colored oils by taxing all yellow margarines, whether colored artificially or not. Margarine makers found a way around that law, too. They discovered that it didn't prohibit consumers from dying their own margarine.

So they provided a yellow "color capsule" free of charge with every purchase of margarine. When consumers got the margarine home, they massaged the dye around inside the cellophane package of margarine until it was a uniform golden color. While this was a minor inconvenience for consumers, margarine sales began to creep up again.

GOTCHA!

Finally margarine got a chance to fight back. During the financial insecurity of the Depression and butter rationing of World War II, consumers flocked to margarine, which was no longer perceived as a low-class, disreputable spread of dubious origin. Many consumers discovered that they preferred the economy and even the taste of margarine to that of "the high-priced spread," (as margarine ads called butter). And consumers began wondering why they had to put up with the mess of coloring margarine at home.

Finally in 1950, pushed by vegetable-oil producers, labor unions, and consumers, Congress narrowly passed a law to rescind the federal tax on colored margarine. States began following suit.

Within five years, every state except Minnesota and Wisconsin had repealed such laws. (Minnesota held out until 1963; Wisconsin, "the Dairy State," until 1967.)

FAT IS FAT

In the 1960s and 1970s, the margarine market suddenly pulled ahead of butter as health-conscious consumers began avoiding animal fats, based on studies that concluded that margarine was less artery-clogging than butter.

But it turned out that the studies were wrong. More recent research showed that hydrogenating vegetable oil to make it semi-solid creates "transfatty acids" that act like saturated fats, raising blood cholesterol levels.

As that word got out to consumers, margarine sales dropped 8% in 1994, while butter sales went up 5.3 percent. Margarine makers, by now resigned to changing their product every few years to match the vagaries of life, law, politics, and consumer demand, scrambled to come up with formulations that tasted good and were free of transfatty acids.

After a century and a quarter, the war between butter and margarine isn't over yet.

* * *

FOR THE BIRDS

The domestic turkey was domesticated by the Aztecs and the Incas, who used them as food and sacrificed them to their gods.

Top four high school hazing sports: swimming, diving, soccer, lacrosse.

TRICK SHOTS: MORE FAKED PHOTOS

A few more historic photographs that people chose to believe, even though they were pretty obvious phonies.

FICTIONAL NEWS

Famous Footage: The "California Election Report"

Trick Shot: In 1934 Upton Sinclair, legendary muckraker and author of *The Jungle*, an exposé of Chicago's meatpacking industry, ran for governor of California. Sinclair's candidacy marked one of the best chances a socialist had ever had of winning a statewide office in the U.S. That's when newsreels like the "California Election Report" appeared. It featured interviews in a railyard with one hobo after another, each saying that "he rode the rails to the Golden State just as soon as he heard that the new governor would be handing out free lunches."

The Real Picture: The newsreels were pure Hollywood, put together by director Irving Thalberg with the support of Samuel Goldwyn. Both considered Sinclair "a dangerous red who wanted to rob the rich to support the poor." The hobos were just actors (Thalberg and his crew wanted real hobos, but couldn't find any in the L.A. railroad yard), and the "railyard" was a set on the MGM back lot. Other newsreels were just as phony.

Development: In the days before television, newsreels were a primary source of news for the public, and this negative coverage— shown repeatedly in California theaters—helped ensure Sinclair's defeat.

ON TOP OF THE WORLD

Famous Photos: Frederick Cook at the North Pole

Trick Shots: On September 6, 1909, an exhausted Robert Peary wired from Labrador, "Stars and Stripes nailed to the Pole—Peary." Peary, 53, had apparently realized a goal he'd set 23 years earlier— to be the first person to reach the North Pole. But it turned out that he was too late: On September 1, explorer Frederick Cook had wired from the Shetland Islands that he'd made it to the

---

In an average minute, 20,900 gallons flow from the Amazon River into the sea.

North Pole the year before. Cook's proof: photographs of him and his Eskimo companions at the Pole. Cook's photographs, which were published all over the world, marked the completion of one of the last great exploratory challenges on earth . . . or did they?

The Real Picture: As it turned out, it was another of Cook's "accomplishments" that got him into trouble. Cook had previously claimed he'd been to the summit of Mount McKinley. "On the day Cook received the keys to New York City for his North Pole trek," write the editors of *Reader's Digest* in *Strange Stories of America's Past,* "the man who'd supposedly climbed McKinley with him admitted they'd never really been *near* the 20,320-foot peak." The Explorer's Club investigated and found that the McKinley 'summit' picture had been taken from a 5,300-foot ridge.

Development: The scandal brought Cook's North Pole claims into question but, amazingly, he so charmed the public that many people sided with him over Peary. His spurious North Pole pictures weren't totally discredited until 1918, two years before Peary's death. (Dr. Cook later served four years in Leavenworth prison for promoting stock in a company owning oil he "discovered" in Wyoming.)

WHO'S WHO IN THE REVOLUTION?

Famous Photos: Spanish Loyalists committing atrocities in the Spanish Civil War (1936–1939)

Trick Shot: In 1936, "when the Spanish Civil War broke out, U.S. newspaper baron William Randolph Hearst jumped into the fray. He ran photos showing atrocities . . . being committed by the pro-democracy Loyalists against Fascist followers of Francisco Franco."

The Real Picture: The Spanish picture was actually Franco's men committing atrocities against the Loyalists.

Development: The controversy helped turn public opinion against the Loyalists and hastened World War II. Without more support from the U.S. and other Allied powers, the Loyalists faltered and the Nazi-supported fascists were able to defeat their enemies—providing momentum for Hitler and Mussolini.

THE PETTICOAT WARS

*The sex scandal involving Monica Lewinsky (the first, and last,
time we mention her name in one of these books) helped
create a crisis in Washington that most Americans think
was unparalleled. Actually, in the early 1800s, there was
a worse one, that did measurable damage: an entire
cabinet was overturned. Newspapers called it
"The Petticoat Wars." Never heard of it?
That's what we're here for.*

FORGOTTEN FIGURE: Peggy O'Neal, a beautiful barmaid, tavern-keeper's daughter, and "woman of easy morals" who worked in her father's Washington, D.C., tavern and lodging house in the 1820s.

CLAIM TO FAME: The most famous and controversial Cabinet wife of the 19th century—inspiration for the "Petticoat Wars" that rocked Washington in the 1820s

BACKGROUND: O'Neal was also the longtime mistress of Senator John Eaton, a wealthy young widower from Tennessee. On January 21, 1829, she and Eaton finally married. That was scandal enough in its own right; but not long after they were married, President Andrew Jackson made Eaton Secretary of War, catapulting the former barmaid into the status of Cabinet wife, the pinnacle of Washington society.

Other Cabinet wives resented the new Mrs. Eaton's sudden elevation in social status. At the instigation of Vice President John C. Calhoun's wife, Floride, they began freezing her out of their social functions. President Jackson was livid about it, and called a special meeting of the Cabinet to defend Eaton's virtue. When the Cabinet wives continued to ostracize Eaton, Jackson purged the entire Cabinet, replacing every appointee except Postmaster General William Barry.

Perhaps the biggest casualty in the Petticoat War was Vice President Calhoun, a southerner who had hoped to ride into the Presidency on Jackson's coattails. His wife's intransigence put an end to those dreams, and Jackson threw his support to Secretary of State Martin Van Buren, a bachelor whose immunity from the

Of the 1,000 varieties of cherries grown in the U.S., only 10 are grown commercially.

pressure of the Cabinet wives, enabled him to remain friendly with the Eatons throughout the crisis.

Van Buren replaced Calhoun as Vice President during Jackson's second term, and succeeded Jackson to the presidency in 1837.

Some historians speculate that had Calhoun, a Southerner, become president instead of Van Buren, a Northerner, he might have been able to soothe the North-South tensions that led to the outbreak of the Civil War in 1860.

INTO THE DUSTBIN: When John Eaton became Minister to Spain, he and Peggy became the toast of Madrid. After Eaton died, Peggy, now in her sixties, married a twenty-something Italian dance instructor, only to watch him run off with her granddaughter and most of her money.

* * *

DON'T MISS THESE!

EXOTIC WORLD
Location: The desert town of Helendale, California, halfway between Los Angeles and Las Vegas.
Background: Probably the only museum in the world run by strippers for strippers. Tours are conducted by Dixie Evans, the "Marilyn Monroe of Burlesque," whose most famous act is an interpretive dance that highlights the major events in Monroe's life.
Be Sure to See: The Exotic World Rolls-Royce, Jayne Mansfield's couch, and thousands of 8x10 photographs of strippers covering the walls in each room. There's also a gift shop that sells T-shirts, lapel pins, and other baubles.

THE MUTTER MUSEUM
Location: Philadelphia College of Physicians
Background: Although intended primarily for medical professionals, it's chock-full of oddities that appeal to the average person.
Be Sure to See: The preserved liver of Chang and Eng, the original Siamese twins; and the Chevalier Jackson Collection of swallowed objects that had to be surgically removed.

The U.S. Treasury mints about 19.5 million pennies a day.

UNFINISHED MASTERPIECE: LEONARDO'S HORSE

*Here's an unfinished masterpiece from one of
the Renaissance's greatest geniuses.*

THE HORSE STATUE. Created by Leonardo da Vinci. Would
have been the largest equestrian monument on earth . . . if it had
ever been built. Leonardo considered it a crowning achievement.

Background: In the 1480s, the Duke of Sforza commissioned
Leonardo to build a huge statue of a horse to honor his father,
Francesco Sforza. Da Vinci worked on it for nearly 17 years, studying
horses exhaustively and then making a series of models, including a
full-sized clay model that was 24 feet tall. Next step: Completing the
molds, into which more than 50 tons of molten bronze would be
poured to create the final horse. Then a war broke out.

Unfinished Masterpiece: On September 10, 1499, before da Vinci
could cast the horse, the French captured Milan. Some soldiers
camped nearby . . . and a company of them used the clay model for
target practice, riddling it with holes. Afterward, the model was
totally destroyed by exposure to the weather. When Leonardo died 20
years later, in 1519, he was "still mourning the loss of his great horse."

Update: In 1977 an American named Charles Dent happened to
pick up a copy of *National Geographic* magazine, which contained
an article on Leonardo and his horse. Dent was an Italian
Renaissance buff and decided that completing Leonardo's horse
would be a fitting way to honor the greatest mind of the period.

Leonardo had left no detailed drawings or other notes that indicated what the final horse was supposed to look like; all that survived
were preliminary sketches. No matter—Dent decided to wing it, and
on September 10, 1999, exactly 500 years to the day that da Vinci
was forced to abandon his dream, his horse (or at least an approximation) was unveiled in Milan. It was intended, Dent explained, as a
gift "to all the Italian people from the American people." But, ironically, few Italians attended the unveiling—mostly Americans showed
up (not Dent, though, he'd died a few years earlier).

The heaviest pumpkin ever recorded weighed 1,061 pounds.

WHY ASK WHY?

Sometimes the answer is irrelevant—it's the question that counts. These cosmic queries are from BRI readers.

Why do we say something is out of whack? What is a whack?

If a pig loses its voice, is it disgruntled?

Why are a wise man and a wise guy opposites?

Why does the word "lisp" have an "s" in it?

Why do women wear evening gowns to nightclubs? Shouldn't they be wearing nightgowns?

If love is blind, why is lingerie so popular?

How does it work out that people always die in alphabetical order?

Why do "overlook" and "oversee" mean opposite things?

"I am" is reportedly the shortest sentence in the English language. Could it be that "I do" is the longest sentence?

If people from Poland are called "Poles," why aren't people from Holland called "Holes?"

If you ate pasta and antipasta, would you still be hungry?

How is it possible to "run out of space"?

If a vegetarian eats vegetables, what does a humanitarian eat?

Why is it that if someone tells you that there are 1 billion stars in the universe you will believe them, but if they tell you a wall has wet paint you will have to touch it to be sure?

If you mixed vodka with orange juice and milk of magnesia, would you get a Phillips Screwdriver?

If Barbie is so popular, why do you have to buy all her friends?

If Fred Flintstone knew that the large order of ribs would tip his car over, why did he order them at the end of every show?

If Superman is so smart, why does he wear underpants over his trousers?

If you jog backward, will you gain weight?

Toto the dog was paid $125 a week for his work in *The Wizard of Oz*.

DRAT, SHE'S DEAD!

You don't always get a Hollywood ending when you're making a Hollywood film. Sometimes the star dies or becomes incapacitated during filming. It happened in these movies. Here's how they handled it.

SARATOGA (1937), *starring Jean Harlow and Clark Gable*
The Situation: The 26-year-old Harlow, "Hollywood's origi-nal platinum blonde," died of kidney failure when the film was only about half complete. MGM wanted to abandon produc-tion and scrap what they had . . . but Harlow's fans protested. So the studio "and a very reluctant Gable" continued filming.
Body Double: Harlow's scenes were filmed with her stand-in, Mary Dees, who was "carefully lit and photographed in long shots, over the shoulder, from behind, looking through binoculars, or under wide-brimmed hats." Ironically, the film, which grossed $3.3 mil-lion, was the most successful of Harlow's career—and also the most critically acclaimed (although the *New York Times* complained that in the film, "Harlow was patently not her tempestuous self ").

THE CROW (1994), *starring Brandon Lee—son of martial-arts star Bruce Lee*
The Situation: A horrible accident occurred just three days before filming was to be completed. In the story, Lee's character is shot and killed. In real life, that's what happened to Lee. The tip of one of the blanks loaded in a .44-caliber handgun hit Lee, 27, in the stomach when the gun was fired during a scene. He died shortly after. Police said it was an accident.
    Producer Ed Pressman says: "We weren't so sure if we wanted to finish it. But Brandon's mother and his girlfriend, whom he planned to marry just after it was finished, wanted it finished and released. So we finished it."
Body Double: The producers altered some existing footage digi-tally and made plans to film new footage using stuntmen who would be wearing special face masks made from a plaster cast of Lee's face. But the stuntmen refused to wear the masks, arguing they were in bad taste. "No one felt good about wearing the masks," says make-up artist Lance Anderson. "The director finally got around that problem by filming long shots instead."

The average cow produces 70,000 glasses of milk in her lifetime.

YOU CAN'T CHEAT AN HONEST MAN (1938), *starring W. C. Fields*

The Situation: Fields was one of Hollywood's legendary drunks. Most of the time that didn't interfere with his films, but *You Can't Cheat an Honest Man* was different—Fields, who was supposed to both write the film and star in it, was too drunk to do either.

Body Double: Director George Marshall compensated by hiring a writing "assistant" named Everett Freeman for Fields, and by casting other stars like Edgar Bergen and Charlie McCarthy in the film to take up some of Fields's screen time. He also hired a double for Fields and filmed him in long shots. That turned out to be a particularly smart move: one afternoon, in the middle of production, Fields shuffled off the set into his limousine (which had a wet bar in the back) and never returned.

Marshall still didn't have all the footage of Fields that he needed to finish the film . . . so he improvised. He combined what he had with shots of Fields's double and put Edgar Bergan and Charlie McCarthy onscreen even longer.

Despite its flaws—or more likely because of them—the movie was a hit and to this day is considered a W. C. Fields classic. "All the critics," says Everett Freeman, "referred to the movie's daring innovations, its departure from formula, and its innovative use of the camera—especially on the long shots intercutting to the close-ups."

THE THREE STOOGES (1955)

The Situation: Shemp Howard replaced his brother Curly in the Stooges in 1949 and co-starred with them for six years. In 1955, while working on several Stooges films, he had a heart attack and died.

Body Double: Moe and Larry considered appearing as a duo, but Columbia Pictures wouldn't hear of it. They also wouldn't scrap the unfinished Shemp episodes. Instead, they hired Joe Palma as a double. His face was never seen—his back was always to the camera.

The four episodes: *Hot Stuff, Rumpus in the Harem, Scheming Schemers,* and *Commotion on the Ocean.* Check them out sometime.

Sound travels a mile in five seconds through the air.

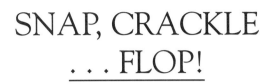

SNAP, CRACKLE
. . . FLOP!

For every successful cereal, there are hundreds of bombs like Banana Wackies and Ooboperoos. We found these legendary cereal flops in Cerealizing America *by Scott Bruce and Bill Crawford.*

KELLOG'S KREAM CRUNCH (1963). Frosted-oat loops mixed with cubes of freeze-dried vanilla-orange or strawberry ice cream. According to a Kellogg's exec: "The product kind of melted into gooey ice cream in milk. It just wasn't appetizing."

SUGAR SMILES (1953). General Mills' first try at sugar cereal. A bizarre mixture of plain Wheaties and sugar-frosted Kix. Slogan: "You can't help smiling the minute you taste it."

DINOS (early 1990s). After the success of Fruity Pebbles, Post tried naming a cereal after the Flintstones' pet dinosaur. "A question that came up constantly," recalls a Post art director, "was 'We've got Cocoa Pebbles and Fruity Pebbles . . . so what flavor is Dino?' . . . It sounds like something Fred would be getting off his lawn instead of something you'd want to be eating."

DAY-O (late 1960s). "The world's first calypso-inspired presweetened cereal," from General Mills.

OOOPS (early 1970s). General Mills had so many bombs, they came up with a cereal they actually said was based on a mistake—jingle: "Ooops, it's a crazy mistake, Ooops, it's a cereal that's great!"

KELLOGG'S CORN CRACKOS (1967). The box featured the Waker Upper Bird perched on a bowl of candy-coated twists. An internal company memo said: "It looks like a bird eating worms; who wants worms for breakfast?"

PUNCH CRUNCH (1975). A spinoff of Cap'n Crunch. The screaming pink box featured Harry S., an exuberant hippo in a sailor suit, making goo-goo eyes at Cap'n Crunch. Many chain stores perceived the hippo as gay and refused to carry the cereal. Marveled one Quaker salesman: "How that one ever got through, I'll never understand."

FAMOUS UNSOLVED DISAPPEARANCES

*Here are two more unsolved
disappearances that have made the news.*

JIMMY HOFFA

Claim to Fame: Ruled the Teamsters Union from 1957 to 1967; turned it into America's biggest, richest, and most corrupt union—with overt connections to the Mafia. In a highly publicized 1967 trial, he was convicted of jury tampering and sent to federal prison. In 1971 he was released—on condition that he not hold union office until 1980.

Hoffa didn't stay inactive long: In 1972 he filed a lawsuit to overturn the arrangement and began a campaign to return to power. By 1975 he'd gained enough support in the union to pose a threat to the leaders who'd replaced him—if his lawsuit succeeded.

Disappearance: On July 30, 1975, Hoffa went to a meeting with two men—an Eastern Teamster official and a Detroit mobster. He never returned. Police dug up fields, ripped up cement floors, and dredged rivers, but besides Hoffa's car—which was discovered at a shopping center near his home—no trace of him was ever found.

What Happened: Most experts, including the FBI, say the Mafia had Hoffa killed. Why? The mob had switched allegiance to Hoffa's successors while he was in prison and didn't want him messing things up. Hoffa's bodyguard, however, insists it was the government that killed the union boss. The reason? They were still trying to cover up the fact that they used the Mafia to try to kill Fidel Castro, and Hoffa knew too much.

MADALYN MURRAY O'HAIR

Claim to Fame: America's most famous (and most vilified) atheist, O'Hair filed the 1963 lawsuit that resulted in the U.S. Supreme Court's decision to ban school prayer, and in the late 1960s founded an organization called American Atheists, Inc.

Disappearance: In 1995 O'Hair, her son Jon, and her granddaughter Robin headed to Virginia for a vacation . . . and were never

---

Poll result: 1 in 6 employees say they got so mad at a co-worker last year . . .

seen again. Several days later, a note appeared on the front door of the American Atheists headquarters informing employees that they'd been laid off and that O'Hair, forced to leave on important business, would eventually return. She never did. The only trace ever found was Robin's abandoned car, discovered six months later in an airport parking lot.

What Happened: Some O'Hair loyalists believe she was assassinated by the CIA or the Pope. Others think the 77-year-old woman disappeared so she could die in private; she was obese and suffered from diabetes, heart disease, and chronic dizziness. She may have chosen to avoid the distasteful (to her) praying that her death would surely generate.

Her enemies, and at least one reporter, have a different theory: They think O'Hair and her family embezzled money and fled. O'Hair's organization was "beset with lawsuits, an IRS investigation, and diminishing membership." And an investigation by *Vanity Fair* magazine turned up circumstantial evidence that after transferring considerable assets to New Zealand, O'Hair and her companions moved there.

Postmortem: Her disappearance preserved her place as a part of contemporary culture. "She was looking for a new role," a biographer wrote, "and she found it: missing person. [Now] she'll be on the mind of the public for centuries."

*   *   *

WHY DO WE FLY FLAGS AT HALF-MAST?

In the days of sailing ships, when someone died on board or a national leader died, ships slackened their rigging, which gave the ship a disheveled look that was supposed to symbolize mourning, "the nautical equivalent of walking around in sackcloth and ashes." Lowering flags partway down the mast was another part of the practice, the only part that survives to this day.

TO SLEEP . . . OR NOT TO SLEEP?

Here are some random facts about sleeping that you may not know. Complied for us by the BRI's own John Darling, who has never met Peter Pan and would like us to stop asking if he has, already.

THE NEED FOR SLEEP

Newborn babies sleep about 16 hours a day; adults average half that. Teens, especially girls, are gluttons for sleep (10 hours average), but it's not because they're lazy, as many parents think. Stanford researchers found it was tied to the complex inner labors of puberty. This hunch is underlined by teen girls' need for extra Z's during their periods.

- We sleep best at certain times and if we stray from our required sleep needs, there's no telling what will happen. The nuclear disasters at both Chernobyl and Three Mile Island, as well as the *Exxon Valdez* wreck and *Challenger* shuttle explosion, have been linked to lack of sleep or altered sleep cycles among key people at key moments.

- "Jet lag" shifts our sleep cycle, often creating confusion, mental dullness, and a desire to sleep at odd times. The Army was disappointed to find that troops flown overseas often require a week to overcome their disorientation. This phenomenon is the bane of passenger jet crews. In one instance, for example, all three members of a jetliner crew fell asleep as they reached the end of their overnight New York-to-Los Angeles flight. While air traffic controllers radioed them frantically, the jet flew 100 miles out over the ocean. Finally, one of the crew woke up and saw the sea in every direction. They had just enough fuel to make it back to LAX.

TO NAP OR NOT TO NAP?

- According to Stanley Coren, in his book *Sleep Thieves*, science has identified the two big peaks in our need for sleep—at 3 a.m. and 3 p.m. The first is dead in the center of our sleep cycle, but the second is smack in the middle of our workday. Shouldn't we

---

The Mona Lisa has no eyebrows. Shaved eyebrows were the fad when she was painted.

be napping in mid-afternoon? At present, only 38% of us do.

- Who's getting the most sleep? Surveys find:
  —In the U.S., Westerners and Southerners sleep longer than Easterners and Midwesterners.
  —Women sleep more than men.
  —Poor people sleep more than the rich.
  —People who work evening or night shifts get far less sleep—about 5.6 hours—than day workers. No matter how hard they try, researchers say, people who sleep out of their normal cycle never fully adjust.

DOES LESS SLEEP = SUCCESS?

- A short sleep cycle is not inherently bad. Some people seek it out and sing its praises. Multi-millionaire magnate Donald Trump boasts of needing only three to four hours a night. Former junk-bond king Michael Milken gets only four to five hours.

- This raises the question: is there a link between sleep and success? Tufts University researcher Ernest Hartmann found that people who sleep less than 5.5 hours tend to be extroverted, ambitious, and efficient, while people who sleep more than 9 hours tend to be anxious, insecure, introverted, and indecisive. Other researchers think this is nonsense, noting that short-sleepers tend to be fast-paced, Type-A personalities (thus prone to heart disease), while long-sleepers include society's creative, alternate-type thinkers and artists.

- Researchers hoped a survey of the CEO's and chairs of the *Fortune* 500 companies would settle the question of whether "the early bird really does get the worm." Apparently, it does. They found that 46 percent of the leaders they surveyed slept an hour less than the national average of 7.5 hours. Fifteen percent slept 5–6 hours and 2 percent slept 4–5 hours.

THE TRICK TO GETTING MORE SLEEP

Most of us, however, aren't looking for ways to sleep less—our focus is on how to get more. Here are some tips from the experts:
- Go to bed about the same time each night.
- Avoid nightcaps, except warm milk.
- Avoid illuminated clocks (they're a reminder you can't sleep).
- Exercise before going to bed.
- A dark and slightly cool bedroom is best (about 65°F).

The average American drinks 3.4 cups of coffee a day.

MORE
STRANGE LAWSUITS

Here are a more real-life examples of unusual legal battles.

THE PLAINTIFF: Janet R.
THE DEFENDANT: Kay-Bee Toys at Valley View Mall, Roanoke, Virginia
THE LAWSUIT: She claimed that while shopping in the mall in 1996, she was hit by a truck—a toy truck. Apparently a customer, playing with a radio-controlled 4 x 4, bumped Robinson in the ankle. She sued for $100,000, asking compensation for "pain, humiliation, aggravation, and disability."
THE VERDICT: Suit dropped by plaintiff.

THE PLAINTIFF: Etta Stephens of Tampa, Florida
THE DEFENDANT: The Barnett Bank
THE LAWSUIT: In 1995 Stephens opened the envelope containing her monthly money market statement . . . and found the account balance listed as zero, instead of $20,000 as she expected. "Upon seeing this," says one report, "Stephens clutched her bosom and fell to the ground" with a heart attack. Officials of the bank said it was a mistake caused by a "printing error" and apologized. But Stephens still sued them for nearly killing her.
THE VERDICT: Unknown.

THE PLAINTIFF: Katherine Balog, 60-year-old Californian
THE DEFENDANTS: Bill Clinton and the Democratic Party
THE LAWSUIT: In 1992 Balog filed suit "to recover damages for the trauma of Clinton's candidacy." She claimed she was suffering "serious emotional and mental stress" because Clinton, a "Communist sympathizer" and "draft dodger," was about to be elected president.
THE VERDICT: Unknown.

Every thousand years, spring gets two-thirds of a day shorter.

THE PLAINTIFF: Bennie Casson
THE DEFENDANT: PT's Show Club, an Illinois strip joint
THE LAWSUIT: In 1997 a stripper named Busty Heart allegedly approached Casson during her act and "slammed" her 88-inch bust (a reported 40 pounds per breast) into his head and neck. He sued for "emotional distress" and claimed an old neck injury had been aggravated by the attack.
THE VERDICT: No lawyer would take the case, so the judge had to dismiss it.

THE PLAINTIFF: Debra Lee Benagh, 44, of Denver
THE DEFENDANT: Elitch Gardens, an amusement park
THE LAWSUIT: In 1997, according to Benagh's suit, she rode on the Mind Eraser roller coaster . . . and actually suffered memory loss. Benagh sued for negligence, contending that the park operators should have known of the ride's hazards.
THE VERDICT: Unknown.

THE PLAINTIFF: Swee Ho, a Chinese merchant in Thailand
THE DEFENDANT: Pu Lin, a rival merchant
THE LAWSUIT: As reported by Gerald Sparrow, once a judge in Bangkok: "Pu Lin had stated sneeringly at a party that Swee Ho's new wife, Li Bua, was merely a decoration to show how rich her husband was. Swee Ho, he said, could no longer 'please the ladies.' Swee Ho sued his rival for slander in the British Consular Court, claiming that Li Bua was his wife in every sense."
THE VERDICT: Swee Ho won . . . without a word of testimony. Swee Ho's lawyer "simply put the blushing Li Bua in the witness box. She was quite obviously pregnant."

* * *

IRONIC TWIST

The Ramses brand condom is named after the great Pharaoh Ramses II, who fathered over 160 children.

If you weigh 120 pounds on Earth, you'll weigh about 20 pounds on the moon.

CELEBRITY MALPRACTICE

Famous spokespeople sell us everything from underwear to cars. We assume they really stand behind the product . . . but as history shows, that's not necessarily the case. Here are four examples of what Newsweek *magazine calls "celebrity malpractice"—good reminders to think twice before you trust someone just because they're well-known.*

CELEBRITY: Pat Boone, former teen idol and squeaky-clean Christian

COMPANY: Karr Preventative Medical Products Inc., maker of Acne-Statin, a mail-order pimple cream

MALPRACTICE: In the 1970s, Boone appeared in TV, magazine, and newspaper ads, claiming that Acne-Statin "had been scientifically found to cure the most severe cases of acne by eliminating certain bacteria and fatty acid from the pores of the skin." But as one critic pointed out, the product actually had "the same facial efficacy as shoe polish." In 1978 Boone was found guilty of false advertising, along with the manufacturer, and was ordered to stop appearing in the commercials and provide refunds to thousands of customers. At the time, it was the stiffest FTC penalty ever given to a celebrity endorsing a product.

CELEBRITY: Johnny Unitas, legendary Baltimore Colts quarterback

COMPANY: First Fidelity Financial Services, Inc., a second-mortgage broker in Hollywood, Florida

MALPRACTICE: In 1981 Unitas appeared on radio ads assuring listeners: "I know what it's like to put your name on the line and make it count. That's where my friends at First Fidelity come in." When First Fidelity went bankrupt and its founder was jailed for fraud, two investors sued Unitas (who'd received only $7,000 for his endorsement) for the $78,000 they'd invested and lost in the company. Their lawyer explained: "They invested their money based upon the belief that someone like Unitas . . . would not be involved in misrepresentation. A celebrity has some obligation

Americans consume 16,000 tons of aspirin every year.

to . . . make sure he is not being used in a scheme of fraud."
Unitas's lawyer protested: "There is nothing in the law to require
an endorser . . . to go through the books to make sure the product
he is putting his picture on is sound." Unitas became the first pro-
football player ever sued for "advertising a bum product."

CELEBRITY: Lloyd Bridges, veteran TV and movie actor
COMPANY: Diamond Mortgage Co. (which lent money at high
rates to people who couldn't get mortgages anywhere else) and an
affiliated company, A.J. Obie & Associates (which found investors
to finance the mortgages)
MALPRACTICE: In 1986 Bridges and another actor, George
Hamilton, appeared in ads promising people that the companies'
"secured investments" would "help them to a better life."
According to court documents, however, the only people who got
a better life out of the deal were the executives who looted the
companies. They kept investors' money instead of putting it into
more mortgages, then, facing claims of more than $40 million,
eventually went bankrupt. Two of them went to jail. Meanwhile,
both Hamilton and Bridges were prosecuted by the state of Illinois
under its consumer fraud law. Hamilton immediately settled, but
Bridges fought the suit, insisting he was merely a spokesman for
Obie "with no special expertise in investments." When an appeals
court rejected his contention, Bridges gave up the fight and settled
the case.

CELEBRITIES: Ed McMahon and Dick Clark
COMPANY: American Family Publishers sweepstakes
MALPRACTICE: The avuncular McMahon and ageless Clark
appeared in 1990s ads telling consumers to watch for the mailing
with Uncle Ed's picture on it. But more than 30 states said the
mailings were outright fraud. For example: Some mailings indicated that a recipient was one of two people vying for the grand
prize, and the first person to return the entry form would win. "In
their zeal to sell magazines," said Florida's attorney general, "AFP
and its high profile pitchmen have misled millions of consumers.
They have clearly stepped over the line from advertising hype to
unlawful deception." States sued AFP, McMahon, and Clark. AFP
settled, paying $50,000 to each state and agreeing to change its
practices.

Angel Falls in Venezuela is 15 times higher than Niagara Falls.

PUN FOR THE MONEY

BRI member Erica Gordon keeps sending Uncle John her horrible puns.
Of course, he loves them—and then insists on "sharing" them with us.
So why are we including them here? Have you ever heard the saying
"Misery loves company?" Heh, heh. Feel free to groan out loud.

TWO ESKIMOS were sitting in a kayak. They got chilly, so they decided to light a fire in the craft. Unfortunately, it sank—proving once and for all that you can't have your kayak and heat it, too.

TWO BOLL WEEVILS grew up in South Carolina. One went to Hollywood and became a famous actor. The other stayed behind in the cotton fields and never amounted to much. The second one became known as the lesser of two weevils.

THERE WAS A MAN who entered a local paper's pun contest. He sent in ten different puns, hoping that at least one of the puns would win. Unfortunately, no pun in ten did.

A WOMAN HAD TWINS, but gave them up for adoption. One of them went to a family in Egypt and was named "Amal." The other went to a family in Spain who named him "Juan." Years later, Juan sent a picture of himself to his mom. When she got the picture, she told her husband wistfully that she wished she also had a picture of Amal. Her husband responded: "But they're twins—if you've seen Juan, you've seen Amal."

SOME FRIARS NEEDED TO RAISE MONEY, so they opened up a small florist shop. Since everyone liked to buy flowers from the men of God, the rival florist across town thought the competition was unfair. He asked the good fathers to close down, but they would not. He went back and begged the friars to close. They ignored him. He asked his mother to plead with them. They ignored her, too. Finally, the rival florist hired Hugh McTaggart, the roughest and most vicious thug in town to "persuade" them to close. Hugh beat up the friars and trashed their store, saying he'd be back if they didn't close shop. Terrified, they did so—thereby proving (are you ready?) that Hugh, and only Hugh, can prevent florist friars.

Is it true that the average person speaks only 10 minutes each day?

THE ORIGIN OF THE SHOPPING CART

*Some modern conveniences seem so simple and logical that it's hard
to believe they actually had to be invented. Take the shopping cart,
for example. You might guess it evolved from some sort of small
wagon people were already using. But it came from the mind of one
man. Here's the story, told in* The Cart That Changed
the World, *by Terry P. Wilson.*

A BIGGER BASKET

In 1937 Sylvan Goldman owned two Oklahoma City
supermarkets. Back then, shoppers carried their food in
wicker baskets provided by the grocer. One day Goldman was
standing around, watching customers, when he realized that as
soon as a basket was either full or too heavy, people stopped shopping. "The thought came to me," Goldman recalled, "that if we
could somehow give a customer two baskets and still leave them
with a free hand to shop, we could do considerably more business."
He came up with a plan:

> In my office I had some folding chairs that salesmen used
> when they called on me. I realized that if I put wheels on
> them, raised the seats so there was room to put another rack
> at the bottom of the chair, and let the back of the chair be
> the handle, customers could be shopping comfortably with
> two baskets.

Goldman worked with a carpenter to adapt the chairs. Their
first effort was a flop—it hit a wooden match on the floor and collapsed. But several months later, they created a collapse-proof
steel-framed "basket carrier." Now Goldman was ready to introduce
it to the public.

IT'S NEW! IT'S SENSATIONAL!

Goldman ran newspaper ads all week, announcing that he would
introduce a brand-new shopping convenience on the weekend. The
ads said: "Can you imagine wending your way through a spacious
food market without having to carry a cumbersome shopping basket

According to one study, 85% of parents use child car-safety seats incorrectly.

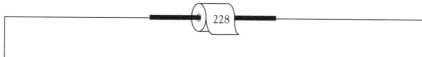

on your arm? . . . Every customer who visits our stores this weekend will see the latest device conceived by the mind of man; and be able to shop with an ease never before known in any Food Store!"

There was no mention of the shopping cart—customers had to come to the store to find out what the new marvel was. And that weekend, plenty of customers came . . . but no one used the cart. As Goldman relates:

> I went to our largest store, and there wasn't a soul using a "basket-carrier." An attractive girl at the entrance was asking them to "please take this cart" to do their shopping with. But the housewives . . . decided, 'No more carts for me. I've been pushing enough baby carriages. I don't want to push any-more.' And the men would say, 'You mean, with my big strong arm I can't carry a darn little basket like that?' And he wouldn't touch it. It was a complete flop.

CONSUMER PSYCHOLOGY

A few days later, Goldman hit on an idea to get people to use the carts.

> For each store, I hired a young lady in her late 20s, another in her 40s, and someone else in her late 50s. I also hired a cou-ple of men about 30 and 50 years old. [I put them] right by the entranceway of the store with basket-carriers, shopping, pushing the cart around with merchandise in the top and bot-tom baskets. I told this young lady who was offering the carts to customers to say, "Look, everybody's using them; why not you?" And when people saw them in use, they started using them, and the carts immediately became a huge success.

Within a few weeks all of Goldman's stores were offering "basket-carriers," and the devices became extremely popular.

SELLING THE SHOPPING CART

Encouraged by the success of his invention, Goldman patented the design and formed the Folding Basket-Carrier Company to manu-facture it. Then he hired his cousin, Kurt Schweitzer, to demon-strate the cart at a meeting of U.S. supermarket operators.

The expo went so well that when he returned, Schweitzer offered to quit his import-export job and sell shopping carts full-time. Goldman agreed, and Schweitzer set out to visit every major

Horse jockeys are the only U.S. athletes legally allowed to bet on themselves.

grocery store between New York and St. Louis. He returned with disastrous news: almost no stores had ordered the cart. Managers were afraid that children would race basket-carriers up and down the aisles, knocking merchandise off shelves and into customers. Cart-related accidents would lead to lawsuits, they said, and the convenience wasn't worth the risk.

GROCER PSYCHOLOGY

Goldman put considerable thought into solving the problem and, once again, came up with an idea that was revolutionary in its time:

> We gathered a group of employees in one of our stores after closing hours and took a movie of them acting as customers shopping . . . [That way, store-owners could see] exactly how this worked—how easily and how well it was accepted, how the problems a lot of them feared didn't materialize at all . . . When the film was finished, I told Kurt, "Now when you go in to try to see the buyer, tell him . . . you have something new and [you have to] show it to them."
> He took his projector in with the film, shut off the light, closed the door, and showed it on a wall . . . Before he got halfway back to New York, we had so many orders for carts, we couldn't have made them in God knows how long a time.

The Folding Basket-Carrier Company bought new equipment and went into mass production. Goldman's basket-carriers evolved into today's shopping cart and quickly became a fixture in nearly every grocery store in America.

* * *

UNUSUAL THEME RESTAURANT

Baked Pig Face (*Seven Locations in Mainland China*)
Theme: Western-style restaurant built around a traditional dish from Northeastern China—baked pig heads
Details: Waitresses wear caps with the restaurant's "Porky Pig-like logo." Main dish: "a whole pig's head, yellow teeth and all, cooked for 12 hours in 20 herbs and spices." The steaming heads are "split in half and laid split-side down on a platter . . . piping hot, with piglet-shaped dumplings as a garnish." Vacuum-sealed heads available for takeout.

If a woodchuck could chuck wood, it would chuck about 700 pounds.

THE MAN WHO INVENTED THE YEAR 2000

Why do we think it's the year 2000 (or 2001, or 2010)? Blame it on an obscure Ukranian monk named Dionysius Exiguus—"Dennis the Short"—who had the idea in the first place. Here are the details from our book Uncle John's Indispensable Guide to the Year 2000.

BACKGROUND

Until Dionysius Exiguus ("Dennis the Short") came up with the *Anno Domini* (A.D.) system, there was no uniform way to number years. Europeans measured time from any number of benchmarks—the founding of Rome (referred to as A.U.C.—short for the Latin *ab urbe condita,* or "from the founding of the city"), the reign of Emperor Diocletian, and other even more obscure dates.

THE NEW CALENDAR

In 1278 A.U.C., Pope John I asked Dennis, the abbot of a Roman church and a respected scholar, to come up with a new calendar based on Jesus's birthday. This was no easy task: no one knew exactly when Jesus had been born.

Working from Gospel accounts, official Roman records, and astrological charts, Dennis finally settled on December 25, 753 A.U.C. Theoretically, December 25 should have been the first day of Dennis's new calendar. But he started the year eight days later, on January 1. The religious rationale was that it was the Feast of the Circumcision—Jesus's eighth day of life. But more likely, it was because January 1 was already New Year's Day in Roman and Latin Christian calendars.

Dennis called his first year 1 A.D. That made the current year 525 A.D.

NO IMMEDIATE IMPACT

The initial response to Dennis's calculations was silence. No one used the new system for centuries. In fact, even he didn't follow his own chronology (he continued to use the A.U.C system).

It took more than 1,000 years for many countries to accept Dennis's system (called *incarnation dating*). It was officially adopted by the Catholic Church at the Synod of Whitby in 664. But no one actually used it until late in the 8th century, when a celebrated English historian known as the Venerable Bede annotated the margins of a book with A.D. dating. This work was widely copied and is probably responsible for spreading knowledge of the system around Europe.

A.D. dating was made "universal" at the Synod of Chelsea in 816 A.D., but it still wasn't widely used by many Catholic countries until the 12th century—and even later for other nations. Britain, for example, didn't adopt the Gregorian calendar until 1752; China accepted it for civil use in 1911.

IMPACT NOW

Hardly anyone today has heard of Dennis, although his calendar is the international standard. In fact, the main reason he gets noticed isn't because of his achievements, but because of his screwups. Dennis made two fundamental mistakes: 1) he got Jesus's birthday wrong (Jesus was probably born between 11 and 4 B.C.), and 2) he started his calendar with 1 A.D. instead of zero.

WHY DID HE DO IT?

It's easy to understand why Dennis got Jesus' birthday wrong—after all, he didn't have much to go on. No reference books, no computer searches.

But starting time with the year 1 goes against common sense. Logic dictates that we count a child's first birthday after a full year—when he or she is one year old—not when they're born. So why did Dennis do it?

Rushworth Kidder of the *Christian Science Monitor* speculates that "nobody wanted to describe the first year of Christianity as a zero." But Stephen Jay Gould says the answer is much simpler: "Western mathematics in the 6th century had not yet developed a concept of zero."

In other words, says futurist Josh Redel, "Dennis didn't really have any choice. He was a prisoner of history, like the rest of us."

The average American kid in daycare catches 10.

BEEN NOWHERE, DONE NOTHING

BRI member Debbie Thornton sent in this list of real-life bumper stickers. Have you seen the one that says . . .

SUBURBIA: Where They Tear Down the Trees and Name Streets After Them

I Have No Idea What I'm Doing Out of Bed

Been Nowhere, Done Nothing

Support Bacteria: It's the Only Culture Some People Have

I Used to Be Indecisive; Now I'm Not Sure

My Reality Check Just Bounced

No Sense Being Pessimistic— It Wouldn't Work Anyway

The More You Complain, the Longer God Lets You Live

Forget About World Peace— Visualize Using Your Turn Signal!

Warning: Dates in Calendar Are Closer Than They Appear

Consciousness: That Annoying Time Between Naps

Age Is a Very High Price to Pay for Maturity

I Doubt, Therefore I Might Be

The Older You Get, the Better You Realize You Were

Dyslexics Have More Fnu

Men Are from Earth. Women Are from Earth. Deal With It.

The Gene Pool Could Use a Little Chlorine

So You're a Feminist . . . Isn't That Cute!

Time Is What Keeps Things from Happening All at Once

Your Kid May Be an Honor Student but You're Still an Idiot

We Have Enough Youth, How About a Fountain of "Smart"?

Your odds of living to age 116: 1 in 2 billion.

HOW TO MAKE A MONSTER, PART II

Here's the second installment of our history of
Uncle John's favorite movie monster . . . Gojira, the original
Japanese name for Godzilla. (Part I starts on page 106.)

DESIGNING A MONSTER

It took the model department three tries to come up with the right design for Gojira. The first model had fishlike scales for skin and a line of pointy spikes running down its back. Producer Tomoyuki Tanaka liked the spikes, but thought the head was too big and the scales too "fishy." Next they created a "warty" Gojira with a smaller head and large rounded bumps on the skin. Tanaka didn't like this treatment either, so they came up with "alligator" Gojira, this time with much smaller, linear bumps arranged in rows like bumps on an alligator's back. Alligator Gojira got the nod.

SUITS ME FINE

Now Tanaka had a name and a look for his monster—but what kind of special effects would he use? Stop-motion animation, (e.g., claymation) used tiny, moveable clay models, and was filmed frame by frame. It produced excellent results—*King Kong* was filmed with stop-motion animation—but was time consuming and expensive. Plus, it limited the amount of detail that could be shown—a big problem, since so much of the script involved the monster knocking down buildings. (It's almost impossible to make a building collapse realistically when filming frame by frame.)

The alternative: use a man in a monster suit. That could be filmed at a larger scale, making higher levels of detail possible. And because the footage would be filmed in "real time" instead of frame by frame, it could be finished in a few weeks instead of several months. The problem with such a low-tech technique was that if the filmmakers weren't careful, the man in the monster suit would end up looking like . . . a man in a monster suit.

In the end, it was scheduling that decided the issue—a monster

---

New data: The average American male laughs 69 times a day; the average woman, 55.

suit was quicker, and Toho studios had only a year to produce the film, so Godjira became a man in a costume.

The special-effects crew built a full-sized Gojira model, which they used to create plaster molds for the monster suit. Then they poured latex rubber into the molds to make Gojira's skin. The skin was then attached to a cloth "inner skin," made of cloth stuffed with polystyrene foam and bamboo to provide the monster's bulk. The fully assembled suit weighed more than 220 pounds.

The actor entered the costume via a zipper that ran along the dorsal fin; he was (barely) able to see out of the costume through four tiny holes in Gojira's neck. The monster's head was then mounted on a brace that rested on the actor's head; an offscreen technician used a radio-controlled mechanism to open and close the mouth.

SWEATY WORK

Gojira's action sequences were filmed at a high speed so that when it was slowed down for viewing, the buildings crumbled more realistically. But this meant that the set had to be lit twice as bright as when filming at normal speed, and the hot lights caused temperatures inside the suit to climb as high as 120°F, with the only ventilation provided by the eyeholes in Gojira's neck.

Under these conditions it was nearly impossible to film for more than a few minutes at a time. Typically, the actor inside the suit would spend 7 to 10 minutes rehearsing a scene in costume with the studio lights turned off. Then the lights came on and the scene was filmed for about 3 minutes, which was all the actor could take before he risked passing out from heat prostration and suffocation. Collapsing mid-scene was not unusual, and two actors who alternated as Gojira sweated so profusely that the crew drained as much as half a pint of sweat from the suit at the end of the day.

The on-screen result of filming in such difficult conditions was a slow, lumbering creature who shuffled and lurched across the tiny cityscapes . . . but that was just the look that Tanaka wanted: in the 1950s, paleontologists incorrectly assumed that most dinosaurs were huge, slow-witted, slow-moving creatures, and Tanaka's quest for dinosaur accuracy dovetailed nicely with the limitations imposed by the heavy suit and hot studio lights.

What sports celebrity appeared simultaneously on *Time*, *Newsweek*, and *Sports Illustrated*?

TINY TOWN

Entire city blocks of downtown Tokyo were reconstructed in elaborate detail for the film. For the scene in which Gojira destroys Tokyo's famous Ginza district, special effects man Eiji Tsuburaya's technicians reproduced a three-square-block section of the district in miniature, complete with interior floors and walls to make sure the buildings would crumble realistically when Gojira smashed them. Tsuburaya also insisted that the tiny automobiles, buses, and trains be handmade from cast iron to ensure that when Gojira stepped on them, the sturdy little vehicles would crush realistically.

MAKING NOISE

Finding a suitable roar for Gojira was one of the trickier aspects of creating the monster. The film's sound-effects team tried numerous actual animal sounds: grunts, growls, roars, and other noises. They played them backward, forward, individually, and in groups, but nothing seemed to work. Then composer Akira Ifukube tried rubbing the strings of a bass violin with the fingers of a resin-coated rubber glove, and reverberating the sound. That did the trick.

OPENING NIGHT

Finally, after 122 days of filming, *Gojira* premiered in Japan on November 3, 1954. The film had cost a fortune to make—the final tally was 60 million yen (about $65 million in 1999 dollars), about 250 times the average cost of a Japanese film at that time.

But it turned out to be a good investment: *Gojira* was one of the most popular films of the year and earned a fortune for Toho.

Gojira was also a critical success. "While American monster-on-the-loose films used radiation to get the monster up and running around," David Kalat writes in *A Critical History and Filmography of Toho's Godzilla Series*, "Honda saw his monster as a narrative device to discuss the terror of the nuclear age." Less than a decade after World War II, Japanese critics understood and appreciated the implicit message.

Turn to page 302 for Part III.

Secretariat, the race horse (in 1973).

MODEL CITIZENS

Some thoughtful commentary from the mouths of "babes."

"I don't have to fake dumb. I am dumb."
—*Jerry Hall*

"I don't wake up for less than $10,000 a day."
—*Linda Evangelista*

"Everywhere I went, my cleavage followed. But I learned I am not my cleavage."
—*Carole Mallory*

"I'm so naive about finances. Once when my mother mentioned an amount and I realized I didn't understand, she had to explain: 'That's like three Mercedes.' Then I understood."
—*Brooke Shields*

"Blah, blah, blah. I'm so tired of talking about myself."
—*Elle Macpherson*

"I don't think I was born beautiful. I just think I was born me."
—*Naomi Campbell*

"I've always been a bit more maturer than what I am."
—*Samantha Fox*

"Everyone should have enough money to get plastic surgery."
—*Beverly Johnson*

"I believe that mink are raised for being turned into fur coats and if we didn't wear fur coats those little animals would never have been born. So is it better not to have been born or to have lived for a year or two to have been turned into a fur coat? I don't know."
—*Barbi Benton*

"People think modeling's mindless, that you just stand there and pose, but it doesn't have to be that way. I like to have a lot of input. I know how to wear a dress, whether it should be shot with me standing up or sitting. And I'm not scared to say what I think."
—*Linda Evangelista*

"I look at modeling as something I'm doing for black people in general."
—*Naomi Campbell*

"I can do anything you want me to do so long as I don't have to speak."
—*Linda Evangelista*

"I wish my butt did not go sideways, but I guess I have to face that."
—*Christie Brinkley*

The U.S. Postal Service owns 176,000 cars and trucks . . .

THE JOKE'S ON US!

Americans tend to overlook an important side to our love affair
with celebrities—they're always trying to sell us something:
an idea, image, or product. And many of them don't
mind lying to us, either. Here are a few examples.

FOR SALE: A Cherished Possession

In the early 1900s Bat Masterson, legendary Wild West lawman, became a New York sports writer. Because he needed the money, he reluctantly agreed to sell his famous sixgun—the "gun that tamed the West."

The Truth: He actually bought old guns at pawnshops or junk stores, carved notches in them (one for each "kill"), and sold them to admirers for a tidy profit. Each time, he swore it was the authentic gun he'd used in Dodge City.

FOR SALE: An Intellectual Image

In 1961 an article in *Time* magazine helped convince Americans that they'd elected an exceptionally bright man as president. It reported that JFK had taken a course in something called "speed-reading" and could zip through an amazing 1,200 words a minute. It became common knowledge—and part of his mystique—that he could read a whole book in one sitting.

The Truth: The number was concocted by Kennedy and *Time* reporter Hugh Sidey. First, JFK told Sidey he could read 1,000 words a minute. Upon reflection, however, he decided that number sounded too low. "How about 1,200?" Sidey asked. "Okay," Kennedy replied. And that's what was printed. Actually, JFK never finished the speed-reading course he took and, at best, could read 800 wpm (still a lot, but not as impressive).

FOR SALE: A Folksy White House Tradition

It was a Yuletide tradition during the Reagan presidency. Gathering with reporters, the Great Communicator would ceremoniously light the National Christmas Tree on the Mall in Washington, D.C., by pushing a button from inside the White House.

... the largest civilian vehicle fleet on earth.

The Truth: The button wasn't connected to anything—a Park Service employee actually lit the tree. The press found out by accident in 1989, when President Bush went to the tree site and lit it in person. Bush's press secretary let it slip that, unlike the Reagan years, "that was the real thing." Cornered, he admitted that Reagan's button was a prop. "Then came the follow-up question," the *Washington Post* reported: "Were all the other buttons disconnected, too?"

FOR SALE: Ultimate Weirdness
In the 1980s a number of strange stories about pop singer Michael Jackson were reported by the media—especially by the tabloids. The press reported, for example, that Jackson . . .

- had bought an oxygen chamber and was sleeping in it. The reason: he wanted to live to be 100.

- had offered to buy the remains of John Merrick, the "Elephant Man," for $500,000. (*Playboy* magazine jokingly responded that "descendants of the Elephant Man have offered $100,000 for the remains of Michael Jackson's nose.")

- was so obsessed with his chimp, Bubbles, that he was learning "monkey language" to communicate with him.

Even more than his music, the constant stream of reports on Jackson's weirdnesses made him a pervasive presence in pop culture. Everyone talked about him.
The Truth: The stories were all false—concocted, it turns out, by Jackson himself. According to one report, Jackson had "learned early how little truth means when seeking publicity" back when he was in the Jackson 5. In private, he even "began reading biographies of hokum-master P. T. Barnum for ideas."

* * *

PROCEED WITH CAUTION

- A black widow's poison is 15 times more powerful than rattlesnake venom.

- Black widows like warm, dark places, and in pre–indoor plumbing days, were "fond of hiding in outhouses, where they often spin webs across toilet seats."

RANDOM ORIGINS

Once again, the BRI asks—and answers—the
question: where did this stuff come from?

THE JOCKSTRAP

T HE JOCKSTRAP
"Millions of male athletes can thank bicycling—and the
cobblestone streets of Boston—for the truss that protects
their masculinity . . . In 1897, those bumpy Beantown byways got
too rough for the nether regions of bike racers. To address this
unexpected need, the BIKE manufacturing company invented the
"bicycle jockey strap"—eventually shortened to 'jock.'" (*Bicycling*
magazine)

THE ROLODEX

Arnold Neustadter invented several devices (the Swivodex, the
Clipodex, etc.) for clerical workers, but they were flops. In 1950, to
clear his own desk clutter, he created the first Rolodex. It wasn't a
big seller at $7.50. But then came Hollywood. The Rolodex was
featured in films as the accessory of powerful men—"The bigger
the Rolodex, the bigger the man," as Neustadter's son-in-law David
put it. At one time, there were hundreds of Rolodex models,
including the 6,000-card, triple-wheel Torque-a-Matic. Today only
a few models are still offered, including a little, handheld, comput-
erized version.

SNEEZING POWDER

In 1905 Sam Adams, a salesman for "a coal-tar product," noticed
that it made people sneeze. *Scribner's* magazine wrote in 1940:
"Adams began fooling with it for his own amusement . . . High
spots included sprinkling the powder through hotel keyholes, in a
cafe where a wandering brass band was serenading, and at a trap-
shooting contest where he unnerved his competitors by dusting it
near them as they took aim . . . In 1906 he formed the Adams
Novelty Company and marketed the powder as Cachoo . . .
Cachoo divided the country like nothing since the Civil War.
Town fathers passed ordinances, school principals preached sermons, editorial writers inveighed against Cachoo. But a laugh-hun-
gry public demanded more." It was the beginning of the modern

Highest consumption of canned beans in the U.S.: New York, Los Angeles, Boston.

novelty industry. Adams went on to invent the Dribble Glass, the Joy Buzzer, and other classics. His biggest regret: in 1930 a Toronto company offered him exclusive rights to the Whoopee Cushion . . . and he turned it down. "The whole idea seemed too indelicate," said the man who invented the Bloody Finger, "so I passed it up."

THE ATLAS
"In the late 16th century French geographer Gerhard Mercator (1512–1594) published a book of maps whose frontispiece was a picture of Atlas holding the world on his back. Almost from then on, any collection of maps has been called an *atlas*." (*Literary Life*)

THE FOOTBALL HUDDLE
"In 1924, Herb McCracken, the coach of the Lafayette College football team, discovered that his hand signals [flashed to players during the game] had been scouted and decoded by Penn, his upcoming opponent. On game day, McCracken countered by ordering his players to gather en masse, several yards behind the line of scrimmage, and talk over the plays in a whisper. It immediately became a ritual." McCracken later helped start the Scholastic publishing company, "but told family members that he was most proud of giving birth to the huddle." (*New York Times*)

THE CASH REGISTER
In 1879 a Dayton, Ohio, saloonkeeper named James J. Ritty was vacationing on a transatlantic steamer when he took a tour of the engine room and saw a machine that counted the number of revolutions of the ship's propeller. He figured a similar machine might help him keep track of his saloon sales, and prevent dishonest bartenders from looting the till. When he got home, he and his brother invented "Ritty's Incorruptible Cashier"—a machine with two rows of keys with amounts printed on them, a clocklike face that added up the amount of money collected, and a bell that rang after every transaction. It was the first product from the business that would become the National Cash Register Company (NCR).

When is it legal for the dead to vote? If they die after mailing in an absentee ballot.

MY BODY LIES OVER THE OCEAN

More stories about miscellaneous body parts
removed from famous people after they died.

EINSTEIN'S EYES

EINSTEIN'S EYES
Where They're Located: Bank vault in New Jersey
How They Got There: It turns out Dr. Harvey wasn't the only sticky-fingered professional at Einstein's autopsy (see p. 146): At about the same time Harvey was absconding with the brain, Einstein's ophthalmologist, a doctor named Henry Abrams, was removing the eyes. He placed them in a jar and locked them away in a bank vault until 1994, when he reportedly began looking for a buyer. "When you look into his eyes, you're looking into the beauties and mysteries of the world," he told Britain's *Guardian* newspaper. "They are clear as crystal; they seem to have such depth."

JOSEPH HAYDN'S SKULL

Where It's Located: In Haydn's marble crypt in Eisenstadt, Austria, after being separated from the rest of the body for more than 145 years
How It Got There: Haydn's patron, the Prince of Esterhazy, saw to it that Haydn's body was buried intact following the composer's death in 1809. But some phrenologists (people who "read" skulls) wanted to see if they could divine the source of the composer's genius by looking at his skull. So they dug up his body, removed the head, took it away for study . . . and then refused to bring it back unless the Prince of Esterhazy paid them a ransom. The prince balked at paying the blackmail, so Haydn was reburied, without his head.

The head eventually ended up in the Musikverein museum in Vienna, Austria, where it was stolen, eventually resurfacing "in the home of an Austrian professor, who displayed it on his piano," and then returned to the museum in 1895. That year the village of Eisenstadt began lobbying for the head's return to Haydn's crypt.

They negotiated until 1935, to no avail. Then, at the end of World War II, they tried again. Negotiations dragged on for nine

People who drink coffee are less likely to commit suicide than people who don't.

years, and finally, in 1954, Haydn's head was reunited with the rest of his body.

SANTA CLAUS'S FINGERS

Where They're Located: "Now on display in the city of Antalya, Turkey"

How They Got There: Saint Nicholas, the Catholic bishop believed to be the inspiration for Santa Claus, died in the fourth century A.D. He was buried in his old church, in what is now the Turkish town of Demre, on the Mediterranean coast. But somehow, his remains ended up in a church in the Italian port of Bari (tradition has it Italian merchants from Bari stole them in 1087), and the town of Demre has been trying to get the bones back for 900 years. All they have left is "a finger or two," on display in a nearby city.

"One reason Christians aren't keen to send the bones back," the *Wall Street Journal* reports, "is because Turkey is now predominantly Moslem. In fact, some believe the 11th-century Christian monks in Myra allowed the Italians to remove the bones in order to save them from the advancing Turkish armies."

Muammer Karabulut, chairman of the Santa Claus Foundation, which seeks the return of the bones, says his group's mostly Moslem membership should not be an issue. After all, he insists, "Santa Claus is [a] universal figure."

STONEWALL JACKSON'S ARM

Where It's Located: The Chancellorville battle site near Fredericksburg, Virginia

How It Got There: On May 2, 1863, as he was returning to camp after engineering an important victory for the Confederacy, the legendary general was accidentally shot by his own troops. Jackson was hit in the right hand and in the left wrist and shoulder, and his left arm had to be amputated above the elbow.

Jackson's chaplain, B. Tucker Lacy, had a brother who owned a house near the hospital, so he took the severed limb to his brother's for burial. Confederate troops buried the arm in a nearby field, complete with a religious ceremony and a marble tombstone. When Jackson died from complications eight days later, he was buried in Lexington, Virginia.

According to *Roadside America*, "The arm was exhumed in 1929 and reburied in a steel box on a plantation known as Ellwood.

First nationwide bestselling book in the U.S.: the memoirs of Ulysses S. Grant.

Around the field in which it now lays, there is only one grave-stone: the one belonging to Jackson's arm."

OTHER CELEBRITY BODY PARTS

- **Thomas Hardy's heart.** "Hardy's heart was to be buried in Stinsford, England, his birthplace, after the rest of his body was cremated in Dorchester. All went according to plan until the great poet's sister's cat snatched the heart off her kitchen table and disappeared into the woods with it."

- **Emanuel Swedenborg's skull.** The famous Swedish philosopher's skull was stolen by a retired sea captain 50 years after Swedenborg's death. It turned up in an antique shop in Wales a century later. When Swedenborg's descendents learned of the skull's existence, they went to Wales and bought it . . . and then auctioned it off at Sotheby's for $3,200.

- **Buddha's teeth.** Tradition has it that two or three teeth (depending on who you ask) were found in Buddha's cremated remains following his death 2,400 years ago. Today the teeth are in temples in Beijing, China; Sri Lanka; and Taipei, Taiwan.

- **Percy Bysshe Shelley's heart.** When he drowned in 1822, Shelley "was cremated on the beach upon which his body had washed. For some reason his heart would not burn and it was taken from the fire and given to his wife, Mary Wollstonecraft Shelley (author of *Frankenstein*), who carried it with her in a silken shroud everywhere she went for the rest of her life."

- **Chang and Eng Bunker's liver.** The two brothers, born in Thailand in 1811, were attached at the chest. P. T. Barnum made them world-famous (coining the term "Siamese twin"). One or both of their livers was apparently removed upon their death, and now sits in a jar at the Mutter Museum in Philadelphia.

* * *

Random Animal Fact: On average, cats spend 30 percent of their waking hours grooming themselves. They purr at 26 cycles per second, about the same frequency as an idling diesel engine.

One mother shark can give birth to as many as 70 baby sharks per litter.

HEY, THAT'S MY NAME ON THE BALLOT!

As people pay less attention to election issues, candidates have to focus more on name recognition. That can lead to some confusion, as it did in these elections.

R USSO FOR CONGRESS!
In 1946 Joseph Russo, a popular Boston city councilman, decided to run for a seat in the U.S. Congress. At first his only opponent in the Democratic primary was a young World War II veteran named John Fitzgerald Kennedy. But at the last minute, another candidate appeared on the ballot: a second Joseph Russo. Who was this new challenger! Turns out he was a family friend of the Kennedys. It's widely believed that JFK's father got Russo #2 into the race to confuse voters and ensure his son's victory. **Election Results:** It worked. Joseph Russo and Joseph Russo split the Russo vote; JFK won the primary by a landslide.

CAROL MOSELEY-BRAUN FOR ALDERMAN!

In 1998, 21-year-old Lauryn K. Valentine asked a court to allow her to change her name to Carol Moseley-Braun. It had nothing to do with politics, she explained—it was a tribute to former U.S. Senator Carol Moseley-Braun, the first African-American woman to serve in the Senate. Valentine claimed that Moseley-Braun "had encouraged me to stay in school when I was considering dropping out." The judge granted her request.

Surprise! In December 1998 the new Moseley-Braun filed papers to run for Chicago city alderman. The real Moseley-Braun and another candidate for alderman both filed legal challenges. Election Results: Unknown. (Anyone out there know what happened?)

JOHN F. KENNEDY FOR STATE TREASURER!

Future president John F. Kennedy had just been elected to the U.S. Senate in 1952; what was he doing running for State Treasurer in 1953? Answer: It was John Francis Kennedy. He was no relation, wasn't rich, didn't attend Harvard—and wasn't even a high school graduate. This Kennedy had quit school at the age of 14 and was working as a stockroom supervisor at the Gillette Razor Blade Company when he decided to cash in on his popular name and run for office. The incumbent treasurer, John Hurley, resigned in 1953, and JFK ran in the special election to replace him. His qualifications? "I got a good name," he said in an interview, "I know a lot of people at Gillette to say 'hi' to, and I want to make money and get ahead in life."

Election Results: Kennedy lost the 1953 race . . . but never underestimate the power of a name. When he ran again in 1954, he won. Total campaign expenses: about $100, "most of which was spent to throw an election-night party." Kennedy served six years as state treasurer. In 1960—the year the other JFK was elected president—he ran for governor, and lost.

WARNER FOR SENATE!
In 1996 John Warner, the incumbent U.S. Senator from Virginia, ran for re-election against a multimillionaire businessman named . . . Warner. The challenger's first name was Mark, but under Virginia law, the ballot did not identify which Warner was the incumbent, or even which one was the Republican (John) or the Democrat (Mark). "Although some analysts figure the name problem will make no real difference in the end," the *Washington Post* reported, "others envision a chaotic scenario in which thousands of votes could be cast unwittingly for the wrong man. Mark Warner . . . figures, at least half seriously, that he could gain a couple of percentage points simply by winning the drawing to determine who will be listed on the ballot first."

Election Results: No contest—John Warner was re-elected.

OTHER RACES
Taylor vs. Taylor, 1886. "Two brothers named Taylor ran against each other for governor of Tennessee, a battle that became known as the 'War of the Roses' because their mother had given each candidate a different color rose." (*San Francisco Chronicle*)

Hansen vs. Hansen vs. Hanson, 1974. "George V. Hansen ousted incumbent Orval Hansen in a Republican primary for a House seat in Idaho, then topped Democrat Max Hanson in the fall."

In Venice, Venetian blinds are known as "Persian blinds."

LOONEY LAWS

Believe it or not, these laws are real.

In Macomb, Illinois, it's illegal for a car to impersonate a wolf.

In Rumford, Maine, it's against the law to bite your landlord.

An ordinance in San Francisco bans picking up used confetti to throw again.

It's against the law in Atlanta, Georgia, to tie a giraffe to a telephone pole or street lamp.

It's against the law in Chicago to eat in a place that is on fire.

In International Falls, Minnesota, it's against the law for a cat to chase a dog up a telephone pole.

It's illegal to catch fish while on horseback in Washington, D.C.

It's illegal to take a lion to the theater in Maryland.

It's against the law to drive more than 2,000 sheep down Hollywood Boulevard.

Brawley, California, passed a resolution banning snow within the city limits.

In Tennessee, it's illegal to drive a car while you're asleep.

Anyone found underneath a sidewalk in Florida is guilty of disorderly conduct.

It's illegal in New Jersey to slurp your soup.

A Texas law states that when two trains meet at a railroad crossing, each must come to a full stop, and neither shall proceed until the other has gone.

It's illegal in Hartford, Connecticut, to kiss your wife on a Sunday.

It's against the law in Kentucky to remarry the same man four times.

In Marshalltown, Iowa, it's illegal for a horse to eat a fire hydrant.

In Tennessee, it's against the law to shoot game other than whales from a moving car.

It's illegal in Fairbanks, Alaska, for two moose to have sex on city sidewalks.

What do gorillas and housecats have in common? Both purr.

BIG, BAD BARBIE

She's the world's favorite doll, a friend to millions of little girls . . . but don't mess with her—she's rough, she's tough, and she'll sue the pants off you for just mentioning her name. How scary can Barbie be? Just ask these former defendants.

BARBIE VS. PAUL HANSEN

Background: Hansen, a San Francisco artist, began selling "Barbie art" in the early 1990s. He took conventional Barbie dolls and turned them into social satire, creating characters like Exorcist Barbie, Tonya Harding Barbie, and Drag Queen Barbie.
Here Comes Barbie: Hansen had sold about 150 of the dolls and earned about $2,000 when Mattel filed suit against him, claiming $1.2 billion in damages.

Art is generally protected as free speech, but Hansen wasn't looking for a fight. He promised to pull his dolls from store shelves, sell them only in art galleries . . . and donate all of the profits to charities. Good enough? Nope. The *Wall Street Journal* reported:

> "Mattel's lawyer still wanted to go to trial to collect damages and win a stricter definition of 'art gallery.' After a year of litigation, even the judge lost patience . . . and granted a partial . . . judgement against Mattel 'for not having a sense of humor.'"

Outcome: Hansen eventually settled out of court and stopped making the dolls. "It was a year from hell," he says.

BARBIE VS. BARBARA BELL

Background: In 1992 Bell, a 44-year-old quiltmaker, claimed that she was receiving psychic messages from Barbie. (Barbie's first message: "I need respect.") For only $3 a pop, she offered to channel Barbie's spirit and answer personal questions from Barbie fans. She also published the *Barbie Channeling Newsletter*.
Here Comes Barbie: Mattel threatened a multimillion-dollar lawsuit against Bell if she didn't shut down her business and cease publication of her newsletter.
Outcome: Bell complied . . . but still doesn't see what all the fuss was about. "Look," she says, "for $3 nobody's getting hurt. I don't claim to be the only voice of Barbie. And I'm sure not taking any

Researchers say: 5% of Americans never get married.

other channeler's business. I've carved out my own niche in the market. There are 700 million Barbie dolls in the world, with no voice."

BARBIE VS. AQUA

Background: In 1997 Aqua, a bubblegum rock band from Denmark, recorded "Barbie Girl" ("I'm a Barbie Girl / in the Barbie world / life in plastic / it's fantastic"). It became a Top 10 hit.

Here Comes Barbie: Mattel filed suit against MCA, the band's U.S. record label, in September 1997, claiming that the song infringed on Barbie trademarks and contained lyrics that "associate sexual and other unsavory themes with Mattel's Barbie products."

MCA fought back, claiming in a countersuit that Mattel had defamed MCA. They also threatened to introduce expert testimony that Mattel had based Barbie on a German "sexpot" doll called Lilli that was marketed to adults in the 1950s. "Mattel's idea in 1959, said their expert, "was to peddle a . . . grown-up sex doll to little girls by dolling it up in designer clothes. What Aqua has done in 'Barbie Girl' is not to make Barbie into a 'sex object' . . . but to point out . . . that she has been one all along."

Outcome: The judge dismissed both suits. Mattel is still appealing.

BARBIE VS. PAUL DAVID

Background: David, a Chillicothe, Ohio, Barbie collector and publisher of a Barbie catalog, remained in Mattel's good graces until the mid-1990s. That's when he wrote in one of his catalogs that "if there were an ugly contest, Elizabethan Queen Barbie would definitely win." He also forgot to put the registered trademark ® symbol on some Barbie photos.

Here Comes Barbie: Mattel swooped down and sued David for copyright infringement, accusing him of copying the company's packaging for his own use.

Outcome: According to the *Wall Street Journal*, "after a lengthy battle, he signed a settlement agreement . . . that stipulates that Barbie may only be portrayed in his catalog as 'wholesome, friendly, accessible and kind, caring and protecting, cheerful, fun loving, talented, and independent.'" David then sold his entire Barbie collection in disgust.

Benjamin Franklin gave guitar lessons.

BARBIE VS. MARK NAPIER

Background: Napier, a New York Web site artist, operated the Distorted Barbie Web site, which featured such "repressed real-world Barbies" as Kate Moss Barbie, Fat and Ugly Barbie, and Dolly Parton Barbie.

Here Comes Barbie: Mattel sent Napier a cease-and-desist letter, telling him to shut down the site.

Outcome: Rather than shut down the site, Napier just blurred the doll's images and replaced the "B" in Barbie with a "$."

BARBIE VS. *HIM AND MEN'S HEALTH*

Background: In 1996 *Him*, a British men's magazine, and the German edition of *Men's Health* published a set of 10 photographs of Ken and Barbie in "improper . . . explicit and offensive positions." The British article promised a new "Position of the Month" in each subsequent issue, and the German magazine posted animated versions of the photographs on its Web site.

Here Comes Barbie: Mattel sued for unspecified damages, accusing the magazines of ruining Ken and Barbie's "wholesome and aspirational" image.

Outcome: Unknown.

* * *

NEWSMAKER BARBIE

"Two former waitresses claim they witnessed the skewering, mutilation, and deep-frying of a Barbie doll at Hoss's Steak & Sea House in Hampton, Oklahoma.

"In March, the women filed a federal sex-discrimination lawsuit against the restaurant, alleging that the Barbie doll incident in September 1994 was a 'satanic ritual,' and that they had to work in a hostile environment. No trial date has been set . . . Both women seek reinstatement with back pay. They also want damages in excess of $25,000. The women contend that after the doll was fried, the grease in the fryer was not changed for seven days and was used to cook food served to patrons at the restaurant. Company officials have denied that the incident occurred or that either woman was harassed or subjected to a hostile working environment."

—**Wire service report**

A hibernating bear can go as long as six months without a bathroom break.

THE DEVIL'S DICTIONARY

Ambrose Bierce was one of the most famous newspaper columnists of the late I 880s—known as "the wickedest man in San Francisco" at a time when S.F. was a pretty rough-and-tumble town. Although not as popular as Mark Twain, his wit was just as satirical and biting. Case in point: The Devil's Dictionary, a caustic set of definitions for otherwise harmless words, written in installments for his column, then compiled in a book. Your library probably has a copy; if you like dark humor, it's great bathroom reading. Here's a sample of what you'll find in it.

Abstainer, *n.* A weak person who yields to the temptation of denying himself a pleasure.

Alone, *adj.* In bad company.

Bequeath, *v.t.* To generously give to another that which can no longer be denied to somebody.

Consult, *v.t.* To seek another's approval of a course already decided on.

Depraved, *p.p.* The moral condition of a gentleman who holds the opposite opinion.

Divorce, *n.* A resumption of diplomatic relations and rectification of boundaries.

Faith, *n.* Belief without evidence in what is told by one who speaks without knowledge, of things without parallel.

Fault, *n.* One of my offenses, as distinguished from one of yours, the latter being crimes.

Forbidden, *p.p.* Invested with a new and irresistible charm.

Governor, *n.* An aspirant to the United States Senate.

Heaven, *n.* A place where the wicked cease from troubling you with talk of their personal affairs, and the good listen with attention while you expound your own.

Homesick, *adj.* Dead broke abroad.

Hypocrite, *n.* One who, professing virtues that he does not respect, secures the advantage of seeming to be what he despises.

Impiety, *n.* Your irreverence toward my diety.

Impunity, *n.* Wealth.

Intimacy, *n.* A relation into which fools are providentially drawn for their mutual destruction.

60% of the country of Liechtenstein's GNP is generated by the sale of false teeth.

Jealous, *adj.* Unduly concerned about the preservation of that which can be lost only if not worth keeping.

Lawyer, *n.* One skilled in circumvention of the law.

Lecturer, *n.* One with his hand in your pocket, his tongue in your ear, and faith in your patience.

Marriage, *n.* The state or condition of a community consisting of a master, a mistress, and two slaves, making in all, two.

Mythology, *n.* The body of a primitive people's beliefs concerning its origin, early history, heroes, dieties and so forth, as distinguished from the true accounts that it invents later.

Novel, *n.* A short story padded.

Once, *adj.* Enough.

Optimism, *n.* The doctrine, or belief, that everything is beautiful, including what is ugly, everything good, especially the bad, and everything right that is wrong.

Pantheism, *n.* The doctrine that everything is God, in contradistinction to the doctrine that God is everything.

Patience, *n.* A minor form of despair, disguised as a virtue.

Piety, *n.* Reverence for the Supreme Being, based upon His supposed resemblance to man.

Politician, *n.* An eel in the fundamental mud upon which the superstructure of organized society is reared.

Pray, *v.* To ask that the laws of the universe be annulled in behalf of a single petitioner, confessedly unworthy.

Rack, *n.* An argumentative implement formerly much used in persuading devotees of a false faith to embrace the living truth . . .

Reporter, *n.* A writer who guesses his way to the truth and dispels it with a tempest of words.

Road, *n.* A strip of land along which one may pass from where it is too tiresome to be to where it is futile to go.

Selfish, *adj.* Devoid of consideration for the selfishness of others.

Senate, *n.* A body of elderly gentlemen charged with high duties and misdemeanors.

Trial, *n.* A formal inquiry designed to prove and put upon record the blameless characters of judges, advocates and jurors.

Twice, *adv.* Once too often.

Year, *n.* A period of three hundred and sixty-five disappointments.

Zeal, *n.* A certain nervous disorder afflicting the young and inexperienced. A passion that goeth before a sprawl.

When medieval Europeans burned witches, the witches' families had to pay for the wood.

POLI-TALKS

More quotes from (and about) our revered politicians.

"I think it's about time we voted for senators with breasts. After all, we've been voting for boobs long enough."
—**Claire Sargent, Arizona senate candidate in 1992, on women candidates**

"Elvis is in fact a Republican."
—**John Kasich (R-Ohio) House budget chief, in 1995**

"They told me to go for the jugular—so I did. It was mine."
—**Bob Dole, on the 1976 failure of the Ford-Dole ticket**

"Most people don't have the luxury of living to be 80 years old, so it's hard for me to feel sorry for them."
—**Phil Gramm, opposing medical treatment for the elderly**

"It's hard for somebody to hit you when you've got your fist in their face."
—**James Carville, on the usefulness of negative campaigning**

"If God had wanted us to vote, he would have given us candidates."
—**Jay Leno**

"Politics is show business for ugly people."
—**Paul Begala, Clinton's campaign adviser**

"Washington is Salem. If we're not lynching somebody 24 hours a day in this wretched town, we're not happy.
—**Tom Korologos, Washington lobbyist**

"That's a good question. Let me try to evade you."
—**Paul Tsongas, presidential candidate, in 1992**

"Look, half the time when I see the evening news, I wouldn't be for me, either."
—**Bill Clinton, in 1995**

"Democracy is the process by which people choose the man who'll get the blame."
—**Bertrand Russell**

"Unlike the president, I inhaled. And then I threw up."
—**Christine Todd Whitman, governor of New Jersey**

"If hypocrisy were gold, the Capitol would be Fort Knox."
—**Sen. John McCain**

Most common phobia in the world: *odynophobia*—the fear of pain.

URBAN LEGENDS

We ran pieces on urban legends in our Great Big *and* Giant Bathroom Readers. *Since then, we've found so many more good ones that we just had to include them here, too. Remember the rule of thumb: if a wild story sounds true, but also sounds too "perfect" to be true, it's probably an urban legend.*

THE LEGEND: The Lego company has started to add a plastic homeless person to some of its kits. The reason: to make Legos more "relevant."
HOW IT SPREAD: By word of mouth in the early 1990s. It made the rounds of toy stores, where some employees apparently accepted the rumor at face value . . . and passed it on to customers. One Toys "R" Us salesperson explained to a reporter that the promotion was designed "to teach kids sensitivity and compassion."
THE TRUTH: In 1992 the *Chicago Tribune* asked the Lego Company directly about the rumors. A spokesperson insisted they were false. "You see," he said, "only happy, smiling people live in Legoland."

THE LEGEND: You can trade soda can pull-tabs for time on kidney dialysis machines. (Each pull-tab is worth one minute of dialysis for someone in need.)
HOW IT SPREAD: Word of mouth
THE TRUTH: This is just the latest version of a classic legend. For more than 40 years, people have been collecting worthless items—empty matchbooks, the little tags on teabags, and even cellophane strips from cigarette packs—as a humanitarian gesture, believing they will provide vital medical treatment (time in an iron lung was popular in the 1960s) or seeing-eye dogs. The definitive word: "There is no pull-tab/kidney dialysis donation program," writes Jan Brunvand in *Too Good to Be True*. "It never existed. Anywhere."

THE LEGEND: There's a slasher at the shopping mall near you. He lies in wait under shoppers' cars . . . and when they approach with their packages, he reaches out from under the car and cuts their ankles and achilles tendons with a knife. When the shopper

---

How do you know when a turkey is panicking? That's the only time it whistles.

falls to the ground, he crawls out from under the car, grabs the merchandise, and runs away.

HOW IT SPREAD: Word of mouth. Supposedly it didn't make the news because your mall is bribing the police and paying off the victims to keep the story quiet.

THE TRUTH: The grown-up equivalent of the monster hiding under the bed has been around as long as shopping malls—about 50 years. It's especially popular during the Christmas shopping season. In fact, in 1989 the rumors about a mall in Tacoma, Washington, were so pervasive that it had to set up police field stations in the parking lot to calm consumers who were too frightened to do their holiday shopping.

THE LEGEND: A man insured his expensive cigars, smoked them, then tried to collect on the insurance policy by claiming they were destroyed "in a series of small fires." The insurance company refused to pay up, so the man sued and won. But when he collected his money, the insurance company had him arrested for arson.

HOW IT SPREAD: The story was posted to the alt.smokers .cigars newsgroup on the Internet in 1996. It was identified as an urban legend and debunked at the outset; nevertheless, it has been circulating as a true story ever since.

THE TRUTH: The cigar story is an example of a classic theme in urban legends: a clever person finds a loophole in some kind of rule or regulation and exploits it, but gets nailed in the end.

* * *

JOB HUNTING
Some entries from real-life job applications:

- "Note: Please don't misconstrue my 14 jobs as job-hopping. I have never quit a job."

- "I have become completely paranoid, trusting completely no one and absolutely nothing."

Four most dangerous steps on most staircases: the two at the top and the two at the bottom.

THE BEST BUSINESS DEAL IN U.S. HISTORY, PART II

When the Dodge Brothers put $3,000 in cash and $7,000 in parts into the Ford Motor Company, they made history. Here's what happened next. (Part I of the story is on page 170.)

TURNAROUND

Four weeks after the Dodge brothers made their deal with Malcomson, the Ford Motor Company was on the verge of bankruptcy. With $223.65 in the bank, not a single car sold, and payroll for the Ford workers due the next day, it looked like the company's stock would be worthless.

Then, on July 15, 1903, a dentist named Dr. E. Pfennig became Ford's first customer, paying $850 cash for a Model A. "Dr. Pfennig's payment of the full cash price through the Illinois Trust and Savings Bank represented a turning point in the fortunes of the Ford Motor Company," Robert Lacey writes in *Ford: The Men and the Machine*. "From $223.65 onwards, its cash flow went one way only."

UP, UP, AND AWAY

When it opened for business in 1903, the Ford Motor Company could only build a few cars at a time. But as orders increased, Henry Ford and his assistants knew that the key to success was to find ways to speed production.

They did. In the year ending September 1906, the company made 1,599 cars; the following year production more than quadrupled to 8,000; and by 1912 Ford was manufacturing 78,000 cars per year. That was only the beginning: production more than doubled the following year and then more than doubled again in 1914, until Ford was manufacturing over 300,000 cars per year, or 1,000 cars for every work day, a production increase of 4,000 percent in just over a decade.

OH, BROTHER

About the only thing that grew faster than the Ford Motor Company's production and sales figures was the value of Ford

It takes 720 peanuts to make a pound of peanut butter.

stock, 10 percent of which belonged to the Dodge brothers. They'd earned back their entire $10,000 in the first year's dividends alone, and since then their Ford stock had paid out millions more.

In addition, since they were still manufacturing most of Ford's mechanical components at their own Dodge Brothers factory (at the time the largest and most modern such manufacturing plant in the world), they profited twice: first by supplying parts to Ford and second, by owning shares in the company.

T-TIME

That changed in 1914, when Henry Ford built his own parts manufacturing plant to replace the one owned by the Dodge brothers. Until then, the Ford Motor Company, like most other auto companies, had focused on assembling cars, leaving the actual manufacturing of the parts to subcontractors. Now that Ford could afford to finance his own manufacturing plant, he didn't need the Dodge brothers any more.

With their business relationship with Ford coming to an end, the brothers had to figure out what do with their plant. Henry Ford had offered to lease the plant and run it himself, and the Dodges gave it serious thought . . . but then they had another idea.

DON'T CHANGE A THING

When it went on sale in October 1908, the Ford Model T was the most advanced car of its day. As the years passed, automotive technology improved, but Henry Ford refused to make any changes to it, stylistically or even mechanically. Unlike other cars, you still had to start the Model T using a hand crank, and since it didn't come with a fuel gauge, the only way to tell how much gas you had was by dipping a stick into the gas tank. Having been with Ford from the beginning, the Dodge brothers knew all of the car's weaknesses, but when they suggested improvements, Ford ignored them.

In the end, the Dodge brothers decided to use their factory to manufacture the car that Henry Ford refused to build: one that was better than the Model T.

Turn to page 366 for Part III.

Q: What do French and African marigolds have in common?

UNCLE JOHN'S
PAGE OF LISTS

*For years, the BRI has had a file full of lists. We've
never been sure what to do with them . . . until now.*

3 REAL EXCUSES USED IN COURT
1. "I was thrown from the car as it left the road. I was later found in a ditch by some stray cows."
2. "The indirect cause of the accident was a little guy in a small car with a big mouth."
3. "To avoid hitting the bumper of the car in front, I struck the pedestrian."

TOP 5 BILL-BOARD SONGS ON APRIL 5, 1964
1. "Can't Buy Me Love" (The Beatles)
2. "Twist and Shout" (The Beatles)
3. "She Loves Me" (The Beatles)
4. "I Want to Hold Your Hand" (The Beatles)
5. "Please Please Me" (The Beatles)

3 CELEBRITIES WHO SAY THEY'VE SEEN A UFO:
1. Muhmmad Ali
2. Jimmy Carter
3. William Shatner

7 WEIRD PLACE NAMES
1. Peculiar, Missouri
2. Smut Eye, Alabama
3. Loudville, Massachusetts
4. Disco, Illinois
5. Yeehaw Junction, Florida
6. Slaughter Beach, Delaware
7. Humptulips, Washington

3 MEN KNOWN BY THEIR MIDDLE NAMES
1. James Paul McCartney
2. William Clark Gable
3. Ruiz Fidel Castro

5 MOST-HATED HOUSEHOLD CHORES

1. Washing dishes
2. Bathroom cleaning
3. Ironing
4. Vacuuming
5. Washing windows
—Gallup Poll

4 WORDS NOBODY USES ANYMORE
1. Podge ("To walk slowly and heavily.")
2. Roinous ("Mean and nasty.")
3. Battologist ("Someone who pointlessly repeats themselves.")
4. Battologist ("Someone who pointlessly repeats themselves.")

3 MOST PRIZED AUTOGRAPHS
1. Shakespeare (6 are known to exist)
2. Christopher Columbus (8 exist)
3. Julius Caesar (None are known to exist)

A: They both come from North America.

WORD ORIGINS

Ever wonder where words come from?
Here are some interesting stories.

JACKPOT
Meaning: A huge prize
Origin: "The term goes back to draw poker, where stakes are allowed to accumulate until a player is able to 'open the *pot*' by demonstrating that among the cards he has drawn, he has a pair of jacks or better." (From *Dictionary of Word and Phrase Origins*, Vol. II, by William and Mary Morris)

GRENADE
Meaning: A small, hand-thrown missile containing an explosive
Origin: "The word comes from the French *pomegrenade*, for pomegranate, because the military missile, which dates from the sixteenth century, both is shaped like the fruit and explodes much as the seeds burst out from it." (From *Fighting Words*, by Christine Ammer)

AMMONIA
Meaning: A potent, odorous cleaning fluid
Origin: "Ammonia is so called because it was first made from the dung of the worshippers' camels at the temple of Jupiter *Ammon* in Egypt." (From *Remarkable Words with Astonishing Origins*, by John Train)

HEATHEN
Meaning: An ungodly person
Origin: "Christianity began as primarily an urban religion; people in rural districts continued to worship older gods. The Latin word for countryman was *paganus*—whence, of course, pagan; the Germanic tongues had a similar word, something like *khaithanaz*, 'dwelling in the heath' (wilderness)—whence heathen." (From *Loose Cannons and Red Herrings*, by Robert Claiborne)

India has an estimated 550 million voters.

CALCULATE
Meaning: Add, subtract, divide, and/or multiply numbers or money
Origin: "In Rome 2,000 years ago, the merchant figured his profit and loss using what he called *calculi*, or little stones' as counters. So the Latin term *calculus*, 'pebble,' not only gave us *calculate* but . . . our word *calculus* . . . one of the most complicated forms of modern mathematics." (From *Word Origins*, by Wilfred Funk, Litt. D.)

MUSEUM
Meaning: Building or collection of art, music, scientific tools, or any specific set of objects
Origin: A shrine to the Greek Muses. "Such a shrine was known as a *mouseion* . . . When the *Museum* at Alexandria was destroyed in the fourth century . . . the word nearly dropped out of use. Three hundred years ago, a scholar rediscovered the word." (From *Thereby Hangs a Tale*, by Charles Earle Funk)

DOPE
Meaning: Drugs
Origin: "This word was originally a Dutch word, *doop*, meaning a sauce or liquid. Its first association with narcotics came when it was used to describe the viscous glop that results from heating opium. Then, by rapid extension, it came to mean any narcotic." (From *Dictionary of Word and Phrase Origins, Vol. III*, by William and Mary Morris)

RIVAL
Meaning: Competitor
Origin: "A *rival* is etymologically 'someone who uses the same stream as another.' The word comes from Latin *rivalis*, meaning 'of a stream.' People who use or live by the same stream are neighbors and, human nature being as it is, are usually in competition with each other." (From *Dictionary of Word Origins*, by John Ayto)

* * *

RANDOM CAT FACT
World-record mouser: "Towser," a tabby who caught mice at a Scottish distillery. She lived to the age of 21, and caught an average of three mice a day. Estimated lifetime haul: 23,000 mice.

In Montreal it's illegal to water a garden in the rain.

TALKING HEADS

*Who says talk show hosts don't have anything
intelligent to say? Oh, never mind.*

"Okay, our focus: 'Are Babies Being Bred for Satanic Sacrifice?' Controversial to say the least. Unbelievable to say the least. Disgusting to say the least. We'll be right back."
—**Geraldo Rivera, just before a commercial break**

"This is the 'Jerry Springer Show'....There is no such thing as class!"
—**Jerry Springer**

"That man is so repugnant. All of these satanic murderers are."
—**Geraldo Rivera, discussing Charles Manson**

"It's always difficult to be meaningful and relevant, because there's just not enough time."
—**Oprah Winfrey**

"Nobody differentiates between one show and another. It's all of us in the same trash can."
—**Sally Jesse Raphael**

"I'd rather be called sleazy than to be identified as intelligent."
—**Phil Donahue**

"There's nothing wrong with skipping your job to come to the 'Ricki Lake Show!'"
—**Ricki Lake**

"Your wife wants you to die. Your reaction, quickly."
—**Geraldo Rivera**

"My show is just plain STU-PID!"
—**Jerry Springer**

"Tonight you'll be looking at some horrible scenes and meeting some horrible people."
—**Geraldo, introducing his TV special "Murder: Live from Death Row"**

"Wow! This story is beyond dysfunctional!"
—**Ricki Lake**

"Oprah's quitting in two years and I will be all you have, so you better be nice to me!"
—**Jenny Jones**

"If you think it was an accident, applaud."
—**Geraldo, speaking about Natalie Wood's drowning**

What do whales and buffaloes have in common? Both stampede.

FOR CYNICS ONLY

Are you the kind of person who always expects the worst—who's never surprised by scandals or heroes who are exposed as phonies? Then this page is for you. Read it and weep . . . or laugh . . . or whatever.

DENNIS THE MENACE
Hank Ketcham, creator of the "Dennis the Menace" comic strip, considers his work a beacon for families. "The Mitchells represent what I hope America is," he said in 1990. But at last report, he was estranged from the real Dennis—his son—who inspired the strip in the first place. "We lead separate lives, there's very little communication," Ketcham told a reporter unapologetically. He added: "I don't want a closer relationship."

At age 46, Dennis was living in an Ohio trailer park with his second wife, working as a tire retreader. The cute kid with the cowlick told People magazine: "Dad can be like a stranger. Sometimes I think that if he died tomorrow, I wouldn't feel anything."

FAMILY VALUES
Nancy Reagan has publicly said she's against premarital sex. But it turns out the former first lady was pregnant when she and Ronald Reagan were married. Apparently, she claimed for years that her daughter Patti had been born prematurely. But in her 1989 autobiography, *My Turn*, she revealed the truth. As UPI reported when the book came out:

For the first time she admitted that her daughter Patti "was born—go ahead and count—a bit precipitously but very joyfully October 22, 1952." The Reagans were married the previous March, two weeks after announcing their engagement. Mrs. Reagan told [reporters] she saw no conflict between her public disapproval of premarital sex and her daughter's conception. "We're not talking about teenagers. And we knew we were going to get married."

Critics have accused the Reagans of hypocrisy for preaching "family values" while having a tangled set of personal relationships.

"It's true that we weren't always able to live up to the things we believed in," she said in the book, "but that doesn't mean we didn't believe in them."

Medical term for earwax: *cerumen.*

IT'S JUST MONEY

From 1989 to 1993, Catalina Vasquez Villalpando was treasurer of the United States—the person in charge of the U.S. Mint whose signature appeared on all paper money until 1993. But in 1994, she pled guilty to "evading federal income taxes, obstructing an independent counsel's investigation, and conspiring to conceal financial links to her former company" while she was serving in her government position. In addition to not reporting income, she concealed information about money she received from a telecommunications firm in which she was a senior vice president. (Coincidentally, the company was awarded several contracts from the federal government while she was in the Treasury Department.)

A WHALE OF A PROPERTY

When the first *Free Willy* film became a hit, kids started asking about the star. To their surprise, the real whale—named Keiko—wasn't doing too well. "The 3-1/2 ton whale spends his days endlessly circling a pool so shallow he has trouble remaining submerged," Ted Bardacke wrote in a 1994 *Washington Post* article. "Three times a day, he does a few tricks at Reino Aventura, the Mexico City amusement park that has owned him for more than a decade....He is sick with a herpes-type skin infection, he is dangerously underweight, and his teeth either never matured or are being worn down by constant contact with the pool's walls and bottom.

Keiko is not the only one with a problem. With the killer whale still in captivity, Warner Bros., the studio behind *Free Willy*, has a public relations disaster swimming around in a Mexico City fish tank. Not only has the studio been unable to follow through on its promise to . . . let the whale go, but Keiko is slated to star—via outtakes from the first film and through robotics—in a sequel, *Free Willy II: The Return Home* . . . If Keiko is still languishing south of the border while in the sequel Willy is out in the wild . . . the new movie could draw more protests than viewers."

Reino Aventura was willing to donate the whale, but not to pay his moving expenses. "Warner has made a lot of money on the film and only paid us $75,000," said a spokeswoman. "Now we have to deal with all this bad publicity. Warner should cough up the dough." Ultimately, the orca was moved to a more appropriate facility in Newport, Oregon and Warner was free—to churn out more *Free Willy* films, videos, and a TV series.

At last count, Minnesota had 99 lakes named Mud Lake.

Q & A:
ASK THE EXPERTS

*Here are some more random questions, with
answers from America's trivia experts.*

THE COLD, WET TRUTH
Q: *Why does your nose run in cold weather?*
A: "It is not necessarily because you have a cold. If very cold air is
suddenly inhaled, the mucous membranes inside your nostrils first
constrict, then rapidly dilate as a reflex reaction. This permits an
excess of mucous to form, resulting in a runny nose or the 'sniffles.'" (From *The Handy Weather Answer Book*, by Walter A. Lyons,
Ph.D.)

HAPPY TRAILS
Q: *Why do jets leave a trail of white behind them?*
A: "The white trail that you see is, in fact, a man-made cloud. At
low altitudes, the air is able to absorb large quantities of water. But
at high altitudes, water has a tendency to come out of the air,
which can form a cloud. This only happens, though, if the air contains small particles—such as dust—on which the water can con-
dense. It also helps the process if the air is agitated.

"Now enter the high-flying jet. Its exhaust fills the air with a
huge supply of spent fuel particles, and at the same time it shakes
or agitates the air . . . leaving a long, narrow cloud behind it."
(From *Ever Wonder Why?*, by Douglas B. Smith)

EURASIA, EURASIA
Q: *Why are Asia and Europe considered two continents even though
they appear to be one?*
A: "The ancient Greeks thought the Eurasian landmass was
divided in two by the line of water running from the Aegean Sea
to the far shore of the Black Sea.

"By the time they found out otherwise, Europeans were not
about to surrender their continental status." (From *Why Things
Are*, by Joel Achenbach)

Top speed of a pigeon in flight: 90 mph.

YOU EXPECT ME TO SWALLOW THAT?

Q: *How do circus sword swallowers do it?*
A: Believe it or not, they really do swallow the sword. The main problem is learning how to relax the throat muscles and stop gagging. This takes weeks of practice . . . But it can be done.

"The sword doesn't cut the sword swallower's throat because its sides are dull. The point is usually sharp, but that's not a problem as long as the sword swallower doesn't swallow any swords long enough to poke him (or her) in the pit of the stomach." (From *Know It All!*, by Ed Zotti)

METHOD TO THE MADNESS?

Q: *How are interstate highways numbered in the United States?*
A: "Believe it or not, this is one government practice that is organized and logical. All east–west interstate highways are even-numbered and increase from south to north. Thus, east–west Interstate 80 is north of I-10. North–south interstates are odd-numbered and increase from west to east. City bypasses and spurs have triple digits and are numbered odd or even depending on their directional orientation." (From *Thoughts for the Throne*, by Don Voorhees)

YOU GET WHAT YOU PAY FOR

Q: *If you dropped a penny from the top of the Empire State Building (or any skyscraper) and it happened to hit someone on the head, would it easily pierce their skull?*
A: "Given that the Empire State Building is 1,250 feet tall and ignoring such factors as wind resistance, a penny dropped from the top would hit the ground in approximately 8.8 seconds, having reached a speed of roughly 280 feet per second. This is not particularly fast. A low-powered .22 or .25 caliber bullet, to which a penny is vaguely comparable in terms of mass, typically has a muzzle velocity of 800 to 1,100 FPS, with maybe 75 foot-pounds of energy.

"On top of this we must consider that the penny would probably tumble while falling, and that the Empire State Building . . . is surrounded by strong updrafts, which would slow descent considerably. Thus, while you might conceivably inflict a fractured skull on some hapless New Yorker, the penny would certainly not 'go through just like that.'" (From *The Straight Dope*, by Cecil Adams)

Hitler had his own private train, complete with 15 railcars. It was named *Amerika.*

MONKEY SEE, MONKEY DO

Do television and movies influence our actions? Of course
(see page 162), but unfortunately, some people take it
to extremes. There's just no cure for stupidity.

MONKEY SEE: In the 1971 film *The Godfather*, Corleone family henchmen intimidate a Hollywood mogul by killing his prize race horse and sticking the horse's head in his bed.

MONKEY DO: In 1997 two New York crooks decided to use a similar method to intimidate a witness scheduled to testify against them at trial: "On the morning the witness was scheduled to testify, they left the head of a slaughtered animal as a death threat. 'We wanted to leave a cow's head because his wife was from India, and they consider cows sacred,' one said. 'But where do you find a cow's head in Brooklyn? So I went to some butcher in Flatbush and found a goat head. I figured it was close enough.'" One crook was sentenced to 4 years in prison; the other got 14 to 42 years.

MONKEY SEE: In the video for Joe Diffie's song "John Deere Green," a boy climbs a water tower and paints a green heart."

MONKEY DO: "This apparently gave some genius in Mississippi the bright idea of scaling his local water tower and painting 'Billy Bo Bob Loves Charlene' in green paint. Perhaps tuckered out from having to write all three of his first names on the water tower, the guy then lost his balance and was seriously injured when he hit the ground." (*Chicago Sun-Times*)

MONKEY SEE: In the 1993 film *The Program*, "drunk college football players lie down in the middle of a busy road to prove their toughness."

MONKEY DO: "A scene in the movie *The Program* will be deleted after one teenager was killed and two others critically injured while apparently imitating the scene, the Walt Disney Co. said Tuesday . . . Sources indicated it will cost $350,000 to $400,000 to re-edit." (*Daily Variety*)

In Athens, Greece, you can lose your driver's license for being "poorly dressed" or "unbathed."

MONKEY SEE: In 1997 Taco Bell introduced a new advertising campaign featuring a talking Chihuahua that has since become known as the "Taco Bell Dog."

MONKEY DO: Since then, sales and adoptions of Chihuahuas have gone through the roof. "Before the Taco Bell commercials became popular, no one wanted Chihuahuas," says Marsha Teague of the Portland, Oregon, humane society. "Now people ask specifically for the 'Taco Bell Dog.'" The dogs, priced from $300 to $600, "sell within two days, faster if their coloration resembles the actual TV star. "We can't even keep them in stock," a pet-shop owner says. "Everybody always comes in and imitates the Taco Bell commercial." (*Portland Oregonian*)

On the other hand, it isn't necessarily all bad . . .

MONKEY SEE: The Nancy Drew series is about a strong-willed, independent teenage detective who constantly finds herself in danger, then has to think her way out of it.

MONKEY DO: In the early 1990s, an eleven-year-old Michigan girl was kidnapped and thrown into the trunk of a car. "Instead of panicking," *The Christian Science Monitor* reported, "she asked herself what Nancy Drew would do in such a situation. Then she found a toolbox, pried the trunk open, made a call from a nearby phone booth, and her assailant was arrested."

* * *

MORE, MORE, MORE!

- In 1997 an employee at a Bangkok hotel was sent to prison for robbing guests' safe deposit boxes. His method: he rubbed his nose on the buttons, making them oily so he could tell which ones the guests had pushed to open the safe. His inspiration: an episode of the TV show *MacGyver*.

- In 1996, 17-year-old Steve Barone was booked for robbing a gun store. He claimed he did it "only because he was taken over by another personality, which was an amalgam of guys from the movies *Pulp Fiction*, *Reservoir Dogs*, and *Goodfellas*." (*News of the Weird*)

When pizza became popular in the U.S. in the 1930s, sales of oregano shot up 5,200%.

"CARMEN, I BESMOOCH YOU!"

*Here's one of the great mistranslations of all time, discovered by
Stephen Pyle and reprinted in his book* Heroic Failures.

BACKGROUND. In 1981 the Genoa Opera Company put
on a production of Bizet's *Carmen*. For tourists in the audience, they translated the program into English. Here's an
excerpt of what they printed.

ACT ONE

"Carmen, a cigarmakeress from a tobago factory loves Don Jose of
the mounting guard. Carmen takes a flower from her corsets and
lances it to Don Jose. (Duet: 'Talk me of my mother.') There was a
noise inside the tobago factory and revolting cigarmakeresses burst
onto the stage. Carmen is arrested and Don Jose is ordered to
mounting guard on her but she subduces him and lets her escape."

ACT TWO

"The tavern. Carmen sings (Aria: 'The sistrums tinkling.') Enter
two smugglers ('Ho, we have a mind in business.') Enter Escamillo,
a Balls fighter. Carmen refuses to penetrate because Don Jose has
liberated her from prison. He just now arrives. (Aria: 'Slop here
who comes.') But here are the bugles singing his retreat. Don Jose
will leave and draws his sword. Called by Carmen's shrieks the two
smugglers interfere with her. Jose is bound to dessert. Final Chorus:
'Opening Sky Wandering Life.'"

ACT THREE

"A rocky landscape. Smugglers chatter. Carmen sees her death in
the cards. Don Jose makes a date with her for the next Balls fight."

ACT FOUR

"A place in Seville. Procession of Ballfighters. The roaring of balls
is heard in the arena. Escamillo enters (Aria and chorus: 'Toreador.
Toreador. All hail the Balls of a toreador.') Enter Don Jose (Aria: 'I
besmooch you.') Carmen repels him. She wants to join with
Escamillio now chaired by the crowd. Don Jose stabbs her. (Aria:
'Oh, rupture, rupture.') He sings: 'Oh, my seductive Carmen.'"

Squirrels cannot see the color red.

I TAWT I TAW A PUDDY-TAT!

Sure, they're cartoon characters, but Tweety and Sylvester are still a classic comedy team—literally made for each other, right? Well, no. It actually took a few years before anyone thought of putting them in the same cartoon. Here's how it happened.

FIRST CAME TWEETY . . .
Created by: Looney Tunes director Bob Clampett
Inspiration: "In school I remember seeing nature films which showed newborn birds in a nest," Clampett recalled. "They always looked funny to me. One time I kicked around the idea of twin baby birds called 'Twick 'n' Tweet' who were precursors of Tweety."

Tweety's basic design and "innocent stare at the camera" were copied from an even more unusual source: a nude baby picture of Clampett himself. That's probably why the original Tweety was pink.
Debut: "Tale of Two Kitties," a 1942 spoof of Abbott and Costello (who appeared as bumbling cats named Babbit and Cat-stello). The little nameless bird's opening line, "I tawt I taw a puddy tat!" made the cartoon—and the character—a hit. The voice was supplied by Mel Blanc (who also did Daffy Duck, Bugs Bunny, Porky Pig, et al.). It was recorded at normal speed but played back faster.

Tweety's next cartoon, "Birdy and the Beast" (1944), gave him a name and personality. In 1946 movie censors decided the pink bird "looked naked" and insisted Clampett put a pair of pants on him. The cartoonist refused; instead, he gave Tweety "yellow feathers and a slimmer body."

THEN CAME SYLVESTER . . .
Created by: Oscar-winning Looney Tunes director Friz Freleng
Inspiration: Freleng designed the cat "to look subtly like a clown. I gave him a big, red nose and a very low crotch, which was supposed to look like he was wearing baggy pants." According to Mel Blanc, the unwitting model was Looney Tunes' "jowly executive producer Johnny Burton."

On average, adults have 2 gallons of air in the space between their skin and clothes.

Debut: A 1945 cartoon, "Life with Feathers." The plot: "A love bird has a major fight with his wife and decides to end it all by letting a cat (Sylvester, before he had a name) eat him." The cat's first words, on finding a bird who wants to be eaten: "Thufferin' thuccotash!"

Sylvester's voice—also supplied by Mel Blanc—sounded more like Blanc's real speaking voice than any of his other characters. It was actually the same voice he used for Daffy Duck, but not sped up. Says Blanc in his autobiography, *That's Not All Folks:*

> Sylvester has always been a favorite of mine. He's always been the easiest character for me to play. When I was first shown the model sheet of Sylvester, with his floppy jowls and generally disheveled appearance, I said to Friz Freleng, 'A big sloppy cat should have a big shthloppy voice! He should spray even more than Daffy.' While recording Sylvester cartoons, my scripts would get so covered with saliva that I'd repeatedly have to wipe them clean. I used to suggest to actress June Foray, who played Tweety's vigilant owner Granny, that she wear a raincoat to the sessions.

Sylvester's first cartoon was nominated for an Oscar, and he appeared (still nameless) in two more before Clampett got permission to team Tweety with him in 1947. However, Clampett left Warners Bros. just as he began working on the project.

TOGETHER AT LAST
Freleng took over the cartoon. He gave the cat a name—Thomas (changed to Sylvester in 1948 by animator Tedd Pierce, who thought a slobbering cat needed a name that could be slobbered) —and made Tweety a little friendlier. "I made him look more like a charming baby, with a bigger head and blue eyes," Freleng explained.

In their first cartoon together, "Tweetie Pie," Thomas catches Tweety, who's freezing in the winter cold. But before he can eat the bird, Thomas's owner saves it and brings it home. Tweety then proceeds to terrorize the cat and take over the house.

"Tweety Pie" earned the Warner Bros. cartoon studio its first Academy Award and the pair made 55 more cartoons together.

According to market research, if a girl owns one Barbie, she probably owns seven.

THE ORIGIN OF BASKETBALL, PART III

We could go on and on about basketball, but we have to leave room for other subjects. So this is the last installment of our b-ball history . . . for this edition. (Part I starts on page 27.)

BY ANY OTHER NAME

In 1891, when James Naismith posted the rules to his new game on the YMCA bulletin board, he didn't bother to give it a name. He just called it "A New Game." One of The Incorrigibles suggested calling it "Naismith Ball" . . . but the phys-ed teacher just laughed.

"I told him that I thought that name would kill any game," Naismith recalled in his memoirs. "Why not call it Basket Ball?" The delighted player spread the word, and it's been basket ball (changed to basketball in 1921) ever since.

SCORE!

The Incorrigibles took to the game right away, and by the end of the week their games were drawing a crowd. Teachers and students from a nearby women's school started showing up on their lunch hour; a few weeks later, they began organizing their own teams.

When The Incorrigibles went home for Christmas a few weeks later, they brought copies of the rules—and their enthusiasm for the game—to YMCA chapters all over the country. In January, a copy of the Springfield school paper, complete with an introduction to basketball (including diagrams and a list of rules), was sent to each of the nearly 200 YMCAs in the U.S. "We present to our readers a new game of ball," the article read, "which seems to have those elements in which it ought to make it popular among the Associations."

In the months that followed, these chapters introduced basketball to high schools and colleges in their communities; YMCA missionaries to other countries began spreading the game all over the world.

Given the opportunity, chimpanzees will hunt ducks.

"It is doubtful whether a gymnastic game has ever spread so rapidly over the continent as has 'basket ball,'" Dr. Gulick wrote proudly in October 1892, before the game was even a year old. "It is played from New York to San Francisco and from Maine to Texas by . . . teams in associations, athletic clubs, and schools."

But just as soon as the rules for basketball began to spread, people began trying to change them. Sometimes they succeeded—even in the face of opposition from its founders—and sometimes they didn't. Overall, the game proved to be extraordinarily adaptable, a factor that has been instrumental in keeping it popular.

THE INVENTION OF DRIBBLING

One of the first rules to come under attack was the no-running-with-the-ball rule. When he invented the game, Naismith wanted the person with the ball to stand still and throw it to another player . . . who then had to stop moving and either shoot or pass.

But players quickly found that when they were cornered and couldn't pass, they could escape by either rolling or throwing the ball a few feet, then running to get it themselves. From there it was just a matter of time before they realized that by repeatedly throwing the ball in the air, they could move across the court alone—even though they weren't supposed to be moving at all. "In the early years," Paul Ricatto writes in *Basket-Ball*, "it was not uncommon to see a player running down the floor, juggling the ball a few inches above his hand. This so closely approximated running with the ball [travelling] that a rule was inserted saying that the ball must be batted higher than the player's head."

DOWN TO EARTH

Players also discovered that it was easy to move with the ball if they repeatedly bounced, or "dribbled," it with both hands. The idea is believed to have been born on the urban playgrounds of Philadelphia; from there it spread to the University of Pennsylvania and beyond. Eventually it became the preferred method of advancing the ball down the court (beating out juggling the ball over one's head).

Dr. Gulick and other basketball powers were not amused. In 1898 they inserted a rule into the official basketball rulebook outlawing two-handed dribbling. "The object of the [new] rule," Dr. Gulick wrote, "is largely to do away with dribbling . . . The game

---

Injured fingernails grow faster than uninjured ones.

must remain for what it was originally intended to be—a passing game. Dribbling has introduced all of the objectionable features that are hurting the game."

Gulick assumed that the issue was dead, since one-handed dribbling was obviously too difficult for anyone to try. But players confounded the doctor. In fact, one-handed dribbling proved so effective that it became the standard.

HOW MANY PLAYERS?

Naismith originally recommended using nine players per team, but said the game could be played with almost any number—depending on the size of the court and how many people wanted to play. Some teams took this advice to extremes: in the early 1890s, Cornell University played a game with 50 people on each side! So many spectators complained about losing sight of the ball at such games that most university teams began scaling back. Then in 1896, the University of Chicago and the University of Iowa played the first collegiate basketball game with only five players on a team. It worked so well that within a year, nearly every college team in the country used five players.

OUT-OF-BOUNDS

In his original list of rules, Naismith wrote that the first player to retrieve a ball after it had gone out-of-bounds got to throw it back into play. But he wasn't sure that rule worked; it seemed to encourage dangerous play: "It was not uncommon," Naismith wrote in his memoirs, "to see a player who was anxious to secure the ball make a football dive for it, regardless of whether he went into the apparatus that was stored around the gym or into the spectators in the bleachers."

The rule ended for good one day while Naismith was supervising a game in Springfield. As occasionally happened, the ball ended up in the balcony that circled the gym. Normally, the teams would race up the stairs to get to the ball first. But on this day, while one team scrambled upstairs, the other showed it had been practicing in secret. They used an acrobatic maneuver, boosting one player up onto the shoulders of another until they were high enough to jump over the railing onto the balcony. Naismith immediately changed the rule to what it is today (the last team to touch the ball before it goes out-of-bounds loses it).

An *exocannibal* is a cannibal who eats only enemies. An *indocannibal* eats only friends.

NOTHING BUT NET

The wooden peach baskets broke easily when players threw balls at them, and within a year the YMCA replaced them with sturdier wire mesh trash cans. But these were a problem, too: every time someone scored, the action had to stop until the referee climbed a ladder and retrieved the ball by hand. (Apparently, nobody thought of removing the bottoms of the baskets.)

Over the next few years, the trash cans were replaced by specially made baskets with trapdoors that opened when the referee pulled a string . . . and then by bare metal hoops, which let the ball drop to the ground by itself.

But the bare hoops went a little too far. When nobody was standing near the basket, it was difficult to tell whether the ball really had gone in. So the YMCA suspended a rope net under the hoop to catch the ball. Believe it or not, these nets were closed at the bottom—the ball was pushed out with a stick. It wasn't until 1912 that they finally cut off the bottom. From then on, the "swish" made it obvious whether the ball had gone in or not.

THE ORIGIN OF BACKBOARDS

It's hard to imagine shooting a basketball without a backboard. But the backboard wasn't created to help players score—it was created to keep fans out.

In gyms like the one at Springfield, the only place for fans to sit was in the balcony. It became common for them to gather near the basket during the game. From there, Robert Peterson writes,

> It was easy for a fervid spectator to reach over the rail and guide the shots of his favorites into the basket or deflect those of his opponents. So for 1895–96, the rules called for a 4-by-6-foot wire or wood screen behind the basket to keep fans from interfering. Wire screens were soon dented by repeated rebounds, giving the home team an advantage because the players knew . . . their own backboard. So wood gradually supplanted the wire mesh boards.

ON THE MAP

From Dr. Gulick's point of view, basketball was an unqualified success. It had helped encourage interest in sports and physical fitness, increased attendance at YMCA chapters all over the country, and

---

Al Capone's older brother Vince Capone was a policeman in Nebraska.

raised the profile of the YMCA in the communities it served. "One of the best solutions to the difficulty of maintaining the interest of the members has been the judicious introduction of the play element into the work," the journal *Physical Fitness* reported in the summer of 1894, "and in this line nothing has been so peculiarly and generally satisfactory as Basket Ball." Thanks in large part to the success of basketball, Dr. Gulick's anti-sports critics were silenced and the YMCA became synonymous with sports and physical fitness.

WAR GAME

For all its successes, basketball was still just a game and might never have become a national pastime if it hadn't been for some bad publicity the U.S. Army generated for itself.

In 1916 Gen. John J. Pershing led the "Punitive Expedition" into Mexico in an unsuccessful attempt to capture Pancho Villa. "The newspapers had made much of the drinking and prostitution that had served to entertain an army with time on its hands," Elliott J. Gorn and Warren Goldstein write in *A Brief History of American Sports*, and when the U.S. entered World War I in 1917, it was determined that such embarrassing publicity would not be generated again.

"For the first time in American history," Gorn and Goldstein write, "sports were formally linked to military preparedness . . . As American troops were deployed overseas in 1917, they were accompanied everywhere by 12,000 YMCA workers who brought sports along with them"—including basketball. More than a million U.S. troops fought in World War I, and tens of thousands of them learned to play basketball while they were in Europe. By the time the war was over, basketball had become an inextricable part of American life.

* * *

OOPS

"In 1994, an Emergency Medical Service crew in New York rushed an abandoned bag of spaghetti to the hospital after they mistook it for a fetus."

—*Esquire,* January 1995

The ancient Greeks played cards. In those days, aces were known as "dogs."

THE RIDDLER

What's white, and black, and read in the middle? This page of riddles. (See the answers on page 750.)

1. What unusual natural phenomenon is capable of speaking in any language?

2. A barrel of water weighs 20 pounds. What do you have to add to it to make it weigh 12 pounds?

3. Before Mount Everest was discovered, what was the highest mountain on Earth?

4. What word starts with an "e," ends with an "e," and usually contains one letter?

5. Forward I am heavy, but backward I am not. What am I?

6. He has married many women, but has never been married. Who is he?

7. How many bricks does it take to complete a building made of brick?

8. How many of each animal did Moses take on the ark?

9. How many times can you subtract the number 5 from 25?

10. If you have it, you want to share it. If you share it, you don't have it. What is it?

11. In Okmulgee, Oklahoma, you cannot take a picture of a man with a wooden leg. Why not?

12. The more you have of it, the less you see. What is it?

13. The more you take, the more you leave behind. What are they?

14. The one who makes it, sells it. The one who buys it, never uses it. The one who uses it, never knows that he's using it. What is it?

15. What can go up a chimney down but can't go down a chimney up?

16. What crime is punishable if attempted, but is not punishable if committed?

17. What happened in the middle of the 20th century that will not happen again for 4,000 years?

18. What is the center of gravity?

19. What question can you never honestly answer "yes" to?

20. You can't keep this until you have given it.

Most-used expression of any language on earth: "OK."

LUCKY FINDS

*Ever found something valuable? It's one of the best feelings
in the world. Here's another installment of a regular
Bathroom Reader feature—a look at some folks who
found really valuable stuff . . . and got to keep it.
We should all be so lucky!*

LOTS OF LUNCH MONEY

The Find: Two paintings
Where They Were Found: At an estate sale
The Story: Carl Rice started buying paintings at thrift stores and garage sales in 1993, imagining they were worth a lot of money. Each time he found one that he thought might be valuable, he'd send a photograph to the famous New York auction house, Christie's. The reply was always the same: worthless.

By 1996 Rice owned a stack of 500 paintings and really couldn't afford to buy any more; his business was about to fold and he would soon be unemployed. But he was hooked. One day in 1996, as he roamed around an estate sale, he noticed a 6-by-12-inch picture of roses that he liked. He bought it for $10. On his way out, he saw a 15-by-24-inch floral picture on the wall and couldn't resist that, either. He bought it for $50. Rice tossed the paintings into his car trunk and headed home to an irritated wife. According to Rice, she said something like, "More of that s***?"

But when they checked the artist's name—Martin Johnson Heade—in a price guide, they found out he was a well-known 19th-century painter. The excited couple sent photos to Christie's again, and this time there was no rejection letter—the auction house sent a New York vice president to authenticate the paintings. In 1998 the $60 investment was auctioned off for over $1 million. The Rices had to borrow money to attend the auction, but left with $600,000 after-tax dollars in their pockets.

BOOK BUYER'S BONUS

The Find: Three sketches
Where They Were Found: In a book

The average computer worker types 90,000 keystrokes in an eight-hour shift.

The Story: In 1999 a woman bought a book for $1 at a flea market in Amsterdam. While flipping through the book on her way home, she found three drawings that looked old.

She took them to an art expert to see what they were. His assessment: two were original drawings by Rembrandt and the third was by one of his students. She sold them to a German collector for $55,000, but oddly enough, didn't feel grateful. In fact, her agent told reporters, "When I asked for my 3 percent commission, [she] said I could have a beating instead."

OH, BABE-Y!
The Find: A baseball
Where It Was Found: In Grandma's attic
The Story: In 1997 a New Jersey boy named Chris Scala dressed up as Babe Ruth for a school project on famous Americans. When his 87-year-old great-grandmother heard about it, she remembered that she had an old ball that had been signed by Ruth, in her attic. It had been given to her husband back in 1927 "as a prize for making the New Jersey all-state high school baseball team."

Her grandson Mark had played in the attic many times as a kid, but had never seen the ball. Skeptical, he drove to his grandmother's house and looked around . . . and was surprised to locate it in an old box "with other discarded baseballs." He was even more amazed to discover an inscription that identified it not only as a Babe Ruth home run ball, but as the very first ball Ruth had ever hit for a home run in Yankee Stadium. He took the ball to the Baseball Hall of Fame in Cooperstown, New York. It was authenticated, and sold at auction in 1999 for $126,500.

LUCKY BUCKET
The Find: "An interesting rock"
Where It Was Found: In a mine in North Carolina
The Story: (From the Richmond, Virginia, *Times-Dispatch*, 1999) "Ten-year-old Lawrence Shields was picking through a bucket of dirt at a commercial gem mine in North Carolina last week when he found an interesting rock. 'I just liked the shape of it,' he says.

"It turned out to be a 1061-carat sapphire. Lawrence and his parents say they've been told it could be worth more than $35,000."

On average, people aged 24 to 35 worry less than adults of any other age group.

SPECIAL UNDERWEAR

More important underwear innovations to keep abreast of.

SIX-DAY UNDERWEAR

S "The Honda Motor Company's bi-annual inventiveness contest for employees has unearthed some unique innovations, but none to match 6-day underwear, the 1987 winner. According to the story in the *Wall St. Journal*, the underwear has three leg holes, which enables it to last for six days without washing. The wearer rotates it 120 degrees on each of the first three days, then turns it out and repeats the process."

—Forgotten Fads and Fabulous Flops

THE ALARM BRA

LONDON—"A newly developed techno-bra—the latest in personal alarm systems—is the brainchild of Royal College of Art design student Kursty Groves. Targeted at young urban women, the bra uses miniature electronics and conductive fabric to monitor the wearer's heart rate. If it detects a sudden change in pulse—one that indicates panic—it radios a distress call to police and identifies the bra's location. And since the electronics are contained in jell-like cushions inside each cup, the bra enhances the wearer's figure. 'You can also have some lift and support if you like,' Groves says."

—Wire Service Report, 1999

SWEAT PANTS

Want to give off a manly, territorial odor without having to sweat for it? Japanese scientists have a new product—sweat-laced underpants.

Apparel and cosmetics maker Kanebo Ltd. says millions of tiny capsules in the fabric contain a synthesized pheromone found in the sweat of a man's underarms. Friction breaks the capsules, releasing the pheromone; an added musk scent intensifies the effect.

"Unfortunately, the power is fleeting—Kanebo estimates the pheromones are completely dissipated after ten washings."

—Parade Magazine, 1998

About 21,000 commercial airline flights are scheduled daily in the United States.

THE RETURN OF ZORRO

Here's the second part of our history of
"the Fox." (Part I is on page 94.)

THE MARK OF ZORRO

When Johnston McCulley created Zorro—the first "super-hero" with a secret identity—in 1919, he didn't have any idea what mark he would leave on pop culture. "Zorro not only became a vehicle for stars such as Fairbanks," Sandra Curtis writes in *Zorro Unmasked*, "the character also directly inspired numerous dual-identity imitators, including the Phantom, the Lone Ranger, the Green Hornet, and Superman."

He was especially important to Batman. Creator Bob Kane saw *The Mark of Zorro* when he was 13, and credits Fairbanks with providing the inspiration for the Caped Crusader:

[Zorro] was the most swashbuckling, derring-do, super hero I've ever, ever seen in my life, and he left a lasting impression on me. And of course later, when I created the Batman, it gave me the dual identity, because Zorro had the dual identity. During the day, he played a foppish count, Don Diego . . . a bored playboy, and at night became Zorro. He wore a mask and he strapped his trusty sword around his waist. He came out of a cave . . . which I made into a bat cave, and he rode a black horse called Tornado, and later on I had the Batmobile. So Zorro was a major influence on my creation of Batman.

THE NEXT ACTION HERO

McCulley went on to write a total of 64 Zorro short stories, many of which were the basis for the 10 feature films, 5 film serials, several TV series, and more than a dozen foreign films that have appeared over 70 years. Tyrone Power played Zorro in the 1940 remake of *The Mark of Zorro*, and nine years later Clayton Moore played the masked man—before going on to find fame as the Lone Ranger. In 1998 *The Mask of Zorro*, starring Antonio Banderas as the young protégé of the original, grossed over $90 million.

THE TWO MOST UNUSUAL ZORRO FILMS:

- *Zorro's Black Whip* (1944). The only female Zorro. "Linda Stirling dons a black outfit and becomes the Black Whip, riding in the hoofprints of her crusading brother [Zorro], who was killed for his just beliefs." (*Video Movie Guide*)

- *Zorro, The Gay Blade* (1981). "Tongue-in-cheek sword play with George Hamilton portraying the swashbuckling crusader and his long-lost gay brother, Bunny Wigglesworth." (*Videohound's Golden Movie Retriever*)

ZORRO ON TV

The most popular post–World War II Zorro was Guy Williams, who played "The Fox" on the Walt Disney TV series from 1957 to 1959.

Disney bought the rights to Zorro in 1953, but spent so much money building Disneyland (which opened in 1954) that he didn't launch the Zorro series until 1957. Disney had been looking for an unknown actor to play the part of Zorro, and found his man in Williams—whose father and uncle were experienced swordsmen. Williams himself had studied fencing since the age of seven.

THE CROCKETT SYNDROME

A few years before (see page 137), Disney's "Davy Crockett" had created TV's first merchandising boom—every kid in America wanted a coonskin cap. Disney was caught off-guard and wasn't able to fill the demand. This time, he vowed not to make the same mistake. At the same time Zorro went on the air, the country was flooded with Zorro lunch boxes, puzzles, watches, pajamas, trading cards, Pez dispensers, and even sword sets—complete with a mask and chalk-tipped plastic sword, with which kids could mark "Z's" all over the house.

Disney had a hit on his hands, but cancelled the show after only two seasons when he couldn't agree with ABC on a price for it. Guy Williams was stunned by the decision, but went on to play Professor John Robinson on TV's *Lost in Space*. (Special note to Zorro fans: We don't know what happened to Sgt. Garcia . . . but we're trying to find out.)

First baseball player to be named Rookie of the Year: Jackie Robinson, in 1947.

MORE "I SPY"
AT THE MOVIES

Here are more of the little in-jokes and gags that moviemakers throw into films for their own amusement. The info comes from Reel Gags, *by Bill Givens, and* Film and Television In-Jokes, *by Bill van Heerden.*

THE BLUES BROTHERS (1980)

I Spy . . . Steven Spielberg
Where to Find Him: He plays the Cook County small-claims clerk. (Note: Spielberg returned the favor to co-star Dan Aykroyd by giving him a cameo role in *Indiana Jones and the Temple of Doom*. He played the English ticket agent at the airport.)

MAVERICK (1994)

I Spy . . . Actor Danny Glover
Where to Find Him: Glover, who appeared with *Maverick* star Mel Gibson in the *Lethal Weapon* series, shows up in a cameo as a bank robber. He and Gibson seem to recognize each other, then shake their heads and say, "Nah." Glover even uses his line from the *Lethal Weapon* films, "I'm too old for this s***."

RESERVOIR DOGS (1992)

I Spy . . . A real-life act of revenge
Where to Find It: The scene in which actor Tim Roth shoots a woman. The actress was his dialogue coach, who had apparently made life difficult for him during the filming. He insisted that she be cast in the role so he could "shoot" her.

TWISTER (1996)

I Spy . . . A tribute to Stanley Kubrick (Jan de Bont, *Twister's* director, is a big Kubrick fan)
Where to Find It: In the characters' names: one is Stanley, another is called Kubrick. And when a drive-in theater is hit by a twister, the movie playing onscreen is Kubrick's *The Shining*.

There is no leading cause of death for people who live past the age of 100.

TRADING PLACES (1983), TWILIGHT ZONE—THE MOVIE (1983), COMING TO AMERICA (1988), and other films directed by John Landis

I Spy . . . The phrase "See You Next Wednesday"

Where to Find It: Landis says it was the title of his first screenplay and he always tries get it into a film somewhere. In *Trading Places* and *Coming to America*, for example, it's on a subway poster. In *The Blues Brothers*, it's on a billboard. In *The Stupids*, it's on the back of a bus. In *Twilight Zone*, someone says it aloud . . . in German.

BACK TO THE FUTURE (1985)

I Spy . . . A nod to *The Rocky and Bullwinkle Show*

Where to Find It: The scene in which Michael J. Fox crashes into the farmer's barn. The farmer's name is Peabody; his son is Sherman. Peabody and Sherman were the brilliant time-traveling dog and his boy in the Jay Ward cartoon show.

WHEN HARRY MET SALLY . . . (1989)

I Spy . . . Estelle Reiner, director Rob Reiner's mother

Where to Find Her: She's the woman who tells the waiter: "I'll have what she's having," when Meg Ryan fakes an orgasm in a restaurant.

RAIN MAN (1988)

I Spy . . . A reference to Dustin Hoffman's family

Where to Find It: When Hoffman recites names from the phone book. Two of them—Marsha and William Gottsegen—are his real-life in-laws.

NATIONAL LAMPOON'S ANIMAL HOUSE (1978)

I Spy . . . A way to get into Universal Studios free

Where to Find It: In the final credits, it says "Ask for Babs"—referring to a character in the film who supposedly became a tour guide there. For many years, if someone really did ask for Babs, they'd get free or discounted admission to the tour. Bad news: Universal doesn't honor the promotion anymore.

IN MY EXPERT OPINION . . .

Think the experts and authorities have all the answers?
Well, they do . . . but often the wrong ones.

"Animals, which move, have limbs and muscles; the Earth has no limbs and muscles, hence it does not move."
—**Scipio Chiaramonti, professor of mathematics,**
University of Pisa, 1633

"Nature intended women to be slaves. They are our property. What a mad idea to demand equality for women! Women are nothing but machines for producing children."
—**Napoleon Bonaparte**

"I must confess that my imagination refuses to see any sort of submarine doing anything except suffocating its crew and floundering at sea."
—**H. G. Wells, 1902**

"You ain't goin' nowhere, son. You ought to go back to drivin' a truck."
—**Jim Denny, manager of the Grand**
Ole Opry, to Elvis Presley, 1954

"If excessive smoking actually plays a role in the production of lung cancer, it seems to be a minor one."
—*The National Cancer Institute,* **1954**

The horse is here to stay, but the automobile is only a novelty—a fad."
—**Marshall Ferdinand Foch, French military strategist, 1911**

"With over 50 foreign cars already on sale here, the Japanese auto industry isn't likely to carve out a big slice of the U.S. market for itself."
—*Business Week,* **1968**

"We don't believe Jackie Robinson, colored college star signed by the Dodgers for one of their farm teams, will ever play in the big leagues."
—**Jimmy Powers,** *New York Daily News* **sports columnist, 1945**

Most common plastic surgery performed on American men: breast reduction.

READ ALL ABOUT IT!

*Two good reasons not to believe everything
you read in the newspapers.*

THE STORY: In the early 1920s, the *Toronto Mail and Empire* reported that two scientists named Dr. Schmierkase and Dr. Butterbrod had discovered "what appeared to be the fossil of the whale that had swallowed Jonah." The whale had a muscle that functioned like a trapdoor, giving access to its stomach.

The next day, evangelists all over Toronto read the story from the pulpit, citing it as confirmation that the Biblical story of Jonah and the whale was true . . . and the day after that, a rival newspaper ran a story reporting on the evangelists' speech.

THE TRUTH: Three days after the original story ran, the *Toronto Mail and Empire* ran a second story exposing the first one as a hoax, the work of a journalist named Charles Langdon Clarke.

Clarke liked to spend his free time cooking up news items based on Biblical stories, and then attributing them to fictional newspapers like the *Babylon Gazette* or the *Jerusalem Times* for added credibility. Anyone who spoke German would have had an inkling that the story was a joke—Dr. Schmierkase and Dr. Butterbrod translates as Dr. Cheese and Dr. Butter Bread.

THE STORY: In January 1927 the *Chicago Journal* reported that a "killer hawk" had been seen preying on pigeons in the downtown area. The next day other Chicago papers ran the story on their front pages, and continued doing so for five consecutive days, igniting considerable public hysteria in the process: A prominent banker offered a reward for capture of the hawk dead or alive; a local gun club sent shooters downtown to stalk the bird, with help of local Boy Scouts troops who joined in the hunt.

THE TRUTH: A week after the *Journal* ran the hawk story, it announced the start of a newspaper serial called "The Pigeon and the Hawk." The other papers, realizing they'd been tricked into publicizing a rival paper's promotion on their front pages for an entire week, never printed another word about the killer hawk.

When William Shakespeare moved into his new home, he named it New Home.

FAMILIAR PHRASES

Where do these familiar terms and phrases come from? The BRI staff has researched them and come up with some interesting explanations.

BUY A PIG IN A POKE
Meaning: Buying something sight unseen
Origin: "The poke was a small bag (the words *pouch* and *pocket* derive from the same roots), and the pig was a small pig. As related in Thomas Tusser's *Five Hundredth Good Pointes of Husbandrie* (1580), the game was to put a cat in the poke and try to palm it off in the market as a pig, persuading the buyer that it would be best not to open the poke because the pig might get away." (From *The Dictionary of Clichés*, by James Rogers)

TOUCH AND GO
Meaning: A risky, precarious situation
Origin: "Dates back to the days of stagecoaches, whose drivers were often intensely competitive, seeking to charge past one another, on narrow roads, at grave danger to life and limb. If the vehicle's wheels became entangled, both would be wrecked; if they were lucky, the wheels would only touch and the coaches could still go." (From *Loose Cannons and Red Herrings*, by Robert Claiborne)

KNOCK OFF WORK
Meaning: Leave work for the day
Origin: "[This phrase] originated in the days of slave galleys. To keep the oarsmen rowing in unison, a drummer beat time rhythmically on a block of wood. When it was time to rest or change shifts, he would give a special knock, signifying that they could knock off." (From *Dictionary of Word and Phrase Origins Vol. 2*, by William and Mary Morris)

DOES THAT RING ANY BELLS?
Meaning: Does that sound familiar?
Origin: "Old-fashioned carnivals and amusement parks featured shooting galleries, in which patrons were invited to test their marksmanship by shooting at a target—often with a bell at the

The average person's skin weighs twice as much as their brain.

center: if something was right on target, it rang the bell. Similarly, to say that something 'doesn't ring any bells' means that it doesn't strike any 'target' (evoke any response) in your mind." (From *Loose Cannons and Red Herrings*, by Robert Claiborne)

BEAT THE RAP

Meaning: Avoid punishment for a wrongdoing
Origin: "It is likely that this slang Americanism originated in another expression, take the rap, in which rap is slang for 'punishment,' facetiously, from a 'rap on the knuckles.' One who takes the rap for someone else stands in for the other's punishment. Beat the rap . . . often carries with it the connotation that the miscreant was actually guilty, though acquitted." (From *The Whole Ball of Wax*, by Laurence Urdang)

BE ABOVEBOARD

Meaning: Be honest
Origin: Comes from card playing. "Board is an old word for table." To drop your hands below the table could, of course, be interpreted as trying to cheat—by swapping cards, for example. "But if all play was above board this was impossible." (From *To Coin a Phrase*, by Edwin Radford and Alan Smith)

* * *

IRONIC DEATH

Thomas Parr was thought to be England's oldest living man in the 17th century. He was supposedly 152 years old in 1635, when King Charles invited him to a royal banquet in hopes of learning the secret to his longevity. Parr's answer: "Simple meals of grains and meats."

Final Irony: According to one account: "'Marvelous,' said the King as he offered Parr goose livers and baby eels basted in butter and onions, followed by fried sheep's eyeballs. Throughout the banquet, Parr regaled the King with stories while the King saw to it that Parr's plate and glass were always full. Unfortunately, Parr, overwhelmed by the food, expired during the meal. The distraught King, feeling responsible, had him buried in Westminster Abbey."

Five percent of Americans say they never make their beds.

MYTH AMERICA:
FROM BAD TO VERSE

In some instances, "common knowledge" about important moments in American history comes from poems that, though dramatic and inspiring, turn out to be complete fiction. Here are two examples.

THE LANDING OF THE PILGRIM FATHERS (1826)

> *The breaking waves dashed high*
> *On a stern and rock-bound coast.*
> *And the woods, against a stormy sky,*
> *Their giant branches toss'd*
>
> *And the heavy night hung dark*
> *The hills and water o'er,*
> *When a band of exiles moor'd their bark*
> *On the wild New England shore . . .*

Significance: According to Bill Bryson in *Made in America*, this poem is responsible for "forming the essential image of the Mayflower landing that most Americans carry with them to this day."

Background: It was written by Felicia Dorothea Hemans, who lived 200 years after the Pilgrims landed, never visited the United States even once, and "appears to have known next to nothing about the country" or the Pilgrims. So how did she come to write the poem? Bryson explains:

> It just happened that one day in 1826 her local grocer in Rhyllon, Wales, wrapped her purchases in a sheet of two-year-old newspaper from Boston, and her eye was caught by a small article about a founders' day celebration in Plymouth. It was probably the first she had heard of the Mayflower or the Pilgrims. But inspired as only a mediocre poet can be, she dashed off a poem.

Myth-understood: The Pilgrims eventually did land at Plymouth, but that was on their fourth trip to shore, not their first. And they didn't land at night, or anywhere near the rocks (including Plymouth Rock).

President McKinley's pet parrot was named Washington Post.

For that matter, the Pilgrims didn't even refer to themselves as "pilgrims"—they called themselves "saints," and would not become known as Pilgrims until 200 years later. (The sailors who brought the Pilgrims to the New World had another name for them: "puke stockings," Bryson writes, "on account of the Pilgrims' apparently boundless ability to spatter the latter with the former.")

PAUL REVERE'S RIDE (1861)

Listen my children, and you shall hear
Of the midnight ride of Paul Revere,
On the eighteenth day of April, in Seventy-five;
Hardly a man is now alive
Who remembers that famous day and year.
He said to his friend, "If the British march
By land or sea from the town to-night,
Hang a lantern aloft in the belfry arch,
Of the North Church tower as a signal light,
One, if by land, and two, if by sea;
And I on the opposite shore will be,
Ready to ride and spread the alarm
Through every Middlesex village and farm,
For the country folk to be up and to arm . . .

Significance: More than any other single source, this poem established the classic elements of the Paul Revere myth: that lanterns were hung in the church tower as signals and that Revere made the difficult journey alone, almost singlehandedly warning the nation of imminent British attack.

Background: Henry Wadsworth Longfellow wrote the poem to serve as an inspiration to Union soldiers fighting in the Civil War, and used considerable dramatic license to achieve that end. "He made the ride into a solitary act," says historian David Hackett Fischer. "Paul Revere for him becomes a historical loner who does almost everything by himself . . . The point was that one man, acting alone, could turn the course of history, and this was an appeal to individuals in the North to do it again in another crisis."

Myth-understood: Historians now believe that as many as 60 men rode that night to warn of the British attack. "That doesn't in any way take away from Paul Revere," Fischer says. "He, more than anybody, set those other people in motion." And while there may

Oregon has the most ghost towns of any state.

have been lanterns in the North Church tower, Fischer points out, Paul Revere wasn't the one who received the signal, he was the one who sent it to others, just in case he wasn't able to get across the Charles River to begin his ride.

In his book *Lies, Legends, and Cherished Myths of American History*, Richard Shenkman isn't so charitable about Revere. He writes:

> Paul Revere rode into the hero's spotlight only in 1863, when Longfellow wrote his famous poem . . . rescuing Revere from virtual obscurity. Historians say before the poem, many Americans were not even familiar with Revere's name. In the early nineteenth century, not a single editor included Revere in any compendium of American worthies . . . [But] by the end of the century, his reputation had improved so immensely that the Daughters of the American Revolution put a plaque on his home in Boston.

And let's not forget, Paul Revere didn't even finish his famous ride—he was captured by the British.

* * *

AMPHI-FACTS

- The largest amphibian in the world is the Chinese giant salamander.

- The largest giant salamander on record: 5 feet—from the tip of the snout to the tip of the tail—it weighed nearly 100 pounds.

- The largest frog in the world is the rare Goliath frog of Africa.

- The largest toad in the world is probably the Marine toad, from tropical South America.

- The smallest known amphibian is the Arrow-poison frog, found only in Cuba.

- The smallest newt in the world—at about two inches—is the Striped newt, from the southeastern U.S.

- There will be a test in the morning.

First U.S. coin to have a president on it: the 1909 Lincoln penny.

NOW HEAR THIS!

If you weren't reading right now, you might be listening to a "personal tape player"—like a Walkman. But then when people started banging on the door, asking what you were doing in there, you wouldn't hear them. Maybe they'd panic and think you were dead, like Elvis. They'd run outside and get a bunch of people to help break down the door. Wham! And there you'd be, completely oblivious. They'd get so mad that they'd attack you with the toilet plunger, which would get stuck to the top of your head. You'd have to go to the emergency room, and well, aren't you glad you're reading Uncle John's Bathroom Reader *instead? Since it's not safe to listen to a Walkman, we'll print a story about it instead. It's by Jack Mingo.*

THE PRESSMAN

In the mid-1970s, a team of Sony engineers headed by Mitsuro Ida created the Pressman—a portable tape recorder that could fit into a shirt pocket. As Sony expected, it quickly became standard equipment for journalists. But there was one small problem: the Pressman recorded in mono, and radio journalists preferred working in stereo. They requested a stereo version.

Sony's engineers put their best into it, shrinking stereo components, trying to get them into a small, pocket-sized case. They almost made it—but could only fit in the playback parts and two tiny speakers. Since the whole point was to come up with a tape recorder, the attempt was an embarrassing and expensive failure. Still, the quality of the sound was surprisingly good. So Ida kept the prototype around the shop instead of dismantling it. Some of the engineers started playing cassettes on it while they worked.

THE MISSING LINK

One day Masaru Ibuka wandered by. Although he'd co-founded the company with Akio Morita, he was considered too quirky and creative to fit into day-to-day operations. So he was made "honorary chairman"—a title that gave him much respect, little authority, and lots of time to wander the halls of Sony.

Ibuka stopped to watch the Pressman engineers working on their design problem. He heard music coming from the unsuccessful

London police photographed the eyes of Jack the Ripper's victims . . .

prototype and asked, "Where did you get this great little tape player?" Ida explained that it was a failure because it couldn't record.

Ibuka spent a lot of his time roaming around, so he knew what was going on all over the company. He suddenly remembered another project he'd seen that was being developed on the other side of the building—a set of lightweight portable headphones.

"What if you got rid of the speakers and added the headphones?" he asked Ida. "They'd use less power and increase the quality of the sound. Who knows, maybe we can sell this thing even if you can't record on it." The engineers listened politely and respectfully— while privately thinking the old man had finally lost it. Why make a tape recorder that can't record?

LISTENING WELL

Ibuka took the gadget, with headphones attached, to Morita. He too was skeptical . . . until he heard the quality of the stereo music. To the shock of the engineering team, Morita gave it a green light. It was dubbed the Walkman, to go along with the Pressman.

The marketing department thought it was a terrible idea. They projected that the company would lose money on every unit sold. Even the name seemed wrong. According to American distributors, "Walkman" sounded "funny" to English ears. So Sony rolled the product out as the "Soundabout" in the U.S. and the "Stowaway" in England. Their 1979 publicity campaign—a low-budget, luke-warm affair aimed at teens—got virtually no results. It seemed as though the Walkman's critics were right.

As it turned out, though, Sony had just targeted the wrong market. Teens had boom boxes . . . it was adults who wanted the Walkman. The little unit was perfect for listening to Mozart while jogging or the Stones while commuting, and was small enough to fit into a briefcase or the pocket of a business suit. To Sony's surprise, while collar workers discovered the Walkman on their own. It became a sudden, raging success. Sony had prepared an initial run of 60,000 units; when the first wave hit, they sold out instantly.

The world still loves the Walkman and its offspring. By 1997, four million personal cassette players were sold a year.

. . . theorizing that his image might be recorded on their retinas.

STRANGE TOURIST ATTRACTIONS

The next time you're traveling across America, you might want to visit these unusual attractions. (From the hilarious book Roadside America.*)*

THE NUT MUSEUM
Location: Old Lyme, Connecticut
Background: In 1973 an artist named Elizabeth Tashjian (now known as "The Nut Lady") crammed her antebellum mansion full of nuts, things made from nuts, things that are used with nuts, and things that are inspired by nuts, including the "Nut Anthem," which she wrote herself. "Oh nutttts," she croons, "have a bee-you-tee-ful his-tory and lorrrre . . ." Her Nut Museum is popular with tourists, despite the fact that the Connecticut Department of Tourism removed it from its official guide in 1988, claiming the house is overrun with squirrels. ("It's a plot," she says.)
Be Sure to See: Large nuts. Small nuts. Nut art. Nuts and nut-crackers living together in peace. "In the outside world, nutcrack-ers are the nuts' mortal enemy. Here," she says, "nuts and nutcrack-ers can be friends."

THE RICHARD NIXON LIBRARY AND BIRTHPLACE
Location: Yorba Linda, California
Background: Richard Nixon was born here in 1913; when he died in 1994, he was buried in the yard. Unlike most presidential libraries, the Nixon Library does not accept funding from the fed-eral government, which means that Nixon's cronies (and Nixon himself when he was alive) were free to put their own alternate-reality spin on his failed presidency.
Be Sure to See: The Watergate: The Final Campaign exhibit, where you can listen to the "Smoking Gun" Watergate tape that forced Nixon from office, and then listen to the narrator distort the truth in your headphones: "It was Nixon's critics who call this 'the smoking gun.' But it is not what it once appeared to be . . . This conversation resulted in no obstruction of justice, and no cover-up resulted from the conversation."

Q: How did black sheep get such a bad rap?

THE ANNUAL COW CHIP TOSS

Location: Beaver, Oklahoma
Background: Every year, dozens of contestants from as far away as Alaska and more than 2,500 spectators gather to see who can throw a cow chip farther than anyone else. Contestants pay $15.00 for two cow chips: The winner gets a jacket, losers get T-shirts, all of which say, "I Slung Dung." (The world record is 182.3 feet, set in 1979.)
Be Sure to See: The different cow chip-tossing techniques on display, including Frisbee, overhead baseball, and sidearm. "Throwing it like a discus above the head with a lot of back-spin works well," says contestant Brock Russell. "Licking your thumb before each toss helps too."

NATIONAL FRESHWATER FISHING HALL OF FAME

Location: Hayward, Wisconsin
Background: Opened in 1970, this Hall of Fame is housed inside the world's largest fiberglass fish (a muskie), half a city block long and standing four and a half stories tall at its highest point. The mouth doubles as an observation deck.
Be Sure to See: The Hall of Outboard Motors, the minnow bucket exhibit, the Examples of Poor Taxidermy wall, and the Primitive Fisherman and Primitive Fisherman's Son displays (fur-covered mannequins that are supposed to show how cavemen fished). If you'd like to honor the memory of a dead fisherman, you can bake their name into a ceramic brick and have it added to the hall's memorial wall.

* * *

KEEP ON TRUCKIN'

According to a poll by American Tours International the "most unexpected" (and unintentional) tourist attractions in the U.S. for foreign visitors are truck stops. Foreigners view truck drivers as "the last cowboys" and like to visit their eating places. Another big attraction: I-90 in South Dakota, "a blacktop with few towns for hundreds of miles."

A: Their wool is harder to dye than the wool of white sheep.

VEGETABLE NAMES

More vegetable facts from BRI member Jeff Cheek.

CABBAGE

Originated in Asia and introduced to Europe by Alexander the Great, about 325 B.C. The name comes from the Latin *caput*, meaning "head." It's high in vitamin C, but contains sulfurous compounds that, when cooked, give off odors similar to rotten eggs or ammonia.

SCALLIONS

These tiny green onions owe their name to the biblical city of Ashkelon. When the Romans conquered the city, they called the tiny onions *caepa Ascolonia* or "onions of Ashkelon," This became "scallions."

JERUSALEM ARTICHOKES

These sweet, starchy roots did not grow in Jerusalem and they are not artichokes. Native Americans used them as bread. The mix-up came when a Spanish explorer thought they were some kind of sunflower. *Girasol* (turn to the sun) is "sunflower" in Spanish. An American heard it as "Jerusalem." No one knows why he also added "artichoke."

BROCCOLI

The word comes from the Latin *bracchium*, or "branch." It was developed about 2,500 years ago on the island of Cyprus and was a popular dish at ancient Roman banquets. (The Roman emperor Tiberius, who ruled from 14 to 37 A.D., once publicly scolded his son for eating all the broiled broccoli at a state banquet.) It was popularized in the U.S. by Italian immigrants.

KIWI FRUIT

Originally from China, they were imported to New Zealand in the early 1900s and renamed "Chinese Gooseberry." They finally made it to the U.S. in 1962, and a Los Angeles distributor named Frieda Caplan named it after the New Zealand national bird, the kiwi. It took 18 years before the American public started buying it.

CANTALOUPE

A type of muskmelon brought to Italy from Armenia in the first century A.D., and grown in the town of Cantalupo, which is where it gets its name.

Why is the Wyoming Valley so difficult to find? It's in Pennsylvania.

STRANGE
ANIMAL LAWSUITS

*In the Middle Ages, it was not unusual for animals to be
put on trial as if they could understand human laws.
These lawsuits were serious affairs.*

THE PLAINTIFFS: Vineyard growers in St.-Julien, France
THE DEFENDANTS: Weevils
THE LAWSUIT: In 1545 angry growers testified to a
judge that the weevils were eating and destroying their crops.
According to one source: "Legal indictments were drawn, and the
insects were actually defended in court."
THE VERDICT: Since the weevils were obviously eating the
crops, they were found guilty. In 1546 a proclamation was issued by
the judge demanding that the weevils desist . . . and amazingly,
they did. The farmers weren't bothered by weevils again until
1587. Once more, the insects were put on trial; however, the outcome is unknown.

THE PLAINTIFFS: The people of Mayenne, France
THE DEFENDANT: Mosquitoes
THE LAWSUIT: In the 1200s, a swarm of mosquitoes were
indicted as a public nuisance by the people of the town. When the
bugs failed to answer the summons, the court appointed a lawyer to
act on their behalf.
THE VERDICT: The lawyer did such a good job pleading their
case that the court took pity. The judge banished them, but gave
them a patch of real estate outside town where they would be
allowed to swarm in peace "forever."

THE PLAINTIFF: The city of Basel, Switzerland
THE DEFENDANT: A rooster
THE LAWSUIT: In 1474 the rooster was accused of being (or
helping) a sorcerer. The reason, according to the prosecutor: it had
laid eggs . . . and as everyone knows, an egg laid by a rooster is
prized by sorcerers. On top of that, it was shown "that Satan

---

First movie ever shown in the White House: *Birth of a Nation,* in 1916.

employed witches to hatch such eggs, from which proceeded winged serpents most dangerous to mankind."

The rooster's lawyer admitted it had laid an egg, but contended that "no injury to man or beast had resulted." And besides, laying an egg is an involuntary act, he said, so the law shouldn't punish it. **THE VERDICT:** The judge refused to allow the lawyer's argument and declared the rooster guilty of sorcery. Both the unfortunate fowl and the egg it had allegedly laid were burned at the stake.

THE PLAINTIFFS: Barley growers in Autun, France
THE DEFENDANTS: Rats
THE LAWSUIT: In 1510 the rodents were charged with burglary, having eaten and destroyed the barley crop. A young lawyer named Bartholomew de Chassenée was appointed to defend them. When the rats failed to appear in court, Chassenée successfully argued that since the case involved all the rats of the diocese (the area under jurisdiction of one bishop), all of them should be summoned. When the rats failed to appear again, Chassenée argued that it was because they were scared by "evilly disposed cats which were in constant watch along the highways." Since, by law, the rats were entitled to protection to and from court, the plaintiffs "should be required to post a bond" that would be forfeited if the cats attacked the rats on their way to court.
THE VERDICT: Unknown, but the publicity from the case helped Chassenée to establish a reputation as a sharp lawyer. In fact, many historians now regard him as one of France's greatest lawyers.

THE PLAINTIFF: The Grand Vicar of Valence, France
THE DEFENDANTS: Caterpillars inhabiting his diocese
THE LAWSUIT: In 1584 the Grand Vicar excommunicated the insects for causing destruction to crops, and ordered them to appear before him. When they didn't appear, a lawyer was appointed to defend them.
THE VERDICT: The lawyer argued his case, but lost. The caterpillars were banished from the diocese. "When the caterpillars failed to leave, the trial continued until the short-lived caterpillars died off. The Vicar was then credited with having miraculously exterminated them."

How can you tell when a panda is roaring? It sounds like it has indigestion.

WEIRD DOLL STORIES

Maybe it's because they look human that dolls seem to inspire such bizarre behavior in people. Here are a few examples.

STAR TREK'S MR. SPOCK DOLL

In 1994 England, under the auspices of the European Union, slapped import quotas on all "nonhuman creature" dolls manufactured in China. The quota did not apply to human dolls, which meant that Captain Kirk dolls were allowed into the country. But the quota did apply to Mr. Spock, since he is a Vulcan and therefore a nonhuman creature (even though Spock's mother was human). "It seems very strange," said Peter Waterman, a spokesperson for the British toy industry, "that we should have customs officials involved in a discussion of whether Mr. Spock is an alien or a human being."

GROWING UP SKIPPER

Introduced by Mattel in the spring of 1975, Skipper—Barbie's little sister—really did grow up. When you cranked her arm, she grew one-quarter inch taller and sprouted breasts and an hourglass figure. The doll was attacked by feminists, who charged that the doll was "a grotesque caricature of the female body," and "caters to psychotic preoccupation with instant culture and instant sex object." The doll sold well anyway.

EARRING MAGIC KEN

In 1993 Mattel introduced Earring Magic Ken, a version of Barbie's boyfriend that came with a lavender mesh shirt, a lavender vest, and an earring. It became an instant camp classic in the gay community—which interpreted Ken's choice of clothing and jewelry to mean that there was a very good reason why, after more than 30 years of dating, Barbie and Ken had never gotten married.

Mattel insisted there was no hidden agenda. "The designers were amazed when all of this surfaced," they claimed. Then they took the doll off the market.

World's actual oldest profession, according to anthropologists: witch doctor.

TALKING BARBIE AND G.I. JOE DOLLS
In 1993 a group calling itself the Barbie Liberation Organization (BLO) claimed it switched the voice boxes on as many as 300 G.I. Joe and Barbie dolls in France, England, and the U.S. at the peak of the Christmas shopping season, to protest "gender-based stereotyping in children's toys." So when kids opened their G.I. Joes, they said things like, "I love school. Don't you?" and "Let's sing with the band tonight" in a female voice; Barbie said "Dead men tell no lies," in a deep, booming male voice.

TELETUBBIES
In 1998—shortly after televangelist Jerry Falwell attacked Tinky-Winky as a stalking-horse for gay culture—a woman who bought a Teletubby at a New York toy store claimed that when she got the doll home, it shouted obscenities like "bite my butt" and whispered anti-gay remarks. A spokesman for the manufacturer said that the doll, named Po, was actually bilingual—and was saying "Faster, faster!" in Cantonese.

THE CABBAGE PATCH SNACKTIME DOLL
The 1996 Snacktime doll came with a motorized set of gears that powered its lower jaw, allowing it to chew and "eat" plastic carrots and cookies. That, however, was not all it liked to eat—in 1997 the Consumer Produce Safety Commission received more than 100 reports of children getting their fingers and hair stuck in the mechanical mouth, "which would not stop chewing until the battery back was removed." Mattel later admitted that it had not fully tested the product, withdrew the doll from the market, and offered to buy back dolls for $40 apiece. Only about 1,000 of the 500,000 dolls sold were returned.

FURBIES
In 1999 the National Security Agency issued a Furby Alert, warning that the dolls—which come with sophisticated computer chips that allow it to record and mimic human speech—might "overhear secret information and 'start talking classified,'" inadvertently passing secret information along to America's enemies. Accordingly, Furbies were banned from sensitive areas in the Pentagon.

When you're looking at someone you love, your pupils dilate.

FAMOUS FOR
15 MINUTES

Here's more proof that Andy Warhol was right when he said that
"in the future, everyone will be famous for 15 minutes."

THE STAR: Scott O'Grady, a U.S. Air Force captain
THE HEADLINE: *Downed Pilot Dodges Serbs, U.S. Media*
WHAT HAPPENED: In June 1995 O'Grady's F-16 was
shot down over Serb-controlled Bosnian territory. He ejected safely
. . . but as he parachuted to the ground, he could see Serb soldiers
watching him float to earth. America held its breath as rescue
operations took place. And somehow O'Grady evaded capture. He
spent the next six days hiding under leaves, surviving on roots and
bugs until the Marines were able to airlift him to safety. His only
injury: "trench foot," from wearing his boots for six days straight.
THE AFTERMATH: O'Grady made a few appearances on network news shows, and was guest of honor at President Clinton's
State of the Union Address in 1996. He also wrote a book describing his experience, but generally avoided media interviews and
kept a low profile. "He just wants his identity back," his father
explained to *Time* magazine. "He wants to be a normal human
being."

THE STAR: Greg Willig, 27-year-old toymaker from Queens
THE HEADLINE: *Toy Man Takes on Twin Towers*
WHAT HAPPENED: One afternoon in 1976, Willig noticed
how beautiful the World Trade Center looked in the afternoon
sun. "The light was reflecting off the building," he says, "and I
thought of climbing it. It was like an epiphany—I was somehow
irresistibly drawn to it."

On May 26, 1977, after about a year of preparation, Willig made
the climb. Using handmade anchoring devices that he stuck into
window-washing tracks, he scaled the 1,350 feet of the World Trade
Center's South Tower in three and a half hours. Practically the
whole time, news helicopters were circling, broadcasting the story.

When Willig got to the 55th floor, two policemen were lowered

When you're looking at someone you hate, they do the same thing.

from the roof in a window-washer's bucket to talk him out of going any farther. When that failed, they quizzed him to see if he was insane. "Every response he gave was reasonable," one of the officers said. "The only thing unreasonable about it was that he was on the outside of the building."

THE AFTERMATH: Willig's brush with fame began the moment he made it to the top, where police asked for his autograph before slapping on handcuffs and taking him to jail. Released on bail, he made appearances on the *Today Show* and *Good Morning America*. He also gave interviews to dozens of newspapers, magazines, and radio stations. But fearing he'd become "a sideshow attraction," Willig turned down offers to climb other buildings for money.

The city of New York charged Willig with criminal trespass, reckless endangerment, and disorderly conduct, and sued him for $250,000 (the cost of police overtime and the fuel used by the police helicopter), to discourage copycat "human flies" . . . but Mayor Abe Beame eventually reduced the amount to $1.10, a penny for each floor. Today Willig limits his climbs to mountains and rocks.

THE STAR: Wilhelm von Struensee
THE HEADLINE: *You've Got Mail! So Does Your Husband! And His Is Better Than Yours!*
WHAT HAPPENED: When Susan von Struensee moved to a new apartment in 1996, she listed both her husband Wilhelm and herself in the telephone directory. The only catch: she didn't have a husband—"Wilhelm von Struensee" was a name she added to her phone listing to discourage crank callers.

Susan didn't get crank calls, but Wilhelm got junk mail—lots of it—and Susan noticed that much of "his" junk mail was better than hers. For example: "I was thinking of joining AAA one winter," she says. "When Wilhelm got a free AAA membership and I didn't, I realized they assumed the men in marriages made all the decisions." Likewise, Cambridge Savings Bank invited Wilhelm (but not Susan) to a branch opening, and the Mt. Auburn Hospital sent him (but not her) a letter promoting its health services.

Susan filed a complaint with the Massachusetts Commission Against Discrimination.

Hot chocolate: In Japan, you can buy cocoa flavored with 2% chili pepper sauce.

THE AFTERMATH: When the story was picked up by wire services, newspapers all over the country published articles about Wilhelm. He became the most famous non-person ever listed in a Massachusetts telephone directory.

THE STAR: Joseph Hazelwood, captain of the *Exxon Valdez*
THE HEADLINE: *Captain's Career, and 1,500 miles of Alaskan Shoreline, Come to Oily End in Prince William Sound*
WHAT HAPPENED: On March 24, 1989, the *Exxon Valdez* oil tanker ran aground off the coast of Alaska, spilling 11 million gallons of oil over 10,000 square miles of water and 1,500 miles of shoreline. It was the worst oil spill in U.S. history. Hazelwood, who admitted to having consumed at least three drinks ashore before boarding the ship, had gone below and left his third mate and helmsman in charge of the ship. He was vilified by media all over the world as "a drunk who left his post."
THE AFTERMATH: Although he flunked the sobriety test administered 11 hours after the accident, Hazelwood was acquitted of operating a tanker while intoxicated. He was, however, convicted of misdemeanor negligence, fined $50,000, and sentenced to 1,000 hours of community service. He also had his captain's license suspended for nine months for leaving the bridge. Then he dropped out of the public eye. Although he was legally qualified to captain any ship on any ocean, he wasn't able to find work; no shipping company would risk the bad publicity. Instead, he worked as a lobster fisherman, boat transporter, and even as an instructor at New York's Maritime College, teaching students "how to stand watch on the bridge of a tanker."

* * *

IRONIC DEATH

Lieutenant Andrew Bright: Credited as "the first Englishman ever to wear suspenders."
Final Irony: "Lieutenant Bright never quite got the hang of them, it seems. Forgetting he had them on one day, Bright tried to take his trousers off while still wearing his jacket. Tangled in the galluses, he knocked over a candle and perished in the ensuing fire."

Pollination experts say: We can thank bees for apples, flies for chocolate, and bats for tequila.

HOW TO MAKE A MONSTER, PART III

Here's the third installment of the Godzilla
story. (Part I starts on page 106.)

COMING TO AMERICA

C OMING TO AMERICA
Gojira's box-office success in Japan caught the attention of American movie studios; in 1955 Joseph E. Levine of TransWorld Films bought the film's U.S. rights for $25,000. The spelling of the monster's name was changed to Godzilla, an approximation of how it was pronounced in Japanese (GO-dzee-la); and the title was changed to *Godzilla, King of the Monsters*.

Levine knew that if he released *Godzilla* with Japanese dialogue, it would appeal only to art-house film crowds—and he wouldn't make back his investment. A subtitled film would miss the youth audience entirely, since many kids were too young to read them. So Levine adapted the film for Americans by dubbing it into English.

MADE IN USA

It wasn't the only change Levine made: The plot was revised, scenes were rearranged or removed entirely, and brand-new scenes were filmed to insert an American character into the previously all-Japanese film. The American, played by Raymond Burr (of TV's *Ironsides* and *Perry Mason*), is a newspaper reporter named Steve Martin who happens to be on assignment in Japan when Godzilla goes on the attack.

Burr couldn't appear on screen at the same time as the Japanese actors in the original version of the film, but numerous scenes of Japanese actors talking to one another were re-edited to make it look like they were talking to him.

FROM A TO B

The effect of Levine's changes was to turn what had been a polished, serious film for adults into a monster movie made for drive-in movie theaters and kiddie matinees. But that was precisely what he wanted: In the mid-1950s, the American film industry was in a

Busiest stretch of highway in the U.S.: New York's George Washington Bridge.

slump. The advent of television, combined with laws that had forced the major studios to sell off their theater chains, caused a dramatic drop in movie attendance and movie profits. Major studios became extremely cautious, making fewer A-films than they had in the 1940s.

As a result, several companies sprang up to make cheapo B-movies for drive-ins and faded downtown movie palaces. Then, along came *Gojira*. "Though a big budget, major studio film in Japan," Stuart Galbraith writes in *Monsters Are Attacking Tokyo!*, "the Americanized *Gojira* was released [solely] as an exploitation feature." Because it was intended for the B-movie market, the changes were done on the cheap, which lowered the quality of the American version of the film. The poor dubbing and sophomoric dialogue made it difficult for Western filmgoers, already used to clichéd American monster movies, to take the film seriously. And they didn't.

SON(S) OF GODZILLA

Say what you will about the changes Levine made to the original *Gojira*, he knew his audience. *Godzilla, King of the Monsters*, opened in the U.S. on April 26, 1956, and made more than $2 million at the box office, an astonishing sum for the 1950s. The American version did so well that it was exported back to Japan under the title *Monster King Godzilla* (Raymond Burr's dialogue was dubbed into Japanese), where it added to the profits already made by the original *Gojira*. And Burr's character was so popular with Japanese audiences that reporter characters became a staple of later Godzilla movies in the 1960s and 1970s.

Enthused by the success of the first *Gojira* film, Toho ordered up the first of what would become more than 20 sequels. *Gojira's Counterattack* (the U.S. version was called *Gigantis the Fire Monster*) was released in 1955. Toho made nine non-Gojira monster movies between 1955 and 1962, featuring such monsters as the Abominable Snowman, and a robot mole named Mogera. But as J. D. Lees writes in *The Official Godzilla Compendium*, the release of *King Kong vs. Godzilla* in 1962 made Godzilla a superstar. "The pairing with the famous ape elevated Godzilla from the swelling ranks of interchangeable atomic monsters of the fifties and placed him among the classic pantheon of cinema creatures."

The world's first golf rule book was published in Scotland in 1754.

GODZILLA FLICKS

- **Godzilla Raids Again** (1955). The first cheesy *Godzilla* sequel, it was brought to America in 1959 as *Gigantis the Fire Monster*, to avoid confusion with the original. Plot: "Yearning for a change of pace, the King of Monsters opts to destroy Osaka instead of Tokyo, but the spiny Angorous is out to dethrone our hero. Citizens flee in terror when the battle royale begins." *Director:* Ishiro Honda (*Videohound's Golden Movie Retriever*)

- **King Kong vs. Godzilla** (1962). Developed from an idea by Willis O'Brien, creator of the original *King Kong*'s stop-motion animation. O'Brien's story was about a fight between Kong and "the Ginko," a monster made by Dr. Frankenstein's grandson. But the only studio willing to make the film was Toho—and they insisted on using Godzilla. The Japanese played it as a satire, with the two monsters wrestling in Tokyo (where else?) and on top of Mt. Fuji. King Kong wins. *Director:* Ishiro Honda (*A Critical History of Godzilla*)

- **Godzilla vs. Mothra** (1964). Released as *Godzilla vs. the Thing*. "When the egg of giant monster Mothra is washed ashore by a storm, a greedy entrepreneur is quick to exploit it. Meanwhile, Godzilla reappears and goes on a rampage . . . Godzilla, who seems to be really enjoying his reign of destruction, shows more personality than in previous appearances . . . Excellent in all departments." *Director:* Ishiro Honda (*Cult Flicks and Trash Pics*)

- **Godzilla vs. Monster Zero** (1965). "Novel Godzilla adventure with the big guy and Rodan in outer space. Suspicious denizens of Planet X require the help of Godzilla and Rodan to rid themselves of the menacing Ghidrah, whom they refer to as Monster Zero. Will they, in return, help Earth as promised, or is this just one big, fat double cross?" *Director:* Ishiro Honda (*Videohound's Golden Movie Retriever*)

- **Godzilla vs. Sea Monster** (1966). "This exercise in cardboard mayhem stars the saucy saurian as a crusty critter suffering a case of crabs when he's attacked by colossal crustaceans (notably Ebirah, a giant lobster) and does battle with the Red Bamboo bad-guy gang." *Director:* Jun Fukuda (*Creature Features Movie Guide Strikes Again*)

Highest bill ever minted by the U.S. Treasury: $100,000 bill. Lowest: 5¢ bill.

- *Godzilla on Monster Island* (1972). "In this harmless, toy-like movie, Godzilla talks, as he and spiny Angillus battle alien-summoned Ghidrah and new playmate Gigan, who has a buzz-saw in his belly." *Director*: Jun Fukuda (*Leonard Maltin's Movie & Video Guide*)

- *Godzilla vs. the Smog Monster* (1972). "A Japanese industrial city has an ecology woe; its bay of waste and rotting animal life breeds Hedorah, which shoots laser beams from its eyepods and flies at will . . . To the rescue comes the flat-footed Godzilla to indulge in a duel-of-the-titans." Godzilla flies in this one, and it looks really cheap—"the army consists of about 10 guys." *Director*: Yoshimitsu Banno (*Creature Features Movie Guide Strikes Again*)

- *Godzilla vs. Megalon* (1973). "The 400-foot-tall green lizard is aided by a jet-packed robot in fighting off Megalon (a giant cockroach with Zap Killer Beam), Baragon the stomper, and a race of underground Earthlings, the Seatopians." *Director*: Jun Fukuda (*Creature Features Movie Guide Strikes Again*)

- *Godzilla vs. the Cosmic Monster* (1974). Japanese sci-fi sukiyaki with the King of Monsters battling a cyborg Godzilla controlled by aliens bent on conquest. A huge rodent creature said to embody Asian spirits comes to the real Godzilla's aid when the languid lizard squares off against antagonistic Angorus." *Director*: Jun Fukuda (*Creature Features Movie Guide Strikes Again*)

- *Godzilla: 1985* (1984). "After 30 years, the Big G recovers from his apparent death . . . and returns to destroy Tokyo all over again. Disregarding the previous fourteen sequels (most of which were set in "the future" anyway), the plot marches along much like a '70s disaster film." *Director*: Kohji Hashimoto. (*Cult Flicks and Trash Pics*)

- *Godzilla vs. Biollante* (1989). "Genetic scientist Surigama uses cells from Godzilla's body to create hardy new crop strains, while also splicing the cells' DNA to that of his dead daughter, using that of her favorite rose as a catalyst. His experiments result in the gigantic plant/animal monster Biollante, a night-mare of creeping vines, snapping teeth, and corrosive sap." *Director*: Kazuki Ohmori (*Cult Flicks and Trash Pics*)

- *Godzilla* (1998). Charmless big-bucks travesty starring Matthew Broderick. Bad career move.

If you're average, you'll move your residence 11 times in your life.

WORD ORIGINS

Here are some more interesting word origins.

PUNCH
Meaning: A fruity drink
Origin: "From Sanskrit *panca* or Hindustani *panch*, which means 'five,' the theory being that there were five ingredients—alcohol, water, lemon, sugar, and spice." (From *The Story Behind the Word*, by Morton S. Freeman)

EAVESDROP
Meaning: Secretly listen to someone else's conversation
Origin: "In Anglo-Saxon England, a house had very wide over-hanging eaves . . . to allow rain to drip safely away from the house's foundation. So the eavesdrip, later the eavesdrop, provided a place where one could hide to listen clandestinely to conversation within the house." (From *Morris Dictionary of Word and Phrase Origins*, by William and Mary Morris)

CHEAT
Meaning: A dishonest person; the act of deceiving someone for gain
Origin: Comes from *escheat*—a medieval legal term for "the reversion of property to the state in the absence of legal heirs, and of the state's rights to such confiscation. The officer who looked after the king's escheats was known as the cheater . . . The dishonest connotations of the word evolved among thieves in the 16th century." (From *Wicked Words*, by Hugh Rawson)

SNOB
Meaning: A snooty person; someone who puts on airs
Origin: "It seems that Oxford freshmen were required to register 'according to rank.' Those not of noble birth added after their names the phrase *sine nobilitate* which was then abbreviated to 's. nob.,' thus creating . . . a perfect definition for the commoner who wishes to mingle with the nobles." (From *Dictionary of Word and Phrase Origins, Vol. III*, by William and Mary Morris)

Mercury is the only metal that is liquid at room temperature.

ZANY

Meaning: Crazy
Origin: "Dates back to the commedia dell'arte in Italy of the 16th century. The *zanni* (as it was spelled in Italian) was a buffoon who mimicked one of the characters, usually the clown. The English changed its spelling to *zany* and used it to refer to any simpleton or bumbling fool." (From *Dictionary of Word and Phrase Origins, Vol. II*, by William and Mary Morris)

AMBITION

Meaning: Single-minded drive toward achieving a goal
Origin: *Ambitio* is the Latin term for "running around." The term originally referred to the way politicians in ancient Rome ran around "in search of voters to persuade or buy." (From *Loose Cannons and Red Herrings*, by Robert Claiborne)

ALCOHOL

Meaning: An intoxicating beverage
Origin: "The word comes from Arabic *al-kuhul*, a powder used as a cosmetic. Borrowed into English, *alcohol* came to mean any distilled substance. *Alcohol of wine* was thus the 'quintessence of wine' . . . by the middle of the 18th century *alcohol* was being used on its own." (From *Dictionary of Word Origins*, by John Ayto)

DIAPER

Meaning: A cloth used to capture a baby's waste
Origin: "From Greek *diaspros*, meaning 'pure white' . . . Originally, a fabric woven of silk, sewn with gold threads, and used for ecclesiastical robes." (From *Thereby Hangs a Tale*, by Charles Earle Funk)

DOODLE

Meaning: Aimless, absent-minded scribbles on scraps of paper
Origin: The word *doodle* comes from the German word *dudeln*, meaning 'to play the bagpipe.' The notion seems to be that a person who spends his time playing bagpipes would be guilty of other frivolous time-wasting activities." (From *Dictionary of Word and Phrase Origins, Vol. III*, by William and Mary Morris)

A STRAIGHT FACE

Ever wonder what the Big Guys of poker know that you don't? They swear it's all in keeping a straight face, and watching the table for the players who don't. Here are a few pointers from the experts.

IT'S ALL IN THE GAME

There are well over 400 great professional poker players in the world today. So if poker is truly a game of "chance," then how can so many people be consistently good at winning? It's not the card itself, say the experts, as much as the flip of the card that gives away the game to people who know what to look for. Players, particularly weaker players, give away "tells," or unconscious reflexes during the game that the tried and true poker player can use to get the edge.

One of the poker greats, the self-proclaimed "Mad Poker Genius," Mike Caro has made a living from poker and a killing from studying the psychology of the game. On his Web site, Mike Caro's World, he talks at length about the various "tells" to watch for in others, and how to avoid them yourself.

#1: WEAK AND STRONG

The first rule of thumb in gauging your fellow players is the "Strong When Weak" guideline.

- In general, players who have lousy hands subconsciously act more aggressively; players with strong hands act indifferent and passively. Why? "Because," Caro says, "deception is fundamental to poker—otherwise we'd play with our hands fully exposed."

- When a player looks down and has a lousy hand, he doesn't want to give away his emotions because then he's lost the game up front. So unconsciously, he usually acts the opposite of the way he is feeling. An experienced player knows this and watches for the cues. An even better player will play off these psychological indicators.

TELL ME TRUE

"Tells" are far more prevalent in weak and mediocre players than in the pros. But watch out—really good players are good actors, and a top-of-the-line poker player knows how to *fake* a "tell" to throw off his opponents. The situation can become so complex that it's next to impossible to tell whether a gulp (for example) was a sign of fear . . . or simply a great acting job. Here, according to Caro, are some of the universal poker tells to watch for.

The Heavy Heart: A sad sigh during the bet usually means a player has a good hand. Be somewhat cautious and don't call unless your hand is very good too.

Shifty Eyes: A glance away from the table once the hand has been dealt. This usually indicates a player who's holding a good hand and wants to hide his excitement.

Stare Down: A direct stare into another player's eyes after the cards have been dealt or during a bet is usually a sign of a weak hand. Staring into anyone's eyes is considered somewhat aggressive and can therefore be read that a player is bluffing.

Pokerclack: Pokerclack is a soft clucking noise that sounds morose or shameful. It's a term coined by Caro, and he describes it as the noise you'd make after saying something like, "I'm feeling terrible today. My old dog Shep ran into the street and got run over."

Flair: An extra flamboyance at the toss of a poker chip during a bet is almost always a sign that a player is trying to hide a bad hand. He's bluffing.

The Jitters: Shaky hands during a bet suggests excitement, nervousness, tension in the player. Even skilled players often mistake this sign and think the shaky player is bluffing and scared he's going to lose. That's almost never the case, however, according to Caro. Players who are bluffing tend to be rock-steady, not jittery. It's the player who's got a monstrously good hand who sometimes can't contain his excitement.

The Big Chill: When a player goes quiet after betting, you can almost guarantee he's got a lousy hand and he's bluffing.

The Babbling Brook: When a talkative player begins babbling somewhat incoherently or absentmindedly during or after a bet, he's usually got a lousy hand. His hand disrupted his normal conversation and he didn't want to go silent for fear he'd give himself away. But this cowboy's almost surely bluffing.

Chip Fondling: The hands have been dealt and the guy on your right is fingering his poker chips. Read it as a sign that he's raring to place his bet; he's got a great hand.

The Stiff: If you see a player suddenly go rigid and hold his breath following a bet, take it as a sign of bluffing. Call him.

TATTLING & TELLING

It's betting time around your Friday night poker table and your buddy flips his chip in the air with flair and a wink. With all of this newfound knowledge, you know you've just spotted a bluff. What should you do when you notice a "tell"? Mike Caro says: "Don't let your pride destroy the profit you could make from tells. Never announce that, 'I knew you were bluffing,' if you successfully call and win with a weak hand. Say, instead, 'I don't know why I called. I almost didn't, but at the last second I decided to test you one time. I guess I got lucky.' That kind of talk will encourage an opponent to try again."

* * *

THE NAME GAME

There are hundreds—maybe thousands—of poker variations . . . and some of them sound downright funny when said out loud. A few of our favorite goofy-sounding poker games:

Change the Diaper	The Good, the Bad, and the Ugly
Cowpie Poker	
Dirty Schultz	Grocery Store Dots
Five Card Stud with a Bug	Howdy Doody
Making Babies	Linoleum
There Can Only Be Juan	Mexican Sweat
Three Legged Race	Navy Nurse
Trash Bin	Pass the Trash
Want It? Want It? Got It!	Screwy Louie

Survey result: 35% of people watching TV yell at it.

ON THE MARK

Quotes from America's great humorist, Mark Twain.

"Eloquence is the essential thing in a speech, not information."

"Good breeding consists in concealing how much we think of ourselves and how little we think of the other person."

"There is no sadder sight than a young pessimist."

"If you pick up a starving dog and make him prosperous, he will not bite you. It is the principal difference between a dog and a man."

"Irreverence is the champion of liberty and its one sure defense."

"Let us endeavor so to live, that when we die, even the undertaker will be sorry."

"Noise proves nothing. Often a hen who has merely laid an egg cackles as if she has laid an asteroid."

"All you need in this life is ignorance and confidence, and then Success is sure."

"Against the assault of laughter, nothing can stand."

"Whenever you find you are on the side of the majority, it is time to pause and reflect."

"You can't depend on your eyes if your imagination is out of focus."

"Golf is a good walk spoiled."

"Let us be thankful for fools. But for them the rest of us could not succeed."

"Everything has its limit—iron ore cannot be educated into gold."

"It is easier to stay out than to get out."

"It is noble to teach oneself, but still nobler to teach others—and less trouble."

"I find that the further I go back, the better things were, whether they happened or not."

"Do the thing you fear most and the death of fear is certain."

According to a Gallup poll, one in seven Americans can't locate the U.S. on a map.

BIRTH OF A GIANT, PART II

They never tell you things like this in school, but the father of the modern bathtub—a real bathroom hero—was also the father of General Motors. Or at least the grandfather. Here's Part II of the story. (Part I starts on page 74.)

ON THE ROAD

In 1904 William Crapo Durant became the head of the Buick Motor Company. Durant was so well known as a successful businessman that when he began his first official task, selling stock in Buick to the public, there was no shortage of takers. In a few short months, he had raised Buick's capital from $75,000 to more than $1.5 million.

Next, Durant set to work designing cars, setting up a network of Buick dealers, and building what was then the largest automobile factory in the U.S. The company grew by leaps and bounds: In 1904 Buick had sold fewer than 30 cars in its entire history. By the end of 1906, it had sold more than 2,000 cars, was building 250 new ones a week, and could not keep up with the new orders that were pouring in.

COME TOGETHER

In 1907 a financial panic rocked Wall Street, and although Buick emerged from the crisis even stronger than it had been before, Durant was convinced that the best way to weather future hard times was for the "Big Four" auto companies—Buick, Ford, REO (founded by Ransom E. Olds after he was forced out of the Olds Motor Works), and Maxwell-Briscoe (co-founded by the Briscoe Brothers with the money they made selling their Buick stock)—to merge into one large company. In Durant's vision, each company would swap its own stock for shares in the new company.

According to *A Most Unique Machine*, the scheme might have worked except that Henry Ford wanted $3 million in cash. Not to be outdone by Ford, Olds changed his mind and also insisted on $3 million in cash. Durant didn't have $6 million in cash, so the deal

---

The world's largest restaurant, the Royal Dragon, in Bangkok . . .

quickly collapsed. On September 1, 1908, Durant created his own new company and called it General Motors.

BOOM AND BUST

Two months after he founded General Motors, Durant bought the Olds Motor Works. The company had fallen on hard times since Ransom Olds had left to found REO, and as Durant soon learned, there weren't even any plans in the works for new Oldsmobiles. "We just paid a million dollars for road signs," he complained to an assistant.

A few days later, Durant came up with an idea for a quick fix: He showed up at the Olds plant with a new Buick and had workers saw the car's chassis into quarters. He moved the left and right sides of the car six inches apart and lengthened it by a foot.

"Make your new car a little longer, a bit wider, and with more leg room than my Buick," he told the workers. "It will look like an Oldsmobile when you put your radiator and hood on it. And there, with paint and upholstery, is next year's Oldsmobile." The new car, priced at $250 more than the Buick, sold so well that the Olds division was making a profit by the end of the year.

Two months later, Durant bought the Oakland Motor Car Company, the predecessor to GM's Pontiac division; six months after that, he bought Cadillac, then one of the most profitable auto manufacturers in the country. In the meantime, he also snapped up a number of companies that supplied GM with auto parts.

BYE-BYE, BILLY

If Durant had stopped there, GM might have remained healthy. But he didn't. "Instead of consolidating his gains around the great Buick and Cadillac potential, and their suppliers such as Weston-Mott and AC Sparkplug," Richard Crabb writes in *Birth of a Giant*, "Durant brought into General Motors a long list of firms that held patents on devices which he thought might provide important improvements for the future . . . He chased patents as some boys chase butterflies."

By the end of 1909, Durant had acquired 13 different auto companies and 10 auto parts companies, most of which were money losers that drained profits from his healthy divisions. Things came to a head in 1910, when sales at Buick and Cadillac slumped to the point where Durant didn't have enough cash to make his payroll and pay his bills.

Durant figured he would need about $7 million to weather the crisis, but he wasn't sure—he had acquired companies so fast and kept so many of the details in his head that GM's financial records were several weeks behind. By the time the records were sorted out, it turned out that Durant actually needed more than $12 million to meet his obligations.

Durant's bankers were aghast at the mess he had made of GM, but the company had grown so big so fast that they could hardly afford to let it fail: if GM crashed, it might take the entire Detroit economy with it. So they lent GM the money it needed . . . on the condition that Durant turn over control of GM to the bankers themselves, who would oversee the running of the company until the loans were repaid.

There was no other way out, so on November 15, 1910, Durant announced his retirement.

For Part III of the GM story, turn to page 343.

* * *

YOUR TAX DOLLARS AT WORK

"A Pentagon inspector general's report released in 1989 revealed that the Navy was sinking its surplus ships without first stripping them of valuable equipment. The report stated, 'We feel confident that public property valued in excess of $17 million was destroyed.' Among the items that could have been retrieved and sold were new mattresses (still in their plastic packaging), band-saws, milling machines, motors, and lathes, as well as all types of furniture, gold and silver (in the communications equipment), brass, copper, ovens, radio equipment, cryptologic equipment, surgical equipment, and pumps. Investigators inspecting retired ships that were destined to be sunk noted the presence on board of numerous spare parts that were still being bought by the Navy."

—John Kohut,
Stupid Government Tricks

American office workers send an average of 36 e-mails a day.

WHAT'S IN A NAME?

Product names don't necessarily reflect the product, but rather the image that manufacturers want to project. Were you fooled by these?

CORINTHIAN LEATHER

Sounds Like: Fancy leather from some exotic place in Europe—specifically, the Greek city of Corinth. The phrase "rich Corinthian leather" was made famous by actor Ricardo Montalban, in ads for Chrysler's luxury Cordoba in the 1970s. (The seats were covered with it.)

The Truth: There's no such thing as Corinthian leather. The term was made up by Chrysler's ad agency. The leather reportedly came from New Jersey.

HÄAGEN DAZS

Sounds Like: An imported Scandinavian product.

The Truth: It was created by Ruben Mattus, a Polish immigrant who sold ice cream in New York City, who used what the *New York Times* called the Vichyssoise Strategy:

> Vichyssoise is a native New Yorker. Created at the Ritz Carlton in 1917, it masqueraded as a French soup and enjoyed enormous success. When Mattus created his ice cream, he used the same tactic . . . He was not the first to think Americans would be willing to pay more for a better product. But he was the first to understand that they would be more likely to do so if they thought it was foreign. So he made up a ridiculous, impossible to pronounce name, [and] printed a map of Scandinavia on the carton.

The ice cream was actually made in Teaneck, New Jersey.

JELL-O PUDDING POPS

Sounds Like: There's pudding in the pops.

The Truth: There isn't. Family secret: One of Uncle John's relatives was involved with test-marketing the product several decades ago. When John asked him about it, he laughed. "Our research shows people think that if it says 'pudding' on the label, it's better quality or better for you. They're wrong. It's really the same."

Bottle-nosed whales can dive 3,000 feet in two minutes.

Anyway, we suppose that's why they still sell it with "pudding" on the label.

PACIFIC RIDGE PALE ALE, *"brewed in Northern California"*
Sounds Like: A small independent brewer in Northern California. The flyer says:

Brewmasters Gery Eckman [and] Mitch Steele . . . always wanted to brew a special ale in Northern California just for California beer drinkers . . . so they created Pacific Ridge Pale Ale. It's produced in limited quantities, using fresh Cascade hops from the Pacific Northwest, two-row and caramel malts and a special ale yeast for a rich copper color . . . Handcrafted only at the Fairfield brewhouse.

The Truth: In tiny letters on the bottle, it says: "Specialty Brewing group of Anheuser-Busch, Inc., Fairfield, California."

SWEET 'N LOW SODA
Sounds Like: The drink was sweetened with nothing but Sweet 'N Low.
The Truth: As Bruce Nash and Allan Zullo write in *The Misfortune 500*, "MBC Beverage Inc., which licensed the Sweet 'N Low name . . . discovered that consumers wanted the natural sweetener NutraSweet rather than the artificial saccharine of Sweet 'N Low. So they sweetened Sweet 'N Low soda with NutraSweet, a Sweet 'N Low *competitor*."

DAVE'S CIGARETTES
Sounds Like: "A folksy brand of cigarette, produced by a down-to-earth, tractor-driving guy named Dave for ordinary people who work hard and make an honest living." According to humorist Dave Barry, here's the story sent to the media when the cigarettes were introduced in 1996:

Down in Concord, N.C., there's a guy named Dave. He lives in the heart of tobacco farmland. Dave enjoys lots of land, plenty of freedom and his yellow '57 pickup truck. Dave was fed up with cheap, fast-burning smokes. Instead of just getting mad, he did something about it . . . Dave's Tobacco company was born.

The Truth: Dave's was a creation of America's biggest cigarette corporation, Philip Morris, whose ad agency unapologetically called the story a "piece of fictional imagery."

Total combined population of the North American colonies in 1610: 350.

ON BROADWAY

Many Broadway hits started out with "no legs," but through the perseverance, pluck, and luck of people who believed in them, managed to get on their feet and become runaway hits.

SOUTH PACIFIC (1949)

When he first read James Michener's *Tales of the South Pacific* in the late 1940s, director Joshua Logan knew it would make a great Broadway show. He told producer Leland Hayward, and Hayward agreed—but warned Logan not to mention it to anyone until they owned the rights. Too late: At a party, Logan tipped his cards to Richard Rodgers—who, with partner Oscar Hammerstein, immediately purchased a controlling 51% interest and went on to write the music and lyrics. (Logan wound up co-producing it with them.)

They cast Mary Martin, fresh from *Annie Get Your Gun*, and famed opera singer Ezio Pinza in the lead roles. Martin was afraid she'd be dwarfed by the Pinza's voice, so the composers avoided duets. Martin had just cut her hair short and, realizing it would dry in three minutes, suggested the song "I'm Gonna Wash That Man Right Out of My Hair," which became a classic.

The play is considered one of the earliest entertainment vehicles promoting racial tolerance in its portrayal of love between a Naval officer and a Polynesian woman. South Pacific won Tonys in all the acting categories, captured a Pulitzer Prize, and was the top-grossing film of 1958.

LIFE WITH FATHER (1939)

The idea for this play comes from a series of autobiographical *New Yorker* articles about growing up in a Victorian household in New York City, written by Clarence Day.

At first, producer Oscar Serlin wanted to adapt it for a movie starring W. C. Fields, but the author's widow was horrified at the thought of the bulbous-nosed comedian playing the title role.

Serlin switched his sights to Broadway, but investors were hohum about such tame fare on the eve of WWII. Serlin brought in two writers, Howard Lindsay and Russel Crouse, who so loved the concept that they worked without payment for two years

---

In the 19th century, India imported ice harvested from ponds in the United States.

developing scenes for the play. When all major actors rejected the title role, writer Lindsay took it himself. And when the company didn't have enough funds to open in a Maine summer stock production, Lindsay and his wife, Dorothy Stickney ("Mother") mortgaged their home to get it going.

On the eve of the Broadway opening, Lindsay said to Crouse, "We've got a nice little comedy here. We might even get six months out of it." It turned out to be the longest-running of all non-musical shows in Broadway history to date (3,224 performances over eight years). In fact, it so engaged audiences that it was made into a movie in 1947 and a TV series that ran from 1953 to 1955.

THE WIZ (1975)

Producer Ken Harper got the idea of retelling *The Wizard of Oz* using African American characters, and got 20th Century Fox to invest $650,000. But after disappointing tryouts in Baltimore, he was advised to close it. The director, Gilbert Moses, quit, so Harper replaced him with actor (and costume designer) Geoffrey Holder, who made big changes in cast and concept.

At its Broadway opening, the mostly white critics were disappointed because it "didn't measure up to the original movie." Closing notices were posted that night. But Harper got Fox to mount a huge advertising campaign—TV ads targeting African Americans. Word of mouth praised the dazzling choreography, staging, and costuming. *The Wiz* stayed open and went on to win seven Tonys, including Best Musical, and was made into a movie in 1978.

THE ODD COUPLE (1965)

"The idea came to me when I was at a party in California," playwright Neil Simon told the *Manchester Guardian*. "There were 24 people there; and do you know that every one of them was a divorcee? The men were either on their second marriage or recently divorced, and the women were in the process of getting divorced. All the men shared apartments because they had to be able to keep up their alimony payments and this was the cheapest method of living . . . I thought it was a good idea for a play"—and a movie . . . and a TV show . . . and a revival of the play . . . and a sequel to the movie . . .

In a recent poll, 23% of workers surveyed said they'd work harder if . . .

YOU'RE MY INSPIRATION

*It's always fascinating to find out who, or what,
inspired cultural milestones like these.*

STAR WARS. According to *Leonard Maltin's Movie Guide*, the 1958 Japanese film that was "acknowledged by George Lucas as a primary inspiration for *Star Wars*" is *Hidden Fortress*, directed by Akira Kurosawa. The comedy-adventure "deals with the adventures of a strong-willed princess—à la Carrie Fisher, in the space fantasy—and her wise, sword-wielding protector—Toshiro Mifune, in the role adapted for Alec Guinness," says *Video Guide*. The two other main characters, a pair of bumbling farmers, are said to have been models for C-3PO and R2-D2.

THE "MAN WITH NO NAME." The character in *A Fistful of Dollars* (1964), who made Clint Eastwood a movie star, was also inspired by Kurosawa. "It is almost a scene-for-scene remake of Akira Kurosawa's *Yojimbo*, the tale of a lone samurai (played by Toshiro Mifune) who comes to a town torn by two rival gangs of fighters. He plays them against each other . . . and in the end finishes off pretty much the whole town and leaves with all the money. Replace a samurai with a gunslinger and replace the Japanese village with a small Western town, and you have *A Fistful of Dollars*." (*Real Video*)

JAMES T. WEST. Robert Conrad, the original star of TV's *Wild, Wild West*, fashioned James West's movements after a favorite actor—Toshiro Mifune.

DOLLY PARTON. Her famous "look" was inspired by a woman in her hometown. (No, not Toshiro Mifune.) Parton says: "There was this tramp that lived in our town, I better not say her name, 'cause she's probably got kids and grandkids now. But back then, she wore these bright-colored clothes and she had this peroxide yellow hair—yellow, not blond—and she used to walk up and down the streets of our hometown and they always said, 'Oh she's just trash, she's just a whore.' But I thought she was beautiful."

their employer offered them a **"$1,000 shopping spree at the store of their choice."**

IT'S A WEIRD, WEIRD WORLD

More proof that truth really is stranger than fiction.

¡YO QUIERO CASA SANCHEZ!

"A Mexican restaurant in San Francisco offered a lifetime of free lunches to anyone willing to get a tattoo of its logo, Jimmy the Corn Man, a sombrero-wearing mariachi boy riding a blazing corn-cob. Amazingly, 38 people have braved the needle for a permanent coupon at Casa Sanchez so far. 'I think people have gotten much stupider tattoos for much stupider reasons,' says tattoo artist Barnaby Williams, who created 30 of the 'body coupons.'"
—*USA Today*, April 13, 1999

TERRORIST VOGUE

"Carlos the Jackal was one of the world's most notorious and elusive terrorists, accused of 83 deaths worldwide and more than a dozen other charges stemming from a 20-year killing spree.

"After two decades of evading the law, he was arrested in a Sudanese hospital while undergoing liposuction and a tummy tuck."
—*San Francisco Chronicle*

NOSING AROUND

"Ruth Clarke, 23, of London, England, underwent surgery to correct a lifelong breathing problem in 1981. She was presented with a tiddlywink, which doctors had removed from her nose.

"Clarke vaguely recalled losing the disk as a tot, but she didn't dream it was right under her nose all the time."
—*Encyclopedia Brown's Book of Strange Facts*

THE POSTMAN RINGS MORE THAN TWICE

"From 1974 to 1976, a young man in Taiwan who wrote 700 love letters to his girlfriend, trying to talk her into marriage. He suc-ceeded—she married the mailman who delivered the letters to her."
—*Weird News and Strange Stories*

If a grasshopper is hungry enough, it will eat the paint off your house.

THEY WENT THATAWAY

Malcolm Forbes wrote the fascinating book, They Went Thataway, *about the deaths of famous people. Here are a few of the stories he found.*

ALEXANDER THE GREAT

Claim to Fame: Greek conqueror who lived from 356 B.C. to 323 B.C.

How He Died: Complications stemming from a drinking contest

Postmortem: In 323 Alexander was in Babylon preparing to lead his troops into battle. One evening at a banquet, he got into a drinking contest with some of his soldiers and is believed to have consumed as much as a gallon and a half of wine. He woke up the next morning feeling miserable; a chill brought on by cold weather only made things worse. Ten days later he was dead.

W. C. FIELDS

Claim to Fame: Film comedian and legendary drunk

How He Died: Drank himself to death

Postmortem: Excessive drinking was the hallmark of Fields's onscreen persona; with his bloated physique and enormous, fleshy red nose, he made a perfect movie buffoon. But if anything, he drank more in real life than in his films. He was notorious for polishing off two quarts of gin a day, and as early as 1936 spent a year in a sanatorium recovering from pneumonia and tuberculosis aggravated by drinking. He cut back on the booze . . . but only until his health returned.

By the early 1940s, decades of hard drinking had damaged Fields's health to the point where he no longer had the strength to appear in feature-length films; he was reduced to making short cameo appearances in heavy pancake makeup that hid the burst veins in his face. When his landlord raised the rent on his house in the fall of 1946, Fields just checked back into the sanatorium. He was failing fast—he had cirrhosis of the liver, cardiac edema, weakened kidneys, and stomach troubles—and the booze that friends

---

When you use your car's brakes, they generate enough heat to warm your house.

smuggled into the sanatorium only made things worse. On Christmas Day in 1946, Fields suffered a massive stomach hemorrhage and died a few hours later. He was 67.

PLINY THE ELDER

Claim to Fame: Preeminent historian and scientist of the ancient Roman Empire. Much of what we know about life in ancient Rome comes from Pliny's numerous writings.

How He Died: Killed by his own curiosity

Postmortem: One day in A.D. 79, Pliny's sister woke him up from a nap to tell him about a huge cloud of smoke that was rising from the top of a nearby mountain. Pliny, an admiral in the Roman Navy, ordered his ship to investigate.

The mountain was Mt. Vesuvius—an active volcano—and the cloud of smoke was part of an eruption that was burying the city of Pompeii, killing thousands of Romans even as Pliny sailed closer, paying no heed to the huge rocks that were raining down into the waters around his ship.

When his ship got close to the beach, Pliny waded ashore to walk along the base of Mt. Vesuvius and get an even closer look. His companions fled in terror when a huge, ominous-looking black cloud began to descend on the beach, but Pliny did not—and moments later he choked to death in a cloud of sulfurous gas.

MARIE CURIE

Claim to Fame: First woman to win the Nobel Prize for discovering the element radium and pioneering the study of radioactivity.

How She Died: Massive radiation poisoning

Postmortem: Although Curie helped discover radioactivity, she never understood its destructive power. She routinely handled radioactive material without any lead shielding, and as a result, suffered from radiation-induced exhaustion and even painful lesions on her hands.

When World War I broke out, Curie went to the battlefields of Europe and exposed herself even further, using primitive X-ray equipment to help surgeons find bullets and shrapnel in wounded soldiers. By the early 1930s, her immune system was so compromised by radiation poisoning that she could no longer fight off common illnesses. In July 1934, she died from anemia, a disease that normally would not have been fatal.

Q: What made the Dickin Medal for Valor unique during World War II?

ZZZZ-Z-Z-Z-Z-Z

According to experts, horses, deer, and giraffes sleep an average of only 3 hours a day, while cats get a whopping 15 hours. Humans sleep an average of 7.5 hours a day. What happens during those 7 or so hours while you're sleeping? It will probably always be a mystery, but we have more answers now than we did half a century ago.

THE MYSTERY OF SLEEP

It wasn't until 1954 that science made a big breakthrough and recognized that REM (rapid eye movement) during sleep was caused by dreaming. Since then, the science of sleep has expanded rapidly, with over 100 distinct sleeping disorders now classified and many doctors devoting their careers exclusively to sleep problems.

INTO THE WAVES

Scientists now recognize four stages of sleep:

Stage 1: After your muscles relax, your brain produces smaller waves of 9 to 12 cycles per second. You think normal, everyday thoughts. Pulse and breathing are regular.

Stage 2: Brain waves get larger with sudden bursts. Your eyes go "off" and wouldn't register anything if they were opened. Eyes may roll slowly back and forth.

Stage 3: Brain waves get slower and bigger, about five times larger than in stage 1.

Stage 4: Profound unconsciousness, with the biggest, slowest brainwaves. It takes over an hour to reach this stage. Most people only go to stage 4 once or twice, then come back to lighter sleep (generally stage 1), and experience REM (dream-state).

THE REM EXPERIENCE

Once you're in REM . . .

- The muscles of your middle ear begin vibrating (science doesn't know why).
- Brain waves resemble a waking state, but you're dreaming.
- Muscles are relaxed, but may twitch or move.
- Pulse and breathing speed up. But we breathe less oxygen and use fewer calories than in other stages of sleep.

A: It was awarded to animals: 32 carrier pigeons, 18 dogs, 3 horses, and a cat.

- Blood flow and brain temperature accelerate.
- Eyes dart all over the place, "seeing" what we're dreaming.

The first REM episode averages 10 minutes; then episodes recur on a 90 to 100-minute cycle, with the deeper sleep stages (3 or 4) getting shorter in between. During REM our bodily processes are not operated by the larger, evolved parts of our brain, but by the brain stem—the "ancient brain" we had millions of years ago when we were arboreal (living in trees) mammals.

REM FACTS

- We can dream without REM, but scientists have established that these dreams are simple and uneventful. REM dreaming, on the other hand, is the more exciting, dramatic kind. We do REM dreaming about two hours a night. In a lifetime, this adds up to 5 or 6 years of REM dreaming.

- You may think that because your body seems to go offline, your mind does too. Not so. Your brain spends the night integrating the info and experiences you've gained during the day, and most of this happens during REM sleep. Laboratory tests showed that if mice learned complex tasks and then were deprived of their REM time, they forgot what they learned. In tests on University of Ottawa students, researchers noticed that the faster students learned things, the more REM time they required. Slower learners needed less REM time.

- Life stresses and changes also increase the need for REM. Using a group of divorcing women in their early 30s as subjects, psycho-analyst Rosalind Cartwright conducted a study that demonstrated they needed more REM time to assimilate their big changes.

- Among people over 65, those who are mentally sharper experience REM more frequently.

- Most people don't reach REM until about an hour and a half after going to sleep; people with depression, however, get to REM in about half this time. They also experience it more intensely.

- REM occupies approximately 22 percent of sleeping time. Pleasant dreams.

Bug rule of thumb: Centipedes are carnivores, millipedes are vegetarians.

BRITS VS. AMERICANS: A WORD QUIZ

People in both countries speak English, but we don't necessarily use the same words. For instance, the British call a raincoat a "mackintosh." See if you can match the British words to their American counterparts.

BRITISH	AMERICAN
1. Knackered	a. Dessert
2. Crumpet	b. Heated argument
3. Stone	c. Moron
4. Nick	d. Umbrella
5. Afters	e. Sandwich
6. Rubber	f. Pleased
7. Lollipop lady	g. An attractive woman
8. Berk	h. Sneakers
9. Pilchards	i. Easy task
10. Chuffed	j. Iffy, suspect
11. Redundant	k. Stupid
12. Yob	l. Exhausted
13. Brolly	m. Run (in stockings)
14. Spot on	n. Crossing guard
15. Naff	o. Worthless, unfashionable
16. Dodgy	p. Diaper
17. Nappy	q. Steal
18. Nutter	r. Kook
19. Butty	s. Sardines
20. Plonk	t. Cheap wine
21. Doddle	u. Unemployed
22. Starkers	v. Eraser
23. Tailback	w. Perfect
24. Wally	x. Naked
25. Gormless	y. Fourteen pounds
26. Wonky	z. Traffic jam
27. Ladder	aa. Nerd
28. Daps	bb. Unstable
29. Argy-bargy	cc. Hooligan

27. m   24. aa   21. i   18. r   15. o   12. cc   9. s   6. v   3. y
29. b   26. bb   23. z   20. t   17. p   14. w   11. u   8. c   5. a   2. g
28. h   25. k   22. x   19. e   16. j   13. d   10. f   7. n   4. q   1. l

If you count things compulsively, you're an *arithmomaniac*.

LAUNCHING AIR JORDAN

If you had to name just one person associated with an athletic shoe, it would be Michael Jordan, right? Here's how he became Air Jordan, from the BRI's long-time pop historian, Jack Mingo.

WALKING ON AIR

The air-filled shoe wasn't Nike's idea. The first air sole was patented in 1882, and over 70 more were registered with the U.S. Patent Office before 1969. They all failed because of technical problems.

In 1969, a designer named Frank Rudy gave it a shot. He left a job at Rockwell International during a downturn in the aerospace industry, and invested his time and money in an effort to develop a running shoe with air soles. After many attempts, he finally succeeded by using a thin polyurethane bag for an air cushion. Then he convinced the Bata shoe company to try it out.

The first prototypes worked great. Unfortunately, it was the middle of the oil embargo of 1974, and Bata's supplier quietly changed its polyurethane formula to use less oil. The new formula wasn't as strong as the old one; when the soles warmed up and air pressure increased, they would explode like a rifle shot. Bata suddenly lost interest.

LAST ATTEMPT

Nearly broke and desperate, Rudy flew to France to show Adidas what he had. He didn't get anywhere with them, but while he was hanging around the Adidas offices, he heard an employee mention a little U.S. company named Nike that was selling running shoes on the West Coast. Rudy made some calls, found out there was a running shoe trade show that weekend in Anaheim, and caught the next flight to Southern California.

He stopped by the Nike booth in Anaheim just as it was closing and got the name of the company's president, Phil Knight. Rudy

Snails have teeth.

immediately found a pay phone and called Knight at Nike's headquarters in Beaverton, Oregon. Knight listened to Rudy's story, then invited him for a visit.

NIKE JUMPS IN

Knight, an amateur runner, personally took Rudy's air-filled shoes for a run. They slowly deflated as he ran, but he saw their potential. "It was a great ride while it lasted," he told Rudy. Then he put Rudy on retainer for six months, to see if he could make the idea work.

After much trial and error, Nike finally came up with something they liked—an inflated midsole that went between the regular sole of a shoe and the runner's foot. Nike called their new creation the Tailwind and rushed it into production at $50 retail—the highest price anyone had ever charged for a mass-produced running shoe. But runners bought them anyway. Unfortunately, a last-minute fabric switch resulted in a shoe that fell apart after a short time, infuriating customers. About half of the shoes were returned as defective.

Nike eventually got the bugs out. This time they decided not to release the shoe directly into the marketplace. They were going to wait and try something special.

LUCKY CHOICE

Meanwhile, Nike was reevaluating its marketing strategy. The company had been paying professional athletes anywhere from $8,000 to $10,000 apiece to wear and endorse their shoes. One day in 1983, Nike execs did an analysis and found they "owned" about half of the players in the NBA—at a cost of millions of dollars a year. In fact, they had 2,000 athletes on their endorsement roster. It was getting more expensive all the time and it wasn't necessarily winning them any more business.

So they decided to switch tactics and find one promising rookie... then sign him to a long-term contract before he got too expensive. They considered Charles Barkley and Patrick Ewing, but finally settled on 20-year-old college junior Michael Jordan. Their plan was to design a brand-new shoe for him, push it hard, and tie the product to the man (and vice versa), so when consumers saw the player, they'd think "shoes!"

Second most-published playwright in history, after Shakespeare: Neil Simon.

LAUNCHING AIR JORDAN

They had just the right product—the air-cushioned sole. Nike offered Jordan $2.5 million for a five-year contract, plus royalties on every Air Jordan shoe sold. But Jordan turned them down. He didn't particularly like Nike shoes. In fact, he loved Adidas and was willing to make concessions to sign with them. He told their representatives, "You don't even have to match Nike's deal—just come close." But Adidas wasn't interested. They offered only $100,000 a year, with no special shoe and no royalties. So, in August 1984, Jordan signed with Nike.

Nike came up with the distinctive black and red design for the Jordan shoe. In fact, it was so distinctive that the NBA commissioner threatened to fine him $1,000 if he wore Air Jordan shoes during games, because they violated the NBA "uniformity of uniform" clause. Jordan wore them anyway, creating an uproar in the stands and in the press...and Nike gladly paid the fine.

FLYING SOLO

It was the beginning of a brilliant advertising campaign. Air Jordan went on to become the most successful athletic endorsement in history, selling over $100 million worth of merchandise in the first year alone. The dark side: Air Jordans became so popular that it became dangerous to wear them in some cities, as teenagers began killing other teenagers for their $110 sneakers. And the company was embarrassed—or should have been—by the revelation that a worker in its Far East sweatshops would have to work for several weeks to make enough money to buy a pair.

Despite occasional bad publicity and considerable competition over the years, however, Air Jordans became so successful that in 1997, Michael Jordan and Nike announced that after his retirement from professional basketball, Jordan would be heading his own division of Nike.

* * *

BET YOU DIDN'T KNOW

The singer Engelbert Humperdinck's real name is Gerry Dorsey. Dorsey didn't make either his first or last name up, though: He borrowed them from a famous German composer. The original Engelbert Humperdinck wrote the opera *Hänsel and Gretel*.

SPACED-OUT SPORTS

They give an awful lot of interviews, but sports stars—and even announcers—aren't always the most articulate people.

"Our similarities are different."
—**Dale Berra, on his father**

"Sutton lost 13 games in a row without winning a ball game."
—**Ralph Kiner**

"It's not so much maturity as it is growing up."
—**Jay Miller, hockey player, asked if his improved play was due to maturity**

"I've got a great repertoire with my players."
—**Danny Ozark**

"Three things are bad for you. I can't remember the first two, but doughnuts are the third."
—**Bill Petersen**

"There comes a time in every man's life, and I've had plenty of them."
—**Casey Stengel**

"Tony Gwynn was named player of the year for April."
—**Ralph Kiner**

"I just talked to the doctor. He told me her contraptions were an hour apart."
—**Mackey Sasser, on his wife's pregnancy**

"Noah."
—**Barry Bonnel, former Seattle Mariner, asked to name his all-time favorite Mariner**

"His reputation preceded him before he got here."
—**Don Mattingly**

"He slides into second with a stand-up double."
—**Jerry Coleman**

"Not true at all. Vaseline is manufactured right here in the U.S.A."
—**Don Sutton, on accusations that he doctored baseballs with a foreign substance**

"You have to be stupid, and this works out well for me."
—**Bubba Baker, on playing in the NFL**

"I'm going to cancel my prescription."
—**Bob Stanley, on being criticized in a Boston paper**

"What would I do that for? It only gets Spanish stations."
—**Jeff Stone, on why he wouldn't bring his TV back to the U.S. after playing in Venezuela**

. . . but nearly 50% say they're "self-conscious about it."

LOST IN TRANSLATION

Have you ever thought you were communicating brilliantly, only to find out that others thought you were a lunatic? That's an especially easy mistake to make when you're speaking a foreign language or dealing with a foreign culture. A few examples:

PRODUCT CONFUSION

Gerber Baby Food: Gerber used the same packaging strategy in Africa that it uses in America—a picture of the Gerber baby on the label. They apparently didn't realize that since many Africans don't read, it's standard practice to put pictures of the contents on jar labels. As you might guess, the product didn't go over well.

The Dairy Association: Taking their "Got Milk?" campaign to Mexico, they translated their slogan into Spanish. Unfortunately, it came out as "Are you lactating?"

Johnson Wax: When Johnson introduced their furniture cleaner Pledge into the Netherlands, they didn't know that, in Dutch, Pledge means "piss."

MEDIA TRANSLATIONS

In the late 1970s, the TV sitcom *Laverne and Shirley* was shown in Bangkok, Thailand—where women did not act like the show's main characters. Each program was preceded by a disclaimer saying: "The two women depicted in the following episode are from an insane asylum."

According to one source, audiences in Lebanon were going to see *Titanic* because the title in Arabic slang translates as *Let's Have Sex.*

MIXED-UP MENUS

These items are from real menus. Bon appétit.
Horse-rubbish sauce (Rome)
Torture soup (Djerba)
Crab Meat Shaag and Botty Kebab (New York)
Terminal soup (Istanbul)
Farte aux Fraises (Turkey)

32% of women and 8% of men say they're better at doing the laundry than their spouse.

Frozen soap with Peccadilloes (Madrid)
Stewed abalone with 3 things and lucky duck (Bangkok)

SCREWED-UP SIGNS
A street sign in London reads: "Dead slow children at play."

When English/Spanish signs were first posted at Sky Harbor International Airport in Phoenix, Arizona, they were full of mistakes. One sign, meant to remind arriving travelers to declare fruits, vegetables, and meats, read "Violadores Seran Finados," which translates as "Violators Will Be Deceased."

DIPLOMATIC SNAFUS
A French ambassador, M. Cambon, once thanked a Chicago mayor for a tour of the city. "Thank you," he said. "But I am sorry so to cockroach on your time." The mayor replied, "But you don't mean 'cockroach,' Mr. Cambon; it is 'encroach' you mean." "Oh, is it?" Cambon asked. "I see, a difference in gender."

An Englishwoman at a French diplomatic party asked a Frenchman for a light. What he heard instead was, "Are you a dung-hill?"

CAMPING INSTRUCTIONS
These regulations were posted at a campground in Italy:
- Cars must enter or go away from the camp with motors out.
- THEN IS STRICTLY FORBIDDEN TO:
    a. Reserve box parking, spaces with chairs, fences, rape, or other means
    b. Dainage of the plants and equipman
    c. Dig simples around tents
    d. Set to go into the camp, not authorized from the direction
- The above listed rules are inappellable. All of the camping personnel are authorized to send away anyone who does follow them.

IT'S JUST A TITLE, AFTER ALL
You have to wonder what Chinese movie audiences think they're going to see when U.S. films are shown in China as (for example):

> **Kindergarten Cop:** *Devil King of Children*
> **Indecent Proposal:** *Peach-Colored Transaction*
> **The Shawshank Redemption:** *Excitement 1995*

City with the largest Polish population: Warsaw. Second largest: Chicago.

GO, GO GOETHE

He's reluctant to admit it, but Uncle John does read things besides
The History of Parking Meters *and* Famous Movie Monsters. *He*
even has a favorite philosopher—Johann Wolfgang von Goethe.

"What is the best government? That which teaches us to govern ourselves."

"Legislators and revolutionaries who promise liberty and equality at the same time are either utopian dreamers or charlatans."

"Only law can give us freedom."

"If a man stops to ponder over his physical or moral condition, he generally discovers that he is ill."

"Preoccupation with immortality is for the upper classes, particularly ladies with nothing to do. An able man, who has a regular job and must toil and produce day by day, leaves the future world to itself, and is active and useful in this one."

"Never tell people how you are: they don't want to know."

"If youth is a fault, one soon gets rid of it."

"Fools and wise men are equally harmless. It is the half-fools and the half-wise who are dangerous."

"A clever man commits no minor blunders."

"Know thyself? If I knew myself, I'd run away."

"Whatever you can do, or dream you can, begin it. Boldness has genius, power, and magic in it."

"Only the artist sees spirits. But after he has told of their appearing to him, everybody sees them."

"You can't understand something if you don't possess it."

"Nothing shows a man's character more than what he laughs at."

"Viewed from the summit of reason, all life looks like a malignant disease and the world like a madhouse."

You can buy horseradish ice cream in Tokyo.

MR. TOAD'S WILD RIDE, PART II

Here's the second part of the story of Kenneth Grahame's classic, The Wind in the Willows—*which has been adapted by everyone from A.A. Milne, who wrote the play* Toad of Toad Hall *in 1930, to Walt Disney, who animated it in 1949. (Part I starts on page 48.)*

SMEDLEY'S WILES

Magazines and publishers regularly begged Kenneth Grahame for articles . . . or perhaps a sequel to *The Golden Age* or *Dream Days*. But Grahame had become a notorious recluse; even getting an interview with him was nearly impossible.

In 1907 an American magazine called *Everybody's* put Constance Smedley on the job. The editors told Smedley to get Grahame to write something—anything. She was clever, and wrote to the author saying she was a relative of Governess Smedley—a fictional character in *The Golden Age* and *Dream Days*—who wanted to visit. Grahame was delighted. The two became good friends . . . but he still wouldn't write for her. Grahame said writing "was like physical torture," and "he hated it."

Smedley visited often. One evening, she overheard Grahame telling Mouse his bedtime story and, as one biographer put it, "moved in for the kill." She insisted that Grahame already had a story—he just needed to write it down. He even had much of the material for the book in the letters he'd written to Mouse. To his own surprise, Grahame agreed, and began expanding the letters into a book—the first professional writing he'd done in nine years.

He finished *The Wind in the Reeds* (as he called it) by Christmas 1907, "and packed it up and sent it to the eager Constance Smedley, who dispatched it to her editors, waiting excitedly in New York."

FALSE START

The New Yorkers were stunned. Grahame's other books had been about children—not wild animals. To Smedley's mortification, they turned the book down flat. The manuscript was sent back to

Grahame, who gave it to his agent. But the agent couldn't find anyone in England who was willing to publish it, either.

The problem seemed to be that adults didn't understand *The Wind in the Willows* (now changed from *Reeds* to avoid confusion with an upcoming book by W. B. Yeats). It was a new genre—a novel-length animal fantasy that was not an allegory and had no human protagonist. "*The Wind in the Willows* had no clear generic predecessor," explains a Grahame biographer. "[It] shifted the identification of the reader to the animals themselves . . . and the first adults to read the work simply couldn't adapt to the change."

When Grahame finally did get his book published, he discovered that critics couldn't relate to his story, either. Some criticized it as a poorly thought-out allegory ("Grown up readers will find it monstrous and elusive"); others assumed that since it expressed such an "intimate sympathy with Nature," it was meant to be natural history. One newspaper commented that *The Wind in the Willows*—a book featuring a toad driving a car—would "win no credence from the very best authorities on biology." Even the *Times of London* wrote irrelevantly: "As a contribution to natural history the work is negligible."

One result of the confusion was that the book sold poorly. Another: Grahame couldn't find an American publisher.

THE PRESIDENT STEPS IN

This is where President Teddy Roosevelt figures in the story. Roosevelt was a big fan of Grahame's work. Years earlier, he had met millionaire book collector Austin Purves and learned that Purves knew Grahame. He sent Purves back to England with a request for autographed copies of *The Golden Age* and *Dream Days*.

Grahame, of course, complied, and Roosevelt wrote back, saying "No one you could have sent those books to would have appreciated them more than Mrs. Roosevelt and I." He invited Grahame to stay at the White House if he visited Washington, but Grahame never did.

When *The Wind in the Willows* was published in England, Grahame sent Roosevelt an autographed copy. But Roosevelt chose not to read it. He had recently written an article denouncing stories that confused animals with human beings, and after

In the 1820s, a temperance movement tried to ban coffee, and nearly succeeded.

seeing the reviews of *Willows*, feared it would ruin his love of Grahame's other books.

However, Roosevelt's wife found the book at the White House and started reading it aloud to their children. Roosevelt overheard her and became fascinated with the story. He later wrote to Grahame:

> For some time I could not accept the mole, the water-rat and the badger . . . But after a while Mrs. Roosevelt and two of the boys, Kermit and Ted, all quite independently, got hold of *The Wind in the Willows* and took such a delight in it that I began to feel that I might have to revise my judgement. Then Mrs. Roosevelt read it aloud to the younger children, and I listened now and then . . . I have since read the book three times, and now all the characters are my dearest friends.

The Roosevelt children sent their copies of the book to England to be autographed by Grahame. Meanwhile, Grahame's agent was still trying to find an American publisher. He had just sent the manuscript to Scribner's—who informed him that they were not interested—when a note arrived at the publisher from President Roosevelt. It said: "*The Wind in the Willows* is such a beautiful thing, Scribner must publish it."

Scribner did. And never regretted it. The book sold slowly at first, but caught on and went through many printings. Its success in the U.S. made it a hit in England, too.

By 1908 Grahame (no longer with the bank) was living comfortably off the royalties from his books. *Willows* changed popular tastes and paved the way for the genre of animal fantasies, which includes everything from Mickey Mouse to *Charlotte's Web*.

NOTE: The story doesn't have a particularly happy ending, however. Like Peter, who inspired *Peter Pan* (see page 436), Mouse committed suicide. One day while he was at college, he went for a walk and never came back. He had been hit by a train. Officials called it an accident, but the wounds showed he had been lying on the tracks when the train came.

In 1912 the Archbishop of Paris declared dancing the tango a sin.

DUMB CROOKS

Here's more proof that crime doesn't pay.

NOTE-ABLY STUPID
"A 24-year-old man was pulled over outside of Buffalo, New York, for driving at night without headlights. When the patrolman asked to see his license, the driver began nervously searching in the car and eventually produced a handful of cards and papers. Among the various identification, the patrolman found a note which contained the message, 'I have a gun. Put all the money in the envelope quickly!' The note was linked to a heist [that occurred] two days earlier in which the man and a 25-year-old accomplice had robbed a Buffalo bank."

—Disorganized Crime

DRIVEN TO TEARS
SPRINGFIELD, OR—"On July 8, a teenage boy approached a 1995 Dodge Neon, pointed a handgun at the driver and ordered all of the passengers out of the car.

"The boy started to drive off, but the vehicle immediately stalled at the intersection . . . because he couldn't drive a stick shift.

"The would-be thief ran off, along with two other hidden accomplices. They were later arrested and charged each with three counts of robbery and kidnapping."

—Medford, Oregon, Mail Tribune, July 9, 1999

RIGHT ON TIME
"Stephen E. Peterson, of Fort Collins, Colorado, was arrested for robbing the same 7-Eleven twice in one day. After the second holdup, he promised the clerk he'd be back in a few hours to clean the place out a third time. True to his word, Peterson returned, and the cops nabbed him."

—Maxim magazine

NO NEED TO DUST FOR PRINTS
"Cary L. Rider, 43, was recently arrested for burglary in Illinois after police found him in the hospital. The burglar had tried to

It takes twice as long to lose new muscle if you stop working out than it did to gain it.

move a safe, but it fell on his left hand—and his glove was found underneath it, still containing the top part of the burglar's middle finger . . . Said one officer: 'He admitted it. What can you do if your finger's there?'"

—*The Portland Oregonian*, **November 21, 1997**

RATS!

"An 18-year-old man walked into a store in Scotland and held a rat up to the cashier's face. The man then instructed the cashier to 'give me all your money or I'll sic my rat on you.' The cashier just laughed."

—*Disorganized Crime*

NOT READY FOR HALLOWEEN

"J. Douglas Cresswell tried to rob a motel while disguised by a black garbage sack over his head. The trouble was that he had forgotten to cut eyeholes in the sack; his frantic efforts to punch holes in the sack with his fingers as he stumbled towards the door delayed his getaway and he was arrested by the police. He was jailed for twenty-five years."

—*Mammoth Book of Oddities*

TIME TO SPARE

"John William Howard, 45, fled Maryland, where he was wanted on sexual assault charges, and headed for Arizona. Passing through Brookshire, Texas, low on gas and cash, he tried to sell his spare tire to raise some money. A local merchant informed him about a police loan program for just such predicaments, so Howard went to the police station to apply. A routine check turned up his fugitive status, according to Police Chief Joe Garcia, who called Howard 'one of the world's dumbest criminals.'"

—*Dumb Crooks* **Web site**

NEW RECYCLING PROGRAM

"A [robber] in Mainz, Germany, got clean away with a bag of rubbish in April 1995. A clerk filled his carrier bag from the wastepaper bin rather than the cash drawer, and the thief dashed off without checking."

—*The Fortean Times Book of Inept Crime*

Q: What's the average age kids begin to use a microwave? A: Seven.

AESOP'S FABLES

Aesop's fables (see page 173) have been told and retold for thousands of years. Here are a few more we've picked to pass on.

THE FOX AND THE GRAPES

A fox was walking along the road, when he spied some delicious-looking grapes growing on a high trellis. "My, they look good!" he said. He jumped up, but couldn't reach them. He tried again and again, but to no avail. Finally he looked angrily at the grapes and said, "Hmmm, who wants the old grapes? They're probably sour anyway."

Moral: *It's easy to despise what you can't have.*

THE SICK LION

A lion, unable from old age and infirmities to provide himself with food by force, resolved to do so by trickery. He returned to his den, and lying down there, pretended to be sick, taking care that his sickness should be publicly known. The beasts expressed their sorrow, and came one by one to his den, where the lion devoured them. After many of the beasts had thus disappeared, a fox, presenting himself to the lion, stood on the outside of the cave, at a respectful distance, and asked him how he was. "I am very middling," replied the lion, "but why are you standing out there? Please come in and talk with me." "No, thank you," said the fox. "I notice that there are many footprints entering your cave, but I see no trace of any returning."

Moral: *The wise person learns from the misfortunes of others.*

THE FOOLISH TRAVELERS

A man and his son were walking along the road to market with their donkey. As they walked, they met a couple. "Did you ever see anything so silly?" the man said to his wife. "Two men walking when they have a donkey with them. What's a donkey for, after all, if not to carry a man?"

Hearing this, the man put his son on the back of the donkey and they went on their way. Soon they met two countrymen. "Did you ever see such a terrible thing?" one cried. "The strong young man rides while his poor father must walk." So the boy dismounted and the father got on instead.

They hadn't gone very far when they met two women. "Look at that heartless father!" exclaimed one of them. "His poor little son must walk while he rides." At that, the man said to his son, "Come up here with me. We'll both ride."

They both rode for a while until they reached a group of men. "Aren't you ashamed?" they called out. "Overloading a poor little donkey like that." So the man and his son both climbed off the donkey.

They thought and thought. They couldn't walk along with the donkey, or ride it one at a time, or ride it both together. Then they had an idea. They got a tree and cut it into a long pole. Then they tied the donkey's feet to it, raised the pole to their shoulders, and went on their way, carrying the donkey.

As they crossed a bridge, the donkey—who didn't like being tied up—kicked one of his feet loose, causing the father and son to stumble. The donkey fell into the water. Because its feet were tied, it drowned.

Moral: *If you try to please everyone, you'll end up pleasing no one.*

THE ASS AND THE FOX

An ass put on a lion's skin, and roamed around the forest amusing himself by scaring all the foolish animals he met. Finally, he met a fox, and tried to scare him, too—but as soon as the fox heard the ass's voice, he said, "Well, I might have been frightened . . . if I hadn't heard your bray."

Moral: *Clothes may disguise a fool, but his words give him away.*

THE THIRSTY PIGEON

A pigeon, overcome by thirst, saw a glass of water painted on a sign. Not realizing it was only a picture, she quickly flew towards it and crashed into the sign. Her wings broken, she fell to the ground . . . and was captured by a bystander.

Moral: *Zeal should not outrun discretion.*

THE SERPENT AND FILE

A serpent wandered into a carpenter's shop. As he glided over the floor he felt his skin pricked by a file lying there. In a rage he turned and attacked, trying to sink his fangs into the file; but he could do no harm to heavy iron and soon had to give over his wrath.

Moral: *It is useless attacking the insensible.*

Face value of a *Titanic* boarding pass auctioned in 1999: $8. It sold for $100,000.

MORE
CLASSIC HOAXES

Here are a few more of our favorite frauds.

THE PSALMANAZAR HOAX

The Set-Up: In 1703 a "converted heathen from Formosa" [now Taiwan] named George Psalmanazar was introduced to the Bishop of London by a local cleric (actually, his confederate). "In eighteenth-century London," as Laura Foreman writes in *Hoaxes and Deceptions*, "a Formosan was as great a sensation as a Martian would be today," and Psalmanazar became the toast of English society.

People were fascinated with his stories. They were shocked to learn, for example, that before he joined the Anglican faith, he was a cannibal—and that snakes, snake blood, and raw meat, including the flesh of executed criminals, were delicacies in Formosa. Divorce customs were similarly barbaric: If a Formosan man grew tired of his wife, "he had only to accuse her of adultery, and he then was entitled to cut off her head and eat her." Psalmanazar taught himself to eat raw meat, and whenever he dined with upper-class hosts, would insist on it.

The Bishop of London sent the "reformed savage" to Oxford University to study and to lecture on Formosan language and history. While he was there, the Anglican Church commissioned him to translate the Bible into Formosan (a language he promptly invented). The following year, Psalmanazar wrote his extremely popular *Historical and Geographical Description of Formosa*, complete with comprehensive descriptions of Formosan art, culture, diet, dress, and language. Among his disclosures: Formosan religion demanded that the hearts of 18,000 Formosan boys under the age of nine were sacrificed to the gods every year, "a population-depleting practice offset by the sparing of eldest sons, and polygamy."

Why It Worked: No one in England had ever been to Formosa, and Psalmanazar was so inventive that when a doubting missionary who really had spent 18 years in China challenged him publicly,

Psalmanazar made him look foolish. Plus, the English of the time were incredibly gullible about other cultures. When, for example, they asked why he didn't he look Oriental, Psalmanazar explained that the ruling class spent all their time in underground houses—it was only the workers whose skin turned "yellow." The public bought it.

Perhaps the real reason Psalmanazar was so successful was religious chauvinism. He roundly criticized Catholic missionary work in Asia and embraced the Anglican Church—confirming as an outsider what many English felt was true anyway. And in 1700, it was considered a real feather in the English church's cap to have converted a cannibal when Catholics couldn't.

What Happened: Psalmanazar's graphic descriptions of life in Formosa were at odds with everyone else's, and skeptics kept attacking until he was finally exposed as a fraud by Dr. Edmund Halley (of comet fame) in 1706. Halley quizzed Psalmanazar on just how much sunlight those underground houses got—and Psalmanazar got this, as well as other phenomena, wrong. He finally admitted having made everything up—including the "language" he spoke—and confessed to being a Frenchman. But he never revealed his true identity . . . it remains a mystery to this day.

THE BARON OF ARIZONA

The Set-Up: In 1883 a man named James Addison Reavis filed legal papers claiming ownership of more than 17,000 square miles of territory in what is now Arizona and New Mexico.

This wasn't as far-fetched as it might sound: when the U.S. government purchased the Arizona Territory from Mexico in 1848, it agreed to honor all Spanish land grants, and according to Reavis, the land had been presented to Don Miguel de Peralta de la Cordoba in 1748 by the King of Spain. Reavis said he'd bought the land and title from the family that had inherited it, and now he was staking his claim.

If Reavis's claim was true, the thousands of people living and working in Arizona were there illegally . . . and could be forced to leave. At the time, there were thousands of land grants being processed and verified by the United States. Reavis's was just the biggest (and most outrageous). Government experts pronounced it real.

"The claim brought panic to the territory," writes one historian, "and an outpouring of riches to the new baron." Railroads, mines, and other businesses began paying him for the right to use his land. Over the next decade, he collected more than $10 million.

Why It Worked: Reavis was an extremely talented forger who had spent years laying the groundwork for his fraud. In particular, he had traveled to Spain where, after getting access to historic documents, he had skillfully altered them to create a record of the (nonexistent) Peralta family and their land grant. Then he produced impeccable copies of the grant itself.

What Happened: There are different accounts of how the hoax was eventually discovered. According to one source, a newspaper publisher noticed that the typestyle on one of the documents was too recent to be authentic, and that the watermark on the paper was from a Wisconsin paper mill that had not even been built when the document was supposedly drafted.

Another says that technology did Reavis in. When he planned his scheme, Reavis knew nothing of scientific innovations that would make it possible for investigators to test the age of paper and ink. By 1893 suspicious officials were able to have the tests done— and they revealed that the 135-year-old documents "were written in the wrong kind of ink on 10-year-old parchment." Reavis was sentenced to six years in prison for his crime, and died penniless in 1908.

* * *

THAT'S ART!

- How slow a painter was Paul Cézanne? So slow that when he painted a bowl of fruit, it wasn't uncommon for the fruit to begin to rot before he finished painting. So he used waxed fruit for models.

- In the 19th century a 26-year-old painter named Richard Dadd went insane, killed his father, and was confined to an asylum. The asylum let him continue his painting . . . and his insanity actually improved his painting ability: *Oberon and Titania*, one of the works he painted at the asylum, is considered one of the greatest paintings of the Victorian era.

What's another word for *minonette*? "Volleyball."

BIRTH OF A GIANT, PART III

By now you know that the patent for the first modern bathtub spawned General Motors. But whatever happened to Billy Durant and David Buick? Read on. Here's Part III of the story. (Part II is on page 312.)

COMEBACK

The bank-appointed executives who took control of GM from Billy Durant made a number of moves that helped restore the company to health. They shut down all of the money-losing divisions and used the money they saved to improve quality at Buick, Oldsmobile, Cadillac, and other divisions that showed promise. In just a few years, they rescued the company from the brink of bankruptcy, paid back all bankers, and built GM into one of the most competitive auto companies in the U.S.

But the executives made a mistake that would cost them dearly: they discontinued the Buick Model 10, a low-priced Buick that Durant had created to compete against Ford's Model T. Short-sighted GM executives were skeptical that smaller, cheaper cars would ever make any money (the Model T would become the bestselling car in American automobile history). So they scrapped the Model 10, despite the fact that it was the most popular car in the Buick lineup, and concentrated on building bigger, more expensive cars.

The decision was a disaster for Buick: sales at the division dropped more than 50 percent in one year, forcing GM to shut down entire assembly plants and lay off hundreds of workers.

SEE THE U.S.A.

The crisis at Buick gave Durant an opening. In 1911 he bought an abandoned Buick factory, staffed it with Buick auto workers who'd been laid off during the sales slump, and announced that he was forming a new company to manufacture and sell cars designed by Louis Chevrolet, one of the most famous race car drivers of the day.

Some of the larger Chevrolets really were designed by Louis

Chevrolet . . . but the new company's bestselling model, introduced in 1915, was basically a Buick Model 10 that had been rechristened the Chevrolet 490 (so named because it sold for $490). Priced just $50 higher than the Model T—but equipped with an electric starter and other features that the Model T lacked—the 490 was poised to give Ford a run for its money.

And thanks almost entirely to the 490, sales at Chevrolet nearly tripled from 5,000 cars to more than 13,500 cars in 1915, making Chevrolet one of the top auto companies in the country. Durant had done it again . . . and he was only getting started.

HE'S B-A-A-A-CK

Even as he was building Chevrolet into an automotive powerhouse, as early as 1913 Durant began secretly acquiring large blocks of General Motors stock. He encouraged friends and associates to do the same, and even convinced the DuPont chemical company to acquire more than 25 percent of GM.

On September 16, 1915, Durant pounced. He showed up at GM's annual shareholders meeting accompanied by several assistants carrying bushel baskets filled with the GM stock certificates that Durant either owned or controlled. "Gentleman," Durant calmly announced to the room, "I now control this company."

DÉJÀ VU

This time Durant managed to stay on at GM until 1920. He inherited a much stronger, more profitable company than the one he'd left in 1910, but as time passed he began to slip into his old habits. He bought the Sheridan and the Scripps-Booth auto companies and added them to the GM fold, but they did little more than steal sales from GM's other divisions. Durant also bought up several tractor companies and merged them all into what he named GM's Samson Tractor Division . . . which went on to lose more than $42 million before it was finally shut down in 1920.

Durant might have even managed to survive these debacles had the U.S. economy not fallen into a deep recession in 1920. As sales of automobiles dropped sharply, GM's stock price began to plummet, prompting Durant to buy shares in an attempt to keep the stock price from sliding further. It didn't work—by the time Durant exhausted his fortune in November 1920, GM's share price had dropped from a high of nearly $50 to under $12.

Only state with official vegetables: New Mexico, with the chili and the frijole.

But Durant wasn't just broke—he was deep in debt. He had purchased the stock using $20 million borrowed from 21 different stockbrokers and three different banks . . . and had no way to pay the loans back.

DuPont and the other major shareholders worried that if the extent of the company's insolvency became known, the value of GM's stock might collapse entirely. Once again, however, GM was too big to fail—DuPont feared that if GM collapsed it might drag the entire country into a depression, not just Detroit. Rather than allow that to happen, DuPont paid off Durant's loans on the condition that he hand over his GM stock and resign.

Once again, Durant had no alternative.

STRIKE THREE

But Durant was no quitter. He contacted 67 of his friends and told them he was starting another auto company. Forty-eight hours later he had raised more than $7 million in cash, and on January 21, 1921—less than two months after he was forced out of GM—he filed papers incorporating Durant Motors, Inc.

Next, he began taking orders for cars and selling shares in the new company. By January 1, 1923, he had collected cash deposits for more than 231,000 cars and had more stockholders than any other U.S. company except AT&T.

As it had been at Chevrolet, the most popular car of the Durant Motors line was the one designed to compete against the Ford Model T. The car was called the Durant Star and sold fairly well . . . until Henry Ford unexpectedly lowered the price of the Model T. Durant was not able to match him.

Two other cars, the Flint and the Durant Six, never caught on with the public, and although Durant Motors held its own through the 1920s, the company finally went under in 1933, during the Great Depression. Durant filed for personal bankruptcy three years later, listing more than $914,000 in debts and only $250 in assets (his clothes).

LAST STOP

A few months later, some reporters located Durant, washing dishes and sweeping the floor in a former Durant Motors salesroom that had been converted into a hamburger restaurant and a Food Market grocery store. Durant owned them both, and he would later

The largest of the Easter Island statues weighs more than 80 tons.

add some bowling alleys to his holdings. It was his final attempt at empire building.

"Mr. Durant is just as enthusiastic over building up the Food Market as he ever was over automobiles," Durant's nephew told reporters. "In fact, he no longer can bear the thought of an automobile." Durant died 11 years later at the age of 86.

BYE, BYE BUICK

David Buick fared worse than William Durant. Although he sat on the Buick Co. board of directors, Buick was so deeply in debt that he owned only one share of Buick Co. stock. When he resigned from the company in 1908, Durant reportedly gave him a severance check for $100,000. Buick quickly burned through the money by investing in a new auto company, a carburetor company, shady oil deals, Florida real estate, and other get-rich-quick schemes. When he died in a Detroit hospital on March 5, 1929, Buick was so broke that, in the words of one reporter, "he could afford neither phone nor Buick."

* * *

THIS SPACE FOR GRAFFITI

The average American uses 730 crayons by the age of 10.

HOMEMADE BESTSELLERS

Some books are published with high expectations but flop. Others have extremely modest beginnings but turn into bestsellers. Here are three.

HOW TO KEEP YOUR VOLKSWAGEN ALIVE

Simple Start: John Muir was an ex-NASA engineer-turned-hippie dropout living in Taos, New Mexico, in the mid 1960s. He supported himself by fixing cars, mostly Volkswagens. But when a friend's Volkswagen broke down while he was too busy to work on it, he typed up some instructions for the friend to follow herself. She got her Volkswagen running again, and Muir decided to turn his instructions into an auto repair manual. He "test-marketed" the book by reading it aloud to people working on their VWs and taking notes on how well they did.

Bestseller: Muir pitched the manuscript to a number of publishers, but they all turned him down, telling him there were already too many auto repair manuals on the market. "I knew there were no manuals like ours," Muir recalled in the 1970s, "so we sold the house in Taos, found a typist, and wrote to printers for bids. The plan was to sell mail order and directly to old book stores." Muir printed 2,500 copies using his own money, threw them in the back of his Volkswagen bus and began selling them store-to-store. Interest in the book began to build via word of mouth. "After that," says Steven Carey, president of John Muir Publications, "*Life* magazine ran a feature article on the book, and it just took off." To date, more than 2.5 million copies have been sold. Old-style Volkswagen Beetles and vans haven't been sold in the U.S. since 1977; even so, *How to Keep Your Volkswagen Alive* still averages sales of more than 30,000 copies a year.

THE CELESTINE PROPHECY

Simple Start: In the mid-1970s, a children's therapist named James Redfield was traveling through the Peruvian Andes when he heard tales of a lost ancient document that supposedly revealed the meaning of life. For some reason the story appealed to him, and

---

The blood vessels of a blue whale are wide enough for an adult trout to swim through.

remained in the back of his mind until 1989, when he quit his counseling job and began writing a novel about just such an ancient text. He wrote much of the book in a Waffle House restaurant. "That helped to keep the story simple," Redfield says.

Bestseller: Nobody wanted to publish Redfield's book, so he formed his own publishing company and spent his entire $13,000 savings printing up 3,000 copies, which he began selling to New Age bookstores across the American South. Redfield credits the book's success to independent bookstore owners, who recommended the book to their readers. *The Celestine Prophecy* bombed with the critics—*The National Review* called it "a tenth-rate melodrama joining Gnostic hubris with flower-child theology"—but it was a smash hit with the New Age crowd. Redfield self-published more than 150,000 copies before selling the rights to Warner Books, which went on to sell 5.5 million more.

LIFE'S LITTLE INSTRUCTION BOOK

Simple Start: When his son Adam was packing up to go to college, H. Jackson Brown decided to write down some observations and advice that he thought his son might find useful. "I started writing," Brown says, "and what I thought would take a few hours took several days." When he was finished, Brown put the notes into a binder and presented it to his son. A few days later, Adam phoned home. "Dad," he said, "I've been reading the book and I think it's one of the best gifts I've ever received. I'm going to add to it and someday give it to my son." Brown figured that if his son found the notes useful, other people would, too; so he made them into a book.

Bestseller: Brown self-published enough copies to sell to bookstores near his Nashville home, and they sold well enough that some bookstore owners encouraged him to sell the manuscript to an established publisher. He approached Rutledge Hill Press, but owner Larry Stone turned the book down. Brown gave him a copy anyway. "I left that copy on my desk for four or five weeks," Stone says, "and everyone who came in my office picked it up, flipped through it, and even read a few things out loud. It caught up to me one day, and I thought, hey, we probably ought to reconsider this book. So I called Jack up and asked if he'd found a publisher. He said, 'No' and I said, 'You have now.'" The book went on to sell more than 5 million copies.

63% of American adults will rent at least one video this month.

WE AIN'T LION: THE MODERN ZOO IS BORN, PART II

Every year more than 120 million people visit zoos, aquariums, ocean-
ariums, and wildlife parks in the United States and Canada—a greater
attendance than that of football, baseball, and hockey games combined!
The story of the origin of the modern zoo is on page 158.

STATUS SYMBOL

In the late 1850s, Philadelphian Dr. William Camac visited the London Zoo. Inspired by what he saw, he founded the Philadelphia Zoological Society. His goal: To build a world-class zoological garden and the first scientific zoo in America.

By the late 1850s, major cities all over Europe either had zoos or were in the process of establishing them. They were status symbols: the citizens of Madrid, Hamburg, and Dublin, for example, regarded zoos as a means of communicating to the rest of world that their cities were to be taken as seriously as London or Paris.

Dr. Camac wanted the same thing for Philadelphia: "When we see cities such as Amsterdam, Frankfurt, and Dublin—cities not so large as Philadelphia—supporting first-class zoological gardens," he wrote, "we see no reason why Philadelphia, with all its taste, wealth, enterprise, and advantages, should not in time possess one of the finest institutions in the world."

SIDESHOW

The United States lagged far behind Europe in the development of zoos. Westward expansion brought pioneers in contact with animals they had never seen before . . . and many animals were captured and brought back to cities to be exhibited to curious crowds. But as late as the 1870s, most animal viewing was limited to spectacles like a bear chained up in the corner tavern, or traveling carnivals put on by sea captains to show off exotic animals captured overseas.

Farthest distance a pumpkin has been hurled without the use of explosives: 3,718 feet.

EARLY AMERICAN ZOOS

New York

By 1861 New York City had a menagerie in Central Park, but this jumble was little more than a dumping ground for private collections and carnivals, including a black bear, two cows, deer, monkeys, raccoons, foxes, opossums, ducks, swans, eagles, pelicans, and parrots. No rational thought was put into the collection; the keepers just accepted whatever animals people gave them.

Still, the menagerie was a popular attraction. "By the late 1800s," Linda Koebner writes in *Zoo*, "it was a center of entertainment both for wealthy Fifth Avenue strollers and for the poor who were looking for a break from their daily working lives. Newly arrived immigrants lived in dark, crowded tenements on the Lower East Side of New York. A trip up to the green of Central Park to see the menagerie was well worth the walk or the nickel fare on the trolley."

Chicago

The menagerie in Chicago's Lincoln Park wasn't much better than the one in Central Park. It got its start when the Central Park menagerie presented them with a gift of two swans. This prompted similar "gifts," and by 1873 the park had 27 mammals and 48 birds.

GENUINE ARTICLE

While these zoos were popular attractions, neither Central Park nor Lincoln Park knew anything about animals or bothered to hire anyone who did; care and feeding of the creatures was left to the parks department, whose main concern was picking up garbage and raking leaves.

As Dr. Camac proposed it, the Philadelphia Zoological Garden would be something completely different: a well-funded, intelligently planned collection of animals housed in permanent facilities and run by a professional, full-time staff. The public would be admitted into the zoo, but it would also serve a more serious purpose: scientists at the University of Pennsylvania, the Academy of Sciences, and other organizations would be able to study and observe the animals up close.

Planning for the facility began in March of 1859, but the outbreak of the Civil War interfered with construction, so it was not completed until 1873.

Highest fast-food restaurant: McDonald's in La Paz, Bolivia, at 11,000 ft above sea level.

THE TOILET ERA

When it opened to the public on July 1, 1874, the Philadelphia Zoo was a state-of-the-art facility, complete with a monkey house, bird house, prairie dog village, and sea lion pool. But the early zookeepers had a lot to learn about caring for animals. Hunters and trappers who captured the animals knew next to nothing about how the animals lived in the wild or what they ate, and thousands died before they could be delivered to the zoo. The zookeepers didn't know much more, and animals that made it to the zoo didn't live much longer.

Because animal behavior was so poorly understood, animals that lived in social or family groups in the wild were often acquired one at a time and lived alone in bare cages—no attempt was made to simulate their natural environment. Animals frequently had nowhere to hide, and climbing animals like monkeys and wildcats had nowhere to go to get off the floor. The emphasis in cage design was on preventing disease by making them easy to clean: enclosures were usually made of concrete and tile and looked so much like bathrooms, Koebner writes, that "this manner of keeping the animals gave rise to the term 'the toilet era.'"

Visitors to the zoos were similarly shortchanged: displays did little to educate the public other than give the name of the animal and the feeding schedule. Scientific aspects of the zoo were played down; the garden's staffers themselves were poorly informed and so could do little to shed light on any of the exhibits.

Where the public was concerned, the emphasis was on entertainment. Elephants paraded, bears danced, and chimpanzees wore clothes and ate with silverware at dinner tables, part of the zoology garden's attempt to show how "humanlike" they were.

A NEW ERA

Things began to improve at the turn of the century, thanks in large part to a German circus trainer named Carl Hagenbeck, considered the "father of modern zoos." For years Hagenbeck had made his living catching and training exotic animals for zoos. In 1907 he expanded his business by opening his own zoo, which he named the Hagenbeck Tierpark.

As an animal catcher, Hagenbeck had seen animals in the wild and was determined that the animals in *his* zoo would never live in cages that looked like restrooms. "I wished to exhibit them not as

---

Humdinger: Hawaii's state fish is the humuhumunukunukuapua'a.

captives, confined to narrow spaces and looked at between bars, but as free to wander from place to place within as large limits as possible."

Hagenbeck put his experience as an animal trainer to work, testing the animals to see how high and how far they could jump, and then dug moats so deep and wide that the animals would not try to escape. He also tried to give the exhibits an authentic appearance so that the animals would be as comfortable as possible.

OPTICAL ILLUSION

Hagenbeck also arranged the exhibits to give them as natural an appearance as possible; it even seemed as if predators and their prey were part of the same exhibit. The lion exhibit was located just in front of the zebra, antelope, and ostriches (safely separated by a moat that was concealed behind bushes and landscape). All of the animals appeared to be together, just as they would be in their natural habitat in Africa. As a result, Koebner writes, "the public could see the interrelationship of animals, begin to picture what the African landscape looked like, and learn about predators, prey and habitats."

The advantages of Hagenbeck's reforms were obvious, and most zoos began adopting his ideas to improve their exhibits. Still, his enclosures had drawbacks: They were expensive, took up more space than cages, and increased the distance between animals and the viewing public from 5 feet to as much as 75 feet. And some zoo directors felt they were too revolutionary. Dr. William Hornaday of the Bronx Zoo, for example, criticized the new enclosures as "a half-baked German fad." But Hornaday was in the minority. Zookeepers from all over the world began making pilgrimages to the Hagenbeck Tierpark to learn as much as they could.

CHANGING TIMES

Hagenbeck's reforms were part of a broader zoological trend: All over the world, zoos were beginning to take better care of their animals. In the old days, the supply of animals in the wild seemed inexhaustible—if an animal in a zoo died, they could just send a hunter into the jungle to get another one. Life was cheap, and animals were expendable.

By the early 1900s, zoos were already beginning to look different. Many animals had been driven to extinction or close to it.

According to Pickle Packers Intl, the crunch of a pickle should be audible from 10 paces.

And foreign governments—realizing how valuable the surviving animals were—started charging zoos for the privilege of hunting in their territories. As the supply of animals went down and the cost of obtaining them went up, zoos became more interested in preserving and extending the lives of the animals they had.

But the practical aspects of running and maintaining a zoo didn't change as fast as the philosophy. "Even with increased difficulties in capture and export, it would still be many decades before capture in the wild slowed significantly," Koebner writes in *Zoo*. Until about the early 1960s, zoos still obtained the majority of their animals from well-funded expeditions into the wild, which amounted to little more than raids upon wildlife areas in Africa and Asia. Barbaric practices, such as killing a mother elephant or hippopotamus in order to capture its child, were still commonplace and widely accepted.

ZOOS TODAY

In the 1960s and 1970s, however, zoos began to make substantive shifts toward conservation—not just of the animals in the zoo, but also those still in the wild. And instead of competing against one another, they began working together to accomplish these goals. This is critical in the case of endangered species that are extinct, or practically so, in the wild . . . and survive only in zoos today.

In cases where only a few dozen animals survive and their numbers are scattered among several zoos, the only way to bring the species back from extinction is to manage the animals as one population.

"Today's zoos have a very specific message to preach," writes Allen Nyhuis in *The Zoo Book*. "By introducing the public to the world's enormous variety of animals and their native habitats, they hope that people will better appreciate the animals and want to help preserve them."

* * *

Since 1984, America's zoos have spent more than $1 billion on upgrading and improvements.

Top speed of an abalone on the move: 5 yards per minute.

HOT STUFF!

*In 1991 America turned a culinary corner—that's the first year
we spent more money on salsa than on ketchup. If you love
"hot" food, this chapter is for you.*

BLAME IT ON COLUMBUS

When Christopher Columbus arrived in the New World, he
thought he'd landed in India. So he called the people he met there
"Indians."

That wasn't the only mistake he made: when his hosts served a
spicy food containing hot chiles, he assumed the chiles were
related to *piper nigrum*, the plant that produces black pepper.

They're actually part of the *Solanaceae*, or nightshade, family
and are more closely related to potatoes, tomatoes, and eggplants.
But chiles have been known as chile "peppers" ever since.

MADE IN BOLIVIA

All varieties of chile peppers descended from prehistoric wild chile
plants that originated somewhere near present-day Bolivia.
Scientists believe that most animals avoided the painfully hot
plants, but birds ate them—apparently because they can't taste
chiles—and spread the seeds all over Central and South America.
Humans began eating the wild peppers as early as 7000 B.C., and
had domesticated them by 2500 B.C.

South American and Latin American peoples, including the
Aztecs, revered the peppers. They were used for everything from
treating upper-respiratory disorders to ritualistic morning bever-
ages. Montezuma, the last Aztec emperor, drank a concoction of
chocolate and hot chiles for breakfast. The Incas took their reverence a step further: Agar-Uchu, or "Brother Chile Pepper" in
English, is one of the four brothers of the Incan creation myth.

Chiles remained exclusive to the New World until Columbus
brought some to Europe. From there they spread via trade routes to
every remaining corner of the globe, and within a century they
were firmly established in the cuisines of India, China, and Africa.
Today an estimated 75% of the world's population eats chiles on a
daily basis. Mexico tops the list—Mexicans consume, on average,
one chile per person, every day.

Checkers used to be known as "chess for ladies."

CHILE SCIENCE
What Makes Them Hot?

- All chiles contain a powerful alkaloid called *capsaicin* (cap-SAY-a-sin), which gives chiles their heat—and which isn't found in any other plant. It's so potent that humans can detect it even when it's diluted to one part per million.

- The "capsaicinoids," as they're also known, are produced in the plant by the *placenta*—the part just below the stem of the chile. That's also where the seeds and the "ribs" grow. On average, these parts are 16 times hotter than the rest of the plant, so it stands to reason that one way to cool down a chile (if that's what you want) is to remove the placenta.

- How hot is capsaicin? It's so strong that it's the main ingredient in a product designed to drive grizzly bears away. It's also the "pepper" in pepper spray, which has replaced tear gas spray in more than 1,200 police departments around the United States. According to *Smithsonian* magazine, when sprayed in the face, "it causes eyes to slam shut and creates a spasm in the respiratory system—an unpleasant experience that lasts 30 to 45 minutes."

What Makes Them So Good?

- When you eat chiles, capsaicin irritates the pain receptor cells in your mouth.

- Some scientists believe the receptors then release something known as "substance P," which rushes to "alert" the brain to the pain. In response, the brain produces chemicals called endorphins that kill the pain and elicit feelings of well-being. Does hot, spicy food taste less hot to you after a couple of bites? Chile enthusiasts say this is the endorphins at work.

- In fact, some experts theorize that it's the addictive nature of endorphins, not the taste of the chiles themselves, that makes the spice so popular.

Cooling Down

- Do you reach for ice water when you eat a hot pepper? It's not a great idea—it not only won't cool your mouth down, it will

---

Iron Age magazine once called Theodore Roosevelt "a drunk." He sued, and won 6¢.

probably make things worse by spreading the capsaicin around. Beer might work (experts aren't sure), but the best way to put out the fire is to drink cold milk . . . or eat any dairy product (e.g., frozen yogurt) with lactic acid. They contain casein, which acts like a detergent to help wash away the capsaicin. Other recommended foods: sugar, salt, tortillas, brandy Alexander, hunks of bread, and corn.

THE SCOVILLE SCALE

In 1912 Wilbur Scoville, a pharmacologist with the Parke Davis pharmaceutical company, needed to test the potency of some chiles he was mixing into a muscle salve. He mixed pure ground chiles into sugar water and had a panel of tasters drink the water, in increasingly diluted concentrations, until the liquid was so diluted that it no longer burned their mouths.

Next, Scoville assigned a number to each chile based on how much it needed to be diluted before the tasters tasted no heat. The "Scoville scale," as it's still known, measures potency in multiples of 100. Here's how some popular chiles are ranked:

Bell and sweet peppers:	0–100 Scoville Units
New Mexican peppers:	500–1000
Española peppers:	1,000–1,500
Ancho & pasilla peppers:	1,000–2,000
Cascabel & cherry peppers:	1,000–2,500
Jalapeno & mirasol peppers:	2,500–5,000
Serrano peppers:	5,000–15,000
De Arbol peppers:	15,000–30,000
Cayenne & Tabasco:	30,000–50,000
Chiltepin peppers:	50,000–100,000
Scotch bonnet & Thai peppers:	100,000–350,000
Habanero peppers:	200,000 to 300,000
Red savina habanero peppers (the hottest chiles ever recorded):	as much as 577,000
Pure capsaicin:	16,000,000

Today the potency of chiles is measured very precisely by machines that calculate the exact amount of capsaicin in each chile. But the scale that is used is still named the Scoville scale in Wilbur Scoville's honor.

HEALTH NOTES

Can eating chiles make you sick? Epidemiologists from Yale University and the Mexico National Institute of Public Health concluded that chile peppers may cause stomach cancer. However, peppers also contain *quercetin*, a chemical shown to reduce cancer risk in lab animals, so who knows?

Other maladies to watch out for if you're a hardcore chile eater:

- Salsa sniffles. "Sweating and rhinitis (runny nose) caused by eating hot peppers."

- Hunan hand. "The skin irritation that comes from chopping chiles."

- Jaloprocitis. "The burn jalapeños leave as they exit the body. On the other hand, according to a book called *The Healing Powers of Chili*:

- A 1986 experiment at Oxford University in England found that eating chiles may assist in burning calories.

- The popular muscle salve Heet is made mostly of capsaicin.

- Chilies are low in fat, high in fiber, and loaded with beta carotene and vitamin C. One half cup of chopped chile peppers offers more than twice the vitamin C of an orange.

- Capsaicin is a natural antibiotic, slowing down bacteria's growth.

- A few more ailments that have been treated with capsaicin: acne, alcoholism, arthritis, bronchitis, cramps, hemorrhoids, herpes, indigestion, low blood pressure, shingles, wounds.

MORE CHILE FACTS

- *Chilli* is the *Nahuatl*, or Aztec, word for the plant.

- According to most accounts, chile peppers were introduced into what is now the United States by Capitan General Juan de Oñante, who also founded Santa Fe in 1598.

If you're an average sleeper, you'll roll over 12 times in bed tonight.

PARLEZ-VOUS DOUBLESPEAK?

See if you can match the terms used by businesses, educators, and advertisers on the left (100 percent guaranteed real!) with the English on the right. From William Lutz's book, Doublespeak Defined.

DOUBLESPEAK	REAL ENGLISH
1. "Urban transportation specialist"	A. Stupid
2. "Adverse weather visibility device"	B. Smell
3. "Renaturalize"	C. Torture
4. "Sea-air interface climatic disturbance"	D. Briefcase
5. "Judgmental lapse"	E. Crime
6. "Maximum incapacitation"	F. Cartel
7. "Physical pressure"	G. Explosion
8. "Nutritional avoidance therapy"	H. Undertaker
9. "Induce adverse reaction"	I. Mistake
10. "Therapeutic misadventure"	J. Censor
11. "Natural amenity unit"	K. Love
12. "Organoleptic analysis"	L. Outhouse
13. "Intuitively counter-productive"	M. Cab driver
14. "Data transport system"	N. Windshield wiper
	O. Medical malpractice

In France, a good snack is pig brain paté spread over crackers.

15. "Implement a lean concept of synchronous organizational structures"

16. "Human kinetics"

17. "Fee for quality"

18. "Producer cooperative"

19. "Suboptimal"

20. "Uncontained engine failure"

21. "Variance"

22. "Personal manual database"

23. "Weed"

24. "Creative altruism"

25. "Grief therapist"

P. Physical education

Q. Failed

R. Hunt

S. Wave

T. Fire someone

U. Death penalty

V. Calendar

W. Diet

X. Harm

Y. Tuition

Answers

1. M; 2. N; 3. R; 4. S; 5. E; 6. U; 7. C; 8. W; 9. X; 10. O; 11. L; 12. Z; 13. A; 14. D; 15. T; 16. P; 17. Y; 18. F; 19. Q; 20. G; 21. I; 22. B; 23. J; 24. K; 25. H. V;

* * *

ROCK GOSSIP

Wretched Excess. "Aerosmith liked to bring a chainsaw with them on tour so that they could chop up hotel rooms with greater efficiency. The musical group also traveled with extra-long extension cords. Why? So that the TVs they threw out of their hotel rooms would keep playing all the way to the ground . . . or the pool."

Sheep snore.

KNOW YOUR BIBLE(S)

You've heard of the King James Version . . . the Revised Standard Version . . . and the New Revised Standard Version. Ever wonder why there are so many different versions of the Bible in the first place? Here's an explanation—as well as a look at some versions you've probably never heard of—from John Dollison's 1993 book, Pope-Pourri.

IN THE BEGINNING

Even by nonreligious standards, the Bible and its various translations are the most significant written works the Western world has ever produced. They are mileposts by which historians measure the progress of European civilization: The Gutenberg Bible (c. 1455), for example, was the first book ever printed on a movable type printing press; Martin Luther's 1534 German translation is considered the birthplace of the modern German language; and the King James Version of 1611 has been described as "the noblest monument of English prose," superior even to the works of William Shakespeare.

No one knows how many Bibles have been distributed over the centuries, but the number easily exceeds 100 million copies—making it by far the most popular book ever printed. (The second-best selling book in history? Dr. Benjamin Spock's *Common Sense Book of Baby and Child Care*.) So far the Bible has been translated into more than 260 different languages, including more than 20 different English versions—most of which are still in print. If there's one thing all of these editions and translations demonstrate, it's that as spoken languages continue to evolve, the Bible needs to be updated regularly so that it remains accurate, understandable, and relevant to the people who read it. Here's a look at some of the most important, most popular, and most unusual updates ever produced:

THE CLASSICS
The Vulgate Bible (405). Written by Saint Jerome (c. 342–420), the first person to translate the ancient Greek, Hebrew, and other texts that make up the Bible into Latin. His version was named the "Vulgate" Bible because Latin was the language of the vulgar or common people, as opposed to Greek, the language of the upper classes and the nobility. The Vulgate is still in use today.

Q: What did all the passengers of the *Mayflower* have in common?

The Wycliffe Bible (1384). Shortly before his death, the English religious reformer John Wycliffe translated the Vulgate Bible into English. However, the Catholic Church forbade English translations, and denounced it as heretical. Wycliffe died before the Church got its hands on him, but in 1415 the Council of Constance ordered his body dug up, burned, and thrown into a river.

The Tyndale Bible (1526). William Tyndale, an English Protestant reformer, published the first English translation of the Bible taken directly from the ancient Hebrew and Greek texts. It too was condemned by the Church. In 1535 Tyndale was arrested on charges of "willfully perverting the meaning of the Scriptures"; a year later he was strangled and burned at the stake. (The first approved English translation, the Douay-Rheims Bible, was finally published in 1582.)

The King James Bible (1616). Commissioned by England's King James I, who wanted an official English translation of the Bible of Protestant Churches. It was translated from a 16th-century Greek text, which was later discovered to contain 14 centuries of copyists' errors. So in 1855 the Anglican Church published an update, the English Revised Version—and in 1901 released the American Standard Version, a special translation for U.S. Protestants. (Its revision, the Revised Standard Version, was published in 1946, which in turn was followed by the *New* Revised Standard Version in 1989.)

WEIRD BIBLES

The Geneva Bible (1560). Nicknamed the "Breeches Bible" because it was the first Bible to depict Adam and Eve wearing pants. Why? The editors thought Genesis 3:7 (the passage where Adam and Eve "sewed fig leaves together and made themselves *aprons*") was too racy . . . so they dumped "aprons" and replaced it with "breeches."

Webster's Bible (1883). Published by Noah Webster, creator of *Webster's Dictionary*. He too thought the Bible was filled with smut: "Many words and phrases," he complained, "are so offensive, especially to females, as to create a reluctance in young persons to attend Bible classes and schools in which they are required to read passages which cannot be replaced without a blush." So he rewrote the entire Bible, removing the "filthiest" passages entirely and cleaning up the less offensive ones. Words such as "whore," "fornication," and "teat" gave way to milder expressions like "lewd woman," "lewdness," and "breast."

ULTRASPECIALIZED BIBLES

The Black Bible Chronicles. In 1993 African American Family Press released *The Black Bible Chronicles: A Survival Manual for the Streets,* a street-language paraphrase of the first five books of the Old Testament. ("Thou shalt not steal" appears as "You shouldn't be takin' from your homeboys"; "Thou shalt not kill" translates as "Don't waste nobody"; and "Thou shalt not commit adultery" emerges as "Don't mess around with someone else's ol' man or ol' lady.") The book was written by P. K. McCary, a Houston, Texas, Sunday school teacher who was having trouble reaching inner-city kids using standard Bible texts. "Over the years, I have found that kids just pick up on this language. For them, it's a kick. As my daughter would say, 'It's tight.'"

The Klingon Authorized Version. Ambrose Bierce once described faith as "belief without evidence in what is told by one who speaks without knowledge, of things without parallel." The folks at the Klingon Bible Translation Project are taking the concept one step further—they're translating the Bible into an imaginary language so that it can be read by a race of people who don't exist . . . except in the minds of *Star Trek* fans. Sample translation: John 3:16 ("For God so loved the world, that he gave his only begotten Son, that whosoever believeth in him should not perish but have everlasting life") reads: "toH qo' muSHa'pu'qu'-mo' JoH'a', wa' puqloDDaj nobpu' ghaH 'ej ghaHbaq Harchugh vay', vaj not Hegh ghaH, 'ach yln jub ghajbeh ghaH."

When finished, the Klingon Authorized Version may prove two things: 1) that the Word of God truly is universal; and 2) that *Star Trek* fans need to get out more often.

* * *

"The young have aspirations that never come to pass, the old have reminiscences of what never happened."

—*H. H. Munro (Saki)*

Your body gives off enough heat in 30 minutes to boil half a gallon of water.

UNCLE JOHN'S "STALL OF FAME"

More members of Uncle John's bathroom pantheon.

Honoree: Glen Dorenbush, formerly of San Francisco
Notable Achievement: Being flushed down the toilets of his favorite bars after he died
True Story: According to news reports, "When Dorenbush died in the summer of 1996, his cronies ended up with eight pounds of his ashes and an interesting predicament. The amiable eccentric left no will when he checked out, but had made it clear to those who knew him best what he wanted done with his remains: he wanted most of his ashes flushed down the toilets of his favorite bars."
The dilemma: "It's technically illegal in California to sprinkle cremated remains down the can, not to mention bad for the plumbing." His friends finally decided to "scatter some ashes on a beach in Puerto Vallarta where he loved to vacation and some more in the ocean off Stinson Cafe on Hyde Street. The rest, it was decided, would go down the latrines at several undisclosed locations."

Honoree: An unnamed homeowner in Fayetteville, Arkansas
Notable Achievement: Creative bathroom-based entrepreneurship
True Story: In 1995 the man bought Jimmy Johnson's former house and had a great idea while renovating his bathroom. He took out an ad in a local paper, offering a great deal for football fans: For only $250, they could own (and sit on) the toilet once used by the ex–Dallas Cowboys coach.

Honoree: Richard List of Berkeley, California
Notable Achievement: Creating a museum (and philosophical statement) featuring painted toilets
True Story: "New York has the MOMA," writes a San Francisco reporter, "Paris has the Louvre. Berkeley has the New Sense Museum, where art is strictly in the eyes of the beholder. The New Sense (say it fast) consists of a vacant, weed-strewn lot studded with weird objects, most notably a flotilla of commodes painted

fluorescent pink, orange, and green." According to Richard List, the museum's guiding force, "People say, 'I don't get the message.' Well, that's the point. Life is a mystery."

Honoree: St. Louis circuit judge Edward Peek
Notable Achievement: Presiding over the first murder trial ever instigated by an argument about toilet paper
True Story: There's nothing funny about this, of course, but it's too weird to leave out. In the late 1980s, a 36-year-old man admitted to the judge that he had shot and killed his younger brother. The reason: He was angry that his brother had "used too much of a new eight-roll package of toilet paper." The man was convicted of second-degree murder.

Honoree: Barney Smith of San Antonio, Texas
Notable Achievement: Created the Toilet Seat Museum in his garage
True Story: Smith, a plumber, asked his customers if he could keep the old toilet seat every time he installed a new one. "Then," says the *Houston Post*, "he would decorate each seat with something special, things like keepsakes from a vacation or mementos from a historic moment . . . Smith has decorated and dedicated about 400 toilet-seat lids, artistically altering the functional commode covers to become hanging history. And he has generously hung them for the world to see."

Honoree: Nelson Camus of Hacienda Heights, California
Notable Achievement: Inventing the world's first urine-powered battery
True Story: The "Argentine-born electrical engineer," says John Kohut in *Dumb, Dumber, Dumbest*, "announced that his battery generates more power than standard acid-reaction batteries and is cheaper. His partner, Ed Aguayo, said 10 urine-powered batteries, each about half the size of a normal car battery, could power a normal house." No word on when the battery will become available.

Top three "problem" employees, according to the *Wall Street Journal:*

IT'S A WEIRD, WEIRD WORLD

More proof that truth really is stranger than fiction.

PERFORMING UNDER PRESSURE

"On September 12, the Great Hurricane of 1938 devastated the New England states. That morning a man in West Hampton Beach received a barometer in the mail. The needle was stuck on "hurricane." Disgusted, and thinking it was defective, he marched back to the Post Office and mailed the instrument back to the store from which he had purchased it. When he returned, his home was gone."

—Our Fascinating Earth

DID HE CROAK?

"Doctors in a Mexican hospital were in the midst of open-heart surgery when a frog fell out of an overhead lamp and landed on the patient."

—The Fortean Times

ROCK YOUR WORLD

"For years, maps have shown that northern Germany's highest mountain, the Brocken, was 3,747 feet tall. But recently, more precise measurements revealed that the peak is only 3,741 feet tall. To avoid correcting the world's maps, a construction company trucked 19 tons of granite to the summit, stacking the rocks in a 6-foot pile."

—Portland Oregonian, **February 28, 1998**

NEXT COMES A STRAIT JACKET

"Despite 18 years working at a Florida fishing camp, Freddie Padgett was so terrified of water that he wore a life jacket to bed on stormy nights. Friends made fun of him, until a twister sucked him out of his RV while he was sleeping and dropped him into Lake Harney over a mile away. He suffered broken ribs and other injuries, but authorities say the life jacket probably saved his life."

—The Skeptic

. . . "The Non-Stop Talker," "The Screamer," and "The Practical Joker."

THE BEST BUSINESS DEAL IN U.S. HISTORY, PART III

Here's the last installment of the story. (Part II is on page 255.)

CAR WARS
On November 14, 1914, the first Dodge rolled off the assembly line. It had a bigger engine than the Model T and a modern stick-shift transmission, as well as features like a speedometer, an electric starter, electric headlights, a windshield, and a spare tire. And it only cost $100 more than the Model T.

THE EMPIRE STRIKES BACK
Naturally, Henry Ford was not amused that Ford dividends were being used to bankroll his competition. But when the Dodge brothers offered to sell him their Ford stock, he refused . . . and instead announced in 1916 that the Ford Motor Company would no longer pay dividends and would instead plow all of its profits back into the business.

The Dodge brothers sued to force Ford to pay dividends, and in 1919 they won: Ford was required to pay $19 million in back dividends (most of which went directly back to Henry Ford, since he owned the lion's share of the stock anyway), but Ford would not give in. On December 1918, he announced that he was "retiring" from Ford and turning control over to his son Edsel.

Henry left for an extended vacation in southern California. Then on March 5, 1919, the *Los Angeles Examiner* broke a story that shook the automobile industry:

HENRY FORD ORGANIZING HUGE NEW COMPANY TO BUILD A BETTER, CHEAPER CAR

According to the report, while his old company had employed 50,000 workers, the new company would hire as many as 250,000 and would have automobile plants all over the world. The scale of production would make it possible to sell cars for between $250 and $350, cheaper than they had ever been sold before. No other auto manufacturer would be able to match the price.

GETTING OUT

The Dodge brothers were in a bind—if Ford was serious, it would probably drive both Dodge Brothers and the Ford Motor Company out of business. Their own company and their Ford stock would be worthless.

"But the Dodge brothers and the other minority shareholders found themselves mysteriously approached in the following weeks by would-be Ford share purchasers," Robert Lacey writes. "It became clear that the threads all led back to Henry, working through Edsel in Detroit. The bidding started at $7,500 per share (the Dodge brothers owned 2,000 shares). The Dodge brothers responded with their $12,500 price—and $12,500, in the end, became the price that Ford had to pay." The "huge new company," it turned out, was just a ploy that Ford used to depress the value of the Dodge brothers stock so that he could buy them out on the cheap.

SO LONG, FELLAS

The Dodge brothers received $25 million for their Ford stock, which came on top of the $9.5 million they had received in dividends between 1903 and 1919, for a total return of $34.5 million on their original $10,000 investment. Even though Ford had gotten the better of the bargain, the Dodges (along with the other original investors in Ford) made so much money that business historians now consider it the most profitable investment in the history of American commerce.

NOTE: Less than a year later, the Dodge brothers were attending the 1920 New York Auto Show when Horace suddenly fell ill with pneumonia. His condition was so grave that John maintained a round-the-clock bedside vigil, only to catch pneumonia himself and die 10 days later. Horace lingered for just a few more months before he died. In 1925 their widows sold the Dodge Brothers Motor Car Company to a New York banking syndicate for $146 million in cash—at the time the largest cash transaction in auto history. In May 1929, the bankers sold Dodge Brothers to automaker Walter Chrysler for $170 million . . . just in time for the Great Depression.

LEGENDARY TV FLOPS

There are plenty of bombs in TV history, ut these three shows are legends.

MELBA
A CBS sitcom starring singer Melba Moore as Melba Patterson, a single mother who ran "the Manhattan Visitors' Center." Premiered as a mid-season replacement on January 28, 1986—the day the *Challenger* space shuttle exploded. Drew the worst ratings of the 1985-86 season and was cancelled immediately. In August, CBS aired the other episodes it had commissioned. The night of its return was CBS's lowest-rated prime-time evening in the network's history.

TURN ON!
A half-hour of skits and jokes that was supposed to be "the second coming of 'Laugh-In'." It premiered on February 5, 1969, and turned out to be "just a bunch of stupid sex jokes." (The longest skit had two actors making faces at each other for several minutes while the word SEX flashed on screen.) Affiliates and sponsors hated it so much that it was cancelled the next day. In fact, the Denver ABC affiliate cancelled it *halfway through* the premiere, with the message: "The remainder of this show won't be seen." How bad was "Turn On!"? We can only speculate. The producers' settlement with the networks and sponsors stipulates that the "tapes would be locked up and never shown again."

YOU'RE IN THE PICTURE.
A game show hosted by Jackie Gleason. Four celebrity panelists sat in back of a 7' x 10' picture frame and stuck their heads through porthole cutouts—making them part of a picture they couldn't see. With clues from Gleason, they tried to guess what the picture was. It debuted January 21, 1961. "Viewers who tuned into the show's third broadcast," writes Maxene Fabe in *Game Shows*, "saw only a bare stage containing an armchair in which Gleason sat. 'I apologize for insulting your intelligence,' he told his astonished viewers. 'From now on I promise to stick to comedy.'" The program was replaced the following week with "The Jackie Gleason Show."

Christopher Columbus's fee for "discovering" America: about $300.

McREVENGE!

Don't let all that happy Ronald McDonald stuff fool you—from the begin-ning, McDonald's has played hardball in the burger business. Not even the company's namesakes, the McDonald brothers, were exempt. Here's a classic revenge story on a sesame seed bun.

SETTING THE STAGE

In 1949, Dick and Mac McDonald opened a drive-in restaurant in San Bernardino, California. By 1954, it was so popular that a salesman named Ray Kroc made a deal to turn it into a national chain and pay the brothers a part of every dollar earned.

That's how McDonald's got started.

Six years later, Kroc offered to buy the brothers out for $1 million apiece. They said yes, but there was a misunderstanding: Kroc thought he was getting the original San Bernardino restaurant as part of the agreement; the McDonalds insisted it wasn't part of the deal.

THE EMPIRE STRIKES BACK

Kroc was furious. He had counted on the cash flow the restaurant would bring. "I closed the door to my office and paced up and down the floor calling the [McDonald brothers] every kind of son of a bitch there was," Kroc recalled. "I hated their guts." Privately, he told co-workers: "I'm not a vindictive man, but this time I'm going to get those sons of bitches." According to John Love in *McDonald's Behind the Arches*, that's exactly what he did.

> The moment the deal was completed, Kroc...hopped on a plane to Los Angeles, bought a piece of property [in San Bernardino] one block away from the brothers' original fast-food drive-in—and ordered the construction of a brand-new McDonald's store. It had only one purpose: to put the McDonald brothers' drive-in out of business.

THE BIG M SINKS

The brothers had already been forced to take down their "McDonald's" sign, because Kroc's company now owned their trade name. They renamed it "The Big M," but in every other way it was the same as it always had been. The problem was, Kroc's restaurant

---

Washington, D.C., has more psychiatrists per capita than any other city in the country.

also looked like the Big M . . . but his had the McDonald's name. Customers were a little confused, but figured that the original restaurant had been moved; they took their business to the new McDonald's. Sales at the Big M plummeted. In 1968, the McDonald brothers finally gave up. They sold their drive-in to a local restauranteur. But he couldn't make it work either. In 1970, Kroc had his final revenge: the birthplace of the fast food industry closed for good.

*   *   *

ANIMAL REVENGE

"An ice fisherman in Edwardsburg, Michigan, hauled a 4-pound beauty out of the lake, cleanly removed the hook from the mackerel's mouth and placed the fish on the ice to re-bait his line. The thrashing mackerel flung itself in the air, locked its teeth on the fisherman's leg and had to be pried loose by two men. The bite required a doctor's attention."

—Oops, by Richard Smith

"In Missouri, Larry Lands was showing off a turkey he had shot and put in his trunk when the not-yet-dead bird started thrashing around and pulled the trigger of Lands's gun, also in the trunk. Lands was shot in the leg. 'The turkeys are fighting back,' said county sheriff Ron Skiles."

**—News from the Fringe,
by John Kohut & Roland Sweet**

*   *   *

CONTINENTAL DRIFT

"In revenge for England's closing of the Libyan embassy in London, Col. Muammar el-Qaddafi ordered that England be deleted from all Libyan maps in the mid-1980s. In its place was put a new arm of the North Sea, bordered by Scotland and Wales."

—More News of the Weird

One in ten children sleepwalk.

POLI-TALKS

Here are some comments about everyone's favorite—and everyone's least favorite—subject. From Ariel Books' compilation called Politics.

"I am the future."
—Dan Quayle

"The first law of politics: Never say anything in a national campaign that anyone might remember."
—Eugene McCarthy

"There is something about a Republican that you can only stand for just so long. On the other hand, there is something about a Democrat that you can't stand for quite that long."
—Will Rogers

"Democrats are the party that says government can make you richer, smarter, taller, and get the chickweed out of your lawn. Republicans are the party that says government doesn't work—and then they get elected to prove it."
P.J. O'Rourke

"It seems to be a law of nature that Republicans are more boring than Democrats."
—Stewart Alsop

"I don't know a lot about politics, but I know a good party man when I see one."
—Mae West

"I'm a fellow that likes small parties, and the Republican party is about the size I like."
—Lyndon B. Johnson

"Republicans sleep in twin beds—some even in separate rooms. That is why there are more Democrats."
—Will Stanton

"I'm a loyal Republican. I support the president [Ronald Reagan] when he's right—and I just keep quiet the other 95 percent of the time."
—John LeBoutiller

"Democrats give away their old clothes; Republicans wear theirs. Republicans employ exterminators; Democrats step on the bugs. Democrats eat the fish they catch; Republicans eat 'em and hang 'em on the wall."
—Sean Donlon

Q: What does an algologist study? A: Seaweed.

GREAT MOMENTS
IN ADVERTISING

It may be hard to believe, but Americans weren't always concerned about bad breath, foot odor, dandruff, etc. It took a concerted effort by advertising agencies to focus our attention on these earth-shattering problems. The BRI salutes this contribution to our way of life by recognizing three memorable ad-chievements.

THE DISCOVERY OF "HALITOSIS" (1926)

Product: Listerine

Story: Listerine antiseptic had been a product of the Lambert Company since the 1880s, but was never particularly successful. By the 1920s—the early years of Prohibition—its most attractive feature to consumers was its 25% alcohol content.

In 1926 the company decided to boost sales by creating an ad campaign around one special feature . . . but what could the product actually do? No one was sure, so they gave it to a chemist to find out. His list of Listerine's benefits included an unfamiliar term: "Removes halitosis."

"What's that mean?" the president asked.

"Bad breath," the chemist replied.

"Perfect!" said the president.

Armed with a scientific-sounding name, Listerine pioneered a new advertising approach: presenting bad breath as a crippling social disease that Listerine could (of course) cure. Their ads showed endless situations in which Halitosis spelled business and romantic ruin.

Sample Ad: (Photo of a woman staring into a mirror) *What Secret Is Your Mirror Holding Back?* "Night after night, she would peer questioningly into her mirror, vainly seeking the reason. She was a beautiful girl and talented, too . . . yet in the one pursuit that stands foremost in the mind of every girl and woman—marriage—she was a failure.

"Many men came and went in her life. She was often a bridesmaid, but never a bride. And the secret her mirror held back

Laid end to end, the blood vessels in your body would wrap around the equator three times.

concerned a thing she least suspected—a thing people will not tell you to your face . . . Halitosis!"
Results: In a few years, the company's profits increased 4,000 percent. Roland Marchand notes in *Advertising the American Dream:*

> Not surprisingly, the company's style and strategy gave rise to a whole new school of advertising practice [of "scare" ads . . . Phrases like "the halitosis style" and "the halitosis appeal" became standard advertising jargon. In unmistakable tribute, copywriters discovered and labeled over a hundred new diseases.

INVENTING "ATHLETE'S FOOT" (1928)
Product: Absorbine Jr.
Story: Until 1928 Absorbine Jr. advertised itself as relief for "sore muscles, muscular aches, bruises, burns, cuts, and abrasions." Then, inspired by Listerine's success, they looked for—and found—a new affliction they could cure: ringworm of the foot. Their masterstroke was making it less scientific sounding. They dubbed it "athlete's foot," and portrayed it as the secret worry of the upper-class.
Sample Ad: (Photo of a man relaxing on a yacht) *"You'd Like to Be in This Man's Shoes . . . Yet He Has* ATHLETE'S FOOT! A yacht . . . a half dozen town houses and country seats . . . a flock of gleaming motors, and a railroad or two—this man has everything the world has to offer—*and* ATHLETE'S FOOT! And he doesn't know what it is! A power among big men, he feels *furtive* about the dry, scaly condition between his little toes. But he will know soon what worries him. For now all medical authority knows that what he has is a form of ringworm infection caused by *tinea trichophyton* and commonly known as 'Athlete's Foot.'"
Results: Hardly anyone paid attention to it before Absorbine Jr.'s ad campaign. Today it's treated as a bona fide medical condition.

COINING THE TERM "B.O." (1928)
Product: Lifebuoy Soap
Story: In 1928 Lifebuoy, described by D. Allen Foster in his book, *Advertising,* as "a liver-colored cake smelling like a hospital after the morning cleaning," found its sales slipping badly. So Lever Brothers hired a new ad agency . . . which took the Listerine approach one step further—to "planned vulgarity." Foster explains:

The Phoenicians invented the world's first phonetic alphabet, in 2000 B.C.

B.O. *(body odor)* was its keynote . . . The copy hammered away at the deodorant theme—"How to play it safe"—with pictures of people practically holding their noses.

In *I Hear America Listening,* Stuart Flexner describes the Lifebuoy campaign as "the hallmark of scare ads against underarm and other body perspiration odors."

Sample Ad: (Picture of anguished office worker peering over his shoulder at two huddled co-workers) *"ONE LITTLE WHISPER SHATTERED MY PRIDE.* I'd given Dick and Bob a cheery good night! They merely nodded in reply—but I was getting used to their unfriendliness. Then, as I walked away—came the whisper— 'B.O.!' That explained it all. In a flash, I understood the coolness of others here at the office . . . my failure to land that promotion I looked forward to.

"Nothing can ruin chances of social and business success as quickly as 'B.O.' Even the faintest hint of it is enough to turn others against you . . . Tests prove that Lifebuoy not only stops 'B.O.' but that you can build increasingly better protection against 'B.O.' by using Lifebuoy every day!"

Results: Of course, it worked. By the early 1930s, "the two-note foghorn warning 'Beee-oohhhh' was known to everyone through radio ads—and Lifebuoy was the best-selling soap in America."

STILL MORE DISEASES!!!

Flexner writes: "With the success of Halitosis and B.O., modern advertising continued to coin and popularize terms for both real and imaginary ailments and embarrassing conditions." Some BRI favorites:

Accelerator Toe
Ashtray Breath
Acidosis ("sour stomach")
Bromodosis ("sweaty foot odor")
Cosmetic Skin
Dishpan Hands
Enlarged Pores
Homotosis ("lack of attractive
   home furnishings")
Incomplete Elimination

Middle-Age Spread
Office Hips
Pink Toothbrush
   ("bleeding gums")
Smoker's Fur
Summer Sluggishness
Tattletale Gray (dirt left
   on clothes by mild
   laundry detergent)
Tell-Tale Tongue

Largest cast ever assembled for a film scene: 300,000, for the funeral scene in *Gandhi.*

THE BIRTH OF THE AMERICAN FLAG, PART II

Here's the second installment of our history
of Old Glory. (Part I starts on page 190.)

GOING THROUGH SOME CHANGES

A flag with 13 stars and 13 stripes made perfect sense for a country with 13 states. In 1791, however, Vermont became a state, with Kentucky following a year later. Congress had to decide whether to change the flag, keeping in mind that it would be expensive. It was estimated at the time that the new flags would cost $60 each for every ship in the country—a cost that opponents warned would have to be borne again and again as new states entered the Union.

In the end, national pride won out over cost considerations. Both the House and Senate passed a bill stipulating that after May 1, 1795, "the flag of the United States be fifteen stripes, alternate red and white; and that the union be fifteen stars, white in a blue field."

A LONG STORY

By 1816 there were 19 states in the Union, with a 20th, Mississippi, on the way. Adding 4 or 5 more stripes would change the look of the flag considerably.

Making matters more confusing, there was little uniformity in American flags flown around the country. The official flag had 15 stars and stripes, but as new states entered the union, some states—the new arrivals in particular—had added new stars and stripes so they would be represented on the flag just as any other state. Some states flew flags with as many as 19 stars and stripes, while one government building in Washington, D.C., had a flag with only 9 stripes. Something had to be done.

In 1817 the Congress asked Capt. Sam Reid, a hero of the War of 1812, to come up with a lasting solution. He proposed returning to the original 13 stripes, but allowing a new star to be added to the blue field for each new state that entered the Union. Acting on his suggestion, Congress drafted and President James Monroe signed into law the Flag Act of 1818. Once again, however, it was

---

What does *genitofemoral neuropahthy* mean? "Jeans are too tight."

not a major issue for many Americans. Some politicians even resented having to "waste" time on the legislation. "A consummate piece of frivolity," huffed one on the Senate floor while the bill was being debated.

STAR SYSTEM
The bill passed by only four votes, and once again left significant details out. As in 1777, the new resolution did not specify the exact size of the flag or how the stars should be arranged. This time, no one did anything about it for 94 years. An investigation conducted in 1912 found that flags of 66 different sizes and proportions were adorning federal offices. President William Howard Taft responded by issuing an executive order that finally established official guidelines for the flag. It commanded that the stars on the flag, which by now numbered 48, be arranged in "six horizontal rows of eight stars each."

ONE MORE TIME
President Taft's 48-star flag remained the standard for nearly 47 years—until 1959, when both Alaska and Hawaii were on the verge of statehood. How would the 50 stars be arranged on the new flag? The House of Representatives introduced three different bills addressing the issue, but in the end President Eisenhower just issued an executive order directing that the stars be arranged in five rows of six, and four rows of five. The changes went into effect at 12:01 a.m. on July 4, 1960, with a special provision allowing existing 48-star flags to remain flying until they wore out, which saved the federal government from having to replace the more than 51,000 flags flown outside government buildings when the new flags went into effect. The flag has been unchanged ever since.

FLAG FACTS
- Capt. Sam Reid, whose flag design led to the Flag Act of 1818, received little recognition (Peter Wendover, the congressman who pushed the Flag Act through Congress, got most of the credit). Not only is the name Sam Reid almost completely unknown today, within a relatively few years after proposing the changes to the flag, he became a forgotten man in his own time. His death in the 1860s went almost unnoticed, and he was buried in a grave that remained unmarked until the 1940s,

Camel rule of thumb: One-humped camels run faster than two-humped camels.

when Congress finally appropriated money for a tombstone and a flagpole for his grave.

- On June 14, 1777, the Continental Congress approved a resolution creating a national flag (which is why we now celebrate Flag Day on June 14). At the time, however, the resolution wasn't exactly the top news of the day. No one outside of the government knew about it until a Pennsylvania newspaper mentioned it in a brief article on September 2, 1777.

- On the other hand, on December 22, 1942, the Code of Flag Display and Use came into being. It more than made up for people's lack of interest in the past by describing, in meticulous detail, everything from what time of day to raise and lower the flag to how to drape it over a casket.

* * *

HOUSEHOLD TIPS

Here are some tips that BRI member Jerry Weinberg e-mailed to our Web site. We don't know if they work or not, but what the heck, we thought we'd pass them along:

- "To get the most juice out of fresh lemons, bring them to room temperature and roll them under your palm against the kitchen counter before squeezing."

- "If you accidentally add too much salt to a dish while it's still cooking, drop in a peeled potato. It absorbs the excess salt."

- "Wrap celery in aluminum foil when putting in the refrigerator—it will keep for weeks."

- "Stuff a miniature marshmallow in the bottom of a sugar cone to prevent ice cream drips."

A *misodoctakleidist* is someone who hates practicing the piano.

WORD ORIGINS

Here are some more interesting word origins.

AMBULANCE
Meaning: A specialized vehicle for transporting the injured to a hospital
Origin: "The name comes from an invention of Napoleon Bonaparte's, *l'hôpital ambulant* (walking hospital), a litter fitted with bandages and other first-aid equipment that served as a field hospital for wounded soldiers. In time, the litters became elaborate and mechanized, yielding first to horse-drawn wagons, eventually to motorized ambulances." (From *Fighting Words*, by Christine Ammer)

TABOO
Meaning: A behavior or activity that is prohibited
Origin: "Originally a Tongan word, *tabu*, meaning 'marked as holy.' The first taboos were prohibitions against the use or even the mention of certain things because of religious belief that to do so would invoke the wrath of the gods. The word gradually was extended in use to cover all sorts of prohibitions or bans based upon social convention." (From *Dictionary of Word and Phrase Origins, Vol. III*, by William and Mary Morris)

BUMPKIN
Meaning: A loutish countryman
Origin: "From the Dutch *boomkin*, small tree—hence, a countryman thought to possess the tree's intelligence." (From *Loose Cannons and Red Herrings*, by Robert Claiborne)

SENATE
Meaning: A representative body in a republic or democracy
Origin: "Literally, 'a gathering of old men.' Like most cultures, ancient Roman society respected age. In the days before the Roman Empire, tribes would gather. The representatives from these clans were usually elders, whose experience led to wiser, more thoughtful deliberation. When the empire flourished, the tradition of the council of elders continued. To this day there are age requirements for our Senate." (From *Where in the Word?*, by David Muschell)

About a third of the human race has perfect 20-20 vision.

UNCLE JOHN'S TOP 10 AMAZING COINCIDENCES

We're constantly finding stories about amazing coincidences, so in this BR, Uncle John listed his 10 favorites. Send us yours, and next edition, we'll do a readers' Top 10.

10. WHAT GOES AROUND . . .
"In 1965, at age four, Roger Lausier was saved from drowning off a beach at Salem, Mass., by a woman named Alice Blaise. Nine years later, in 1974, on the same beach, Roger paddled his raft into the water and pulled a drowning man from the water. The man was Alice Blaise's husband."

—*The Book of Lists*

9. NUMBER NINE, NUMBER NINE . . .
Beloit, Wisconsin—"Nicholas Stephen Wadle was born at 9:09 a.m. on the ninth day of the ninth month of 1999. But the string of coincidences doesn't end there. He weighed 9 pounds, 9 ounces.

"A spokeswoman for Beloit Memorial Hospitals said the mother 'couldn't believe it,' but 'the most surprised were the professionals involved . . . As the nines started to stack up, they were going crazy.'

"The baby was due Sept. 15, but complications with the births of Mrs. Wadles's two older children led her doctor to schedule a cesarean section for Thursday, to be safe. The delivery was set for 8:00 a.m. but there was an emergency, which allowed the 9:09 birth."

—**Appleton, Wisconsin, *Post Crescent*, September 10, 1999**
(Contributed by Julie Roeming)

8. ARE YOU MY DADDY?
"Wilf Hewitt, 86, a widower from Southport, wanted to look through a list of registered voters in the library, and asked the woman who had the list if she was going to be long. Vivien Fletoridis replied that she was looking for a man named Hewitt.

Odds of winning if you challenge a traffic ticket in court: about 1 in 3.

She was his daughter, whom he had not seen for 46 years. Wilf had had a wartime love affair with Vivien's mother, who had died in 1983. Their daughter was adopted in 1941 and went to Australia with her foster parents. In July 1987 she traced her two brothers and sister through an agency, and then set out to find her father."

—*The Fortean Times*

7. REINCARNATED SURVIVOR

"On three separate occasions—in 1664, 1785, and 1860—there were shipwrecks where only one person survived the accident. Each time that one person's name was Hugh Williams."

—*The Book of Useless Information*

6. I DO, I THINK

"A woman in Kissimmee, Florida, should have no trouble remembering her new husband's name. But, following a bizarre chain of coincidences surrounding the couple's wedding, she might have trouble remembering what he looks like.

"Ronald Legendre married his girlfriend, Hope, in August 1995. The best man—who wasn't related to the groom in any way—was also named Ronald Legendre. And the ceremony was performed by someone who wasn't connected to either man: Judge Ronald Legendre."

—*Knuckleheads in the News*

5. SECRET-AGENT KID

"James Bond, 15, a pupil at Argoed High School, North Wales, and a candidate for examinations in 1990, was given the examination number 007 by a computer quirk."

—*The World's Most Incredible Stories*

4. HER NAME IS MY NAME, TOO

"A computer mix-up that gave two American women the same social security number was responsible for highlighting a further series of incredible coincidences. Patricia Kern of Colorado and Patricia di Biasi of Oregon were brought together by the blunder. "The women discovered they had both been born Patricia Ann Campbell with fathers called Robert. They were born on the same date, too: March 13, 1941. Both Patricias married military men in 1959, within eleven days of one another, and had children aged

The first thing Thomas Edison filmed with his movie camera was a person sneezing.

nineteen and twenty-one. They also shared an interest in painting with oils, had studied cosmetics, and worked as bookkeepers."

—*One in a Million*

3. AND HER NAME IS MY NAME, TOO

"Mother of two, Michelle Samways, was caught up in a spot of trouble—with mother of two, Michelle Samways. The two women moved into numbers 5 and 6 Longstone Close, Portland, England, in Oct. 1994 and hardly a day goes by without a mix-up of some kind. They discovered that they share the same name only when they entered a raffle at a toddlers' group. The two Michelles, aged 26 and 27, were both named after the 1965 Beatles song. They are the same height and build, [and have] similar hair color."

—*The Fortean Times*

2. BABIES KEEP FALLING ON MY HEAD

"Joseph Figlock was passing an apartment block in Detroit in 1975 when he was knocked unconscious. A baby had fallen fourteen stories and landed on him. Both survived. One year later, Figlock was passing the same apartment block—and once again he was hit by a falling child . . . and survived!"

—*One in a Million*

And the #1 coincidence is . . .

1. CIVIL SERVANT

"One of the lesser-known figures of American history is Wilmer McLean, a Virginia farmer who took little interest in politics.

"In 1861, most of the Rebel army marched onto McLean's land. The Union forces attempted to bar their way, and the first full-scale battle of the Civil War (Battle of Bull Run), got underway—right on his farm. Thirteen months later, it happened again. The second battle at Bull Run destroyed McLean's land. McLean had had enough. He packed his wagons and moved two hundred miles away from the war.

"Three years later, in a weird twist of fate, two men confronted each other in Wilmer McLean's parlor. These two men talked and signed a document on McLean's best table; for he had moved to a little village called Appomattox Court House—where Robert E. Lee and Ulysses S. Grant negotiated the end of the Civil War."

—*Ripley's Believe It or Not*

Q: What do olives and tomatoes have in common? A: They're both fruits.

ANYTHING FOR PUBLICITY

After Princess Diana's death on August 31, 1997, a Wall Street Journal *reporter kept a watch on the press releases sent to newspapers. He was amazed at how quickly (and crassly) people tried to use her death as a PR "hook." Here are some of the press releases his office received.*

August 31
PSYCHOLOGIST CALLS [FOR] SELF-EXAMINATION OF TABLOID VOYEURISM

Los Angeles, Entertainment Wire
A psychologist in Hollywood reacting to the tragedy in Paris today in which Princess Diana was involved in a serious automobile accident allegedly exacerbated by pursuing paparazzi said: "We are all to blame if this accident is a result of Princess Diana fleeing from tabloid photographers. The photographers are paid huge sums for these photos because we are addicted to them . . . "

Psychologist Robert R. B___, Ph.D., has assisted radio, TV and print media since 1984 to find answers and provide insight to enhance understanding of psychological issues.

AMERICAN PHYSICIANS MOURN DEATH OF

PRINCESS DIANA

Chicago, PR Newswire
Physicians of the American Medical Association are saddened at the tragic death of Diana, Princess of Wales . . .

Although we never worked with Princess Diana directly, the AMA is nevertheless proud of our mutual commitment to the campaign for a worldwide ban on anti-personnel land mines . . . As the world mourns this stunning loss, the AMA urges physicians everywhere to remember Princess Diana as a woman of courage, compassion and grace.

HOLLYWOOD PUBLICIST TO LEAD LAW CHANGE FOR PAPARAZZI STALKINGS

Los Angeles, PR Newswire
In response to the death of Princess Diana and producer Dodi Al-Fayed, Hollywood publicist Michael Levine has

---

You can sweat as much as 3 gallons of water a day in a hot climate.

pledged to lead an effort to change laws to . . . punish the criminal behavior of stalking tabloid journalists.

Levine, who represented Hollywood producer Fayed for a year in the early '90s, expressed outrage at the "totally unnecessary loss of innocent life."

"I have witnessed the behavior of the tabloids go from obnoxious to criminal in the last few years," said Levine. "I'm frankly surprised that something like this didn't happen sooner."

DIANA'S DEATH—THE TRAUMA HER CHILDREN WILL EXPERIENCE

Los Angeles, Entertainment Wire
A psychologist reacting to the tragedy in Paris . . . says that another tragedy is just beginning. "The trauma faced by her two children and the psychological reactions they will face today and live with the rest of their lives . . .

"There is no way we can begin to describe what these children are feeling but it's most likely a combination of shock, anger, denial, and depression. We might have lost a princess but they lost a mother and they need the help of experienced professionals to sort it out . . . " Contact: Robert R. B____ Ph.D.

September 1
STATEMENT BY THE REV.

BILLY GRAHAM ON THE DEATH OF DIANA, PRINCESS OF WALES

Minneapolis, PR Newswire
Like almost everyone else in the world, the unexpected death of Diana, Princess of Wales, came as a profound shock to my wife Ruth and me. I know that Her Majesty The Queen and the other members of the Royal Family especially [are] carrying a heavy burden during this time, and we are praying for them and for all those who were touched by this tragedy.

This tragedy should remind us again of how fragile life is, and how we should each be ready to enter eternity and meet God at any moment.

September 3
FTD ADDS OPERATORS TO HANDLE CALLS FOR FLOWER ORDERS IN MEMORY OF PRINCESS DIANA

Chicago, PR Newswire
[In] response to numerous calls regarding sending flowers for Princess Diana's London funeral this Saturday, FTD has added additional customer service representatives to process these international flower orders.

"Even given the extraordinary tragedy of the Princess's recent death, we are taken aback by the sheer volume of calls and inquiries we are receiving," said Bob Norton, President and CEO of FTD.

Big year: Dr. Pepper, Coca-Cola, and Hires Root Beer were all invented in 1886.

"We are seeing to it that all orders received are processed with the utmost expediency and care."

September 4
PRINCESS DIANA TRAGEDY REINFORCES THE IMPORTANCE OF ESTATE PLANNING

Philadelphia, Business Wire
The recent tragedy involving the death of Princess Diana has left the world stunned and concerned for her two sons, Princes William and Henry.

It was reported that Diana has willed close to 90 percent of her $30 million dollar estate to her sons, which will include money, property, and jewelry.

In light of this tragedy, the Pennsylvania Institute of CPAs suggests that everyone prepare a will for the sake of their heirs. Estate planning is important because it gives you control over how your wealth is distributed and can prevent unnecessary and expensive disputes about the disposition of your assets—as well as the caretaking of your children—upon your death.

September 5
MICHIGAN FOOD TRADE ASSOCIATION CALLS ON FOOD STORES TO STOP SELLING SLEAZE PUBLICATIONS EXPLOITING PRINCESS DIANA

Warren, Mich., PR Newswire
The Michigan Food & Beverage Association (MFBA) is asking all of its 2,900 members on a voluntary basis to refuse to sell certain supermarket tabloids or similar newspapers or magazines which exploit Princess Diana's death for a minimum period of four weeks effective immediately.

"Enough is enough," said Ed Deed, president of Michigan's largest food trade association.

"Exploiting Princess Diana's death is unconscionable."

* * *

JOB HUNTING

Some entries from real-life job applications:

- REASON FOR LEAVING LAST JOB: "I was working for my mom until she decided to move."
- PERSONAL INTERESTS: "Donating blood—14 gallons so far."
- REFERENCES: "None. I've left a path of destruction behind me."

John Scott Harrison's father, William Henry Harrison, was a U.S. president . . .

AIR FORCE ONE

You've heard of Air Force One, but what do you really, know about it? Here's a short history of what's now considered the "flying White House."

HOMEBOUND

Nowadays we take it for granted that traveling around the world is part of the president's job. But that wasn't always the case: As late as the 1930s, it was considered the president's duty not to leave the country—he was expected to remain on U.S. soil for his entire term of office . . . and wasn't even supposed to stray far from Washington, D.C. This tradition was left over from the pre-telephone age, when the only way a president could command the government on a moment's notice in an emergency was to be physically in or near the nation's capital at all times. Leaving town literally meant leaving power, and presidents aren't supposed to do that. For the first 130 years of the Republic, not a single American president left the United States while in office, not even once. (Well, okay, once. Grover Cleveland briefly sailed across the U.S.-Canada border in the 1890s.)

So in January 1943, when Franklin Roosevelt flew to North Africa to meet with Winston Churchill and plan the Allied invasion of Southern Europe, he became only the third president to leave the country (the others: cousin Teddy Roosevelt inspected the Panama Canal in 1906 and Woodrow Wilson attended the Paris Peace Conference at the end of World War I).

SMALL WORLD

FDR hated airplanes, but German submarines were patrolling the Atlantic and sinking American ships, so the Secret Service forbade him from traveling by sea. He flew in a chartered PanAm Flying Boat seaplane called the *Dixie Clipper*. That changed everything. When FDR's historic trip became publicized weeks later, it turned out to be an important psychological boost not just for the war effort, but also for the fledgling airline industry. If it was safe enough for President Roosevelt to fly during the war, people reasoned, it would be safe enough for anyone else to fly in times of peace. Furthermore, Americans realized that with planes, the president could travel almost anywhere in the world in a matter of days

. . . So was his son Benjamin Harrison.

and return just as quickly if need be. And thanks to radio and telephone communications, it was possible to remain in fairly close contact with the government at all times. Within weeks of Roosevelt's historic journey, the U.S. Army Air Corps (precursor to the Air Force) began making plans to provide a custom-made plane for the president's exclusive use. Since then, each president has had an official plane, and today the president's airplane is considered an extension of the White House.

THE NAME

- Technically speaking, although there is a special presidential airplane, it doesn't have the radio call sign *Air Force One*. The call sign is attached to the president himself; it is given to whatever Air Force plane in which he happens to be flying. Likewise, any plane in which the vice president flies is known as *Air Force Two*.

- In fact, before JFK, each presidential aircraft had its own name: President Roosevelt's plane was nicknamed the "Sacred Cow" by the White House Press Corp; President Truman's plane was the *Independence* (Truman named it himself, out of fear that it might otherwise become the "Sacred Cow II"); and President Eisenhower's was the *Columbine*.

- Then, in 1962, President Kennedy took delivery of a Boeing 707, the first presidential jet airplane . . . and never bothered to name it. With no other name to go by, the media began referring to the plane by its call sign. The term *Air Force One* has been used for presidential aircraft ever since.

- In 1971 Richard Nixon renamed his plane *The Spirit of '76* in advance of the U.S. Bicentennial, but the name never took hold.

MADE TO ORDER

- One of the perks of being president is that you get to have *Air Force One* remodeled to suit your own tastes. President Truman had his plane painted to look like a giant eagle, with stylized blue feathers, cockpit windows that looked like eyes, and a nose painted to look like a big brown beak. (The nose was later repainted yellow, out of fear the White House Press Corps might nickname the plane "Brown Nose.")

Your fingernails are made from the same substance as a bird's beak.

- President Lyndon Johnson had all of the passenger seats unbolted and turned around so that they faced the rear of the plane—toward his compartment. He also ripped out the cherry wood divider separating his compartment from the rest of the plane and replaced it with clear Plexiglas, Jerry Ter Horst writes in *The Flying White House,* "so that he could keep an eye on everybody—and they on him."

- LBJ also installed a secret taping system, which, ironically, President Nixon ordered removed after he took office.

CODE NAME: PROJECT LIDA ROSE

The most extensive makeover for *Air Force One* came in the late 1950s and was proposed by Allen Dulles, director of the CIA. Not long after he inaugurated the super-secret, high-altitude U-2 spy plane program, Dulles proposed outfitting the president's airplane with hidden spy cameras for an upcoming trip to the Soviet Union. Unlike U-2 spy planes, which flew at altitudes as high as 70,000 feet, President Eisenhower's plane would be flying under 5,000 feet, and was the only Western aircraft allowed into Russian airspace. Why not take advantage of the trip to take much closer pictures of Soviet defenses?

Whether or not Eisenhower was informed of the plan (many historians suspect he wasn't), it was approved, and his aircraft was fitted with a camera inside a hidden compartment in the fuselage. The controls were carefully disguised to look like the co-pilot's fresh-air vent, so that they would be undetectable even if a Soviet pilot was riding shotgun in the cockpit.

The cameras on board the presidential plane might well have provided the U.S. with the biggest intelligence coup of the Cold War . . . had they ever been put to use. But they weren't—on May 1, 1960, pilot Francis Gary Powers was shot down in his U-2 sky-plane over Soviet airspace, and Nikita Khrushchev used the incident to scuttle Eisenhower's visit to the USSR. The cameras were removed when John F. Kennedy was elected president.

HELP YOURSELF

- Stealing objects stamped with the presidential seal has long been one of the perks of being invited to fly aboard *Air Force One*. Still, not every president has approved: President Carter was so offended by the practice that he ordered the plane's

---

Coconut shells can absorb more impact than most crash helmets.

expensive engraved crystal ashtrays, candy dishes, and wine glasses removed and had them replaced with plastic containers and paper cups.

- Lyndon Johnson took the opposite approach—he filled the plane with expensive trinkets so that his guests would have something to steal. "It was useful to him to have people brag about flying with LBJ—and to have a souvenir with which to prove it," one aide remembers.

- True to form, when LBJ returned home to Texas on his last official trip aboard *Air Force One,* he reportedly stole everything that wasn't nailed down . . . and a few items that were, recalls pilot Ralph Albertazzie:

When I took over the plane after it came back from Texas, I found an empty larder. We had no presidential china, no *Air Force One* silverware, no *Air Force One* cigarettes, no cocktail napkins, no towels—not even any paper products like toilet tissue. They were all gone. Even LBJ's special executive chair—the one we called "the throne"—was unbolted from the floor and taken away. The presidential stateroom was bare of pillows, blankets, and everything else that bore the presidential seal. I couldn't believe my eyes.

* * *

DRIVE-IN FOOD

The first drive-in restaurant was Kirby's Pig Stand, opened by J. G. Kirby on a highway between Dallas and Fort Worth in 1921. But it turns out that the idea of restaurant service to an automobile is almost as old as cars themselves.

It started as a way for the upper-class of Boston to show off. In 1904 Mrs. "Jack" Gardner of Boston, a social-climber famous for outrageous stunts like walking a lion around the city streets, organized a special "motoring event." She and four carloads of friends went to the Hotel Touraine, where, at her insistence, they were served oysters by waiters "compelled to run out with their trays to the autos." Next, the party motored to Adams House, where they were served soup in the street, and then to eight more establishments for eight more courses, the last of which was chop suey at a Chinese restaurant, for dessert.

One in every 5 potatoes grown in the U.S. end up as french fries.

THE NEWSPAPER HOAX THAT SHOOK THE WORLD

The media's power to "create" news has become a hot topic in recent years. But it's nothing new. This true story, from a book called The Fabulous Rogues, *by Alexander Klein, is an example of what's been going on for at least a century. It was sent to us by BRI member Jim Morton.*

Most journalistic hoaxes, no matter how ingenious, create only temporary excitement. But in 1899 four reporters in Denver, Colorado, concocted a fake story that, within a relatively short time, made news history—violent history at that. Here's how it happened.

THE DENVER FOUR
One Saturday night the four reporters—from Denver's four news-papers, the *Times*, *Post*, *Republican*, and *Rocky Mountain News*—met by chance in the railroad station where they had each come hoping to spot an arriving celebrity around whom they could write a feature. Disgustedly, they confessed to one another that they hadn't picked up a newsworthy item all evening.

"I hate to go back to the city desk without something," one of the reporters, Jack Toumay, said.

"Me, too," agreed Al Stevens. " I don't know what you guys are going to do, but I'm going to fake. It won't hurt anybody, so what the devil."

The other three fell in with the idea and they all walked up Seventeenth Street to the Oxford Hotel, where, over beers, they began to cast about for four possible fabrications. John Lewis, who was known as "King" because of his tall, dignified bearing, interrupted one of the preliminary gambits for a point of strategy. Why dream up four lukewarm fakes, he asked. Why not concoct a sizzler which they would all use, and make it stick better by their solidarity.

The strategy was adopted by unanimous vote, and a reporter named Hal Wilshire came up with the first suggestion: Maybe they

---

An adult horse eats 15 pounds of hay and 9 pounds of grain every day.

could invent some stiff competition for the Colorado Fuel and Iron Company by reporting the arrival of several steel men, backed by an independent Wall Street combine, come to buy a large site on which they planned to erect a new steel mill. The steel mill died a quick death; it could be checked too easily and it would be difficult to dispose of later.

Stevens suggested something more dramatic: Several detectives just in from New York on the trail of two desperados who had kidnapped a rich heiress. But this story was too hot; the editors might check the wire services or even the New York police directly.

Thereupon Toumay and Lewis both came up with the obvious answer. What they needed was a story with a foreign angle that would be difficult to verify. Russia? No, none of them knew enough about Russia to make up an acceptable story. Germany was a possibility or perhaps, a bull-ring story from Madrid? Toumay didn't think bull-fighting was of sufficient interest to Denverites. How about Holland, one of the reporters offered, something with dikes or windmills in it, maybe a romance of some sort.

THE PLOT THICKENS

By this time the reporters had had several beers. The romance angle seemed attractive. But one of the men thought Japan would be a more intriguing locale for it. Another preferred China; why the country was so antiquated and unprogressive, hiding behind its Great wall, they'd be doing the Chinese a favor by bringing some news about their country to the outside world.

At this point, Lewis broke in excitedly. "That's it," he cried, "the Great Wall of China! Must be fifty years since that old pile's been in the news. Let's build our story around it. Let's do the Chinese a real favor, let's tear the old pile down!"

Tear down the Great Wall of China! The notion fascinated the four reporters. It would certainly make the front page. One of them objected that there might be repercussions, but the others voted him down. They did, however, decide to temper the story somewhat.

A group of American engineers had stopped over in Denver en route to China, where they were being sent at the request of the ruling powers of China, to make plans for demolishing the Great Wall at minimum cost. The Chinese had decided to raze the

A runner consumes about 7 quarts of oxygen while running a 100-yard dash.

ancient boundary as a gesture of international good will. From now on China would welcome foreign trade.

By the time they had agreed on the details it was after eleven. They rushed over to the best hotel in town, and talked the night clerk into cooperating. Then they signed four fictitious names to the hotel register. The clerk agreed to tell anyone who checked that the hotel had played host to four New Yorkers, that they had been interviewed by the reporters, and then had left early the next morning for California. Before heading for their respective city desks, the four reporters had a last beer over which they all swore to stick to their story and not to reveal the true facts so long as any of the others were alive. (Only years later did the last survivor, Hal Wilshire, let out the secret.)

GREAT CHINESE WALL DOOMED!
PEKING SEEKS WORLD TRADE!

THE SNOWBALL EFFECT

Within a few days Denver had forgotten all about the Great Wall. So far, so good, But other places soon began to hear about it. Two weeks later Lewis was startled to find the coming destruction of the Great Wall spread across the Sunday supplement of a large Eastern newspaper, complete with illustrations, an analysis of the Chinese government's historic decision—and quotes from a Chinese mandarin visiting in New York, who confirmed the report.

The story was carried by many other papers, both in America and in Europe. By the time it reached China it had gone through many transformations. The version published there—and the only one that probably made sense in view of the absence of any information on the subject from the Chinese government—was that the Americans were planning to send an expedition to tear down the Chinese national monument, the Great Wall.

Such a report would have infuriated any nation. It led to particularly violent repercussions in China at that time. The Chinese were already stirred up about the issue of foreign intervention—European powers were parceling out and occupying the whole country. Russia had recently gotten permission to run the Siberian railway through Manchuria. A year previously German marines had seized the port town of Kiachow, and set up a military and naval base there. France followed by taking Kwangchowan.

When you pop a champagne cork, it can travel as fast as 100 mph.

England had sent a fleet to the Gulf of Chihli and bullied China into leasing Weihaiwei, midway between the recent acquisitions of Russia and Germany.

Faced with this danger of occidental exploitation, possibly even partition, the Chinese government under Emperor Kwang-Hsu began to institute radical reforms, to remodel the army along more modern lines, and to send students to foreign universities to obtain vital technical training.

An important segment of Chinese society bitterly resented not only foreign intervention, but all foreign cultural influences, as well as the new governmental reforms. In 1898 Empress Tsu Hsi made herself regent and officially encouraged all possible opposition to Western ideas. A secret society known as the Boxers, but whose full name was "The Order of Literary Patriotic Harmonious Fists," took the lead in verbal attacks on missionaries and Western businessmen in China by openly displaying banners that read "Exterminate the foreigners and save the dynasty."

THE SPARK THAT LIT THE FIRE

Into this charged atmosphere came the news of America's plan to force the demolition of the Great Wall. It proved the spark that is credited with setting off the Boxer Rebellion. A missionary later reported: "The story was published with shouting headlines and violent editorial comment. Denials did no good. The Boxers, already incensed, believed the yarn and now there was no stopping them."

By June 1900, the whole country was overrun with bands of Boxers. Christian villages were destroyed and hundreds of native converts massacred near Peking. The city itself was in turmoil, with murder and pillage daily occurrences and the foreign embassies under siege.

Finally, in August, an international army of 12,000 French, British, American, Russian, German, and Japanese troops invaded China and fought its way to Peking. There, the troops not only brought relief to their imperiled countrymen, but also looted the Emperor's Palace and slaughtered innumerable Chinese without inquiring too closely whether they belonged to the "Harmonious Fists" or just happened to be passing by. The invading nations also forced China to pay an indemnity of $320 million and to grant further economic concessions. All this actually spurred the reform movement, which culminated with the Sun Yat-Sen revolution in 1911.

Thus did a journalistic hoax make history. Of course, the Boxers might have been sparked into violence in some other fashion, or built up to it of their own accord. But can we be sure? The fake story may well have been the final necessary ingredient. A case could even be made that the subsequent history of China, right up to the present, might have been entirely different if those four reporters had been less inventive that Saturday night in the Hotel Oxford bar.

*   *   *

And Now It's Time For A Little...WEIRD MUSIC

Here are some real (no kidding) albums you can get:

- "Music to Make Automobiles By"

Volkswagen made this recording "to inspire their workers." It features the sounds of an auto assembly line backed with an orchestra.

Not to be confused with:

- "Music to Light Your Pilot by," from the Heil-Quaker Corporation (a heater and air-conditioner manufacturer),

- "Music to Relax By in Your Barcalounger"

- "Music to Be Murdered By" (from Alfred Hitchcock)

- "The American Gun: A Celebration in Song"

A late-night TV special, not available in stores. Rage International offered this country music classic with a free oiled plastic rifle case. Songs include: "Thank you, Smith & Wesson," "America Was Born with a Gun in Her Hand," "Never Mind the Dog, Beware the Owner," and the ever-popular "Gun Totin' Woman."

OOPS!

Everyone's amused by tales of outrageous blunders—probably because it's comforting to know that someone's screwing up even worse than we are. So go ahead and feel superior for a few minutes.

HOT CLUE
PHILADELPHIA—"A former Philadelphia fireman, in Federal Court here trying to overturn his dismissal for long hair, set his head on fire.

"William Michini apparently tried to dramatize that his locks were not a safety threat to his job. 'Hair is self-extinguishing. It doesn't burn,' he boasted. With that he struck a match and held it to his head, which caught fire. 'It must have been the hairspray I used,' said the sheepish firefighter."
—Remarkabilia, by John Train

. . . AND HOW'S YOUR WIFE, CARLY?
"Kathie Lee Gifford inadvertently stumbled into talk-show hell on a recent 'Live with Regis and Kathie Lee.'

"Singer-songwriter James Taylor was one of the guests, and the perky one, just making conversation, asked how his older brother, Alex, was doing well. . . . Alex died about four years ago.'

"The *Washington Post* noted: 'Mortification hung in the air for a few long moments.' Blues singer Alex Taylor died of a heart attack in 1993, at age 46."
—The Portland Oregonian, May 1, 1997

WHAT ARE YOU DOING HERE?
"The Aldo Oliveri Stadium was meant to be the perfect memorial for one of Italy's greatest sports heroes: a stadium in Verona, dedicated to the memory of the goalie who led Italy to victory in the 1938 World Cup. Everything went smoothly right up to the weekend before it was due to open, when a small problem was discovered. Aldo Oliveri wasn't dead; he was alive, 86, and by all accounts, in the best of health. Plans are now afoot to open the stadium late, under a different name."
—The Fortean Times, 1997

Bagpipes were invented in Iran and brought to Scotland by the Romans.

... AND WHAT ARE YOU DOING HERE?

"In 1964 Gary Grannai escorted Tricia Nixon to the International Debutante Ball in New York City. Seven years later President Nixon was justifying his prosecution of the Vietnam War, despite the family's loss of a friend: 'Gary was a second lieutenant. He was on patrol duty when it happened. You feel the personal tragedy when it comes into your own home. Yet there is no alternative to the war's going on.' Publication of these remarks was followed by the [embarrassing] reappearance of Gary Grannai, who was very much alive and happily married."

—Oops, by Richard Smith and Edward Recter

WELL, IN FRANCE KIDS LIKE IT

"French broadcasting system Canal France International blamed a 'technical glitch' that sent an X-rated film instead of children's programming to Arab countries last Saturday. 'We deeply regret this unacceptable incident, and we share in the high feelings prompted in Saudi Arabia and more widely in the Arab world,' a foreign ministry spokesman said. An investigation is under way."

—USA Today, July 23, 1997

SURE IT WAS A MISTAKE

TORONTO—"Proofreaders at Canada's postal service let a royal error slip through in the production of a souvenir stamp book—a reference to 'the Prince of Whales.'

"Much to Canada Post's chagrin, the book was printed with a passage describing a visit by the 'Prince of Whales' to the snowy shores in 1860. He eventually became King Edward VII.

"It was human error and there was no intended slight to the Royal Family or to Prince Charles, said a spokesman. He also said Canada Post will not pull the book from shelves."

—Reuters News Service, 1997

ALPHABET SOUP

In the 1980s, the Pfeiffer Brewing Company decided to use its successful print ad campaign on the radio. They realized it was a mistake when they heard the announcer say their written slogan aloud: "Pfeiffer's . . . the beer with the silent P."

THE FIRST LADY

Many Americans don't recall that Eleanor Roosevelt was the first modern first lady (1933–1945) to take an active interest in America's political life, supporting causes and speaking out about issues.

"Courage is more exhilarating than fear, and in the long run it is easier."

"We started from scratch, every American an immigrant who came because he wanted a change. Why are we now afraid to change?"

"For a really healthy development of all the arts, you need an educated audience as well as performers."

"People grow through experience if they meet life honestly and courageously. That is how character is built."

"Every effort must be made in childhood to teach the young to use their own minds. For one thing is sure: If they don't make up their own minds, someone will do it for them."

"It is curious how much more interest can be evoked by a mixture of gossip, romance, and mystery than by facts."

"The important thing is neither your nationality nor the religion you professed, but how your faith translated itself in your life."

"In this world, most of us are motivated by fear—governments more, perhaps, even than individuals."

"Remember always that you have not only the right to be an individual; you have the obligation to be one. You cannot make any useful contribution in life unless you do this."

"The idea of rugged individualism, completely divorced from the public interest, has a heroic sound, a kind of stalwart simplicity. The only trouble is that for many years it has been inapplicable to American life."

"The function of democratic living is not to lower standards, but to raise those that have been too low."

Hardest substance in your body: the enamel in your teeth.

PAUL IS DEAD!

The biggest, most widely discussed rumor about rock bands and performers ever was—appropriately—about the Beatles. In 1969 millions of fans were convinced that Paul McCartney was dead, and spent months trying to prove it. Here's the inside story.

HAVE YOU HEARD THE NEWS?

Although no one knows precisely when or how it started, sometime in 1969 a rumor began circulating that Paul McCartney of the Beatles was dead. The idea really took off one Sunday that September, when an Eastern Michigan University student identifying himself as "Tom" called the "Russ Gibb Show" on WKNR-FM.

The caller told Gibb he'd heard that McCartney had been dead for some time, that the rest of the Beatles knew about it, and that they had started inserting "hints" of McCartney's death into their most recent record albums. Why were they keeping McCartney's death a secret? Maybe it was to let fans down easily . . . maybe it was to make as much money as they could before the death became public and the band had to dissolve.

But that was beside the point. The point was that Paul was dead, the caller told Gibb, and the proof was in the music.

GETTING IT BACKWARD

Gibb had been in the radio business for some time, and this wasn't the first dead-rock-star story he'd ever heard. Celebrity-death rumors were as common as they were unfounded, and Gibb initially dismissed this one as being just as ridiculous as the others . . . until Tom told him to play the Beatles' song "Revolution 9" backward to hear one of the "clues."

When Gibb played back the part of the song where the voice says "Number Nine" over and over, he thought he could hear the words, "Turn me on, dead man." He began to wonder if Paul McCartney really was dead, and he shared his suspicions with his listeners. Within minutes the switchboard was lit up with calls. Everybody wanted to know if McCartney was really dead.

Armadillos can catch malaria.

PAPER TRAIL

The rumors might never have amounted to anything more, if someone named Fred LaBour hadn't been listening to the "Russ Gibb Show" that Sunday afternoon.

LaBour, a University of Michigan sophomore who wrote for his college newspaper, *The Michigan Daily*, was supposed to write a review of the Beatles' new *Abbey Road* album for an upcoming issue. But he was still looking for some kind of angle that would make the article more interesting.

As LaBour listened to Tom and Russ Gibb discussing whether Paul McCartney was dead, he knew he had his angle—turn the rumor into a full-length article, a satire that pretended to take the whole idea seriously. LaBour thought it would make an interesting and amusing read. He had no idea how right he was.

The next day, LaBour wrote up his "review" of *Abbey Road* and turned it in to John Gray, the arts editor for the *Michigan Daily*. Gray was so impressed that he decided to give it an entire page in the paper. "Just how long did it take you to come up with this masterpiece?" he asked.

"It only took an hour and a half," LaBour said, "and it's the best bull**** I ever wrote."

HOT OFF THE PRESSES

LaBour's article ran on page 2 of *The Michigan Daily* with the headline "McCartney Dead; New Evidence Brought to Light." The article claimed that Paul had been dead for nearly three years:

> Paul McCartney was killed in an automobile accident in early November, 1966, after leaving EMI recording studios tired, sad, and dejected. The Beatles had been preparing their forthcoming album, tentatively titled *Smile*, when progress bogged down in intragroup hassles and bickering. Paul climbed into his Aston-Martin, sped away into the rainy, chill night, and was found hours later pinned under his car in a culvert with the top of his head sheared off. He was deader than a doornail.

The article claimed that the surviving Beatles decided "to make the best of a bad situation," because "Paul always loved a good joke," LaBour quoted John Lennon as saying. The surviving Beatles decided to replace Paul with a body double and continue as if he hadn't died. To that end, the group held a "Paul Look-Alike

---

Aspirin has never been approved by the FDA. It has never been rejected, either.

Contest" and found a living substitute in Scotland, a man named William Campbell.

Thanks to extensive voice training, lip-synching, and a moustache (which John, George, and Ringo also grew), Campbell had somehow managed to pass himself off as Paul McCartney for more than three years, despite the fact that the band had been inserting clues into their songs and onto their album covers all along. The *Abbey Road* album cover, for example, shows the four Beatles crossing the street: McCartney is the only one walking out of step, the only one who's barefoot ("the way corpses are buried in Italy," LaBour claimed), and is holding a cigarette in his right hand, when everybody knows he is left-handed. On top of that, the license plate on one of the cars parked on the road reads "28IF"—which LaBour claimed was a coded way of saying that McCartney would be 28 if he were still alive.

CLUE ME IN

LaBour probably never intended for his joke to travel beyond the University of Michigan, but by the end of the day the story had spread to other nearby colleges, and from there to the rest of the country over the next several days. Wherever the rumor spread, people began studying the Beatles' recent album covers and listening to their albums backward . . . and finding their own "clues," which only added to the story's credibility and caused it to spread even further.

"In terms of media coverage," Andru J. Reeve writes in *Turn Me On, Dead Man*, "the rumor reached an apex during the last two weeks of October. Major newspapers and network television had avoided comment up to this point, for they assumed that, like rumors of the past, the story would fade before the presses had a chance to warm up."

SILENT PARTNER

So did Paul McCartney: Recently married and burned out from the difficult *Abbey Road* recording session, McCartney was holed up with his wife and kids in Scotland and wasn't coming out for anything, not even to prove he wasn't dead. Like a lot of people, when he first heard the rumor, he figured it would soon pass.

But the rumor refused to die, and McCartney finally consented to giving Apple Records a written statement that he wasn't dead. But he still refused to make a public appearance. For many people, the fact that a written statement was all the Beatles' own record company could come up with was further proof that he really was dead.

WHEW!

It's probably fitting that *Life* magazine provided the most convincing evidence that death had not taken McCartney. *Life* sent a reporter and two staff photographers to McCartney's farm to "bring back any visual evidence of Paul's existence, even if he refused to be interviewed." McCartney not only refused, he heaved a bucket of water at them. Once he calmed down, however, McCartney let the photographers take some pictures of him with his family. *Life* ran one on the cover the next issue.

Amazingly, some skeptics saw the *Life* magazine article as further proof that McCartney was dead—when you hold the magazine cover up to a bright light, the car in the Lincoln Continental ad on the reverse side appears to be impaling McCartney. For most fans, though, seeing the pictures of Paul with his family was enough, and the rumor receded as quickly as it had spread.

FOR THE RECORD

The only unresolved question was whether the rumors were orchestrated or fueled by the Beatles themselves, perhaps to increase sales of *Abbey Road.*

"One undeniable fact became apparent," Andru Reeve writes: "sales of Beatles albums did increase." Priced $2 higher than earlier Beatles albums, *Abbey Road* sold slowly at first . . . until about the time that the rumors started circulating. Then, Reeve writes, it "rocketed to number one and the other albums germane to the rumor (*Sgt. Pepper's, Magical Mystery Tour,* and the "White Album" resurfaced on the Billboard Top 200 LP chart after absences of up to a year and a half."

* * *

"I did not attend his funeral, but I wrote a nice letter saying I approved it."

—*Mark Twain*

In her entire life, Queen Berengaria of England never once visited England.

URBAN LEGENDS

Word to the wise: If a story sounds true, but also seems too good to be true, it's probably an "urban legend." Here's the inside poop.

WHAT MAKES A GOOD URBAN LEGEND?

People who study urban legends point to several characteristics that contribute to their believability and chances of survival.

- **They contain "details" that create the impression the story is true.** Take the story about the woman who tries on an imported coat at the mall, feels a sting on her wrist . . . and later dies from the bite of a poisonous baby snake that had hatched in the lining of the coat. The name of the mall (it's almost always nearby), the item of clothing, its price, and other seemingly corroborative details are usually included in the story.

- **They may contain a grain of truth, which implies that the entire story is true.** No word on what would happen if someone really did put a dog in a microwave oven, but if you've ever tried to hardboil an egg in one, you know it would probably be ugly.

- **The story reflects contemporary fears.** The poodle-in-the-microwave story dates back to the days when few people owned microwaves, and fewer still understood how they worked. Other legends may be inspired by fear of attack, embarrassment, ghosts, or science.

- **The person telling the story believes he knows the person who knows the person who witnessed or is involved in the story.** The listener thereby accepts it on faith, and when they tell the story, they can also claim a personal connection that makes the story more believable.

- **The story is reported in the media, either as fact or a rumor.** It doesn't really matter whether the news story gives it credibility or labels it a myth; either way, the legend is often given new life. In 1917, columnist H.L. Mencken published a fictional history of the bathtub in the New York *Evening Mail* that claimed President Millard Fillmore installed the first White House bathtub in 1851. The story isn't true—Andrew Jackson

---

Odds that you will become famous enough to merit mention in a history book: 1 in 6 million.

installed the first indoor plumbing, complete with bathtub, in 1833. Mencken later admitted the hoax. But it continues to appear in print to this day.

FIVE URBAN LEGENDS
1. THE STORY: On October 10, 1995, the U.S. Chief of Naval Operations released the following transcript of what the story claims is "an actual radio conversation."

> NAVY: Please divert your course 15 degrees to the north to avoid a collision.

> CIVILIAN: Recommend you divert YOUR course 15 degrees to south to avoid a collision.

> NAVY: This is the captain of a U.S. Navy ship. I say again, divert YOUR course.

> CIVILIAN: No, I say again, you divert YOUR course.

> NAVY: THIS IS THE AIRCRAFT CARRIER ENTERPRISE. WE ARE A LARGE WARSHIP OF THE U.S. NAVY. DIVERT YOUR COURSE NOW!

> CIVILIAN: This is a lighthouse. Your call.

How It Spread: On the Internet.
The Truth: According to Patrick Crispen, who co-writes The Internet Tourbus (http://www.tourbus.com), "It turns out the Navy story is a very old urban legend," made fresh by new exposure on the Internet.

2. THE STORY: A traveler visiting New York City meets an attractive woman in a bar and takes her back to his hotel room. That's all he remembers—the next thing he knows, he's lying in a bathtub filled with ice; and surgical tubing is coming out of two freshly stitched wounds on his lower chest. There's a note by the tub that says, "Call 911. We've removed your left kidney." (Sometimes both are removed). The doctors in the emergency room tell him he's the victim of thieves who steal organs for use in transplants. (According to one version of the story, medical students perform the surgeries, then use the money to pay off student loans.)
Note: Uncle John actually heard this from a friend, Karen Pinsky,

Originally, the "five golden rings" in the Twelve Days of Christmas

who sells real estate. She said it was a warning given by a real estate firm to agents headed to big cities for conventions.

How It spread: French folklorist Veronique Campion-Vincent has traced the story to Honduras and Guatemala, where rumors began circulating in 1987 that babies were being kidnapped and murdered for their organs. The alleged culprits: wealthy Americans needing transplants. From there the story spread to South America, then all over the world. Wherever such stories surfaced—*including* the United States—newspapers reported them as fact. The New York version surfaced in the winter of 1991, and in February 1992, the *New York Times* "verified" it. Scriptwriter Joe Morgenstern, thinking it was true, even made it the subject of an episode of the NBC-TV series "Law and Order."

The Truth: National and international agencies have investigated the claims, but haven't been able to substantiate even a single case of organ theft anywhere in the world. The agencies say the stories aren't just groundless, but also implausible. "These incredible stories ignored the complexity of organ transplant operations," Jan Brunvald writes in *The Baby Train and Other Lusty Urban Legends*, "which would preclude any such quick removal and long-distance shipment of body parts."

3. THE STORY: One of the most potent forms of marijuana in the world is "Manhattan White" (also known as "New York Albino"). The strain evolved in the dark sewers of New York City as a direct result of thousands of drug dealers flushing their drugs down the
toilet during drug busts. The absence of light in the sewers turns the marijuana plants white; raw sewage, acting as a fertilizer, makes it extremely potent.

The Truth: Most likely an updated version of the classic urban myth that alligators live in the New York sewers.

4. THE STORY: A young woman finishes shopping at the mall and walks out to her car to go home. But there's an old lady sitting in the car. "I'm sorry ma'am, but isn't your car," the woman says.

"I know," the old lady replies, "but I had to sit down." Then she asks the young woman for a ride home.

The young woman agrees, but then remembers she locked the car when she arrived at the mall. She pretends to go back into the

weren't rings. They were ringed pheasants.

mall to get her sister, and returns with a security guard. The guard and the old lady get into a fight, and in the struggle the old lady's wig falls off, revealing that she's actually a man. The police take the man away, and under the car seat, they find an axe. (The story is kept alive by claims that the mall has bribed reporters and police to keep the story quiet.)

The Truth: The modern form of the tale comes from the early 1980s and places the action at numerous malls . . . New York, Las Vegas, Milwaukee, Chicago, and even Fresno, California, depending on who's telling the story. Folklorists speculate the tale may date all the way back to an 1834 English newspaper account of "a gentleman in his carriage, who on opening the supposed female's reticule [handbag] finds to his horror a pair of loaded pistols inside."

5. THE STORY: Two young men are driving home from a party one rainy night and notice a beautiful young woman standing by the side of the road. She doesn't have a raincoat or umbrella, so they stop and offer her a ride. She accepts, and while they drive her to her house, one of the young men gives her his jacket to wear.

About a block from the young woman's house, they turn around to say something to her . . . but she is gone. They drive to her house anyway, knock on the door, and the woman who answers tells them, "that was my daughter. She was killed two years ago on the same spot you picked her up. She does this all the time."

The next day the young men look up the girl's obituary in the library. There it is—complete with a picture of the girl they picked up. Then they go to the cemetery . . . and find the jacket she borrowed resting on her tombstone.

The Truth: Another oldie-but-goodie. According to folklorist Richard Dorson, it predates the automobile. The story "is traced back to the 19th century," he writes, "in America, Italy, Ireland, Turkey, and China; with a horse and wagon picking up the benighted traveler." In the Hawaiian version, the girl hitches a ride on a rickshaw.

UNFINISHED MASTERPIECE: THE BEACH BOYS' *SMILE*

*Today they're thought of as a golden-oldies pop band, but at
their peak the Beach Boys were America's #1 rock band and
considered the creative equivalent of the Beatles. Here's the story
of the never-completed album that might have kept them on top.*

UNFINISHED MASTERPIECE: *Smile*, by Brian Wilson,
Van Dyke Parks, and the Beach Boys

WHAT IT IS: An unfinished Beach Boys album.
Considered by many who have heard bootleg tapes to be among
the best albums in the history of rock 'n' roll, *Smile* might have had
the same impact on the Beach Boys' career that *Sergeant Pepper's
Lonely Hearts Club Band* had on the Beatles' (it was released a few
months after Brian Wilson ended work on *Smile*).

THE STORY: Before they'd even graduated from high school, the
three Wilson brothers (Brian, Carl, and Dennis), their cousin Mike
Love, and a friend named Al Jardine had hit it big with good-time
pop music about Southern California surfing, cars, and girls.

The man behind the music was the oldest brother, Brian, who
wrote most of their songs, arranged their harmonies, and worked
with studio musicians to get exactly the right sound. In the
Beatlemania mid-1960s, when it seemed like only British Invasion
groups could make the charts, the Beach Boys successfully matched
the Beatles, with hit after hit.

BATTLE OF THE BANDS

A rivalry developed between the Beach Boys and Beatles. When
one group released a new album, it prompted the other to see if
they could top it, a process that intensified as both bands' music
became more serious and complex. Wilson, though, was at a disad-
vantage: The Beatles had two great songwriters, John Lennon and
Paul McCartney (three if you include the less-prolific George).

And they had a brilliant producer, George Martin. The Beach Boys essentially had just Brian. "From the point of view of his family," David Leaf writes in *The Beach Boys and the California Myth*, "Brian was almost a benefactor rather than an artist. He wrote the hits and made the records, and the group sang them and toured and were rich and lived in the manner they had become accustomed to, all thanks to Brian Wilson."

For several years, Brian managed to write virtually all the songs on the three albums a year the band released, while also performing in concerts all over the world. But with such an unrelenting schedule, something was bound to give, and in December 1964, Brian had a nervous breakdown on an airplane while en route to a concert tour. He recuperated, but he and the band decided to hire a replacement for him for touring, so Brian could stay home and work full-time in the studio, creating songs that would be ready for the boys to add their voices to whenever they returned from the road.

Brian made the studio his instrument and created a unique pop sound. But the new songs began to take the Beach Boys in a new direction, away from the surfing, cars, and girls that had made them America's #1 rock 'n' roll act. It was a direction the other members of the band weren't sure they wanted to go.

PET SOUNDS

In May 1966, the group released an album called *Pet Sounds*, which many critics consider the best Beach Boys album ever. It served as a wake-up call to the Beatles, a warning that their rivalry with the Beach Boys was escalating to a new level. Paul McCartney was floored by what he heard. "No one is educated musically until they hear *Pet Sounds*," he said later. "It is a total classic record that is unbeatable in many ways . . . *Pet Sounds* was our inspiration for making *Sergeant Pepper's*. I just thought, 'Oh dear me, this is the album of all time. What are we going to do?'"

For all the praise it received, *Pet Sounds* was a commercial disappointment. "What many critics consider to be one of the best and most important albums in rock history never was embraced by American record buyers," Leaf writes. "It never sold enough to become a gold record . . . It took many listenings for a fan to finally appreciate and absorb what Brian had accomplished. In terms of record sales, this was damaging, because the fan underground quickly passed the word to 'stay away from the new Beach Boys album, it's weird.'"

Elvis owned $60,000 worth of prescription sunglasses when he died.

Pet Sounds' weak sales took its toll on Wilson. "*Pet Sounds* was not a big hit," Brian's ex-wife Marilyn says. "That really hurt Brian badly. He couldn't understand it. It's like, why put your heart and soul into something. I think that had a lot to do with slowing him down."

GOOD VIBRATIONS

The rivalry continued. The Beatles' "All You Need Is Love" inspired Brian Wilson to piece together a complex single called "Good Vibrations." Today "Good Vibrations" is considered a pop oldie, but in its day it was a revolutionary piece of music, a "pocket symphony," as Brian Wilson called it, that took more than six months of recording time and 90 hours of recording tape to create. Brian created 11 different versions of the song before he finally found one he liked, a process that caused production costs to balloon to more than $50,000, a fortune in the mid-1960s.

The expense was worth it. Unlike *Pet Sounds*, "Good Vibrations" was a huge hit. It sold 400,000 in the first four weeks alone and went on to become the Beach Boys' first million-selling single. "By the fall of 1966," Leaf writes, "the Beach Boys led by Brian Wilson, had musically gone past the Beatles . . . With 'Good Vibrations,' Brian surpassed everything current in popular music . . . It firmly established Brian as the foremost producer on the music scene."

"Jesus, that ear," Bob Dylan once remarked about Brian Wilson, "he should donate it to the Smithsonian."

SMILE

Brian Wilson's next project was an album tentatively titled *Dumb Angel*, which he told a friend would be a "teenage symphony to God." The album, a deeply personal statement, which was later renamed *Smile*, was poised to take the Beach Boys even deeper into the realm of "experimental" music, something that worried Brian Wilson's friend David Anderle. "I said, 'Don't have them as part of *Smile*. Do it on your own, man. Make it a Brian Wilson album.'" Perhaps out of loyalty to his brothers and his cousin Mike Love, Brian decided not to go off on his own. The band remained intact; *Smile* was slated as their next album.

By the time the other members returned from a concert tour of England, Brian had much of the background music for *Smile* finished; all the band would have to do was record the vocals. Lyrics

It isn't a "big band" unless it has 14 different instruments.

for many of the songs had been written by Van Dyke Parks, a composer and lyricist known for his obscure, Bob Dylan-esque style.

The other Beach Boys were anything but Bob Dylan-esque, so they began arguing with Brian as soon as they got into the studio. "When they came back from England," David Anderle says, "the last thing they wanted to do was become experimental. From where they were coming from, the Van Dyke Parks influence was not a healthy influence for them lyrically. They were hearing things they'd never heard before. It was not Beach Boys lyrics." Mike Love was the most resistant. "Don't f*** with the formula," he groused during one recording session. The other members of the band dreaded another commercial disappointment like *Pet Sounds*.

FROWN

"The group resisted the experimentation," Leaf writes, "and resented the way Brian treated them as a musical instrument, but most of all, they didn't like Van Dyke Parks's words. It was the fighting over Parks's lyrics that eventually made Brian, who loved what Van had created, begin to question the songs."

As the arguments continued, Brian began to lose confidence, and *Smile* fell behind schedule. Pressure was mounting. Then, suddenly in February 1967, Van Dyke Parks left to sign a solo contract with Warner Bros., leaving Brian to finish the remaining songs alone and fend for himself against the rest of the band. Rather than fight for his ideas, he began to withdraw. "He really did back away from it, just back off and go to the bedroom or whatever," Anderle says. "He just wouldn't face up to it."

Capitol Records pushed *Smile*'s release date back repeatedly; meanwhile, the Beatles, with much fanfare, came forth with *Sergeant Pepper's Lonely Hearts Club Band*. Brian bought a copy and put on the headphones. He played it over and over again into the night; and as he marvelled at the Beatles' accomplishment, what little self confidence he still had was shattered. He withdrew into his room and never finished his album. "*Smile* was destroying me," he explained in 1976.

"Had *Smile* been concluded and put out," David Anderle says, "I think it would have been a major influence in pop music. I think it would have been as significant if not a bigger influence than

---

Most popular TV show in Venezuela: the "Miss Venezuela Pageant."

Sergeant Pepper was . . . That album was startling. And I think *Smile* would have been even more startling."

BEACHED BOYS

Within months after *Smile* bit the dust, the Beach Boys' reluctance to experiment caught up with them. The rock music world was changing all around them, and they weren't changing with it.

In June 1967 they cancelled their appearance at the Monterey Pop Festival at the last minute. The festival, which served as a springboard to superstardom for new artists like Janis Joplin, Jimi Hendrix, and The Who, was a major turning point in rock 'n' roll, and the Beach Boys weren't a part of it. "Instead," Leaf writes, "they alienated the hip audience that had just begun to accept them because of music like *Pet Sounds* and 'Good Vibrations.' By not appearing, the Beach Boys quickly found themselves in exile as pop relics."

Within months of releasing "Good Vibrations," the Beach Boys had fallen so far out of step with where rock 'n' roll was heading that it had actually become fashionable to hate them. "In person, the Beach Boys are a totally disappointing group," *Rolling Stone* founder Jann Wenner wrote in December 1967. "The Beach Boys are just one prominent example of a group that has gotten hung up in trying to catch the Beatles. It is a pointless pursuit . . . Their surfing work continued for about ten albums with little progress."

While reproduced and rerecorded versions of some of the *Smile* material appeared on subsequent Beach Boys albums over the next five years, it wasn't the same. The magical moment for what might have been the greatest rock album of all time was lost.

POST-MORTEM

In the fall of 1989, I was working with a band who turned me on to the bootlegged recordings of Brian Wilson's legendary, aborted *Smile* sessions. Like a musical burning bush, these tapes awakened me to a higher consciousness in record making. I was amazed that one, single human could dream up this unprecedented and radically advanced approach to rock 'n' roll. How could a talent so great be so misunderstood and underappreciated?

—**Record producer Don Was**

Black sheep have a better sense of smell than white sheep.

THE BIRTH OF THE CADILLAC

Unless you're a car buff, you may not know that the Cadillac was first built by Henry Ford . . . or that it was considered the car that made driving safe for women . . . or that it was directly connected to the Lincoln. Here's the story, from John "I can't get my MG running" Dollison.

OH, HENRY

On October 10, 1901, Alexander Winton, a well-known race car driver, arrived in Grosse Point, Michigan, and challenged all comers to a race. The only man who took him up on the offer was a country boy named Henry Ford. Ford, whose Detroit Automobile Company had failed a year earlier, was racing a car he had designed and built himself.

Earlier that day, Winton had broken the world automobile speed record, driving a mile in 1 minute, 12.4 seconds—just under 50 miles per hour. Few people thought Ford, a local, had a chance to win . . . but when Winton's car developed engine trouble in the seventh lap, Ford shot past him to win the race. It was a significant victory.

As Robert Lacey observes in *Ford: The Men and the Machine:*

> It was a great and famous victory, thoroughly earned. A driver who wins a modern motor race through the mechanical failure of his rivals might feel less than satisfied. But on October 10, 1901 . . . the ability of Henry Ford's racer to keep going reflected directly on each man's ability to address the problem that mattered more to early motorists than maneuverability and speed. Mechanical reliability was the real challenge . . . Henry Ford won hands down.

BACK TO WORK

The victory was so impressive that five local businessmen who had seen the race chipped in $10,000 each to set Ford up in a new auto company. They even named the firm the Henry Ford Company to capitalize on Ford's newfound fame.

As head of the company, Ford's first job was to design a passenger car that could be sold to the public. But he "did not seem

Q: What do all of the characters in Shakespeare's plays have in common?

inclined to settle down to a small car production plan," one contemporary remembered. "He talked mostly about wanting to build a larger and faster racing car," and he began sneaking off to work on it.

A CHANGE IN PLANS

Ford's playing hooky was not a new problem—it was the same thing that had forced the Detroit Automobile Company to close its doors the year before. Rather than let that happen again, the investors hired Henry Leland, owner of Detroit's most respected machine shop, to supervise both the shop and Ford.

But Ford refused to take orders from Leland, and a few days later quit the company that bore his name, leaving Leland to take over. With Ford out of the picture, the investors renamed the company in honor of Antoine Laumet de Lamothe Cadillac, the French explorer and soldier of fortune who founded the city of Detroit. The Cadillac Automobile Company was born.

The investors who hired Leland "would not regret their decision," George S. May writes in A Most Unique Machine. "In a short time there could have been no doubt in their minds that in Henry Martin Leland they had found the man they had earlier hoped Henry Ford would turn out to be."

Today automotive historians consider Leland to be as important and indispensable a figure in the creation of the modern automobile industry as Henry Ford himself.

STRAIGHT SHOOTER

Leland had gotten his start in the firearms industry as a teenager in the 1860s. Too young to fight, he spent the Civil War years working in factories that mass-produced rifles for the Union Army, then after the war made revolvers at the Colt firearms factory. Whereas early firearms had been made and assembled one part at a time by highly skilled master craftsmen, the adoption of mass-production techniques and precisely engineered, fully interchangeable parts had made it possible for unskilled workers to assemble rifles by the thousands.

Just as Henry Ford was responsible for pioneering the use of the moving assembly line in automobile production, it was Leland, more than any other man, who introduced mass-production techniques to the automobile industry. When he arrived at Cadillac in

A: None of them smoke.

1902, most auto parts were manufactured to a precision of no more than 1/16 of an inch—which meant that even after parts were made, they still had to be filed, ground down, and sometimes even hammered by hand so they would fit properly into place. All this extra work was time-consuming and expensive, and added to the cost of a car.

Drawing from his experience in the firearms industry and in his own precision machine shop, Leland made automobile parts accurate to within 1/10,000 of an inch, something that had never been done before. Parts fit so well together that they could be assembled rapidly without special hand fitting. And because the parts were manufactured to such high levels of precision, the completed engines ran more smoothly, quietly, and reliably than had ever been possible before.

HIGH TECH

At first, Cadillac was marketed as a low- to mid-priced automobile; The first luxury Cadillac, the Model 30, wasn't introduced until 1905. Even so, thanks to Leland's manufacturing improvements, the company quickly acquired a reputation for offering higher quality than was available in any other car at any price.

The company also developed a reputation as a pioneer in automotive technology. Some of the most important innovations came about as the result of a tragedy. In 1910 a friend of Leland's named Byron Carter stopped to assist a woman motorist whose car had stalled. When Carter knelt down to start the woman's car using the hand-crank, the car backfired and the hand-crank shot out of Carter's hand, shattering his arm and his jaw. The injuries did not heal properly, and Carter later died from gangrene.

START ME UP

Devastated by his friend's death, Leland ordered his engineers to drop what they were doing and figure out a better way to start a car. "The Cadillac car," he told them, "will kill no more men."

A few months later, his engineers came back with a revolutionary electric self-starter powered by a battery so strong that it could also power an electric ignition system and electric headlights. From 1912 on, all Cadillacs started with the push of a button on the dashboard and featured headlights so bright that for the first time, it was truly safe to drive at night. These improvements ushered in a new era in the automotive age, as Richard Crabb writes in *Birth of a Giant*:

> The self-starter and electric lights greatly extended the potential use of the motorcar. So long as it was necessary to crank the engine by hand and endure the hazards of either acetylene or magneto powered lights, women could make only limited use of the motorcar. With the addition of these two features, introduced by Cadillac, women could drive, as well as men.

MOVING ON

When General Motors purchased Cadillac for $4.5 million in 1909, Leland agreed to stay with the company, but only after GM president William Durant promised that Leland could continue running the company with a free hand.

Leland stayed with Cadillac after Durant was forced into retirement . . . and though he'd grown wary of Durant's haphazard management style, even stayed with the company after Durant seized back control of GM in 1915. But when Durant, a pacifist, refused to allow GM to participate in the war effort at the outbreak of World War I, Leland resigned and formed a company to manufacture airplane engines.

TOP OF THE LINE

Leland, now in his mid-70s, had spent his career making cars better than anyone thought cars could be made. But he believed that his best cars were still ahead of him, and at the war's end, he returned to the auto industry.

Leland was the Grand Old Man of the auto industry, and his friends and colleagues urged him to finally put his own name on a car. But Leland would have none of it—his new car was going to be the greatest ever built, he explained, and should be named after the greatest American who ever lived. Leland named his car after Abraham Lincoln, the president for whom he'd cast his first vote, in 1864.

The 1921 Lincoln was an excellent car, but Leland had paid more attention to the car's engineering than to its styling, and it looked out of date. "Automotive writers were entranced by its ability to accelerate smoothly from walking speed to about 75 mph without vibration, without fuss," Ralph Stein writes in *The American Automobile*. "Aesthetically, the Lincoln was a disaster. In

1921, people paying up to $6,600 for a new car did not wish to drive around in cars that looked like 1914, no matter how well they had been constructed."

THE END

That wasn't the only bad news: In the fall of 1920, just as Leland was bringing his Lincolns to market, the postwar boom petered out and the country slid into a deep recession. Sales stalled, and Lincoln filed for bankruptcy.

The situation at the Ford Motor Company was much different. Ford earned record profits in 1921, and when the Lincoln Motor Company was put up for auction in January 1922, he bought it for $8 million, barely half its estimated worth.

Ford publicly acknowledged Leland as "one of the greatest motorcar men in America," and when he bought Lincoln, he kept Leland on and promised that he would be allowed to run the company as freely under Ford ownership as he had before.

But less than 24 hours after Lincoln reopened for business, Ford executives began interfering in the running of the plant. Four months later, a frustrated Leland confronted Henry Ford personally and offered to buy the company back for the original $8 million, plus interest.

Ford refused. "Mr. Leland," he replied, "I wouldn't sell the Lincoln plant for $500 million. I had a purpose in acquiring that plant, and I wouldn't think of letting it go." Two weeks later, Ford, acting through intermediaries, forced Leland to resign. Leland spent the rest of his life battling Ford in court to win his company back, but never succeeded. He died in 1932 at the age of 89.

BOYTOY

What was Henry Ford's "purpose" in buying Lincoln at auction? Ford's son Edsel had pestered him for years to get him to replace the Model T, which had been in production since 1908, with something more modern. Buying Lincoln and letting Edsel run it may have been Henry Ford's way of preventing Edsel from meddling with his beloved Model T—which remained in production until 1927.

PAYBACK

But the real motive may simply have been revenge:

Had Henry Ford really walked off the job at the Henry Ford Company in 1902, leaving Henry Leland to pick up the pieces at the company that would soon be renamed Cadillac? Or was Ford fired—by Henry Leland? "According to a story that has appeared in a variety of versions," George May writes in *A Most Unique Machine*:

> Henry Ford did not really resign from the Henry Ford Company. He had, in effect, been fired by his backers, whose growing suspicions regarding Ford's capabilities had been confirmed by criticisms of various aspects of Ford's work. They had received the evaluations from an unimpeachably qualified source, the brilliant mechanic, Henry M. Leland.

Twenty years later, Ford, by then the world's most successful and wealthiest automaker, bought Leland's precious Lincoln Motor Company at a bankruptcy auction . . . and then promptly reneged on his promise to allow Leland to continue at the helm. According to May: "This, it has been said, was Henry Ford's revenge for what Henry Leland had done to him in 1902."

* * *

7 EXCUSES FOR SLEEPING ON THE JOB
(courtesy of the Internet)

1. "They told me at the blood bank this might happen."

2. "Whew! I musta left the top off the liquid paper."

3. "This is one of the seven habits of highly effective people!"

4. "This is in exchange for the six hours last night when I dreamed about work!"

5. "Darn! Why did you interrupt me? I had almost figured out a solution to our biggest problem."

6. "Boy, that cold medicine I took last night just won't wear off!"

7. "I wasn't sleeping. I was trying to pick up my contact lens without my hands."

More babies are conceived in December than in any other month.

THE GREAT PEDESTRIAN

Over the years, sports have changed. Back in the 1860s, before the NBA, NFL, or NHL, you might have been cheering for your favorite pedestrian! Here's the story of the Babe Ruth of professional walking.

WALKING FEVER

America's number-one pedestrian, Edward Payson Weston, walked his way to fame and fortune in the late 1860s and infected the sports world with a "walking fever" that raged for half a century. Largely because of Weston, walking contests for a time rivaled prize fighting and horse racing as an early big-money pro sport.

Foot racing had been common at country fairs, and distance walkers were setting records before he took up the sport, but Weston's endurance feats that attracted huge crowds of fans, filled the pages of sporting journals, and turned pedestrianism into an international craze.

AN HISTORIC WALK

Weston first gained attention at the age of 22 when he carried out a bet to walk 478 miles from Boston to Washington in 10 consecutive days, to attend Lincoln's inauguration. He started from Boston's State House on February 22, 1861, followed by a swarm of fans riding in buggies, and walked the first 5 miles in 47 minutes before settling down to a steadier pace.

Crowds cheered him town by town, and reporters covered every mile of his marathon. A snowstorm slowed him some, and he slipped and fell several times, but plodded on through New England and got as far as New York the morning of February 27. Most of the time he ate as he walked, although he did manage to sit down to one solid meal each day. Sleep was in catnaps by the roadside or in farmhouse kitchens, and he began each new walking day at midnight.

By the time he reached Philadelphia, Weston was ahead of schedule, so he bedded down for a day in a hotel room. He then

---

25% of men wait until "a few weeks" before Christmas to do their holiday shopping.

walked all night from Philadelphia to Baltimore, had breakfast, and started out in pouring rain to hike the final lap over muddy roads. He made it to Washington at 5 p.m. on March 4, 1861, too late to see Lincoln sworn in as president but still in time to enjoy dancing at the Inaugural Ball that night.

A WALKING PRO

According to the terms of the wager, he collected only a bag of peanuts for his long walk. But he also collected reams of publicity and decided to turn professional. He got his first big fee as a pro, and also created an international sensation, by walking from Portland, Maine, to Chicago in 1867 for a prize of $10,000. To win he had to cover the distance of more than 1,200 miles within a month, not including Sundays, which were eliminated to prevent a public outcry against sporting on the Sabbath.

Nattily dressed in a short jacket, tight-fitting knee breeches, colored belt, silk derby, buff gloves, and red-topped brogans, he took off from Maine on October 29 and covered the distance in 26 walking days, with enough time to spare not only to attend church services but also to make speeches to crowds of admirers along the way. Weston carried a walking stick to chase away hostile dogs, and at one point had to use his fists to beat off a man who attacked him in an attempt to halt the contest. He received threatening letters from gamblers who had bet against him, two attempts were made to poison his food, and he was warned that the only way he would reach Chicago would be "in a coffin." But he arrived the morning of Thanksgiving Day, his feet hardly swollen, and was still fit enough to address a cheering crowd at the Crosby Opera House that evening on the benefits of walking as outdoor exercise.

THE MAIN ATTRACTION

For most of his long life, Weston crisscrossed the country's roads on endurance walks against time for fat wagers and big prizes. He also competed against hundreds of other pros in walking contests at race courses and indoor tracks, where he drew such crowds that he was often paid as much as three-fourths of the gate receipts. Some walkers beat him on level tracks in six-day matches, but few equaled his remarkable feats on the open roads.

15% of women start Christmas shopping in July.

He staged an endurance contest walking through snow in New England in 1869, covering 1,058 miles in 30 days. At St. Louis in 1871, he walked part of 200 miles backward and still covered the distance in 41 hours. In 1874 in Newark, New Jersey, he footed 500 miles in just under 6 days after doing the first 115 miles of it in 24 hours.

Weston went to Europe in 1876 to cash in on his international fame and spent eight triumphal and profitable years there in crowd-drawing exhibitions, mainly in England. In London in 1879 he won the Astley Belt, emblematic of world supremacy, by defeating British champion "Blower" Brown in a 6-day "go as you please" match that allowed both jogging and heel-and-toe walking. He covered 550 miles in 141 hours, 44 minutes.

OLD MAN WESTON

At the age of 68 in 1907, after constant years of grueling competition, Weston repeated the walk he had made 40 years before, from Portland, Maine, to Chicago. He walked 1,345 miles in 24 days 19 hours to beat his own early record by some 29 hours. He celebrated his 70th birthday two years later with the longest endurance walk of his life, across the United States from New York to San Francisco.

Weston started from New York on March 15, 1909, hopeful that he could cross the country by "a rather devious route" that would let him cover more than 4,000 miles in 100 days. By then there was a motorcar instead of a horse-drawn carriage to transport the judges and supplies. But Weston disdainfully rejected most of the "modern" comforts offered him along the way and also held to his own ideas as to what was a proper diet.

He began his days at 3:30 each morning with a breakfast of oatmeal and milk, two slices of buttered toast, three poached eggs, three cups of coffee, a bowl of strawberries, two oranges, and half a dozen griddle cakes. On the road during the day he consumed 18 eggs, each beaten up in a pint of milk with a tablespoon of sugar. "If I want a piece of pie while I'm on a walk, I'll eat it, or griddle cakes or pudding," he said. "The stomachs that can't digest ordinary food are those that are spoiled by high living or no exercise."

On average, your left hand does 56% of your typing.

STILL WALKING

Weston was still at it in 1914 when, at the age of 74, he tramped 1,546 miles from New York to Minneapolis in 51 days. Even after that he walked in some contests and exhibitions, but devoted more of his time to encouraging others to walk for health, competition, and the "joy of discovering the open road," warning that motorcars were making people more indolent than ever.

Ironically, the first great pedestrian was hit by a car while he was walking on a street in Brooklyn, New York, in 1927. He suffered injuries that kept him in a wheelchair most of the last two years of his life, and he died in 1929 at the age of 90.

* * *

OTHER GREAT PEDESTRIANS

- Daniel O'Leary was an Irish-born Chicagoan who did his first endurance walking as a door-to-door salesman. Inspired by Weston, O'Leary became his greatest rival. O'Leary's greatest performance was in 1907 in Cincinnati, where at the age of 63 he walked a mile at the beginning of each hour for 1,000 consecutive hours. During the 42 days it took to complete the test, O'Leary's longest period of uninterrupted sleep was 50 minutes.

- In 1910 John Ennis, crossed the country from New York to San Francisco. Ennis added a showmanly flair by taking time out for exhibition swims along the way. After a plunge into the Atlantic Ocean at a Coney Island amusement park, Ennis started walking on May 23, 1910. He swam in Lake Erie and later swam the Mississippi on a day he had walked 45 miles. As he made his westward way over the roads, he swam seven other rivers and lakes before reaching the Pacific at San Francisco on August 24. His total cross-country walking time was 80 days, 5 hours.

- A group known as the Kansas City Hikers made pedestrianism a family affair in 1913. Mr. and Mrs. Morris Paul teamed up with Mr. and Mrs. Gus Kuhn and their five-year-old daughter, Ruth, to walk from Kansas City, Missouri, to San Francisco. They took their time, stopping for as long as five days at some places, and spent a total of 227 days in walking the 2,384 miles.

About 8% of students at the Dunkin Donuts Training Center fail the six-week course.

AS SEEN ON TV!

We've all seen them—those cheesy TV ads for products no one needs, but millions of people buy. You've probably forgotten all about them. Well, heh-heh, we're here to remind you about . . .

GLH#9: Hair-in-a-can from the infamous Ron Popeil (GLH stands for "great looking hair.") A spray can of some sort of powdered pigment that sticks to your head. Just hold a few inches from your bald spot and spray! Comes in nine colors and according to the free brochure, you can use it on your dog!

THE CLAPPER: "Clap on, clap off!" From Joseph Industries, makers of the Chia Pet. "Clap twice and a lamp goes on, clap twice and it goes off. Only $19.95!"

INSIDE THE EGGSHELL SCRAMBLER: A piece of plastic with a curved needle attached. Impale the egg on the needle and it activates a motor. The needle spins inside the shell and *scrambles the egg!* "Outperforms a fork or whisk in every way! Scrambles the yolk and white of an egg right inside the shell in less than five seconds! You'll use it a lot and every time you do, you'll save washing a bowl and fork!"

THE GINSU KNIFE: From Dial Media. Ads showed a karate expert shattering bricks and kicking a watermelon, then fuming because he couldn't cut as well as the "amazing Ginsu knife!" Sounds vaguely Asian, but it's not—it was originally brought to the company by a salesperson who thought it was great because it never needed sharpening. But it was still just a knife . . . until the creative vice president of Dial came up with a Japanese-sounding name, a karate-theme ad, and the tag line: "But wait, there's more!"

THE VEG-O-MATIC: "This is Veg-O-Matic, the world-famous food appliance. Slice a whole potato into uniform slices with one motion . . . Simply turn the ring and change from thin to thick slices. Isn't that amazing? Like magic, you can change from slicing to dicing. No one likes dicing onions. The Veg-O-Matic makes

Strom Thurmond was the only person ever elected . . .

mounds of them fast. The only tears you'll shed will be tears of joy. You can make hundreds of French fries in one minute. Isn't that sensational? Here's your chance to own one for only $9.99!" From Ronco.

THE SMOKELESS ASHTRAY: A plastic ashtray with a little fan that sucks smoke *in*. "Does cigarette and cigar smoke offend you? Does smoke irritate your eyes? If it does, you need the new Smokeless Ashtray . . . Helps clear the air you breathe. If you smoke, buy one and be considerate of those who don't smoke. If you don't smoke, buy one for those who do. Buy two or three. They really do make great Christmas gifts. And they're only $9.98!"

POCKET FISHERMAN: A fishing rod and reel that fold into a small carrying case. "Attaches to your belt . . . or fits in the glove compartment of your car!"

MIRACLE MOP: For $19.95 you get the original self-wringing mop "with a twistable shaft that lets you wring out the head without putting your hands into the dirty water!"

THE BUTTONEER: "The problem with buttons is they always fall off. *The problem with buttons is they always fall off.* And when they do, don't sew them on the old-fashioned way with needle and thread. Use The Buttoneer, the new automatic button fastener that attaches any kind of button! . . . Repair upholstery, pleat draperies, attach appliqués, ribbons, decorate toys, dolls . . . it's The Buttoneer!"

THE RONCO BOTTLE AND JAR CUTTER: "An exciting way to recycle throwaway bottles and jars into decorative glassware, centerpieces, thousands of things! . . . A hobby for Dad, craft for the kids, a great gift for Mom. The Ronco Bottle and Jar Cutter. Only $7.77!"

THE RONCO RHINESTONE AND STUD SETTER: A gizmo that attaches rhinestones and studs to jackets and jeans. "It changes everyday clothing into exciting fashions! . . . For young or old, the Ronco Rhinestone and Stud Setter is great fun!" Later marketed on TV as The Bedazzler.

. . . to a U.S. Senate seat as a write-in candidate (1954).

MORE
STRANGE LAWSUITS

More bizarre lawsuits from contemporary news reports.

THE PLAINTIFF: William H. Folwell, Episcopal bishop of Central Florida
THE DEFENDANT: U.S. government
THE LAWSUIT: The bishop hurt his knee while playing tennis at the Naval Training Center. He claimed the injury "prevented him from genuflecting," and sued for $200,000. The Feds counter-sued, saying the holy man had been sneaking onto the tennis courts and had no right to be there in the first place. They said he owed them $5,200 for use of the courts over the last five years.
THE VERDICT: Case dismissed. Neither side got any cash.

THE PLAINTIFF: Continental Airlines
THE DEFENDANT: Deborah Loeding, former wife of Continental pilot William Loeding
THE LAWSUIT: In 1994 William Loeding took a random drug test administered by the airline. Marijuana was detected, and Loeding was fired—although he swore he'd never gone near the stuff. He filed grievance after grievance with his union—and finally, during his third hearing, his ex-wife admitted she was responsible. To vent her anger at her ex-husband, she'd put pot in a loaf of rye bread she baked for him. Continental sued her for endangering passengers and causing her ex-hubby "significant distress in his personal and professional life."
THE VERDICT: Pending.

THE PLAINTIFF: Paul and Nancy Marshall, baseball fans
THE DEFENDANTS: San Diego Padres baseball team
THE LAWSUIT: In 1993, in a cost-cutting move, the Padres began trading high-salaried star players to other teams. When former batting champ Gary Sheffield was traded, the Marshalls filed a suit charging the Padres with deceiving season ticket holders.

On an average night, it takes an average person seven minutes to fall asleep.

(The team had sent out a letter saying players like Sheffield and Fred McGriff, an all-star first-baseman, "create the core of an excellent team for years to come.") The Marshalls asked for punitive damages and a promise that the Padres wouldn't trade McGriff.

THE VERDICT: Settled out of court. The Padres agreed to a more liberal ticket refund policy, and the Marshalls' suit was dropped. McGriff was traded to the Atlanta Braves five days later.

THE PLAINTIFF: James Houston
THE DEFENDANT: Northern Arizona University
THE LAWSUIT: According to news reports, Houston "is suing his alma mater because he believes that getting a doctorate was too easy." He is asking for $1 million.
THE VERDICT: Pending.

THE PLAINTIFF: Ethyln Boese, of Portland, Oregon
THE DEFENDANT: Restlawn Funeral Home
THE LAWSUIT: On July 25, 1996, a closed-casket funeral was held for Boese's husband, James. When it was over, Ethyln asked for a last look at the man she'd been married to for 50 years. When the casket was opened, she saw a stranger—in her husband's suit. At first, the funeral director wouldn't believe it was the wrong body. Finally he did, and found the right one. The family quickly got a different suit for the corpse, held a new funeral, and filed a lawsuit for $500,000 for "emotional distress."
THE VERDICT: Unknown

THE PLAINTIFF: Katie Rose Sawyer, age 11
THE DEFENDANT: Cody Finch, age 10
THE LAWSUIT: Fifth-graders Sawyer and Finch were "married" on the school playground in the fall of 1996. Then a few months later, they were "divorced" (another fifth-grader wrote up "Divores" papers). Katie said Cody kept bothering her, so she sued him under the New Mexico Family Violence Protection Act. "My mom told me, 'Don't get married again until you're an adult,'" Katie told reporters.
THE VERDICT: Unknown.

The English sparrow isn't a sparrow. And it comes from Africa, not England.

THE STRANGE DISAPPEARANCE OF AUGUSTIN LE PRINCE

Why do history books credit Thomas Edison with inventing the movie camera and ignore Augustin Le Prince? That was our question—until Uncle John found a copy of The Missing Reel, *by Christopher Rawlence, which lays out the circumstances of Le Prince's life and disappearance. Is this story true? And if it is, why isn't it more famous?*

BACKGROUND

Augustin Le Prince was a French inventor who studied with Louis Daguerre, one of the fathers of photography. In the early 1880s, Le Prince began experimenting with a new idea—a motion-picture camera. By 1885 he had a working prototype, and by 1886 he'd applied for a U.S. patent. In 1888 he received the first patents ever granted for a movie camera, in both France and the United States.

In March 1890 Le Prince demonstrated his camera to officials at the Paris Opera house. It was an amazing feat. For the first time ever, moving pictures were projected onto a screen. Recognizing Le Prince's genius, they encouraged him to show his invention to the public right away. But Le Prince was bothered that the picture was flickery and hard to make out. So instead of making a name for himself, he returned to his workshop in Leeds, England, to perfect his machine.

In September of that same year, after a weekend visit with his brother in Dijon, Le Prince boarded a train for Paris to meet with his friends, the Wilsons. They planned to travel to England together, but Le Prince never arrived. The Wilsons waited awhile, then "assuming he had been detained on business, decided to go on to London without him."

Meanwhile, Le Prince's wife and children were living in New York. Le Prince planned to visit them in October and promised to bring his single-lens movie camera and projector—which he felt were now completed and ready to patent.

Napoleon's writing was so unreadable . . .

But he didn't show up and didn't send any word of explanation. Le Prince's wife, Lizzie, frantically cabled their home in Leeds. When she got no reply, she contacted Richard Wilson. Wilson had no idea what had happened and went to Le Prince's house to investigate. He found it locked up and deserted.

GONE!

Lizzie called in Scotland Yard and the French Missing Persons Bureau. They searched every morgue and asylum between Dijon, Paris, London, and Leeds. Every railway station along the route was visited. Messages were placed in all the French national newspapers. They even looked into the possibility that Le Prince had lost his mind and enlisted with the Foreign Legion. But no trace of Le Prince was ever found.

What became of Le Prince's work? Unfortunately, Wilson cleaned out Le Prince's studio. While he saved some items, he threw out the bits and pieces that may, in fact, have provided unqualified proof of Le Prince's great achievements. Three months after Le Prince's disappearance Thomas Edison applied for—and ultimately received—a patent for the first practical "motion-picture machine." Today he's considered the father of the movie camera.

SUSPICIOUS FACTS

- Le Prince had not yet patented the latest designs of his movie camera and projector—he was worried that if he went public with his discoveries before they were perfected, someone would find a loophole in the patent and capitalize on his invention before he could.

- As a result, he revealed it only to a close circle of friends . . . including his lawyer, Clarence Seward. Le Prince didn't know it, but Seward and his partner also worked for Thomas Edison—who, only months later, claimed to have invented the motion-picture camera.

- In the process of applying for a previous U.S. patent, Le Prince's lawyers (Seward & Guthrie)—without informing him—dropped a crucial clause that would have given him broad protection. Le Prince never had time to correct it—he was too busy writing more detailed British and French patents and perfecting his projector.

. . . that many of his letters were mistaken for battlefield maps.

WHAT HAPPENED?

Theory #1: *Le Prince's patent lawyer betrayed him. He was kidnapped and/or murdered to prevent him from filing for the patent on his newest camera (or so that others could steal the valuable patents he was presumed to be carrying)—which was at least a decade ahead of its time.*

Interesting points:

- Edison's invention (presented with great fanfare as a huge breakthrough but actually more rudimentary than Le Prince's machine) infringed on Le Prince's patents. But when Lizzie Le Prince tried to sue Edison, she learned she couldn't: under U.S. law, someone is not declared dead until seven years after they have disappeared, and as long as the holder of a patent is living, only he can sue for infringement.

- Edison had a reputation for ruthlessness among fellow inventors. There were invariably bitter patent battles involving his inventions, with someone always claiming Edison had stolen them. Edison himself once said: "Everyone steals in industry and commerce. I've stolen a lot myself. The thing is to know how to steal."

- Le Prince, in fact, had wanted to collaborate with Edison but had been strongly warned against it and decided to keep his distance.

- After Le Prince disappeared, Lizzie Le Prince accidentally found out that Seward's partner, Guthrie, had been in Europe at that time. He could have engineered the disappearance . . . and Lizzie suspected that he had.

On the other hand . . .

- Inventors are often involved in patent battles—because inventions are usually built upon the work of many people. And occasionally, two inventors turn out to have developed the same idea simultaneously but independently.

- Also: While Edison had a reputation for patenting inventions not clearly his own, he didn't have a reputation for violence. One modern investigator concluded after a thorough investigation that "not a shred of evidence [has been found] to suggest Edison . . . had anything to do with Le Prince's disappearance."

Average speed of a golf ball in flight during the PGA Tour: 160 mph.

Theory #2: *Le Prince had lied—the camera and/or projector were not perfected. Depressed, nearly bankrupt, and out of options, he committed suicide.*

Interesting Points:

- Despite having a working model, Le Prince could not perfect the projector, and refused to demonstrate his invention until he could. (Ironically, Edison didn't have a projector either—people looked through a small peephole. Further irony: only months after Le Prince's disappearance, high-quality celluloid—the material that would have allowed Le Prince to perfect his projector—became available.)

- We have only Lizzie Le Prince's say-so that her husband claimed to have solved his projector problems.

- Le Prince was plagued by debt and constantly feared that his laboratory would be raided by creditors. Though his mother had recently died and left a considerable inheritence, there was a bitter dispute with his brother over his claim to the money. Le Prince had been visiting him in Dijon, trying to work things out. But it is believed that his brother thought Augustin had gotten all the money he deserved from the estate.

- Faced with failure after years of grueling work, Le Prince may have felt life was not worth the struggle anymore.

Some Possible Explanations:

- Le Prince's lawyers may have dropped the important part of his American patent application only because they didn't understand his revolutionary work—in fact, the patent office itself didn't understand Le Prince's patent until he went down and explained it to them in person.

- Though Seward, Le Prince's patent lawyer, worked for Edison, it may have been plain coincidence—he was a prominent patent lawyer of the day.

- It may have been just a lucky break for Edison that Le Prince—who could have challenged him for patent infringement—disappeared.

And then again . . .

If it happened before A.D. 476, it's "ancient." After A.D. 476, it's "medieval."

THE TONIGHT SHOW, PART IX

The feature story in our Giant 10th Anniversary Bathroom Reader *was the history of* The Tonight Show. *But we never finished it—it was interrupted by a guest host, Professor Pear, and then Johnny Carson went on vacation. Well, we finally got the rest of the story. For all of you BR fans who've been waiting for Part IX, here, at long last, it is.*

NO CONTEST

By 1973 Johnny Carson was the undisputed king of late-night television. With the timeslot virtually to itself, *The Tonight Show* grossed an estimated $100 million a year for NBC. This gave Carson a lot of power. When his contract came up for negotiation, he used his heavyweight status to push for shorter workweeks and huge salary increases.

The biggest battle came in 1979, when Carson announced he was quitting the show. NBC finally lured him back, but only after tripling his salary and cutting the length of the show from 90 minutes to an hour. Carson did make one concession: he agreed to go back to a four-day workweek. But from then on, he—not NBC—would own *The Tonight Show.*

GROWING OLD

In its early years, *The Tonight Show* defined hipness for the viewing audience, but as the years passed, what had seemed so fresh and lively in 1962 inevitably began to show its age. *The Tonight Show* still got huge ratings, but there was little new about the show: same host, same sidekick, same bandleader wearing loud sport jackets, same guests, same formula jokes, same skits with Aunt Blabby, Ed Fern, and other stale characters.

Carson came under increasing criticism for being stale in the 1980s, but he sill managed to defeat all challengers without difficulty. Comedian Alan Thicke launched *Thicke of the Night* in the fall of 1983 (his sidekick: Arsenio Hall); he lasted nine months. In 1986 comedian David Brenner began a syndicated talk show called *Nightlife*. It was dead within a year. In the fall of 1986, New York newspaper columnist Jimmy Breslin started an interview show on ABC called *Jimmy Breslin's People*. Like the others, Breslin could not compete with Carson's ratings. He quit after four months.

The problem with *The Tonight Show* wasn't that it was losing established viewers, it was that it wasn't gaining any new ones. Younger viewers—the ones advertisers want the most—got their comedy elsewhere, including *Saturday Night Live* and *Late Night with David Letterman*.

Because of this (and also because Carson had a penchant for talking about retiring whenever his contract came up for renegotiation), NBC spent a lot of time mulling over who would fill his shoes when he finally left the show.

CAN WE TALK?

In the mid-1980s, the leading candidate to take over Carson's chair was comedian Joan Rivers, who had signed on as Carson's "permanent guest host" in 1983. Rivers bested Carson's own ratings many nights, and she helped attract younger audiences to the show with guests like Cher, Elvis Costello, and Pee Wee Herman.

Things changed in 1986, when Carson (once again) hinted to NBC that he was thinking of retiring in 1987, marking 25 years on the job. The network circulated a secret memo listing possible replacements . . . and Rivers found out she wasn't on the list.

JUMPING SHIP

Meanwhile, TV executive Barry Diller had been hard at work trying to create a "fourth network" for Fox Broadcasting. Diller played poker with Carson occasionally . . . but that didn't stop him from going after Rivers when he heard she was unhappy at NBC.

Diller needed a flagship show to launch the Fox network, and he figured a late-night talk show hosted by Rivers would have a good shot at stealing Carson's crown. He offered the job to Rivers, and she took it . . . without telling Carson beforehand. It was the biggest mistake of her career.

The day after she signed the contract with Fox, Rivers called Carson with the news. But word had already leaked out, and Carson was furious. He refused to speak to Rivers when she called, and he hung up on her a second time the next day.

Doc Severinsen and others have speculated that Carson would have been supportive if Rivers had told him about the move

---

In Tucson, Arizona, potholes are officially known as "pavement deficiencies."

sooner. "He probably would have plugged her show, or even done a walk-on for her," Severinsen says. "But he and others were disappointed nothing was said to them until the last minute."

The Carson-Rivers split was on the front page of newspapers all over the country, but Carson—who immediately tore up Rivers's *Tonight Show* contract—maintained an icy silence on the show. He never brought the subject up again, except for the occasional joke in his monologue. "I hope Reagan runs again," he joked in June 1986. "If he doesn't, he'll probably start his own talk show." But things continued to happen behind the scenes, Bill Carter writes in *The Late Shift:*

> In a demonstration of just how powerful Carson still was, Rivers found herself one step removed from leper status in Hollywood. Guests had to risk the wrath of the *"Tonight"* show to go on with Joan. She did herself no favors by trying to turn into a hipster, booking rock-and-roll acts half her age and singing "The Bitch Is Back" with Elton John. The show was doomed and disappeared in months.

FADING AWAY
Not long after Joan Rivers left *The Tonight Show,* comedian Jay Leno replaced her as permanent guest host. Like Rivers, Leno's ratings matched and many nights even bested Carson's ratings, and he attracted younger, more ethnically diverse viewers to the show— just what the advertisers wanted.

Carson was still the undisputed King of the Night and *The Tonight Show* was the biggest moneymaker in the history of television, but his hold was slipping. The show's audience dropped 47% between 1978 and 1992, and the viewers who kept watching were mostly older than the 20- and 30-somethings advertisers increasingly coveted.

HEAD START
It was just a matter of time before Carson retired . . . or was pushed aside for a younger, fresher face. Other networks smelled blood. They figured that if they could get a talk show up and running by the time Carson finally did retire, they'd have a shot at capturing the late-night audience for themselves.

CBS struck first by luring Pat Sajak away from *Wheel of Fortune* to host the *Pat Sajak Show* in January 1989. They were sure he'd

By the time the king of Siam died in 1910, he had fathered 370 children.

bring his 43-million-strong *Wheel of Fortune* audience with him to late-night TV.

They were wrong—Sajak appealed to the same audience that watched *The Tonight Show*, but those viewers were perfectly happy with Carson. Sajak actually beat Carson in ratings his first week on the air, but that lead evaporated and the show went into a death spiral. In the months to come, Sajak's staffers had trouble even finding a studio audience, let alone a television audience, and by the end of the year, more than 50 CBS stations around the country dumped him in favor of the *Arsenio Hall Show*, an independently produced program which had also premiered in January 1989.

Arsenio appealed to the younger viewers who'd abandoned *The Tonight Show* over the years, and as Pat Sajak went into the tank, Arsenio began building an audience.

TAKING IT ON THE CHIN

Things were so bad at CBS that the network approached Jay Leno about starring in a *Jay Leno Show* that would keep the affiliates from defecting to Arsenio Hall. Sure, they said, Leno was guest hosting *The Tonight Show*, but who knew when Carson would retire . . . or if Leno would still be on the job when he did.

Leno mulled over the offer for a couple of months . . . then turned CBS down. Why take over Sajak's failing show when he was so close to inheriting Carson's? Leno wanted to follow in Carson's footsteps, not Joan Rivers's, so he stayed put. The *Pat Sajak Show* went off the air in April 1990.

But that didn't stop Leno from using the CBS offer to cement his position at NBC. He already had a "penalty payment" in his contract that paid him a large settlement if Carson left the show and Leno wasn't named as his replacement; now he renegotiated for a higher salary and an unwritten promise from NBC that he would take over *Tonight* when Carson retired.

In May 1991, the network made it official—they signed a contract guaranteeing that Leno would be named Carson's successor when he finally retired . . . but how long away was that? Weeks? Months? Years?

BATTLING THE SYNDICATES

Nobody at NBC knew it at the time, but it would take exactly seven days. Leno signed the new contract on May 16; on

Lions are the only cats that live in packs.

May 23, Carson announced he was quitting.

The announcement came as a total surprise to NBC—Carson hadn't told anyone at the network. In fact, he timed it to embarrass NBC, announcing his decision at the annual NBC affiliates' convention as stunned network officials sat openmouthed in the front row. "This is the last year that I am doing *The Tonight Show*," he said simply, "and it's been a long, marvelous run . . . My last show is going to be May 22, 1992."

WHAT ABOUT DAVE?

When NBC gave Leno the nod for *The Tonight Show*, it did so with the expectation—or at least the hope—that David Letterman would stay put in the 12:30 a.m. slot, where *Late Night with David Letterman* had been since 1982. But Letterman wanted the *Tonight Show* job . . . and he felt that his 11 years on NBC had earned him the right. Hosting *The Tonight Show* had been his goal since childhood. "I've had one dream in my life," he later explained to his agent, "All I want is *The Tonight Show*."

But as Letterman himself admitted, he had never told anyone at NBC how badly he wanted the job. He later recalled,

> When Johnny was still there, it would have hurt my feelings if he'd thought that I was politicking for his job . . . So what I did was take every opportunity, if asked, to go on the record as saying, "Yes I would like to be considered for the job." I wasn't comfortable with anything more than that.

Letterman had hoped that his success with his own show would be enough to get him the job. It wasn't.

SECOND CHANCE

Letterman spent the next few months after Carson's announcement in a funk, convinced that his entire career had boiled down to playing second fiddle to Jay Leno . . . or getting out of show business entirely. "My market value is zero," he complained to his friends.

But his mood began to improve late in the summer of 1991, when he hired Michael Ovitz, chairman of Creative Artists Agency (CAA), and then the most powerful agent in Hollywood. Letterman's NBC contract kept him at the network through April 1993, and forbade him from considering other offers until February of that year, still 17 months away. But Ovitz began sounding out networks and syndication companies behind the scenes to see who would be interested when Letterman finally became available.

THE SEDUCTION OF DAVE
Everyone wanted Letterman: CBS, ABC, Fox, Paramount, Columbia Television, Walt Disney, Viacom, and others all made pitches to Ovitz. But Letterman refused to consider any timeslot later than 11:30, which knocked out ABC (it wasn't about to move *Nightline*), and Fox, which had committed to creating a late-night show starring Chevy Chase. The syndicates, which sell shows to one television station at a time, were out too because they had no control over when or where a show would air. That left CBS and NBC, which had the right to keep Letterman at the network by matching the highest offer.

CBS offered Letterman a contract paying a $12.5 million-a-year salary, plus an $82 million budget for the show over three years. Like Carson, Letterman would retain ownership of the show, plus production rights for an hour-long show that would run from 12:30 a.m. to 1:30 a.m.

NBC had until January 15, 1993, to match CBS's offer. But to do so, they had to fire Leno, who was finally settling into the job and earning decent ratings, after months of turmoil. The company split along regional lines: executives in Burbank, where *The Tonight Show* was taped, sided with Leno; New York wanted Letterman.

GUY NEXT DOOR
In the end, reputation—Letterman's for being impossible to work with, and Leno's for being a team player—played as big a role in deciding their fates as any other factor. While Letterman was insulting NBC executives—*by name*—on the air, banning them from *Late Night* staff parties and squabbling over control of *Late Night* reruns, Leno, on his own initiative, was making appearances at affiliates all over the country to shore up support for his show.

NBC ultimately decided that even if Leno's ratings dipped a little when he went up against Letterman, he was a team player; Letterman, on the other hand, was a pain in the ass. As Bill Carter writes in *Night Shift:*

> Jay had done his groundwork exceptionally well. All that campaigning through affiliates and advertisers, every appearance at an NBC event . . . had made an impression . . . And

All of them are named Jim Smith.

then there was Dave: recalcitrant, irritable, uncooperative Dave.

NBC refused to match CBS's offer point by point, but it did offer to make Letterman host of *The Tonight Show* when Leno's current contract expired (even sooner if Leno quit in disgust), at roughly the same salary he would get at CBS. NBC refused to give him ownership of the show. The CBS offer was better, and Letterman was free to accept it if he wanted to.

THANKS, JOHNNY
Letterman wasn't sure he wanted to go to CBS—he'd spent a lifetime working toward hosting *The Tonight Show*, and he wasn't sure he wanted to give it up just because NBC was offering to make him filthy rich a little more slowly than CBS was.

Letterman couldn't make up his mind . . . so he called Johnny Carson and asked him what he would do in the same situation. "I'd probably walk," Carson told him. So Letterman did.

STARTING OVER
The Late Show with David Letterman premiered on CBS on August 30, 1993; to no one's surprise, Letterman thumped Leno's ratings on opening night.

NBC hoped that Letterman's ratings would peak and then drop off after a few weeks; even if Leno stayed in second place, he wouldn't be too far behind Letterman. They were wrong—Letterman whipped Leno in the ratings night after night, month after month, for nearly two years. Leno didn't beat Letterman in the ratings even once in more than 90 consecutive weeks.

REVERSAL OF FORTUNE
But in 1995 things began to change, thanks to two factors:

1. The collapse of CBS's programming schedule. When Letterman joined CBS in 1993, the network was #1 in prime-time ratings; it was broadcasting the NFL, the World Series, and the Olympics, and it had the strongest station lineup in the country.

By July 1995 all of that had changed. CBS was mired in third place and had lost the broadcast rights to the NFL and the World Series. Its ratings were so bad that some affiliate stations even jumped ship and signed with Fox. The Tiffany Network hit rock bottom in September 1995 and became the first of the Big Three networks to slip into fourth place in the ratings behind Fox.

2. A revamping of *The Tonight Show* format. In May 1994 Leno took his show to New York, and realized that by imitating the format created to support Carson's strengths, he'd been undermining his own. "I'm a night-club comic," he explains. "Prior to [our New York trip], we were doing the show exactly as it was for Johnny. People meant well, but I ended up doing a *Tonight Show* by committee, instead of the one I wanted to do." As Ed Bark of the *Dallas Morning News* wrote:

> On Sept. 27 of that year, *Tonight* unveiled a new, more intimate set that allowed Mr. Leno to do his monologue virtually in the midst of a gaggle of audience members seated in a small, floor-level section. Comedy bits were stretched out and sourpuss bandleader Branford Marsalis gave way to the considerably more congenial Kevin Eubanks . . . *Tonight* slowly made headway against the *Late Show*.

On July 10, 1995, Hugh Grant went on *The Tonight Show* with his first post–Divine Brown public appearance. As ratings soared, Leno leaned over and asked, "What the hell were you thinking?" That week, *Tonight* had its first ratings win against the *Late Show*.

By the beginning of 1997, the *Late Show* had slipped to third place behind both *The Tonight Show* and *Nightline*; as late as the summer of 1999 it was still there. *Tonight* had regained its place as King of the Night, but it was no longer the monolith that it had been under Allen, Paar, and Carson. Late-night television is now more competitive than it has ever been, and it is likely to remain so for years to come.

* * *

Random fact: What did Mexican War hero General Winfield Scott remember most about the time he ate dinner at the White House? A pickpocket stole his wallet, which contained $800.

THE DARK SIDE OF PETER PAN

"All children except one, grow up. They soon know that they will grow up . . . this is the beginning of the end." The first paragraph of James Barrie's classic story, Peter Pan, *introduced its central theme. It sounds innocent, but a look at Barrie's life gives it a more sinister twist.*

I WON'T GROW UP

"All of James Barrie's life led up to the creation of *Peter Pan*," wrote one of his biographers.

A pivotal point came in 1866 when Barrie, the youngest in a Scottish family of 10 children, was six: his brother David, the pride of the family, died in a skating accident. Barrie's mother was devastated. To comfort her, little James began imitating David's mannerisms and mimicking his speech. This bizarre charade went on for years . . . and only got weirder: when James reached 13, the age at which David had died, he literally stopped growing. He never stood taller than 5', and didn't shave until he was 24. He always had a thin, high-pitched voice.

SUCCESS AND FAILURE

From childhood, Barrie's main interest had been creating stories and plays. After graduating from college, he moved to London to pursue a career as a writer, and soon his work was being published. In the 1880s, his novels about a "wandering little girl"—his mother—captured the public's imagination and put him on the road to fame and wealth. He soon became one of England's most famous writers.

Despite his professional success, the gawky Barrie was painfully shy with women, and the thought of marriage terrified him. After a nightmare, he wrote in his journal: "Greatest horror, dream I am married, wake up screaming." But that didn't stop him from putting lovely actresses on a pedestal. Barrie became enamored of leading lady Mary Ansell, who appeared in his early plays. Motherlike, she nursed him through a life-threatening bout of pneumonia. And when he recovered, they decided to marry.

Folk wisdom: If you refrigerate your rubber bands, they'll last longer.

It was a disaster. Barrie wasn't capable of an intimate relation-ship and was probably impotent as well—stuck, physically and emotionally in a state of perpetual boyhood. Eventually, Mary fell in love with a young writer named Gilbert Cannan and demanded a divorce. Barrie refused, because his marriage had provided him with the appearance of being normal. But when Mary threatened to tell the world that he was impotent and had never consum-mated their marriage, Barrie gave in.

THE LOST BOYS

In 1899, while still unhappily married, Barrie befriended young George, John, and Peter Davies and their mother, Sylvia, in London's Kensington Park. The boys' father, Arthur Davies, was too busy tending to his struggling career as a lawyer to spend much time with his family. Childless Barrie was happy to play with the Davies boys. He became a frequent caller at their home, and even rented a cottage nearby when they went on vacations in Surrey.

Barrie idolized the children's beautiful mother. But it was with the children that he could truly be himself. He met with them daily in the park or at their home. They played Indians together, or pretended to be pirates, forcing each other to "walk the plank." Barrie made up stories for the boys, featuring talking birds and fairies, and acted them out.

PETER IS BORN

In 1901 Barrie ordered a printing of only two copies of a photo-essay book of his adventures with the Davies boys. He entitled it *The Boy Castaways of Black Lake Island* and gave one copy to the boys' father (who promptly left it on a train). The next year, Barrie published these adventures in a novel called *The Little White Bird*.

In a story-within-a-story, the narrator of *The Little White Bird* tells "David" (George Davies) about Peter Pan, a seven-day-old boy who flies away from his parents to live with fairies. All chil-dren start out as birds, the story goes, but soon forget how to fly. Peter eventually flies home, and tearfully sees through the nursery window that his mother is holding a new baby and has forgotten him. Now Peter Pan can never go home and will never grow up.

The Little White Bird was popular, and readers begged Barrie to give them more of that new character, Peter Pan.

Barrie knew exactly how to bring Peter Pan back. He had often

There are 250,000 sweat glands in a pair of human feet.

taken the Davies boys to pantomimes—dazzling Christmastime musical dramas put on for children. The plays always featured a young hero and heroine (both played by actresses), a Good Fairy, a Demon King, fight scenes, characters flying (on invisible wires), and a "transformation scene," in which the ordinary world became a fairyland. During the performances, Barrie carefully observed the boys' reactions. They seemed to love every moment.

So why not, Barrie thought, put Peter Pan in a similar children's play for the London stage?

THE DARLINGS

Barrie always acknowledged that the Davies boys' free-spirited youth was his inspiration for Peter Pan. "I made Peter by rubbing the five of you together, as savages with two sticks produce a flame," he wrote on the dedication page of the printed version of the play. More than that, however, the Davies family—loving mother, impatient father, and adorable sons—served as Barrie's model for the Darlings in the play. He even used their names:

- Mr. Darling was named after the eldest boy, George Davies.

- Jack Davies became John Darling.

- Michael and Nicholas became Michael Nicholas Darling.

- Peter Davies's name went to Peter Pan.

As for the author, he appears as Captain James Hook, whose right hand is gone. Barrie suffered paralysis of his right hand from tendonitis. Hook is relentlessly pursued by a crocodile who has swallowed a ticking clock, which biographers say was "a metaphor of Barrie stalked by cruel time." Porthos, his St. Bernard, became nurse-dog Nana, who exasperated the stuffy father (in real life, he was exasperated not with the dog, but with Barrie).

Barrie added a sister, Wendy, modeled after Margaret Henley, the deceased daughter of Barrie's friend, M. E. Henley. The six-year-old girl had called Barrie her "fwendy" (friend), and from that child-word, Barrie invented the name Wendy. It rapidly became one of England's most popular girl's names.

Worldwide, the average woman is 5 inches shorter than the average man.

WILL PETER PAN FLY?

Peter Pan posed a radical departure for adult theater. Barrie had an agreement with producer Charles Frohman to deliver a play manuscript. He offered Frohman another play gratis if he would only produce his "dream child," *Peter Pan.* "I'm sure it will not be a commercial success," Barrie said.

But Frohman, a wealthy American who liked risky ventures, said he would produce both plays. After reading the manuscript of *Peter Pan,* Frohman was so excited, he would stop friends on the street and force them to listen to passages from it. With an American staging now secured, it was easier for Barrie to find backing for a London opening.

The play was first performed at the Duke of York's Theatre on December 27, 1904, with an actress, Nina Boucicault, as Peter Pan. Having an actress play the boy—a tradition that continues to this day—began as a practical matter. The role was too demanding for a child; only an adult could handle all of the lines. And only an adult female could pass for a boy.

Peter Pan was an immediate hit, quelling Barrie's misgivings that an audience of adults wouldn't go for a play he'd originally written for children. One review compared Barrie's genius with that of George Bernard Shaw. Later, Barrie would cash in on the play's popularity by writing the novels *Peter Pan in Kensington Gardens* (1906) and *Peter and Wendy* (1911).

THE FATE OF THE LOST BOYS

But this story has no happy ending. Arthur Davies died of cancer, which left Barrie and Sylvia free to marry. Barrie went so far as to give her an engagement ring, but then she, too, died of cancer. Suddenly Barrie was the legal guardian of five boys, ages 7 to 17.

He devoted his life to them, imagining them as his own, but the boys felt he was overbearing in his possessiveness. Some biographers claim that the Davies brothers grew uncomfortable with their lives because they were always badgered about their relationship with the famous James Barrie. (On the other hand, he had little affection to bestow on his real family. Barrie was also named guardian of his brother's grandchildren when their parents died . . . but although he paid for their education, he refused to see them.)

George, the eldest Davies child and Barrie's favorite, died in World War I in 1915. Michael drowned in a pool at Oxford while

It takes 345 squirts from a cow's udder to get a gallon of milk.

being taught to swim by a close friend; there were rumors of a suicide pact. John married and distanced himself from Barrie. Peter Davies committed suicide as an adult in an attempt to escape, some say, from forever being called "Peter Pan."

Barrie ended up famous and rich, but a sad and lonely man. He was described as looking prematurely old and withered. Just before he died in 1937, he willed all proceeds from the copyright of *Peter Pan* to London's Great Ormond Street Hospital for Sick Children. Millions of dollars were realized from this bequest. Under British law, copyrights may extend no longer than 50 years before becoming public property. In this special case, Parliament made an exception and allowed the hospital to continue offering the world's best pediatric care because of the boy who never grew up.

* * *

THE CLAPPING GAMBLE

The play's most original and magical moment comes when the fairy Tinkerbell, in an attempt to save Peter's life, drinks poison that Captain Hook had intended for the boy. Boldy, Peter addresses the audience and calls on them to save the fairy's life. "Clap if you believe in fairies," he begs. Nina Boucicault, the first Peter, asked James Barrie, "Suppose they don't clap? What do I do then?" Barrie had no answer. The director told orchestra members to start the clapping if the audience sat on their hands. But the ploy was not necessary: the audience suspended disbelief with a vengeance and Nina-Peter wept openly with Tink's return to life.

* * *

A "lost boy" was a Victorian
euphemism for one who died young.

Space Age soufflé: In France, the Big Dipper is called the "casserole."

THE OTHER SIDE
OF PETER PAN

Now that you know something about James Barrie and the origins of Peter Pan, how does it change the way you perceive the story? Here are some quotes from the original book.

ALL CHILDREN, EXCEPT ONE, grow up. They soon know that they will grow up, and the way Wendy knew was this. One day when she was two years old she was playing in a garden, and she plucked another flower and ran with it to her mother. I suppose she must have looked rather delightful, for Mrs. Darling put her hand to her heart and cried, "Oh, why can't you remain like this forever!" This was all that passed between them on the subject, but henceforth Wendy knew that she must grow up. You always know after you are two. Two is the beginning of the end.

* * *

MRS. DARLING FIRST HEARD of Peter when she was tidying up her children's minds. It is the nightly custom of every good mother after her children are asleep to rummage in their minds and put things straight for next morning, repacking into their proper places the many articles that have wandered during the day. If you could keep awake (but of course you can't) you would see your own mother doing this, and you would find it very interesting to watch her. It is quite like tidying up drawers. You would see her on her knees, I expect, lingering humorously over some of your contents, wondering where on earth you had picked this thing up, making discoveries sweet and not so sweet, pressing this to her cheek as if it were as nice as a kitten, and hurriedly stowing that out of sight.

When you wake in the morning, the naughtiness and evil passions with which you went to bed have been folded up small and placed at the bottom of your mind; and on the top, beautifully aired, are spread out your prettier thoughts, ready for you to put on.

The Earth is turning to desert at a rate of 40 square miles per day.

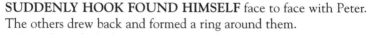

* * *

SUDDENLY HOOK FOUND HIMSELF face to face with Peter. The others drew back and formed a ring around them.

For a long duck the two enemies looked at one another; Hook shuddering slightly, and Peter with the strange smile upon his face.

"So, Pan," said Hook at last, "this is your doing."

"Ay, James Hook," came the stern answer, "it is all my doing."

"Proud and insolent youth," said Hook, "prepare to meet thy doom."

"Dark and sinister man," Peter answered, "have at thee."

Without more words they fell to and for a space there was no advantage to either blade. Peter was a superb swordsman, and parried with dazzling rapidity . . . Hook, scarcely his inferior, forced him back, hoping suddenly to end all with a favorite thrust . . . but to his astonishment he found his thrust turned aside again and again . . .

"Pan, who art thou?" he cried huskily.

"I'm youth, I'm joy," Peter answered . . . "I'm a little bird that has broken out of the egg."

This, of course, was nonsense; but it was proof to the unhappy Hook that Peter did not know in the least who or what he was, which is the very pinnacle of good form.

"To't again!" he cried despairingly.

He fought now like a human flail, and every sweep of that terrible sword would have severed in two any man or boy who obstructed it; but Peter fluttered around him as if the very wind it made blew him out of the danger zone.

* * *

"PETER," WENDY SAID, "are you expecting me to fly away with you?"

"Of course; that is why I have come . . ."

"I can't come," she said apologetically, "I have forgotten how to fly."

"I'll soon teach you again."

"Oh Peter, don't waste the fairy dust on me . . ."

Then she turned up the light, and Peter saw. He gave a cry of pain . . . "What is it?" he cried again.

She had to tell him. "I am old, Peter . . . I grew up a long time ago . . . I couldn't help it."

Walt Disney was afraid of mice.

COURT TRANSQUIPS

Do court transcripts make good bathroom reading? Check out these quotes from a little book called Disorder in the Court. *They're things people actually said in court, recorded word for word.*

Q: "What is your date of birth?"
A: "July fifteenth."
Q: "What year?"
A: "Every year."

Q: "What gear were you in at the moment of impact?"
A: "Gucci sweats and Reeboks."

Q: "Are you sexually active?"
A: "No, I just lie there."

Q: "This myasthenia gravis—does it affect your memory at all?"
A: "Yes."
Q: "And in what ways does it affect your memory?"
A: "I forget."
Q: "You forget. Can you give us an example of something that you've forgotten"

Q: "How old is your son—the one living with you."
A: "Thirty-eight or thirty-five, I can't remember which."
Q: "How long has he lived with you?"
A: "Forty-five years."

Q: "What was the first thing your husband said to you when he woke up that morning?"
A: "He said, 'Where am I, Cathy?'"
Q: "And why did that upset you?"
A: "My name is Susan."

Q: "And where was the location of the accident?"
A: "Approximately milepost 499."
Q: "And where is milepost 499?"
A: "Probably between milepost 498 and 500."

Q: "Sir, what is your IQ?"
A: "Well, I can see pretty well, I think."

Q: "Did you blow your horn or anything?"
A: "After the accident?"
Q: "Before the accident."
A: "Sure, I played for ten years. I even went to school for it."

Q: "Do you know if your daughter has ever been involved in the voodoo or occult?"
A: "We both do."
Q: "Voodoo?"
A: "We do."
Q: "You do?"
A: "Yes, voodoo."

Q: "Trooper, when you stopped the defendant, were your red and blue lights flashing?"
A: "Yes."
Q: "Did the defendant say anything when she got out of her car?"
A: "Yes, sir."
Q: "What did she say?"
A: "'What disco am I at?'"

The saguaro cactus does not grow its first arm until it's at least 75 years old.

YOUR GOVERNMENT AT WORK

BRI member Tim Harrower found most of these in a book called Goofy Government Grants & Wacky Waste. Now you can breathe a sigh of relief that your tax dollars are well spent on things like . . .

SCIENTIFIC RESEARCH

- Using bikini-clad women as bait, the National Science Foundation spent $64,000 to study whether distractions such as sex would decrease the honking of drivers stuck in traffic jams.

- Researchers from the National Institute on Alcohol Abuse and Alcoholism spent $102,000 to learn whether sunfish that drink tequila are more aggressive than sunfish that drink gin.

- University of Washington scientists used a government grant to monitor worm defecation. They discovered that all their worms were constipated.

- The National Institutes of Health spent more than $1 million to study cervical cancer using two test groups: nuns who were virgins and "nuns who are sexually active."

BUILDING A STRONG MILITARY

- Martin Marietta, a Department of Defense contractor, was caught charging the government $263,000 for tickets to a Smokey Robinson concert in Denver and $20,194 for professional-quality golf balls.

- In 1981 the U.S. Air Force said it could build 132 B-2 bombers for $22 billion. After eight years it had spent the money and had only one plane. A year of tests showed that the B-2 could perform its missions only 26% of the time . . . and it deteriorated in rain, heat, and humidity. The Air Force said it didn't want any more B-2s; Congress authorized contractors to build 21 of them anyway, at a cost of $44.7 billion.

But It's Not Just Us: The government of Japan recently financed a seven-year study to determine whether earthquakes are caused by catfish wiggling their tails.

The Apaches referred to horses as "God dogs."

SUPERSTITIONS

Here's where some common superstitions come from.

FINDING A FOUR-LEAF CLOVER

The belief that four-leaf clovers are good luck comes from the Druids, ancient residents of the British Isles. Several times a year, they gathered in oak groves to settle legal disputes and offer sacrifices . . . then they ended their rituals by hunting for four-leaf clovers. Why? They believed a four-leaf enabled its owner to see evil spirits and witches—and therefore avoid them.

THROWING PENNIES INTO A WELL

Ancient people believed spirits living in springs and fountains demanded tribute—usually flesh. Young Mayan girls, for example, were sometimes tossed into the Well of Sacrifice (where they would "marry" the spirits). Today we just toss the spirits a penny or two for luck.

KNOCKING ON WOOD

In the Middle Ages, churchmen insisted that knocking on wood was part of their tradition of prayer, since Christ was crucified on a wooden cross. They were right . . . but the tradition started several thousands of years earlier, with a different deity. Both Native Americans and ancient Greeks developed the belief (independently) that oak trees were the domain of an important god. By knocking on an oak, they were communicating with him and asking for his forgiveness. The Greeks passed their tradition on to the Romans, and it became part of European lore. The oak's "power" was eventually transferred to all wood.

NAILING A HORSESHOE OVER A DOOR

This "good luck charm" is a combination of two superstitions:

1. In early times, horses were considered magical. Because they can find their way in the dark, for example, people believed they could foresee danger or could guide souls through the underworld, so anything connected with a horse was lucky.

The last U. S. train robbery took place in 1933.

2. Horseshoes are made of iron, which was considered protective. The Norse god of battle wore iron gloves and carried an iron hammer. Romans nailed pieces of iron over their doors, believing it could ward off evil spirits.

In the 10th century, Christians added their own twist to the superstition—the tale of a blacksmith named Dunstan, who later became Archbishop of Canterbury. Dunstan had an unusual customer one day, a man with cloven feet who requested iron shoes. Dunstan pretended not to recognize him and agreed to make the shoes. But he knew who the fellow was—he shackled the Devil to the wall, treating him so brutally that Satan cried for mercy. Dunstan released him only after extracting a promise to never enter a dwelling with a horseshoe on the door.

OPENING AN UMBRELLA INDOORS
One of the few superstitions that isn't ancient or irrelevant. In the 18th century, spring-loaded, metal-spoked umbrellas were new and unpredictable. Opening one indoors was courting disaster—it could fly out of control and damage property . . . or people. It was a practical impulse to regard it as bad luck.

PULLING ON A WISHBONE
Over 2,000 years ago, the Etruscans (an early Italian civilization) believed that chickens—which squawk before they lay their eggs—could tell the future. The powers extended to part of the chicken's skeleton, too, so when a sacred hen died, the Etruscans put its collarbone in the sun until it dried out. Then people would pick it up, rub it, and make a wish. It became known as the "wishbone." Why this particular bone? Apparently because the V-shape looks a little like a human crotch.

Later, as more people wanted to get in on the wishing, the rubbing turned into a symbolic tug-of-war. Not everyone was going to get their wish; it became a contest to see whom the gods favored.

THE STORK BRINGING BABIES
In Scandinavia, storks—gentle birds with strong family ties—habitually nested on top of people's chimneys. So when Scandinavian parents needed to explain to youngsters how babies arrived, the stork was a handy answer. This traditional tale was spread in the 1800s by Hans Christian Andersen, in his fairy tales.

Q: What color is a purple finch? A: Crimson.

HOW THE SPIDER WAS CREATED

Here's the ancient Greek story of the creation of the spider—and the reason we call spiders "arachnids."
From Myths and Legends of the Ages.

There was a maiden named Arachne who was so skillful at weaving and embroidery that people would come from far and near to marvel at her work. Not only was the work itself beautiful, but Arachne's movements as she wove were so graceful and lovely that people would say, "Minerva herself must have taught you!"

But Arachne had become so vain about her skill that she couldn't bear to hear even the goddess Minerva praised.

"Is that so," scoffed Arachne. "Let Minerva try her skill with me. If I don't surpass her, I will pay the penalty!"

Minerva, hearing this, was angry. But she was also merciful. She disguised herself as an old woman and came to Arachne. "I am an old woman," she said, "and I have learned much in my long lifetime. Challenge your fellow mortals, if you want, but don't

challenge a goddess. If I were you, I would beg Minerva's forgiveness and hope she'll pardon you."

But Arachne laughed scornfully. "I am not afraid," she said. "I meant what I said. Let Minerva come down and compete with me . . . if she dares!"

"She comes!" answered Minerva. And dropping her disguise, she stepped forward.

Arachne paled, but only for a moment. "Let us begin," she said. So the contest began. Minerva wove scenes showing the immense power of the gods. The beauty of her work was so great that the watchers were breathless with admiration.

Then Arachne began to weave. She purposely chose to weave pictures showing the weakness and errors of the gods. Her pictures were so lifelike they almost seemed to move. She wove so marvelously that even Minerva admired her art. But

There is no bread in shortbread. It's a cookie.

furious at Arachne's insults, Minerva struck her shuttle and it fell apart. Then she touched Arachne's forehead and made her feel guilt and shame.

Arachne, in remorse, rushed away and hung herself. Then Minerva took some pity on her and said, "Live, guilty woman. But from now on, you and your children shall continue to hang."

As she spoke, Arachne's form shriveled up, while her arms and legs grew thinner, until finally she was changed into a spider. Her descendants can be seen to this day, hanging from the thread which they weave into webs.

* * *

TARANTULA ATTACK!

The poor tarantula is misunderstood—some people still believe its bite is fatal. (In *Dr. No*—the first James Bond film—for example, villains try to kill 007 by putting a tarantula on his pillow.)

- Actually, some species are not poisonous at all. And those that are have a bite generally no more harmful than a bee sting. Unlike bees, however, tarantulas give warnings before they attack—they rear up and bare their fangs. If that doesn't work, they sting.

- John Browning writes in *Tarantulas*, a pet guide for tarantula owners, "Tarantulas have never been known to kill a human being with their venom." However, he suggests caution: just as some people are allergic to bee stings, some can have severe allergic reactions to tarantula bites.

- Of more concern than a bite: Some species have poisonous hairs that can temporarily blind their enemies—including humans. If a tarantula feels threatened, it will rub its abdomen with its hind legs until some strands of hair fall off, then throw the strands at its enemy. (A tarantula with a large bald spot on its abdomen is either old, or under a lot of stress!)

Q: What's the seabird with the zoological name *Puffinus puffinus?*

WHY ASK WHY?

Sometimes, answers are irrelevant—it's the question that counts. These cosmic queries are from the Internet.

Why is *abbreviation* such a long word?

Why are there interstate highways in Hawaii?

Why is there an expiration date on sour cream?

Why is it that when you transport something by car, it's called a shipment, but when you transport something by ship, it's called cargo?

Why do we drive on parkways, and park on driveways?

If you're driving in a vehicle at the speed of light, what happens when you turn on the headlights?

Why don't you ever hear about *gruntled* employees?

What is a "free" gift? Aren't all gifts free?

Why do they call it *necking*?

Why isn't *phonetic* spelled the way it sounds?

If you tied buttered toast to the back of a cat and dropped it from a height, what would happen?

Have you ever imagined a world with no hypothetical situations!

If he's arrested, does a mime need to be told he has a right to remain silent?

Why do they call it a TV "set" when you only get one?

What was the best thing *before* sliced bread?

If you throw a cat out a car window, does it become kitty litter?

If one synchronized swimmer drowns, do the rest have to drown, too?

If a cow laughed, would milk come out her nose?

What's another word for *synonym?*

What is the speed of dark?

A: Not the puffin. The Manx shearwater.

FAMILIAR PHRASES

Where do these familiar terms and phrases come from? Etymologists have researched them and come up with these explanations.

ACID TEST
Meaning: A test of whether something is true or valuable.
Origin: In the past, gold was traded as currency. To find out if it was genuine, a gold coin could be tested with nitric acid. If the piece was counterfeit, the acid decomposed it. If it was genuine, the gold remained intact.

BUILD A FIRE UNDER SOMEONE
Meaning: Get someone to take action.
Origin: Mules can be stubborn. They sometimes splay all four legs out and refuse to move . . . and no amount of coaxing or beating will budge them. "When farmers wanted them to move and everything else failed," explains Nigel Rees in *Why You Say It*, "a small fire was built under the mule's belly in hopes that once in action the animal could be guided and kept moving.

BEFORE YOU CAN SAY "JACK ROBINSON"
Meaning: At once; instantly.
Origin: According to lore, the original Jack Robinson was a gentleman who kept his unannounced visits on his neighbors so short that they hardly had a chance to speak before he was gone. The term appears in Dickens's *A Christmas Carol* and Twain's *Huckleberry Finn*.

A FALSEHOOD
Meaning: A lie.
Origin: Before hats came into vogue, men wore hoods of cloth or fur attached to their cloaks. Many professionals—e.g., doctors and priests—wore distinctive hood styles. If a con man wanted to set himself up as a professional in a town where he wasn't known, all he had to do was put on the right hood. This deception came to be labeled a *falsehood*.

In the Middle Ages, you were supposed to throw eggs at the bride and groom.

MODERN MYTHOLOGY

*These mythological characters may be as famous
in our culture as Hercules or Pegasus were in
ancient Greece Here's where they came from.*

SNAP!, CRACKLE!, & POP! In 1933 commercial artist
Vernon Grant was working at his drawing board when he
heard this Rice Krispies ad on the radio:
Listen to the fairy song of health, the merry chorus sung by
Kellogg's Rice Krispies as they merrily snap, crackle, and pop in
a bowl of milk. If you've never heard food talking, now is your
chance.
Inspired, he immediately drew three little elves—which he named
after the noises the cereal supposedly made. Then he took the
sketches to N.W. Ayer, the Philadelphia ad agency that handled
Kellogg's advertising; they bought the cartoons on the spot. They
also hired Grant to keep illustrating the little trio for cereal boxes,
posters, and ads. He made a good living working for Kellogg's over
the next decade, but wasn't happy with the arrangement. So he
decided to sue Kellogg's for sole ownership of the characters. Bad
move: he lost, Kellogg's fired him, and Grant never made another
cent off the characters he'd created.

THE SUN-MAID RAISIN GIRL. "The sun-bonneted woman
. . . who smiles on every box of Sun-Maid raisins was a real person," writes Victoria Woeste in *Audacity* magazine. "Her name was
Lorraine Collett and in 1915 she was sitting in her front yard letting her hair dry before participating in Fresno's first Raisin Day
parade. A Sun-Maid executive was passing by and was struck by
the sight. He had a photographer come take her picture, then had
artist Fanny Scafford paint the picture from it." All Collett made
from it was a $15 modeling fee and a bit part in a 1936 film called
Trail of the Lonesome Pine. The original bonnet is now in the
Smithsonian.

MR. PEANUT. Amadeo Obici founded the Planters Nut &
Chocolate Company in 1906, in Wilkes-Barre, Pennsylvania.
Roasted and salted peanuts were still new to most Americans, and

the company was an immediate success. As it got bigger, Obici decided he needed a logo. In 1916 he sponsored a contest to find one. The winner: 13-year-old Antonio Gentile, from Suffolk, Virginia, who submitted a drawing of "a little peanut person" and got $5 for it. A commercial artist took Gentile's sketch, added a hat, cane, and monocle (to lend a touch of class to the lowly legume), and Mr. Peanut was born. The elegant gentle-nut made his debut in 1918, in *The Saturday Evening Post*.

MCGRUFF THE CRIME DOG. In the late 1970s, the Ad Council made a deal with the U.S. Justice Department to create an anti-crime ad campaign. Their first task: invent a spokes-character (like Smokey the Bear) to deliver the message in commercials. Adman Jack Keil began riding with the New York police to get ideas. He remembers:

> We weren't getting anywhere. Then came a day I was flying home from the West Coast. I was trying to think of a slogan—*crunch crime, stomp on crime.* And I was thinking of animal symbols—*growling at crime, roaring at crime.* But which animal? The designated critter had to be trustworthy, honorable, and brave. Then I thought, you can't crunch crime or defeat it altogether, but you can snap at it, nibble at it—*take a bite out of crime.* And the animal that takes a bite is a dog.

A bloodhound was the natural choice for a crimefighter, but they still needed a name . . . so they sponsored a nationwide name-the-dog contest. The most frequent entry was Shure-lock Bones. Others included: Sarg-dog, J. Edgar Dog, and Keystone Kop Dog. The winner was submitted by a New Orleans police officer. In the ads, Keil supplies McGruff's voice.

TONY THE TIGER. In 1952 Kellogg's planned to feature a menagerie of animals—one for each letter of the alphabet—on packages of its Sugar Frosted Flakes. They started with K and T: Katy the Kangaroo and Tony the Tiger. But they never got any further. Tony—who walked on all fours and had a much flatter face than today—was so popular that he became the cereal's official spokes-character. In the first Frosted Flakes commercials, only kids who ate Tony's cereal could see him. His personality has changed a number of times since then, but his voice hasn't. It's Thurl Ravenscroft, an ex-radio star who jokingly claimed to have made a career out of just one word: "Grr-reat!"

In Equatorial Guinea, it's illegal to name your child Monica.

FAMOUS FOR 15 MINUTES

Here it is again—our feature based on Andy Warhol's prophetic comment that "in the future, everyone will be famous for 15 minutes." Here's how a few people have been using up their allotted quarter-hour.

THE STAR: Pete Condon, 1989 graduate of the University of Georgia

THE HEADLINE: *Case Clothes'd: Job Seeker Wears Résumé, Gets Calls*

WHAT HAPPENED: Condon had graduated from college with a 3.5 grade average, but couldn't get the marketing/advertising job he wanted. Finally, in February 1992, the 25-year-old blew up his résumé, put it on a sandwich board, and stood on an Atlanta street corner during rush hour with a sign saying: "I will work for $25,000 a year." An *Atlanta Constitution* reporter spotted him. The next day his photo and story were in newspapers all over the country.

AFTERMATH: In the next two months, Condon got more than 500 job offers from as far away as Japan and Panama. He was the subject of college lectures and term papers, and women sent photos asking to meet him. Condon finally took a job at Dean Witter . . . at a salary of considerably more than $25,000.

THE STAR: John (or Tom) Helms

THE HEADLINE: *Lucky Leaper Lands Lightly on Ledge, Likes Life*

WHAT HAPPENED: Just before Christmas in 1977, Helms—a 26-year-old down-and-out artist—decided to commit suicide by jumping off the Empire State Building. He took the elevator to the 86th floor observation deck (more than 1,000 feet up), climbed over the safety rail, and let go. He woke up half an hour later, sitting on a ledge on the 85th floor. Miraculously, a 30-mph wind had blown him back against the building. He knocked on a window, and an astonished engineer in the NBC-TV transmitter room helped him in. "I couldn't believe it," the engineer said. "You don't see a lot of guys coming in through the window of the 85th floor. I poured myself a stiff drink." The story made national news.

How can you tell when a porpoise is searching for a mate? It swims upside down.

AFTERMATH: Helms decided life was okay after all, and got hundreds of offers from families who wanted to take him in for the holidays. Two years later a similar incident occurred. On December 2, 1979, Elvita Adams climbed over the 86th floor's safety rail and jumped. She fell about 20 feet before she was blown back onto a 2 1/2-foot ledge, breaking her hip. A guard heard her yelling in pain and rescued her.

THE STAR: Graham Washington Jackson, a Navy musician
THE HEADLINE: *Sobbing Soldier Shows Symbolic Sorrow*
WHAT HAPPENED: President Franklin D. Roosevelt died on April 12, 1945, at the "Little White House" in Warm Springs, Georgia. Jackson was there to see FDR's body taken away. "It seemed like every nail and every pin in the world just stuck in me," he said later. As tears streamed down his face, he spontaneously began playing a tune called "Goin' Home" on his accordion. Edward Clark, a photographer, noticed Jackson and snapped a shot that was published in *Life* magazine. The picture captured the nation's shock and grief so well that both the photo and Jackson became world-famous.
AFTERMATH: Over the next four decades, Jackson was invited to the White House to play for every president. In fact, Jimmy Carter—who regarded the *Life* photo as one of the best ever taken—had Jackson named Georgia's "Official State Musician" when Carter was governor. Jackson died in 1983, at age 79.

THE STAR: Leon Henry Ritzenthaler, possible half-brother of President Bill Clinton
THE HEADLINE: *Surprise Sibling Surfaces in Paradise*
WHAT HAPPENED: In June 1993, a few months after Clinton took office, The *Washington Post* announced that Ritzenthaler—a retired janitor in Paradise, California—was the president's long-lost half-brother.

Clinton's mother had married William Blythe in 1943. Ritzenthaler's mother had married Blythe eight years earlier, in 1935. She and Blythe had divorced in 1936, but continued to "visit" after the divorce; Leon was born in 1938, the result—his mother claimed—of one of those visits. The *Post* spent four months checking, and sure enough, Leon's birth certificate listed Blythe as his father. But Blythe's sister insisted that it was *another* member of the family who was really the father—that Blythe had merely covered for him.

Meanwhile, the press camped on Ritzenthaler's doorstep. Leon said he wanted nothing from the president except their father's health records, so he could pass them on to his kids. (Although he admitted he wouldn't mind meeting his brother.) Clinton said he'd comment after talking to Ritzenthaler.

The president did call Leon a few days later; they chatted for 15 minutes. And in August, Clinton sent a note that said, "I look forward to meeting you before too long."

AFTERMATH: The story simply died. Clinton seems never to have mentioned Ritzenthaler again, and the press apparently lost interest.

Sidelight: In August 1993, a woman named Wanetta Alexander surfaced, swearing to reporters that the William Blythe she'd married in 1941 was the same man who'd fathered Clinton. That would have made her daughter the president's half-sister . . . but more interesting, it would have made Clinton "illegitimate." Alexander hadn't divorced Blythe until 1944, and Clinton's mother had married him in 1943. It was apparently never proved.

THE STAR: Ruth Bullis, a waitress at Stanford's Restaurant in Lake Oswego, Oregon

THE HEADLINE: *Tip Tops Charts*

WHAT HAPPENED: In November 1995 a customer ordered a gin-and-tonic and a sandwich from Bullis, paid for it with a credit card, and wrote in a $40 dollar tip. Then he ordered another gin-and-tonic and left $100. Four hours later, after a third gin-and-tonic, he left a whopping $1,000 tip. Bullis said he insisted: "I can leave you whatever I want . . . I'm a big spender." But she put the tips aside, waiting to see if he'd have second thoughts. A few weeks later, he showed up again . . . and left $100. She decided it was okay to spend the money. But she was wrong. In February American Express notified Stanford's that the customer wanted his money back.

AFTERMATH: When the story was picked up by national news media, the company that owned Stanford's decided on its own to avoid further publicity and refund the tip to the customer. Bullis kept $1,000 *and* her job.

It takes around 200,000 frowns to create a permanent brow line.

REEL QUOTES

Here are some of our favorite lines from the silver screen.

ON DATING
Allen: "What are you doing Saturday night?"
Diana: "Committing suicide."
Allen: "What are you doing Friday night?"
—*Play It Again, Sam*

ON LOVE
Darrow: "You ever been in love, Hornbeck?"
Hornbeck: "Only with the sound of my own voice, thank God."
—*Inherit the Wind*

"Jane, since I've met you, I've noticed things I never knew were there before: birds singing . . . dew glistening on a newly formed leaf . . . stop lights . . . "
—**Lt. Frank Drebin,**
Naked Gun

ON ANATOMY
Nick Charles: "I'm a hero. I was shot twice in the *Tribune*."
Nora Charles: "I read where you were shot five times in the tabloids."
Nick: "It's not true. They didn't come anywhere near my tabloids."
—*The Thin Man*

ON GOLF
"A golf course is nothing but a poolroom moved outdoors."
—**Barry Fitzgerald,**
Going My Way

ON RELIGION
Sonja: "Of course there's a God. We're made in his image."
Boris: "You think I was made in God's image? Take a look at me. Do you think he wears glasses?"
Sonja: "Not with those frames . . . Boris, we must believe in God."
Boris: "If I could just see a miracle. Just one miracle. If I could see a burning bush, or the seas part, or my Uncle Sasha pick up a check."
—**Woody Allen's**
Love and Death

ON BEING CLEAR
Ted Striker: "Surely, you can't be serious."
Dr. Rumack: "I *am* serious. And don't call me Shirley."
—*Airplane!*

Chief, the U.S. Cavalry's last horse, died in 1968. He was 36.

READ ALL ABOUT IT!

*We've all heard the expression "Don't believe everything
you read." Here are a few examples of why that's true.*

PLAINFIELD TEACHER'S COLLEGE WINS AGAIN!
(*New York Herald Tribune* and other papers, 1941)
   The Story: In 1941 the *Tribune*, the *New York Post*, and a
number of other New York papers began reporting the scores of a
New Jersey football team called the Plainfield Teachers College
Flying Figments as it battled teams like Harmony Teachers College
and Appalachia Tech for a coveted invitation to the first-ever
"Blackboard Bowl."
The Reaction: As the season progressed and the Figments
remained undefeated, interest in the small college powerhouse
grew, and so did the press coverage. Several papers ran feature articles about Johnny Chung, the team's "stellar Chinese halfback who
has accounted for 69 of Plainfield's 117 points" and who "renewed
his amazing strength at halftime by wolfing down wild rice."
The Truth: Plainfield, the Flying Figments, and its opponents were
all invented by a handful of bored New York stockbrokers who
were amazed that real teams from places like Slippery Rock got
their scores into big-city newspapers. Each Saturday, the brokers
phoned in fake scores, then waited for them to appear in the
Sunday papers. The hoax lasted nearly the entire season, until
Time magazine got wind of it and decided to run a story. In the few
days that remained before *Time* hit the newsstands, the brokers
sent in one last story announcing that "because of a rash of flunk-
ings in mid-term examinations, Plainfield was calling off its last
two scheduled games of the season."

PETRIFIED MAN FOUND IN NEVADA CAVE!
(Virginia City *Territorial Enterprise*, 1862)
The Story: According to the article, a petrified man with a
wooden leg was found in a cave in a remote part of Nevada. The
man was found in a seated position, with

> the right thumb resting against the side of his nose, the left
> thumb partially supported the chin, the forefinger pressing the

inner corner of the left eye and drawing it partially open; the right eye was closed, and the fingers of the right hand spread apart.

The article claimed the man had been dead for at least 300 years.

The Reaction: The story spread to other newspapers in Nevada, from there to the rest of the country, and from there around the world. The archaeological "find" was even reported in the London scientific journal *Lancet*.

The Truth: The story was the work of the *Territorial Enterprise's* local editor, Samuel Clemens (later known by his pen name, Mark Twain). Clemens figured people would know it was a hoax by the description of the stone man's hand positions. [Uncle John's note: Try doing it yourself.] But he was wrong. "I really had no desire to deceive anybody," he explained later. "I depended on the way the petrified man was sitting to explain to the public that he was a swindle . . . [It was] a delicate, a very delicate satire. But maybe it was altogether too delicate, for nobody ever perceived the satire part of it at all."

NOISY GHOST HAUNTS SAN DIEGO BANK BUILDING!
(*The San Diego Metropolitan*, 1987)

The Story: The article claimed that the Great American Bank Building, one of San Diego's best-known landmarks, was plagued by mysterious footsteps heard late at night, creepy voices, ghostlike images materializing out of thin air; just about all of the classic ghost clichés. The article even claimed the ghost or ghosts had reduced janitorial costs 25% by helping the building's custodians do the vacuuming. The article included a photo of the ghost, and quoted a "parapsychologist" calling it "one of the finest examples of spiritual photography I've ever seen."

The Reaction: The public took the story seriously, and when the tenants of the Great American Bank Building learned of the incidents, they began reporting their own sightings—including power failures, carpeting that had been "mysteriously vacuumed," and cleaning equipment that moved from one floor to another; one electrician even reported seeing his tools float in midair and ghosts walking in the hallway.

The Truth: The article was the brainchild of *Metropolitan* publisher Sean Patrick Reily, who later admitted it had been inspired by Mark Twain's "petrified man" work.

Siberia means "sleeping land."

WEIRD CELEBRATIONS

One of Uncle John's bathroom stalwarts is Stabbed with
a Wedge of Cheese, *by Charles Downey. There's a lot
of offbeat stuff in it, including info on these festivals.*

THE ANNUAL FIRE ANT FESTIVAL
Location: Marshall, Texas
Background: Fire ants are red ants that swarm and bite—a
real problem in South Texas. People in Marshall decided that since
they couldn't get rid of the ants, they might as well have some fun
with them.
Special Events: Fire Ant Call, Fire Ant Roundup, and a Fire Ant
Chili Cookoff in which entrants must certify in writing that their
fixins contain at least one fire ant. The ending to the festivities is
the Fire Ant Stomp—not an attempt to squash the ants, but an
old-fashioned street dance.

THE INTERNATIONAL STRANGE MUSIC FESTIVAL
Location: Olive Hill, Kentucky
Background: Founded to honor people who make music from non-
musical items.
Special Events: Every act is a special event. Performers have
included:

- A Japanese trio playing "My Old Kentucky Home" on a table
  (upside down, strung like a cello), tea pot (a wind instrument),
  and assorted pots and pans (bongo drums)
- A 15-piece orchestra of automobile horns
- A seven-foot slide whistle requiring three people to operate it
- A "Graduated Clanger"—a system of ever-smaller fire alarm
  bells, played like a xylophone

THE ANNUAL CHICKEN SHOW
Location: Wayne, Nebraska
Background: Held on the second Saturday in July, featuring a
crowing contest for roosters, a free omelet feed for humans, and a

Fish cough.

chicken-flying meet, fully sanctioned by the International Chicken Flying Association.

Special Events: A "Most Beautiful Beak" contest, chicken bingo, and an egg drop (participants risk egg-on-the-face by trying to catch a raw egg dropped from a fully extended cherry picker). The National Cluck-Off selects the person with the most lifelike cluck and most believable crow. Another contest offers prizes to the man and woman who sport the most chickenlike legs.

THE WORLD GRITS FESTIVAL

Location: St. George, South Carolina

Background: World's only celebration honoring the South's staple food. Special grits dishes are offered for all meals of the day. Also featured are a grits mill, a grits-eating contest, and a grits cooking contest. The event was born when someone discovered that the 2,300 citizens of St. George went through about 1,800 pounds of grits a week.

Special Events: "The Roll-in-Grits Contest." A kids' wading pool is filled with hot water and several hundred pounds of grits, then stirred with a canoe paddle till done. Each contestant: 1) weighs in, 2) gets in the pool and wallows in it for seven seconds, 3) gets out and weighs in again. The object: To see how many pounds of grits can stick to your body. All-time winner had 26 pounds stuck to him.

THE UGLY PICKUP PARADE AND CONTEST

Location: Chadron, Nebraska

Background: In 1987 newspaper columnist Les Mann wrote an homage to his junker 1974 pickup, "Black Beauty," claiming it was the ugliest truck on the planet. Irate ugly-truck owners wrote in, saying they could top him. So the first Ugly Truck Contest was born.

Special Events: Experts pick the Ugly Pickup of the Year. An Ugly Pickup Queen leads the three-block parade through town. Official rules: Trucks have to be street-legal, and over a decade old. They have to be able to move under their own power; a majority of the surface area has to be rust and dents; and, most important, they've got to have a good Ugly Truck name. Contestants get extra points for something *especially* ugly on their truck.

Moscow is closer to Washington, D.C., than Honolulu is.

UNCLE ALBERT SAYS...

Cosmic question: What would Albert Einstein think if he knew we consider his comments great bathroom reading?

"Only two things are infinite, the universe and stupidity—and I'm not sure about the former."

"God is subtle, but He is not malicious."

"'Common sense' is the set of prejudices acquired by age eighteen."

"Nationalism is an infantile disease. It is the measles of mankind."

"I never think of the future. It comes soon enough."

"Try not to become a man of success, but rather, a man of value."

"I experience the greatest degree of pleasure in having contact with works of art. They furnish me with happy feelings of an intensity such as I cannot derive from other realms."

"To punish me for my contempt for authority, Fate made me an authority myself."

"Why is it that nobody understands me, and everybody likes me?"

"A life directed chiefly toward fulfillment of personal desires sooner or later always leads to bitter disappointment."

"My political ideal is that of democracy. Let every man be respected as an individual, and no man idolized."

"Whatever there is of God and goodness in the Universe, it must work itself out and express itself through us. We cannot stand aside and let God do it."

"Science without religion is lame, religion without science is blind."

"I am a deeply religious non-believer . . . This is a somewhat new kind of religion."

"With fame I become more and more stupid, which of course is a very common phenomenon."

FLUBBED HEADLINES

These are 100% honest-to-goodness headlines.
Can you figure out what they were trying to say?

Kids Make Nutritious Snacks

ENRAGED COW INJURES
FARMER WITH AXE

Red Tape Holds Up New
Bridge

BILKE-A-THON NETS
$1,000 FOR ILL BOY

PANDA MATING FAILS;
VETERINARIAN TAKES
OVER

Eye Drops Off Shelf

HELICOPTER POWERED
BY HUMAN FLIES

Circumcisions Cut Back

POPE TO BE ARRAIGNED
FOR ALLEGEDLY BUR-
GLARIZING CLINIC

City wants Dead to pay for
cleanup

MOORPARK RESIDENTS
ENJOY A COMMUNAL
DUMP

Montana Traded to Kansas
City

International Scientific
Group Elects Bimbo As Its
Chairman

Storm delayed by bad weather

LEGISLATORS TAX
BRAINS TO CUT DEFICIT

Study Finds Sex, Pregnancy
Link

DEAD GUITARIST NOW
SLIMMER AND TRIMMER

Trees can break wind

RANGERS TO TEST
PEETERS FOR RUST

Cockroach Slain, Husband
Badly Hurt

LACK OF BRAINS
HINDERS RESEARCH

Two Sisters Reunited After 18
Years At Checkout Counter

MISSOURI WOMAN BIG
WINNER AT HOG SHOW

PANTS MAN TO
EXPAND AT THE REAR

Pontius Pilate was born in Scotland.

ANONYMOUS STARS

You've watched them work, you've heard them speak—but you've probably never heard their names. They're the actors inside the gorilla suits, the voices of talking animals, etc. We think they deserve a little credit.

THE VOICE OF E.T.

- E.T.'s voice was created by combining the voices of three people, a sea otter, and a dog. But the person who spoke the most famous lines—"E.T. phone home" and "Be good"—was Patricia A. Welsh, a former radio soap opera star who'd been involved in only one other movie (*Waterloo*, with Robert Taylor, in 1940).

- By contract, she was forbidden to say her lines (which are copyrighted) even casually in conversation; Steven Spielberg said he "didn't want kids to get confused about E.T.'s image." Her name isn't even listed in the credits.

DARTH VADER

- David Prowse is a 6'6", 266-pound former heavyweight wrestling champion. George Lucas saw him in A *Clockwork Orange* and offered him his choice between two parts— Chewbacca or Vader. Prowse chose Vader because he didn't like the idea of going around in a "gorilla suit" for six months.

THE "LOST IN SPACE" ROBOT

- Bob May, a stuntman, had a few small parts in a TV series called *Voyage to the Bottom of the Sea*. The producer, Irwin Allen, told May he was the right size for a part in a new TV series and asked if he'd be interested. May said yes; Allen said: "Fine, you have the part, go try on the robot costume."

- Cast members goofed on May a lot. One time they locked him in the robot suit and left him there during a lunch break. He tried yelling, but no one was around . . . so he had a cigarette. Irwin Allen wandered in, saw smoke coming from the robot, and thought it was burning up. He went to get a fire extinguisher while May yelled from inside the suit. Later, Allen decided he liked the effect and had May smoke a cigar in the suit for a story about the robot burning out.

Mosquitos have 47 teeth.

MR. ED'S VOICE

- When *Mr. Ed* debuted in 1960, the horse's voice was credited to "an actor who prefers to remain nameless."

- *TV Guide* sent a reporter to the studio to figure out who it was. The reporter found a parking space on the *Mr. Ed* set assigned to an old 1930s movie cowboy named Alan "Rocky" Lane.

- Lane admitted it was his voice (he'd been too embarrassed to let people know). He dubbed Ed's voice off-camera, while the horse was "mouthing the words." A nylon bit concealed in Ed's mouth made him move his lips.

R2-D2

- Kenny Baker, 3'8" tall, was hired simply because he fit into the robot suit. "They made R2-D2 small because Carrie and Mark were small . . . My agent sent me down. They looked at me and said, 'He'll do!'

- "I thought it was a load of rubbish at first. Then I thought, 'Well, Alec Guinness is in it; he must know what's going on.'"

THE VOICE OF THE DEMON IN THE *EXORCIST*

- Mercedes McCambridge, an Academy Award–winning actress, was a Catholic. So when she was offered the role, she was uncertain about whether to take it. She consulted Father Walter Hartke at Catholic University, and he approved.

- In the film, the demon's voice is heard as Linda Blair vomits green gunk. According to one report: "A tube was glued to each side of Blair's face and covered with makeup. Two men knelt on either side of Blair holding a syringe filled with the green stuff, ready to shoot on cue."

- "McCambridge had to coordinate her sound effects with the action. A prop man lined up a row of Dixie cups in front of her containing apple pieces soaking in water, and some containing whole boiled eggs. McCambridge held the soft apple chunks in her jaws as she swallowed a boiled egg. On cue, in precise coordination with the screen action, she flexed her diaphragm and spewed everything on the microphone . . . 'It was hard,' she said. 'I sometimes had to lie down after those scenes.'"

Short people have fewer back problems than tall people do.

FORGOTTEN HISTORY

A few tidbits of obscure history from Keep Up
with the World, *a 1941 book by Freling Foster.*

X-RAY-PROOF UNDERWEAR

"A short time after X-rays were discovered in 1895 and news of their penetrating power had spread throughout the world, the women of England believed—and were horrified by—the rumor that a British firm was about to make X-ray spectacles that would enable the wearer to look right through clothing. Within a few months, a manufacturer and a London department store made a small fortune with their new 'X-ray-proof underwear.'"

APE HANGED AS A FRENCH SPY

"In 1705, during Queen Anne's War between France and England, a small vessel was wrecked in the North Sea off the English coast village of West Hartlepool and the sole survivor, a pet ape belonging to the crew, was washed ashore on a plank and captured by fishermen. The villagers had never before seen such a peculiar character, but they were not to be fooled by his hairy disguise and outlandish chatter. The following day, the monkey was tried by court martial, found guilty, and hanged as a French spy."

THE FIRST MOVIE STAR

"The first film star was John Bunny of New York City, who made approximately 100 one-reel comedies for the Vitagraph Company between 1911 and his death in 1915. As his pictures were shown in numerous countries, Bunny's short fat figure soon became more widely known than that of any other living individual. When he went on a world tour in 1913, he became the first movie star ever to be recognized and surrounded by huge crowds in every city he visited."

THE AMPERSAND

"The oldest symbol representing a word is "&," known as the *ampersand*. Originally, it was one of the 5,000 signs in the world's first shorthand system, invented by Marcus Tiro in Rome in 63 B.C."

The longest-surviving Civil War veteran died in 1959.

THE TRUTH
ABOUT LOVE

*If you want to know something important, ask a kid. These
quotes about love were submitted by BRI member Alan Reder,
who got them from the Internet and e-mailed them to us.*

HOW DO TWO PEOPLE WIND UP FALLING IN LOVE?

Andrew, age 6: "One of the people has freckles and so he finds somebody else who has freckles too."

Mae, age 9: "No one is sure why it happens, but I heard it has something to do with how you smell . . . That's why perfume and deodorant are so popular."

Manuel, age 8: "I think you're supposed to get shot with an arrow or something, but the rest of it isn't supposed to be so painful."

WHAT IS FALLING IN LOVE LIKE?
John, age 9: "Like an avalanche where you have to run for your life."

Glenn, age 7: "If falling in love is anything like learning how to spell, I don't want to do it. It takes too long."

HOW IMPORTANT IS BEAUTY IN LOVE?
Anita, age 8: "If you want to be loved by somebody who isn't already in your family, it doesn't hurt to be beautiful."

Brian, age 7: "It isn't always just how you look. Look at me. I'm handsome like anything and I haven't got anybody to marry me yet."

Christine, age 9: "Beauty is skin deep. But how rich you are can last a long time."

At Old English weddings, guests threw shoes at the groom.

WHY DO LOVERS HOLD HANDS?

Gavin, age 8: "They want to make sure their rings don't fall off because they paid good money for them."

John, age 9: "They are just practicing for when they might have to walk down the aisle someday and do the matchimony thing."

WHAT'S YOUR PERSONAL OPINION ABOUT LOVE?

Jill, age 6: "I'm in favor of love as long as it doesn't happen when *Dinosaurs* is on television."

Floyd, age 9: "Love is foolish . . . but I still might try it sometime."

Dave, age 8: "Love will find you, even if you are trying to hide from it. I've been trying to hide from it since I was five, but the girls keep finding me."

Regina, age 10: "I'm not rushing into being in love. I'm finding the fourth grade hard enough."

WHAT'S A SUREFIRE WAY TO MAKE A PERSON FALL IN LOVE WITH YOU?

Del, age 6: "Tell them that you own a whole bunch of candy stores."

Camille, age 9: "Shake your hips and hope for the best."

Carey, age 7: "Yesterday I kissed a girl in a private place . . . We were behind a tree."

REFLECTIONS ON THE NATURE OF LOVE

Greg, age 8: "Love is the most important thing in the world, but baseball is pretty good, too."

* * *

"To love a thing means wanting it to live."

—*Confucius*

Clams can live as long as 150 years.

THE BIRTH OF
THE TONIGHT SHOW,
PART I

*The Tonight Show is a television institution that's been around
longer than a lot of you readers. It's also the forerunner of most
of today's TV talk shows—and it's got a fascinating history.
So we've decided to include parts of it throughout the book.
Tune it in one day at a time, the way you might watch the show.*

GOODNIGHT, AMERICA

If you flip through the TV channels between 11:30 p.m. and 1:00 a.m., you'll see a lot of talk shows.

But it wasn't always that way. Before 1950, there weren't many TV shows of *any* kind on that late. Networks ended their programming at 11:00 p.m., and many affiliate stations went off the air, too. If they didn't, chances are they played old movies—*bad* ones. Hollywood, threatened by the inroads TV was making into their business, refused to give them anything good.

Bad movies and test patterns—no wonder hardly anyone was watching.

LEAVE IT TO WEAVER

In 1950 an NBC executive named Sylvester "Pat" Weaver, who'd successfully launched the *The Today Show* and *Your Show of Shows* (a 90-minute variety show starring comic Sid Caesar), turned his attention to late-evening programming.

Weaver (whose daughter, by the way, is actress Sigourney Weaver) figured that a program like *Your Show of Shows,* with vaudeville or Broadway review acts, would be successful between 11:30 p.m. and 12:30 a.m.—especially since there was so little competition. He passed around a memo outlining his idea to other NBC executives. It would be called *Broadway Open House,* he wrote, and would be "zany, light-hearted . . . for people in the mood for staying up . . . It would have the glitter and excitement of Broadway, but the backstage ambience of a party." Through the medium of television, viewers could hobnob with the rich and

---

Can you flare your nostrils? Only 30% of humans can.

famous. Some NBC executives thought it was the dumbest idea they'd ever heard.

"Late night?" one of them supposedly asked at a meeting. "Eleven thirty? At that hour, people are either sleeping or . . . "

"Most people aren't that lucky," another NBC exec said, to which Weaver replied: "Let's do something for 'most people.'"

HOST OF PROBLEMS

Finding the right host has always been a problem for talk shows—even from the beginning. *Your Show of Shows* had done well with a comedian for a host, and Weaver thought it would work again with *Broadway Open House.* His first choice was a nightclub comic named Jan Murray . . . but Murray decided to emcee a TV game show instead.

Second choice was Don "Creesh" Hornsby, a cross between Robin Williams and PeeWee Herman. On his own L.A. show, he performed magic tricks, played the piano, ran around the stage shouting "Creesh! Creesh!," and pulled brassieres out of women's blouses. "His stuff was really wild," Weaver remembered years later. "We reasoned, 'What the hell, it'll be late at night and who cared?'"

Creesh took the job, moved his family to New York . . . and then died suddenly the weekend before *Broadway Open House* was to premiere. NBC executives were shocked by his death, but weren't completely unprepared: his act was so weird that they'd already thought about replacements in case he bombed.

Broadway Open House went on the air May 22, 1950, hosted by Tex and Jinx, a husband-and-wife team with their own radio interview show. They were terrible. So Weaver quickly replaced them with comic actor Wally Cox (*Mr. Peepers*) . . . who lasted only a few days. Then he tried Dean Martin and Jerry Lewis. They were better, but were so overbooked that they couldn't work as regular hosts.

Weaver's next choice was a comedian named Jerry Lester. He took the job . . . but would only agree to work three nights a week—Monday, Wednesday, and Friday. So NBC hired Morey Amsterdam (who later became famous on *The Dick Van Dyke Show*) to fill in on Tuesdays and Thursdays. A young Neil Simon was hired as a writer.

Longest word in Japanese: *Chi-n-chi-ku-ri-n.* It means "very short person."

KEEPING ABREAST

Today, the "sidekick" is a standard part of late-night talk shows. But in 1950, it was a new idea. Few people recall that the first side-kick was Dagmar, a beautiful blonde woman with huge breasts.

Dagmar had an even smaller job on the show than Ed McMahon had on *The Tonight Show*—all she had to do was look stupid on camera. She didn't even talk. "For the first two or three months," Robert Metz writes in *The Tonight Show*, "Dagmar sat on a stool right in front of the band with an off-the-shoulder dress and an enormous overhang that may have influenced the wit who dubbed television the boob tube. Dagmar seemed to fit that phrase on both counts. She was a stereotypical dumb blonde. A large sign under the stool read, 'Girl Singer,' but she never opened her mouth and never sang."

BOOM . . . AND BUST

Broadway Open House quickly built a following. Within two months, Jerry and Dagmar were national celebrities. When the show made a trip to Cleveland, 45,000 people turned out to watch the taping, paying $2.50 apiece for the privilege.

But NBC still had problems with the show: Morey Amsterdam's performance didn't measure up to Lester's, and in November 1950, he quit. Lester still refused to work more than three days a week, so NBC had to find someone to fill in on the other days. They tried a number of young comics, but none of them caught on.

Then Lester and Dagmar—who turned out to have true comic talent—began feuding. The fight got so bad that Lester added a second, less-threatening blonde named Agathon to the show to help with the magic tricks.

Open House became increasingly stale. Critics who'd lauded it a few months before started attacking it. Finally, in May 1951, Lester quit. The show limped along for three more months as NBC searched frantically for another host . . . but they never found one. It went off the air on August 23, 1951. Three more years would pass before NBC would attempt another late-night show.

That's just the beginning. See page 547 for Part II.

The Earth is 100 million years older than the moon.

CURSES!

*Even if you're not superstitious, it's hard to resist tales of
"cursed" ships, tombs, and so on. Here are some of our favorites.*

THE CURSE OF JAMES DEAN'S PORSCHE

Curse: Disaster may be ahead for anyone connected with James Dean's "death car." It seems to attack people at random.

Origin: In 1955 Dean smashed his red Porsche into a another car and was killed. The wreckage was bought by George Barris, a friend of Dean's (and the man who customized cars like the Munsters' coffin-mobile for Hollywood). But as one writer put it, "the car proved deadly even after it was dismantled." Barris noticed weird things happening immediately.

Among Its Victims:

- The car slipped while being unloaded from the truck that delivered it to Barris, and broke a mechanic's legs.

- Barris put its engine into a race car. It crashed in the race, killing the driver. A second car in the same race was equipped with the Porsche's drive shaft—it overturned and injured its driver.

- The shell of the Porsche was being used in a Highway Safety display in San Francisco. It fell off its pedestal and broke a teenager's hip. Later, a truck carrying the display to another demonstration was involved in an accident. "The truck driver," says one account, "was thrown out of the cab of the truck and killed when the Porsche shell rolled off the back of the truck and crushed him."

Status: The Porsche finally vanished in 1960, while on a train en route to Los Angeles.

THE PRESIDENTIAL DEATH CYCLE

Curse: Between 1840 and 1960, every U.S. president elected in a year ending in a zero either died in office of natural causes or was assassinated. By contrast: Since 1840, of the 29 presidents who were not elected in the 20-year cycle, only one has died in office and not one has been assassinated.

Origin: The first president to die in office was William Henry Harrison, elected in 1840. In 1960, when John Kennedy was shot, people began to realize the eerie "coincidence" involved.

The most popular Easter egg color is blue. Next are purple and pink.

Victims:

- William Henry Harrison, dead in 1841 after one month in office
- Abraham Lincoln (elected in 1860), fatally shot in 1865
- James Garfield (1880), assassinated in 1881
- William McKinley (re-elected in 1900), fatally shot in 1901
- Warren G. Harding (1920), died in 1923
- Franklin D. Roosevelt (elected for the third time in 1940), died in 1945
- JFK (1960), assassinated in 1963
- Ronald Reagan (1980) was nearly the eighth victim. He was shot and badly wounded by John Hinckley in 1983.

Status: Astrologers insist that 1980 was an aberration because "Jupiter and Saturn met in an air sign, Libra." That gave Reagan some kind of exemption. They say we still have to wait to find out if the curse is over.

THE CURSE OF THE INCAN MUMMY

Curse: By disturbing a frozen mummy's remains, authorities brought bad luck to the region where it had been buried.

Origin: Three Andean mummies were discovered by an archaeologist/mountaineer in October 1995. They had been undisturbed in snow at the top of 20,000-foot Mount Ampato, in Southern Peru, for at least 500 years. Then an earthquake exposed them. One of the mummies was the remains of a young woman, referred to by local shamans as "Juanita." She had apparently been sacrificed to Incan gods.

Among Its Victims:

- Within a year of the discovery, a Peruvian commercial jet crashed and killed 123 people near the discovery site.
- Thirty-five people were electrocuted when a high-tension cable fell on a crowd celebrating the founding of the city of Arequipa (which is near the discovery site).

Status: Local shamans said these were the acts of the angered "Ice Princess." To break the curse, they gathered in the city of Arequipa in August 1996 and chanted: "Juanita, calm your ire. Do not continue to damn innocent people who have done nothing to you." Apparently it worked—we've heard nothing of it since 1996.

THE BIRTH OF THE MICROWAVE

To a lot of us, microwave ovens are "magical mystery boxes." We're not sure how they work . . . but after a while we can't live without them. Uncle John swore he'd never use one—until he had children. Now he blesses it every time he hauls out an emergency frozen pizza and manages to feed the kids before they kill each other. If you use a microwave, you might be interested to know more about it.

Chances are, you'll use a microwave oven at least once this week—probably (according to research) for heating up leftovers or defrosting something.

Microwave ovens are so common today that it's easy to forget how rare they once were. As late as 1977, only 10% of U.S. homes had one. By 1995, 85% of households had at least one. Today, more people own microwaves than own dishwashers.

MICROWAVE HISTORY

Magnetrons, the tubes that produce microwaves, were invented by British scientists in 1940. They were used in radar systems during World War II . . . and were instrumental in detecting German planes during the Battle of Britain.

These tubes—which are sort of like TV picture tubes—might still be strictly military hardware if Percy Spencer, an engineer at Raytheon (a U.S. defense contractor), hadn't stepped in front of one in 1946. He had a chocolate bar in his pocket; when he went to eat it a few minutes later, he found that the chocolate had almost completely melted.

That didn't make sense. Spencer himself wasn't hot—how could the chocolate bar be? He suspected the magnetron was responsible. So he tried an experiment: He held a bag of popcorn kernels up to the tube. Seconds later they popped.

The next day Spencer brought eggs and an old tea kettle to work. He cut a hole in the side of the kettle, stuck an egg in it, and placed it next to the magnetron. Just as a colleague looked into the kettle to see what was happening, the egg exploded.

The world's most popular car color is red.

BRINGING MICROWAVES TO MARKET

Spencer shared his discovery with his employers at Raytheon and suggested manufacturing magnetron-powered ovens to sell to the public. Raytheon was interested. They had the capacity to produce 10,000 magnetron tubes a week . . . but with World War II over, military purchases had been cut back to almost nothing. "What better way to recover lost sales," Ira Flatow writes in *They All Laughed*, "than to put a radar set disguised as a microwave oven in every American home?"

Raytheon agreed to back the project. (According to legend, Spencer had to repeat the egg experiment in front of the board of directors, splattering them with egg, before they okayed it.) The company patented the first "high-frequency dielectric heating apparatus" in 1953. Then they held a contest to find a name for their product. Someone came up with "Radar Range," which was later combined into the single word—*Radarange*.

DEVELOPING THE PRODUCT

Raytheon had a great product idea and a great name, but they didn't have an oven anyone could afford. The 1953 model was 5 1/2 feet tall, weighed more than 750 pounds, and cost $3,000. Over the next 20 years, railroads, ocean liners, and high-end restaurants were virtually the only Radarange customers.

- In 1955 a company called Tappan introduced the first microwave oven targeted to average consumers; it was smaller than the Radarange, but still cost $1,295—more than some small homes.

- Then in 1964, a Japanese company perfected a miniaturized magnetron. For the first time, Raytheon could build a microwave oven that fit on a kitchen countertop. In 1967 they introduced a Radarange that used the new magnetron. It sold for $495. But that was still too expensive for the average American family.

- Finally, in the 1980s, technical improvements made it possible to lower the price and improve the quality enough to make microwave ovens both affordable and practical. By 1988, 10% of all new food products in the United States were microwaveable. Surveys showed that the microwave oven was America's favorite new appliance—and it still is today.

How does a microwave oven work? See page 628 to find out.

It takes about 21 pounds of milk to make 1 pound of butter.

Q&A: ASK THE EXPERTS

*Everyone's got a question or two they'd like answered.
Here are a few of those questions, with answers from
some of the nation's top trivia experts.*

HOLY COW!

Q: *Why are there holes in Swiss cheese?*
A: Because of air bubbles. "During one of the stages of preparation, while it is still 'plastic,' the cheese is kneaded and stirred. Inevitably, air bubbles are formed in the cheese as it is twisted and moved about, but the viscous nature of the cheese prevents the air bubbles from rising to the surface and getting out. As the cheese hardens, these air pockets remain, and we see them as the familiar 'holes' when we slice the wheel of cheese." (From *A Book of Curiosities*, compiled by Roberta Kramer)

PHOTO FINISH

Q: *Why do eyes come out red in photographs?*
A: "The flash from the camera is being reflected on the rear of the eyeball, which is red from all the blood vessels." The solution: "Use a flash at a distance from the camera, or get your subjects to look somewhere else. Another trick is to turn up the lights in the room, making them as bright as possible, which causes the subject's pupil to contract and admit less of the light from the subsequent flash." (From *Why Things Are*, by Joel Aschenbach)

READ OIL ABOUT IT

Q: *What do the numbers (like 10W-30) mean for motor oil?*
A: "Oil is measured in terms of *viscosity*, which is a measure of a liquid's ability to flow. There are 10 grades, from 0W to 25W for oils . . . meant for winter weather use (the W stands for winter), and from 20 to 60 for oils rated to work at 212°F. The lower the number, the thinner the oil. Multigrade oils, like 10W-30, were developed to stay thin at low temperatures and still work well at high temperatures. Most experts recommend 5W-30 for very cold weather, 10W-30 for warmer weather." (From *Numbers*, by Andrea Sutcliffe)

Which language has the most words? English—nearly 1 million.

HOT STUFF

Q: *How can you cool off your mouth after eating hot peppers?*
A: "Drink milk, says Dr. Robert Henkin, director of the Taste and Smell Clinic in Washington, D.C. Casein, the main protein in milk, acts like a detergent, washing away capsaicin, the substance in hot peppers responsible for their 'fire.'" (From *Parade* magazine, November 14, 1993)

SOMETHING FISHY

Q: *Do fish sleep?*
A: Hard to tell if they sleep in the same sense we do. They never look like they're sleeping, because they don't have eyelids. "But they do seem to have regular rest periods . . . Some fish just stay more or less motionless in the water, while others rest directly on the bottom, even turning over on their side. Some species . . . dig or burrow into bottom sediment to make a sort of 'bed.' Some fish even…prefer privacy when they rest; their schools disperse at night to rest and then reassemble in the morning." (From *Science Trivia*, by Charles Cazeau)

PICK A BALL OF COTTON

Q: *Should you toss out the cotton after opening a bottle of pills?*
A: Yep. "The cotton keeps the pills from breaking in transit, but once you open the bottle, it can attract moisture and thus damage the pills or become contaminated." (From *Davies Gazette*, a newsletter from Davies Medical Center in San Francisco)

SLIPPERY QUESTION

Q: *A few years ago, we started seeing foods containing "canola oil." What is it?*
A: A variety of rapeseed—which, until recently, was only grown for industrial oils. "Scientists in Canada were able to breed new varieties of rapeseed that were suitable for cooking. They named their creation *canola* to honor Canada. Canola seed contains 40% to 45% oil, of which 6% is saturated fatty acids. Canola oil contains less fat than any other oil: 50% less than corn oil and olive oil, 60% less than soybean oil." (From *Why Does Popcorn Pop*, by Don Voorhees)

The German language has about 185,000 words. French has less than 100,000.

TOP-RATED TV SHOWS, 1949–1954

These were the most popular programs of TV's early years. Most weren't filmed, so unless you remember them, they're gone forever.

1949–1950

1. Texaco Star Theater
2. Toast of the Town (Ed Sullivan)
3. Arthur Godfrey's Talent Scouts
4. Fireball Fun for All
5. Philco Television Playhouse
6. Fireside Theatre
7. The Goldbergs
8. Suspense
9. Ford Theater
10. Cavalcade of Stars

1950–1951

1. Texaco Star Theater
2. Fireside Theatre
3. Your Show of Shows
4. Philco Television Playhouse
5. The Colgate Comedy Hour
6. Gillette Cavalcade of Sports
7. Arthur Godfrey's Talent Scouts
8. Mama
9. Robert Montgomery Presents
10. Martin Kane, Private Eye

1951–1952

1. Arthur Godfrey's Talent Scouts
2. Texaco Star Theater
3. I Love Lucy
4. The Red Skelton Show
5. The Colgate Comedy Hour
6. Fireside Theatre
7. The Jack Benny Program
8. Your Show of Shows
9. You Bet Your Life
10. Arthur Godfrey and His Friends

1952–1953

1. I Love Lucy
2. Arthur Godfrey's Talent Scouts
3. Arthur Godfrey and His Friends
4. Dragnet
5. Texaco Star Theater
6. The Buick Circus Hour
7. The Colgate Comedy Hour
8. Gangbusters
9. You Bet Your Life
10. Fireside Theatre

1953–1954

1. I Love Lucy
2. Dragnet
3. Arthur Godfrey's Talent Scouts
4. You Bet Your Life
5. The Bob Hope Show
6. The Buick-Berle Show
7. Arthur Godfrey and His Friends
8. Ford Theater
9. The Jackie Gleason Show
10. Fireside Theatre

1954–1955

1. I Love Lucy
2. The Jackie Gleason Show
3. Dragnet
4. You Bet Your Life
5. Toast of the Town (Ed Sullivan)
6. Disneyland
7. The Bob Hope Show
8. The Jack Benny Program
9. The Martha Raye Show
10. The George Gobel Show

Brain food: You can think 625 thoughts on the caloric energy of one Cheerio.

WHAT'S A BLUE MOON?

You've heard the saying "once in a blue moon." And you've probably heard the song "Blue Moon." So what are these guys talking about? The diligent staff of the BRI has been searching the skies for the answer.

THE EXPRESSION

According to the *Dictionary of Word and Phrase Origins*, the term "blue moon" first appeared in England in 1528. The source: A book (or booklet) entitled *Read Me and Be Not Wroth*, which said: "If they say the mone is blew / We must believe that it is true."

The term *once in a blue moon* was apparently derived from this sarcastic little rhyme about the upper class. It originally meant "never." But by the early 1800s it was used to describe "a very rare occurrence." This meaning is actually more correct, because two kinds of blue moons really do exist.

THE FACTS

- The moon does occasionally appear blue. In *The Moon Book*, Kim Long writes:

  This phenomenon [is] associated with unusual atmospheric conditions. A blue-colored moon, or one with a green color, is most likely to be seen just before sunrise or just after sunset if there is a large quantity of dust or smoke in the atmosphere. These particles can filter out colors with longer wavelengths, such as red and yellow, and leave green and blue wavelengths to temporarily discolor the moon.

- The term "blue moon" was once commonly used to describe a full moon that appears twice in one month. "This occurs approximately every 32 months," says Christine Ammer in *Seeing Red or Tickled Pink*. "A full moon comes every 29 1/2 days, when the earth's natural satellite is opposite the sun in the sky. Thus any month except February could see two full moons." However, in 1999 *Sky and Telescope* magazine admitted this was a mistake.

The water we drink is 3 billion years old.

FREEZE-DRIED CATS AND COTTAGE CHEESE

Uncle John was drinking some freeze-dried coffee when he suddenly got up and started asking everyone in the office what "freeze-drying" is. No one could tell him. So we did some research and wrote this article. We figured if we didn't know, you might not either.

FREEZER BURN

If you've ever had a freezer, you've probably seen "freezer burn"—the discolored, dried-out crust that forms on food when it's been in the freezer too long or isn't wrapped correctly.

What causes it?

Evaporation. Even when something is frozen solid, the water molecules are still moving. And some of them move fast enough to fly right off the surface of the food. Then one of three things happens:

1. They get pulled back by the food's gravitational field.

2. They slam into air molecules and bounce back onto the food.

3. They fly off into space.

Over time, so many water molecules will fly off into space that the surface of the food actually becomes dehydrated. That's freezer burn. It's also known as *sublimation*, the process by which ice evaporates without first turning into water.

That's what freeze-drying is—drying something out while it's still frozen.

FREEZER SCIENCE

In the 19th century, scientists studying sublimation discovered that the process happened faster in a jar when the air was pumped out. (The jars are called *vacuum chambers*.) This is because when you remove air, you're removing the air molecules. The fewer air molecules there are to bump into, the greater the chance that the water molecules will escape into space—which speeds the drying.

But the freeze-drying process still took too long. So over the next half-century, scientists tried to find ways to speed it up. They succeeded . . . and then began freeze-drying anything and everything to see what would happen. The first practical applications

A light-year (the distance light travels in a year) is about 6 trillion miles.

they found were in the medical field: many microscopic organisms—including bacteria, viruses, vaccines, yeasts, and algae—could actually survive the process; so could blood plasma.

By World War II, freeze-dried blood plasma and penicillin (which could be reconstituted with sterile water) accompanied soldiers onto the battlefield. And by the end of the war, freeze-dried instant coffee tablets were included in U.S. troops' K rations.

FREEZE-DRIED FOODS

After the war, food companies poured money into making freeze-dried food palatable. It took 10 years, but they finally figured out that when food is "flash frozen" (i.e., frozen as quickly as possible), followed by freeze-drying, much of the flavor is preserved.

The prospects for freeze-dried food seemed limitless: In 1962 *The Reader's Digest* hailed it as "the greatest breakthrough in food preservation since the tin can," and food technologists predicted that sales of freeze-dried food products would rival sales of frozen foods by 1970. Hundreds of food companies rushed new products to the markets. A few, like freeze-dried coffee, were successes. But most wound up in the "fabulous flop" category. For example:

- **Corn flakes with freeze-dried fruit.** As we told you in the first *Bathroom Reader*, in 1964 Post introduced Cornflakes with Strawberries and Kellogg's introduced Cornflakes with Instant Bananas. Both predicted that sales would hit $600 million in a few years. Both were wrong. It turned out that freeze-dried fruit gets soft on the outside when soaked in milk, but stays crunchy on the inside. And by the time the fruit is soft enough to eat, the cereal is soggy. Millions of families bought the cereals once, but never came back for a second helping.

- **Kellogg's Kream Krunch.** Cereal with chunks of freeze-dried ice cream. Different product, same problem: the cereal turned soggy before the ice cream reconstituted.

- **Freeze-dried steak.** "It looks like a brownish sponge," *Business Week* wrote in 1963, "but plop it into hot water and in a few minutes the 'sponge' blossoms into a sirloin steak that tastes almost as good as one from the butcher's." Wishful thinking. It cost as much as a good T-bone, but tasted like a beef sponge.

- **Freeze-dried scrambled eggs.** "Can be prepared by simply cooking with water," *Consumer Reports* wrote in 1962. But that was the only good news. Their tasting panel "came up with a luke warm 'neither like nor dislike' . . . and at current egg prices, two dozen fresh eggs cost the same as two freeze-dried servings."

Other Freeze-Dried Flops

- Freeze-dried mushrooms in a box, from Armour foods
- Freeze-dried cottage cheese ("with cultured sour cream dressing"), from Holland Dairies
- Freeze-dried milkshake mix, from Borden

PET PROJECTS

- The process of freeze-drying is now widely used in taxidermy (stuffing and mounting dead animals). In the late 1950s, scientists at the Smithsonian Institution discovered that by freeze-drying animals instead of skinning and stuffing them, they could produce more lifelike specimens while reducing labor costs by as much as 80%. Today more than a third of all museums in the United States have freeze-dryers, and some companies will even freeze-dry pets.

- The process is the same as with freeze-drying food, with one exception: the animals are bent into lifelike poses, such as "dining on prey," "fetching a stick," or "resting by fire," before they are frozen.

- Since the internal organs remain in place, animals retain virtually the same shape and dimensions when they're freeze-dried. The only difference is their weight—a freeze-dried animal has roughly the same consistency as styrofoam.

- The process is effective, but is impractical with large animals. Animals weighing as little as 65 pounds can take as long as a year to lose all of their moisture, so most large animals are still skinned and stuffed the old-fashioned way.

NEWS FLASH

"Mrs. Oramae Lewis of Bedford, Ohio, had her cat Felix freeze-dried by a local veterinarian after it was run down by an 18-wheel tractor trailer. The veterinarian used a freeze-drying machine once used by a coffee company. 'Now I can have Felix just like I did when he was alive,' she said. 'He's just like he was in real life, only flatter.'"

—*The Washington Post,* June 27, 1983

American travelers' favorite foreign cities: 1) London, 2) Paris, 3) Vancouver.

MARK TWAIN SAYS...

No one else in the history of American literature has combined sardonic wit, warmth, and intelligence as successfully as Mark Twain.

"All you need in this life is ignorance and confidence and then success is sure."

"What a talker he is—he could persuade a fish to come out and take a walk with him."

"The lack of money is the root of all evil."

"Why shouldn't truth be stranger than fiction? Fiction, after all, has to stick to possibilities."

"Be careful about reading health books. You may die of a misprint."

"But who prays for Satan? Who in eighteen centuries, has had the common humanity to pray for the one sinner who needed it most?"

"There are two times in a man's life when he should not speculate: when he can afford to and when he can't."

"Thousands of geniuses live and die undiscovered—either by themselves, or by others."

"We do not deal much in facts when we are contemplating ourselves."

"Envy . . . the only thing which men will sell both body and soul to get."

"If we had less statesmanship, we would get along with fewer battleships."

"If I cannot swear in heaven I shall not go there."

"It takes me a long time to lose my temper but once lost, I could not find it with a dog."

"Virtue has never been as respectable as money."

"I wonder how much it would take to buy a soap-bubble if there was only one in the world."

In 1997 about one-third of American homes had computers.

THE BEST THINGS EVER SAID?

From The 637 Best Things Anybody Ever Said,
edited by Robert Byrne.

"If God lived on Earth, people would break his windows."
—*Jewish proverb*

"I have an intense desire to return to the womb. Anybody's."
—*Woody Allen*

"When you don't have any money, the problem is food. When you have money, it's sex. When you have both, it's health. If everything is simply jake, then you're frightened of death."
—*J. P. Donleavy*

"Is sloppiness in speech caused by ignorance or apathy? I don't know and I don't care."
—*William Safire*

"When you have got an elephant by the hind legs and he is trying to run away, it is best to let him run."
—*Abraham Lincoln*

"In the end, everything is a gag."
—*Charlie Chaplin*

"One of the symptoms of an approaching nervous breakdown is the belief that one's work is terribly important."
—*Betrand Russell*

"When ideas fail, words come in very handy."
—*Goethe*

"Victory goes to the player who makes the next to last mistake."
—*Savielly Grigorievitch*

"After all is said and done, more is said than done."
—*Unknown*

"Three o'clock is always too late or too early for anything you want to do."
—*Jean-Paul Sartre*

"A little inaccuracy sometimes saves tons of explanation."
—*H. H. Munro*

"The best way to get praise is to die."
—*Italian prove*

In the 1600s in Europe, "fashion" wigs were often made of plaster of I

STRANGE LAWSUITS

These days, it seems that people will sue each other over practically anything. Here are a few real-life examples of unusual legal battles.

THE PLAINTIFF: Wendy Potasnik, a nine-year-old from Carmel, Indiana
THE DEFENDANT: The Cracker Jack Division of Borden, Inc.
THE LAWSUIT: In 1982 Wendy and her sister Robin each bought a box of Cracker Jack. Robin got a prize in her box, but Wendy didn't . . . which made her "really mad."

"They advertise a free toy in each box," she told a reporter. "I feel that since I bought their product because of their claim, they broke a contract with me." So she sued, asking the court to make Borden "pay court costs and furnish a toy."
THE VERDICT: Wendy dropped the suit after Borden apologized and sent her a coupon for a free box of Cracker Jack . . . even though the company refused to pay the $19 that Potasnik had spent on court costs.

THE PLAINTIFF: Alan Wald
THE DEFENDANT: The Moonraker Restaurant in Pacifica, California
THE LAWSUIT: In 1993 Wald went to the Moonraker for an all-you-can-eat buffet. He'd already eaten between 40 (Wald's count) and 75 (the restaurant's count) oysters—and was still at it—when the restaurant cut him off. Apparently, other customers were complaining that there were no oysters left. The restaurant offered to refund Wald's $40 to get him to go, but Wald insisted he was within his rights—he hadn't had all he could eat yet. He demanded $400 for "humiliation and embarrassment."
THE VERDICT: Wald was awarded $100 by the judge—but the restaurant was the real winner. "It was great publicity," said the owner. "We're going to get a shovelful of oysters and present them to [Wald] at his table. He can come back anytime."

Poll results: Baby boomers now say that "old age" begins at 79.

THE PLAINTIFF: The Swedish government
THE DEFENDANT: Elisabeth Hallin, mother of a five-year-old boy named Brfxxccxxmnpcccclllmmnprxvclmnckssqlbb11116 (which she pronounces "Albin")
THE LAWSUIT: For five years the Hallins, who say they believe in the surrealist doctrine of "pataphysics," refused to give their son a name. Then Swedish tax officials informed them it was a legal requirement. They chose Brfxxccxxmnpcccclllmmnprxvclmnckssqlbb11116—which was immediately rejected by the authorities. The couple insisted that the "typographically expressionistic" name was merely "an artistic creation," consistent with their pataphysical beliefs.
THE VERDICT: The government disagreed. The Hallins were fined 5000 kronor (about $735) and ordered to come up with a different name.

THE PLAINTIFF: Lorene Bynum
THE DEFENDANTS: St. Mary's Hospital in Little Rock, Arkansas
THE LAWSUIT: In 1992 Bynum visited her husband, a patient at the hospital. She wanted to use the bathroom, but the toilet seat was dirty—and there wasn't enough toilet paper to spread out on it. So she took off her shoes and tried to go to the bathroom standing on the toilet seat. Unfortunately the seat was loose. Bynum fell, spraining her lower back. She sued the hospital for negligence.
THE VERDICT: A jury awarded Bynum $13,000. But the Arkansas Supreme Court overturned the verdict. "The injuries resulted from her act of standing on the commode seat, which was neither designed nor intended to be used in that way," they explained.

THE PLAINTIFF: Victoria Baldwin
THE DEFENDANT: Synergy, a hair salon in Sydney, Australia
THE LAWSUIT: In July 1996 Baldwin had her hair cut at the salon. The result was so bad, she complained, that it made her "look like Hillary Clinton." She sued for damages, plus reimbursement for money spent on hats to cover her head until the hair grew back.
THE VERDICT: Baldwin won $750, plus $234 for the hats.

It's estimated that 75% of all U.S. dollars contain traces of cocaine.

THE FOOLISH HUNTER

Here's a chance to soak up a little wisdom while you're just sitting around. This is an old Hebrew tale, from a longtime favorite book of Uncle John's called Myths and Legends of the Ages.

A hunter once caught a bird in a trap. "Let me go," the bird pleaded. "It won't do you any good to kill me—I'm not very big. If you roast me, all you'll get is a mouthful or two at the most. And if you lock me in a cage, I can promise you right now that I'll never sing a note for you. But if you let me go, I'll give you three pieces of wisdom which will bring you great happiness and success."

The hunter pondered over the bird's speech. "All right," he said. "Tell me your three pieces of wisdom, and I'll let you go."

"First," said the bird, "never believe a story that goes against your common sense. Secondly, don't regret what is done and cannot be undone." Then, cocking his head to one side, the bird concluded, "And the third piece of wisdom is, don't try the impossible."

"There's nothing so wise about that," scoffed the hunter. "I practice those teachings all the time. But since you're not much use to me anyway, I'll let you go."

No sooner was the bird released, than he flew to a high branch of a nearby tree. "Foolish man!" he said. "Did you think I was just an ordinary bird? Oh no! Now I can tell you that I am much different from other birds. My heart is made of a precious ruby. If you had cut me open and taken out my heart, you might have been the richest man in the world."

When the man heard this, he cursed his folly in letting the bird go. He shook his fist at the bird in the tree. I'll catch you, you rogue!" he cried in a rage of disappointment.

The hunter quickly started to climb the tree. But the bird flew to the tip of a high branch, well out of the man's reach. The hunter leaned far out, trying to lay his hands on the bird. But he lost his balance, fell out of the tree, and was badly hurt.

"So!" cried the bird. "You said there was nothing wise

In June 1989 two original carbon scripts of *Citizen Kane* sold for $231,000.

about my words—that what I told you is only what you always practice! But the first thing I told you was never to believe anything that was contrary to common sense. Did anyone ever hear of a bird whose heart was made of a ruby? No. Yet you instantly believed my story.

"The next thing I said was don't regret what has been done and cannot be undone. You let me go—but then you instantly regretted it!

"The last piece of wisdom was, don't waste your energies pursuing the impossible. How could you ever hope to catch me, a bird who can fly—just by climbing a tree? Yet, you persisted in your folly and tried to snare a winged bird with your bare hands."

The shaken hunter got to his feet . . . a bruised but wiser man.

* * *

AND SPEAKING OF FOOLISHNESS . . .

The Etruscan Warrior

Background: In 1918 New York's Metropolitan Museum of Art paid $40,000 for the fragments of a 2,500-year-old, 7-foot-tall statue of an Etruscan warrior that predated the Roman Empire. (The Etruscans were conquered by the Romans in 396 B.C.) The museum reassembled the fragments into a nearly intact statue—only the left thumb was missing. The museum made the statue a centerpiece of its Etruscan warrior display, which opened in 1933. **The Truth:** In 1936 rumors began circulating that an Italian stonemason had made the statue at the turn of the century . . . but the exhibit was so popular that the museum refused to investigate. Finally, in 1960, the museum had the statue's glaze tested chemically and proved conclusively that it was a fake.

A few months later, Alfredo Fioravanti (an Italian stonemason, of course) confessed to making the statue . . . and produced the warrior's missing left thumb as proof.

The fingerprints of humans and koalas are virtually identical.

WHAT'S FOR BREAKFAST?

We take it for granted that bacon, eggs, orange juice, and coffee are breakfast foods. But it's really just a matter of tradition.

COFFEE AND TEA. People started drinking coffee and tea in the morning not because they were pleasant, but because they were hot, dark, and mysterious. Until the 17th century, it was common for Europeans to start their day with alcohol. Queen Elizabeth, for example, had a pot of beer and a pound of beefsteak for breakfast every day. Scottish breakfasts routinely included a dram of whiskey. Coffee, tea, and sugar had the same illicit appeal as alcohol when they reached Europe in the 1600s—so they became suitable substitutes for booze.

EGGS & BACON, SAUSAGE, OR HAM. Colonists brought chickens and pigs with them to America because they were easy to transport by ship, and could provide food on the long voyage. Besides that, it was traditional to eat meat in the morning—and pork was the colonists' first choice. (It was so popular that one writer suggested they rename the U.S. "the Republic of Porkdom.") Eggs probably became a staple at breakfast because "they're freshest when just gathered from the previous night's roosting."

CITRUS FRUIT / ORANGE JUICE. Believe it or not, people started eating oranges in the morning because they thought it would warm them. The ancient Greeks taught that some foods heat your body, and other foods cool it—regardless of the temperature at which they're served. Peas were cold, for example, onions were hot...and oranges were very hot. People still believed this in the Middle Ages, which is why the Spanish began eating candied orange peels the first thing in the morning. The habit was picked up by the British, who brought it to the Colonies. (In Scotland, the orange peel became orange marmalade, which they put on toast with butter—starting another breakfast tradition.)

Orange juice became a staple of the American breakfast table in the 1920s. In 1946 concentrated orange juice was introduced.

In her films, Shirley Temple always had 56 curls in her hair.

THE BIG DIPPER

What's the one constellation everyone knows? The Big Dipper. After you read this article you'll be able to sound like a know-it-all the next time you're stargazing with someone.

THE NIGHT SKY

The Big and Little Dippers are probably the best-known star groups in the northern hemisphere. They're both parts of larger star groups, or constellations, named after bears. The Big Dipper belongs to the constellation Ursa Major, "The Greater Bear," and the Little Dipper is part of Ursa Minor, "The Lesser Bear."

- Ursa Major is the most ancient of all the constellations. For some reason, early civilizations all over the world seem to have thought of it as a bear. This is remarkable, since Ursa Major doesn't look anything like a bear. It's even more remarkable when you consider that most of the ancient world had never seen a bear.

THE NATIVE AMERICAN SKY

In the New World, the Iroquois, who had seen plenty of bears, called it Okouari, which means . . . bear. The Algonquin and Blackfoot tribes called it "The Bear and the Hunters." For them, the three stars in the handle of the Big Dipper were three hunters going after the bear.

- In a typical Native American story, a party of hunters set out on a bear hunt. The first hunter carried a bow and arrow. The second hunter brought along a pot or kettle to cook the bear in. The faint star Alcor, which you can just see above the middle star of the Dipper's handle, was the pot. The third hunter carried a bundle of sticks with which to build a fire to cook the bear.

- The bear hunt lasted from spring until autumn. In the autumn, the first hunter shot the bear. Blood from the wounded animal stained the autumn leaves in the forest. The bear died, was cooked, and was eaten. The skeleton lay on its back in the den through the winter months. The bear's life, meanwhile, had entered into another bear, which also lay on its back, deep asleep for the winter.

The average meteor is no larger than a grain of sand.

- When spring returned, the bear came out of the den and the hunters started to chase her again, and so it went from year to year.

THE GREEK SKY

Greek mythology offers another version of how the Bears got into the sky. Calisto, the beautiful daughter of the King of Arcadia, caught the eye of Zeus, the king of the gods. Zeus took her by surprise, leaving her to become the mother of his child. In time, Calisto gave birth to a son, whom she named Arcas. Hera, queen of the gods, changed Calisto into a bear in a jealous rage.

After a number of years had passed, Arcas was out hunting when he saw a bear. Not knowing the bear was his mother, Arcas raised his spear, ready to kill the animal. Before Arcas could throw his spear, Zeus quickly rescued Calisto by placing her in the skies— where she remains today. Arcas also became a constellation, Ursa Minor, next to his mother.

- Some say Zeus swung both bears around by their tails and flung them into the sky, which explains why their tails are so long.
- The Greeks called Ursa Major Arktos, which means "Bear." This is where we get our word *Arctic*. The Greek poet, Homer, described the Bear as keeping watch from its Arctic den looking out for the hunter Orion. Homer also remarked that in his day, the Bear never sank into the ocean, which meant that it never set. Hera was responsible for this, having persuaded the ocean gods not to allow the two Bears to bathe in their waters.

HIPPOS AND PLOWS

But not everyone has thought of these constellations as bears. The Egyptians saw the seven stars of the Big Dipper as a bull's thigh or a hippopotamus. Because its stars circled around the north pole of the sky without setting, or "dying," below the horizon, this constellation was a symbol of immortality and figured in rebirth rituals at funerals. Ursa Minor was the Jackal of the god Set that participated in rites for the dead taking place in the Egyptian underworld.

In Mesopotamia, Scandinavia, Italy, and Germany, people referred to the Big Dipper as a wagon, chariot, or cart. In England it was "Charles' Wain" (the word wain meant "wagon" and

---

The average American buys 17 yards of dental floss each year.

Charles stood for Charles the Great). The Little Dipper was the "Smaller Chariot," or "Little Wain." The four stars that make up the bowl of the dipper are the carriage part of the wain, and the dipper's handle is the part of the wain attached to the horses that pull it.

In some parts of England (and elsewhere), people saw the Big Dipper as "The Plough." The four stars of the dipper's bowl form the blade of the plough, behind which stretches its three-starred handle.

DIPPER DIRECTIONS

At the tip of the handle of the Little Dipper is the most celebrated star in the sky, Polaris, the North Star. While not the brightest star in the heavens, Polaris is certainly the most valuable. It has provided directions to countless travelers. The two stars at the end of the bowl of the Big Dipper, called "The Pointers," point to the North Star.

The Greeks used the Greater Bear and the Phoenicians used the Lesser Bear to find north. American slaves called the Big Dipper "The Drinking Gourd" and followed it northward to freedom.

Seen from the spinning Earth, the sky appears to move during the night, carrying all the stars along with it. Only the North Star stands in the same spot at the hub of the dome of the sky. The Greeks called this star *Cynosure*, a word that has found its way into our language meaning the center of attraction or interest. Others called the North Star the "Lodestar," most likely referring to the magnetic rock lodestone, used in mariners' compass needles to find north.

* * *

"It is easier to accept the message of the stars than the message of the salt desert. The stars speak of man's insignificance in the long eternity of time. The desert speaks of his insignificance right now."

—*Edwin Way Teale*

In 1995, 8,000 kids were poisoned by eating cigarette butts.

GROUCHO MARX, ATTORNEY AT LAW

Here's a script from a recently rediscovered radio show featuring Groucho and Chico Marx. It's from Five Star Theater, *which aired in 1933.*

(*Phone rings*)
MISS DIMPLE: Law offices of Beagle, Shyster, and Beagle . . . No, Mr. Beagle isn't in yet, he's in court . . . I expect him any minute.

(*Door opens*)
MISS DIMPLE: Good morning, Mr. Beagle.

GROUCHO: Good morning. Have I any appointments today?

MISS DIMPLE: No, Mr. Beagle.

GROUCHO: Well, make some. Do you expect me to sit here alone all day? Don't you think I ever get lonesome? What do you take me for? (Pause.) Well, go on—make me an offer.

(*Phone rings*)
MISS DIMPLE: Beagle, Shyster, and Beagle . . . Just a second. Mr. Flywheel, a man says he found the book you lost.

GROUCHO: (*Takes phone*) Hello . . . Yes, this is Flywheel . . . You found my book? . . . Oh, don't bother bringing it over—you can read it to me over the phone. Start at page 150. That's where I left off . . . Hello! Hello! (*Sneers*) He hung up on me. After I go to the trouble of putting aside legal business to talk to him!

MISS DIMPLE: Legal business? Why Mr. Flywheel, you were doing a crossword puzzle.

GROUCHO: Well, is doing a crossword puzzle illegal? Now how about mailing this letter?

MISS DIMPLE: But it has no stamp on it.

GROUCHO: Well, drop it in the box when nobody's looking.

MISS DIMPLE: Anyway, this letter is too heavy for one stamp. I think we'd better put two stamps on it.

GROUCHO: Nonsense. That'll only make it heavier. On second thought, never mind the letter. It's just a note to my friend, Steve Granach, asking for a loan . . . but he's probably got his own troubles. I hardly think he can spare it. And even if he had it, I think he'd be a little reluctant to lend me the dough. He's kind of tight that way. Why, I don't think he'd let me have it if I was going hungry. In fact, that guy wouldn't give me a nickel if I were starving. And he calls himself a *friend* . . . the cheap, four-flushing swine. I'll show *him*

The most costumes ever used for one film was 32,000—for *Quo Vadis* in 1951.

where to get off. Take a letter to that snake and tell him I wouldn't touch his money. And if he ever comes near this office again, I'll break every bone in his body.

(Knock on door)

MAN: Excuse me. Are you Mr. Flywheel or Mr. Shyster?

GROUCHO: I'm both Flywheels. And Shyster doesn't belong to the firm.

MAN: Then why is his name up there on the door?

GROUCHO: Well, Shyster ran away with my wife. And I put his name on the door as a token of my gratitude.

MAN: Oh. Well, Mr. Flywheel, permit me to introduce myself. I'm Bertram T. Bardwell. I suppose you've been hearing about my charity work and my fight against crime?

GROUCHO: Oh yes, I've been hearing about it for a number of years, and I'm getting pretty sick of it, too.

MAN: Why . . . er . . . I happened to be in court this morning when your thrilling address to the jury sent that man to prison for five years, where he belongs.

GROUCHO: My speech sent him to prison? *(Laughs)* That's a good one on the jury. I was defending that guy. As I was . . .

MAN: Just a moment, Mr.

Flywheel. Let me ask you a question.

GROUCHO: No, I'll ask you one. What has eight legs and sings?

MAN: Why . . . er . . . I don't know.

GROUCHO: A centipede.

MAN: But a centipede has a hundred legs.

GROUCHO: Yes, but it can't sing.

MAN *(Annoyed)*: Mr. Flywheel, my organization is waging an intensive fight against crime in this city, and I feel you're a man who can help us drive the crooks out of town.

GROUCHO: Drive them? Why not let them walk? *(Dramatically)* Bardwell, you've come to the right man. There isn't room enough in this town for gangsters and me . . . However, we're putting up a big hotel this spring. Now if you'll excuse me, I have a director's meeting at the poolroom across the street.

MAN: Mr. Flywheel! How can you go out to a poolroom?

GROUCHO: I have to go out. I can't play pool in here—there's no table! Miss Dimple, I'll be back in an hour." *(Door closes)*

Groucho will be back on page 689, after a few words from our sponsor.

Shirley Temple won an honorary Oscar in 1934, when she was only 5 years old.

UDDERLY SIMPLE

We all know these terms, but if someone were to ask you what they actually mean, would you be able to tell them? Here's the difference between the different kinds of milk sold in most supermarkets.

Whole Milk. Milk as it comes from the cow. The USDA requires it to contain at least 3.25% fat and 8.25% other solids. It's also about 88% water.

Low-Fat Milk. Milk with some fat (cream) removed. Depending on how it's labeled, it can contain 0.5% to 2.5% fat *by weight*. By percentage of calories, it's more. E.g., "1% milk" gets 24% of its calories from fat; "2% milk" gets 36% from fat. Vitamins A and D are found in the cream; when the cream is removed, the USDA requires dairies to "fortify" milk by putting the vitamins back in.

Evaporated Milk. Milk that has had 60% of its water removed. Sometimes it has a caramelized flavor, a result of the heating process used to remove the liquid.

Condensed Milk. Whole milk, mixed with as much as 40% to 45% sugar, then evaporated over heat.

Cream. When it's taken from skim or low-fat milk, cream is made into four different products: *regular cream* (18% milk fat by weight—not calories); *light whipping cream* (30%–36% milk fat); *heavy whipping cream* (36% or more milk fat); and *half-and-half* (half milk, half cream—10%–12% milk fat).

Buttermilk. When cream is agitated, or "churned," the globules of fat separate out from the cream and clump together, forming butter. The globules are removed from the liquid, which is called "buttermilk."

Acidophilus Milk. When milk is pasteurized to kill bad bacteria, a lot of beneficial bacteria is killed along with it. In acidophilus milk, the lactobacillus acidophilus bacteria, which aids digestion by regulating bacteria in the digestive system, is put back in after pasteurization.

Soy Milk. Made from whole soybeans, which are pureed, boiled, filtered, and sometimes sweetened.

It's estimated you'll eat some 35,000 cookies in your lifetime.

WRIGHT ON

Existential wisdom from Steven Wright.

"We had a quicksand box in our backyard. I was an only child, eventually."

"My theory of evolution is that Darwin was adopted."

"I was walking down the street wearing glasses when my prescription ran out."

"I put instant coffee in my microwave oven and almost went back in time."

"My grandfather invented *Cliff's Notes*. It all started back in 1912 . . . Well, to make a long story short . . . "

"I'm writing an unauthorized autobiography."

"I wrote a few children's books. Not on purpose."

"Curiosity killed the cat, but for awhile, I was the suspect."

"If all the nations in the world are in debt, where did the money go?"

"If the pen is mightier than the sword, in a duel I'll let you have the pen."

"I own the erasers for all the miniature golf pencils."

"Anywhere is walking distance if you've got the time."

"Ever notice that irons have a setting for 'Permanent Press'? I don't get it . . ."

"You can't have everything. Where would you put it?"

"I went fishing with a dotted line and caught every other fish."

"I stayed up all night playing poker with Tarot cards. I got a full house and four people died."

"First time I read the dictionary I thought it was a poem about everything."

The first cereal to come in boxes? Shredded Wheat.

FOR YOUR READING PLEASURE

Recently, we stumbled on Bizarre Books, a collection of weird-but-true book titles, compiled by Russell Ash and Brian Lake. Hard to believe, but these titles were chosen and published in all seriousness. How would you like to spend your time reading . . .

How to Avoid Intercourse with Your Unfriendly Car Mechanic, by Harold Landy (1977)

Sex After Death, by B. J. Ferrell and Douglas Edward Frey (1983)

The Unconscious Significance of Hair, by George Berg (1951)

Wall-Paintings by Snake Charmers in Tanganyika, by Hans Cory (1953)

The Inheritance of Hairy Ear Rims, by Reginald Ruggles and P. N. Badhuri (no date given)

A Toddler's Guide to the Rubber Industry, by D. Lowe (1947)

The Baron Kinvervankotsdorsprakingatcdern. A New Musical Comedy, by Miles Pewter Andrew (1781)

Manhole Covers of Los Angeles, by Robert and Mimi Melnick (1974)

The Gentle Art of Cooking Wives, Anon. (1900)

The History and Romance of Elastic Webbing Since the Dawn of Time, by Clifford A. Richmond (no date given)

Frog Raising for Pleasure and Profit, by Dr. Albert Broel (1950)

Eat Your House: Art Eco Guide to Self-Sufficiency, by Frederic Hobbs (1981)

The Urine Dance of the Zuni Indians of New Mexico, by Captain John G. Bourke (1885)

Constipation and Our Civilization, by James Charles Thomson (1943)

Harnessing the Earthworm, by Thomas J. Barrett (1949)

Swine Judging for Beginners, Joel Simmonds Coffey (1915)

Fish Who Answer the Telephone, by Yuri Petrovich Frolov (1937)

Wampum was once legally used as money in the United States.

THEY WENT THATAWAY

Malcolm Forbes wrote a fascinating book about the deaths of famous people. Here are a few of the stories he found.

BENJAMIN FRANKLIN
Claim to Fame: American statesman
How He Died: Complications from sitting in front of an open window
Postmortem: Franklin was a big believer in fresh air, even in the middle of winter. He slept with the windows open year-round and, as he wrote, "I rise almost every morning and sit in my chamber without any clothes whatever, half an hour or an hour, according to the season." In April 1790 Franklin, 84, developed an abscess in his lungs, which his doctor blamed on too many hours spent sitting at the open window. The abscess burst on the 17th, sending him into a coma. He died a few hours later.

JOSEPH STALIN
Claim to Fame: Soviet dictator, 1929–1953
How He Died: Stroke
Postmortem: Stalin, who had murdered tens of millions of his own country people, may have been the last victim of his own reign of terror. On the evening of March 1, 1953, Stalin, 74, stayed up drinking with his cronies until 4:00 a.m. His normal habit was to rise again around noon, but that day he didn't.

As the hours passed and Stalin did not emerge from his private quarters, his aides began to panic. They didn't want to risk his wrath, but they were worried. At 10:30 p.m., they finally worked up the nerve to enter his apartments, where they found him sprawled on his living room floor, paralyzed by a stroke and unable to speak. The terrorized aides still did not know what to do . . . so they didn't call for the Kremlin doctors until 8:30 a.m. the following morning. By then it was too late: according to Stalin's daughter Svetlana, the dictator "died a difficult and terrible death" four days later.

The only rock that floats in water? Our experts say pumice.

KING GEORGE V

Claim to Fame: King of England, grandfather of Queen Elizabeth
How He Died: Euthanized with morphine and cocaine . . . to meet a newspaper deadline
Postmortem: The king, a heavy smoker, was in the final stages of lung disease on January 20, 1936. His death was imminent: the date of the State Funeral had been set, and the *London Times* had been instructed to hold the presses—a death announcement would be coming soon. "That night, however, the old king lingered on," Sarah Bradford writes in *The Reluctant King*, and the king's doctor, Lord Dawson,

> seeing that his condition of "stupor and coma" might last for many hours and could easily disrupt all arrangements, therefore "decided to determine the end" . . . Dawson later admitted that the moment of the King's death was timed for its announcement to be made in the respectable morning papers, and the *Times* in particular, rather than "the less appropriate evening journals."

The king's "last words" as reported to the media: "How is the Empire?" His actual last words: "Goddamn you!"

DIAMOND JIM BRADY

Claim to Fame: Turn-of-the-century millionaire, collector of fine gems (hence the nickname), one of the world's all-time great eaters
How He Died: He ate himself to death. A typical day started with a breakfast of steak, eggs, cornbread, muffins, pancakes, pork chops, fried potatoes, and hominy, washed down with a gallon or more of orange juice. Breakfast was followed with snacks at 11:30, lunch at 12:30, and afternoon tea; all of which involved enormous quantities of food (but no alcohol—Diamond Jim didn't drink). Dinner often consisted of 2 or 3 dozen oysters, 6 crabs, 2 bowls of turtle soup, 7 lobsters, 2 ducks, 2 servings of turtle meat, plus steak, vegetables, a full platter of pastries, and a 2-pound box of chocolate.
Postmortem: When Brady suffered an attack of gallstones in 1912, his surgeons opened him up and found that his stomach was six times normal size and covered in so many layers of fat they couldn't complete the surgery. Diamond Jim ignored their advice to cut back, yet hung on another five years—albeit in considerable pain from diabetes, bad kidneys, stomach ulcers, and heart problems. He died of a heart attack in 1917, at the age of 61.

Who's won the most Oscars? Walt Disney: 20 statuettes, 12 plaques and certificates.

DEMOCRACY IN ACTION

*A democracy is only as weird as the people who participate
in it—and you know what that means: anything
can happen in an election. Here's proof.*

ABSENTEE BALLOT

WESTMORELAND, KS—"What if they held an election and nobody came? It happened in Pottawatomie County. Nobody, not even the candidate, showed up to vote in the Rock Creek School Board election Tuesday. 'I don't understand it,' County Clerk Susan Figge said Wednesday. 'I really don't.' Three hundred twenty-seven people were eligible to vote, but none showed up—not even the candidate, Mike Sotelo, who was running unopposed." The school board wound up appointing a new member themselves.

—Associated Press, April 1997

ELECTING A CORPSE

"A dead man was elected mayor of a small town in Colorado in 1983. The voters of Ward, population 125, elected as the mayor of this old mining town, a resident who died a week before the election. Some of the voters were undoubtedly paying tribute to the man and the community, for as one resident quipped, 'Ward's a ghost town, and we decided to elect a dead man to represent the silent majority.' But not everyone shared this sentiment; another voter was heard to say, 'When he won, I just about died.'"

—The Daily Planet Almanac, 1985

ELECTION FRAUD?

YPSILANTI, MI—"When City Councilman Geoffrey Rose turned over a voter list to a college freshman to help get out the vote, it didn't occur to him to ask the kid whom he was getting out the vote for. It turns out, the 18-year-old Eastern Michigan University student was looking out for No. 1." Instead of encouraging voters to cast their ballots for Rose, Frank Houston went door to door urging people to write in *his* name. And he won.

The most widely used surname in the world is Li. About 87 million people have it.

"Rose, who thought he was running unopposed in Monday's primary, said: 'Frank is 18 years old, and he's already acting like what most people in the country can't stand in elected officials.' Houston, who's thinking about majoring in political science, said he didn't lie to Rose. 'All I ever said was that I was going to get people to vote,' he told reporters."

—*Christian Science Monitor*, April 1994

TIE VOTE

NOV. 14, 1994—"In Rice, Minnesota, Virgil Nelson and Mitch Fiedler, who tied 90 to 90 in the November 1994 election for a city council seat, settled the race by drawing cards. On the first try, both drew eights, and on the second, both drew aces. Then Nelson drew a seven, and Fiedler drew an eight for the victory."

—*News of the Weird*

AND ELSEWHERE . . .

- COPENHAGEN, DENMARK—"Danish comedian Jacob Haugaard, promising better weather, shorter lines, and the right of men to be impotent, got the shock of his life by being elected to parliament in a general election. A stunned Haugaard, the first independent member of parliament elected in Denmark, told crowds of reporters: 'It was all a practical joke, honestly.' He won with 23,211 votes after spending his official campaign money on free hot dogs and beer for voters and providing kettles for old age pensioners."

  —*Reuters*, September 1996

- "In Britain's April elections, the usual fringe parties were in evidence—such as the Blackhaired, Medium-Build Caucasian Party—but the longest-standing alternative, the Monster Raving Loony Party, ran the most candidates. Its main platform this year was to tow Britain 500 miles into the Mediterranean Sea to improve the country's climate. (Other years, platforms have included setting accountants in concrete and using them as traffic barriers, and putting all joggers on a giant treadmill to generate electricity.)

  "Fifty other MRLP candidates made proposals such as requiring dogs to eat phosphorescent food, so pedestrians could more easily avoid stepping in their poops."

  —*"The Edge"* in *The Oregonian*, May 1997

Most-performed rock song in history: "You've Lost That Lovin' Feeling."

A YEN FOR EGG ROLLS

Do the recipes they serve at your local Chinese restaurant really come from China? Don't bet on it. Here are a few food facts to munch on.

Today, Chinese Americans make up less than 1% of the U.S. population, but roughly a third of all ethnic restaurants in the U.S. are "Chinese," and every supermarket carries a line of "Chinese" food.

NEW-FANGLED FOOD
It started with the Gold Rush of 1849. As thousands of "Forty-Niners" streamed into California in search of gold, whole boom-towns—including a tent city named San Francisco—sprang up to supply their needs.

- One merchant who set up shop in San Francisco was a Chinese American named Norman Asing (described by one historian as a "cadaverous but keen old fellow" with a long ponytail and stovepipe hat). He opened a restaurant called, "The Macao and Woosung" and charged $1 for an all-you-can-eat Chinese buffet.

- It was the first Chinese restaurant on U.S. territory, and it was a hit with miners and other San Franciscans. Asing's success inspired dozens of other Chinese immigrants to open restaurants, called "chow chows."

MADE IN CANTON
Over the next three decades, hundreds of thousands of Chinese migrated to the United States. By 1882—when Congress curtailed Chinese immigration—there were more than 300,000 Chinese nationals living on the West Coast.

- Most came from Kwangtung Province, whose capital city was Canton. So most Chinese restaurants served Cantonese-style food.

- In Cantonese cuisine, very little goes to waste: nearly every part of an animal that can be eaten is used in one dish or another.

- So, says John Mariani in *America Eats Out*, "'Going for Chinese' was considered adventurous eating for most white Americans at the turn of the century." Typically, one food critic who ate in San Francisco's Chinatown in the late 1800s wrote

---

As a boy, young Ian Fleming also gave his mother the nickname "M."

that he was served "Pale cakes with a waxen look, full of [strange] meats . . . Then giblets of you-never-know-what, maybe gizzards . . . perhaps toes." "Before long, however," Mariani writes, "Chinese cooks learned how to modify their dishes to make them more palatable to a wider American audience." The result: Chinese-American cuisine, food that looked and tasted "Chinese," but was actually invented in the U.S. and was unknown in China. Some examples:

- **Chop Suey.** No one knows for sure when it was invented, or how it got its name. The likely start: In 1850 a bunch of hungry miners busted their way into a chow-chow late at night and demanded to be fed. The chef just stirred all the table scraps and leftovers he could find into a big mess and served it. The miners loved it. When they asked what it was, the chef replied, "chop sui," which means "garbage bits" in Cantonese. The dish remained virtually unheard of in China until after World War II; today, it's advertised there as American cuisine.

- **Chow Mein.** A mixture of noodles and Chinese vegetables, probably served to railroad crews in the 1850s. From a Mandarin dialect word that means "fried noodles."

- **Egg Foo Yung.** From a Guangdong word that means "egg white." Translated literally, Egg Foo Yung means "egg egg white."

- **Fortune Cookies.** Invented in 1916 by David Jung, founder of the Hong Kong noodle factory in Los Angeles.

"By the 1920s," says Mariani, "Chinese restaurants dotted the American landscape, and a person

was as likely to find a chop suey parlor in Kansas City as New York, even though the typical menu in such places bore small resemblance to the food the Chinese themselves ate . . . Won ton soup, egg rolls, barbecued spareribs, sweet-and-sour pork, and beef with lobster sauce were all concocted to whet Americans' appetites . . . To this day it is standard procedure for an American in a Chinese restaurant to be handed a 2-column menu written in English, while a completely different menu printed in Chinese will be given to a Chinese patron."

Note: Until the 1970s, Chinese-American cuisine was almost exclusively Cantonese. If you're a fan of Szechuan or Hunan cooking, thank Richard Nixon. He opened the People's Republic of China to the West in the '70s . . . which brought us new Chinese cuisines.

In Italy, James Bond is known as "Mr. Kiss-Kiss-Bang-Bang."

GO ASK ALICE

When Charles Lutwidge Dodgson met a four-year-old girl named Alice Liddell in 1856, he wrote in his diary, "I mark this day with a white stone"—which meant it was a particularly wonderful day for him. It turned out to be a pretty good day for children all over the world: Charles Dodgson became famous as Lewis Carroll . . . and Alice Liddell was the child who inspired him to write Alice in Wonderland.

BACKGROUND

Charles Lutwidge Dodgson was a deacon and professor of mathematics at Christ Church College in Oxford. He was also a poet and photographer who drew his inspiration from children—especially little girls. In fact, he chose teaching as a career because it left him time to pursue photography and poetry.

- In 1856, the same year Dodgson began teaching at Christ Church, a new dean arrived—Henry George Liddell. He had four children, and Dodgson quickly became friendly with them. He especially enjoyed taking them on outings and photographing the girls. The youngest, 4-year-old Alice, had a special relationship with Reverend Dodgson—perhaps because her favorite expression was "let's pretend."

DOWN THE RABBIT HOLE

On what he recalled as a "golden July afternoon" in 1862, Dodgson took the three Liddell girls boating on the river for a picnic.

- As they rowed lazily downstream, Alice begged Dodgson to tell them a story . . . so he made one up.

- He called his heroine Alice to please her. Then he "sent her straight down a rabbit-hole to begin," he later explained, "without the least idea what was to happen afterwards."

- Amazingly, he made up most of *Alice in Wonderland* on the spot.

SAVING A TREASURE

Alice liked the story so much that she asked Dodgson to write it down. He agreed. In fact, that night—as a gift for his favorite little girl—he sat up and wrote the whole thing out in longhand, adding his own illustrations. He called it *Alice's Adventures Underground*.

Most types of lipstick contain fish scales as an ingredient.

- Dodgson had already decided he needed a pseudonym for the humorous poems and stories he'd been contributing to magazines. (He also wrote academic articles on mathematics, and was afraid people wouldn't take him seriously if they knew he was writing nonsense rhymes.)

- He came up with the name Lewis Carroll by scrambling letters in his first two names, and used it for the first time when he signed *Alice's Adventures Underground* for Alice.

A BOOK IS BORN

Fortunately for us, before Dodgson brought the handwritten manuscript to Alice, he happened to show it to a friend named George MacDonald, who read it to his children. If he hadn't, Alice's adventures might have been nothing more than a personal gift to one little girl. But the entire MacDonald family loved the story so much that they urged Carroll to publish it.

- After giving the original to Alice Liddell as promised, Dodgson decided to take their advice. He revised the story, added to it, then hired John Tenniel, a well-known cartoonist, to illustrate it.

- The book was published in 1865 as *Alice's Adventures in Wonderland*. It became so popular that in 1871 Carroll published the further adventures of Alice, entitled *Through the Looking Glass*.

THE ALICE MYSTERY

Shortly after Dodgson presented Alice with the handwritten story, something happened that ended his relationship with the Liddell family. No one knows what it was. But the abruptness of the split has led to speculation about Carroll's sexuality. Why was he so interested in little girls in the first place?

- In fact, however, there's no evidence that his relationships with children were in any way improper. His biographers interviewed many of the women Carroll entertained as children and they always spoke of him with great respect and fondness. It's more likely, say some biographers, that Carroll broached the subject of marriage to one of the Liddell girls and was rejected.

- At any rate, the lazy days of games and stories were over for Alice and Dodgson. By the time Alice received her copy of the

A Midsummer Night's Dream **takes place between April 29 and May 1.**

published edition of *Alice's Adventures in Wonderland*, the author was no longer a part of her life.

In 1926 Alice Liddell sold the original manuscript of *Alice's Adventures Underground* to an American book dealer for $25,000. He resold it to a group of Americans. They took it to England and presented it as a gift to the British people in gratitude for their bravery in World War II. It remains there today, in the British Museum.

* * *

FAMILIAR FACES

Many of the now-classic characters in Carroll's stories were easily recognizable to the Liddell children. For example:

The White Rabbit: Was modeled after Carroll himself. Like the rabbit, he was very proper, usually dressed in an old-fashioned formal black suit and top hat. He always wore gloves—no matter what the weather—which he frequently misplaced.

The Dodo: Carroll had taken the girls to a museum, where they were fascinated by a stuffed Dodo bird. He incorporated the bird into the story as himself because he stammered and his name came out: as "Do-Do-Dodgson."

The Duck, Lory, and Eaglet: The Duck was Carroll's friend, Robinson Duckworth, who'd accompanied him on many of the outings with the children. The Lory was Lorina Liddell, the Eaglet, Edith Liddell. The three sisters show up again in the Dormous's story as Elsie (from L.C., Lorina's initials), Lacie (an anagram for Alice), and Tillie (a family nickname for Edith).

The Mock Turtle's Song: "Beautiful Soup" was a parody of one of the children's favorite songs, "Star of Evening," and the way they sang in their childish voices.

The Mad Hatter: Supposedly modeled after an eccentric man named Theophilus Carter, who'd been at Christ Church but became a furniture dealer.

Buyer's tip: The slowest time for car dealers is just before Christmas.

THE WORLD
ACCORDING TO ALICE

*The Alice books are among the most quotable children's stories
ever written. There's a gem on practically every page—and some
passages are packed with them. In the 1st and 6th Bathroom
Readers we included a few sections of Lewis Carroll's
work. Here are some more.*

In that direction," the Cheshire Cat said, waving its right paw
round, "lives a Hatter: and in that direction," waving the other
paw, "lives a March Hare. Visit either you like: they're both
mad." "But I don't want to go among mad people," Alice remarked.

"Oh, you can't help that," said the Cat: "we're all mad here. I'm
mad. You're mad."

"How do you know I'm mad!" said Alice.

"You must be," said the Cat, "or you wouldn't have come here."

*　　*　　*

"It was much pleasanter at home," thought poor Alice, "when one
wasn't always growing larger and smaller, and being ordered about
by mice and rabbits. I almost wish I hadn't gone down that rabbit
hole and yet it's rather curious, you know, this sort of life! I do
wonder what can have happened to me! When I used to read fairy
tales, I fancied that kind of thing never happened, and now here I
am in the middle of one! There ought to be a book written about
me, that there ought! And when I grow up, I'll write one but I'm
grown up now," she added in a sorrowful tone, "at least there's no
room to grow up any more here."

*　　*　　*

"Alice took up the fan and gloves, and, as the hall was very hot,
she kept fanning herself all the time she went on talking: 'Dear,
dear! How queer everything is today! And yesterday things went
on just as usual. I wonder if I've been changed in the night? Let me

---

Poll results: 44% of Americans think God is a man; only 1% think God is a woman.

think: was I the same when I got up this morning? I almost think I can remember feeling a little different. But if I'm not the same, the next question is, Who in the world am I? Ah, that's the great puzzle!' And she began thinking over all the children she knew, that were of the same age as herself to see if she could have been changed for any of them."

*   *   *

"Who are you?" said the Caterpillar.

This was not an encouraging opening for a conversation. Alice replied, rather shyly, "I, I hardly know, sir, just at present at least I know who I was when I got up this morning, but I think I must have been changed several times since then."

"What do you mean by that?" said the Caterpillar sternly. "Explain yourself!"

"I can't explain myself, I'm afraid, sir," said Alice, "because I'm not myself, you see."

"I don't see," said the Caterpillar.

"I'm afraid I can't put it more clearly," Alice replied very politely, "for I can't understand it myself to begin with; and being so many different sizes in a day is very confusing."

"It isn't," said the Caterpillar.

"Well, perhaps you haven't found it so yet," said Alice; "but when you have to turn into a chrysalis—you will some day, you know—and then after that into a butterfly, I should think you'll feel a little queer, won't you?"

"Not a bit," said the Caterpillar.

"Well, perhaps your feelings may be different," said Alice; "all I know is, it would feel very queer to me."

"You!" said the Caterpillar contemptuously. "Who are you?"

*   *   *

"The two *Alices* are not books for children; they are the only books in which we *become* children."

—Virginia Woolf

The average lightning bolt is only an inch in diameter.

IT'S A MIRACLE!

They say the Lord works in mysterious ways. Do you believe it?
These people obviously do . . . In fact, they may be the proof.

THE GLASS MENAGERIE

The Sighting: A 35-foot-high image of the Virgin Mary on the side of a building in Clearwater, Florida

Revelation: In 1996 workers chopped down a palm tree in front of the Seminole Finance Company building. Not long afterward, a customer noticed a discoloration in the building's tinted windows that resembled the Madonna. The discovery was reported on the afternoon news. By the end of the week, an estimated 100,000 people visited the site . . . including a Baptist minister who was ejected after he "condemned the crowd for worshipping an image on glass."

Impact: The city set up a "Miracle Management Task Force" to install portable toilets at the site, arrange police patrols, and erect a pedestrian walkway over the adjacent road (Route 19) to stop the faithful from dodging in and out of traffic. "That's the busiest highway in Florida," one policeman told reporters. "You want to know the real miracle? Half a million people have crossed that intersection and nobody's been injured or killed."

STRANGE FRUIT

The Sighting: The words of Allah in a sliced tomato in Huddersfield, England

Revelation: In June 1997, 14-year-old Shasta Aslam sliced a tomato in half for her grandparents' salad and saw what appeared to be the Koranic message "There is no God but Allah" spelled out in Arabic in the veins of one half of the tomato, and the words "Mohammed is the messenger" written in the other half. "There were some letters missing and it was hard to decipher," her grandmother told reporters, "but the message was clear."

Impact: Hundreds of Muslims from all over the United Kingdom went to view the tomato. "They knock on the door and I take them through to the kitchen and open the fridge door for them to have a look," the grandmother explained. The tomato has since been moved to the freezer.

World leaders: The U.S. is #1 in gun ownership per capita; Finland is #2.

NICE BUN

The Sighting: The face of Mother Teresa in a cinnamon bun in Nashville, Tennessee

Revelation: In the fall of 1996, bakers at the Bongo Java coffeehouse were baking cinnamon buns when they noticed one that bore a striking resemblance to Mother Teresa.

Impact: Bongo Java owner Bob Bernstein shellacked the bun and put it in a display case beneath the coffeehouse's cash register. The story was reported in newspapers and on national television. The coffeehouse, now a tourist attraction, set up a Web site and began selling "Immaculate Confection" T-shirts, mugs, cards, and "Mother Teresa's Special Roast" coffee beans. More than 2 million people from 80 different countries have visited the Web site, and many have left messages. "I hate to burst your bubble," one visitor wrote, "but to me, it looks more like Abe Vigoda in a hooded sweatshirt."

When Mother Teresa—who didn't even allow her own order to use her image in fundraising—learned of the bun, her lawyers asked the coffeehouse to remove it from display. "If it were sacrilege, we'd stop," a Bongo spokesman said. "But it's not."

THIRSTY FOR ENLIGHTENMENT

The Sighting: A statue of Lord Ganesh, the elephant-headed Hindu god of wealth and power, drinking milk through its trunk

Revelation: On September 21, 1995, a Hindu in India had a dream that Ganesh, the god of wealth and power, "wanted some milk." So he held an offering of a teaspoonful of milk up to the trunk of his Ganesh statue . . . and it drank it. As word spread over the next few days, the same phenomenon was observed in Hindu communities in England, Hong Kong, Malaysia, Nepal, the Netherlands, and the United States. (Skeptics point to capillary action—the ability of porous stone and metals to absorb liquids—as a likely culprit.)

Impact: According to Indian news reports, "So many Hindus were caught up in the mass hysteria that milk supplies were depleted and shopkeepers raised the price of milk 20 times. The military used bamboo canes to control the worshippers flooding Hindu temples." The phenomenon spread to other religions. "After reading news reports," one man in Kuala Lumpur wrote, "I tried the same thing on Mother Mary and baby Jesus. They drank a whole spoonful."

The firefly is the official insect of the state of Pennsylvania.

OLYMPIC MYTHS

Every two years, we're treated to another round of Olympics. Whether you watch them or not, it's impossible to avoid all the hype—which, it turns out, isn't all true. Next time someone refers to "Olympic tradition," read this to them.

THE MYTH: Athletes who competed in the ancient Greek Olympics were amateurs.

THE TRUTH: Technically, maybe. But in fact, they were handsomely rewarded for their victories. "Contrary to popular belief," says David Wallechinsky in his *Complete Book of the Olympics*, "the Ancient Greek athletes were not amateurs. Not only were they fully supported throughout their training, but even though the winner received only an olive wreath at the Games, at home he was amply rewarded and could become quite rich." Eventually, top athletes demanded cash and appearance fees—even back then.

THE MYTH: In ancient Greece, the Olympics were so important that everything stopped for them—even wars.

THE TRUTH: No war ever stopped because of the Olympics. But wars didn't interfere with the games because: 1) participants were given nighttime safe-conduct passes that allowed them to cross battlefields after a day's fighting was done and 2) the Olympics were part of a religious ceremony, so the four Olympic sites—including Delphi and Olympia—were off-limits to fighting.

THE MYTH: To honor ancient tradition and discourage commercialism, organizers of the modern Olympics decided that only amateur athletes could compete.

THE TRUTH: Not even close. It was "amateurs only" strictly to keep the riff-raff out. Baron Coubertin, the man responsible for bringing back the Olympics in 1896, was a French aristocrat who wanted to limit competitors to others of his social class. "He saw the Olympics as a way to reinforce class distinctions rather than overcome them," writes one historian. Since only the rich could afford to spend their time training for the games without outside support, the best way to keep lower classes out was to restrict them to amateurs.

More than half of Americans say they regularly watch TV while eating dinner.

THE MYTH: The torch-lighting ceremony that opens the games originated with the ancient Greeks.
THE TRUTH: It has no ancient precedent—it was invented by the Nazis. The 1936 Olympics took place in Berlin, under Hitler's watchful eye. Carl Diem, who organized the event for the Führer, created the first lighting of the Olympic flame to give the proceedings "an ancient aura." Since then, the ceremony has become part of Olympic tradition . . . and people just assume it's much older than it really is.

THE MYTH: The 5-ring Olympic symbol is from ancient Greece.
THE TRUTH: The Nazis are responsible for that myth, too. According to David Young's book, *The Modern Olympics,* it was spread in a Nazi propaganda film about the Berlin Games.

THE MYTH: Adolf Hitler snubbed U.S. runner Jesse Owens at the 1936 Olympics in Berlin.
THE TRUTH: This is one of the enduring American Olympic myths. Hitler, the story goes, was frustrated in his attempt to prove Aryan superiority when Owens—an African American—took the gold. The furious Führer supposedly refused to acknowledge Owens's victories. But according to Owens himself, it never happened. Hitler didn't congratulate anyone that day because the International Olympic Committee had warned him he had to congratulate "all winners or no winners." He chose to stay mum.

THE MYTH: The Olympic marathon distance was established in ancient times to honor a messenger who ran from Marathon to Athens—about 26 miles—to deliver vital news . . . then died.
THE TRUTH: The marathon distance—26 miles, 385 yards— was established at the 1908 games in London. It's the distance from Shepherd's Bush Stadium to the queen's bedroom window.

THE MYTH: Drugs have always been taboo in the Olympics.
THE TRUTH: Drugs weren't outlawed until 1967. In fact, according to the *Complete Book of the Olympics,* drugs were already in use by the third modern Olympic Games: "The winner of the 1904 marathon, Thomas Hicks, was administered multiple doses of strychnine and brandy *during* the race."

The largest fossilized dinosaur turd ever found measures 22" x 8" x 7.5".

FAMILIAR PHRASES

More unusual origins of everyday phrases

CARRY A TORCH FOR SOMEONE

Meaning: Be devoted to (in love with) someone
Origin: During the 19th century, a dedicated follower showed support for a political candidate by carrying a torch in an evening campaign parade. Only enthusiastic followers took part in such rallies. A fellow who carried a torch didn't care who knew that he was wholeheartedly behind his candidate. Later, the term was applied to someone publicly (and obsessively) in love.

SELL LIKE HOTCAKES

Meaning: Go over big; have a big commercial success
Origin: In the early 1800s, hotcakes were *the* popular fast food at carnivals and country fairs. Anyone who set up a hotcake stand was sure to make a killing.

PUT THE SCREWS TO SOMEONE

Meaning: Pressure someone mercilessly
Origin: According to Robert Claiborne in *Loose Cannons and Red Herrings*, "The screws aren't those used to fasten a piece of woodwork together, but the much larger screws used to compress such things as cotton bales. If someone's putting the screws on you, they're squeezing you for all you're worth."

BAWL SOMEONE OUT

Meaning: Berate (or yell at) someone for doing something wrong
Origin: "The word *bawl* for a loud, rough cry goes back to the fifteenth century and probably derives from the Latin for *baulare*, to bark like a dog, the word first meant to bark or howl the way a dog does, but it was also applied to the sounds of other animals, especially cows and bulls. This supports the theory that to *bawl out* originated as ranch slang, suggested by the bawling or bellowing of angry bulls." (*Animal Crackers*, by Robert Hendrickson)

The Elvis Presley hit "Hound Dog" was written in about ten minutes.

PULL YOUR OWN WEIGHT
Meaning: Do your share
Origin: Surprisingly, a rowing term. "Each member of a crew must pull an oar at least hard enough to propel his or her own weight." (*Have a Nice Day No Problem*, by Christine Ammer)

DEAD SET AGAINST SOMETHING
Meaning: Unalterably opposed to something
Origin: An industrial term. When a machine is bolted down or fastened so it can't move, it's said to be "dead set."

DRUM UP BUSINESS
Meaning: Find a way to sell things
Origin: "Before the practice of advertising in printed media became so common, traveling hawkers of various wares would enter a village in their wagons and attract an audience by beating a drum." (*The Whole Ball of Wax*, by Lawrence Urdang)

A BOOBY TRAP
Meaning: A hidden hazard, designed to surprise the victim
Origin: Literally a trap for a *booby* (or *boob*)—a term that probably came from the Spanish word *bobo*, meaning stupid.

FIT AS A FIDDLE
Meaning: In tip-top shape
Origin: "The phrase was originally 'fit as a fiddler,' and referred to the stamina of fiddlers, who could play for a dance all night long without even getting tired." (*Why Do We Say It*, by Castle Books)

MONKEY SUIT
Meaning: Formal wear; a tuxedo
Origin: "The organ grinder's monkey, dressed in a little jacket and given a hat in which to collect coins, was a familiar sight in the 18th and 19th centuries. About 1820 a close-fitting, short jacket was called a *monkey jacket* for its resemblance to the street musician's monkey; toward the end of the 19th century this name was also used for tuxedo jacket." Eventually the tux itself was nicknamed *monkey suit*. (*Raining Cats and Dogs*, Christine Ammer)

President Dwight Eisenhower helped popularize Izod alligator shirts.

COURT TRANSQUIPS

Here are some more great moments in American jurisprudence.
(These quotes are taken from actual court transcripts.)

Q: "How many trucks do you own?"
A: "Seventeen."
Q: "Seventy?"
A: "Seventeen."
Q: "Seventeen?"
A: "No, about twelve."

Q: "Tell us your full name, please.
A: "Mine?"
Q: "Yes, sit."
A: "555–2723."
Q: "Mr. Daniels, do you have any problems hearing me?"
A: "Not really."
Q: "Where do you live?"
A: "Pardon?"

Q: "Do you wear a 2-piece bathing suit now that you have a scar?"
A: "I don't wear a bathing suit at all now.
Q: "That can be taken two ways."

Q: "What device do you have in your laboratory to test alcohol content?"
A: "A dual column gas chromatograph, Hewlett Packard 5710A with flame analyzation detectors."
Q: "Can you get that with mag wheels?"
A: "Only on the floor models."

Q: "Do you recall examining a person by the name of Rodney Edgington at the funeral chapel?"
A: "Yes."
Q: "Do you recall approximately the time that you examined the body of Mr. Edgington?"
A: "It was in the evening. The autopsy started at about 8:30 p.m."
Q: "And Mr. Edgington was dead at that time, is that correct?"
A: "No, you dumb asshole. He was sitting on the table wondering why I was doing an autopsy."

Q: "Where do you live?"
A: "LaPosta Tailer Court."
Q: "How do you spell that trailer court?"
A: "T-r-a-i-l-e-r C-o-u-r-t."

Texas-born President Lyndon Johnson inspired a boom in cowboy hats.

BRAND NAMES

You already know these names—
here's where they come from.

ACE BANDAGES. When World War I broke out in 1914, the Becton Dickinson Company had to stop importing German elastic bandages and start making them in the U.S.A. They held a contest to give the new product a name. The winners: a group of doctors who called it ACE, for All Cotton Elastic.

ALPO. The original canned dog food, introduced in 1937 as All-Pro. Shortened in 1944 to *Alpo*.

ARM & HAMMER. In the 1860s the Church family owned the Vulcan Spice Mills. Their logo was an arm and a hammer, representing the Roman god Vulcan (who was a blacksmith). When the family formed a baking soda company in 1867, they used the same logo . . . and eventually named the company after it.

DELTA AIRLINES. Huff-Daland Dusters, formed in 1924, was the world's first crop-dusting service. When they moved to Louisiana a year later, they changed the name to Delta Air Service (because they were serving the Mississippi Delta). In 1929 they began their first passenger route, between Dallas and Jackson.

GRAPE-NUTS. The first Post cereal, introduced in 1897. The reference to *grapes* comes from the baking process, in which part of the starch in the dough is converted to dextrose—commonly called "grape sugar." And C. W. Post thought the cereal's small granules looked like nuts.

SARA LEE. Charles Lubin and his brother-in-law owned three bakeries in the Chicago area. But Lubin dreamed of bigger things—he wanted a product that would be distributed nationally. In 1949 he created a cheesecake that he could sell through supermarkets, and named it after his daughter, Sara Lee Lubin. Within five years the company had developed a way to quick-freeze Sara Lee cakes and was selling them all over the U.S.

It figures: Brain cells are the only human cells that don't reproduce.

WORD GEOGRAPHY

Did you know that many words are taken from place names? Here are some examples, from a book called Toposaurus, *by John D. Jacobson.*

BUNGALOW
From: Bengal, India
Explanation: England's 200-year occupation of India led to many borrowed Hindi words. An Indian *bangla* is a one-story house, often with a roofed porch (in Hindi, a *veranda*). *Bangla*—which literally means "from Bengal"—was anglicized to *bungalow*.

BIBLE
From: Byblos (a city now called Jubayl in present-day Lebanon)
Explanation: The ancient city of Byblos was where the Phoenicians converted a plant called papyrus into a type of paper. Greeks called the paper *biblios*, after the city, and soon a *biblion* meant "a little book." In 400 A.D. Greeks started using the word *Bible* to refer to the Christian scripture. Lower-case *bible* today means any authoritative source work.

SLEAZY
From: Silesia, Poland
Explanation: The Eastern European region of Silesia was known for its fine cloth. Eventually, so many low-quality imitations wound up on the market that *Silesian* turned into *sleazy*.

JEANS
From: Genoa, Italy
Explanation: Genoa—called *Gene* by 16th-century Europeans—was the first city to make the denim cloth used for jeans. The pants were named after the city.

SPA
From: Spa, Belgium
Explanation: The Belgian resort town of Spa was known for its healthful mineral springs. As a result, the term *spa* became associated with mineral water. Today it means "a place to rejuvenate."

Eagles can't hunt when it's raining.

THE EIFFEL TOWER, PART I

*It's hard to believe now, but when the Eiffel Tower was proposed
in the late 1800s, a lot of Parisians—and French citizens in
general—opposed it. Here's a look at the story behind one
of the most recognizable architectural structures on earth.*

REVOLUTIONARY THINKING

In 1885 French officials began planning the Great
Exposition of 1889, a celebration of the 100th anniversary
of the French Revolution. They wanted to build some kind of
monument that would be as glorious as France itself.

The Washington Monument, a masonry and marble obelisk, had
recently been completed. At 557 feet high, it was the tallest building on earth. The French decided to top it by constructing a 1,000-
foot-tall tower right in the heart of Paris.

Now all they had to do was find somebody who could design
and build it.

OPEN SEASON

On May 2, 1886, the French government announced a design contest: French engineers and architects were invited to "study the
possibility of erecting on the Champ de Mars an iron tower with a
base 125 meters square and 300 meters high."

Whatever the contestants decided to propose, their designs
had to meet two other criteria: 1) the structure had to be self-
financing—it had to attract enough ticket-buying visitors to the
exposition to pay for its own construction; and 2) it had to be a
temporary structure that could be torn down easily at the end of
the Exposition.

MERCI . . . BUT NON, MERCI

More than 100 proposals were submitted by the May 18 deadline.
Most were fairly conventional, but some were downright weird.
One person proposed building a huge guillotine; another suggested
erecting a 1,000-foot-tall sprinkler to water all of Paris during

---

Rule of thumb: The right rear tire on your car will wear out before the others do.

droughts; a third suggested putting a huge electric light atop the tower that—with the help of strategically placed parabolic mirrors—would provide the entire city "eight times as much light as is necessary to read a newspaper."

NO CONTEST
The truth was, none of them had a chance. By the time the contest was announced, Alexandre-Gustave Eiffel—a 53-year-old structural engineer already considered France's "master builder in metal" had the job sewn up. (He would later become known as *le Magicien du Fer*—"the Iron Magician.")

Weeks earlier he had met with French minister Edouard Lockroy and presented plans for a wrought iron tower he was ready to build. Eiffel had already commissioned 5,329 mechanical drawings representing the 18,038 different components that would be used. Lockroy was so impressed that he rigged the contest so only Eiffel's design would win.

JOINT VENTURE
In January 1887 Eiffel signed a contract with the French government and the City of Paris. Eiffel & Company, his engineering firm, agreed to contribute $1.3 million of the tower's estimated $1.6 million construction cost. In exchange, Eiffel would receive all revenues generated by the tower during the Exposition . . . and for 20 years afterward. (The government agreed to leave the tower up after the Exposition.) Afterward, full ownership reverted to the City of Paris. They could tear it down if they wanted.

MONEY MACHINE
Unlike other public monuments, the Eiffel Tower was designed to make money from the very beginning. If you wanted to take the elevator or the stairs to the first story, you had to pay 2 francs; going all the way to the top cost 5 francs (Sundays were cheaper). That was just the beginning: restaurants, cafés, and shops were planned for the first story; a post office, telegraph office, bakery, and printing press were planned for the second story. In all, the tower was designed to accommodate up to 10,416 paying customers at a time.

A horse expends more energy lying down than it does standing up.

GROUNDBREAKING

Construction began on January 26, with not a moment to spare. With barely two years left to build the tower in time for the opening of the Exposition, Eiffel would have to build the tower more quickly than any similar structure had been built before. The Washington Monument, just over half the Eiffel Tower's size, had taken 36 years to complete.

PARISIAN PARTY POOPERS

A 1,000-foot tower would dwarf the Parisian skyline and overpower the city's other landmarks, including Notre Dame, the Louvre, and the Arc de Triomphe. When digging started on the foundation, more than 300 prominent Parisians signed a petition protesting the tower. They claimed that Eiffel's "hollow candlestick" would "disfigure and dishonor" the city. But Eiffel and the city ignored the petition, and work continued uninterrupted.

OTHER FEARS

The tower still had its critics. A French mathematics professor predicted that when the structure passed the 748-foot mark, it would inevitably collapse; another "expert" predicted that the tower's lightning rods would kill all the fish in the Seine.

The Paris edition of the *New York Herald* claimed the tower was changing the weather; and the daily newspaper *Le Matin* ran a headline story claiming, "The Tower Is Sinking." "If it has really begun to sink," *Le Matin* pontificated, "any further building should stop and sections already built should be demolished as quickly as possible." As the tower's progress continued unabated, however, a sense of awe began to replace the fear.

Part II of the story begins on page 695.

Part II of the story begins on page 695.

*   *   *

INTERESTING SIDELIGHT

August Eiffel also designed and built the iron skeleton that holds up the Statue of Liberty.

Female spiders spin better webs than males do.

HOW ABOUT A WILSON SANDWICH?

Every sport has its own language. Here's a bit of basketball lingo, inspired by the book How to Talk Basketball, *by Sam Goldpaper and Arthur Pincus.*

Aircraft carrier: Big gun. Player you bring in to win the battle—a franchise center like Kareem Abdul-Jabbar.

Belly-up: Play tight defense, right up against your opponent.

Brick: Lousy shot, tossed up with no idea where it's going. "Usually hits the backboard with a thunk."

Curtain time: Point at which there's no way one of the teams can win. "No miracle is big enough to make it happen."

East Cupcake: Hometown of a team's easiest possible opponent.

Fire the rock: Shoot well, as in "John Stark can fire the rock."

French pastry: Making an easy shot look tough and a tough shot look tougher.

Garbage man: Player who only seems to score when unguarded.

Garbage time: End of the game, when players just toss the ball up "without any pattern, grace, or apparent skill." (See *Curtain time*.)

Hatchet man: Heavy fouler, often the one who goes after the opponent's star player to take him out of the game.

Ice: "Coolest player on the court." One who is never fazed.

Kangaroo: Player who's such a good jumper you figure he or she must be related to one.

Leather breath: What players have when a shot has been blocked right back in their face.

Nose bleeders: Players who jump so high they "can suffer nose bleeds from the change in altitude."

Shake and bake: Taking it to the hoop using every move and fake imaginable.

Submarine: Getting under players after their feet have left the floor for a shot to knock them off-balance.

Suburban jump shot: Classic shot using perfect form. Used by players who grew up playing a less physical game in suburban gyms.

Three-sixty: Showy move involving dunking the ball while spinning in a full circle.

Wheel and deal: Making amazing offensive moves (wheel) and then passing the ball off (deal).

Wilson sandwich: What players eat when a shot's blocked back in their face. Other meals: Spalding sandwich, Rawlings sandwich, etc.

Among other things, ancient Egyptian embalmers preserved mummies with cinnamon.

SPACED-OUT SPORTS

*Our friend Tim Harrower, an awesome talent in sniffing out
Bathroom Reader material, came up with these quotes from sports
announcers and interviews and graciously sent them our way.*

"We have only one person to
blame, and that's each other."
    —*Barry Beck,*
    N.Y. Ranger, explaining
    how a brawl started

"Winfield goes back to the
wall. He hits his head on the
wall—and it rolls off! It's
rolling all the way to second
base! This is a terrible thing
for the Padres."
    —*Jerry Coleman,*
    S.D. Padres radio
    announcer, describing a fly
    ball hit by a member of the
    opposing team

"We are experiencing audio
technicalities."
    —*Ralph Kiner,*
    N.Y. Mets announcer

"If I wasn't talking, I wouldn't
know what to say."
    —*Chico Resch,*
    N.Y. Islanders goalie

"Arnie, usually a great putter,
seems to be having trouble
with his long putt. However,
he has no trouble dropping
his shorts."
    —*Golf broadcaster,*
    during a tournament

"He fakes a bluff!"
    —*Ron Fairly,*
    S.F. Giants announcer

"Kansas City is at Chicago
tonight—or is that Chicago at
Kansas City? Well, no matter
. . . Kansas City leads in the
eighth, 4 to 4."
    —*Jerry Coleman,*
    Padres announcer, going
    through the scoreboard
    on air

"His reputation preceded him
before he got here."
    —*Don Mattingly, N.Y.*
    Yankees' star, on new
    pitcher Dwight Gooden

"Lintz steals second standing
up! He slid, but he didn't
have to."
    —*Jerry Coleman,*
    Padres announcer

"I don't want to tell you any
half-truths unless they're completely accurate."
    —*Dennis Rappaport,*
    boxing manager, explaining
    his silence regarding boxer
    Thomas Hearns

Only 1% of people suffering from night blindness are females.

CANINE QUOTES

A few thoughts about man's best friend.

"You can say any fool thing to a dog, and the dog will give you this look that says, 'My God, you're right! I never would have thought of that!'"
—**Dave Barry**

"They say the dog is man's best friend. I don't believe that. How many friends have you had neutered?"
—**Larry Reeb**

"My dog is half pit bull, half poodle. Not much of a guard dog, but a vicious gossip."
—**Craig Shoemaker**

"Outside a dog, a book is man's best friend. Inside a dog it's too dark to read."
—**Groucho Marx**

"If a dog will not come to you after he has looked you in the face, you should go home and examine your conscience."
—**Woodrow Wilson**

"Dogs laugh, but they laugh with their tails."
—**Max Eastman**

"Acquiring a dog may be the only opportunity a human ever has to choose a relative."
—**Mordecai Siegal**

"Every dog should have a man of his own. There is nothing like a well-behaved person around the house to spread the dog's blanket for him, or bring him his supper when he comes home man-tired at night."
—**Corey Ford**

"To his dog, every man is Napoleon; hence the constant popularity of dogs."
—**Aldous Huxley**

"To err is human, to forgive is canine."
—**Anonymous**

"Dogs have more love than integrity. They've been true to us, yes, but they haven't been true to themselves."
—**Clarence Day**

"Every dog is entitled to one bite."
—**English proverb**

What do foxes and bees have in common? They both pollinate plants.

AFTER THE FUNERAL

Your grave is supposed to be your final resting place. But that isn't always the case, especially if you're famous. Take a look at what happened to these unfortunate folks.

ABE LINCOLN
Claim to Fame: 16th president of the United States
How He Died: Assassinated by John Wilkes Booth on April 14, 1865
After the Funeral: On April 21, his body was laid to rest in a temporary vault in Springfield, Illinois, while a permanent mausoleum was under construction. The body was moved three more times, then entombed in the National Lincoln Monument on October 15, 1874. But in 1876 a ring of counterfeiters made two attempts to kidnap the body and hold it hostage until an accomplice was freed from prison; the second attempt was nearly successful—it was foiled just as the conspirators were prying open the sarcophagus.

Between 1876 and 1901, Lincoln's body was moved *14 more times*—sometimes for security reasons, other times to repair the dilapidated crypt. In 1901 Old Abe was laid to rest a final (so far) time. As his son Robert supervised, the coffin was encased in steel bars and buried under tons of cement. As far as anyone can tell, Abe hasn't been moved since.

FRANCISCO PIZARRO
Claim to Fame: 16th-century Spanish explorer and conquistador of the Incas
How He Died: Stabbed to death by his countrymen in 1541 in a feud over Incan riches
After the Funeral: Pizarro's body was buried behind the cathedral in Lima on the night he died, where it remained for 2 1/2 years. In 1544 his bones were exhumed, placed in a velvet-lined box, and deposited under the main altar of the cathedral.

Pizarro's remains were moved repeatedly over the next 350 years because of earthquakes, repair work on the cathedral, and other reasons. On the 350th anniversary of his death, in 1891, a mummified body authenticated as his was placed in a glass and marble sarcophagus, which was set out for public display.

The world's oceans have risen an average of 6 inches in the past 100 years.

Then, in 1977, some workers repairing a crypt beneath the main altar found two boxes—one lined with velvet and filled with human bones. The other box bore the Spanish inscription "Here is the skull of the Marquis Don Francisco Pizarro who discovered and won Peru and placed it under the crown of Castile."

Which body was Pizarro's? In 1984 forensics experts from the United States flew to Peru to compare the two sets of remains and determined that the bones in the boxes were those of Pizarro. (The box itself fit the historical description, and of the two sets of bones, the ones in the boxes were the only ones with stab wounds.)

Aftermath: When Pizarro's bones were positively identified, they were placed in a box in the glass sarcophagus, and the "impostor" mummy (who was never identified) was returned to the crypt underneath the altar.

JOHN PAUL JONES

Claim to Fame: Revolutionary War hero, founding father of the U.S. Navy, and the man who said, "I have not yet begun to fight"

How He Died: Kidney disease and bronchial pneumonia. Jones was one of the greatest heroes of the American Revolution, but that counted for little when he died in Paris on July 18, 1792. Rather than pay to ship the body back to the United States for burial, the American ambassador to France instructed Jones's landlord to bury him "in the most private manner, and at the least possible expense."

After the Funeral: In 1899, 107 years later, another U.S. ambassador to France, Horace Porter, became obsessed with locating Jones's grave and returning it to the United States for a proper hero's burial. Nobody knew where in Paris Jones was buried, but after six years of searching, Porter was pretty sure he was buried in a cemetery for Protestants. The cemetery, abandoned decades earlier, had since had an entire neighborhood built on top of it.

Acting on information that Jones had been buried in a lead casket, Porter hired a digging party to tunnel under the neighborhood and search for a lead casket among the hundreds of rotting and exposed wooden caskets. They found three lead coffins—and Jones was in the third. His body was so well preserved that it was identified by comparing the face to military medals inscribed with Jones's likeness. An American Naval Squadron returned him to

The right whale's eyeball is about as big as an orange.

the U.S. Naval Academy in July 1905 . . . where the body was stored under a staircase in a dormitory for seven more years until Congress finally appropriated enough money to build a permanent crypt.

JESSE JAMES
Claim to Frame: Wild West bank and train robber
How He Died: Shot by one of his gang members on April 3, 1882
After the Funeral: In the years after his death, several men came forward claiming to be the "real" Jesse James, arguing that the person in the grave was someone else. In September 1995 the remains were exhumed and their DNA was compared with James's living descendants. Result: It was him.

ZACHARY TAYLOR
Claim to Fame: 12th president of the United States
How He Died: On July 4, 1850, Taylor ate a bowl of fresh cherries and iced milk. Hours later, he complained of stomach pain and diarrhea; on July 9 he died.

Historians have always assumed Taylor died of natural causes; but rumors that he was poisoned with arsenic have persisted since his death. Taylor opposed the extension of slavery into newly admitted states; conspiracy theorists speculated he was murdered by pro-slavery forces.
After the Funeral: In 1995 Taylor's heirs consented to an exhumation to settle the controversy once and for all. Result: The tests were negative. "President Taylor had in his remains only minuscule levels of arsenic—consistent with any person who lived in the 19th century," forensic anthropologist Dr. William Maples writes in *Dead Men Do Tell Tales*. "The possibility that another poison was used to kill Taylor is extremely remote . . . On the face of this evidence, the verdict of history must be that Zachary Taylor died of natural causes."

A *selenologist* is someone who studies the moon.

WILDE ABOUT OSCAR

Wit and wisdom from Oscar Wilde, one of the most popular—and controversial—writers of the 19th century.

"When people agree with me I always feel that I must be wrong."

"I never put off till tomorrow what I can possibly do the day after."

"I sometimes think that God, in creating man, somewhat overestimated His ability."

"As long as a woman can look ten years younger than her own daughter, she is perfectly happy."

"Women are meant to be loved, not to be understood."

"After a good dinner one can forgive anybody, even one's own relations."

"I like men who have a future, and women with a past."

"Women give to men the very gold of their lives, but they invariably want it back in small change."

"Nowadays people know the price of everything and the value of nothing."

"The Americans are certainly great hero-worshipers, and always take their heroes from the criminal classes."

"No great artist sees things as they really are. If he did he would cease to be an artist."

"In this world there are only two tragedies. One is not getting what one wants and the other is getting it."

"Experience is the name everyone gives to their mistakes."

"A gentleman is one who never hurts anyone's feelings unintentionally."

"The basis of action is lack of imagination. It is the last resource of those who know not how to dream."

Back to nature: You can't get athlete's foot if you never wear shoes.

FART FACTS

You won't find trivia like this in any ordinary book.

THE NAME

The word *fart* comes from the Old English term *foertan*, to explode. *Foertan* is also the origin of the word *petard*, an early type of bomb. *Petard*, in turn, is the origin of a more obscure term for fart—*ped*, or *pet*, which was once used by military men. (In Shakespeare's *Henry IV*, there's a character whose name means fart—Peto.)

WHY DO YOU FART?

Flatulence has many causes—for example, swallowing air as you eat and lactose intolerance. (Lactose is a sugar molecule in milk, and many people lack the enzyme needed to digest it.) But the most common cause is food that ferments in the gastrointestinal tract.

A simple explanation: The fats, proteins, and carbohydrates you eat become a "gastric soup" in your stomach. This soup then passes into the small intestine, where much of it is absorbed through the intestinal walls into the bloodstream to feed the body.

But the small intestine can't absorb everything, especially complex carbohydrates. Some complex carbohydrates—the ones made up of several sugar molecules (beans, some milk products, fiber, etc.) can't be broken down. So they're simply passed along to the colon, where bacteria living in your intestine feed off the fermenting brew. If that sounds gross, try this: the bacteria then excrete gases into your colon. Farting is how your colon rids itself of the pressure the gas creates.

FRUIT OF THE VINE

So why not just quit eating complex carbohydrates?

First, complex carbohydrates—which include fruit, vegetables, and whole grains—are crucial for a healthy diet. "Put it this way," explains Jeff Rank, an associate professor of gastroenterology at the University of Minnesota. "Cabbage and beans are bad for gas, but they are good for you."

Diamonds have been worth more than pearls for only about a century.

Second, they're not the culprits when it comes to the least desirable aspect of farting: smell.

Farts are about 99% odorless gases—hydrogen, nitrogen, carbon dioxide, oxygen, and methane (it's the methane that makes farts flammable). So why the odor? Blame it on those millions of bacteria living in your colon. Their waste gases usually contain sulfur molecules—which smell like rotten eggs. This is the remaining 1% that clears rooms in a hurry.

AM I NORMAL?

Johnson & Johnson, which produces drugs for gas and indigestion, once conducted a survey and found that almost one-third of Americans believe they have a flatulence problem.

However, according to Terry Bolin and Rosemary Stanton, authors of *Wind Breaks: Coming to Terms with Flatulence*, doctors say most flatulence is healthy. What's unhealthy is worrying about it so much.

NOTABLE FARTERS

Le Petomane, a 19th-century music hall performer, had the singular ability to control his farts. He could play tunes, as well as imitate animal and machinery sounds rectally. Le Petomane's popularity briefly rivaled that of Sarah Bernhardt.

A computer factory in England, built on the site of a 19th-century chapel, is reportedly inhabited by a farting ghost. Workers think it might be the embarrassed spirit of a girl who farted while singing in church. "On several occasions," said an employee, "there has been a faint girlish voice singing faint hymns, followed by a loud raspberry sound and then a deathly hush."

Joseph Stalin was afraid of farting in public. He kept glasses and a water pitcher on his desk so that if he felt a wind coming on, he could mask the sound by clinking the glasses while pouring water.

Martin Luther believed, "on the basis of personal experience, that farts could scare off Satan himself."

It takes about 2 1/2 gallons of oil to make a car tire.

BATHROOM BEGINNINGS

*A few interesting odds and ends from under
the sink and in the medicine cabinet.*

AUTOMATIC TOILET BOWL CLEANER. A guy named Eisen cleaned the toilets in his house because his wife wouldn't—but he hated it. One day in 1977, while hanging out at a swimming pool, he started thinking that if chlorine keeps pools sanitary, it could do the same for his toilets—and then he wouldn't have to scrub them. But how to keep the bowl water chlorinated? Later at dinner, Eisen was inspired by the sour cream on his baked potato: he figured that if he put chlorine in a sour cream container, punched holes in it, and put it in his toilet tank, it would get a dose of chlorine every time it was flushed. It worked. He turned it into a product called 2000 Flushes, now the best-selling toilet cleaner in America.

BRECK SHAMPOO. In 1898, at age 21, John Breck became America's youngest fire chief. It didn't make him happy, though—he was obsessed with the fact that he was going bald. He decided to take chemistry classes at a nearby college to see if he could save his hair. There, he hit on a solution: liquid shampoo. (At the time, Americans used bar soap on their hair—shampoos were used only in Europe.) The shampoo he developed didn't save his hair, but in 1908 it did become the inspiration for America's first shampoo company.

DRAMAMINE. In 1949 a woman with a bad case of hives went to the Johns Hopkins Allergy Clinic in Baltimore. Her doctor gave her a prescription for a new drug he thought was an antihistamine. On her next visit, the woman's hives were just as bad . . . but she was in good spirits. For once, she said, the motion of the streetcar she took to get there hadn't made her sick. The doctor suspected the drug had something to do with it. So he gave her a placebo to see if she'd get motion sickness again. She did. He gave her the drug again—the motion sickness vanished. The clinic got the army to try it on soldiers "making a rough trans-Atlantic crossing via ship." Worked fine. The drug—Dramamine—became the standard treatment for motion sickness.

The first golf course to have 18 holes was St. Andrews in Scotland, in 1764.

OTHER PRESIDENTIAL FIRSTS

We all know the first president (Washington), the first president to serve more than two terms (FDR), and so on. But who was the first to be cloned? For that info, you need to turn to the Bathroom Reader.

The president: Gerald Ford
Notable first: First president to be a fashion model. In the late 1930s, he was a student at Yale Law School. His girl-friend, a model, convinced him to put $1,000 into a modeling agency. His reward: He got to pose in skiwear ads with her.

The president: Richard Nixon
Notable first: First president to host a rock concert at the White House. Unlikely as it seems, Nixon invited the Guess Who and the Turtles to Washington to play for his daughters.

The president: Abraham Lincoln
Notable first: First president to be cloned. Someday this may be big news. Now it's just a curiosity. In 1990 a group of research scientists got permission to duplicate the DNA from Lincoln's hair, blood, and skull (which they got from the National Museum of Health and Medicine in Washington, D.C.), to find out whether he had a disease called Marfan's syndrome.

The president: John Quincy Adams
Notable first: First president with a pet reptile. Adams kept a pet alligator in the East Room of the White House. Historians say he enjoyed "the spectacle of guests fleeing from the room in terror."

The president: George Washington
Notable first: First president to use "help wanted" ads to hire staff. Washington moved to New York—the U.S. capital—in 1789 and put a classified ad in the *New York Daily Gazette* requesting a coachman and a cook "for the Family of a President." Apparently it was no great honor to work for a First Family—the ads ran for six weeks before the jobs were filled.

The word *alligator* comes from *el lagarto*—Spanish for "the lizard."

FOUNDING FATHERS

You already know the names. Here's who they belonged to.

Godfrey Keebler. Opened a bakery in Philadelphia in 1853. His family expanded it. Today Keebler is the second-largest producer of cookies and crackers in the U.S.

Linus Yale, Jr. Invented the first combination locks and the first flat-key cylinder locks, in the 1860s. In 1868 the Yale Lock Company was formed to mass-produce his creations.

Joseph Campbell. A fruit merchant, he opened a canning factory in 1869. His specialties included jellies, salad dressing, and mince-meat—but not soup. The company added condensed soup in 1897. (First variety: tomato.)

Pleasant and John Hanes. Brothers who built a tobacco business in the late 1800s, then sold it in 1900. Each invested his profits in a textile company. John's made socks and stockings; Pleasant's made new-fangled two-piece men's underwear. They were separate companies until 1962, when the families joined forces.

Carl Jantzen. Part owner of the Portland Knitting Mill. In 1910, at the request of a member of the Portland Rowing Club, he developed the first elasticized swimsuits. They became popular around the country as "Jantzens." In 1920 the company changed its name to Jantzen.

John M. Van Heusen. Started the Van Heusen Shirt Company. In 1919 it became the first to sell dress shirts with collars attached. He developed a way to weave cloth on a curve in 1920, which made one-piece collars possible . . . and revolutionized the shirt industry.

Arthur Pitney and Walter Bowes. In 1901 Pitney created a machine that could stick postage stamps on letters. In 1920 he joined forces with Bowes. Because of World War I, there was a letter-writing boom, and the post office needed a machine to keep up. In 1920 Congress passed a bill allowing the Pitney-Bowes machine to handle the mail.

First two kitchen utensils: the ladle and the apple corer, in that order.

HERE COMES THE SUN

Some facts about that big lightbulb in the sky, from
astronomer (and BRI member) Richard Moeschl.

It takes 8.3 minutes for the sun's light—traveling at 186,282 miles a second—to reach Earth. (At that speed, light can travel around the Earth seven times in one second.)

The sun looks yellow-gold because we're viewing it through the Earth's atmosphere. Judging from its surface temperature, the sun's color is probably closer to white.

The temperature of the sun at its core is around 73 million degrees F. It takes 50 years for this energy to reach the sun's surface, where we can see it as light.

The total energy output of the sun is 1.92 calories per minute per square centimeter, or 3.83 x 1,000,000,000,000,000, 000,000,000,000 watts.

The amount of power that falls on each square foot of the Earth's surface per minute is about 126 watts, enough to light two standard 60-watt lightbulbs.

With every passing day, the sun is losing energy—but it still has about 5 billion years of life left in it.

The sun contains 99.9% of the matter in the solar system.

The English astronomer James Jeans once figured that if you placed a piece of the sun's core the size of the head of a pin on Earth, its heat would kill a person 94 miles away.

The temperature of the sun's photosphere, the part that sends us light, is about 10,000 degrees F.

The sun produces more energy in one second than human beings have produced in all of our history. In less than a week, the sun sends out more energy than we could make by burning all the natural gas, oil, coal, and wood on Earth.

The surface gravity on the sun is 28 times that of Earth. If you weigh 120 pounds on Earth, on the sun you would weigh 3,360 pounds.

Ouch! There are 1,000 barbs in a single porcupine quill.

CELEBRITY GOSSIP

Here's the BRI's cheesy tabloid section—
a bunch of gossip about famous people.

ALBERT EINSTEIN
He applied to the Federal Polytechnic Academy in Zurich, but flunked the entrance exam. When his father asked his headmaster what profession Albert should adopt, he got the answer, "It doesn't matter, he'll never amount to anything."

For many years, Einstein thought of his work in physics as something of a hobby. He regarded himself as a failure because what he really wanted to do was play concert violin. Einstein was uncharacteristically intense when he played his violin, cussing a blue streak whenever he made a mistake. One evening, while playing violin duets with Queen Elizabeth, Einstein suddenly stopped in the middle of the piece and unceremoniously told her she was playing too loudly.

MUHAMMAD ALI
For some reason, as a child, he always walked on his tiptoes. When he got older, he played touch football, but wouldn't play tackle because he thought it was too rough.

Because he was afraid to fly, Ali (then going by his original name, Cassius Clay) almost didn't make it to the 1960 Rome Olympics, where he won the gold medal that launched his career.

JANIS JOPLIN
In 1965, when she was on the verge of becoming a blues star, strung out on heavy drugs, hanging out with Hells Angels, Joplin wrote to her parents and asked them to send her one present for Christmas: "a *Betty Crocker* or *Better Homes and Gardens* cookbook."

She once went on a blind date with William Bennett. He was apparently so traumatized that he eventually became drug czar under Ronald Reagan, and a conservative "family values" advocate.

GENERAL GEORGE PATTON

On the way through Europe during World War II with his troops, Patton was continuously in danger from shelling, strafing, and bombing. In the middle of one scorched, scarred, and burning landscape, with the sound of explosions around him, he threw out his arms and looked to the skies as if bathing in a warm spring rain. "Could anything be more magnificent?" he shouted to the soldiers all around him. "Compared to war, all other forms of human endeavor shrink to insignificance. God, how I love it!"

MICHAEL JACKSON

Jackson's favorite song? He told a group of reporters that it was "My Favorite Things," performed by Julie Andrews.

His opinion of other singers: Paul McCartney? Okay writer, not much of an entertainer. "I do better box office than he does." Frank Sinatra? "I don't know what people see in the guy. He's a legend, but he isn't much of a singer. He doesn't even have hits anymore." Mick Jagger? "He sings flat. How did he ever get to be a star? I just don't get it. He doesn't sell as many records as I do." Madonna? "She just isn't that good . . . She can't sing. She's just an OK dancer . . . She knows how to market herself. That's about it."

FIDEL CASTRO

For Castro's first revolutionary attack on a military post, he forgot his glasses. As a result, he could barely drive to the post, much less aim his gun accurately.

Castro fancies himself quite a lady's man. In fact, there are dozens of children in Cuba who claim him as father. His technique? One purported lover, a dancer at the Tropicana Hotel, said he read while making love. A French actress complained that he "smoked his damned cigar." An American woman said he never took his boots off. Other women said he took them to romantic spots and then talked for hours on end about things like agricultural reform.

ALFRED HITCHCOCK

When he sat on a public toilet and another man entered the room, he'd quickly raise his legs in the stall "so that no one could tell anyone was there."

Einstein couldn't read until the age of nine.

LUCKY FINDS

In our last Bathroom Reader, we included a section about valuable things people have found. Since then we've found many more stories. Hey—maybe it's not such a rare occurrence. It could happen to you!

GARAGE SALE TREASURE

The Find: Two Shaker "gift" paintings

Where They Were Found: Inside a picture frame

The Story: In 1994 a retired couple from New England bought an old picture frame for a few dollars at a garage sale. When they took the frame apart to restore it, two watercolor drawings—dated 1845 and 1854—fell out.

A few months later, the couple was traveling in Massachusetts and noticed a watercolor on a poster advertising the Hancock Shaker Village Museum. It was similar to the two they'd found. Curious, they did some research and found out the works were called "gift paintings."

It turns out that the Shakers, a New England religious sect of the 1800s, did not allow decorations on their walls; Shaker sisters, however, were permitted to paint "trees, flowers, fruits and birds . . . to depict the glory of heaven." The paintings were then "gifted" to other sisters and put away as holy relics. And one of the couple's paintings was signed by the most famous of all "gift" artists, Hannah Cohoon.

They called a curator of the Hancock Museum with the news, but he didn't believe them. Only 200 Shaker "gift" paintings still exist . . . and very few are of the quality they described. Moreover, all known paintings were in museums—none in private hands. Nonetheless, in January 1996, the couple brought the paintings to the museum, where they were examined and declared authentic. A year later, in January 1997, Sotheby's sold them for $473,000.

BIZARRE BITE

The Find: A diamond

Where It Was Found: In a plate of pasta

The Story: In October 1996 Liliana Parodi of Genoa, Italy, went to her favorite restaurant for some pasta. The meal was uneventful

. . . until she bit down on something hard and it wedged painfully between her teeth. She complained to the management, then left. The next morning, she went to a dentist, who extracted the object—a one-carat, uncut diamond worth about $3,000. Parodi took it to a jeweler and had it set in a ring. How it got into the pasta is still a mystery.

A BEATLE'S LEGACY
The Find: Dozens of sketches by John Lennon
Where They Were Found: In a notebook
The Story: In 1996 a man named John Dunbar—who'd been married to British singer Marianne Faithfull in the 1960s—was going through some old belongings and came across a notebook he hadn't seen in over 25 years. He'd had it with him at a London party in 1967, on a night when he and his friend John Lennon were taking LSD together. But he'd stashed it away and forgotten about it.

During that week in 1967, Lennon had seen an ad in the newspaper offering "an island off Ireland," for about $2,000. At the party, the drugged-out Beatle suddenly decided to buy it. He and Dunbar immediately flew to Dublin, traveled across Ireland in a limousine, and hired a boat to get there. "The island was more like a couple of small hills joined by a gravelly bar with a cottage on it," Dunbar recalled. "When we got there, John sat down and started drawing." The pair stayed on the island for a few days. Lennon did buy it, but never lived there. (In fact, he gave it away a few years later, to a stranger who showed up at Apple Records.)

Dunbar kept the notebook as a memento of the trip, and today, experts estimate the drawings at about $165,000. The incredulous Dunbar can always look at it as a belated "thank you"—he was the fellow, it turns out, who introduced Lennon to Yoko Ono.

LOTTERY TICKET
The Find: A wallet with $224
Where It Was Found: On a street in Adelaide, Australia
The Story: In the 1970s Joan Campbell found a wallet and tracked down the owner, hoping for a nice reward. She was disappointed—all the man gave her was a 55¢ lottery ticket. Later, she cheered up: the ticket paid $45,000.

If an octopus is hungry enough, it will eat its own arms.

BOND...JAMES BOND

*Here's a shaken—not stirred—history of the most popular (and prof-
itable) British secret agent in Hollywood history . . . and of the former
World War II intelligence officer who brought the character to life.*

SPY STORY

Even before World War II started, Great Britain knew it
would never be able to patrol the entire northern Atlantic
and defend all its ships against the German Navy. But the British
also knew that if they could learn the locations of Nazi ships and
submarines by deciphering coded German radio communications,
they'd be able to reroute convoys of food and weapons around
German patrols. In 1939 they launched a massive effort, code-
named Ultra, to do just that.

The Enigma. The Germans sent coded messages using an encryp-
tion machine called the "Enigma." By September 1940 the British
had managed to put together a working model of the Enigma using
parts captured in several raids on German ships. But the Enigma
was so sophisticated that even when the British had one in their
possession, they couldn't crack the German codes. They needed a
copy of the Nazis' special codebook.

FLEMING . . . IAN FLEMING

How were they going to get one? The wildest suggestion came from
the assistant to the Director of Naval Intelligence, a man named
Ian Fleming. On September 12, 1940, Fleming wrote the following
memo to his boss:

Director of Naval Intelligence:

I suggest we obtain the loot [codebook] by the following means:

1. Obtain from Air Ministry an air-worthy German bomber.

2. Pick a tough crew of five, including a pilot, wireless telegraph
operator, and a word-perfect [fluent] German speaker. Dress
them in German Air Force uniform, add blood and bandages to
suit.

3. Crash plane in the Channel after making S.O.S. to rescue
service in plain language.

A *puwo* is an animal that's a cross between a poodle and a wolf.

4. Once abroad the rescue boat, shoot German crew, dump over-board, bring rescue boat back to English port.

In order to increase the chances of capturing a small or large minesweeper, with their richer booty, a crash might be staged in mid-[English] Channel. The Germans would presumably employ one of this type for the longer and more hazardous journey.

OPERATION RUTHLESS
The Director of Naval Intelligence passed the plan along to Prime Minister Winston Churchill, who gave it his personal approval. A German twin-engine Heinkell 111, shot down during a raid over Scotland, was restored to flying condition and a crew was recruited to fly it. "Operation Ruthless" was ready to go . . . But as David Kahn writes in *Seizing the Enigma*:

> In October, Fleming went to Dover to await his chance. None came. Air reconnaissance found no suitable German ships oper-ating at night, and radio reconnaissance likewise found nothing . . . The navy awaited favorable circumstances. But they never materialized, and the plan faded away.

Even though Great Britain never did attempt a raid as daring as Fleming proposed, it did manage to capture codebooks from German ships. By 1943 they were cracking Enigma codes regularly; and by May of that year the Battle of the Atlantic was effectively over.

A NOVEL IDEA
After the war Fleming got out of the intelligence business and became an executive with the company that owned the London *Sunday Times*. He never forgot his wartime experiences.

First Person. By 1952 Fleming was in his forties and about to be married for the first time. He was apparently tense at the thought of giving up his bachelorhood, and his future wife suggested he try writing a novel to ease the strain. Fleming had wanted to write a novel for years, so he decided to give it a try. Drawing on his intel-ligence background, he wrote a spy thriller called *Casino Royale* during his two-month winter vacation in Jamaica.

Picking a Name. The book was filled with murders, torture, and lots of action. It was an autobiographical fantasy, the adventures of a British secret agent named James Bond that Fleming—who spent World War II stuck behind a desk in London—wanted to be, but couldn't.

Fleming thought that giving the agent an unexciting name would play off well against the plot. But what name? As Fleming later recounted, he found it "in one of my Jamaican bibles, *Birds of the West Indies* by James Bond, an ornithological classic. I wanted the simplest, dullest, plainest-sounding name that I could find. James Bond seemed perfect."

ON HIS WAY

Casino Royale was published in England in April 1953, and in the U.S. a year later. The book was a critical success, but sales were disappointing. Luckily for Fleming, he took a two-month vacation in Jamaica every year, and in each of the next several years he wrote a new Bond novel during his vacation, including *Live and Let Die* (1954), *Moonraker* (1955), and *Diamonds Are Forever* (1956).

Live and Let Die became a bestseller in England, and Fleming began building a considerable following in the U.K. But in America, sales remained sluggish for the rest of the 1950s.

Thanks, JFK. The Bond bandwagon got rolling in the United States beginning in 1961, when *Life* magazine published a list of President John F. Kennedy's favorite books. Among the scholarly tomes was one work of popular fiction—*From Russia, With Love.* "This literally made Bond in America overnight," Raymond Benson writes in *The James Bond Bedside Companion.* "From then on, sales improved almost immediately . . . It was good public relations for Kennedy as well—it showed that even a President can enjoy a little 'sex, sadism, and snobbery.'"

*　　*　　*

The first push-button phones were installed November 18, 1963. They were put into service between Carnegie and Greensburg, Pennsylvania.

Boris Yeltsin's favorite Elvis song: "Are You Lonesome Tonight?"

ALLENISMS

Thoughts from one of America's leading wits, Woody Allen.

"My success has allowed me to strike out with a higher class of women."

"My parents put a live teddy bear in my crib."

"When I was kidnapped, my parents sprang into action. They rented out my room."

"The world is divided into good and bad people. The good ones sleep better . . . while the bad ones seem to enjoy the working hours much more."

"Life is full of loneliness, misery, and suffering, and it's all over much too soon."

"I do not believe in an afterlife, although I am bringing a change of underwear."

"How is it possible to find meaning in a finite world, given my waist and shoe size?"

"The difference between sex and love is that sex relieves tension and love causes it."

"My parents stayed together for forty years, but that was out of spite."

"Basically my wife was immature. I'd be at home in the bath and she'd come in and sink my boats."

"Don't pay attention to what your schoolteachers tell you. Just see what they look like and that's how you know what life is really going to be like."

"If God would only give me some clear sign. Like making a large deposit in my name in a Swiss bank account."

"Eternal nothingness is fine, if you happen to be dressed for it."

"I think crime pays. The hours are good, you travel a lot."

"It is a gorgeous gold pocket watch. I'm proud of it. My grandfather, on his death-bed, sold me this watch."

It takes an estimated 2,893 licks to get to the center of a Tootsie Roll pop.

FORGOTTEN POP HISTORY

Here are a few tidbits of obscure Americana, from the 1941 book Keep Up with the World, *by Freling Foster.*

INSTANT HEIRLOOMS

In 18th-century America, before cameras, portrait painters traveled from town to town with an assortment of pictures of men and women, complete except for the face and hair. People who wanted an oil portrait of themselves merely had to select the body they liked best. The head and features would then be painted in by the artist.

THE CORPSE WOULDN'T TALK

As late as the 17th century, America held "trials by touch," in which the defendant in a murder case was made to touch the corpse. If the accused was guilty, the dead man was supposed to move or to indicate the fact in some other way.

BANANAS IN TINFOIL

Bananas were virtually unknown in this country until 1876, when they were featured at the Philadelphia Centennial Exposition. Wrapped individually in tinfoil, they were sold as novelties at 10¢ apiece.

I GET A WHOLE BED TO MYSELF?

The greatest event in hotel history was the opening of Boston's Tremont House in October 1829. It surpassed every other inn and tavern in size (it had 180 rooms), furnishings, and accommodations. Instead of making four or five people—usually strangers to one another—sleep together in one bed in an unlocked room, the Tremont gave each guest a whole room with a lock on the door and clean linen on the bed. Instead of having to use an outside pump to wash, the guest was supplied with a bowl and a pitcher of water. Moreover, the Tremont was the first to install a device in its rooms to signal the office for service; and it was the first hotel to employ bellboys who, at that time, were known as "rotunda men."

Central Park, in New York City, is almost twice as big as Monaco.

WHY A RABBIT'S FOOT?

Good question. When we were kids, they sold rabbits' feet at the local variety store "for luck." We always wondered how a rabbit's foot could be lucky for us, since it obviously didn't do the rabbit any good. Anyway, one day someone wondered aloud where the idea came from, and we went to our BRI library to look it up. To our surprise, no two books gave the same answer. After a while, we were just looking to see how many "reasons" we could find. Here are some favorites.

ORIGINS AND FIRSTS, by Jacob M. Braude
"The rabbit's foot originated as a good luck symbol in show business, where it was used as a powder puff in makeup, and when lost or misplaced, it might delay a performance . . . bad luck. Hence the reverse when it wasn't."

SUPERSTITIOUS!, by Willard Heap
"The rabbit is a prolific animal, producing large numbers of off-spring. For that reason, it was thought to possess a creative power superior to other animals, and thus became associated with prosperity and success. If a person carries a rabbit's foot, preferably the left hind foot, good luck is sure to follow. True believers stroke their hands or faces with it, so they will have success in a new venture."

SUPERSTITIOUS? HERE'S WHY, by Julie Forsyth Batchelor and Claudia De Lys
"The first fears and superstitions developed about the European hare . . . Since most of the habits of these two are alike, superstitions about the hare also apply to the bunny.
"The ancients noticed many things about these timid creatures that they couldn't explain, so they considered them both good and evil. They saw how rabbits came out at night to feed, and how they gathered in bands on clear moonlit nights to play as if influenced by the moon. Another astonishing fact was that northern hares were brown in summer and white in winter.

There are an estimated 28 million Jennifers in the United States.

"But one thing especially impressed primitive man, and that was how the rabbit used his hind legs. There are only two other animals, the greyhound and cheetah, whose rear feet hit the ground in front of the forefeet when running swiftly. Also, rabbits thump the ground with their hind legs as if 'speaking' with them. So their hind feet came to be looked upon as a powerful charm against evil forces."

SUPERSTITIONS, by Peter Lorie
"The idea of a hare's foot as a lucky charm . . . arose out of the primitive medical belief that the bone of a hare's foot cured gout and cramp, though the bone had to be one with a joint in it intact, to be effective. Carrying a hare's foot bone, with joint, would keep away all forms of rheumatism."

ENCYCLOPEDIA OF SUPERSTITIONS,
by Edwin and Mona Radford
"The origin of the superstitions concerning the luck of the rabbit's foot lies in the belief that young rabbits are born with their eyes open, and thus have the power of the Evil Eye, and can shoo away the Evil One."

EXTRAORDINARY ORIGINS OF EVERYDAY THINGS,
by Charles Panati
"The rabbit's habit of burrowing lent it an aura of mystery. The Celts, for instance, believed that the animal spent so much time underground because it was in secret communication with the netherworld of numinia. Thus, a rabbit was privy to information humans were denied. And the fact that most animals, including humans, are born with their eyes closed, while rabbits enter the world with eyes open, imbued them with an image of wisdom for the Celts; rabbits witnessed the mysteries of prenatal life. (Actually, the hare is born with open eyes; the rabbit is born blind. And it is the rabbit that burrows; hares live aboveground. Confusion abounded.)"

President Clinton's favorite movie: *High Noon.*

BUILDING A BETTER SQUIRT GUN

When Uncle John was a kid, he had squirt guns that shot 5 to 10 feet at most, and that was only if you pulled the trigger so hard it hurt. Today, there are water toys that shoot 50 feet or more. Here's the story.

BOY WONDER

Lonnie Johnson loved to tinker. As a kid, he used to take his brothers' and sisters' toys apart to see how they worked. By high school, he'd graduated to mixing rocket fuel in the family kitchen. One year he used scrap motors, jukebox parts, and an old butane tank to create a remote-controlled, programmable robot . . . which won first prize in the University of Alabama science fair. Not bad for a kid from the poor side of Mobile, Alabama.

UNDER PRESSURE

Johnson got an engineering degree from Tuskeegee Institute and wound up working at the Jet Propulsion Lab in Pasadena, California. But he still spent his spare time tinkering. He recalls that one evening in 1982, "I was experimenting with inventions that used water instead of freon as a refrigeration fluid. As I was shooting water through a high-pressure nozzle in the bathtub, I thought "Wow, this would make a neat water pistol."

He built a prototype squirt gun out of PVC pipe, plexiglass, and a plastic soda bottle. Then he approached several toy companies . . . but none of them thought a squirt gun with a 50-foot range would sell. Johnson even looked into manufacturing the toys himself, but couldn't afford the $200,000 molding cost.

BREAKTHROUGH

In March 1989 he went to the International Toy Fair in New York and tried to sell his invention again. This time, the Larami Corporation was interested. They arranged a meeting with Johnson at their headquarters in Philadelphia. When everyone was seated, Johnson opened his suitcase, whipped out his prototype, and shot a burst of water across the entire room. Larami bought the gun on the spot. Within a year, the "Super Soaker" was the best-selling squirt gun in history.

A third of the population of Sweden immigrated to the United States in the 1800s.

IN DREAMS . . .

People have always been fascinated by dreams. Where do they come from? What do they mean? D. H. Lawrence put it perfectly when he said, "I can never decide whether my dreams are the result of my thoughts or my thoughts are the result of my dreams." On occasion, art, music, and even discoveries and inventions have resulted directly from information received in a dream. Here are some examples.

THE SEWING MACHINE

Elias Howe had been trying to invent a practical lock-stitch sewing machine for years, but had been unsuccessful. One night in the 1840s, he had a nightmare in which he was captured by a primitive tribe who were threatening to kill him with their spears. Curiously, all the spears had holes in them at the pointed ends. When Howe woke up, he realized that a needle with a hole at its tip—rather than at the base or middle (which is what he'd been working with)—was the solution to his problem.

DR. JEKYLL AND MR. HYDE

Since childhood, novelist Robert Louis Stevenson had always remembered his dreams and believed that they gave him inspiration for his writing. In 1884, he was in dire need of money and was trying to come up with a book. He had already spent two days racking his brain for a new plot when he had a nightmare about a man with a dual personality. In the dream, "Mr. Hyde" was being pursued for a crime he'd committed; he took a strange powder and changed into someone else as his pursuers watched. Stevenson screamed in his sleep, and his wife woke him. The next morning he began writing down *The Strange Case of Dr. Jekyll and Mr. Hyde.*

INSULIN

Frederick Banting, a Canadian doctor, had been doing research into the cause of diabetes, but had not come close to a cure. One night he had a strange dream. When he awoke, he quickly wrote down a few words that he remembered: "Tie up the duct of the pancreas of a dog . . . wait for the glands to shrivel up . . . then cut it out, wash it . . . and filter the precipitation." This new approach to extracting the substance led to the isolation of the hormone

---

Watches get their name because they were originally worn by night watchmen.

now known as insulin, which has saved millions of diabetics' lives. Banting was knighted for his discovery.

LEAD SHOT

James Watt is remembered for inventing the steam engine, but he also came up with the process for making lead shot used in shotguns. This process was revealed to him in a dream. At the time, making the shot was costly and unpredictable—the lead was rolled into sheets by hand, then chopped into bits. Watt had the same dream each night for a week: He was walking along in a heavy rainstorm—but instead of rain, he was being showered with tiny pellets of lead, which he could see rolling around his feet. The dream haunted him; did it mean that molten lead falling through the air would harden into round pellets? He decided to experiment. He melted a few pounds of lead and tossed it out of the tower of a church that had a water-filled moat at its base. When he removed the lead from the water, he found that it had hardened into tiny globules. To this day, lead shot is made using this process.

THE BENZENE MOLECULE

Friedrich A. Kekule, a Belgian chemistry professor, had been working for some time to solve the structural riddle of the benzene molecule. One night while working late, he fell asleep on a chair and dreamed of atoms dancing before him, forming various patterns and structures. He saw long rows of atoms begin to twist like snakes until one of the snakes seized its own tail and began to whirl in a circle. Kekule woke up "as if by a flash of lightning" and began to work out the meaning of his dream image. His discovery of a closed ring with an atom of carbon and hydrogen at each point of a hexagon revolutionized organic chemistry.

JESUS (as many people think of Him)

Warner E. Sallman was an illustrator for religious magazines. In 1924 he needed a picture for a deadline the next day, but was coming up blank. Finally, he went to bed—then suddenly awoke with "a picture of the Christ in my mind's eye just as if it were on my drawing board." He quickly sketched a portrait of Jesus with long brown hair, blue eyes, a neatly trimmed beard, and a beatific look—which has now become the common image of Christ around the world. Since 1940, more than 500 million copies of Sallman's "Head of Christ" have been sold. It has been reproduced billions of times on calendars, lamps, posters, etc.

About three-quarters of American adults wear some kind of fragrance.

THE BIRTH OF *THE TONIGHT SHOW*, PART II

On page 468 we told you the story of Broadway Open House, *the first late-night TV talk show. The show had its problems and was cancelled after 13 months, but it led to* The Tonight Show, *the most successful talk show in history. Here's the next installment in the story.*

SILENT NIGHT

Broadway Open House went off the air on August 24, 1951, and NBC's late-night airwaves remained dark for three years. But Pat Weaver was still convinced that a late-night talk show could be successful. In 1954 he gave it another shot.

This time, rather than create a show himself, he hired comedian Steve Allen, a panelist on the CBS quiz show *What's My Line*, to do it for him.

MR. TONIGHT

Allen had been working on his own talk-show format off and on for several years. In the 1940s he was the midnight disc jockey on L.A.'s CBS radio affiliate. He spent so much time telling jokes between songs—and building a huge following in the process—that the station changed the show's format to live comedy, complete with a studio audience.

Before Allen went on the air, hardly anyone in Los Angeles had listened to radio late at night. But the show quickly became an institution. Big celebrities began dropping by to plug upcoming movies and do interviews.

CBS recognized Allen's promise and brought him to New York, where he briefly hosted a daytime TV show. But CBS didn't have a whole lot more for him to do. He was cooling his heels on *What's My Line* when he got the call from NBC.

"THE TONIGHT SHOW" IS BORN

On September 27, 1954, *The Tonight Show* premiered. Gene Rayburn (who later hosted *Match Game*) was the announcer, Steve Lawrence and Eydie Gorme made regular appearances, and Skitch Henderson conducted the orchestra—which even then included Doc Severinsen on the trumpet. Don Knotts, Tom Poston, and

---

The most common word spoken by a dying person is "Mother" or "Mommy."

other comedians performed skits, and Bill Dana, one of Allen's writers, invented his character Jose Jimenez on the show.

JUST PLAIN FOLKS

Allen also had several ordinary—albeit odd—folks who made regular appearances, including Mr. Shafer, a fast-talking farmer from upstate New York; Mrs. Sterling, an elderly woman who pestered Allen for presents; and Professor Voss, a quack who advocated bare-chested walks in the snow and drinking a gallon of water before breakfast each morning.

But the highlight of the show was Steve Allen and his improvisational comedic style. Today ad-lib gags are a staple of late-night talk shows, but in the early 1950s *everything* was scripted in advance—and Allen's make-it-up-as-you-go-along format was revolutionary. He conducted man-on-the-street interviews with pedestrians walking past his studio; he dressed up as a border patrol officer and flagged down motorists to inspect their cars for illegal fruit. A few minutes later he flagged a taxi, threw a salami into the back, and told the driver to take it to Grand Central Station. (He did.)

THANKS, STEVE

David Letterman's freewheeling style is more like Allen's than Johnny Carson's. And the similarity is no accident. Letterman, only seven years old when the first segment of *The Tonight Show* aired, grew up watching the program. Years later, he sent his writers to the Museum of Television and Radio in New York to screen old Steve Allen shows and look for ideas. Allen covered himself in tea bags and was dunked in a huge teacup; Letterman covered himself in Alka-Seltzer tablets and got dunked in a huge glass of water. Allen jumped in huge vats of Jell-O, so did Letterman. Allen sent a camera out the back door and into the street, and then ad-libbed with the people who walked by; Letterman did the same, making neighborhood merchants some of the biggest stars of his show.

END OF THE ROAD

As *The Tonight Show* grew in popularity, Allen began to feel constrained in his late-night hours. He wanted to prove himself in prime time. So NBC created *The Steve Allen Show* in October 1956 and ran it directly against the popular Ed Sullivan's *Toast of the Town* on Sunday night at 8:00 p.m. on CBS.

About 4% of Americans are vegetarians.

Allen kept working at *The Tonight Show* three nights a week, with comedian Ernie Kovacs and announcer Bill Wendell (who also announced *Late Night with David Letterman*) replacing him on Monday and Tuesday. NBC also cut *The Tonight Show* from 90 to 60 minutes.

By the end of the year, Allen recalls, "I realized I'd bitten off more than I could chew. One show had to go." The choice was simple: *The Tonight Show* had an audience of about 3 million; *The Steve Allen Show* had an audience of 35 million, and paid five times as much. Besides, Allen admits, "in those days none of us connected with *The Tonight Show* thought it was a big deal at all. It's amazing. It seems a big deal now. It's now part of the national psychological furniture."

The Tonight Show went off the air on January 25, 1957. No one knew if it would return.

* * *

INTERLUDE

In 1956 Pat Weaver had been forced out of NBC. The reason: General David Sarnoff, head of RCA (NBC's parent company), wanted to make his son, Robert, chairman of the network.

When Steve Allen quit *The Tonight Show*, the new chairman replaced it with his own idea—*America After Dark*, a combination news and entertainment show. It was a disaster. Sleepy viewers just couldn't get used to the jarring shifts between light entertainment and hard news reports. "A typical night might have coverage of a new jazz club, followed by a live report from the site of an airplane crash," Ronald Smith writes in *The Fight for Tonight*. "It was as if someone was flicking the dial back and forth between David Letterman and Ted Koppel . . . At that hour of the night, bewildered viewers simply turned the set off and went to sleep."

Chastened, Robert Sarnoff decided to resurrect *The Tonight Show* with a new host. But who was the right person for the job?

To find out, turn to page 598 for Part III of the story.

Abraham Lincoln hated being called "Abe."

DUMB CROOKS

Many Americans are worried about the growing threat of crime, but the good news is that there are plenty of crooks who are their own worst enemies. Want proof? Check out these news reports.

CAREFUL, THIS FINGER'S LOADED
MERCED, CA—"A man tried to rob a bank by pointing his finger at a teller, police said.

"Steven Richard King just held up his finger and thumb in plain sight and demanded money. The Bank of America teller told Mr. King to wait, then just walked away. Mr. King then went across the street to another bank . . . jumped over the counter, and tried to get the key to the cash drawer. But an employee grabbed the key and told him to 'get out of here.'

"Police officers found Mr. King sitting in the shrubs outside the bank and arrested him."

—*New York Times*, April 1997

STRANGE RESEMBLANCE
OROVILLE, CA—"Thomas Martin, former manager of a Jack In the Box restaurant, reported that he'd been robbed of $307 as the store was closing. He provided police sketch artist Jack Lee with a detailed description of the suspect. When Lee put his pad down, he observed that the drawing looked just like Martin. When questioned, Martin confessed."

—*Parade* magazine, December 1996

KEYSTONE KROOK
OAKLAND, CA—"According to the Alameda County District Attorney's office, in 1995 a man walked into an Oakland bank and handed the teller a note reading: *This is a stikkup. Hand over all yer mony fast.*

"Guessing from this that the guy was no rocket scientist, the teller replied, 'I'll hand over the cash as long as you sign for it. It's a bank policy: All robbers have to sign for their money.'

"The would-be robber thought this over, then said, 'I guess that's OK.' And he signed his full name and address.

"That's where the cops found him a few hours later."

—*Jay Leno's Police Blotter*

Bears don't hibernate in caves. They like hollow stumps or logs.

SHAKE YOUR BOOTIES

WICHITA, KS—"Charles Taylor was on trial for robbing a shoe store at knifepoint, accused of taking a pair of tan hiking boots and $69. As he listened to testimony in court, he propped his feet on the defense table. He was wearing a pair of tan boots.

"'I leaned over and stared,' the judge told a reporter later. 'I thought, Surely nobody would be so stupid as to wear the boots he stole to his own trial.' But when an FBI agent called the shoe store, he found out that the stolen boots were size 10, from lot no. 1046—the same size and lot number as the boots Taylor was wearing. The jury found Taylor guilty, and officers confiscated the boots. 'We sent him back to jail in his stocking feet,' the judge said."

—**From wire service reports, March 1997**

NEXT WEEK HE'S COMING BACK FOR BRAINS

"In March 1995, a twenty-six-year-old inmate walked away from his community release facility in South Carolina. He was recaptured a week later when he went back to pick up his paycheck."

—*Knuckleheads in the News,* **by John Machay**

OH, JUST BAG IT

"Not wishing to attract attention to himself, a bank robber in 1969 in Portland, Oregon, wrote all his instructions on a piece of paper rather than shouting.

"'This is a hold-up and I've got a gun,' he wrote and then held the paper up for the cashier to read.

"The bemused bank official waited while he wrote out, 'Put all the money in a paper bag.'

"This message was pushed through the grille. The cashier read it and then wrote on the bottom, 'I don't have a paper bag,' and passed it back. The robber fled."

—*The Book of Heroic Failures,* **by Stephen Pile**

Out of this world: 12% of Americans think they've seen UFOs.

PRESIDENTIAL INFLUENCE

Public service is only a part of our presidents' importance to us—they're also pop icons. Their clothes, their hobbies, and so on have an impact on our lives, too. Here are some examples.

THE ROCKING CHAIR
President: JFK

Influence: Until the 1960s, Americans only thought of rocking chairs as furniture for old folks or porches. Then Kennedy's physician recommended he use a rocking chair whenever possible for back therapy. In 1961 he was photographed at the White House sitting in an "old-fashioned cane-backed porch rocker." Overnight, the company that made the chair was inundated with orders. Sensing a hot fad, furniture makers started cranking out rockers. B. Altman, a New York department store, even devoted an entire floor to them. The result: rocking chairs became furniture for living rooms.

BROCCOLI
President: George Bush

Influence: In 1992 Bush commented that he didn't like broccoli when he was a kid, and he didn't like it now. "I'm president of the United States," he said, "and I'm not going to eat any more broccoli." The story was reported worldwide. Feigning outrage, a major broccoli producer shipped the White House 10 tons of the veggie. The arrival of the truck was carried *live* by CNN.

Campbell's Soups and *Women's Day* magazine co-sponsored a recipe contest called "How to Get the President to Eat Broccoli." With all the publicity, broccoli sales shot up 40%. "I can't begin to tell you how wonderful this has been for us," a broccoli industry spokesperson said. "The asparagus people were saying they wished Bush had picked on them instead."

PAINT-BY-NUMBERS
President: Dwight D. Eisenhower

Influence: Painting-by-numbers was already becoming popular

On average, Americans buy 1.5 toothbrushes a year.

when Ike was elected in 1952. He helped turn it into a national craze. As the media reported, Ike loved to paint, but didn't care about originality (his paintings were copied from postcards, photos, etc.) or results ("They're no fun when they're finished," he said). Plus, he couldn't draw—so he often had other artists outline pictures on his canvas. Naturally, he thought paint-by-numbers kits were great, and gave them his "official" endorsement in 1953 by handing out sets to his staff as Christmas presents. The craze peaked around 1954, but thanks in part to Ike, they're still with us.

GOING HATLESS
President: JFK
Influence: Believe it or not, kids, in 1960 "respectable" men were still expected to wear hats in public. (Not baseball caps but fedoras—the kind you see in old movies.) JFK ignored tradition and usually went hatless. When other men began copying him, there were storms of protest from the fashion industry. The *New York Times*, for example, reported on July 6, 1963:

> A British fashion magazine today stepped up its campaign to persuade President Kennedy to wear a hat and pointedly asked him how a hatless man could properly greet a lady. "How does the president acknowledge such an encounter?" asked *Tailor & Cutter* in an editorial . . . "The deft touch of a raised hat, politely pinched between thumb and forefinger . . . would bring a bright spark of gallantry to modern diplomatic moves."

JFK ignored their entreaties, and the hat industry ultimately bowed to the inevitable.

THE SAXOPHONE
President: Bill Clinton
Influence: When he was running for office, Clinton played his sax on TV—and received a ton of favorable publicity. At his inauguration he did it again, playing "Your Mama Don't Dance." In 1993 the *Wall Street Journal* noted that "thanks in part to President Clinton's willingness to toot his horn on national television, sales of saxophones are way up." Music teachers also reported a big increase in sax students . . . and CD sales of sax music—from Kenny G to John Coltrane—went through the roof.

Alaska has the highest percentage of Baby Boomers; Utah the lowest.

FASHIONABLE MATERNITY CLOTHES

First Lady: Jacqueline Kennedy

Influence: Before 1960 most pregnant women resigned themselves to staying out of public, and to looking embarrassingly dowdy when they ventured out. In the early 1960s Jackie Kennedy brought maternity clothes out of the closet. Although she was pregnant, she remained visible in public life, wearing stylish clothes adapted for her. As *Newsweek* commented:

> *Vogue* and *Harper's Bazaar* view [pregnancy] as mere plump frumpery, too impossibly unchic and rarely, if ever, mentionable. But with Jacqueline Kennedy being [as important as she is], the issue can hardly be obscured much longer. Pregnancy is fashionable; at the very least, it is no longer an excuse for looking *un*fashionable.

Clothesmaker Lane Bryant cashed in on the publicity with their new First Lady Maternity Fashion Ensemble. It was a hit, and maternity clothes have never been the same.

MISCELLANEOUS INFLUENCE

George Bush loved playing horseshoes. During his presidency, sales of the game went up 20%.

In 1962 *Newsweek* wrote: "When Jackie Kennedy sported Capri pants, women raced to buy them. When Jackie appeared in a roll-brimmed hat, millinery shops were rocked with orders for copies. So it was inevitable that when the president's wife took to wraparound sunglasses, a fad would follow. Indeed, despite a recent White House request that merchants not use the presidential family to push products, many of the fast-selling wraparounds still managed to focus their promotion on the First Lady. A big seller, for example, is the $15 *Jaqui*."

President Eisenhower helped popularize TV trays. Every night, reporters told the nation, Ike and his wife "eat supper off matching tray-tables in front of a bank of special TV consoles built into one wall of the White House family quarters." Ordinary families followed suit.

President Kennedy publicized the fact that he had taken the Evelyn Wood speed-reading course. For a time, enrollment at Evelyn Wood—and other courses—boomed.

In 1776 there were 2 million people in the United States.

VIDEO TREASURES

*How many times have you found yourself at a video store
staring at the thousands of films you've never heard of,
wondering which ones are worth watching? It happens to us
all the time—so we decided to offer a few recommendations
for relatively obscure, quirky videos you might like.*

DREAMCHILD (1985) *Drama*
Review: "A poignant story of the autumn years of Alice Hargreaves, the model for Lewis Carroll's *Alice in Wonderland*. Film follows her on a visit to New York in the 1930s, with fantasy sequences by Jim Henson's Creature Shop." (*Video Hound's Golden Movie Retriever*) Stars: Coral Brown, Ian Holm, Peter Gallagher. Director: Gavin Millar.

THE STUNT MAN (1980) *Mystery / Suspense*
Review: "Nothing is ever quite what it seems in this fast-paced, superbly crafted film. It's a Chinese puzzle of a movie and, therefore, may not please all viewers. Nevertheless, this directorial tour de force by Richard Rush has ample thrills, chills, suspense, and surprises for those with a taste for something different." (*Video Movie Guide*) Stars: Peter O'Toole, Steve Railsback, Barbara Hershey. Director: Richard Rush.

SUGAR CANE ALLEY (1984; French, with subtitles) *Drama*
Review: "Beautifully made drama about an 11-year-old boy and his all-sacrificing grandmother, surviving in a Martinique shantytown in the 1930s. Rich, memorable characterizations; a humanist drama of the highest order." (*Leonard Maltin's Movie & Video Guide*) Stars: Gary Cadenat, Darling Legitimus. Director: Edwin L. Marian.

SMILE (1975) *Satire*
Review: "Hilarious, perceptive satire centering around the behind-the-scenes activity at a California 'Young American Miss' beauty pageant, presented as a symbol for the emptiness of American middle-class existence." (*Leonard Maltin's Movie & Video Guide*) Stars: Bruce Dern, Barbara Feldon. Director: Michael Ritchie.

Only pharoahs were allowed to eat mushrooms in ancient Egypt.

WRONG IS RIGHT (1982) *Comedy*
Review: "Sean Connery, as a globe-trotting television reporter, gives what may be the best performance of his career, in this outrageous, thoroughly entertaining end-of-the-world black comedy, written, produced, and directed by Richard Brooks. An updated version of *Network and Dr. Strangelove.*" (*Video Movie Guide*)
Stars: Sean Connery, Robert Conrad. Director: Richard Brooks.

MIRACLE MILE (1988) *Thriller*
Review: "A riveting, apocalyptic thriller about a mild-mannered misfit who . . . standing on a street corner at 2 a.m., answers a ringing pay phone. The caller . . . announces that bombs have been launched for an all-out nuclear war . . . A surreal, wicked farce sadly overlooked in theatrical release." (*VideoHound's Golden Movie Retriever*) Stars: Anthony Edwards, Mare Winningham.
Director: Steve DeJamatt.

TIME BANDITS (1981) *Fantasy*
Review: "This subversive kid's adventure teams a youngster with a criminally minded pack of dwarves on the run from the Supreme Being through holes in time. A highly imaginative, quirky mix of Monty Python humor, historical swashbuckler, and kid's gee-whiz adventure." (*Seen That, Now What?*) Stars: Sean Connery, David Warner. Director: Terry Gilliam.

DEFENSE OF THE REALM (1985) *Thriller*
Review: "A British politician is accused of selling secrets to the KGB through his mistress and only a pair of dedicated newspapermen believe he is innocent . . . They discover a national cover-up conspiracy. An acclaimed, taut thriller." (*Video Hound's Golden Movie Retriever*) Stars: Gabriel Byrne, Greta Scacci. Director: David Drury.

NIGHT MOVES (1975) *Mystery*
Review: "While trying to deal with his own sour private life, a P.I. is hired by a fading Hollywood star to track down her reckless daughter, involving him in art smuggling, murder, and sex on Florida's Gulf Coast. This incisive psychological drama manages to be both intelligent and entertaining." (*Seen That, Now What?*) Stars: Gene Hackman, Jennifer Warren. Director: Arthur Penn.

Poll results: 15% of Americans wet their toilet paper before using it.

LITTLE SHOP OF HORRORS

In this chapter, we feeeed you the story of one of the most unlikely—but most popular—cult films of all time.

ALL SET TO GO

A few days after he finished work on a film called *A Bucket of Blood* in 1959, director Roger Corman had lunch with the manager of Producers Studio, the company that rented him office space. The manager mentioned that another company had just finished work on a film, and the sets were still standing.

"I said, just as a joke, 'If you leave the sets up, I'll come in for a couple of days and see if I can just invent a picture, because I have a little bit of money now and some free time,'" Corman recalled years later. "And he said, 'Fine.' The whole thing was kind of a whim. I booked the studio for a week."

TO B OR NOT TO B

Corman, 32, had only been directing films for five years. (*The Monster from the Ocean Floor* and *Attack of the Crab Monsters* were two early titles.) But he was already developing a reputation for making profitable movies very quickly on minuscule budgets—a skill that would later earn him the title "King of the B films."

He had filmed *A Bucket of Blood*, a "beatnik-styled horror comedy" in only five days, a personal record. He bet his friend at Producers Studio that he could make this next film in 48 hours.

COMING UP WITH A SCRIPT

Corman called scriptwriter Chuck Griffith, who'd written *A Bucket of Blood*, and told him to write a new variation of the same story. The only limitations: it had to be written for the existing sets, and Corman had to be able to rehearse all the scenes in three days . . . and then film them in two.

Griffith took the assignment. He and Corman went bar-hopping to brainstorm an outline for the film. It was a long night: Griffith got drunk, then got into a barroom brawl. Somehow, he and

---

Vitamin C is also important because it helps us absorb iron.

Corman still managed to come up with a story about a nerdy flower shop employee and his man-eating plant.

DEJA VU
Griffith turned in the final script a week later. It was essentially a warmed-over version of A Bucket of Blood.

- In A Bucket of Blood, a well-meaning sculptor accidentally kills his landlord's cat, then hides the evidence by turning it into a sculpture, which he titles Dead Cat. When the sculpture brings him the notoriety he's always sought, he starts killing people and making them into sculptures, too.

- In Little Shop of Horrors, a well-meaning flower shop employee becomes a local hero after he accidentally creates a man-eating plant (which he names Audrey Jr., after his girlfriend) by crossbreeding a Venus flytrap with a buttercup. He then begins killing people to keep the plant—and his fame—alive.

LOW BUDGET
The filming took place between Christmas and New Year's Eve 1959. Corman spent a total of $23,000 on the film, including $800 for the finished script and $750 for three different models of Audrey Jr.: a 12-inch version, a 6-foot version, and a full-grown 8-foot version.

Corman pinched pennies wherever he could. Jack Nicholson, 23 years old when Corman hired him to play a masochistic dental patient named Wilbur Force, remembers that Corman wouldn't even spend money making copies of the script: "Roger took the script apart and gave me only the pages for my scenes. That way he could give the rest of the script to another actor or actors."

Corman also paid a musician named Fred Kat $317.34 for the musical score . . . but as John McCarty and Mark McGee write in The Little Shop of Horrors book,

> Katz simply used the same score he'd written for A Bucket of Blood, which has also been used in another Corman film, The Wasp Woman, and would be used yet again in Corman's Creature from the Haunted Sea. Whether or not Corman was aware he was buying the same score three times is unknown.

There are 31,557,600 seconds in a year.

Even if a shot wasn't perfect, Corman would use it if he could. In the first day of shooting, Jackie Haze and Jack Nicholson accidentally knocked over the dentist's chair, spoiling the shot and breaking the chair. When the property master said it would take an hour to fix the chair so they could reshoot the scene, Corman changed the script to read, "The scene ends with the dentist's chair falling over."

Corman was legendary for getting as much work out of his actors and writers as he could. One example: Chuck Griffith, who wrote the script, also played a shadow on a wall, the man who runs out of the dentist's office with his ear bitten, and the thief who robs the flower shop. He also directed the Skid Row exterior shots and provided the voice for Audrey Jr. (Griffith's voice wasn't supposed to make it into the final film—he was just the guy who stood off camera and read the plant's lines so the actors would have something to react to. Corman had planned to dub in another actor's voice later. "But it got laughs," Griffith says, "so Corman decided to leave it the way it was.")

Corman also saved money by filming all of the Skid Row exteriors actually in Skid Row, and using "real bums to play the bums." Griffith, who directed the scenes, paid them 10¢ per scene, using the change he had in his pocket.

THAT'S A WRAP

Corman finished all of the interior shots in the required two days, then spent a couple more evenings filming the exterior shots. To this day, *Little Shop of Horrors* is listed in the *Guinness Book of World Records* for "the shortest shooting schedule for a full-length, commercial feature film made without the use of stock footage."

In this original release, *Little Shop of Horrors* was only a modest success. It didn't develop its cult following until the late 1960s, when it became a Creature Feature classic on late-night TV. It was adapted into an off-Broadway musical in 1982, which was itself adapted into a new $20 million film in 1987.

"*Little Shop of Horrors* is the film that established me as an underground legend in film circles," Corman says. "People come up to me on the street who have memorized parts of the dialogue. I suppose you could say it was *The Rocky Horror Picture Show* of its time."

PUBLIC PROPOSALS

Asking someone to marry you used to be a solemn, private matter. No longer. Now it's a public event, complete with trumpeters, billboards, and an audience—ranging from a few passersby to hundreds of thousands of TV viewers. (Incidentally, the answers to these proposals were all "yes"!)

DAN CAPLIS
Proposed: On television
Story: Caplis and Aimee Sporer worked for Channel 4 news in Denver—he was the legal expert, she was the anchorwoman. One night they were sitting next to each other during a broadcast. After explaining how judges decide on criminal sentences, Caplis looked at the camera and told the audience that since they were like family, he wanted to share an important moment with them. He took a ring out of his pocket and put it in front of Sporer. Choked up, she said, "I would love to marry you," then turned away from the camera. The quick-thinking cameraman cut for a commercial break.

LOU DROESCH
Proposed: At a city council meeting
Story: Pam Ferris, the city clerk of Louisville, Colorado, was taking notes at the council meeting when Droesch, a local mortgage banker, went up to the microphone to voice his opinion about an issue. It wasn't the issue anyone expected. He said: "I'm crazy about your city clerk. And I ask that the city fathers approve my asking for her hand in marriage." Then he got down on one knee and popped the question.

NEIL NATHANSON
Proposed: In a crossword puzzle
Story: Neil and his girlfriend, Leslie Hamilton, liked doing the San Francisco *Examiner* crossword puzzles together. "One Sunday," writes Michael Kernan in *Smithsonian* magazine, "Leslie noticed that many of the puzzle answers struck close to home.

The Canary Islands are named after a breed of large dogs.

"State or quarterback" turned out to be MONTANA, which is where she came from. "Instrument" was CELLO, which she plays. "I was about halfway through the puzzle," she remembers, "when I figured out that a string of letters running across the middle of the puzzle said 'DEAR—WILL YOU MARRY ME NEIL.' . . . Sure enough, it was Leslie."

Neil, it turns out, had been working with Merl Reagle, the *Examiner's* puzzlemaker, for four months. They invited him to the wedding. "I never did finish the puzzle," Leslie added.

JIM BEDERKA

Proposed: During a college graduation ceremony
Story: Paige Griffin was sitting with her class, ready to graduate from Ramapo College in Mahwah, New Jersey, when her boyfriend, Jim, showed up and asked her to leave the group for a minute. She said no—she didn't want to cause a disturbance. He kept insisting, getting more and more aggravated. Finally she gave in. As she stepped into the aisle, she saw two trumpeters decked in medieval garb standing at the stage. Between them: a sign reading "Paige, will you marry me?" When she accepted, the trumpeters held up a "She said yes" sign; 1,500 people applauded.

MARK STEINES

Proposed: At an AIDS benefit
Story: Leanza Cornett, 1993's Miss America, paused during her performance at a 1994 AIDS benefit in Los Angeles to select a raffle winner. She stuck her hand in a bag, pulled out a piece of paper, and read: "Let's get married. Wanna? Check the appropriate response: Yes or Yes." She thought it was a joke . . . until she realized there was a ring attached.

BOB BORNACK

Proposed: On a billboard
Story: In the Chicago suburb of Wood Dale, Bornack put up a billboard that read: "Teri, Please Marry Me! Love, Bob." The sign company immediately got 10 calls from women named Teri who wanted to know if it was "their" Bob. "One Teri called in a total panic because she's dating two Bobs," said an employee. "She didn't know which one to answer." (It wasn't either of them.)

Flush away! The average toilet will last about 50 years before it has to be replaced.

BRAND NAMES

Here are more origins of commercial names.

ADIDAS. Adolph and Rudi Dassler formed Dassler Brothers Shoes in Germany in 1925. After World War II, the partnership broke up, but each brother kept a piece of the shoe business: Rudi called his new company Puma; Adolph, whose nickname was "Adi," renamed the old company after himself—Adi Dassler.

PENNZOIL. In the early 1900s two motor oil companies—Merit Oil and Panama Oil—joined forces and created a brand name they could both use: Pennsoil (short for William Penn's Oil). It didn't work—consumers kept calling it Penn-soil. So in 1914 they changed the s to a z.

DIAL SOAP. The name refers to a clock or watch dial. The reason: It was the first deodorant soap, and Lever Bros. wanted to suggest that it would prevent B.O. "all around the clock."

WD-40. In the 1950s the Rocket Chemical Company was working on a product for the aerospace industry that would reduce rust and corrosion by removing moisture from metals. It took them 40 tries to come up with a workable Water Displacement formula.

LYSOL. Short for *lye solvent*.

MAZDA. The Zoroastrian god of light.

NISSAN. Derived from the phrase *Nissan snagyo*, which means "Japanese industry."

ISUZU. Japanese for "50 bells."

MAGNAVOX. In 1915 the Commercial Wireless and Development Co. created a speaker that offered the clearest sound of any on the market. They called it the *Magna Vox*—which means *great voice* in Latin.

According to some sources, Crisco makes a good makeup remover.

TELEVISION HOAXES

*A majority of Americans say they get their info and opinions on
world events from TV news and documentaries. When you consider
how easy it is to fake TV "news," that's a pretty scary thought.*

THE TAMARA RAND HOAX

Background: On March 30, 1981, President Ronald Reagan
was shot by John Hinkley Jr. A few days later KNTV in Las
Vegas ran a segment of the *Dick Maurice and Company* show that
had been taped on January 6, 1981—nearly two months earlier.

Incredibly, the tape showed a psychic named Tamara Rand pre-
dicting that Reagan would be shot in March or April "by a young,
fair-haired man who acted alone" and had the initials "J.H." The
prediction-come-true was so amazing that a few days later ABC's
Good Morning America and NBC's *Today* also broadcast it.

The Truth: An Associated Press reporter noticed that Rand was
wearing different rings on her fingers during the assassination segment than on the rest of the show. Her microphone was attached
to her shirt a different way, too. The reporter did some investigating . . . and discovered that the day *after* the assassination, Rand
and Maurice had sneaked back to the TV studios wearing the same
clothes they'd worn in the first interview, and taped a new one.
Then they combined the two videotapes to make it look as if Rand
had predicted the assassination.

What Happened: Maurice and Rand admitted the hoax. Maurice
was suspended from his show; Rand faded back into obscurity.

BLOOD SPORT

Background: On April 29, 1991, Denver's Channel 4 KCNC
News began airing "Bloodsport," a four-part series on Denver's dogfighting underworld. Exhibit A was an anonymous home video
that someone had mailed to KCNC reporter Wendy Bergen. The
footage showed dogs working out on treadmills and fighting one
another. The story launched a police investigation into illegal dogfighting in Denver.

Chew gum while peeling onions. It may keep you from crying.

The Truth: On May 2, 1991, the broadcasting columnist for the *Rocky Mountain News* reported that the "anonymous home video" was actually footage of a dogfight that had been staged for KCNC. Bergen and her cameraman denied the charge, but a few days later the man who staged the fights agreed to cooperate with the police in exchange for immunity. It turned out that the fights had been staged, and that the workout scenes had even been filmed on the cameraman's own treadmill.

As Bob Tamarkin writes in *Rumor Has It,* "After finding out that attending a dogfight was a felony punishable by up to four years in prison, Bergen re-edited the tape to make it look like a home video. She sent it to herself and told executives that it had arrived anonymously."

What Happened: Bergen and her cameraman eventually confessed; both were fired and each was indicted on felony charges. Bergen was found guilty of conspiracy, being an accessory, and one count of dogfighting. She was fined $20,000.

THE PREGNANT MAN OF THE PHILIPPINES

Background: In May 1992 newspapers in the Philippines began running stories about "Carlo," a male nurse who was actually a hermaphrodite—a person born with complete sets of both male and female sexual organs. Carlo claimed he was six months pregnant, and he had a bulging belly to prove it. "I feel proud that I'm going to be the mother of a baby boy," he told reporters. "I'm happy now that I'm really feeling fulfilled like a complete woman." NBC's *Today* picked up the story, and Bryant Gumbel interviewed Carlo on the air.

The Truth: A few days after the *Today* interview, a gynecologist examined Carlo and quickly discovered that 1) he wasn't pregnant, 2) he wasn't a hermaphrodite, and 3) he looked pregnant because he was wearing a fake belly under his shirt. "Carlo" was actually Edwin Bayron, and the pregnancy was part of a scheme to have his gender legally changed to female so that he could marry his male lover, a 21-year-old Army officer, in the Catholic Church.

What Happened: Bayron went underground after the hoax was exposed; Gumbel apologized on the air.

Research reports: An average 4-year-old child asks 437 questions a day.

DATELINE NBC

Background: On November 17, 1992, *Dateline NBC* aired a story attacking the safety record of GM trucks that had "sidesaddle" gas tanks. The story included NBC's own crash tests, which showed two of the trucks exploding into flames when hit by another car in a side impact.

The Truth: As a multi-million-dollar lawsuit filed by GM later alleged, NBC had attached tiny model rocket engines to the trucks to make them burst into flames. Furthermore, the lawsuit alleged, "NBC did not disclose that the fire lasted only 15 seconds, that gasoline had leaked from an ill-fitting cap, and that its own correspondent had argued that the tests were unscientific and should not be aired."

What Happened: NBC settled the lawsuit with GM in February 1993 and as part of the settlement, apologized to GM publicly for staging the crash. NBC News president Michael Gartner was fired 21 days later, and the incident became famous as "a video-age symbol of irresponsible journalism."

*   *   *

LIFE'S LITTLE IRONIES

- Astronaut Buzz Aldrin's mother's maiden name was *Moon*.

- The only member of the band ZZ Top without a beard has the last name *Beard*.

- On January 4, 1971, Geroge Mellendorf, a soldier in Vietnam, sent Pres. Richard Nixon this letter: "Dear President Nixon: It seems nobody cares if we get our mail. We are lucky to get it twice a week. Sir, someone is not doing their job." It was delivered to Mr. Nixon in February 1978, seven years later.

- On January 2, 1997, famous psychic Jeanne Dixon made this celebrity prediction: "A famous entertainer [will] leave a nation in mourning within weeks." On January 25, three weeks later, she died of a heart attack.

FAMOUS FOR BEING NAKED

We know—this sounds a little off-color. Butt . . . er . . . we mean but . . . it's just another way to look at history.

LADY GODIVA, wife of Earl Leofric, lord of Coventry, England, in the 1100s

Famous for: Riding horseback through Coventry, covered only by her long blonde hair.

The bare facts: Lady Godiva was upset by the heavy taxes her husband had imposed on poor people in his domain. When she asked him to give the folks a break, he laughingly replied that he'd cut the taxes if she would ride through the town naked. To his shock, she agreed. But she requested that townspeople stay indoors and not peek while she rode through the streets. Legend has it that they all complied expect for one young man named Tom, who secretly watched through a shutter . . . which gave us the term "peeping Tom."

ARCHIMEDES (287–212 B.C.), a "classic absent-minded professor" and one of the most brilliant thinkers of the Ancient World

Famous for: Running naked through the streets of ancient Syracuse, screaming "Eureka!"

The bare facts: Archimedes' friend, King Hieron II of Syracuse, Sicily, was suspicious that his new crown wasn't solid gold. Had the goldsmith secretly mixed in silver? He asked Archimedes to find out. As Peter Lafferty recounts in his book, *Archimedes:*

> Archimedes took the crown home and sat looking at it. What was he to do? He weighed the crown. He weighed a piece of pure gold just like the piece the goldsmith had been given. Sure enough, the crown weighed the same as the gold. For many days, he puzzled over the crown. Then one evening . . . the answer came to him.
>
> That night, his servants filled his bath to the brim with water. As Archimedes lowered himself into the tub, the water overflowed onto the floor. Suddenly, he gave a shout and jumped

---

No surprise: People laugh least in the first hour after waking up in the morning.

out. Forgetting that he was naked, he ran down the street to the palace shouting "Eureka!" ("I have found it!")

Archimedes, presumably still wearing his birthday suit, explained his discovery to the king: "When an object is placed in water," he said, "it displaces an amount of water equal to its own volume."

To demonstrate, he put the crown in a bowl of water and measured the overflow. Then he put a lump of gold that weighed the same as the crown into the bowl. "The amount of water was measured," writes Lafferty, "and to the king's surprise, the gold had spilled less than the crown." It was proof that the goldsmith really *had* tried to cheat the king. The secret: "Silver is lighter than gold, so to make up the correct weight, extra silver was needed. This meant that the volume of the crown was slightly larger than the gold, so the crown spilled more water."

Archimedes became famous for his discovery. We can only guess what happened to the goldsmith.

RED BUTTONS, popular red-headed actor of the 1940s and 1950s

Famous for: Being the first person ever to appear naked on TV.

The bare facts: In the early 1950s Red did a guest spot on the *Milton Berle Show*, which was broadcast live. One skit featured Berle as a doctor and Buttons as a shy patient who wouldn't disrobe for his exam. Buttons wore a special "breakaway" suit—the coat, shirt, and pants were sewn together so they'd all come off when Berle yanked on the shirt collar. As he explained in *The Hollywood Walk of Shame:*

> When my character refused to get undressed, Milton was supposed to grab my shirt front and rip the entire thing off—and I'd be left standing there in old-fashioned, knee-to-neck piece underwear.
>
> Well, Milton reached for my shirt and accidentally grabbed me *under* the collar. And when he yanked at my breakaway suit, everything came off—including my underwear! We were on live television and there I stood—nude in front of a studio audience and all the people watching at home. When I realized what had happened, I got behind Milton, who was as shocked as I was, but had the presence of mind to announce the next act and have the curtain closed.

Buttons said he turned "as red as my hair."

A bee has 5,000 nostrils. It can smell an apple tree that's 2 miles away.

LITTLE THINGS MEAN A LOT

"The devil's in the details," says an old proverb. And in the profits too. The littlest thing can mean big bucks. Here are a few examples.

A MINUS SIGN

The story: In 1962 an Atlas-Agena rocket that was carrying the Mariner 1 satellite into space was launched from Cape Canaveral. Unfortunately, the rocket went off course and ground controllers had to push the self-destruct button. The whole thing exploded. Investigators found that someone had left a minus sign out of the computer program. Cost to U.S. taxpayers: $18.5 million.

A LETTUCE LEAF

The story: In 1993 Delta Airlines was looking for ways to reduce costs to compete in the cutthroat airline industry. They discovered that by just eliminating the decorative piece of lettuce served under the vegetables on in-flight meals, they could save over $1.4 million annually in labor and food costs.

A SHOE

The story: On September 18, 1997, the Tennessee Valley Authority had to close its Knoxville nuclear power plant. The plant stayed shut for 17 days, at a cost of $2.8 million. Cause of the shutdown: "human error." A shoe had fallen into an atomic reactor.

A DECIMAL POINT

The story: In 1870 the government published a table of nutritional values for different foods. According to the charts, spinach had ten times as much iron as other vegetables. Actually, a decimal point had been misplaced; spinach has about the same amount as other veggies. But a popular misconception had already taken hold that spinach promotes strength. Long-term benefit: It ultimately gave us Popeye the Sailor, who's "strong to the finish,'cause I eats my spinach."

The Indian hero Geronimo was once kicked out of church for gambling.

FAMILIAR PHRASES

*Where do these familiar terms and phrases come from? Etymologists
have researched them and come up with these explanations.*

WHAT A SUCKER!

Meaning: A pushover, an easy mark for a con
Origin: Early settlers in the New World found a strange
fish that fed along the bottom of rivers and streams. They called
it a *sucker*. Soon, any fish that resembled it was referred to as a
sucker—and this included so many types of fish that practically
any time someone threw a hook in the water, they caught "a
sucker." Eventually, the term was applied to a person who'd fall
for anything.

TO HECKLE SOMEONE
Meaning: To disturb a speaker, jeer at
Origin: In medieval times, a brush with iron teeth, called a *heckle*,
was used to split and comb the fibers from flax stalks in clothmak-
ing. By the 15th century the word had become a verb meaning "to
scratch with a steel brush" or "to look for weak points."

DIDDLY-SQUAT
Meaning: Very little of something; small change
Origin: Carnival lingo. Carny barkers referred to nickels and
dimes—the going rate for games of chance—as "*Diddle-e-squat*,"
yelling to passers-by: "Step right up . . . All it costs is diddle-e-
squat."

FROM PILLAR TO POST
Meaning: Driven from one difficulty to another
Origin: The sport of tennis arrived in England in the early 1600s.
It was played in grassy estate courtyards. The gate was at one end
of the court and the mansion was at the other. So a spirited game
would see competitors running back and forth between the pillars
of the mansion and the post of the gate.

Denny's restaurants used to be known as "Danny's" restaurants.

THE SPIDER DANCE

Here's an interesting little tale about a classic folk dance.

DANCE FEVER

Over the last 2,000 years there have been occasional instances of mass hysteria that scientists call "epidemic dancing." Entire towns or provinces will begin wild, spontaneous dancing, often accompanied by hallucinations.

Perhaps the most serious outbreak took place in July 1374, in the French town of Aix-la-Chapelle. As Frederick Cartwright writes in *Disease and History,*

> The sufferers began to dance uncontrollably in the streets, screaming and foaming at the mouth. Some declared they were immersed in a sea of blood, others claimed to have seen the heavens open to reveal Christ enthroned with the Virgin Mary . . . Streams of dancers invaded the Low Countries, moved along the Rhine, and appeared throughout Germany . . . In the later stages, the dancers often appeared to be entirely insensible to pain, a symptom of hysteria.

Today, scientists and historians speculate the dancing was caused by eating rye bread contaminated with "ergot," a fungus that infects bread cereals. One of the chemical compounds created by ergot is lysergic acid diethylamide—LSD. So the dancers were essentially high on LSD. And long after the effects of the drug had worn off, mass hysteria kept them going.

We know about the hallucinogenic effects of LSD today . . . but until a few decades ago, no one had any idea what caused the mysterious outbreaks. In the 16th century, when a similar incident took place near Taranto, Italy, the townspeople blamed the *tarantula*, a local spider named after the town.

The tarantula was known for its painful bite, which was thought to be deadly. So when the dancers survived, the Tarantans were surprised. "In due course," John Ayto notes in *The Dictionary of Word Origins*, "the dancing came to be rationalized as a method of counteracting the effects of the spider's bite, and so the dance was named the *tarantella*."

Italians don't dance away their spider bites anymore, but they still have a lively folk dance called the *tarantella*.

The White House was originally called the "Presidential Palace."

UNLUCKY STARS

They had successful acting careers . . . but might have been even
more successful if it hadn't been for one single decision. Here
are some stories about "the one that got away."

BUDDY EBSEN
Background: Ebsen eventually became famous as Jed
Clampett in the 1962–1971 sitcom *The Beverly Hillbillies*. But
in the 1930s he was an up-and-coming young singer/dancer.
The story: After appearing in several films as an MGM contract
player, Ebsen got his big break in 1938 when he got the part of the
Scarecrow in *The Wizard of Oz*. But Ray Bolger, cast as the Tin
Man, was determined to play the Scarecrow instead. He launched
a relentless campaign for the part . . . and Ebsen, tired of saying no,
finally agreed to swap roles.

It was a costly decision. The make-up department was using aluminum powder to make the Tin Man's face look metallic; Ebsen
developed a severe allergy to it. Nine days after the film went into
production, Ebsen wound up in an oxygen tent at Good Samaritan
Hospital; he'd inhaled so much of the powder that his lungs were
coated with aluminum. Unsympathetic studio execs kept calling
the hospital, wondering when he was coming back to work. Finally
director Mervyn LeRoy simply hired another actor (Jack Haley) to
play the Tin Man.

Ebsen recovered from the aluminum allergy in a few weeks. His
career didn't bounce back as fast, though. He appeared in a handful
of movies in the 1940s, but didn't make a real impression until
1955, when he played Davy Crockett's sidekick in Disney's *Davy*
Crockett, King of the Wild Frontier. He became a TV star in *Hillbillies*
in 1962, but never made it big in the movies.

ELVIS PRESLEY
Background: Elvis left a legacy of about 30 movies, most of them
inane formula films like *Harum Scarum* and *Tickle Me*. But at the
end of his career, the King came close to doing something really
special onscreen.
The story: In Joe Esposito's book *Good Rockin' Tonight*, he reveals
that in 1974, Barbra Streisand offered Elvis "the kind of part he'd

---

A brown bear can run faster than a horse at full gallop.

dreamed of." Elvis was performing at the Las Vegas Hilton. After the show, Streisand and her boyfriend, Jon Peters (then a well-known Hollywood hairdresser), visited him backstage.

"Elvis, can we go someplace where we can talk in private?" she asked. "I have something I would like to tell you about." I suggested the room next to his dressing room, where Elvis rested between shows. Elvis asked me to come in with them. Barbra and Jon sat on the two chairs, Elvis on the bed, and I sat on the floor . . .

Barbra explained the purpose of her visit.

"Elvis, I bought the rights to the Judy Garland movie, A *Star Is Born*," she said. "I'm going to remake it, and I thought you might be interested in starring in it with me." Elvis hadn't been interested in making movies for a long time, but Barbra explained the entire story. Two hours later, he was hooked.

"I'll have to think about it. [My agent], the Colonel, will get back to you," he told her before she left. But to the guys he was more enthusiastic. "I'm going to do it!" he vowed.

It never happened. First, Presley's pals suggested that since Peters was going to produce the film, he'd make sure it showcased Barbra—not Elvis. Then they pointed out that Elvis and Barbra might have a hard time getting along. Elvis was shaken. He called his manager, Colonel Tom Parker, the next night and said he wanted to do the film—but had a few reservations. "Colonel, you think I'm going to take orders from that hairdresser?" he asked.

"I've got news for you," the Colonel said. "I guarantee that they'll turn the contract down because I'm going to request that you get top billing."

A few days later, the Colonel reported back to Elvis. He'd asked for top billing. "That took care of that," the Colonel said. Streisand and Peters never even responded to his offer.

Elvis, who never made another film, lost what he described as "an opportunity parallel to Frank Sinatra's performance in *From Here to Eternity*." That performance won Sinatra an Oscar in 1954 and revived his sagging career. Who knows? If Elvis had made the film, it might have turned his life around.

In the 1880s waterskiing was known as "plankgliding."

BURT WARD
Background: In 1966 Ward was playing Robin on ABC's phenomenally popular TV series *Batman* (produced by 20th Century Fox). He was one of the hottest properties in the country—quoted, copied, and mobbed by fans wherever he went—and he was ready to break into the movies.

The Story: "My agents submitted me to Larry Turman, a talented producer who was getting ready to produce *The Graduate* for Fox," Ward wrote in his autobiography, *Boy Wonder: My Life in Tights.*

I met with Larry and he told me that he wanted me for the lead role in his upcoming movie. The timing was perfect. The film was set to shoot during my hiatus from "Batman." Wow, was I ever excited.

Unfortunately, not only did Fox not want me to work for any other studio, but they refused to let me star in Larry's film. I was told that "Batman" was such an important series to Fox that they didn't want any dilution of Robin's character by having the same actor portray a movie role whose character wasn't the Boy Wonder.

At the time, I was sad and disappointed. When the movie was released and made a superstar out of the actor who replaced me—[Dustin Hoffman]—I wanted to jump off a building without my Batrope.

Batman went off the air about a year after *The Graduate* was filmed. Dustin Hoffman became one of America's best-known actors; Ward quickly faded from sight. "Over the course of the last 20 years," he writes, "I have run into Larry three times. Each time he said the same thing: 'Burt, I wanted you for that role.' I WANTED THAT ROLE! Pardon me while I scream."

TOM SELLECK
Could have starred in: *Raiders of the Lost Ark* (1981)
Background: After years of bouncing around Hollywood, Selleck got his break as a guest on *The Rockford Files* in the 1979–80 TV season. He was brought back for several episodes "by popular demand." But as the season ended, *Rockford* star James Garner quit. That left CBS with a hole in its schedule where a successful detective program had been . . . and a distaste for unmanageable "big stars." The network also had an empty studio in Hawaii, since the

long-running *Hawaii Five-O* had just ended. CBS's solution was *Magnum, P.I.*—a detective show based in Hawaii, starring new-comer Tom Selleck. It was scheduled for the 1980–81 season.

The story: As Cherry Moch and Vincent Virga describe it in their book *Deals*:

> Then the actor's dream became the actor's nightmare. [He was offered] two sensational jobs at once. Steven Spielberg and Geroge Lucas cast him [as Indiana Jones] in *Raiders of the Lost Ark*. They wanted a new face. They asked CBS to postpone "Magnum" . . . *Ark* would most likely make Selleck a superstar, a big plus for any aspiring TV series. Selleck held his breath when he wasn't praying.

> CBS refused, fearful of losing the already announced "Magnum" idea to a competitor and worried about the demands superstars make. The two jobs conflicted and Selleck belonged to CBS. He packed for Hawaii. As it happened, an actor's strike delayed [the 'Magnum'] production for three months. *Raiders*, shooting abroad, was exempt. "I could have gone to Europe and Africa," Selleck said with a sigh, "done *Raiders*, then come back to Hawaii to do 'Magnum.'"

Magnum ran for eight years and made Selleck famous, but he never really made it as a movie star. *Raiders of the Lost Ark*, starring Harrison Ford, became one of the top-grossing films of all time and helped establish Ford as the biggest box-office attraction in history.

*   *   *

RANDOM INFO: FIVE FOOD FLOPS

1. Cold Snap. An imitation ice cream mix introduced by Proctor & Gamble in the 1960s. "It had the taste of cold Crisco, took hours to prepare, and had directions similar to a model airplane."

2. Prest-O-Wine. Like alcoholic Kool-Aid. Just add sugar and water to a purple powder (secret ingredient: yeast), and wait a month.

3. Square Eggs. Introduced in 1989, a French company called Ov'Action, Inc. "Fully cooked, reconstituted egg cubes," 2/3" square. Had a 21-day shelf life and could be microwaved.

4. Spudka. A vodkalike beverage from Idaho potato-growers.

5. Whisp Spray Vermouth. "Good news for martini-drinkers"—vermouth in an aerosol spray container. Also recommended as a seasoning "for fresh fruit, meat, and seafood!"

Human beings have 46 chromosomes. Goldfish have 96.

YOU SHOULD NEVER...

A *few pearls of wisdom from* 599 Things You
Should Never Do, *edited by Ed Morrow.*

"Never argue with an idiot—
folks might not be able to tell
the difference."
—*Anonymous*

"Never believe anything until
it's been officially denied."
—*Antony Jay*

"Never sell the sheep's hide
when you can sell the wool."
—*German adage*

"Never say 'that was before
your time,' because the last
full moon was before their
time."
—*Bill Cosby*
(on talking to children)

"Never cut what you can
untie."
—*Joseph Joubert*

"Never slap a man who chews
tobacco."
—*Willard Scott*

"Never be flippantly rude to
elderly strangers in foreign
hotels. They always turn out
to be the King of Sweden."
—*Hector Hugh Munro*

"Never whisper to the deaf or
wink at the blind."
—*Slovenian adage*

"Never test the depth of a
river with both feet."
—*African adage*

"Never fight an inanimate
object."
—*P. J. O'Rourke*

"Never think you've seen the
last of anything."
—*Eudora Welty*

"Never eat anything whose
listed ingredients cover more
than a third of the package."
—*Joseph Leonard*

"Never play leapfrog with a
unicorn."
—*American adage*

"Never try to outsmart a
woman unless you are another
woman."
—*William Lyon Phelps*

"Never judge a book by its
movie."
—*J. W. Eagan*

Paradise, South Dakota, was named by two residents named Adam and Eve.

A GOLDEN TURKEY...
WITH WINGS!

There are bad movies . . . and then there are bad movies. Years ago the Medved brothers reintroduced stinkers like Plan 9 From Outer Space *to the public in their groundbreaking books,* The 50 Worst Films of All Time *and* The Golden Turkey Awards. *Then Mystery Science Theater 3000 gave us a chance to watch the best of the worst on TV. Today there are millions of bad movie buffs . . . and Uncle John is one of them.*

THE GIANT CLAW
Director: *Fred F. Sears*
Starring: *Jeff Morrow, Mara Corday, Morris Ankrum, Robert Shayne, Louis Merrill, Edgar Barrier, Clark Howat, Ruell Shayne*

The Plot: Mitch (Jeff Morrow), an electrical engineer, is testing aircraft for the military (huh?) when he spots a UFO that doesn't seem to show up on radar. Then, coincidentally, he and his girl-friend, Sally, are in a plane that's captured by the same UFO—which turns out to be a giant puppet . . . er, bird. The plane crash-lands, but Mitch and Sally are saved by a French-Canadian named Pierre—coincidentally, the guy on whose land the giant bird is nesting. See, that's the secret—the giant puppet . . . er, bird, pro-tected by an anti-matter shield, has flown all the way from another galaxy to lay an egg on Earth. Luckily, Mitch and Sally figure it out in time, find the nest, and come up with the only weapon that can defeat the Giant Puppet . . . er, Claw—a "mu-meson" projector. As Air Force General Buzzkirk looks on, they blow up the bird and save the Earth.

Commentary:

- *From **Badmovies.org**:* "One of the great B-movies of all time, I must say, this film made quite an impression. Any movie bold enough to feature a GIGANTIC ANTIMATTER SPACE BUZZARD (Hehehehehe!) is awesome! . . . To top it all off the winged terror is really absurd looking. Forget the premise, forget the execution—who the heck came up with that puppet? A terrific B-movie, it makes me giggle constantly."

Count for yourself: The average dictionary contains entries for 278,000 words.

- From **Creature Features:** "Inane, incredulous, incompetent—
  one of the truly laughable sci-fi turkeys of the '50s and a classic
  low-water mark for schlockmeister producer Sam Katzman . . .
  the titular talon is attached to a giant bird from space, which
  resembles a stuffed Thanksgiving turkey and is obviously pulled
  by wires . . . The asinine avian avenger, with long neck, bulging
  eyeballs and a plucked look, will have you rolling in the aisles."

- From **And You Call Yourself a Scientist!:** "For the most part,
  The Giant Claw is a run-of-the-mill little film, indistinguishable
  from most of its low-budget contemporaries. It has all the usual
  features: the Earth threatened with destruction, an initially
  antagonistic couple who fall in love, a fair mix of scientists and
  the military, pages of pseudo-scientific gobbledygook posing as
  dialogue, stock footage and stock music . . . For the first twenty-
  five minutes, a casual viewer might [suspect] that it's nothing
  more than a time-waster . . . But then we hit the twenty-sixth
  minute, and . . . we realize *The Giant Claw* has something that
  lifts it . . . into the rarefied atmosphere of the truly, unforget-
  tably awful: its monster, without exception the silliest monster
  in all fifties science-fiction, and a sure finalist in any all-time-
  silliest list."

- From **Jabootu's Bad Movie Dimension** (Ken Begg): "The Giant
  Claw has the distinction of featuring perhaps the silliest looking monster of any 1950s Sci-Fi flick. Genre vets Jeff Morrow
  and Mara Corday had no idea what they were in for when they
  signed on for this cheapie." That's literally true. Years later,
  Morrow confessed to a critic:

  We poor, benighted actors had our own idea of what the giant
  bird would look like—our concept was that this was something
  that resembled a streamlined hawk, possibly half a mile long, flying at such speeds that we could barely see it. That was the way
  we envisioned it. Well, the producer, Sam Katzman, decided for
  economic reasons not to spend the $10–$15,000 it would take
  to make a really good bird—he had it made in Mexico, probably
  for $19.98! [My family and I] went to a sneak preview in
  Westwood Village, and when the monster appeared on the
  screen it was like a huge plucked turkey, flying with these
  incredible squawks! And the audience went into hysterics.

  "Morrow was so mortified by what he was acting terrified of on

The world's first recorded tonsillectomy was performed in the year 1000 B.C.

the screen that he slunk out of the theater and met his family in the parking lot when the movie was over. [Then he] hastily retreated to his house" to avoid talking to anyone in the audience.

GREAT DIALOGUE

Narrator: "Once more a frantic pilot radios in a report on a UFO. A bird. A bird as big as a Battleship."

General Buzzkirk: "Three men reported they saw something. Two of them are now dead."

Mitch: "That makes me Chief Cook and Bottle Washer in a one-man Bird Watchers' Society!"

First Pilot: "This is Easy Baker Squadron Leader. Target below and to the side. See it?"

Second Pilot: "Yee-ow! Holy Toledo! I've seen some mighty big chicken-hawks back on the farm, but man, this baby takes the cake! Honest to Pete, I'll never call my mother-in-law an old crow again!"

Sally: "Will it work, Mitch?"

Mitch: "I don't know. I honestly don't have the faintest, foggiest idea. It's one of those cockeyed concepts that you pull down out of Cloud Eight somewhere in sheer desperation."

Scientist: "That bird is extra-terrestrial! It comes from outer space—from some godforsaken anti-matter galaxy millions and millions of light years from Earth. No other explanation is possible."

Narrator: "No corner of the Earth was spared the terror of looking up into God's blue sky and seeing, not peace and security, but the feathered nightmare on wings!"

Mitch: "The explosion was no accident! I did it on purpose! I used the mesic atom projector!"

Scientist: "What!"

Mitch: "Sure! We had the basic wiring all fouled up. It was a simple matter of adjusting the polarity on the main condensor terminals!"

The word *hussy* originally meant "housekeeper."

CLASSIC RUMORS

*Some rumors have been around so long that they deserve a
special place in the annals of gossip. Have you heard any of these?*

ORIGIN: Mid-1940s
RUMOR: The Harvard School of Medicine will buy your
body for $500. All you have to do is let them tattoo the
words "Property of Harvard Medical School" on the bottom of your
feet. When you die, your body will be shipped C.O.D. to Harvard.
HOW IT SPREAD: By word of mouth, back when $500 was a lot
of money.
THE TRUTH: Harvard says it has never paid people for their
bodies, and only accepts donations from people who specify in
their wills that they want their bodies to go to the school. Even
then, surviving relatives have to agree with the bequest. To this
day, the school receives several calls a week asking about the
program.

ORIGIN: The 1950s, heyday of big hair
RUMOR: A teenager got a beehive hairdo, and liked it so much
that she didn't wash it out—not even after a couple of weeks. She
sprayed it every morning with hair spray . . . and suddenly one
morning got a terrible stabbing pain on the top of her head. She
went to the doctor, who found a black widow that had stung the
woman on her scalp. She died from the sting a few days later.
THE TRUTH: This story changes with fashion trends. In the
1960s it was a mouse that tunneled into the brain of a "dirty hippie"; in the 1970s a man died on the floor of a disco when the
cucumber he stuffed down the front of his tight pants cut off circulation to his legs. Most versions have two morals: 1) bathe regularly and 2) avoid loony fashion fads.

ERA: The 1970s, during the energy crisis
RUMOR: The oil companies have a pill that can make a car go
100 miles on one gallon of gas. But they're sitting on it to keep
gasoline sales high. (Similar stories abounded about super-
carburetors and experimental cars that went 1,000 miles on
a gallon of gas.)

The Netherlands used to be known as the United States.

HOW IT SPREAD: Word of mouth, perhaps as an explanation for the fuel crisis, and/or a manifestation of public fear and suspicion of huge corporations.

THE TRUTH: Oil companies scoff at the idea, and no one has ever produced a shred of evidence. The story can be traced to an old gas station con, when hucksters would pull into a gas station, fill a fake gasoline tank with water, and then convince the gas station owner that the car ran on water and a magic pill. The con man then sold the owner a jar of the pills for all the cash he had.

ORIGIN: Late 1930s

RUMOR: If the wrapper of your Tootsie Roll Pop has a picture of the Indian aiming his bow and arrow at a star (called "Shooting Star" by the company) on it, you can send it in for a free bag of candies.

HOW IT SPREAD: From one kid to another since the Tootsie Roll Pop was introduced in 1936.

THE TRUTH: The Tootsie Roll Company has never redeemed an Indian wrapper for bags of candy. Even if it wanted to, it couldn't afford to, since nearly half of all Tootsie Roll Pops have the Indian on the label. The company responds to such requests with a legend of its own: in a special form letter, it explains that Shooting Star is the one who invented the process of putting the Tootsie Pop inside the lollipop. Every once in a while, Shooting Star returns to the factory and inspects the candy to make sure the company is following his instructions. The Indian on the wrapper is Shooting Star's seal of approval: it shows that he has personally inspected that piece of candy himself.

ORIGIN: The 1960s

RUMOR: It's against the law to kill a praying mantis. If you're caught, you can be fined.

THE TRUTH: Praying mantises are good for gardens, but there's no law protecting them—they're not endangered. (In fact, this rumor predated the Endangered Species Act by many years.) The tale was probably invented years ago by a gardener trying to keep kids from destroying the weird-looking, but beneficial, bugs.

J, the youngest letter in the English alphabet, was not added until the 1600s.

THE RESURRECTION OF ELVIS, PART 1

Since his death in 1977, Elvis's popularity has grown. Once he was just a singer. Now he's an icon with his own church (the Church of Elvis), and his own holy site (Graceland). It's an amazing phenomenon—but it hasn't been entirely accidental. Behind the scenes, a handful of people have orchestrated Elvis's return from the dead for their own benefit. Here's part of the inside story. For a more complete story, we recommend Elvis, Inc., by Sean O'Neal. It's entertaining bathroom reading.

BACK FROM THE DEAD

Ironically, the tale of Elvis's resurrection begins with the story of a vampire.

In 1960 Universal Studios dusted off a number of its classic horror films and released them for TV broadcast. It was the first time baby boom kids had ever seen the original *Frankenstein* (starring Boris Karloff), *The Wolfman* (starring Lon Chaney), or *Dracula* (starring Bela Lugosi)—and the films were phenomenally popular. In fact, a huge "monster" fad swept America . . . and Universal cashed in by licensing its characters for T-shirts, posters, lunch boxes, etc. One of the most popular images was Bela Lugosi in his Count Dracula costume.

Courting Universal

When Lugosi's window and son found out about the merchandising deals, they filed a suit to block them. Their argument: Lugosi's name and likeness should be passed on to his family, as his worldly assets had been. At the very least, they had a right to share in the profits.

The Lugosis won their lawsuit. But Universal appealed the decision. The second time around, appellate judges reasoned that if the names and likenesses of famous people could be inherited, the relatives of all public figures—past and present—could sue for royalties. Even George Washington's descendants could charge the federal government for the right to use his image on the $1 bill. The judges ruled in favor of Universal.

In Nepal, Mt. Everest is known as "Gauriosankar."

Laurel and Hardy

In 1975, after Laurel and Hardy's old films became popular on TV, the heirs of Stan Laurel and Oliver Hardy filed a similar lawsuit against the Hal Roach Studios. This time, the *heirs* won, throwing the entire issue of posthumous "intellectual property" into chaos.

Based on legal decisions, it was impossible to tell who owned the rights to a dead celebrity's image—the public . . . or the celebrity's family.

ELVIS PRESLEY

That was the situation when Elvis died from a drug overdose on August 16, 1977. His death was announced at 3:30 that afternoon; within a few hours, newspapers were speculating about his estate's value.

The media figured the King *had* to be worth a bundle: in his more than 20 years as a performer, he'd recorded 144 Top 40 songs, starred in more than 30 films (at one point he was the highest-paid actor in Hollywood), performed in hundreds of sold-out concerts, and sold more than 600 *million* records. No other recording artist had ever even come close to his accomplishments.

Estimates of Presley's fortune were as high as $150 million. (When John Lennon was assassinated three years later, he left an estate valued at more than $200 million.) But they were way off.

The Awful Truth

What the media failed to take into account was that Elvis was one of the most poorly managed and morbidly self-indulgent superstars in entertainment history. True, he had generated more than $4 billion in revenues during his career. But surprisingly little of the money found its way into his pockets—and even less stayed there.

Bad management and bad financial advice ate up about 60¢ of every dollar Elvis earned; letting the IRS fill out his tax forms (he really did—Elvis hated audits) took an extra 20¢ on the dollar. And the King had no trouble finding ways to blow the rest.

BUT WAIT! THERE'S MORE . . .

Unfortunately, that turned out to be just the tip of the iceberg. It turned out that his manager, Colonel Tom Parker, had made a deal that cost Elvis more than $500 million in potential earnings— including $320 million in lost royalties from records sold *after*

The word *mattress* originally meant "place to throw things."

Elvis's death alone. In March 1973 he'd sold RCA the royalty rights to all of Elvis's songs up to that point for $5.4 million. After Parker extracted his usual 50% commission, Elvis was left with $2.7 million—$1.35 million after taxes—for virtually his entire life's work. (Nearly all of that went to pay off ex-wife Priscilla Presley, who divorced him in October 1973.)

As Sean O'Neal writes in *Elvis, Inc.*, "The final agreement signed by Colonel Parker . . . may have been the single most financially damaging contract in the history of the music industry . . . Elvis sold the rights to the greatest master catalog in music history and was left with virtually nothing to show for it. Thereafter, his estate received no royalties at all for any songs Elvis recorded prior to March 1973."

ALL THE KING'S WEALTH

When the probate court tallied up the King's assets, all they found was Graceland, two airplanes, eight cars, two trucks, seven motorcycles, guns, jewelry, and miscellaneous other personal property. Total value: about $7 million. Elvis left everything to his 9-year-old daughter, Lisa Marie, who would inherit when she turned 25. Elvis's father, Vernon Presley, a man with a seventh-grade education, was charged with keeping the estate solvent until then.

Going, Going . . .

What little was left of the King's estate dwindled fast: In February 1978 the National Bank of Commerce sued the estate to collect $1.4 million in unpaid loans to the King. A short time later, the IRS upgraded its estimate of the estate's value and slapped it with millions in new inheritance taxes—payable immediately. Security and upkeep on Graceland ate up $500,000 a year.

Vernon Presley sold off the airplanes, jewelry, and Cadillacs, and even the house that Elvis had bought him, in a desperate scramble to keep the estate off the auction block. But the Presley estate was edging closer and closer to bankruptcy.

How was Graceland saved? To find out, turn to page 714.

The book *Green Eggs and Ham* contains only 50 different words.

THE FORTUNE COOKIE

Confucius says: "Good book in bathroom
is worth ten on library shelf."

HISTORY

"Legend has it," a TV reporter told CNN viewers recently, "that the first secret message was sent hundreds of years ago during the Teng Dynasty. A pastry chef was in love with the daughter of the Lotus Queen, and slipped her rice-paper love notes in baked wontons."

It's a romantic idea—but fortune cookies are actually American, not Chinese. They were invented by George Jung, a Los Angeles noodlemaker, in 1916, who gave them to customers at his Hong Kong Noodle Company to distract them while they waited for their orders.

HOW THEY'RE MADE

A mixture of rice flour and other ingredients is squirted onto small griddles and forms a little pancake. While it's still pliable, it's taken off the grill and folded around a paper fortune.

Traditionally, it was folded by hand. But in 1967 Edward Louie, owner of the Lotus Fortune Cookie Co., invented a machine that automatically inserts the fortunes as the cookies are folded. The strips of paper are sucked in by a vacuum.

THE FORTUNES

The first fortunes were sayings from Confucius, Ben Franklin, etc. But today they're upbeat messages. "Basically," says Edward Louie's son Gregory, "we're in the entertainment business. We give people what they want."

Edward Louie was once asked the secret of his success. He answered: "Nobody can resist reading their fortune, no matter how corny it is."

Louie's favorite fortunes were, "If you see someone without a smile, give them one of yours" and "Don't wait any longer, book that flight."

The U.S. mints $335,000 worth of nickels and $1.1 million worth of dimes a day.

Overall, the ten most popular fortunes are: 1. You will have great success; 2. You will soon be promoted; 3. You will step on the soil of many countries; 4. Your destiny is to be famous; 5. Your love life will be happy and harmonious; 6. Your present plans are going to succeed; 7. Good news will come to you from far away; 8. Now is the time to try something new; 9. Be confident and you will succeed; 10. You will be rich and respected.

A REAL FORTUNE COOKIE

Some fortunes have lottery numbers on the other side. Believe it or not, some people have played those numbers and won.

According to one account: "In March 1995 Barbara and Scott Turnbull got a fortune cookie at a China Coast restaurant in the Texas town of McAllen. They both bought tickets with the same numbers—and won $814,000 each. Meanwhile, Nealy LaHair got a fortune cookie with the same numbers from a China Coast restaurant in Dallas. She played the numbers and won $814,000 for herself."

BACK IN ASIA . . .

In 1989 an entrepreneur in Hong Kong began importing fortune cookies and selling them as luxury items. They were offered as "Genuine American Fortune Cookies."

On December 27, 1992, the Brooklyn-based Wonton Foods signed a joint venture agreement with a company in mainland China to build a fortune cookie plant there. The cookies had never been sold there before! Chinese fortunes are less direct than American ones. So instead of predictions, they offer comments like "True gold fears no fire," "The only way to catch a tiger cub is to go into the tiger's den," and "Constant grinding can turn an iron rod into a needle."

THE UNFORTUNATE COOKIE

In the 1970s a company in New England called the Unfortunate Fortune Cookie Company offered "dismal forebodings . . . for misanthropes, masochists, or what some might regard simply as realists."

What happened to them? They went out of business.

Crab-eating seals don't eat crabs.

MR. MOONLIGHT

*Some facts about our night-light in the sky, from astronomer
(and BRI member) Richard Moeschl.*

It takes 29 days, 12 hours, 44 minutes, and 3 seconds for the moon to go through all of its phases (from one full moon to the next). This is close to the length of a month—which is why the word *month* means "moon."

The light that comes from the moon is sunlight reflected off the moon's surface. It takes 1 1/4 seconds for the light to travel to Earth.

The moon is 2,160 miles in diameter—about a quarter of the Earth's diameter.

If the Earth were as big as a fist, the moon would be the size of a stamp . . . placed 10 feet away.

Astronauts have brought over 843 pounds of moon samples back to Earth.

The side of the moon we always see is called "the near side." The side we never see from Earth is "the far side." That's probably where Gary Larsen got the name of his comic strip.

There is no sound on the moon. Nor is there weather, wind, clouds, or colors at sunrise and sunset.

The average temperature on the moon is -283° to 266°F.

If you weigh 120 pounds on Earth, you would weigh 20 pounds on the moon—1/6 of your Earth weight.

A 3-foot jump on Earth would carry you 18 feet, 9 inches on the moon.

Since the moon spins once on its axis every 27 1/3 days—the same amount of time it takes to go around the Earth once—we end up seeing only one side of the moon (about 59% of its surface).

The moon is moving away from the Earth at the rate of about 1/8 inch a year.

The moon is smaller than any planet in the solar system, but relative to the size of the planets they orbit, our moon is the largest of the moons.

Florida's Disneyworld is larger than the entire city of Buffalo, New York.

LEMONS

*At one time or another just about everyone has owned a car
that they thought was a lemon. But chances are, your car
was nothing compared to these losers.*

THE WOODS SPIDER (1900)

In 1900 the Woods Motor Vehicle Company of Chicago came out with a carriage powered by a tiny electric motor. Like in horse-drawn taxicabs of the day, the driver sat in an elevated back seat, behind the passengers (who sat in the front seats).

Fatal Flaw: The steering. Horses *pulled* a carriage, so they easily turned the wheels when they changed direction. But in the Woods Spider, the driver had to wrestle the wheels himself to get them to turn—which was nearly impossible, since he was sitting in the rear of the car, behind the center of gravity. Bad weather was another problem. The passenger seat had its own convertible top. When it was closed, it blocked the driver's view—he had to crouch and peek through a tiny window, over the passengers' shoulders, to see the road ahead. If passengers were too tall or fat, he couldn't see at all. In 1901 Woods succumbed to logic and moved the driver up front.

THE MACDUFF AEROPINION/PNEUMOSLITO (1904)

Impressed by early aeroplanes, the folks at MacDuff designed a propeller-driven car. (The prop was placed in back, like a giant fan.) In heavy snow, you could slap small wooden skis onto each tire and—voila! The Aeropinion became the Pneumoslito, a propeller-driven sled that flew over frozen turf.

Fatal Flaw: First and foremost, it was tough to handle. But it was a menace, too. In summer, the propeller kicked up enough dust on dirt roads to blind everyone behind it for about a block and a half—a big problem when nearly all roads were unpaved. And the whirling blades were also potential disasters: they could make sausage out of any pedestrian who walked into them, or easily fly off in a car accident. The car was produced for just one year.

About 75% of all the gold mined each year is made into jewelry.

THE ARTHUR SELDEN CAR (1908)

The Arthur Selden Car was a front-wheel-drive car with an unusual feature: the front wheels didn't turn . . . and neither did the rear wheels. Instead, the car itself was hinged in the middle, with the steering connected to the hinge instead of the wheels.

Fatal Flaw: The car jackknifed easily, and the hinges wore out quickly. Besides, the car was so goofy-looking that nobody would have bought it even if it was easy to steer. Selden made a couple of prototypes, then quickly went out of business.

THE LE ZEBRE (1916–1920)

The Le Zebre was a cheap, stylish two-seat convertible that appealed to drivers who wanted expensive sports cars but couldn't afford them. It had a four-cylinder engine, slender lines, a fancy horn, and a spare wheel that sat on the running board. Ooh-la-la!

Fatal Flaw: Quality control at the factory was so bad that the car was like a prop in a slapstick comedy—it fell apart, piece by piece. For example, the axles shattered like clockwork every 200 miles, and the wheel nuts—frequently followed by the wheels themselves—popped off even at low speeds. People bought them anyway, because they were low-priced. The model lasted for four years.

THE DAVIS (1947–1949)

Produced by the Davis Motor Car Company of Van Nuys, California, the Davis was a three-wheeled car, shaped like a gumdrop, that looked like something out of *The Jetsons*. Power was provided via the two rear wheels; the driver steered the single front wheel. The company also made a special military version. (No word on whether the Pentagon actually bought any.)

Fatal Flaw: Bizarre looks and unconventional design would surely have killed the Davis, but they didn't have the chance. Misleading claims made by the company's founder, G. G. "Gary" Davis, beat them to it. Davis swore the car got 116 mpg on the highway, and that it could make sudden, sharp turns at speeds as high as 55 mph. Actual fuel economy turned out to be 65 mpg (not bad, but not as advertised). And in high-speed turns, one of the rear wheels lifted off the ground and spun freely, causing the speedometer to register artificially high speeds. The company was shut down following financial scandal in 1949.

There have been 1,500 "well-documented" sightings of Bigfoot since 1958.

THE WRITING ON THE WALL

At some time, all bathroom readers have found themselves in a public stall with nothing to read. Your eye starts to wander . . . and then you spot—graffiti! Here's a tribute to that emergency reading material.

You might be surprised to learn that graffiti isn't new . . . or even recent. The term comes from the Italian word for "scribbling" . . . and it was coined by archeologists to describe wall-writing found in ancient ruins. It has been discovered in the catacombs of Rome, the Tower of London, medieval English ale-houses, and even Mayan pyramids.

Some of the earliest examples of graffiti were preserved on the walls of Pompeii when Mt. Vesuvius erupted in A.D. 79. As you can see from the following examples, it hasn't changed much in nearly 2,000 years:

Appolinaris, doctor to the Emperor Titus, had a crap here

NO ONE'S A HANDSOME FELLOW UNLESS HE HAS LOVED

Whoever loves, goes to hell. I want to break Venus's ribs with blows and deform her hips. If she can break my tender heart, why can't I hit her over the head?

HULLO, WE'RE WINESKINS

Artimetus got me pregnant

IN NUCERIA, NEAR PORTA ROMANA, IS THE DISTRICT OF VENUS. ASK FOR NOVELLIA PRIMIGENIA

He who sits here, read this before anything else: If you want to make love ask for Attice. The price is 16 asses.

LOVERS, LIKE BEES, ENJOY A LIFE OF HONEY. WISHFUL THINKING

O Chius, I hope your ulcerous pustules reopen and burn even more than they did before

IN NUCERIA VOTE FOR LUCIUS MUNATIUS CAESARNINUS: HE IS AN HONEST MAN

Romula tarried here with Staphylus

Average number of days each year when no major league sports are played: 5.

A RECORD OF HISTORY

People have been studying and collecting graffiti for centuries. Hurlo Thrumbo, an English publisher, put out the first printed collection in the 1700s. In the early 1900s, German sociologists collected scrawls from public toilets and turned them into the first academic study of graffiti. In America, the Kinsey researchers collected bathroom messages as part of their study of men's and women's sex habits. But it wasn't until the 1960s, when graffiti became an outlet for the counterculture and anti-Vietnam protest movement, that academics really started to pay attention.

Now these "scribblings" are regarded as important adjuncts to the "official" history of a culture. They provide a look at what the average person was thinking and give evidence of the social unrest, political trends, and inner psychology of a society.

COLLECTING INFO

After decades of study, experts have decided that graffiti fit into four major categories.

- **Identity graffitists:** Want to immortalize themselves or a part of their lives (a romance, an accomplishment)
- **Opinion or message graffitists:** Want to let the world know what they think: "UFOs are real—the Air Force doesn't exist."
- **Dialogue graffitists:** Talk back to other graffitists. "I've got what every woman wants." (Underneath) "You must be in the fur coat business."
- **"Art" graffitists:** The most recent trend, with spray cans of paint used to create intricate designs signed with pseudonyms. Either vandalism or modern design, depending on your point of view.

THE GRAFFITI HERO

The most famous graffitist in history was Kilroy. Beginning in World War II, the line "Kilroy was here" started showing up in outrageous places. Kilroy left his signature on the top of the torch of the Statue of Liberty, on the Marco Polo Bridge in China, and even on a Bikini atoll where an atomic bomb was to be tested. The original Kilroy was an infantry soldier who was sick of hearing the Air Force brag about always being first on the spot. But the phrase has appeared for so many years in so many places that "Kilroy was here" has become synonymous with graffiti.

There were 16 contestants in the 1996 Arkansas Mosquito Cook-Off.

MORE WRITING ON THE WALL

A sampling of contemporary graffiti, collected since the 1960s.

Q: How do you tell the sex of a chromosome? A: Pull down its genes.

If Love is blind, and God is love, and Ray Charles is blind, then God plays the piano.

Mafia: Organized Crime
Government: Disorganized Crime

Flush twice, it's a long way to Washington.

Death is just nature's way of telling you to slow down.

How come nobody ever writes on the toilet seats?

Things are more like they are now than they have ever been before.

I can't stand labels, after all, I'm a liberal.

Although the moon is smaller than the earth, it's farther away.

Free Chile!
. . . Free tacos!
. . . Free burritos!

Only Jackie knows what her Onassis worth.

Did you ever feel like the whole world was a white wedding gown, and you were a pair of muddy hiking boots?

Standing room only. [written on top of a men's urinal]

The chicken is an egg's way of producing another egg.

If you think you have someone eating out of your hands, it's a good idea to count your fingers.

The typical Stanford undergrad is like a milkshake: thick and rich.

Blessed is he who sits on a bee, for he shall rise again.

Please remain seated during the entire program.
—The Management

There are those who shun elitism.
Why?
. . . Because it is there.
. . . It's the elitist thing to do.

Please do not throw cigarette butts in the toilet, as they become hard to light.

You can lead a horticulture, but you can't make her think.

Charles Darwin's cousin invented the IQ test.

FAMOUS PUBLISHING HOAXES

They say you shouldn't judge a book by its cover—and sometimes, as these hoaxes reveal, you can't even judge them by what's inside.

NAKED CAME THE STRANGER

The Book: In 1966 Mike McGrady, editor of the Long Island newspaper *Newsday*, interviewed "sex-novelist" Harold Robbins and was shocked to learn that Robbins had received a $2 million advance for a book he hadn't even written yet. McGrady decided to see if he could repeat Robbins's success: he deliberately set out to write a bad book, just to see how it would be received by publishers and the public. He came up with a title: *Naked Came the Stranger*, and a pen name: Penelope Asche.

Next, McGrady wrote up a story outline about a suburban housewife who gets even against her philandering husband by seducing married men. He recruited twenty-four *Newsday* reporters to write one chapter apiece, complete with two sexual encounters per chapter, one of which had to be bizarre. "There will be an unremitting emphasis on sex," he explained. "Also, true excellence in writing will be blue-penciled into oblivion."

When the book was finished, McGrady gave it to his sister-in-law, who, posing as Penelope Asche, shopped it around to several New York publishing houses. Dell Publishing paid $37,500 for it, and published it in 1970.

What Happened: *Naked Came the Stranger* became a bestseller—it sold 20,000 copies in the first month alone, thanks in part to McGrady's sister-in-law, who made TV and radio appearances promoting the book. McGrady eventually revealed the hoax, but sales remained strong, eventually topping well over 100,000 copies. McGrady, et al. were offered $500,000 to write a sequel; instead, he wrote a book called *Stranger Than Naked, or How to Write Dirty Books for Fun and Profit*.

Kangaroos are lactose-intolerant.

THE MAN WHO WOULDN'T TALK

The Book: At the end of World War II, George DuPre, a Canadian, returned from Europe and began telling neighbors of his exploits in the secret service. DuPre said he was part of the anti-Nazi French underground until he was captured by the Germans, who tortured him to get him to talk. At one point, DuPre said, they even gave him a sulphuric acid enema—but somehow he managed to keep silent, and later escaped.

As word of DuPre's exploits spread, he became a Canadian national hero. *Reader's Digest* printed an interview with him, which inspired Random House to publish *The Man Who Wouldn't Talk*, the story of his experiences, in 1953.

What Happened: Not long after his book was published, DuPre broke down during an interview with the *Calgary Herald* and admitted he'd made up the entire story. He'd actually spent the entire war in Canada and England. Random House realized it had been fooled and pulled *The Man Who Wouldn't Talk* from its non-fiction list. But rather than destroy the books, the publisher changed the title to *The Man Who Talked Too Much* and began selling it as fiction. Sales went up 500%.

THE MEMOIRS OF LEE HUNG CHANG

The Book: In 1913 Houghton Mifflin posthumously published *The Memoirs of Li Hung Chang*, the autobiography of one of the most famous Chinese statesmen of the era. The book was praised by many China experts—including John W. Foster, Secretary of State under Benjamin Harrison, who had worked with Li Hung Chang during an 1897 peace conference. Chapters of the work were serialized in the *London Observer* and the *New York Sun*.

What Happened: American Chinese experts praised the book. But Chinese experts immediately denounced it as a fake. They pointed out so many inaccuracies and discrepancies that Houghton Mifflin finally had to admit a problem and "look into the matter." They discovered that the book's "editor," a man named William Mannix, was actually its author. Using books on China sent to him by friends, and a typewriter sent to him by the Governor of Hawaii, Mannix had written the book in 1912—while serving time for forgery in a Honolulu prison.

Strangely enough, the book can still be found in many university and public libraries today.

Why are boxing rings called rings? Because they used to be round.

MOTHERS OF INVENTION

There have always been women inventors—even if they've been over-looked in history books. Here are a few you may not have heard of.

MELITTA BENTZ, *a housewife in Dresden, Germany*
Invention: Drip coffeemakers
Background: At the beginning of the 20th century, people made coffee by dumping a cloth bag full of coffee grounds into boiling water. It was an ugly process—the grounds inevitably leaked into the water, leaving it gritty and bitter.

One morning in 1908, Frau Bentz decided to try something different: she tore a piece of blotting paper (used to mop up after runny fountain pens) from her son's schoolbook and put it in the bottom of a brass pot she'd poked with holes. She put coffee on top of the paper and poured boiling water over it. It was the birth of "drip" coffeemakers—and the Melitta company. Today, Melitta sells its coffeemakers in 150 countries around the world.

LADY ADA LOVELACE, *daughter of British poet Lord Byron*
Invention: Computer programming
Background: The forerunner of modern computers—called the "analytical engine"—was the brainchild of a mathematical engineer named George Babbage. In 1834 Babbage met Lady Lovelace, and the two formed a partnership, working together on the engine's prototype. In the process, Lovelace created the first programming method, which used punch cards. Unfortunately, tools available to Babbage and Lovelace in the mid-1800s weren't sophisticated enough to complete the machine (though it worked in theory). Lovelace spent the rest of her life studying cybernetics.

LADY MARY MONTAGUE, *a British noblewoman*
Invention: Smallpox vaccine
Background: In 1717, while traveling in Turkey, she observed a curious custom known as *ingrafting*. Families would call for the services of old women, who would bring nutshells full of "virulent"—live smallpox—to a home. Then it would be "ingrafted" into a patient's open vein. The patient would spend a few days in bed with a slight illness but was rendered immune to smallpox.

Alexander Graham Bell's father-in-law invented the burglar alarm.

This technique was unknown in England, where 30% of smallpox victims died. Montague convinced Caroline, Princess of Wales, to try it on her own daughters. When it worked, she anonymously published *The Plain Account of the Inoculating of the Small-pox by a Turkish Merchant*. Despite vehement opposition from the church and medical establishments, the idea took hold. Lady Montague lived to see England's smallpox death rate drop to 2%.

MARGARET KNIGHT, *an employee of the Columbia Paper Bag Company in the late 1800s*
Invention: The modern paper bag
Background: Knight grew so tired of making paper bags by hand that she began experimenting with machines that could make them automatically. She came up with one that made square-bottomed, folding paper bags (until then, paper sacks all had V-shaped bottoms). But her idea was stolen by a man who'd seen her building her prototype. A court battle followed in which the main argument used against Knight was her "womanhood." But she proved beyond a doubt that the invention was hers and received her patent in 1870. Knight was awarded 27 patents in her lifetime, but was no businesswoman—she died in 1914 leaving an estate of only $275.05.

BETTE NESMITH GRAHAM, *a secretary at the Texas Bank & Trust in Dallas in the early 1950s*
Invention: Liquid Paper
Background: Graham was a terrible typist . . . but when she tried to erase her mistakes, the ink on her IBM typewriter just smeared. One afternoon in 1951, while watching sign painters letter the bank's windows, she got a brilliant idea: "With lettering, an artist never corrects by erasing but always paints over the error. So I decided to use what artists use. I put some waterbase paint in a bottle and took my watercolor brush to the office. And I used that to correct my typing mistakes." So many other secretaries asked for bottles of "Mistake Out" that in 1956 she started a small business selling it. A year later, she changed the formula and founded Liquid Paper, Inc. In 1966 her son, Michael Nesmith, made more money as a member of the Monkees than she did with Liquid Paper. But in 1979, she sold her company to Gillette for $47 million.

In a single day, a pair of termites can produce as many as 30,000 offspring.

MISSED IT BY THAT MUCH

Often success and disaster are a lot closer than we'd like to think. Here are some classic "near misses."

AN ASSASSINATION

Theodore Roosevelt: On October 14, 1912, the former president was on his way to a speech in Milwaukee when a man named John Schrank drew a revolver, pointed it at Roosevelt, and pulled the trigger. Roosevelt staggered but didn't fall. No blood could be detected, but Roosevelt's handlers begged him to go to the hospital. He refused and delivered a 50-minute speech to a cheering throng. However, when he pulled the 100-page speech out of his vest, he noticed a bullet hole in it. It turned out that the bullet had ripped through the paper and penetrated four inches into Roosevelt's body, right below his right nipple. If the written speech hadn't slowed the bullet down, he would have been killed. After speaking, Roosevelt was treated for shock and loss of blood.

A PLACE IN HISTORY

Elisha Gray: Gray was an electrical genius who independently developed his own telephone. Incredibly, he filed a patent for the invention on February 14, 1876—the *exact same day* that Alexander Graham Bell did—but a few hours *after* Bell. "If Bell had been a few hours late," says one historian, "what we know of as the Bell System would have been the Gray System." Gray was successful with other inventions, but was bitter for the rest of his life about not receiving credit for the telephone.

James Swinburne: Leo Baekeland patented the first modern plastic on June 14, 1907; he called it "Bakelite." A day later, a Scottish electrical engineer named James Swinburne filed a patent for almost exactly the same thing. He'd been experimenting with the same chemicals on his own halfway around the world, and had come up with the substance completely independently. Unlike Gray, though, he made peace with his near-miss and wound up chairman of the Bakelite company.

Karate was invented in India.

A CAREER-ENDING "INJURY"

Frank Sinatra: "Gangster Sam Giancana once ordered a hit on Frank Sinatra. He was going to have Sinatra's throat cut to ruin his voice. But on the night the hit was supposed to go down, Giancana was enjoying an intimate moment with [his girlfriend] Phyllis McGuire, who played Sinatra records to heighten the romantic mood. After listening for a while, Giancana decided he couldn't in good conscience silence that voice. He cancelled the hit." (*The Portland Oregonian*, August 29, 1997)

MILITARY DEFEAT

George Washington: "On Christmas night, 1776, Washington was preparing to cross the Delaware with his army to attack the British. The commander of forces at Trenton, Colonel Rall, was German. He was drinking and playing cards when he received a note from a British loyalist warning him of the attack. But the note was in English, which Rall couldn't read, and he was groggy anyway, so he put it in his pocket. At dawn, Washington attacked and because the British were unprepared, he won. As Rall lay dying on the battlefield, the note was translated into German and Rall admitted if he'd read it, 'I would not be here.'" (From *Oh Say Can You See?*)

THE PRESIDENCY

John Janney: "In 1840, Janney was chairman of the Whig Party Convention in Virginia. This convention nominated William Henry Harrison for president. John Janney and John Tyler were the nominees for vice president. When the vote of the convention was a tie, Janney, as chairman, did the "honorable" thing and voted for Tyler. Harrison won the election but died soon after, and John Tyler became president. John Janney lost the presidency by one vote—his own." (From *Dear Abby*, December 17, 1996)

Sen. Ben Wade: When Lincoln was shot in 1865, Andrew Johnson became president. In 1867 the Republican Congress tried to impeach him, but was one vote shy of the two-thirds majority needed to remove him from office. Wade, as president of the Senate, would have become the 18th American president. He became the second man in history to miss the U.S. presidency by one vote.

Take your weight and divide by three. That's how much your legs weigh.

THE TONIGHT SHOW, PART III: JACK PAAR

In his day, Jack Paar left as big a mark on The Tonight Show as Johnny Carson. But he only hosted the show for five years, and it's been more than 35 years since he left the stage . . . so his contribution is largely forgotten. Here's Part III of The Tonight Show. (Part II is on page 547.)

STARTING OVER

With *America After Dark* going down in flames, NBC began looking for someone to host a new version of *The Tonight Show*. The search didn't take long: when Steve Allen had cut back to three days a week in 1956, two comedians had been contenders for the Monday and Tuesday slots: Ernie Kovacs (who got the job) and Jack Paar, an out-of-work television personality.

This time, NBC decided to give Paar a chance. They weren't confident he could pull it off—with good reason. He seemed to have a knack for turning opportunity into disaster.

Army Brat

• Paar first attracted notice in the Army during World War II. He performed as part of the Special Service Company at USO shows, and was notorious for his satirical putdowns of military brass. Enlisted troops loved him, and he drew bigger applause than Jack Benny or Bob Hope when he appeared with them. But the act nearly got him court-martialed after he insulted a commodore.

• After he was discharged, he moved to Hollywood. In 1947 Jack Benny took time off from his radio program and arranged for Paar to fill in over the summer. It might have been a big break, but Paar let his ego and his temper get in the way. Three of his four writers walked out one afternoon after he insulted them once too often. Then he was quoted in *Time* magazine referring to Jack Benny's style of humor as "old hat" and pledging to bring a fresh approach to radio comedy.

- "When the summer ended," Robert Metz writes in *The Tonight Show*, "so did Jack's Hollywood career. He had made lots of enemies there, partly because of unbending attitudes, and, his critics say, his unwillingness to show humility."
- Paar moved on to New York and did a number of TV game, news, and variety shows, but none worked. Then he got a job as Walter Cronkite's replacement on *The Morning Show*, which ran on CBS against *The Today Show*. *The Morning Show*'s ratings went up during Paar's tenure, but he developed a reputation for being "uncooperative." CBS fired him after he refused to attribute his wife's "newfound" beauty to a sponsor's lipstick.
- Paar lost his job, but won an important fan—NBC executive Mort Werner . . . who hired him for *The Tonight Show*.

THE JACK PAAR STYLE

At first, Paar tried to mimic Steve Allen's format. "The first night," he recalled years later, "I grappled with a heavyweight wrestler, threw vegetables at the audience, and fed catnip to a lion." But where Allen had been a gifted and very physical comedian, Paar was uncomfortable and wooden. The critics panned the July 29, 1957, premiere.

Paar struggled with Allenesque skits and physical humor for another six months before he finally told his writers that from now on, he would open with a short monologue, then move to his desk, where he would chat with his guests. Paar was a strong conversationalist, and he wanted to make that the backbone of the show. He also figured that dumping the hijinks would help him attract more serious guests, such as politicians and journalists.

UP, UP, AND AWAY

The Tonight Show was building an audience even before the changes in format, and this helped it grow even more. "Before long," Paar remembered years later, "we had 154 stations, an estimated 30 million viewers weekly, and so many sponsors I felt guilty when I interrupted the commercials with the program." By the end of the second year, Paar's ratings were higher than Steve Allen's had been.

For the first time in its difficult history, *The Tonight Show* was selling out its advertising. And because the show was cheap to produce by TV standards—Paar had only three writers and a weekly budget of $50,000—it made big profits for NBC.

King Henry VIII owned tennis shoes.

TALK SHOW

Guests were booked on the show not because they had a new movie or television show coming out (as most guests are booked today), but because Paar found them interesting to talk to. Some big celebrities never got on, while Betty White, then an unknown comedian, appeared more than 70 times. "Jack was fascinated [by the guests on the show]," says Hal Gurnee, who directed Paar's show and years later would also direct David Letterman's. "He was good at talking to people and convincing them he was interested in what they had to say."

HOT TALENT

It wasn't just Paar's talent for conversation that followed him to *The Tonight Show*. His ego, stubbornness, and bad temper also came along. Ironically, these qualities—which had nearly derailed his career several times—became an important part of *The Tonight Show*'s success. If he was mad about something, he'd vent his anger onstage. If he was emotional, he'd cry. If he didn't like a guest, he'd insult them to their faces, right on national TV. Sometimes he even chewed out his staff on the air. Audiences, which were used to the tightly scripted TV shows of the 1950s, were mesmerized. There was nothing else like it on TV.

Unlike today's talk-show hosts, who tend to keep personal disputes off the air and wage their wars through publicists, Paar fought his feuds on camera and in person. He attacked columnists who criticized his show and could become jealous of any guests who got bigger laughs than he did. One night comedian Jack E. Leonard scored big with the studio audience. Paar told him, "Keep going. You're doing great!" throughout his routine, but a few days later, he announced that Leonard was history. "You'll be seeing a lot of him in the future," Paar told viewers, "but not on my show!"

Even regular guests had to watch their step. Dody Goodman was a ditsy comedian Paar discovered on the first week of the show. She was so funny that he made her a regular. But one night when she got too many laughs, he dumped her.

MR. NICE GUY

Paar could also be a sentimental family man—especially during his monologues, which he peppered with stories about his wife and daughter. When his daughter got her first training bra, he told the

President Chester A. Arthur once sold a pair of Abe Lincoln's pants at auction.

world. And when the family vacationed in foreign countries, Paar always packed a movie camera to record their trips for the show.

"Paar was in essence hosting a nightly gathering at his 'house,'" Ronald Smith writes, "complete with home movies, guests who should not have been invited, and the atmosphere that 'anything might happen.' Some guests were quietly invited to leave, the subject of catty insults. Others were embraced and urged to come back over and over, long overstaying their welcome."

A NATIONAL HABIT

Viewers didn't just *want* to watch *The Tonight Show*, they felt they *had* to, out of fear that they'd miss something if they didn't.

"Jack in all his work let his own quirks, neuroses, suspicions, and dislikes play freely on the surface," Dick Cavett (a writer on the show) recalled in his autobiography. "There was always the implied possibility in his manner that he would explode one day, and you might miss seeing a live nervous breakdown viewed from the comfort of your own bedroom."

As viewers flocked to *The Tonight Show*, so did celebrities from all walks of life. Richard Nixon played piano accompanied by an orchestra of "15 Democratic violinists"; Liberace tickled the ivories while a young Cassius Clay read poetry. "For a change, do that one about you," he goaded the champ. Even Eleanor Roosevelt and Albert Schweitzer made appearances.

A LITTLE POLITICS ON THE SIDE

The Tonight Show may even have helped decide the outcome of the 1960 presidential election. Both Kennedy and Nixon made appearances on the show to explain their positions, and on the eve of the election, Paar invited Bobby Kennedy, JFK's campaign manager, on the show to explain "in three minutes" why his brother should be president. (Nixon, of course, was not pleased.) As James Reston of the *New York Times* put it, there were two litmus tests in the 1960 campaign: "Who can stand up to Nikita Khrushchev. And who can sit down with Jack Paar."

Want to hear a censored joke?
Turn to page 646 for Part IV.

The bullfrog is the only animal that never sleeps.

CELEBRITY ALSO-RANS

It helps to be a celebrity if you want to run for political office. In the recent past, there's been a member of the Love Boat cast, a Hall of Fame pitcher, even a former rock star. Here are four famous Americans who aren't known as politicians . . . because they lost.

HENRY FORD
Ran for: U.S. Senate seat from Michigan
The Story: Ford was one of the richest, most famous men in America when Woodrow Wilson called him into the White House in 1918 and asked him to run for the open senate seat in Michigan. He agreed to do it.

It was a bizarre campaign. Although he had unlimited cash, Ford refused to spend any. He also refused to make any public speeches. And while Ford said nothing, his opponent—Truman H. Newberry—attacked the carmaker mercilessly for his pacifism.
Outcome: Surprisingly, Ford lost by less than 5,000 votes. *Then* he got interested in the election. He demanded a recount and hired private detectives to prove Newberry had cheated. Over the next four years, Ford had more than 40 investigators scouring Michigan, looking for proof that Newberry had spent money on his campaign illegally. This, he claimed (and perhaps believed), would be proof that Wall Street had conspired to beat him.

In the end, he got the revenge he wanted. The Democrats regained control of the Senate in 1922 and announced they were reopening "the Newberry case." Newberry gave in to the inevitable and resigned. Ford never ran for office again.

P.T. BARNUM
Ran for: U.S. House of Representatives
The Story: In 1865 the world-famous showman (known for his alleged comment: "There's a sucker born every minute") ran for—and won—a seat in the Connecticut state legislature. The reason: he wanted to have a hand in abolishing slavery permanently. He was rewarded in 1867 with the Republican nomina-

One of the most popular soups in 1929: peanut butter soup.

tion for U.S. Congress. Strangely, his opponent was also named Barnum.

The rest of the country seemed appalled by the idea. In a typical editorial, *The Nation* called him a "depraving and demoralizing influence" and said Connecticut should be ashamed of itself. Barnum himself noted that by the election time, "half the Christian community" believed he wore "horns and hoofs."

Outcome: A Democratic landslide swept Connecticut, and Barnum was soundly defeated. The man responsible for innumerable hoaxes said he wanted nothing more to do with "oily politicians." But in 1875 he was elected mayor of Bridgeport; and in 1877 he was again elected to the state legislature.

HUNTER THOMPSON

Ran for: Sheriff of Aspen, Colorado

The Story: In 1970 Thompson, the infamous "Gonzo" journalist, jokingly ran for sheriff of the glitzy ski resort as a "freak power" candidate. His platform: He promised to ban cars, tear up the roads and turf them, rename Aspen "Fat City," and put stocks on the courthouse lawn to punish "dishonest" dope dealers.

Outcome: Amazingly, he lost the race by less than 1,000 votes.

SHIRLEY TEMPLE BLACK

Ran for: U.S. House of Representatives

The Story: In the 1930s little Shirley Temple was one of the world's most famous movie stars. In 1966 she was Shirley Temple Black, a committed conservative Republican.

In 1967 the U.S. representative from her district died, and she ran for the Republican nomination in a special election. She started out as the odds-on favorite . . . but lost steam as her positions seemed more and more at odds with her compassionate little-girl movie character. In a magazine interview, for example, she belittled funds spent on rat control in slums, scoffing, "I'd like to know who *counted* the rats." She was also a Vietnam hard-liner, while her opponent—a Vietnam vet with a war injury—was a moderate.

Outcome: She lost the primary, 69,000 to 35,000, and was bitter about it for years. For some reason, she thought that if she'd had two more weeks to campaign, she would have won.

Baby pigs can be housebroken in as little as 3 days.

INFORMAL WRITING

Can't find anything to write on when you get a brainstorm? Do what these people did—grab whatever's in front of you and start scribbling.

WRITTEN ON: A cocktail napkin
BY: Rollin King and Herb Kelleher
THE STORY: Kelleher was a lawyer. King was a banker and pilot who ran a small charter airline. In 1966 they had a drink at a San Antonio bar. Conversation led to an idea for an airline that would provide short intrastate flights at a low cost. They mapped out routes and a business strategy on a cocktail napkin. Looking at the notes on the napkin, Kelleher said, "Rollin, you're crazy, let's do it," and Southwest Airlines was born.

WRITTEN ON: Toilet paper
BY: Richard Berry
THE STORY: Berry, an R&B performer, was at a club in 1957 when he heard a song with a Latin beat that he liked. He went into the men's room, pulled off some toilet paper, and wrote down the lyrics to "Louie, Louie."

WRITTEN ON: The back of a grocery bill
BY: W.C. Fields
THE STORY: In 1940 Fields needed money quickly. He scribbled down a plot idea on some paper he found in his pocket, and sold it to Universal Studios for $25,000. Ironically, the plot was about Fields trying to sell an outrageous script to a movie studio. It became his last film, *Never Give a Sucker an Even Break* (1941). Fields received screenplay credit as Otis Criblecoblis.

WRITTEN ON: The back of a letter
BY: Francis Scott Key
THE STORY: In 1814 Key, a lawyer, went out to the British fleet in Chesapeake Bay to plead for the release of a prisoner. The British agreed, but since Key had arrived as they were preparing to attack, they detained him and his party until the battle was over. From this vantage point Key watched the bombardment, and "by

---

In Yukon, Oklahoma, it's illegal for patients to pull their dentist's teeth.

the dawn's early light" saw that "our flag was still there." He was so inspired that he wrote the lyrics to "The Star Spangled Banner" on the only paper he had, a letter he'd stuck in his pocket.

WRITTEN ON: A cocktail napkin
BY: Arthur Laffer
THE STORY: In September 1974 Arthur Laffer (professor of business economics at USC) had a drink at a Washington, D.C., restaurant with his friend Donald Rumsfeld (an advisor to President Gerald Ford). The conversation was about the economy, taxes, and what to do about the recession. Laffer moved his wine glass, took the cocktail napkin, and drew a simple graph to illustrate his idea that at some point, increased taxes result in decreased revenues. The graph, known as the "Laffer Curve," later became the basis for President Reagan's "trickle-down" economics.

WRITTEN ON: A napkin
BY: Roger Christian and Jan Berry
THE STORY: In the early 1960s Roger Christian, one of the top DJs in Los Angeles, co-wrote many of Jan and Dean's hits with Jan Berry. One night he and Jan were at an all-night diner and Christian began scribbling the lyrics to a new song, "Honolulu Lulu," on a napkin. When they left the restaurant, Jan said, "Give me the napkin . . . I'll go to the studio and work out the arrangements." "I don't have it," Christian replied. Then they realized they'd left the napkin on the table. They rushed back in . . . but the waitress had already thrown it away. They tried to reconstruct the song but couldn't. So the two tired collaborators went behind the diner and sorted through garbage in the dumpster until 4 a.m., when they finally found their song. It was worth the search. "Honolulu Lulu" made it to #11 on the national charts.

WRITTEN ON: The back of an envelope
BY: Abraham Lincoln
THE STORY: On his way to Gettysburg to commemorate the battle there, Lincoln jotted down his most famous speech—the Gettysburg Address—on an envelope. Good story, but just a myth. Several drafts of the speech have been discovered—one of which was written in the White House on executive stationery.

Pearls are made of calcium carbonate, the active ingredient in antacids.

THE DUSTBIN
OF HISTORY

Think your heroes will go down in history for something they've done? Don't count on it. These folks were VIPs in their time . . . but they're forgotten now. They've been swept into the Dustbin of History.

FORGOTTEN FIGURE: Fanny Elssler, Viennese ballerina
CLAIM TO FAME: A superstar of the 1840s, Elssler toured America for two years and inspired what newspapers referred to as "Elssler Mania." Wherever she went, "The Divine Fanny" drew hordes of admirers. They rioted outside her hotel in New York and mobbed her carriage in Baltimore. In Washington, Congress adjourned so lawmakers wouldn't miss her performance. Poems and songs were written about her. At the end of her tour, she went back to Europe and (as far as we know) never returned.

FORGOTTEN FIGURE: Peter Francisco, American soldier
CLAIM TO FAME: Every war has its working-class heroes. During the Revolutionary War, this 19-year-old, known as the "strongest man in the Colonies" and "the American Samson," was the people's favorite. They told stories of Private Francisco's exploits—like the time in 1780, during retreat, when he "lifted a 1,100-pound cannon and *carried* it to the rear"; the time when he was ordered by a British cavalryman to drop his musket and he used his bayonet to "lift the hapless horseman from the saddle"; the time in 1781 at Guilford Courthouse when, "with his thigh laid open by a bayonet, Francisco chopped down 11 British troops before collapsing." By the end of the war, he had become the most famous regular soldier in the Continental Army. After the war, he was rewarded with a job as sergeant at arms for the Virginia legislature.

FORGOTTEN FIGURE: Belva Ann Lockwood (née Bennett), pioneering crusader for women's rights
CLAIM TO FAME: One historian writes: "Lockwood's entire career was a living example of women's potential, even in the stifling atmosphere of the 19th century." In 1873, at age 43, she

Food fact: "Exocannibals" eat their enemies. "Indocannibals" eat their friends.

became an attorney; and in 1879 she was the first woman to plead a case before the United States Supreme Court. She persuaded male lawmakers in Washington to pass a bill awarding equal pay to women employed by the federal government. In 1884 and 1888 she ran for president as the candidate of the National Equal Rights Party . . . and won Indiana's electoral votes—something no woman candidate has done since (at least, not yet).

FORGOTTEN FIGURE: Dr. Mary Edwards Walker, Civil War soldier, the only woman to receive the Congressional Medal of Honor

CLAIM TO FAME: Achieved national prominence during the Civil War, serving as a nurse and later as a spy and surgeon (she was the first woman to hold a medical commission). In the field she dressed like male officers, wearing gold-striped trousers, a felt hat encircled with gold braid, and an officer's greatcoat. She always wore her hair in curls, though, so that "everyone would know that I was a woman." For her service to the sick and wounded, president Andrew Johnson awarded Walker the Congressional Medal of Honor; she was the first and only woman in history thus recognized.

"Immediately after the war," writes one historian, "her attire was so notorious that she was arrested on several occasions for 'masquerading as a man.' However, Walker was never prosecuted, since a grateful Congress had passed a special act granting her the right to wear trousers, in recognition of her wartime services."

Walker avidly campaigned for women's political rights . . . and for their right to wear pants. She also campaigned against cigarettes; she always carried an umbrella "with which she batted offending cigarettes from the mouths of startled men."

She wore her medal proudly, but in 1917, when Walker was 85, a government review board revoked it (along with the medals of 911 other Civil War veterans) on the grounds that "nothing in the records show the specific act or acts for which the decoration was originally awarded." When asked by the Army to return her medal, she replied, "Over my dead body!" "She wore the medal every day, and was wearing it when she took a bad fall on the Capitol steps" on her way to petition Congress for one of her reform causes. A few months later she died . . . and when she was buried, the medal was still pinned securely to her Prince Albert coat.

The *Dick Van Dyke Show* pilot was bankrolled by Joseph Kennedy, JFK's father.

THERE'S EGG ON YOUR FACE!

*Businesses spend plenty of time and plenty of money
setting up elaborate promotions. Sometimes they backfire so
badly that they're funny (to us—not them). A tip of the BRI hat
to Nash and Zullo's* Misfortune 500 *for much of the info here.*

Company: **United Airlines**
Promotion: "Fly Your Wife for Free"
Businessmen were invited to buy a ticket and bring their
wives along at no charge. Part of the promotion included a letter
from the airline thanking people for taking advantage of the offer.
Soon letters poured in to United from angry wives saying they
hadn't been their husbands' companions, and demanding to know
who had.

Company: MCA Records, Canada
Promotion: Press kit for the *Miami Vice* soundtrack
The cops on TV's *Miami Vice* nailed a lot of drug smugglers in the
1980s. When the show's soundtrack was released, MCA Canada
sent reviewers copies of the tape . . . plus a small bag of white powder (it was sugar). Bad idea. Critics howled that MCA was promoting cocaine use. MCA Canada tried to blame the idea on their
California parent company. Then they found out it came from
their own promotions department. "Well," a spokesman explained,
sheepishly, "normally our promotions staff isn't that creative."

Company: Rival Dog Food
Promotion: A media event to publicize Rival's new dog food
In the mid-1960s the president of Rival invited the press to lunch.
He brought along a special guest—a pedigreed collie—which sat at
the main table with him and was served Rival's new "all-beef dinner" for its meal. A clever way to get attention, except that the
dog wouldn't eat it. Wouldn't even sniff it. "In desperation," write
Nash and Zullo, "the Rival president reached into the dog's bowl
and ate the stuff himself—to the cheers of reporters. The next

---

Sneakers get their name because they don't squeak like leather shoes do.

day, newspapers carried stories with headlines such as RIVAL PRESIDENT EATS DOG FOOD, BUT DOG WON'T." "I've never used an animal since," said the chairman of Rival's PR firm, who was fired the next day.

Company: Charleston RiverDogs (a class A minor league baseball team in South Carolina)
Promotion: "Free Vasectomy Day"
The RiverDogs announced they'd be offering a free vasectomy to anyone who showed up at the ballpark on June 15, 1997—Father's Day. The idea didn't go over too well with the general public, particularly the Roman Catholic Diocese of Charleston.

The RiverDogs' marketing VP defended the idea—"Some men find it very useful," she claimed—but less than 24 hours later, the promotion was canceled.

Company: Kellogg Co.
Promotion: They put a photo of Miss Venezuela (19-year-old Alicia Machado), winner of the 1996 Miss Universe contest, on boxes of Special K cereal in her native country.
"In Venezuela," said news reports, "where beauty queen titles launch careers, Special K cereal boxes featured the 19-year-old brunette sitting on an inflatable globe above the slogan, 'Nothing to hide.' Buyers who stocked up on the cereal in the hope of keeping their figures trim now want their money back."
The reason: Four months after winning the crown, Machado had gained 11 pounds and had acquired the nickname "the eating machine." Local newspapers were flooded with angry letters, and after a slew of bad publicity, Kellogg's discontinued the promotion.

Company: Weight Watchers
Promotion: An ad campaign featuring Weight Watchers spokeswoman Sarah Ferguson, the former Duchess of York.
Ferguson appeared on brochures and in ads saying that losing weight is "harder than outrunning the paparazzi." A week later her former sister-in-law, Princess Diana, was killed in a car wreck while trying to outrun the paparazzi. The ad campaign was quickly withdrawn.

The word *longshoreman* is derived from "along-the-shore-man."

ANIMALS FAMOUS FOR 15 MINUTES

When Andy Warhol said, "In the future, everyone will be famous for 15 minutes," he obviously didn't have animals in mind. Yet even they haven't been able to escape the relentless publicity machine that keeps cranking out instant celebrities.

HEADLINE: *Cat Makes Weather Forecasters Look All Wet*
THE STAR: Napoleon, a cat in Baltimore, Maryland
WHAT HAPPENED: A severe drought hit Baltimore in the summer of 1930. Forecasters predicted an even longer dry spell, but Frances Shields called local newspapers and insisted they'd have rain in 24 hours. The reason: Her cat was lying down with his "front paw extended and his head on the floor," and he only did that just before it rained. Reporters laughed . . . until there *was* a rainstorm the next day.
AFTERMATH: Newspapers all over the country picked up the story, and Napoleon became a feline celebrity. He also became a professional weather-cat and newspaper columnist. His predictions were printed regularly—and he did pretty well. All told, he was about as accurate as human weather forecasters.

HEADLINE: *Nuts to Him! California Dog Wins Nutty Contest*
THE STAR: Rocky, a 100-pound male Rottweiler
WHAT HAPPENED: In 1996 a Fresno radio station ran a contest offering free Neuticles to the dog submitting the best ghost-written essay on why he wanted them. (Neuticles are artificial plastic testicles, implanted after a dog is neutered, that supposedly make the dog feel better about itself.) The appropriately named Rocky won.
AFTERMATH: The contest made national news. *Parade* magazine called it the "Best Canine Self-Improvement Story" of 1996.

HEADLINE: *Dog Makes List of Notable Americans*
THE STAR: Otis P. Albee, family dog of the Albees, in South Burlington, Vermont (breed unknown)

---

233 Dalmatians were used in the filming of the movie *101 Dalmatians*.

WHAT HAPPENED: In the 1980s George Albee, a professor at the University of Vermont, was invited to submit biographical information for a book called *Community Leaders and Noteworthy Americans*. Instead, he filled out the forms for his dog—"a retired explorer, hunter, and sportsman with a Ph.D. in animal husbandry." **AFTERMATH:** Otis made it into the book. When this was reported nationwide, Albee announced that Otis had no comment. Apparently, neither did the book's publishers.

HEADLINE: *A Dog Is Man's . . . Best Man?*
THE STAR: Samson, a six-year-old Samoyed mix
WHAT HAPPENED: In 1955 Dan Anderson proposed to Lori Chapasko at the Wisconsin animal shelter where they both volunteered. She said yes . . . and approved when Dan chose their dog Samson to be "best man" at the wedding. "He epitomizes everything a best man should be," Anderson explained to reporters. **AFTERMATH:** The dog was news, but apparently the wedding wasn't. Reporters seem to have ignored it.

HEADLINE: *World Gets Charge from Nuclear Kittens*
THE STARS: Four black kittens—Alpha, Beta, Gamma, and Neutron—who were living at the shut-down San Onofre Nuclear Power Plant in San Diego, California
WHAT HAPPENED: How do you make a nuclear power plant seem warm and fuzzy? Find some kittens there. In February 1996, just as the owner of the San Onofre power plant was kicking off a pro-nuclear PR campaign, a worker happened to find four motherless kittens under a building. A pregnant cat, the story went, had slipped through security at the shut-down power plant, given birth to a litter of kittens, and disappeared. When the worker tried to carry them off the grounds, alarms went off. It turned out that the cute little animals were slightly radioactive . . . though officials explained that they were in no danger. The story was reported worldwide. *The Nuclear News*, a nuclear industry publication, called it "the biggest nuclear story in years." **AFTERMATH:** Seven months later, the Atomic Kittens were pronounced "radiation-free" . . . proving that nuclear power isn't so bad after all. Offers to adopt the pets flooded in from all over the world, but workers at the plant decided to keep them.

Termites are blind.

THE DISCOVERY OF THE PLANETS

As early as kindergarten, we're taught that there are nine planets. But 200 years ago, even scholars were sure there were only six planets. Here's how we got the three new ones.

THE END OF THE SOLAR SYSTEM

People have always known about Mercury, Venus, Mars, Jupiter, and Saturn. Early civilizations named the days of the week after each of these planets, plus the sun and moon. The Greeks watched them move through the night sky, passing in front of the stars that make up the constellations of the zodiac, and called them *planetes*—which means "wanderers."

As recently as the 1700s, people still believed that the planet Saturn was at the farthest extent of the solar system. That there might be other planets wasn't even a respectable idea. But as technology and science became more sophisticated, other members of the solar system were discovered.

URANUS

In 1781 a self-taught astronomer, William Herschel, was "sweeping the skies" with his telescope. By March he had reached the section that included the constellation Gemini, and he spotted an object that appeared as a disk rather than a glowing star. Because it moved slightly from week to week, Herschel thought it was circular . . . and came to the shocking conclusion that it wasn't a comet, but an unknown planet. People were astonished.

Finding a Name

No one since ancient times had named a planet. Herschel felt that it should be called "Georgium Sidus" (George's Star) in honor of his patron, George III—the king of England who reigned during the American Revolution. Some people wanted to name it "Herschel" after its discoverer. But one influential astronomer suggested they call it "Uranus," after the Greek god of the heavens. That made sense, since this new planet was certainly the limit of the skies of the solar system. Or so they thought.

New York's Times Square was originally known as "Acre Square."

NEPTUNE

The newly found planet had a slight variation in its orbit, almost as if something were tugging at it. Could there be another planet affecting Uranus? A century earlier, Isaac Newton had come up with laws describing the effects that the gravitational forces of planets have on one another. Using Newton's laws, two young scientists set out independently in 1840 to find the unknown planet whose gravitational forces might be pulling on Uranus. One of the scientists was a French mathematician, Jean Leverrier. The other was an English astronomer, John Couch Adams. Both hoped the unknown planet would be where their calculations said they could find it.

The Hidden Planet

Adams finished his calculations first, in September 1845. The following August, Leverrier completed his. Neither had access to a large telescope, so they couldn't verify their projections—and no one would make one available to them. Finally, Leverrier traveled to the Berlin Observatory in Germany, and the young assistant manager, Johann Gottfried Galle, agreed to help search for the planet.

That was September 23, 1846. That night, Galle looked through the telescope, calling out stars and their positions while a young student astronomer, Heinrich Louis d'Arrest, looked at a star chart, searching for the stars Galle described. Finally Galle called out an eighth-magnitude star that d'Arrest couldn't locate on the charts. They had found the unknown planet! It had taken two years of research—but only a half hour at the telescope. The honor of the discovery belongs to both Adams and Leverrier, who had essentially discovered the new planet with just a pen and a new set of mathematical laws. The greenish planet was named after Neptune, god of the sea.

VULCAN

Leverrier was on a roll. He started looking for other planets . . . and became convinced that there was one between the sun and Mercury. He called his planet "Vulcan," the god of fire, because it was so close to the sun. Leverrier noted that, like Uranus, Mercury experienced disturbances that caused it to travel farther in one point in its orbit. Since Neptune was one of the causes of similar

---

The first American car theft took place in St. Louis in 1905.

pulls on Uranus, it made sense that another planet was affecting Mercury.

Leverrier never found Vulcan, but people believed it was there until 1916, when Einstein's general theory of relativity was published. Einstein gave a satisfactory explanation for the discrepancies in Mercury's orbit, so scientists no longer needed Vulcan. It thereby ceased to exist . . . until decades later, when Gene Roddenberry, creator of *Star Trek*, appropriated the planet and made it the home of Spock.

PLUTO

The discovery of Neptune did not completely account for the peculiar movements of Uranus. Once again, scientists considered the pull of another planet as a cause and set out to find "Planet X." Using the telescope at his observatory in Flagstaff, Arizona, Percival Lowell searched for Planet X for 10 years. After he died in 1916, his brother gave the observatory a donation that enabled it to buy a telescope-camera. The light-sensitive process of photography allowed astronomers to capture images of dim and distant stars that they couldn't see, even with the aid of a telescope.

In 1929 the Lowell Observatory hired Clyde Tombaugh, a young self-taught astronomer from Kansas, to continue the search for Planet X. Lowell had suggested that the unknown planet was in the Gemini region of the sky. Using an instrument called the *blink microscope*, Tombaugh took two photographs of that area of the sky a few days apart and placed them side by side under the microscope. If something moved in the sky, as planets do, it would appear as a speck of light jumping back and forth as Tombaugh's eyes moved from one photograph to the other, looking through the microscope.

That's just what happened. The observatory announced the discovery of the ninth planet on March 13, 1930. An 11-year-old girl, the daughter of an Oxford astronomy professor, chose the name Pluto—the god of the netherworld—for the new planet.

For years before his death, Tombaugh repeatedly declared that there were no more planets in our solar system. If there were, he said, he would have found them.

British anatomist Richard Owen invented the word *dinosaur* in 1841.

OOPS!

More goofs, blunders, and dumb mistakes.

CHURCH MUSIC

"A funeral in 1996 in an English church ended with Rod Stewart singing:

> If you want my body,
> And you think I'm sexy,
> C'mon baby let me know.

The vicar admitted that when he was recording the deceased's last request—a hymn—he'd apparently failed to erase the entire cassette tape."

—*Fortean Times*, **1996**

UNPLUGGED

"In 1978 workers were sent to dredge a murky stretch of the Chesterfied-Stockwith Canal. Their task was to remove all the rubbish and leave the canal clear . . . They were disturbed during their tea-break by a policeman who said he was investigating a giant whirlpool in the canal. When they got back, however, the whirlpool had gone . . . and so had a 1 1/2-mile stretch of the canal . . . A flotilla of irate holidaymakers were stranded on their boats in brown sludge.

Among the first pieces of junk the workers had hauled out had been the 200-year-old plug that ensured the canal's continued existence. 'We didn't know there was a plug,' said one bewildered workman . . . All the records had been lost in a fire during the war."

—*The Book of Heroic Failures,* **by Stephen Pile**

YIKES!

"Defense lawyer Phillip Robertson, trying to make a dramatic point in front of the jury at his client's recent robbery trial in Dallas, pointed the pistol used in the crime at the jury box, causing two jurors to fling their arms in front of their faces and others to gasp.

240 of the world's 450 different types of cheese come from France.

Though Robertson was arguing that his client should be sentenced only to probation, the horrified jury gave him 13 years."
—"The Edge," in the Portland *Oregonian*, September 10, 1997

THE WRONG NOTE

"A 61-year-old woman and her daughter made a deposit at the drive-up window of an Albuquerque, New Mexico, bank Thursday, and were waiting for a receipt when police cars surrounded them and officers ordered them out of their vehicle at gunpoint. It turned out the New Mexico grandmother had accidentally held up the bank; she'd handed in a deposit slip on which a prankster had scrawled a hold-up message. The FBI said investigators believe someone wrote the note on the deposit slip and left it in a pile inside the bank, where the woman picked it up and used it, unaware of what was written on the back."

—*Washington Post*, May 24, 1997

A PAIR OF BIRDBRAINS

"Each evening, birdlover Neil Symmons stood in his backyard in Devon, England, hooting like an owl—and one night, an owl called back to him.

"For a year, the man and his feathered friend hooted back and forth. Symmons even kept a log of their 'conversations.'

"Just as Symmons thought he was on the verge of a break-through in interspecies communication, his wife had a chat with next-door neighbor Wendy Cornes.

"My husband spends his night in the garden calling out to owls,' said Mrs. Symmons.

"'That's odd,' Mrs. Cornes replied. 'So does my Fred.'

"And then it dawned on them."

—"The Edge," in the Portland *Oregonian*, August 29, 1997

GOVERNMENT EFFICIENCY

"In 1977 a government clerk in Australia made a slight error in paperwork. As a result, a $300,000 police headquarters was built in St. Arnaud's (population 3,000) instead of in St. Alban's (population 40,000). Part of the new construction was a 50-car parking lot. It is currently being used by the two cars and two bicycles of the St. Arnaud's police department."

—*Encyclopedia Brown's Book of Facts*, by Donald Sobol

Ratio of adult bookstores to McDonald's restaurants in the U.S.: 3-to-1.

GREAT MOMENTS IN TELEPHONE HISTORY

Everyone's got a telephone—but it seems the only thing anyone knows about it is that Alexander Graham Bell invented it. Here's a little more history.

FEBRUARY 14, 1876. Beating out a competing inventor by only a few hours, Alexander Graham Bell arrives at the U.S. patent office and patents the telephone in his name. Three days later, he builds the first telephone that actually works. Hoping to earn a page in the history books, he memorizes lines from Shakespeare to use in the world's first telephone conversation. But when the magic moment arrives, he spills acid on himself and barks out, "Mr. Watson, come here. I want you."

Fall 1876. Bell offers to sell the rights to his invention to the Western Union Telegraph Co. for $100,000. He is laughed out of the office.

- Stage fright becomes a significant obstacle in expanding telephone sales. To reassure the public, Bell takes out ads claiming that "Conversations can be easily carried on after slight practice and with occasional repetitions of a word or sentence."

1877. Charles Williams of Somerville, Massachusetts, becomes the first American to install a telephone in his house. (But since no one else had a phone, he couldn't call anyone. So he installed a telephone in his office, where his wife could reach him during the day.)

1877. A woman named Emma Nutt becomes the first female telephone operator in the United States. Initially the phone company preferred to hire young boys as operators, but eventually had to phase them out because of their foul language and penchant for practical jokes.

Some breeds of vultures can fly at altitudes as high as 36,900 feet.

1879. In the middle of a measles epidemic in Lowell, Massachusetts, a physician, worried about what would happen if the town's operators succumbed to the disease, suggests to the local phone company that it begin issuing the nation's first phone numbers to telephone subscribers. At first the public resists the idea, attacking phone numbers as being too impersonal.

1881. Thomas Edison comes up with a new way to answer the telephone. "Originally," writes Margaret Cousins in *The Story of Thomas Edison,* "people wound the phone with a crank, which rang a bell, and then said: 'Are you there?' This took too much time for Edison. During one of the hundreds of tests made in his laboratory, he picked up the phone one day, twisted the crank and shouted: 'Hello!' This became the way to answer the telephone all over America, and it still is."

* * *

GREAT MOMENTS IN EMERGENCY DIALING

In 1995 a woman in Devizes, England, was awakened from a sound sleep by a phone ringing. Upon answering it, she was greeted by moans, groans, and yelling. The woman dismissed the call as a prank and hung up.

A short while later the phone rang again. This time the woman heard outright screaming, followed by a female shouting, "Oh my God!" Terrified, the woman hung up. There was no mistaking it: the voice on the other end belonged to her daughter, who lived about a hundred miles away.

The woman phoned the police. They sent squad cars to the daughter's house, broke down the door, and stormed the bedroom.

There they found the daughter making love to her boyfriend on the bed.

Apparently, during two wild moments of passion, the daughter's big toe accidentally hit the speed-dial button on the phone, which was on a nightstand by the bed.

"This is a warning for other people," a police spokesman said. "If you're going to indulge in that sort of thing, move the phone."

—*Knuckleheads in the News*

"Whale harassment" is a federal offense. It's punishable by up to $10,000 in fines.

THE LEANINGEST TOWER ON EARTH

The Leaning Tower of Pisa is one of the most recognizable buildings in the world, a visual symbol of Italy itself. Here's a look at its unusual history.

CIVIC RIVALRY

In 1155, builders in Venice, Italy, finished work on a bell tower next to the Cathedral of San Marco. Legend has it that citizens in the seaport town of Pisa—determined not to be outdone by the Venetians—decided to build their own bell tower next to the Cathedral of Pisa.

Work began in 1173. The plans called for a seven-story marble tower with more than 200 columns, plus a belfry with seven large bells at the top. The building would be 184 feet tall but only 52 feet in diameter.

The entire building was supposed to stand on a foundation less than 10 feet deep. But as it turned out, the ground—largely sandy soil and waterlogged clay—was too spongy to support it.

BACK AND FORTH

By the time the second floor was finished, the building had already begun leaning slightly to the north. But rather than start over, the builders just lengthened the northern walls on the third floor and shortened the southern ones, leveling off the top of the building in the process. That way, they figured, the rest of the building would be level, too.

STOP AND GO

As luck would have it, political unrest in Pisa forced builders to stop work on the building for 90 years. That meant the clay soil beneath the tower was allowed to compact and strengthen over time. Soil experts now believe that if it hadn't, the tower would have collapsed when the upper floors were added.

But they didn't. Six more stories were successfully added between 1270 and 1278. This time, however, the added weight

---

Ants have five noses. Each one smells a different odor.

caused the building to lean to the *south*, the direction it still leans today. The builders applied the same solution to the fifth floor that they'd used on the third, only in reverse: they lengthened the southern walls and shortened the northern ones, giving the building a slight banana shape. Once again, the top was level.

FINAL ADDITION

Political unrest halted construction again, this time until 1360. By now the building was terribly off-center, but builders added the belfry anyway—again making the southern walls taller than the northern ones, to level out the roof. One hundred eighty-seven years after it was begun, the tower was finally finished.

But the tilt was only beginning. Over the next six centuries, the building moved a fraction of an inch each year. By the early 1990s, it was more than 14 feet off-center.

SAVING THE TOWER

By 1900 the Leaning Tower of Pisa had already become one of the world's great tourist attractions. So the Italian government just appointed a commission to figure out how to keep it from falling over.

The commission wasn't much help—except to the government, which was able to take credit for actively trying to save the tower. After that, whenever scientists speculated that the tower was falling, the government just appointed another commission. The only one that had any lasting impact was the 1933 commission . . . which made things worse. They drilled 361 holes in the ground surrounding the tower and filled them with 1,800 tons of concrete. Instead of stabilizing the ground, the concrete added weight to the tower's foundation, causing it to tip six times faster.

THE FINAL FIX

In 1989 the Italian government appointed its 15th commission. This time, it actually helped. In 1992 scientists began implementing a three-phase plan to halt the tilting:
1. In April 1992 five steel bands were strapped around the second floor of the building (judged to be weakest part). The belts act like girdles—when a masonry building collapses at the base, the part that gives way bursts *outward*, not inward. The bands hold everything in place.

There are 20 days in the Aztec week.

2. In the summer of 1993, scientists began placing 75 eight-ton weights on the north side of the tower, hoping that by compressing the earth to the north, the building would stop leaning so much to the south. By November the tower had actually straightened up about a quarter of an inch.

3. In 1995 the scientists began removing clay soil from beneath the tower, extracting the water, and replacing it all in a process they called "controlled subsistence." When they're finished, the tower will be resting on a drier, firmer soil base that will be better able to support the building.

The End?

In April 1997 John Burland, the British soil mechanics expert who devised the plan, announced that the Leaning Tower of Pisa had finally stopped its tilt. Has the tower been saved? Only time—a lot of it—will tell.

TOWER FACTS

- Six of the tower's eight floors are without safety rails. More than 250 people have fallen to their deaths since 1174.

- According to Italian officials, there's little danger anyone will be hurt if the tower does come crashing down. They predict that a collapse won't be sudden—that there will be plenty of rumbling and groaning in the building ahead of time to warn people. Besides: The building has been closed to the public since 1990.

- Restoration officials get an average of two letters a week with suggestions on how to keep the tower upright. Some of the weirdest: building an identical tower to lean against the first one; building a huge statue of a man who looks like he's holding the tower up; tying helium balloons to the roof; anchoring the top of the tower to a hillside several miles away with a large steel cable.

- Of course, officials could tear the tower down, stone by stone, and rebuild it—this time perfectly vertical—on a strengthened foundation. But there's no chance of that—the tower brings in $300 million a year from tourists. "Let's face it, the tower would have no significance if it were straight," caretaker Spartacom Campani admitted in 1983. "Its lean is Pisa's bread and butter."

Cats have two sets of vocal chords: one for purring, one for meowing.

FIRST FILMS

People like Arnold Schwarzenegger would probably just as soon
you forgot about the films they had to make before hitting it big. But
Jami Bernard didn't forget—she wrote First Films, a book we used
to research this section. We recommend it. The best of its kind.

MERYL STREEP
First Film: *Julia* (1976)
The Role: She plays a snooty, shallow friend of the lead
characters (played by Jane Fonda and Vanessa Redgrave). If you
blink, you might miss her—her two scenes last a total of 61 seconds and her back is to the camera most of the time. She's also
wearing a black wig (which she hated).
Memorable Line: "Oooh . . . you're so famous."

PAUL NEWMAN
First Film: *The Silver Chalice* (1954)
The Role: Newman plays Basil, a Roman slave selected to make
the chalice for Jesus' last meal because he can whittle better than
anyone in Jerusalem. Publicity posters called it *The Mightiest Story*
of Good and Evil Ever Told, Ever Lived, Ever Made into a Motion
Picture! Newman called it "the worst film made in the entirety of
the 1950s." At one point, he even took out a magazine ad urging
people not to see it.

ARNOLD SCHWARZENEGGER
First Film: *Hercules in New York* (1969)—rereleased on video as
Hercules Goes Bananas
The Role: Arnold plays Hercules, of course. Viewers got their first
look at his pumped-up body (including a ludicrous scene in which
he "bounces one pectoral muscle at a time"). But they never heard
his voice. The 22-year-old Austrian's accent was so thick, no one
could understand him. Result: His entire part (but only his) had to
be dubbed. The film is so bad that Schwarzenegger—who was originally billed as "Arnold Strong"—won't acknowledge it.
Memorable Line (When a cabbie demands payment): "Bucks?
Doe? What is all this zoological talk about the male and female
species?"

On average, females hear better than males at every age.

JANE FONDA

First Film: *Tall Story* (1960)

The Role: Not what you'd expect. The future feminist plays June, a 21-year-old home economics major and cheerleader who's got her sights set on the school's basketball star and top scholar (Anthony Perkins). Once she gets him—about a third of the way through the film—she fades into the background. The story then focuses on Perkins's basketball dramas.

Memorable line: (On why she came to college) "The same reason that every girl, if she's honest, comes to college—to get married."

NICOLAS CAGE

First Film: *Fast Times at Ridgemont High* (1982)

The Role: "Brad's Bud"—a part so small that the writers didn't even bother giving him a name (or any lines). Most of his part was cut out, but you can still see him looking miserable behind the grill at All-American Burger. He was billed as Nicolas Coppola, but got so much flak from the cast about being director Francis Coppola's nephew that by his next film he'd changed his name to Cage.

MICHELLE PFEIFFER

First Film: *Hollywood Knights* (1980)

The Role: "Sporting her old nose and too much eye-liner . . . she [plays] Suzy Q, a carhop at Tubby's Drive-In, where her job requires her to wear tall, white go-go boots." On the side, she's an aspiring actress and girlfriend to Tony Danza—who also makes his screen debut in this "low-rent ripoff of *American Graffiti*."

Memorable line: "I have an audition in the morning."

TOM HANKS

First Film: *He knows You're Alone* (1980)

The Role: Hanks is on for 3 1/2 minutes in this low-budget psycho-slasher film. He plays a college student who meets two of the killer's future victims and takes them on a date to a Staten Island amusement park. That's about it.

Memorable line: "Want a goober?"

Genetically speaking, a guinea pig is more closely related to a cow than it is to a rat.

IT'S SO BAD, IT'S...

*Well . . . funny, anyway. Here's some dialogue from B sci-fi films.
No kidding, someone actually got paid to write this stuff.*

Scientist: "They took five death row inmates and injected them with a genetic code of sorts, taken from different species of fish, primarily salmon. It essentially fuses with the genetic material already existing."

Astonished Listener: "Fish-men!?"

Scientist: "You could say that. The goal was to create an amphibious soldier, but . . . something went wrong."

—Humanoids from the Deep

Dr. Wagner: "But you're sacrificing a human life!"

Dr. Brandon (mad scientist): "Do you cry over a guinea pig? This boy is a free police case. We're probably saving him from the gas chamber."

Dr. Wagner: "But the boy is so young, the transformation horrible . . ."

Dr. Brandon: "And you call yourself a scientist! That's why you've never been more than an assistant."

—I Was a Teenage Werewolf

Teenager: "You know something? Those things, whatever they are—they're smarter than all of us put together."

—The Eye Creatures

Dr. Durea: "Oh, she's a lucky young woman, [Dr.] Groton. We have desperate need of her blood. She has survived decapitation and is manufacturing the right type of vital fluid for us. We are not butchers, Groton! We don't have this young lady here to merely drain her body and cast her aside! No. We are scientists! And we must have others to experiment with!"

—Dracula vs. Frankenstein

More than 50% of all the lakes in the world are in Canada.

First Scientist: "You say you made a close examination of this light?"

Second Scientist: "Not as close as I would have liked. It was being guarded by a . . . a sea serpent! A hideous beast that defies description!"

First Scientist: "Oh, doctor, if I didn't know you were a scientist of high standards, I'd say you were a victim of the ridiculous 'Phantom' stories that are running wild around the village!"
—*The Phantom from 10,000 Leagues*

Steve (hero scientist): "Who are you? What do you want?"

Evil alien brain: "I am Gor! I need your body as a dwelling-place while I am here on your planet Earth!"

Steve: "Why me?"

Gor: "Because you are a recognized nuclear scientist. Because you have entrée to places on Earth I want to go. I chose your body very carefully, even before I knew about Sally—a very exciting female!"

Steve: "Leave Sally out of this!"

Gor: "Why? She appeals to me! There are some aspects of the life of an Earth savage that are exciting and rewarding! Things that are missed by the brains on my planet, Arous."
—*The Brain from Planet Arous*

Dr. Marvin (hero scientist): "General, we saw a strange thing this afternoon. We saw what appeared to be a flying saucer."

General Hanley: "A flying saucer!?"

Carol Marvin (scientist's new wife): "It nearly ran us off the road."

Hanley: "You're sure of that?"

Dr. Marvin: "Both Carol and I are subject to the same atmospheric disturbances that may have affected other observers, but there is a quantitative difference, when you're a scientist."

Dr. Marvin: "What do you want with me?"

Alien: "Arrange for your world leaders to confer with us in the city of Washington, D.C."

Dr. Marvin: "They may not listen! I'm only a scientist!"
—*Earth Versus the Flying Saucers*

Most snails travel at the speed of 25 miles per day.

THE PERSONALS

We admit it—we like to sneak a peek at the personal ads every once in a while. Even when they're completely serious, they're fascinating. And when they're strange, they're irresistible. Most of these ads were collected by Kathy Hinckley for her book Plain Fat Chick Seeks Guy Who Likes Broccoli.

WOMEN SEEKING MEN

Me: Buxom blonde with blue eyes. You: elderly, marriage-minded millionaire with bad heart.

I like driving around with my two cats, especially on the freeway. I make them wear little hats so that I can use the carpool lane. Way too much time on your hands too? Call me.

Lonely Christian woman has not sung Glory Hallelujah in a long time. Write soon!

Cute guy with snowplow sought by head-turnin', zany, brainy, late-30s Babe to share happy time in the big drive-way of love. A rake for spring-time a big plus!

Coldhearted, insensitive unconscionable, selfish, hedo-nistic, drunk liar seeks next gullible male without enough sense to stay away from me.

MEN SEEKING WOMEN

Mentally ill? Are you restrained in a straight-jacket? Do you think you're a chicken? Did you kill and eat your last boyfriend? I don't mind. This tall, educated, pro-fessional SWM would like to meet an interesting woman!

I drink a lot of beer, smoke a lot of cigars, and watch foot-ball non-stop from September to January. I seek a woman, 18–32, to share this with.

If it takes a three-legged ele-phant with one tusk five days to cross the Sahara Desert, how many times do I have to put an ad in to get one call?

Award-winning poet, 27 yrs., seeks short-term, intense, doomed relationship for inspi-ration. Must be attractive, sensual, articulate, ruthless, 21–30 yrs., under 5'6". Break my heart, please.

The Chilean Pudu, the smallest member of the deer family, is no larger than a rabbit.

WHY ASK WHY?

Here are more cosmic queries you don't need to answer,
from the Internet and our friends at "The Edge."

Who needs rhetorical questions?

Why do they sterilize the needles for lethal injections?

How do they get the deer to cross the road at the yellow sign?

Why do kamikaze pilots wear helmets?

What do you do when you discover an endangered animal that eats only endangered plants?

If women wear a pair of pants and a pair of glasses, why don't they wear a pair of bras?

Twenty-four hours in a day . . . twenty-four beers in a case . . . coincidence?

Why do they put braille dots on the keypad of the drive-up ATM?

When you're sending someone Styrofoam, what do you pack it in?

Do witches run spell-checks?

If 7-11 is open 24 hours a day, 365 days a year, why are there locks on the doors?

If someone with multiple personalities threatens to kill himself, is it considered a hostage situation?

How can there be self-help groups?

What's another word for *thesaurus?*

If it's tourist season, why can't we shoot them?

Is it true that cannibals don't eat clowns because they taste funny?

When you choke a Smurf, what color does it turn?

If dolphins are so smart, why did Flipper work for television?

If you haven't understood me to this point, why do I bother? If you have understood me, why are you listening?

Top speed attained in the first American auto race in Chicago in 1895: 7.5 mph.

HOW A MICROWAVE WORKS

We gave you a brief history of the microwave oven on page 473. Now here's the rest of the story—the science that makes it work.

WHAT ARE MICROWAVES?

Here's the first thing you should know about "microwaves": Like visible light, radio waves, and X-rays, they are waves of electromagnetic energy. What makes the four waves different from one another? Each has a different length (wavelength) and vibrates at a different speed (frequency).

- Microwaves get their name because their wavelength is much shorter than electromagnetic waves that carry TV and radio signals.

- The microwaves in a microwave oven have a wavelength of about four inches, and they vibrate 2.5 billion times per second—about the same natural frequency as water molecules. That's what makes them so effective at heating food.

- A conventional oven heats the air in the oven, which then cooks the food. But microwaves cause water molecules in the food to vibrate at high speeds, creating heat. The heated water molecules are what cook the food.

- Glass, ceramic, and plastic plates contain virtually no water molecules, which is why they don't heat up in the microwave.

MICROWAVE MECHANICS

- When the microwave oven is turned on, electricity passes through the magnetron, the tube which produces microwaves. The microwaves are then channeled down a metal tube (waveguide) and through a slow rotating metal fan (stirrer), which scatters them into the part of the oven where the food is placed.

- The walls of the oven are made of metal, which reflects microwaves the same way that a mirror reflects visible light.

First U.S. president born outside the original 13 states: Abe Lincoln.

So when the microwaves hit the stirrer and are scattered into the food chamber, they bounce off the metal walls and penetrate the food from every direction. Some ovens have a rotating turntable that helps food cook more evenly.

- Do microwave ovens cook food from the inside out? Some people think so, but the answer seems to be no. Microwaves cook food from the outside in, like conventional ovens. But the microwave energy only penetrates about an inch into the food. The heat that's created by the water molecules then penetrates deeper into the food, cooking it all the way through. This secondary cooking process is known as "conduction."

- The metal holes in the glass door of the microwave oven are large enough to let out visible light (which has a small wavelength), but too small to allow the microwaves (which have a larger wavelength) to escape. So you can see what's cooking without getting cooked yourself.

YOU CALL THAT COOKING?

According to legend, shortly after Raytheon perfected its first microwave oven in the 1950s, Charles Adams, the chairman of Raytheon, had one installed in his kitchen so he could taste for himself what microwave-cooked food was like. But as Adams's cook quickly discovered, meat didn't brown in the oven, french fries stayed limp and damp, and cakes didn't rise. The cook, condemning the oven as "black magic," quit.

When sales of microwave ovens took off in the late 1980s, millions of cooks discovered the same thing: microwaves just don't cook some foods as well as regular ovens do. The reason: Because microwaves cook by exciting the water molecules in food, the food inside a microwave oven rarely cooks at temperatures higher than 212°F, the temperature at which water turns to steam.

Conventional ovens, on the other hand, cook at temperatures as high as 550°F. High temperatures are needed to caramelize sugars and break down proteins, carbohydrates, and other substances and combine them into more complex flavors. So microwave ovens can't do any of this, and they can't bake, either.

Some people feel this is the microwave's Achilles heel. "The name 'microwave oven' is a misnomer," says Cindy Ayers, an executive with Campbell's Soup. "It doesn't do what an oven does."

It takes about 30 minutes for aspirin to find a headache.

"It's a glorified popcorn popper," says Tom Vierhile, a researcher with *Marketing Intelligence*, a newsletter that tracks microwave sales. "When the microwave first came out, people thought they had stumbled on nirvana. It's not the appliance the food industry thought it would be. It's a major disappointment."

Adds one cooking critic: "Microwave sales are still strong, but time will tell whether they have a future in the American kitchen." In the meantime, Uncle John isn't holding his breath—he's too busy heating up leftovers.

MICROWAVE FACTS

- Have you heard that microwave ovens are dangerous? In 1968 the Walter Reed Hospital tested them to see if the microwaves leaked out. They did—and the government stepped in to set the first federal standards for microwave construction. Today all microwaves sold in the U.S. must be manufactured according to federal safety standards.

- If you microwave your foods in a square container and aren't happy with the results, try cooking them in a round one. "Food cooks better in a round container than in a square one," says Jim Watkins, president of the company that makes Healthy Choice microwave food products. "No one really knows why."

- Irregularly shaped foods, such as a leg of chicken that is thick at one end and thin at the other end, cook unevenly.

- Food that has been cut up will also cook faster than a single, large piece of food, for the same reason: the microwaves penetrate completely through smaller pieces of food, but not through larger pieces.

- Aluminum foil reflects microwave energy the same way mirrors reflect light energy. That's why you can't use foil in a microwave.

MYTH-CONCEPTIONS

*Common knowledge is frequently wrong. Here are a few examples
of things that most people believe . . . but just aren't true.*

Myth: Watching TV in a dark room is bad for your eyesight.
Fact: As Paul Dickson and Joseph C. Goulden write in
Myth-Informed, "The myth was created in the early 1950s by an
innovative Philadelphia public relations man named J. Robert
Mendte, on behalf of a client who manufactured lamps."

Myth: For every cockroach you see in your house, there are 10
more you don't see.
Fact: According to studies conducted by the Insects Affecting Man
and Animals Laboratory of the U.S. Department of Agriculture,
the number is actually closer to 1,000 to 1.

Myth: Flamingos are naturally pink.
Fact: Flamingos are grey when chicks. They turn pink as adults
because the sea creatures they eat turn pink during digestion. The
pigment is then absorbed by the bird's body and colors its feathers.
If flamingos are fed a different diet, they're white.

Myth: Johnny Weissmuller's famous Tarzan yell was his own voice.
Fact: His voice was combined with a high C sung by a soprano,
and a hyena's howl recorded on tape and played backward.

Myth: All your fingernails grow at the same rate.
Fact: If you're right-handed, nails on your right hand grow faster; if
you're left-handed, nails on your left will.

Myth: Tonto's nickname for the Lone Ranger, Kemo Sabe, means
"faithful friend."
Fact: In Apache *Kemo Sabe* means "white shirt," and in Navaho it
means "soggy shrub." But George Trendle, who created the Lone
Ranger, didn't know that. He took the name from a summer camp
he went to as a boy.

Caterpillars fast during the day.

Myth: The artist Vincent Van Gogh cut off his entire ear.

Fact: The famous episode followed two months of hard work, hard drinking, and an argument with his best friend, Paul Gauguin. Van Gogh was despondent and cut off only a small part of his earlobe.

Myth: Hens cannot lay eggs without a rooster.

Fact: Almost all eggs we buy in the store are unfertile eggs, laid by hens with no help from a rooster.

Myth: More women in the U.S. have had face lifts than any other type of cosmetic surgery.

Fact: Nope, the cosmetic surgery performed most frequently on women in the U.S. is liposuction. The second most popular process: collagen injections.

Myth: John Kennedy is one of many presidents buried in Washington, D.C.

Fact: Actually, there are only three. William Howard Taft (27th president) and Woodrow Wilson (28th president) are the other ones.

Myth: The largest pyramid in the world is in Egypt.

Fact: The Quetzalcoatl pyramid southeast of Mexico City is 177' tall, with a base covering 45 acres and a volume of 120 million cubic feet. Cheops, the largest in Egypt, though originally 481' tall, has a base covering only 13 acres and a volume of only 90 million cubic feet.

Myth: Giraffes have more vertebrae in their necks than other mammals.

Fact: They're the same as the rest of us. Although giraffes have the longest neck of any animal—10 to 12 feet—they have the same number of vertebrae as all mammals, including humans. The giraffe's neck bones are farther apart, though.

Myth: Air fresheners remove offending odors from the air.

Fact: Not even close. Actually, they either cover smells up with a stronger scent, or make your nose numb so you can't smell the bad stuff. The only way you can get rid of odors is with expensive absorption agents like charcoal or silica gel.

Leading cause of death in Papua, New Guinea: falling out of trees.

SEINFELD-OLOGY

Commentary from one of America's most popular comedians.

"Now they show you how detergents take out bloodstains, a pretty violent image there. I think if you've got a T-shirt with bloodstains all over it, maybe laundry isn't your biggest problem. Maybe you should get rid of the body before you do the wash."

"Nothing in life is 'fun for the whole family.'"

"It's amazing that the amount of news that happens in the world every day just exactly fits the newspaper."

"Seventy-five percent of your body heat is lost through the top of your head. Which sounds like you could go skiing naked if you got a good hat."

"My parents didn't want to move to Florida, but they turned sixty, and that's the law."

"Let me ask you something. If someone's lying, are their pants really on fire?"

"A date is like a job interview that lasts all night. The only difference between the two is that there are very few job interviews where there's a chance you will wind up naked at the end of it."

"One of the powers of adulthood is the ability to be totally bored and remain standing. That's why they could set up the DMV that way."

"Where lipstick is concerned, the important thing is not what color to choose, but to accept God's decision on where your lips end."

"Why does McDonald's have to count every burger that they sell? What is their ultimate goal? Do they want cows to surrender voluntarily?

"You know why dogs have no money? No pockets. 'Cause they see change on the street all the time and it's driving them crazy when you're walking them. He is always looking up at you: 'There's a quarter . . .'"

THE FIGHT FOR SAFE MILK, PART I

"Milk and kids" are virtually synonymous in our culture with "good health." But that wasn't always the case. Until the early 1900s, milk was often adulterated with foreign substances, taken from sick cows, or mishandled during milking and storage. As a result, it was often host to tuberculosis, cholera, typhoid fever, and other life-threatening diseases. But few people knew that the milk made them sick. It wasn't until the late 19th century, when scientists began to understand germ theory, that they realized diseases were being transmitted through milk—and that they could do something to eliminate the hazard. Here's a fascinating but little-known story from American history.

THE GOOD OLD DAYS

In the days before registration, farmers who lived near towns delivered milk the old-fashioned way: They brought a cow into town and went door to door looking for customers. Anyone who wanted milk could step out into the street with a pitcher or a bucket, and watch the farmer milk the cow right before their eyes.

Since customers were standing only a few feet away, it paid for the farmer to take good care of his cows. Nobody wanted to buy milk from a beast that looked mistreated, dirty, or sick. So although there was a risk of buying bad milk, it was kept to a minimum.

CITY SLICKERS

But in cities, where door-to-door cow service wasn't practical or possible, buying milk was another matter. "Milk sellers" acted as middlemen between farmers and townspeople. Like used car dealers today, they were widely mistrusted and said to possess "neither character, nor decency of manner, nor cleanliness." Whether or not the reputation was deserved, they were notorious for diluting milk with water to increase profits. People said their milk came from "black cows," the black cast-iron pumps that provided towns

---

Humphrey Bogart's first line as an actor: "Tennis, anyone?"

with drinking water. And if the pump was broken, horse troughs were always a handy source of water.

Although it actually spread serious diseases, watered-down milk was seen as more of an annoyance than a health hazard, and nothing much was done about it. It wasn't until the 1840s that scandals in the *liquor* industry led to the first demands for milk reform.

THE SWILL MILK SCANDALS

In the mid-1800s it was common for whiskey and other liquor distillers to run dairy and beef businesses on the side. The manufacture of grain alcohol requires huge amounts of corn, rye, and other fresh grains, which are cooked into a mash and then distilled. Once the distillation is complete, the remaining "swill" can be discarded . . . or, as the distilleries discovered, it could be fed to cows.

Profit, not quality, was the priority with "swill herds." As a result, conditions in many distillery-owned dairies were atrocious. The cows spent their entire lives tied up in tiny pens, which were rarely cleaned. They received no food other than the swill—and no fresh water at all since, distillers thought, there was already plenty of water in the swill.

SPOILED MILK

With no exercise, no real food, and no water, even the hardiest cattle sickened and died in about six months. The failing herds were milked daily until the very end; when a cow became too weak to stand on its own, it was hoisted upright with ropes so that it could be milked until it died.

Milk produced by swill herds, as muckraking journalist Robert Hartley wrote in 1842, was "very thin, and of a pale bluish color," the kind nobody in their right mind would buy. So distilleries added flour, starch, chalk, plaster of Paris, or anything else they could get away with to make the milk look healthy. This adulteration only increased the amount of bacteria in milk that was already virtually undrinkable.

TAKING NOTICE

The toll that adulterated milk took on public health was severe: in New York City, where five million gallons of swill milk were produced and sold each year, the mortality rate of children under five tripled between 1843 and 1856.

The speed of a roller coaster increases an average of 10 mph when it's raining.

No one knew for sure what was causing the child mortality rate to soar, and there was probably no single cause. But people began to suspect that bad milk was at least partially to blame. In May 1858 *Frank Leslie's Illustrated Newspaper*, one of the most popular journals of the day, published a series of articles describing in graphic detail the conditions in some of New York's swill dairies.

REFORMS
Public exposure had a devastating impact on the industry. Some distilleries got out of the milk business entirely; others cleaned up their act. Those that remained were forced out of business in 1862, when the state of New York outlawed "crowded or unhealthy conditions" in the dairy industry. Two years later, the state outlawed the industry outright, declaring that "any milk that is obtained from animals fed on distillery waste, usually called swill, is hereby declared to be impure and unwholesome."

Several other states followed suit, including Massachusetts, Pennsylvania, Illinois, Kentucky, and Indiana. As they took action, the spiraling infant death rate in the U.S. leveled off—and even began to decline. But there was still plenty of work to be done to ensure that milk was safe.

For the next part of the story, turn to page 744.

For the next part of the story, turn to page 744.

* * *

TWO-LETTER SCRABBLE WORDS

Some unusual two-letter words that are acceptable to use in Scrabble.

aa	ba	er	ka	na	oy
ae	bo	es	la	ne	pe
ag	da	et	li	nu	pi
ai	de	ex	lo	od	re
al	ef	fa	mi	oe	sh
ar	eh	hm	mm	op	si
aw	em	ho	mo	or	ta
ay	en	jo	mu	os	ti

Honolulu is Hawaiian for "sheltered harbor."

LOVE POTION #9

People have been looking for aphrodisiacs since the beginning of recorded time. Most of the concoctions they've come up with are pretty weird and basically worthless. But some, it turns out, may actually work.

ORIGIN OF THE TERM

The word *aphrodisiac* comes from *Aphrodite*, the Greek goddess of love and beauty (also known as *Kallipygos*, or "Beautiful Buttocks" in Greek).

- Aphrodite was originally supposed to be the embodiment of pure beauty and heavenly love. But over the years she came to represent great prowess in sexuality and seduction as well.
- Eventually, according to the *Dictionary of Word and Phrase Origins*, her name was used "to describe any drug or other substances used to heighten one's amatory desires."

APHRODISIACS IN HISTORY

As sex therapist Dr. Ruth Westheimer says—and history proves—"an aphrodisiac is anything you think it is."

- In the Middle Ages people believed that "eating an apple soaked in your lover's armpit is a sure means of seduction." Others drank the urine of powerful animals to increase sexual powers.
- A 15th-century Middle Eastern book entitled *The Perfumed Garden for the Soul's Delectation* suggested that lovers eat a sparrow's tongue, and chase it down with a cocktail made of honey, 20 almonds, and parts of a pine tree.
- People once thought that eating any plant that looks phallic would increase male virility—carrots, asparagus, and mandrake root were especially popular. Bulbs and tubers—e.g., onions—which people thought resembled testicles, were also believed to increase sexual potency, And peaches, tomatoes, mangos, or other soft, moist fruits were considered aphrodisiacs for women.
- In *Consuming Passions*, Peter Farb and George Armelagos write that during the 1500s and 1600s, "Europe was suddenly flooded with exotic plants whose very strangeness suggested the existence of secret powers." For example: Tomatoes brought back from South America were at first thought to be the forbidden

A *cremnophobe* is someone who is afraid of falling down the stairs.

fruit of Eden, and were known as "love apples." And when potatoes first arrived in Europe—the sweet potato probably brought back by Columbus and the white potato somewhat later—they were immediately celebrated as potent sexual stimulants . . . A work dated 1850 tells the English reader that the white potato will "incite to Venus."

- In the 20th century everything from green M&M's to products like Cleopatra Oil and Indian Love Powder have been passed off as aphrodisiacs. Even in 1989 a British mail-order firm called Comet Scientific was offering an aerosol spray that it claimed made men "irresistible to women."

DANGEROUS APHRODISIACS

- Spanish fly, one of the most famous aphrodisiacs, is also one of the most dangerous. It has nothing to do with Spain or flies. It's really the dried, crushed remains of an insect known as the "blister beetle." Although it can constrict blood vessels, and thus may appear to be a sexual stimulant, it's actually a deadly poison. It can do irreparable damage to the kidneys.

- For thousands of years, people (especially in the Far East) have believed that by eating part of a powerful animal, a man can absorb its sexual vitality. This has led to the ingestion of such weird stuff as dried and powdered bear gallbladders, camel humps, and rhinoceros horns. (In fact, animal horns have been considered sexual stimulants for so long that the term "horny" became slang for "a need for sex.") It has also had a drastic effect on some endangered species. *U.S. News & World Report* noted in 1989 that "with a kilo of rhino horn fetching $42,800 in Taiwan, poachers have slaughtered rhinos so relentlessly that barely 11,000 survive." And in North America, poachers have killed thousands of black bears to get their golf ball–sized gallbladders.

THE REAL THING

Traditionally, scientists have dismissed aphrodisiacs as frauds. But new research into medicinal herbs and pheromones (chemical messengers) has produced some interesting results. Experts now believe that some aphrodisiacs may really work. Here are seven "maybes."

1. Yohimbe: The bark of a West African tree thought for centuries to produce passion in African men. Research has found that

Chili comes from an Aztec word that means "bowl of red."

the chemical yohimbine can in fact excite men by increasing blood flow. The drug was approved by the FDA 10 years ago as a prescription treatment for impotence.

2. Oysters: Traditionally considered an aphrodisiac because of their association with the sea and their resemblance to female sex organs. However, now we also know that they're very rich in zinc—a mineral necessary to male sexual health. A man deficient in zinc is at high risk for infertility and loss of libido.

3. Chocolate: Contains PEA, a neurotransmitter that is a natural form of the stimulant amphetamine. It has been shown that either love or lust increases the level of PEA in the bloodstream and that with heartbreak, the levels drop automatically.

4. Caffeine: Research has shown that coffee drinkers are more sexually active than non-drinkers, but no one's sure if that's because of something in the caffeine, or just because it keeps people awake, and therefore interested, after bedtime.

5. DHEA: This hormone has been called the "natural aphrodisiac" by doctors. It's been shown in studies that blood levels of DHEA predict sexual thoughts and desire. DHEA became a food-supplement fad when it was hyped in the media as a way to increase energy and maybe even prevent cancer or heart disease (as well as boosting the libido).

6. Cinnamon: According to Dr. Alan Hirsch, director of the Smell and Taste Research Foundation, the aroma of cinnamon has the ability to arouse lust. As reported in Psychology Today, "Hirsch fitted male medical students with guages that detected their excitement level, and then exposed them to dozens of fragrances. The only one that got a rise was the smell of hot cinnamon buns."

7. Androstenone: This is a pheromone. Scientists conducting research with animals found that androstenone produced by boars had a very positive effect on the sexual receptivity of sows. Androstenone is also found in human sweat.

FINAL THOUGHT
"Power is the great aphrodisiac."

—*Henry Kissinger*

The average cigar smoker can smoke an average cigar in about an hour and a half.

GIVE 'EM HELL, HARRY

A few words from Harry Truman, our 33rd president.

"It isn't polls or public opinion at the moment that counts. It is right and wrong and leadership—men with fortitude, honesty, and a belief in the right that makes epochs in the history of the world."

"We're going to lick 'em just as sure as you stand there!"

"Whenever the press quits abusing me, I know I'm in the wrong pew."

To his daughter: "Your dad will never be reckoned among the great. But you can be sure he did his level best and gave all he had to his country. There is an epitaph in Boot Hill Cemetery in Tombstone, Arizona, which reads 'Here lies Jack Williams; he done his damnedest.' What more can a person do?"

"If they want to ask me some impudent questions, I'll try to give them some impudent answers."

"You won't get any doubletalk from me. I'm either for something or against it."

"This is your fight. I am only waking you up to the fact that this is your fight. You better get out and help me win this fight, or you're going to be the loser, not I."

"I hope you will join me in my crusade to keep the country from going to the dogs."

"Some of the presidents were great, and some weren't. I can say that because I wasn't one of the great presidents, but I had a good time trying."

"I don't believe in anti-anything. A man has to have a program; you have to be for something, otherwise you will never get anywhere."

My favorite animal is the mule. He has more sense than a horse. He knows when to stop eating—and when to stop working."

One Swedish slang expression for "How are you?" is "Who stole the cash box?"

LET'S ROCK!

We'll bet you didn't know your favorite rock singers could talk, too. Here's some of the profound things they have to say, from The Great Rock 'n' Roll Quote Book, *by Merrit Malloy.*

"I'd rather have ten years of super-hypermost than live to be seventy by sitting in some goddamn chair watching TV."
—*Janis Joplin*

"When you're as rich as I am, you don't have to be political."
—*Sting*

"People used to throw rocks at me for my clothes. Now they wanna know where I buy them."
—*Cyndi Lauper*

"I'd rather be dead than singing 'Satisfaction' when I'm forty-five."
—*Mick Jagger*

"People have this obsession: They want you to be like you were in 1969. They want you to, because otherwise their youth goes with you, you know?"
—*Mick Jagger*

"Nobody loves me but my mother, and she could be jivin', too."
—*B. B. King*

"Rock journalism is people who can't write interviewing people who can't talk for people who can't read."
—*Frank Zappa*

"There are no more political statements. The only thing rock fans have in common is their music."
—**Bob Pittman, Vice President, MTV**

"Some American kid recognized who I was and he says, 'Your dad eats cow's heads.' My daughter says, 'You don't, Daddy. I've never seen you eat a cow's head.' I thought that was kind of sweet."
—*Ozzy Osbourne*

"I would think nothing of tipping over a table with a whole long spread on it just because there was turkey roll on the table and I had explicitly said, 'No turkey roll.'"
—*Steven Tyler, Aerosmith*

"Mainly, I helped wipe out the sixties."
—*Iggy Pop*

Woodrow Wilson was the last president to type all of his own letters.

OH, FRANKIE!

You might be surprised at the role that trickery played in helping an up-and-coming singer get the "lucky break" he needed.

BACKGROUND
In 1942 a young singer named Frank Sinatra gave a performance at New York's Paramount Theater. Until then, his career had gotten little attention. But that night was different— Sinatra played to a packed house and gave such a powerful performance that about 30 bobby-soxers passed out and had to be taken away in an ambulance. The publicity that the incident generated helped catapult Sinatra to superstardom in less than a year.

BEHIND THE SCENES
The decisive moment in Sinatra's career actually came a few weeks *before* the Paramount show, when his press agent, George Evans, saw a teenage girl throw a rose on stage while Sinatra was singing. "I figured if I could pack the theater with a bunch of girls screaming, 'Oh, Frankie,' I'd really have something," he recounted later.

So Evans paid a dozen teenage girls $5 each to sit in the front rows during the performance and swoon. Rehearsing with them in the basement of the Paramount, he taught some of them to faint in the aisles during the slow songs, and taught others to scream 'Oh, Daddy,' when Sinatra sang "Embraceable You." He made sure the theater was full by giving away free passes to schoolkids on vacation. He even rented the ambulance that waited in front of the theater to take the girls away.

MASS HYSTERIA
Evans paid only 12 girls, but in a classic moment of mass psychosis, hundreds of others got caught up in the "excitement." About 20 girls who *hadn't* been paid to pass out fainted . . . and the whole crowd went crazy. The next time he played the Paramount, recalls a promoter, "they threw more than roses. They threw their panties and their brassieres. They went nuts, absolutely nuts." Sinatramania was born. Ol' Blue Eyes went on to become the most popular singer of his generation. But Evans wasn't around to enjoy it. Sinatra fired him a few years later in a dispute over money.

69% of cake eaters eat the cake first, then the frosting.

WHAT HAPPENED AT ROSWELL? PART I

The "incident at Roswell" is probably the biggest UFO story in history. Was it a military balloon . . . or an alien spacecraft? You be the judge.

THE FIRST FLYING SAUCERS

In 1947 a U.S Forest Service pilot name Kenneth Arnold was flying over the Cascade Mountains in Washington State in search of a missing plane when he spotted what he claimed were nine "disc-shaped craft." He calculated them to be moving at speeds of 1,200 miles per hour, far faster than any human-built aircraft of the 1940s could manage.

When he talked to reporters after the flight, Arnold said the crafts moved "like a *saucer* skipping over water," and a newspaper editor, hearing the description, called the objects "flying saucers." Thus, the expression "flying saucer" entered the English language, and a UFO craze much like the one that followed Orson Welles's 1938 broadcast of *War of the Worlds* swept the country. "Almost instantly," Dava Sobel writes in her article *The Truth About Roswell*, "believable witnesses from other states and several countries reported similar sightings, enlivening wire-service dispatches for days."

THE ROSWELL DISCOVERY

It was in this atmosphere that William "Mac" Brazel made an unusual discovery. On July 8, 1947, while riding across his ranch 26 miles outside of Roswell, New Mexico, he came across some mysterious wreckage—sticks, foil paper, tape, and other debris. Brazel had never seen anything like it, but UFOs were on his mind. He'd read about Arnold's sighting in the newspaper and had heard about a national contest offering $3,000 to anyone who recovered a flying saucer. He wondered if he'd stumbled across just the kind of evidence the contest organizers were looking for.

Brazel gathered a few pieces of the stuff and showed it to his neighbors, Floyd and Loretta Proctor. The Proctors didn't know what it was, either. And neither did George Wilcox, the county sheriff. So Brazel contacted officials at the nearby Roswell Army Air Force base to see if they could help.

The Cambodian language has 72 letters in its alphabet, the most of any language.

The next day, an Army Intelligence Officer named Jesse Marcel went out to Brazel's ranch to have a look. He was as baffled as everyone else. "I saw . . . small bits of metal," he recalled to reporters years later, "but mostly we found some material that's hard to describe." Some of it "looked very much like parchment" and some of it consisted of square sticks as long as four feet. Much was metallic.

The stuff was also surprisingly light—Brazel later estimated that all the scraps together didn't weigh more than five pounds. Marcel and his assistant had no trouble loading all the debris into their cars and driving it back to the Roswell base. The next day, Marcel took it to another base, in Fort Worth, Texas, where it was examined further.

SUSPICIOUS FACTS
Was the Wreckage from Outer Space?

- Brazel and the Proctors examined some of the debris before surrendering it to the military. Although it seemed flimsy at first, it was extremely resilient. "We tried to burn it, but it wouldn't ignite," Loretta recalls. "We tried to cut it and scrape at it, but a knife wouldn't touch it . . . It looked like wood or plastic, but back then we didn't have plastic. Back then, we figured it doesn't look like a weather balloon. I don't think it was something from this Earth."

The Military's About-Face

- The morning after the military took possession of the wreckage, the media relations officer at Roswell hand-delivered a news release to the two radio stations and newspapers in town. The release stated that the object found in Brazel's field was a "flying disc," which in the 1940s was synonymous with "flying saucer." It was the first time in history that the U.S. military had ever made such a claim.

- A few hours later, though, the military changed its story: it issued a new press release claiming that the wreckage was that of a weather balloon carrying a radar target, not a "flying disc." But it was too late—the newspaper deadline had already passed. They ran the first news release on the front page, under the headline

AIR FORCE CAPTURES FLYING SAUCER
ON RANCH IN ROSWELL REGION

Other newspapers picked up the story and ran it as well; within 24 hours, news of the military's "capture" spread around the globe.

Babe Ruth wore a cabbage leaf under his baseball cap to keep cool during games.

- Interest in the story was so great that the next day, Brig. Gen. Roger Ramey, commander of the U.S. Eighth Air Force, had to hold a press conference in Fort Worth in which he again stated that the recovered object was only a weather balloon and a radar target that was suspended from it. He even displayed the wreckage for reporters and allowed them to photograph it.

Mr. Brazel's Unusual Behavior

- Mac Brazel refused to talk about the incident for the rest of his life, even with members of his immediate family, except to say that "whatever the wreckage was, it wasn't any type of balloon." Why the silence? His son Bill explains: "The Air Force asked him to take an oath that he wouldn't tell anybody in detail about it. My dad was such a guy that he went to his grave and he *never* told anyone."

- Kevin Randle and Donald Schmitt, authors of *UFO Crash at Roswell*, claim that shortly after Brazel made his famous discovery, "His neighbors noticed a change in his lifestyle . . . He suddenly seemed to have more money . . . When he returned, he drove a new pickup truck . . . he also had the money to buy a new house in Tularosa, New Mexico, and a meat locker in Las Cruces." Randle and Schmitt believe the military may have paid Brazel for his silence.

TRUST ME

Today, if the government announced it had captured a UFO—even if it was mistaken—and tried to change its story a few hours later by claiming it was really a weather balloon, nobody would buy it. But people were more trusting in the years just following World War II. Amazingly, the story died away. As Dava Sobel writes:

> The Army's announcement of the "weather balloon" explanation ended the flying saucer excitement. All mention of the craft dropped from the newspapers, from military records, from the national consciousness, and even from the talk of the town in Roswell.

Even the *Roswell Daily Record*—which broke the story in the first place—was satisfied with the military's explanation. A few days later, it ran a headline that was even bigger than the first one:

GENERAL RAMEY EMPTIES ROSWELL SAUCER

And that was the end of it . . . or was it? See page 731 for more.

60% of pets in Great Britain have some form of health insurance.

THE TONIGHT SHOW PART IV: JACK PAAR'S NEARLY FATAL BATHROOM JOKE

Did you know that bathroom humor nearly killed The Tonight Show *in 1960? It was a big story that year—if you're old enough to have watched* The Tonight Show *back then, you probably remember it well. If not, here's the tale. (Part III is on page 598.)*

FEBRUARY 10, 1960

It began like any other night on *The Tonight Show*. Jack Paar walked out onstage, greeted the audience, and began his monologue.

On this night, however, things would be different. Paar wanted to tell a joke he'd heard from a friend. The friend had learned it from his daughter, who learned it when her junior high school teacher told it to the class. After telling the joke, the teacher passed out typewritten copies of it for the kids to share with their parents. The girl's father liked the joke so much that he gave his copy to Paar.

The joke was slightly risqué by 1960 TV standards. But Paar figured that if it was appropriate for a junior high school class, it was appropriate for his television audience. "I could have read it in church," he joked years later. "Not on Sundays, but I could read it during choir practice on Wednesday."

Paar told the audience that he had debated reading the joke on the show, and hinted that it might not appeal to everyone. "There's a slight question of taste involved here," he said. "I do this only with full knowledge that we're an adult group gathered at this hour, and we're not here to do anyone any harm." And then he told the joke.

The Ford Motor Co. earned an average of $2 profit on each Model T it manufactured.

THE JOKE

"An English lady, while visiting Switzerland, was looking for a room, and she asked the schoolmaster if he could recommend any to her. He took her to see several rooms, and when everything was settled, the lady returned to her home to make the final preparations to move.

"When she arrived home, the thought suddenly occurred to her that she had not seen a W.C. That's a water closet to the British. We would call it a bathroom or ladies' room, men's room. I guess a bathroom.

"So she immediately wrote a note to the schoolmaster asking him if there were a W.C. around. The schoolmaster was a very poor student of English, so he asked the parish priest if he could help in the matter. Together they tried to discover the meaning of the letters W.C. and the only solution they could find for the letters was a 'Wayside Chapel.' The schoolmaster then wrote to the English lady the following note:

DEAR MADAM:

I take great pleasure in informing you that the W.C. is situated nine miles from the house you occupy, in the center of a beautiful grove of pine trees surrounded by lovely grounds. It is capable of holding 229 people and it is open on Sunday and Thursday only. As there is a great number of people and they are expected during the summer months, I would suggest that you come early, although there is plenty of standing room as a rule.

You will no doubt be glad to hear that a good number of people bring their lunch and make a day of it, while others who can afford to go by car and arrive just in time. I would especially recommend that your ladyship go on Thursday when there is musical accompaniment.

It may interest you to know that my daughter was married in the W.C. and it was there that she met her husband. I can remember the rush there was for seats. There were ten people to a seat usually occupied by one. It was wonderful to see the expressions on their faces.

The newest attraction is a bell donated by a wealthy resident of the district. It rings every time a person enters. A bazaar is to be held to provide plush seats for all the people, since they feel it is a

Smallest U.S. town: Hove Mobile Park City, ND, with a population of two.

long-felt need. My wife is rather delicate, so she can't attend regularly.

I shall be delighted to reserve the best seat for you if you wish, where you will be seen by all. For the children, there is a special time and place so that they will not disturb the elders. Hoping to have been some service to you, I remain

Sincerely,
The Schoolmaster

THAT'S NO JOKE

The joke got a hearty laugh from the audience. Paar thanked them and said, "You're my kind of people."

But apparently they weren't NBC's kind of people. Then, as now, *The Tonight Show* was taped in the afternoon, and broadcast at 11:30 p.m. after NBC censors had a chance to look it over. They had never made any substantive changes in the show before . . . but that night they excised the entire water closet joke without telling Paar in advance. "Some idiot got concerned about the words 'water closet,'" he later explained.

Paar was angry when he found out what had happened, but he thought the controversy would make for an interesting discussion on his show. He proposed airing the censored joke the following evening, to "let the viewers decide for themselves" whether it was appropriate. NBC refused. Paar was furious—he felt the censorship was damaging to his reputation, since it implied that he had told a smutty joke on TV.

THAT'S ALL FOLKS

The following evening, Paar walked out onto the stage as usual . . . but rather than deliver his monologue, he vented his rage at NBC. Calling the censorship "a question of free speech," Paar announced that he was quitting *The Tonight Show*. "There must be a better way to make a living than this," he said. "I love NBC, and they've been wonderful to me, but they let me down." Then he bade farewell to the audience, telling them, "You've always been peachy to me, always."

He walked off the stage and went home, leaving his shocked sidekick, Hugh Downs, to finish the show alone. "Is he gone?" Downs asked in amazement, telling the audience, "Jack frequently does things he regrets."

If you feed a wild moose often enough, it will begin to attack people who don't feed it.

HIDING OUT

The incident made headlines all over the country. But Paar was nowhere to be found—he and his wife, Miriam, had escaped to Florida, where they hid out in a half-finished luxury hotel that a friend was building.

The Paars didn't have a phone at the hotel, but NBC somehow learned of their hiding place, and network president Robert Kintner flew down to talk things out. He eventually talked Paar into coming back . . . but only after he and Robert Sarnoff, the chairman of NBC, both publicly apologized for censoring the joke. Paar returned on March 7 after being absent nearly a month. "As I was saying before I was interrupted . . ." he joked with the audience. "There must be a better way of making a living than this. Well, I've looked. And there isn't!"

PAAR'S NO. 1 PROBLEM

Paar's protest increased his celebrity status and made him a hero of sorts with the public. Ironically, however, the bathroom joke that nearly ended his career was now making it almost impossible for him to use public restrooms, because wherever he went—even to the bathroom—admirers would approach him and congratulate him on his victory.

"Finally you reach the porcelain," he lamented, "and find that—with all eyes on your performance—you cannot! What to do? They are all watching! You panic because now they might think you are some kind of weirdo or voyeur looking around. You press the handle of the urinal, you whistle, and you wish you could get the battery-jump starter from the trunk of your auto . . . I tell you, it's very hard being a star in a men's room."

Turn to page 681 for Part V of The Tonight Show's *history.*

* * *

PRECISE DEFINITION

"Egotist: A person more interested in himself than me."
—*Ambrose Bierce*

FORGOTTEN POP HISTORY

*Here are a few tidbits of obscure Americana, from the
1941 book* Keep Up with the World, *by Freling Foster.*

DRAWERS ON SALE? DISGRACEFUL! A New York dry goods
store shocked America in 1876 with the announcement that it would
thereafter carry a full line of ladies' underwear. Until that time, all
such garments were made in the home, being considered too intimate
to be purchased in public. Besides, these unmentionables, when hung
to dry on an outdoor clothesline, were always covered by a sheet to
protect them from the vulgar gaze of passing males.

THE FIRST TALKING DOLL. A doll developed by Thomas A.
Edison about 1888 is believed to be his least-known invention and
the only toy of its time that ever actually talked. The doll had a
small phonograph in its body that enabled it to recite nursery
rhymes, a dozen of which were recorded for its mechanism. After
making several hundred of these dolls, Edison was informed that,
years before, his company had sold the right to manufacture
phonograph toys to another firm. Edison stopped production and
had the dolls destroyed. Of the few he saved and presented to
friends, only two are believed to be in existence today.

OLD-FASHIONED FAMILY VALUES. In the early 1870s in
Corinne, Territory of Utah, a law firm had so many divorce cases
that it developed a slot machine and, through it, sold the necessary
papers for $2.50 a set. At that time in the territory, no grounds for
divorce were required, and these papers were so complete that they
became legal when signed by the couple involved.

TAKE IT OFF! The strip tease is one of the only forms of theatrical entertainment that originated in the United States. It was
introduced in New York. burlesque houses in the late 1920s to
regain the patrons they'd lost to the new musical shows on
Broadway that were featuring nudity.

On the day *The Wizard of Oz*'s Judy Garland died, a tornado touched down in Kansas.

OOPS—FALSE ALARM!

With people so nervous about bomb threats these days,
it's inevitable that there are going to be some pretty bizarre
false alarms. At the BRI, we've been keeping a file on them.
Here's what we've collected so far.

A LIQUOR PROBLEM

Background: In 1978 security personnel at Pan American Airlines suspected that either maintenance crews or flight attendants were stealing miniature liquor bottles, which cost 35¢ apiece, from airplanes. So they attached a clock device to the liquor cabinet to record the times of the alleged thefts.

False Alarm: "While airborne," write Nash and Zullo in *The Misfortune 500*, "a flight attendant heard the ticking and thought it was a bomb. She alerted the captain, who rerouted the plane to the nearest airport, where passengers were quickly evacuated by emergency exits. The unscheduled landing cost Pan Am $15,000."

DIAL B FOR BOMB

Background: In November 1995 a Royal Jordanian Airlines plane en route to Chicago was forced to land in Iceland when it received a bomb threat.

False Alarm: It turned out that the culprit was a Chicago woman who was trying to keep her mother-in-law, a passenger on the plane, from visiting her.

HIT OR MISSILE

Background: On October 17, 1995, Joanna Ashworth heard a thud outside her Level Plains, Alabama, home. "She opened the door," reported the local Daleville *News Ledger*, "and saw a white object sticking out from the roof of the shed behind her home." It was an 18-inch missile. She called the police.

Level Plains officer Lt. Ralph Reed arrived shortly after 6 a.m. and climbed a ladder to look at the missile . . . He saw markings that could have been military, so he decided to leave it where it was. "My mother didn't raise no fool," Reed said. "I wasn't gonna touch it."

The kitty-litter capital of the world is Quincy, Florida.

Reed contacted officials at nearby Fort Rucker, who decided to evacuate people from the area. They closed the roads nearby and called the bomb squad from Fort Benning in Georgia.

False Alarm: Fort Benning's Ordnance Explosive Detachment (OED) arrived four hours later. For about half an hour, they carefully worked on getting the object out of Ashworth's roof. Then they announced to the press that it was a cardboard model that could be purchased at any toy store.

Local police vowed to get to the bottom of things. "The investigation is not closed," Lt. Reed said as the story made national news. A few days later a 14-year-old dropped by the police station to let them know it was his rocket. He'd shot it off at a nearby playground and had been wondering what happened to it.

BRITISH FARCE

Background: According to the *Fortean Times*: "A suspicious-looking cardboard box was found outside a Territorial Army centre in Bristol (England) in 1993."

False Alarm: "The TA called the police, who in turn called an Army bomb-disposal unit, who blew up the box—to find it full of leaflets on how to deal with suspicious-looking packages."

ANIMAL CRACKERS

Background: On May 28, 1996, an employee at the Wal-Mart Superstore in Enterprise, Alabama, found a suspicious-looking box in the parking lot. Police were called. Taking no chances, they roped off the area, then called the bomb squad at Fort Benning, Georgia.

False Alarm: A few hours later, their Ordnance Explosive Detachment (the same ones who showed up in Level Plains) arrived by helicopter. They X-rayed the package and determined that it contained suspicious-looking wires. The store and surrounding area were evacuated. Then the package was blown up. It turned out to contain a dead armadillo.

*   *   *

"My license plate says PMS. Nobody cuts me off."

—*Wendy Liebman*

Big surprise: About 60% of U.S. kids say they "don't want to be like their parents."

RUMORS: BASED ON A TRUE STORY

Some rumors are straight fiction, but some have a kernel of truth at the core—which makes them a little more believable. Have you heard any of these?

Rumor: The baby face on Gerber baby food belongs to Humphrey Bogart, who modeled for the label as an infant. **Hidden fact:** Bogart's mother was a commercial illustrator, and may have done some work for Gerber.
The truth: The Gerber company credits artist Dorothy Hope Smith with designing the Gerber baby. Besides: Bogart was already 29 when Gerber baby food hit store shelves in 1928.

Rumor: After World War II the Japanese renamed one of their cities Usa, so products manufactured there could be exported with labels that read, "made in USA." (We reported this in BR #5.)
Hidden fact: There really is a town in Japan called Usa, just as there are Usas in Russia, Tanzania, and Mozambique.
The truth: Usa predates the war. The town is very small, so it doesn't show up on every map of the country—which may contribute to the notion that it suddenly "popped up" out of nowhere. But even if a country wanted to pull such a stunt, U.S. Customs regulations wouldn't allow it: Imported goods must be stamped with the *country* of origin, not the city.

Rumor: If you write to the H.J. Heinz company in advance of your 57th birthday, they'll send you a free case of Heinz products. They do it to plug their "57 Varieties" slogan.
Hidden fact: The company actually did at one time send free cases of food to people who wrote in to say they were turning 57.
The truth: They stopped in the 1950s. Now they won't send you anything, except maybe a form letter.

Rumor: "Mama" Cass Elliot of the Mamas and the Papas choked to death on a ham sandwich in 1974.
Hidden fact: When Cass died in 1974, it took a week for the autopsy reports to be released. In the meantime, her personal

---

George Washington's favorite tooth whitener: household chalk.

physician did speculate in newspaper interviews that she could have choked on a sandwich.

The truth: The autopsy showed that the cause of death was actually a heart attack caused by her obesity, not choking.

Rumor: Recently, a man somewhere in the South was chomping on an unusually hard plug of chewing tobacco. He took it out of his mouth . . . and discovered he'd been chewing on a human thumb.

Hidden fact: There was a real lawsuit filed in Mississippi in 1918 that resembles this rumor. Plaintiff Bryson Pillars bought some Brown Mule chewing tobacco, chewed the first plug without incident, then started chewing the second plug. According to court records, "when the appellant tackled the second plug it made him sick, but not suspecting the tobacco, he tried another chew, and still another . . . while he was getting 'sicker and sicker.' Finally, his teeth struck something hard. On examination, he discovered a human toe." The Supreme Court of Mississippi ruled against the R.J. Reynolds Tobacco Company, owner of the Brown Mule brand, arguing, "We can imagine no reason why, with ordinary care, human toes could not be left out of tobacco. If toes are found in chewing tobacco, it seems to us that somebody has been very careless."

The truth: The rumor has been circulating for more than 50 years.

Rumor: In the 1960s the U.S. military forced the recall of U.S.S. *Nautilus* plastic submarine models. The models were so accurate that the government feared Soviet spies would buy them and learn our submarine secrets.

Hidden fact: In 1961 Vice Admiral Hyman Rickover did complain that a model kit of the Polaris nuclear submarine, made by the Revell Toy Company, revealed too much—including detailed floor plans of the engine and missile compartments. (Defense contractors that made the real submarine's missiles even used the models to demonstrate how their weapons systems worked.)

The truth: The military complained . . . but the model was never recalled. Super-accurate models annoy the military even today; In 1986 the Testor Model Company offered a surprisingly accurate model of the F-19 Stealth fighter—even before the U.S. Air Force acknowledged the plane existed.

Aardvarks eventually stop growing . . . but their teeth never do.

A HISTORY
OF THE YO-YO

What's it like being in the yo-yo business? They say it has its ups and downs. Here's a brief history of one of the world's most enduring toys.

WHODUNNIT?
•The yo-yo is believed to be the second-oldest toy in the world, after dolls. No one knows for sure when or where it was invented: some think China, others the Philippines.

- Most yo-yo experts agree that a version of the yo-yo was used as a weapon in the Philippines as far back as prehistoric times. Hunters wrapped 20-foot leather straps around heavy pieces of flint and hurled the rock at prey. If a hunter missed, he could pull the rock back and try again. (The name "yo-yo" comes from a Filipino expression that means "come come" or "come back.")

- Even when it fell into disuse as a weapon, the yo-yo retained an important role in Filipino culture: people used yo-yo contests to settle disputes. Yo-yoing became the national pastime of the islands. "To this day," says one game historian, "young, rural Filipinos spend weeks creating their own custom yo-yos out of rare wood or a piece of buffalo horn."

YO-YOS IN EUROPE
- The ancient Greeks played with yo-yos as far back as 500 B.C. They even portrayed yo-yoers in their art. In *World on a String*, Heliane Zeiger writes that terra-cota yo-yos and "a piece of decorated pottery showing a youngster in a headband and tunic, playing with a yo-yo—both from the classical period in Greece—are currently on display in the Museum of Athens.

- "In 1790," Zeiger continues, "the yo-yo made its way from the Orient to Europe, where it became popular among the British and French aristocracies . . . and inherited some new names. In England the yo-yo was known as the *bandalore, quiz, or Prince of Wales's toy.* (A painting from the 1700s shows King George IV, then Prince of Wales, whirling a bandalore.)"

Christopher Columbus introduced lima beans to Europe.

- "In France, the yo-yo picked up the nicknames *incroyable*, *l'emigrette*, and *jou-jou*. One contemporary account of the French Revolution notes that several French noblemen were seen yo-yoing in the carts hauling them off to the guillotine." And Napoleon's soldiers amused themselves with yo-yos between battles.

Coming to America

Bandalores appeared in the United States in the 19th century. For about 100 years, they occasionally popped up as local fads in areas on the East Coast . . . then faded in popularity each time. They never disappeared completely but didn't attain greater success until the early 20th century.

ENTER DONALD DUNCAN

The turning point for the yo-yo came in 1928, when a businessman named Donald Duncan happened to see Pedro Flores, owner of the Flores Yo-Yo Corporation, demonstrating yo-yos in front of his store. Duncan was impressed with the huge crowds that had gathered to watch the tricks. He figured that a mass-produced yo-yo, if heavily promoted, would make a lot of money—so in 1929 he and Flores began manufacturing yo-yos on a larger scale. A year later Duncan bought Flores out for $25,000 and renamed the company after himself.

No Strings Attached

Yo-yo historians disagree on whether Flores or Duncan deserves credit for the innovation, but the yo-yos that Duncan manufactured in 1929 boasted an important new feature: the yo-yo string was looped loosely *around* the axle (the center post between the two halves of the yo-yo), rather than being firmly secured to it. This allowed a Duncan Yo-Yo to spin freely at the end of the string. It transformed the yo-yo from a device that could only go up and down to one that could perform an endless number of tricks.

Duncan started out with just one model—the O-Boy Yo-Yo Top—but by the early 1930s had a whole line of yo-yo products . . . and a trademark on the name "yo-yo." Legally, his company was the only one in the United States that could call its toy a yo-yo.

Elephants breathe 12 times a minute.

SALES HYPE

But it took more than a technical innovation to make the yo-yo a national fad. It took promotion—and Duncan was a promotional genius. He immediately created:

- The "Yo-Yo Champion." Many Filipinos living in the United States had played with yo-yos since they were kids. Duncan hired 42 of them (including his former business partner, Pedro Flores), gave them each the title "Champion," and sent them on tour to demonstrate yo-yos all over the country. At its peak, the company had one demonstrator on the road for every 100,000 people in America.

- The yo-yo contest. To drum up local support, Duncan sponsored neighborhood yo-yo contests all over the country, awarding new yo-yos, "All American Yo-Yo Sweaters," baseballs, gloves, bicycles, and other prizes to winners.

HELP FROM HEARST

But Duncan's most productive effort came one afternoon in 1929, when he walked uninvited into the San Simeon mansion of newspaper press baron William Randolph Hearst, talked his way past the butler, and made a quick sales pitch to Hearst, telling him how he could use yo-yo contests to boost newspaper circulation.

Duncan's idea was simple: Hearst's newspapers would publicize his yo-yo competitions, and in exchange for the free publicity, Duncan would require all entrants to sell three Hearst newspaper subscriptions as the price of admission to the contests. Hearst knew a good idea—and a good product—when he saw one. He took Duncan up on the offer. The promotions worked; in 1931, for example, one month-long effort in Philadelphia helped sell three million yo-yos.

Picture Perfect

To make newspaper coverage of his product as exciting as possible, Duncan arranged to photograph as many actors, professional athletes, and other celebrities playing with yo-yos as he could. He got lucky: two of the first stars who agreed to the photos were Douglas Fairbanks and Mary Pickford—then Hollywood's biggest stars. Their superstar status guaranteed that other celebrities would enthusiastically follow suit.

Some celebrity endorsements went beyond mere photographs: he got Bob Hope to perform yo-yo tricks for U.S. troops during

---

More roses are grown in the state of Texas than in any country on earth.

World War II, and talked a young singer named Bing Crosby into singing promotional songs for the company, including this one:

> What is the dearest thing on earth, that fills my soul with joy and mirth? My yo-yo.

> What keeps my sense in a whirl, and makes me break dates with my best girl? My yo-yo.

THAT'S A LOT OF YO-YOS

These promotional efforts paid off. By the early 1930s annual sales had shot from thousands of yo-yos to millions. The yo-yo craze spread all over the world. Demand became so great that in 1946 Duncan had to build a huge plant in Luck, Wisconsin, to keep up. The factory could turn out 3,600 yo-yos an hour—but at times Duncan still couldn't fill all the orders . . . even running the plant 24 hours a day.

Still, long-term sales were unpredictable. In boom years, the demand for yo-yos was insatiable. Other years, the demand declined by as much as 90%.

UPS AND DOWNS

The biggest yo-yo craze in history took place in the 1960s. In 1962 alone, according to news reports, 45 million were sold—despite the fact that there were only 40 million kids in the country. This should have been the Duncan Yo-Yo Company's finest hour—but it was their undoing. Why?

1. To meet the demand, they expanded and got too far into debt.

2. They stuck with wood when they should have switched to plastic. Wood had to dry for as long as six months, so they couldn't increase production fast enough.

3. They lost their "yo-yo" trademark. There was so much money to be made selling yo-yos that competitors challenged the trademark in court. As proof that the term had become generic, they pointed to a billboard Duncan itself had erected near its factory: *Welcome to Luck, Wisconsin, Yo-Yo Capital of the World.* If there was a *yo-yo capital*, that must mean yo-yos were made elsewhere, too. In 1962 a Federal Court of Appeals ruled that the trademark was invalid because the word yo-yo was the name of the toy itself.

These problems, combined with increasing costs and competition from Frisbees, skateboards, and other toys, sent the company into a tailspin. In 1965 the Duncan Co. filed for bankruptcy.

Three years later, the Flambeau Plastics Corporation bought the rights to the Duncan name and began cranking out plastic yo-yos. The Duncan name survives to this day (its yo-yos still have an 80% to 85% market share), and yo-yo fads still come and go; Donald Duncan, Jr. is even still in the business, producing yo-yos for the educational market under the name Playmaxx. But for purists, the end of the era came in 1965.

YO-YO FACTS

- Donald Duncan applied his promotional genius to other products: he also invented the Eskimo Pie, originated the Good Humor ice cream truck, co-patented the first four-wheel hydraulic automobile brake, and was the first person to successfully market the parking meter to cities and towns. (At one point, his parking meter company manufactured 80% of all meters in the United States.)

- In the early 1900s Hubert Meyer of Toledo, Ohio, patented an edible yo-yo.

- The Lego company built yo-yos for sale in the 1930s, but like Duncan, it sometimes found itself with huge inventories and low demand. One year it had so many unsold yo-yos in its warehouses that it sawed them in half and used them for wheels on toy trucks and cars.

- In 1984 astronaut David Griggs brought a yo-yo on board the Space Shuttle as part of NASA's "Toys in Space" experiments. His finding: yo-yos don't "sleep" in space—they just reach the end of their string and bounce right back up.

- The world's record for yo-yoing was set by John Winslow of Gloucester, Virginia. He started on November 23, 1977 and didn't stop for five days—120 hours.

- The world's largest yo-yo, Big-Yo, is 50" tall and 31 1/2" wide, and weighs 256 pounds. The string is 3/4" braided Dacron rope. In 1980 the *You Asked for It* TV show launched it off Pier 39 in San Francisco. But the string accidentally got wet before the launch and Big-Yo kept spinning in a "sleeper" position until its axle overheated and the string burned through. The yo-yo plunged 30 feet into San Francisco Bay and frogmen had to keep it from drifting away until it could be retrieved and towed to shore.

16th century French doctors prescribed chocolate as a treatment for venereal disease.

CELEBRITY SUPERSTITIONS

They're only human, after all.

John Madden: As Oakland Raiders coach, he wouldn't let his team leave the locker room until running back Mark van Eeghen belched.

Confederate General Stonewall Jackson: Jackson always charged into battle with his left hand held over his head, for "psychic balance."

Alfred Hitchcock: The cameo appearance he made in each film he directed was for good luck.

Michael Jordan: Always wore his North Carolina shorts under his Bulls uniform. "As long as I have these shorts on . . . I feel confident," he said.

The Barrymores: Lionel, Ethel, and John always gave each other an apple on the night of a show's premiere.

Jimmy Connors: Wouldn't compete in a tennis match without a little note from his grandma tucked into his sock.

Jack Lemmon: Whispered "magic time" as filming started.

Thomas Edison: Carried a staurolite, a stone that forms naturally in the shape of a cross. Legend has it that when fairies heard of Christ's crucifixion, their tears fell as "fairy cross" stones. Also a lucky piece for Theodore Roosevelt and Woodrow Wilson.

Greta Garbo: Wore a lucky string of pearls.

Mario Andretti: Won't use a green pen to sign autographs.

Kichiro Toyoda: A fortune-teller told him it was good luck to change his product's name to *Toyota* and only use car names beginning with "C" (Celica, Camry, etc.).

John Wayne: Considered it lucky to be in a movie with actor Ward Bond.

Randy Johnson: Eats pancakes before pitching.

More thunderstorms—3,000 a day—hit the tropics than any other place on earth.

FAMILIAR PHRASES

More unusual origins of everyday phrases.

PARTING SHOT

Meaning: A final cutting remark or severe look at the end of an argument.

Origin: Unlikely as it seems, this term apparently evolved from the term *Parthian shot* or *Parthian shaft*. In about 1 B.C. in Western Asia, Parthian warriors were known for firing arrows *backward* as they were retreating from an enemy.

TO LICK SOMETHING (OR SOMEONE) INTO SHAPE

Meaning: Improve something/someone; make them presentable

Origin: Comes from the old belief that bear cubs were born featureless, as "shapeless masses of flesh and fur" and needed constant licking from their parents to achieve their final shape.

NO-MAN'S LAND

Meaning: Any desolate or dangerous place.

Origin: A thousand years ago in London, retribution for criminal acts was swift and severe. Most crimes were punishable by death. It was customary to transport condemned men just outside of the north wall of the city, where they would be hanged, impaled, or beheaded, and their bodies disposed of . . . Long after the surrounding territory was settled, no one laid a claim to the land where the executions had been held. Since no one owned it, it was designated as no-man's land.

TAKE WITH A GRAIN OF SALT

Meaning: Be skeptical; examine something carefully before accepting a statement's accuracy.

Origin: In ancient times, salt was rare and people thought it had special powers. Among other uses, they sprinkled it on food suspected of containing poison. It became customary to eat a questionable dish only if it was accompanied with a dash of salt.

Whales can get lice.

IT'S THE LAW!
. . . OR IS IT?

Most of us think we know more about the law than we actually do. We challenge you to take the BRI's version of the Bar Exam. Can you tell the difference between legal myths and legal reality? Answers are on page 751.

PROBLEM #1

Bill and his wife get divorced, and he's socked with a hefty alimony payment. His drinking buddy tells Bill to get out of it by declaring bankruptcy. Can he do it?

a) Yes—if he moves around a lot and doesn't hold a steady job.

b) Nope. In his case, love may be temporary . . . but alimony is forever.

c) Of course. Once the bankruptcy is final, all of his debts will be erased.

PROBLEM #2

Susan and Tom are first cousins who've fallen in love. They want to get married and raise a family. Tom's brother tells them they're out of luck—it's not legal. So they do some research and find out:

a) Tom's brother is right. It's illegal in the United States for first cousins to marry.

b) They can get married, but first they'll have to undergo psychological and genetic testing to evaluate the chances of insanity or birth defects. If the results are okay, a court will grant permission.

c) They should start packing and head for Georgia.

PROBLEM #3

Speed-limit signs of 5 mph are posted at the local mall. One of the mall's security officers calls the local police to have some teenagers arrested for speeding through the parking lot. The police dispatcher tells the security officer to forget it—he's not sending out an officer. Why not?

a) The security guard didn't have a radar gun, so the case would be thrown out of court for lack of evidence.

Sonny Bono had only one big solo hit: "Laugh at Me."

b) It's not the police's problem.

c) Speeding violations are a low priority for local police.

PROBLEM #4

You bounce a check at the corner grocery store. Legally, what can they do about it?

a) They're required to request payment as soon as the check is returned to them. If you make good on it immediately, they can only charge you for the amount of the check.

b) They can stick it to you and charge you for up to ten times the amount of the check.

c) If they wanted to, they could have you arrested for theft.

PROBLEM #5

Sally loses her bank card, but doesn't notice it's gone until a couple of days have gone by; then she calls the credit card company right away. What's her maximum liability?

a) $50.

b) None—the card is automatically insured.

c) $500.

PROBLEM #6

You have a great idea for a new product. Your friends advise you to get it patented right away. Is that the best idea?

a) Yes, it's always the best protection for your idea.

b) You can't get a patent for something until you're ready to produce it, so you'll have to get manufacturing deals set up first.

c) Not always. If you apply for a patent, you might be limiting your ability to make money from it.

PROBLEM #7

Your friend dies in a climbing accident in Yosemite National Park in California. Before he left, he told you, "If anything happens to me you can have my guitar." Do you have any legal claim to the instrument?

a) Sorry, no. Wills have to be in writing, signed by witnesses, and notarized.

b) Yes—as long as there were credible witnesses to the promise.

c) Sure, if he hasn't already promised the guitar to someone else.

Karate was not introduced to Japan until about 1917.

Q&A:
ASK THE EXPERTS

More random questions, with answers from America's trivia experts.

A LOT OF BULL

Q: *Do animals see color?*

A: We often act as if they do, but the truth is, most don't. "Apes and some monkeys perceive the full spectrum of color, as may some fish and birds. But most mammals view color only as shades of gray." So, for example, "bulls don't charge because a cape is red. They charge because of the movement of the cape." (From *The Book of Answers*, by Barbara Berliner)

CARROT TRICK

Q: *What are the "baby carrots" sold in plastic bags at supermarkets?*

A: "Take a closer look. Right there on the bag, it says clearly: 'baby-cut.' These aren't now and never were baby carrots. In the early 1990s a carrot packer in Bakersfield, California, thought of a clever way to use his misshapen culls. Mechanically he cut them into short pieces, then ground and polished them until they looked like sweet, tender young carrots.

"Baby-cut packers today don't rely on culls . . . They use a hybrid carrot called 'Caropak' that grow long and slender; it doesn't taper much and has little or no core. In the processing shed, the carrots are cleaned, cut into pieces, sorted by size, peeled in abrasive drums, then polished. Bagged with a little water and kept cold, they stay crisp and bright orange." (From the *San Francisco Chronicle*)

THREAD OF TRUTH

Q: *Is fiberglass really made of glass?*

A: "It is, literally, tiny strands of glass that are anywhere from .0004 inches to two-millionths of an inch in diameter. They can be from six inches to more than a mile long.

"It's made by either of two processes. The longer, thicker fibers are made by melting glass marbles, then drawing melted strands

---

First meal ever eaten in space: "pureed applesauce."

through holes in a platinum bushing. Shorter, thinner fibers are made by an *air-stream* or *flame blowing process* that pulls bits of melted glass into tiny fibers. As the glass fibers cool, they are sprayed with a polymer that protects their surface and keeps the fibers strong." (From *Everything You Pretend to Know and Are Afraid Someone Will Ask*, by Lynette Padwa)

THAT JUMPY FEELING
Q: *How far can a kangaroo jump?*
A: "One large kangaroo, at a single desperate bound, is reported to have cleared a pile of timber 10 1/2 feet high and 27 feet long." (From *Can Elephants Swim?*, compiled by Robert M. Jones)

STEEL AWAY
Q: *"What makes stainless steel stainless?"*
A: "Stainless steel is coated with a thin, transparent film of iron oxide and chromium. This prevents soap, food, water, and air from getting to the metal below and eating it away. Since its coating is smooth, stainless steel is [also] very sanitary. Bacteria, fungi, and dirt have nowhere to hide and are easily washed away . . . [Ironically, the metal] was developed in 1913 by British metallurgist Harry Brearly, who was searching for a better lining for cannons." (From *The Book of Totally Useless Information*, by Don Voorhees)

QUESTION WITH A-PEEL
Q: *Are most of a potato's nutrients in the peel?*
A: "In most cases, the vitamins are spread evenly throughout the potato. But eating the peel is still a good idea. Certain minerals that your body needs, such as calcium and zinc, are found in larger amounts in the peel . . . In baked potatoes, the peel does contain more than its share of vitamins. Baking causes vitamins and other nutrients to pile up in the peel . . . [However], potatoes are members of the nightshade family. The stems, seeds, and skins of this family are poisonous—some more so than others . . . While the flesh of the potato (the white part) is okay, the leaves and skin contain [a small amount of] substances called glycoalkaloids . . . That's why you should never eat potato eyes—that's where the glycoalkaloids concentrate." (From *Know It All*, by Ed Zotti)

Fewer people golf on Tuesday than on any other day of the week.

NEAR-DEATH EXPERIENCES

Death may be lurking closer than you think. Judging from these stories, it might be a good idea to have a box of Tuna Helper on hand, just in case. Here are a few classic "near misses."

TUNA SURPRISE

"During a robbery at a grocery store in Chicago, employee Vincente Arriaga was shot by the robber at a distance of 20 feet. According to a report in the *Chicago Sun-Times*, the bullet barely broke Arriaga's skin because it was slowed down as it passed through a box of Tuna Helper he was holding."

—*News of the Weird,*
January 10, 1996

A STIRRING STORY

"Someone fired a .45 caliber bullet into Ava Donner's kitchen. Luckily, she was holding a spoon. Donner was stirring a pot of macaroni and cheese when a bullet hit the stem of the stainless steel spoon, ricocheted off the refrigerator and landed on the kitchen counter . . . 'If it had been an inch either way, it would have been in her chest,' said Donner's husband. Police suspect the shot was fired by youths target shooting in a nearby vacant lot."

—*San Francisco Chronicle,*
February 26, 1996

RADAR RANGE

"Two members of the British traffic police were in Berwickshire with a radar gun, checking for speeding motorists, when suddenly their equipment locked up with a reading of over 300 miles per hour. Seconds later a low flying Harrier jet flew over their heads and explained the mystery. When the policemen complained to the RAF, they were informed they were lucky to be alive. The jet's target-seeker had locked onto their radar gun as 'enemy' radar . . . which triggered an automatic retaliatory air-to-surface missile attack. Luckily for the traffic cops, the Harrier was unarmed."

—*Pilot* **magazine**

Roughly $20 million in counterfeit U.S. currency is circulating at any given time.

NOTABLE BOOKS

We can't identify the first book ever read in the bathroom,but we have been able to find the stories behind a few other publishing milestones.

THE FANNIE FARMER COOKBOOK

Originally, cookbooks didn't give precise measurements for recipes—they just told readers to use a "pinch" of this, a "heaping spoonful" of that, and a "handful" of something else. Fannie Merrit Farmer, a domestic servant in the late 1850s, had no trouble following such recipes herself—but she found it almost impossible to give instructions to the young girl who helped her in the home where she worked. So she began rewriting the family's recipes using more precise measurements.

Forty years later, she had become the assistant principal of the prestigious Boston Cooking School. In 1896 she decided to publish her first book of "scientific" recipes, *The Fannie Farmer Cookbook*. Her publisher was so worried it wouldn't sell that he forced Farmer to pay for the printing costs herself. She did. It sold four million copies and permanently changed the way cookbooks are written.

DR. SPOCK'S BABY AND CHILD CARE

Dr. Benjamin Spock was a New York pediatrician with a background in psychology when Pocket Books approached him about writing a childcare book for new mothers. It wasn't the first time he'd gotten such an offer: in 1938 Doubleday had asked him to write a similar book, but he'd turned them down, saying he was inexperienced and wasn't sure he could write a good book. He almost rejected Pocket Books for the same reason—until the editor explained that it didn't *have* to be a very good book, "because at 25¢ cents a copy, we'll be able to sell a hundred thousand a year."

Feeling reassured, Spock accepted the offer and wrote *The Pocket Book of Baby and Child Care*. He began with the admonition "Trust yourself"—and wrote a book that was unlike any child-rearing book that had been written before. "The previous attitude in child-rearing books was, 'Look out, stupid, if you don't do as I say, you'll kill the baby,'" Spock recalls. "I leaned over backward not to be alarming and to be friendly with the parents."

His warm, supportive voice paid off; *The Pocket Book of Baby and*

"As the crow flies"? Crows don't fly in straight lines.

Child Care became the second-bestselling book in American history, second only to the Bible. It has sold an average of one million copies a year *every year* since it was published in 1946. Its impact on American culture has been profound. According to *The Paperback in America*: "For two generations of American parents, it has been the bible for coping with their newborns . . . A comparison of new mothers to the number of books sold during the baby boom's peak years—from 1946 to 1964, when nearly 75 million babies were born in the United States—put the estimate of 'Spock babies' at one in five, and that failed to account for the number of women who shared or borrowed the book or used it to raise more than one child."

THE COMPLETE BOOK OF RUNNING

Jim Fixx was a part-time author and full-time editor at *Horizon* magazine . . . until 1976, when his boss "suggested" he find another job. Fixx didn't want another magazine job, but all he knew how to do was write, and he had four kids to support. He'd been running for about eight years, and knew there was no book that gave practical advice for beginning runners, so he came up with an idea to make a quick $10,000—a "breezy, superficial" book called *The Lazy Athlete's Look Younger Be Thinner Feel Better & Live Longer Running Book* (later retitled *The Complete Book of Running*).

As it happened, one of the last things he did for *Horizon* magazine was meet with Pulitzer Prize–winning author Jerzy Kozinski. "As Kozinski and I sat talking in his studio in midtown Manhattan," Fixx recalled, "the conversation turned to my book."

"You have a big job ahead of you," Kozinski said. "To write a book like that, you have to read everything that's been written on the subject." Until then I hadn't thought of doing anything of the sort. All I wanted to do was get the book written quickly and collect my check. But I realized that Kozinski was right. The conversation turned a modest and easily manageable plan into a two-year obsession.

The book came out in 1977. It immediately hit the bestseller list, and became the bible of one of the biggest sports in America. Years later, Fixx died of a heart attack while jogging.

Most popular target for shoplifters: food stores.

REEL QUOTES

Here are some of our favorite lines from the silver screen.

ON INTELLIGENCE

Doc: "This kid is so dumb he doesn't know what time it is."
Golfer: "By the way, what time is it?"
Doc: "I don't know."
—**W.C. Fields,**
The Dentist

ON MARRIAGE

"If love is blind . . . marriage must be like having a stroke."
—**Danny De Vito,**
War of the Roses

"What's marriage anyhow? Just a tradition started by cavemen and encouraged by florists."
—**Olivia de Haviland,**
The Strawberry Blonde

"Marriage is forever—like cement."
—**Peter Sellers,**
What's New Pussycat?

ON SEX

"I like my sex the way I play basketball: one on one, and with as little dribbling as possible."
—**Lt. Frank Drebin,**
The Naked Gun

ON RELIGION

Luna: "Do you believe in God?"
Miles: "Do I believe in God? I'm what you'd call a theological atheist. I believe that there is an intelligence to the universe, with the exception of certain parts of New Jersey. Do *you* believe in God?"
Luna: "Well, I believe that there's somebody out there who watches over us."
Miles: "Unfortunately, it's the government."
—**Woody Allen's** *Sleeper*

ON RELATIONSHIPS

"She dumped me 'cause she said I wasn't paying enough attention to her, or something. I don't know, I wasn't really listening."
—**Jeff Daniels,**
Dumb & Dumber

"A guy'll listen to anything if he thinks it's foreplay."
—**Susan Sarandon,**
Bull Durham

The diesel cruise liner *Queen Elizabeth II* gets 6 inches to the gallon.

THE DISAPPEARANCE OF THE MARY CELESTE

One of the most famous unexplained disappearances ever recorded is the case of the Mary Celeste. *In 1872 it was found drifting aimlessly in the Atlantic, in seaworthy condition and fully provisioned. But the entire crew had vanished without a trace. To this day, no one knows what happened.*

BACKGROUND

On November 5, 1872, the *Mary Celeste* set off from New York carrying a cargo of 1,701 barrels of commercial alcohol. Her captain was Benjamin Spooner Briggs, a well-known seaman who allowed no drinking on his ship and regularly read the Bible to his men. The crew had been carefully chosen for their character and seamanship, especially because the captain had brought along his wife and two-year-old daughter. He was looking forward to a safe and pleasant voyage.

DISAPPEARANCE

One month later, on December 5, Captain Morehouse of the *Dei Gratia*—another cargo ship bound for Gibraltar—noticed a vessel on the horizon. It looked like it was in trouble, so he changed course to see if he could be of assistance. After calling out to the ship and getting no reply, Morehouse lowered a boat and sent two men to board. It was immediately evident that the ship, which turned out to be the *Mary Celeste*, was deserted. The men looked for underwater damage, but the vessel was not leaking, and was in no danger of sinking. There was evidence that the *Mary Celeste* had encountered bad weather, but on the whole she was in perfectly good condition and should have had no problem continuing her journey.

Stranger yet, there were six months' worth of provisions aboard and plenty of fresh water. All of the crew's personal possessions were intact—even the ship's strongbox. In fact, absolutely nothing was missing except some of the ship's papers and the ship's lifeboat. Captain Briggs, his family, and the crew had obviously abandoned

Carrots come from Afghanistan.

the ship in a hurry . . . but why? What could have frightened them so much that they'd desert a seaworthy vessel for an overcrowded yawl and take their chances in the stormy Atlantic?

INVESTIGATION
Still puzzled by the disappearance of the crew, Captain Morehouse decided to claim the *Mary Celeste* as salvage. He put three men aboard her and proceeded with both ships to Gibraltar.

Officials in Gibraltar were suspicious of Morehouse when he showed up with a "salvage" ship in such good condition, still carrying valuable cargo. They investigated and discovered that:

- The *Mary Celeste*'s hull was perfectly sound, indicting she had not been in a collision. Nor was there any evidence of explosion or fire.

- The cargo of commercial alcohol seemed to be intact and complete.

- A phial of sewing machine oil was standing upright, spare panes of glass were found unbroken, and the furniture in the captain's cabin was in its proper place—all indications that the ship hadn't endured particularly rough weather.

- The fact that the crew had left behind all their possessions— even their tobacco—indicated that they had left the ship in a panic, afraid for their lives, but the investigators could see no reason for this.

- The most mysterious item aboard was a sword found under the captain's bed. It seemed to be smeared with blood, then wiped. Blood was also found on the railing, and both bows of the ship had strange cuts in them that could not be explained.

THE OFFICIAL WORD
Solly Flood, attorney general for Gibraltar, found the bloodstains suspicious and was convinced there had been violence aboard the *Mary Celeste*. However, the Vice Admiralty Court issued a verdict clearing Morehouse and his crew of any suspicion. After the ship's owners paid Morehouse a reward, the *Mary Celeste* was given a new crew, and went on to Italy, where her cargo was delivered. She continued to sail for 12 years but was known as a "hoodoo ship," so most seamen refused to set foot on her.

One escalator carries as many people as 13 elevators.

WHAT HAPPENED?

The mysterious disappearance of the *Mary Celeste*'s crew had people all over the world imagining possible scenarios.

- Some believed a mutiny had occurred—the crew murdered the captain and his family, then took the ship. But if that were true, why did they abandon their prize?

- Perhaps an outbreak of disease panicked those left alive. But why would they subject themselves to the close quarters of the smaller boat, where the crowding would *guarantee* that everyone caught the disease?

- The most outrageous explanation offered was that the ship had been attacked by a giant squid several times, until everyone was killed. But a squid wouldn't have been interested in the ship's papers. And a squid wouldn't need the ship's lifeboat.

Because the story of the *Mary Celeste* got so much publicity, phony survivors started popping up and selling their stories to newspapers and magazines. But they all checked out false—no one who claimed to have been on board had their facts straight.

ONLY ONE EXPLANATION?

The mystery of the *Mary Celeste* has puzzled people for over a century. In all that time, say experts, only one feasible explanation has been proposed. This postulates that four things happened, in succession:

1. The captain died of natural causes while the ship was caught in bad weather.

2. A crew member misread the depth of the water in the hold, and everyone panicked, thinking the ship was going down.

3. They abandoned ship in such a hurry that they took no food or water.

4. Everyone in the lifeboat either starved or drowned.

Is that what happened? No one will ever know.

Largest empire in all of human history: the British empire of the 19th century.

HARD-BOILED: CLASSIC FILM NOIR QUOTES

Film noir—French for "black film"—generally refers to the tough-guy detective movies of the 1940s and 1950s. Peggy Thompson and Saeko Usukawa put together a collection of great noir lines called Hard Boiled. *Some samples:*

"I've met a lot of hard-boiled eggs in my time, but you—you're twenty minutes."
——**Jan Sterling,**
The Big Carnival (1951)

Charles McGraw: "You make me sick to my stomach!"
Marie Windsor: "Yeah? Well use your own sink."
——**The Narrow Margin (1952)**

"What do you want, Joe, my life history? Here it is in four words: big ideas, small results."
——**Barbara Stanwyck,**
Clash by Night (1952)

"I treated her like a pair of gloves. When I was cold, I called her up."
——**Cornel Wilde,**
The Big Combo (1955)

Psycho crook (Lee Marvin): "Hey, that's a nice perfume."
Moll (Gloria Grahame): "Something new. Attracts mosquitoes and repels men."
——**The Big Heat (1953)**

"She was giving me the kind of look I could feel in my hip pocket."
——**Robert Mitchum**
Farewell, My Lovely (1975)

Reporter (Audrey Totter): "I don't like your manner."
Detective (Robert Montgomery): "I'm not selling it."
——**Lady in the Lake (1947)**

"I felt pretty good—like an amputated leg."
——**Dick Powell**
Murder, My Sweet (1944)

"I don't pray. Kneeling bags my nylons."
——**Jan Sterling,**
Ace in the Hole (1951)

"What kind of a dish was she? The sixty-cent special—cheap, flashy, strictly poison under the gravy."
——**Charles McGraw,**
The Narrow Margin (1952)

"Personally, I'm convinced that alligators have the right idea. They eat their young."
——**Eve Arden,**
Mildred Pierce (1945)

Fight manager (William Conrad): "Everybody dies. Ben, Shorty, even you."
Boxer (John Garfield): "What's the point?"
Manager: "No point—that's life."
——**Body and Soul (1947)**

The first tennis balls were stuffed with human hair.

QUEEN OF THE NILE

*She's one of the most famous queens in history . . . but
how much do you really know about her?*

For centuries, people have been enthralled by stories of
Cleopatra. She was a tragic heroine in Shakespeare's *Antony
and Cleopatra*; a scheming vamp in *Cleopatra*, Theda Bara's
classic 1917 silent film; a buxom babe in Elizabeth Taylor's 1963
film flop. But most people know very little about the real Queen of
the Nile. And much of what they think they know is false.

Belief: There was only one Cleopatra.
Truth: There were seven Queen Cleopatras in the Egyptian
dynasty that began with King Ptolemy I in 323 B.C.; Cleopatra,
who reigned from 15 B.C.–30 B.C. was the seventh and last. Her
eldest sister was Queen Cleopatra VI, and her daughter (who never
became queen) was also named Cleopatra.

Belief: She was Egyptian.
Truth: She was considered Greek. Cleopatra was one of king
Ptolemy I's direct descendants; *he* had been a Greek staff officer of
Alexander the Great before becoming king of Egypt following
Alexander's death. Like the Egyptian pharaohs before them, the
Ptolemaic dynasty adopted an incestuous brother-sister marriage as
a way to keep their bloodline "pure"; historians believe it's unlikely
Cleopatra had any Egyptian blood at all. For that matter, she was
the first Ptolemaic ruler who could even *speak* Egyptian.

Belief: She was one of the most beautiful women in the world.
Truth: At best, she had ordinary features; at worst, she was decid-
edly unattractive. "Her coins," Lucy Huges-Hallett writes in
Cleopatra: History, Dreams and Distortions, "minted on her orders
and therefore more likely to flatter than otherwise, show a strong,
bony face with a hooked nose and a jutting chin, pretty neither by
the standards of Cleopatra's day nor by those of ours." The ancient
Roman historian Plutarch describes her as being not particularly
good-looking, although her intellect, beautiful voice, and strong
character made her desirable and enjoyable company.

Long shot: Only one person in 2 billion will live to the age of 116.

Belief: She was a great seductress.
Truth: This is based on her well-known affairs with Julius Caesar and Marc Antony. But in the days of ancient Rome, affairs between rulers were a common means of cementing alliances. Caesar is known to have had liaisons with several other queens and at least one king (one of his contemporaries described him as "every woman's man and every man's woman"); Marc Antony was also a notorious womanizer. Cleopatra, on the other hand, was completely celibate for more than half her adult life and is believed to have had only two lovers: Caesar and Marc Antony.

Belief: Caesar and Marc Antony were madly in love with her.
Truth: It is possible Caesar fell in love with Cleopatra (no one knows); but he really stayed in Egypt to get his hands on her fortune. And historians say he made her queen of Egypt because he didn't want to appoint a Roman who might become his rival.

Cleopatra's relationship with Marc Antony was also based on politics. At their first meeting, when they supposedly fell in love, they made a deal: Antony agreed to kill Cleopatra's sister so she'd have no challenge to her authority; Cleopatra became a loyal ally. Then he went back to Rome and his wife. When his wife died, he didn't marry Cleopatra—he hooked up with the sister of a political rival. Years later, he finally visited Cleopatra and the twins he'd fathered with her. Coincidentally, he also needed her treasure and her navy at the time.

Antony did commit suicide and die in Cleopatra's arms, but it wasn't for love; he was despondent because they'd been defeated in battle. Cleopatra committed suicide, too. For love? No. The Romans told her she was going to be paraded in disgrace through Rome in chains, and she couldn't take that.

Belief: She committed suicide by getting herself bitten by an asp.
Truth: Nobody knows for sure how she killed herself. "Plutarch had read the memoirs of her private physician, but even he was not sure," Huges-Hallett writes in *Cleopatra: History, Dreams and Distortions*. "It seems likely to have been the bite of a snake brought to her in a basket of figs, but it may be that she had some poison ready prepared and hidden in a hollow hair comb, or that she pricked herself with a poisoned hairpin. The only marks found on her body were two tiny scratches on her arm."

The foreign city most visited by Americans is Tijuana.

LET THERE BE LITE, PART I

At first glance, it seems incredible that the "lite" phenomenon—a 1980s diet food craze—started with beer. But after you read this two-part BRI report, it should make more sense. We can't help wondering if the whole notion of "diet food" isn't essentially a fraud. What do you think?

AN UNLIKELY BEGINNING

According to beer industry studies, 30% of American beer drinkers—mostly blue-collar males between the ages of 18 and 49—drink 80% of the beer produced in the country. That means that every major U.S. brewery is trying to attract the same customers.

Traditionally, it meant that "diet beer" was a recipe for losing money. Heavy beer drinkers weren't interested in dieting, and dieters weren't very interested in drinking beer. Why make a beer for people who won't drink it?

Those few breweries gutsy (or stupid) enough to brew a low-calorie beer were sorry they tried. In 1964, for example, the Piels Brewing Co. introduced Trommer's Red Letter, "the world's first diet beer." It lasted about a month and a half. Three years later, Rheingold Brewing Co. of New York introduced a low-cal brew called Gablinger's—described by critics as "piss with a head." One company exec lamented: "Everyone tried it—once." At about the same time, the Meister Brau Brewing Co. of Chicago came out with Meister Brau Lite. For some reason, they targeted it at calorie-conscious women. "It failed so badly," said one report, "that it practically took the entire Meister Brau Co. down with it."

LUCKY STRIKE

In the early 1970s Miller Brewing Co. bought the rights to Meister Brau's brands. They got Lite Beer (which was still in limited distribution in the Midwest) as part of the deal, but no one at Miller paid much attention.

In fact, Lite Beer probably would have been quietly dumped right away if company executives hadn't stumbled on something

---

What's the longest English word you can type with only the left hand? *Stewardesses.*

surprising in Meister Brau's sales reports: Lite was actually popular in Anderson, Indiana, a steel town dominated by the same blue-collar workers who were supposed to hate "diet beer." Why did they like Lite? Nobody knew. Curious, the company sent representatives to find out. As Miller advertising executive Jeff Palmer recalls:

> The workers drank Lite, they said, because it didn't fill them up as much as regular beers. As a result, they could drink more. And drinking more beer without having to pay more penalty in feeling filled up, is beer drinker heaven.

According to Palmer, the company did more research, and found that male beer drinkers were interested in a good tasting "light" beer but were "clear, if not vehement, that the concept of a *low calorie* beer was definitely feminine and negative."

So if Miller could figure out how to make Lite taste better, and at the same time think of a way to get rid of the beer's "sissy" image, the company just might find a market for the brew.

LITE CHANGES

Miller president John Murphy decided it was worth a try. He ordered his brew masters to come up with a beer that tasted like other Miller brands, but still cut the calories per can from around 150 to 96. It took them a little over a year.

Meanwhile, ad people went to work on positioning Lite as a "manly" brew that beer-lovers could drink without being ashamed. They decided to build an advertising campaign around "regular guy" celebrities, famous people with whom beer drinkers would be comfortable having a beer in their neighborhood bars. The first guy they picked was Eddie Egan, the detective whose life was portrayed in *The French Connection*. "Unfortunately," one ad exec remembers, "he was under indictment at the time so we couldn't use him." Their next choice: journalist Jimmy Breslin. But he wasn't available either. The executives' third option: a few professional athletes . . . But Miller had a problem there, too—federal law prohibits using professional athletes in beer ads.

Miller was stuck. Who could they use?—who was left? While riding on a New York City bus, Bob Lenz, the ad executive in charge of Miller's account, came up with the answer. He noticed a poster of former New York Jet star Matt Snell, and it occurred to him that although advertising codes prohibited Miller from using

A snail breathes through its foot.

active athletes to sell beer, there was no reason they couldn't employ retired ones. He called Snell.

"We taped him," Lenz recalls, "and once we saw the result, we knew we were onto something." Miller ultimately signed up dozens of ex-athletes for their ad campaign—from baseball players like Boog Powell and Mickey Mantle to bruisers like football's Deacon Jones and hockey's Boom-Boom Geoffrion.

SELLING THE BEER

As it turned out, using ex-jocks was a masterstroke. Because they were a little older (and paunchier) than their contemporaries, they were easier for beer drinkers to relate to. Plus, they had nothing to prove—they were established heroes. If they said it was okay to drink "sissy" beer, no one was going to argue. "When Joe Frazier, Buck Buchanan, or Bubba Smith stroll into the bar and order Lite," wrote *Esquire* magazine in 1978, "you know you can too."

Every spot ended with the celebrities heatedly arguing about Lite's best quality—was it that it's "less filling" or that it "tastes great"—followed by the tag line: "Everything you always wanted in a beer. And less."

When test marketing of Lite exceeded sales projections by an unprecedented 40%, it was attributed largely to the advertising campaign. Blue-collar workers not only felt comfortable drinking a "diet" beer, they also understood that "a third fewer calories" meant that drinking three Lites was only as filling as drinking two regular beers. So rather than cut calories, most Lite drinkers drank more beer, and the sales figures showed it.

LITE BONANZA

Lite was introduced nationally in 1975, and had an astounding effect on the Miller Brewing Co.

- In 1972 the company was the eighth-largest brewer, selling 5.4 million barrels of beer—compared to #1 Anheuser-Busch's 26.5 million barrels.

- By 1978—three years after the introduction of Lite—Miller was in second place and gaining, selling approximately 32 million barrels to Anheuser-Busch's 41 million. Schlitz, Pabst, Coors, and other brewers were left in the dust.

An alligator has a brain the size of your thumb.

As *Business Week* put it, Lite became "the most successful new beer introduced in the United States in this century." Its ads became as well known as the most popular television shows. Some of its spokesmen became better known for their work with Lite than for their sports accomplishments.

THE LIGHT REVOLUTION

It was only a matter of time before other beer makers got into the act. In 1977 Anheuser-Busch brought its muscle "to light" when it introduced Natural Light beer.

Miller fought back, suing to keep any brewers from using the words *Lite* or *Light* in their brand names. But the company only won a partial victory. The court's verdict: Miller's competitors couldn't use the term *Lite*, but were free to use *Light*—since it's a Standard English word and can't be trademarked.

Enthusiastic brewers started bottling their own light beers, and "light" became the hottest product in the beer business. By 1985 it made up 20% of the overall market. By 1994 it was a $16 billion business and comprised 35% of the market.

BACK TO THE FUTURE

Ironically as the "light" category grew, Lite's revolutionary ad campaign began to look out of date. The market had changed, and new light brews were aimed at young, health-conscious Americans—not blue-collar beer-guzzlers. "Light" had gone full circle; it was essentially being sold as a "diet" beer again.

The term "light" gradually took on a life of its own, too. It became a buzzword for any food that was lower in calories, or better for you, than the usual fare. This set the stage for an even bigger "lite" fad.

For Part II of "Let There Be Lite," turn to page 739.

*   *   *

SAD BUT TRUE

"If you're in jazz and more than ten people like you, you're labeled 'commercial.'"

—*Wally Stott*

The Malaysian expression for "take a walk" translates as "eat the wind."

YIDDISH-AMERICAN SLANG

A handful of Yiddish words have become common in the U.S. If you've been wondering what they mean, here's the answer.

Chutzpa (hootz-pah): Clever audacity. Classic definition: "A child who kills both parents, then pleads for mercy because he's an orphan."

Drek: Junk. The bottom of the barrel.

Shtick: An act or a routine. (Usually associated with show business.)

Tchatchke (chotch-key): Toy, knick-knack, worthless gizmo.

Shiksa: A non-Jewish woman.

Schmuck: A fool; sometimes refers to an obnoxious person.

Schlemiel: Hapless individual. A person who always has bad luck; a fool.

Shlep: To haul around.

Shlock: Something that's poorly made, or made for low-class taste.

Kibitz: To offer unsolicited advice.

Noodge: A pest. As a verb, "to pester or coax."

Klutz: Clumsy or inept person. From the German word for "wooden block."

Shmooze: To chat.

Meshugah (me-shoo-ga): Crazy

Mensch: Compassionate, decent person. Someone both strong and kind.

Putz: Dope, fool, schmuck.

Nosh: A snack. (As a verb, "to snack.")

Nudnik (nood-nik): A boring pest. A nudnik can even bore himself.

Bupkis: Nothing.

Shmo: A fool; a dumbo.

Shnook: A meek fool; sad sack.

Shpritz: To squirt. As a noun, a squirt of something.

Oregon has more ghost towns than any other state.

THE TONIGHT SHOW PART V: PAAR'S EXIT

By 1961 Jack Paar was one of the most celebrated
stars in America. Who would have suspected that his job
was making him sick? (Part IV is on page 646.)

END OF THE ROAD

One of the gifts of a skilled performer is the ability to make a difficult task seem effortless, to make it seem like anyone could do it.

So when Jack Paar announced in late 1961 that he was quitting *The Tonight Show* after only five years as host, viewers were surprised. Why would he give up such a great job? After all, he was such a natural at it.

But behind the scenes, it was a different story: people were amazed he'd lasted as long as he did.

BUTTERFLIES

Few people who watched Paar delivering his monologue and talking to guests understood how grueling an experience it was for him:

- Rather than just wing it through his monologues, Paar committed them to memory each night before going to bed by writing them out in longhand, over and over again, until he knew every word by heart. The process often took hours.

- He began to show serious signs of stress: he mumbled, washed his hands compulsively, and paced for hours worrying about the show.

- But the biggest secret was that, despite all his years as a performer, Paar had never gotten over his stage fright. "Jack used to duck under his desk in between commercials and throw up because he was so nervous," recalls Lew Hunter, the director of programming at NBC in the early 1960s. "It was amazing to watch him. That man went through hell to entertain people, and he'd already been on the air over two years when he was still doing that."

Venetian blinds aren't—they were invented in Japan.

As Paar's tenure neared its end, he described his feelings about leaving. "I can't help but feel an overwhelming sense of relief that the ordeal is nearly over," he said. "The end is in sight at last, a release from days of living on my nerve ends and nights of sheer terror, going out before an audience of millions of viewers armed with nothing but a few notes . . . There never was a moment when I wasn't scared to death."

CHOOSING A REPLACEMENT

Two people were under serious consideration for Paar's job: Merv Griffin, host of the NBC game show *Play Your Hunch*, and Johnny Carson, host of *Who Do You Trust?* on ABC.

In the end, of course, NBC chose Carson. They figured that like Paar, Carson was a strong ad-libber and would be able to keep the show moving. They had no idea how good a choice they'd made.

For Part VI, "He-e-ere's Johnny," turn to page 703.

* * *

RANDOM ORIGINS

THE JACUZZI

In 1943 Candido Jacuzzi's fifteen-month-old son suddenly contracted rheumatoid arthritis. The boy was in constant pain; the only thing that made him feel better was hydrotherapy treatments he got in the hospital. Condido decided to build a device that would enable him to have treatments at home. At the time his company, Jacuzzi Bros., Inc., was one of the world's largest manufacturers of submersible pumps. He adapted one so it would work in his bathtub. In 1955 they began manufacturing them as whirlpool baths. They were sold through drugstores at first—but when Hollywood discovered them, they became a symbol of luxury.

THE THIMBLE

"The thimble was originally called a 'thumb bell' by the English, because it was worn on the thumb; then it was referred to as a "thumble," and finally its present name. It was a Dutch invention, and was first brought to England in 1695."

—from *Origins*, by J. Braude

Five U.S. presidents have had the first name James, more than any other name.

LUCKY FINDS

Here are three more stories of people who found something valuable. It could happen to you . . .

A HIDDEN VALUE
The Find: An 1830 painting
Where It Was Found: At an auction
The Story: In the mid-1990s Wanda Bell paid $25 for an old print depicting the signing of the Declaration of Independence. One day, as she was cleaning the print, she noticed something underneath it. She removed it . . . and found an oil painting of a man. Bell was curious to know more about it. In August 1997 she heard that an "antiques roadshow" was offering free appraisals with experts from Sotheby's, so she took the painting there. Their assessment: It's an early portrait painted by a famous New England artist named Sheldon Pect. Estimated value: $250,000.

A ROLL OF FILM
The Find: The pilot show of *I Love Lucy*
Where It Was Found: Under a bed
The Story: In 1949 CBS offered Lucille Ball her own TV show, to be based on her successful radio program, *My Favorite Husband*. She agreed . . . as long as they'd let her real-life husband, Desi Arnaz, co-star. CBS called the idea preposterous. "Who'd believe you were married to a Cuban bandleader?" they said.

Lucy was determined. She and Desi decided to create a live show and take it on the road to prove that audiences would accept them together. "Desi moved quickly to assemble a first-rate vaudeville act," write Steven Coyne Sanders and Tom Gilbert in their book, *Desilu*.

He called in an old friend, the renowned international Spanish clown Pepito, to devise some physical-comedy sketch material. Pepito rigorously coached the couple, as Desi recalled, "eight to ten hours a day" at the Coronado Hotel in San Diego.

The stage show was a huge success, so CBS agreed to film a sitcom pilot. The synopsis: "Ricky goes to a TV audition. Pepito the

As far as anyone can tell, only humans get headaches.

Clown, due to an accident, fails to appear and Lucy takes his place for the show." It was filmed on March 2, 1951.

I Love Lucy, of course, became one of the most successful TV programs in history. But along the way, the pilot episode was lost. Fans and TV historians tried over the years to locate it, but it appeared to be gone for good. Then one day in 1989, Pepito's 84-year-old widow (he'd died in 1975) looked under a bed in her Orange County home and came across a can of film labeled "Lucy-Desi-Pepito" audition. It was the long-lost *Lucy* pilot. Desi, it turns out, had given it to Pepito as a thank-you for his help. The film, with an estimated value of over $1 million, was quickly turned into a TV special and home video.

A LUCKY MISTAKE

The Find: A unique coin

Where It Was Found: At a flea market

The Story: In 1970 Guy Giamo came across an interesting 1969 penny at a Northern California flea market. "What made it intriguing," reported the *San Francisco Chronicle*, "was that it seemed to be a 'double die' stamping, a Bureau of the Mint manufacturing error that gave the legends Liberty and In God We Trust a blurred, double-image look."

There are a lot of double-dies from 1955, worth more than $500 apiece. But double-die coins are easy to fake, and many are counterfeit. Giamo bought it anyway Cost: about $100.

In 1978 he sent it to the U.S. Mint to find out if it was real. A few months later a Secret Service agent called and said simply: "The Treasury Department has determined your coin to be counterfeit, and it will be confiscated and destroyed." "That's it?" Giamo asked. "Affirmative," the agent replied, and hung up.

But that's not the end. A year later Giamo was surprised by *another* call from the Treasury Department. "What the hell do you want now?" he asked bitterly. "We have a coin for you," he was told. Someone had re-examined his penny before it was melted down, and decided it was genuine. "We goofed," they told him.

Giamo's coin is the only double-die 1969-S penny in existence. Its estimated value: as much as $50,000.

ALPO AND GREEN SLIME

"The world of pizza is a world full of anger, anxiety, and anchovies,"
says pop historian Tim Harrower. Literary scholar Gwen Foss
invested years of research to create a glossary of pizza-maker's
slang in an issue of Maledicta, The International Journal of
Verbal Aggression. *Here's some of the more colorful lingo:*

Alpo: Italian sausage, also known as *dog food, Puppy Chow, Kibbles 'n' Bits, and Snausages.*

Beef darts: A game played during slow times, in which employees hurl bits of raw beef against the walls.

Birthday cake: A pizza with way too many items on it.

Blue quarters: Another kitchen game in which coins are heated in a 550°F oven until they turn blue.

Bondage pie: A pizza with S and M (sausage and mushrooms).

Carp: Anchovies, also known as *guppies* and *penguin food.*

Cheese off!: A friendly expletive meaning "Go away!"

Crispy critter: A burnt pizza.

Edgar Allen Pie: A pizza with PO (pepperoni and onions)

Shroomers: Mushrooms.

Flyers and fungus: Pepperoni (because raw slices fly like Frisbees) and mushrooms.

Green slime: Green peppers, especially those that become slippery and slimy. Also known as *lizards* and *seaweed.*

Hemorrhage: Pizza with extra tomato sauce.

Master-baker: An oven tender.

Panty liner: The absorbent cardboard placed under a pizza when it's boxed.

Spoodle: A saucing tool that looks like a combination spoon/ladle.

Starver: A customer who orders a pizza then tells the driver that they didn't order one but offers to buy it at a discount.

Zap zits: Pop the bubbles in a pizza crust as it cooks.

10% of all Dalmatians are born deaf.

BASEBALL CURSES

These "curses" are just fun . . . right?

THE CURSE OF WRIGLEY FIELD

Curse: The Cubs will never make it to a World Series again. Origin: "As the story goes, the late Bill Sianis, founder of the Billy Goat's Tavern, tried to bring his pet goat into Wrigley Field [during the World Series] in 1945," wrote Mike Royko in the *Chicago Tribune*. "He was turned away because the goat smelled. That's when the curse was placed . . . and they haven't been in a World Series since."

The curse at work: Most years since 1945, the Cubs haven't even been in contention for a National League pennant. The club hasn't put together consecutive winning seasons since 1972.

- They finally won a division championship in 1984 and took the first two games in the best-of-five playoff series with the Padres.
- They went back to the playoffs in 1989 and lost again.
- In 1997 the Cubs gave a beer company permission to use the curse as part of an ad campaign. They opened the season with a record-breaking 0-14 losing streak, their worst start in 121 years.

Status: Curse-lifting has been attempted on a number of occasions. The then-current owner of the Billy Goat Tavern once went on *The Tonight Show* with a goat; it didn't work. In Royko's column, he blamed the "curse" on racism. The Cubs were slow to bring in black players in the late '40s, he said, which doomed them to poor teams in the '50s. Weird coincidence: Royko's column on the Cubs' curse was the last he ever wrote. He died shortly after.

THE CURSE OF THE BAMBINO

Curse: The Boston Red Sox will never win a World Series again. **Origin:** On Jan. 5, 1920, Red Sox owner Harry Frazee announced he'd sold Babe "the Bambino" Ruth to the New York Yankees. Frazee got $100,000, plus a $300,000 loan for a mortgage at Fenway Park. The New York Yankees got the best player in baseball—a national treasure. The punishment for exchanging a gift of the gods for cold, crass cash? This curse.

The curse at work: Since then, the Yankees have won 34 pennants

IQ of the average police officer: 104

and 23 World Series. The Red Sox have won four pennants and lost all four World Series in heartbreaking fashion.

- 1946. After leading three games to two (in a best-of-seven series), Boston lost two in a row.
- 1967. They took the series to seven games against the Cardinals . . . and lost.
- 1975. In Game 6, Carlton Fisk's homer in the 12th inning gave Boston a 7–6 victory against Cincinnati in one of the most dramatic moments in baseball history. But the Reds still won Game 7, 4–3.
- 1986. Boston led the New York Mets three games to two. They were winning 5–4 in Game 6, with two outs and two strikes on the Met batter. It looked like the curse was about to be broken. Then disaster hit: The Mets tied the game on a wild pitch by the Red Sox pitcher, and the batter hit a grounder that went through Red Sox first-baseman Bill Bucker's legs; the Mets won the game, 6–5. Naturally, the Red Sox lost Game 7, too.

Status: The Red Sox finally broke the curse in 2004, beating the New York Yankees to win the World Series.

THE CURSE OF COLAVITO

Curse: For trading slugger Rocky Colavito in 1960, the Cleveland Indians were doomed to bad baseball and bad luck.

Origin: April 17, 1960, was known as "the day Cleveland baseball died." That's the day the 26-year-old Colavito, hero of Indians fans, was dealt to the Detroit Tigers for a fading shortstop.

The curse at work: From 1960–93, the Indians finished no higher than third place—and that happened only once, in 1968.

- Bad luck ranged from player troubles (in 1961 top young pitcher Sam McDowell, in his first major league start, broke two ribs throwing a fastball) to fan troubles (in June 1974 they tried a 10¢ Beer Night; drunk fans poured onto the field, forcing a forfeit).
- July 1994. With Cleveland poised to reach the postseason for the first time since 1954, the players went on strike.

Status: Is it over? Hard to tell. The Indians made it to the World Series in 1995, but the best-hitting team in baseball batted .179 and lost in six games. Cleveland led the majors with 99 wins in '96, but choked against Baltimore in the divisional playoffs. As we write this, the Indians are in the World Series again. Maybe this time . . .

The first product Motorola developed was a record player for cars.

WRETCHED REVIEWS

Doesn't it bother you when a movie you love gets a thumbs-down from those two bozos on TV? Us, too. The Critics Were Wrong, by Ardis Sillick and Michael McCormick, compiles hundreds of misguided movie reviews like these.

THE WIZARD OF OZ

"Displays no trace of imagination, good taste or ingenuity . . . It's a stinkeroo."
—*The New Yorker*, 1939

LOVE ME TENDER

(*Elvis's first film*)
"[Presley is] a young man of hulk and probably flabby muscle, with a degenerate face, who sings emasculated innuendos in a southern drawl as he strums guitar. The weak mouth seems to sneer, even in repose, and the large, heavy-lidded eyes seem open only to be on the lookout for opportunities for self-indulgence . . . How a society as dynamic as our own throws up such a monstrosity is beyond the scope of this review."
—*Films in Review*, 1956

STAR WARS

"O dull new world! It is all as exciting as last year's weather reports . . . all trite characters and paltry verbiage."
—*New York*, 1977

JAWS

(*The ads showed a gaping shark's mouth.*) "If sharks can yawn. That's presumably what this one is doing. It's certainly what I was doing all through this picture."
—*The New Republic*, 1975

SNOW WHITE AND THE SEVEN DWARFS

"*Snow White* is a failure in every way. As a moving figure she is unreal, as a face and body she is absurd, and what she does is ludicrous . . . Another *Snow White* will sound the Disney death-knell."
—*Current History*, 1938

THE EMPIRE STRIKES BACK

"Malodorous offal . . . Everything is stale, limp, desperately stretched out, and pretentious. Harrison Ford offers loutishness for charm, and becomes the epitome of the interstellar drugstore cowboy."
—*National Review*, 1980

You're more likely to be struck by lightning than eaten by a shark.

GROUCHO MARX ATTORNEY AT LAW

Here's more dialogue from a recently rediscovered radio show featuring Groucho and Chico Marx—Five Star Theater, which aired in 1933.

(*Phone rings*)

MISS DIMPLE: Law offices of Beagle, Shyster, and Beagle . . . Mr. Beagle? I expect him back from court any minute . . .

(*Door opens; footsteps heard.*)

MISS DIMPLE: Good morning, Mr. Beagle. How did you make out in court?

GROUCHO: Splendid, splendid, Miss Dimple. I got my client off.

MISS DIMPLE: You got him off?

GROUCHO: Yes, I got him off the streets for six months. They put him in the workhouse.

MISS DIMPLE: Oh . . . Well, there's a man out here who wants to talk to you about a job. (*Footsteps approach*)

GROUCHO: Tell him I'll take it. But I won't work for less than a hundred dollars a week.

MISS DIMPLE: You misunderstand. He wants a job here.

GROUCHO: Oh, he wants a job. I think I can put him to work.

CHICO: I don't wanna work. I just wanna job.

GROUCHO: Hmm-m. How about references?

CHICO: Aw, that's awright. You don't need no references. I like your face.

GROUCHO: And I like your face—if it is a face. Have you had any experience?

CHICO: You bet. For 15 years I've been a musician.

GROUCHO: A musician? What do you get an hour?

CHICO: Well, for playing I get ten dollars an hour.

GROUCHO: What do you get for not playing?

CHICO: Twelve dollars an hour.

GROUCHO: That's more like it.

CHICO: Now for rehearsing I make a special rate—that's 15 dollars an hour.

GROUCHO: What do you get for not rehearsing?

CHICO: Oh, you couldn't

King George VI's first name is Albert.

afford that. You see, if I no rehearse I no play. And if I no play, that runs into money.

GROUCHO: What would you want to run into an open man-hole?

CHICO: Just the cover charge.

GROUCHO: Well, drop in some time.

CHICO: Sewer.

GROUCHO: I guess we've cleaned that up. Now go out and find some clients.

CHICO: Hey! We no speak about money.

GROUCHO: That suits me fine. If you promise not to say anything about it, I won't mention it either.

CHICO: Alright, but I gotta have more money.

GROUCHO: I'll tell you what I'll do. I'll give you 50 dollars a week and you can bring your own lunch.

CHICO: Well . . .

GROUCHO: Ok, I'll go even further, I'll give you 50 dollars a week and you can bring lunch for me too.

CHICO: I can't live on fifty dollars a week.

GROUCHO: That will make me very happy. You're hired.

CHICO: When do I start?

GROUCHO: Well, it's one o'clock now. If you start now you can be back here at three with lunch. Bring me a cheese sandwich on white bread.

CHICO: I no gotta white bread, but I can give you rye.

GROUCHO: All right, then I'll take a quart of rye.

(*Applause; commercial break.*)

GROUCHO: Today is Monday. What have we got on the books besides red ink? What's on the court calendar for this afternoon?

MISS DIMPLE: You know you have a suit on today.

GROUCHO: Certainly I have a suit on today. Do you expect me to come in my nightshirt? I only wear that for night court. Where's that assistant I hired last week?

MISS DIMPLE: Oh, Mr. Ravelli. He just phoned.

GROUCHO: Oh, he phoned, did he? Where did he get the quarter? He's been holding out on me. Say, I thought I told him to go out and find some clients.

MISS DIMPLE: He said as soon as he finds a client he'll come see you.

GROUCHO: Oh, so he'll come in to see me. I suppose he doesn't think I'm good enough to go out and see him! Maybe

How many hairs in an average beard? About 15,500

he's ashamed to let me see where he lives. Where does he live?

MISS DIMPLE: He's been living here in the office ever since you hired him.

GROUCHO: No wonder he's ashamed.

MEANWHILE . . .
(*street noises*)

CHICO (*yelling*): Anybody want a lawyer? Nice fresh lawyer today? You want a lawyer, lady? Alright, it don't hurt to ask, you know. Hey, mister, how about you? You wouldn't want a lawyer, would you?

MAN: How do you know I wouldn't?

CHICO: Well, you wouldn't want this one.

MAN: As a matter of fact, I want a lawyer and I want one bad.

CHICO: I got just the man for you. He's terrible.

MAN: Well then, leave me alone. I got no use for your lawyer.

CHICO: Well, I got no use for him either, but I gotta get a client.

MAN: Say, what are you trying to do? Lay off me or I'll call a cop.

CHICO: You want to sue me? I got a good lawyer for you.

MAN: Oh, you . . . Officer, will you keep this nuisance away from me?

COP (Irish): Here you . . . move along, you're obstructing traffic.

CHICO: You want a lawyer?

COP: What would I be wantin' a lawyer for?

CHICO: I don't know. Take him home, wash him up, show him to the kids.

COP: Listen, what are you trying to do?

CHICO: My boss sent me down here to get clients.

COP: Well, you're not going to get any clients for a lawyer standing around here.

CHICO: At'sa fine. How am I gonna get clients?

COP: Hustle around . . . Use your imagination . . . But move along.

LATER . . .

(*door opens; footsteps heard*)

CHICO: Hey, Mr. Flywheel! I gotta client. This lady, she wants to see you.

We'll be back in a few pages with the conclusion. Check out page 735.

The Aztecs restricted the smelling of certain flowers to the upper classes.

ROSEANNE SEZ . . .

A few choice thoughts from Roseanne Barr.

"My husband said he needs more space. So I locked him outside."

"You may think you married the man of your dreams . . . but 15 years later, you're married to a reclining chair that burps."

"My husband and I found this great new method of birth control that really, really works . . . Every night before we go to bed, we spend an hour with our kids."

"Men can read maps better than women, because only the male mind could conceive of one inch equaling one hundred miles."

"The other day on *Donahue*, they had men who like to dress up as women. When they do, they can no longer parallel park."

"I quit smoking. I feel better. I smell better. And it's safer to drink out of old beer cans laying around the house."

"The day I worry about cleaning my house is the day Sears comes out with a riding vacuum cleaner."

"My son is into that nose-picking thing. The least he can do is act like an adult— buy a car and sit in traffic."

"You get a lot of tension. You get a lot of headaches. I do what it says on the aspirin bottle. Take two and keep away from children."

"The way I look at it, if the kids are still alive when my husband comes home from work, then I've done my job."

"Women are cursed, and men are the proof."

"Women complain about premenstrual syndrome, but I think of it as the only time of the month I can be myself."

"It's okay to be fat. So you're fat. Just be fat and shut up about it."

Gadsby, a 50,000-word novel by Ernest Wright, contains no words with the letter "e."

STRANGE CELEBRITY LAWSUITS

*Here's a "strange lawsuits" for celebrity junkies—
people who read* People *magazine.*

THE PLAINTIFF: Elton John
THE DEFENDANT: The *Sunday Mirror*, an English
newspaper
THE LAWSUIT: In 1992 the *Mirror* claimed that John had been
spitting out chewed hors d'oeuvres at a Hollywood party, calling
it a "new diet." The singer had recently gone public about his
bulimia; he sued because "the story implied he was a sham" . . . and
because he wasn't even at the party.
THE VERDICT: The singer was awarded $518,000 in damages.
The *Mirror* issued a formal apology admitting the story was bogus.

THE PLAINTIFF: Catherine Deneuve, French movie star
THE DEFENDANT: Outspoken Enterprises, Inc., a San
Francisco magazine publisher
THE LAWSUIT: For five years Outspoken Enterprises published
Deneuve magazine. By 1996 it had 200,000 readers—making it one
of the largest magazines for lesbians in the United States. The edi-
tor claimed the title was inspired by "the name of her first love,"
not the actress. But Catherine Deneuve didn't believe it. In
January 1996 she sued for trademark infringement.
THE VERDICT: The suit was apparently dropped when the mag-
azine voluntarily changed its name to *Curve.*

THE PLAINTIFFS: French sexpot Brigitte Bardot and her neigh-
bor, Jean-Pierre Manivet
THE DEFENDANTS: Jean-Pierre Manivet and Brigitte Bardot
THE LAWSUIT: Not surprisingly, it's about sex. In 1989 Bardot
and Manivet lived next to each other on the French Riviera.
Bardot owned a female donkey, Mimosa, and a mare, Duchesse;
Manivet had a male donkey named Charly. Bardot, an animal
activist, agreed to let Charly graze with her animals. But when
Charly "began to show male instincts toward the old mare," he lost

Women blink nearly twice as much as men.

his rights—Bardot had him castrated. Manivet was out of town at the time; when he returned, he sued Bardot for 4,500 francs (about $950) in damages, plus 10,000 for "moral prejudice." Bardot countersued, claiming Manivet's publicity about the case had harmed her image.

THE VERDICT: Everyone lost. The court ruled it was within Bardot's rights to "fix" the donkey, but not to protect her "image."

THE PLAINTIFF: Richard Belzer, of TV's *Homicide: Life on the Street*

THE DEFENDANTS: Hulk Hogan and Mr. T., professional wrestlers

THE LAWSUIT: In 1985 Belzer hosted a cable talk show called *Hot Properties*. Hogan and Mr. T. appeared on one program as guests. According to news reports, the interview was "merely awkward" until Belzer asked them to show him some wrestling moves.

"I'm going to make him squeal," Hogan chuckled as he stood up." Mr. T. urged "the Hulkster" to show Belzer a "Pipsqueak Sandwich."

While the band played Chopin's funeral march in the background—and a Manhattan studio audience, including 50 children in wheelchairs, who had been invited to the show, watched in horror—Hogan demonstrated his "front chin lock." After a few seconds, the comedian collapsed. He recovered briefly—long enough to break for a commercial—and then he was taken by ambulance to Mount Sinai Hospital, where nine stitches were taken in his scalp.

Belzer sued the two wrestlers for $5 million.

THE VERDICT: In 1988 the case was settled out of court.

THE PLAINTIFF: Michael B. Mukasey, stepfather of singer Mariah Carey

THE DEFENDANT: Mariah Carey

THE LAWSUIT: In 1993 Mukasey filed suit claiming that Carey had promised to let him market "singing dolls that looked like her." Underlying the lawsuit: His contention that he deserved a share of her earnings because "he helped her achieve stardom by . . . providing transportation to rehearsals and paying for dental work."

THE VERDICT: Case dismissed.

If a female ferret goes into heat and can't find a mate, she'll die.

THE EIFFEL TOWER, PART II

Room with a view: Among amenities that Gustave Eiffel designed for the tower was a penthouse apartment at the top, complete with a grand piano and spotlights for shining on other Paris monuments. He built it for his own use. (Part I appears on page 517.)

EIGHTH WONDER OF THE WORLD

Most advances in architecture and engineering are incremental. If, for instance, you wanted to build the world's first 10-story building, you'd expect to study the construction techniques of 8- and 9-story buildings first.

But Gustave Eiffel didn't have that luxury. No one had ever built an iron tower like his of any size . . . let alone one that was twice as tall as the tallest building on earth.

AN ENGINEERING GENIUS

To accomplish his task, Eiffel devised some incredibly ingenious techniques:

- Unlike other massive engineering projects of the day, he had nearly all of the parts used in the tower prefabricated off-site in his workshops. This meant that when they arrived at the tower, the parts could be quickly riveted into place with a minimum of fuss.

- The rivet holes themselves were predrilled to a tolerance of one-tenth of one millimeter, making it possible for the twenty riveting teams to drive an average of 1,650 rivets a day.

- None of the girders used in the tower was permitted to weigh more than three tons. This made it possible to use smaller cranes to lift everything into place. As Joseph Harris writes in *The Tallest Tower*:

Eiffel had learned that using small components was faster and safer, even if this method did require more riveting, for cranes could be smaller and more mobile. The chances of accidents were reduced, and if one did occur the consequences were less serious. Use of bigger girders would have slowed the entire

More than 25 percent of the world's forests are in Siberia.

operation and required more expensive and complicated construction methods.

Thanks to these and other safety measures, the Eiffel Tower—the world's tallest construction site—was also one of the safest. Of the hundreds of people who worked on the tower, only one, a riveter's assistant named Dussardin, fell to his death.

THE PIERS
In the early days of the project there were actually four construction sites at the Eiffel Tower, one for each foot, or "pier." These piers did not join together until the 180-foot level . . . and once this point was reached, they had to be set *perfectly* level with one another to create a perfectly horizontal platform on which the remaining 800 feet of the tower could be built. If the piers were even slightly out of alignment, the tiniest discrepancy at the base of the tower would be magnified at the top: it would appear to lean.

Eiffel knew there was no way he could *guarantee* the piers would be vertical when finished—the margin for error was too great. So he installed temporary hydraulic pistons in the base of each of the feet. That way, as work on the tower progressed, he could "fine-tune" the entire tower into perfect alignment by slightly raising or lowering each foot. When the tower was properly aligned, workers could drive iron wedges into the piers to secure them permanently.

As it turned out, Eiffel had little to worry about. Even at the 180-foot level, the worst of the four massive piers was less than 2 1/2 inches out of alignment. All four were easily adjusted and secured in place. Even today, the tower is perfectly vertical.

FINIS
The Eiffel Tower was a marvel—not just for its ingenuity of design, but also because it was completed ahead of schedule and under budget. The Exposition was scheduled to open on May 6; work on the tower was finished on March 31.

Eiffel & Company earned back its money in record time. During the six months of the Exposition alone, the tower earned back more than $1.4 million of its $1.6 million construction cost; that, combined with the $300,000 subsidy provided by the French government, pushed the tower into the black even before the Exposition closed.

The tower was such a magnificent structure that it won over

Americans throw away an estimated 27% of their food every year.

many of its earlier critics. Among them was French prime minister Tirard. He had opposed the project at its inception, but awarded Eiffel the medal of the Legion of Honor after it was finished. The tower, a symbol of France's unrivaled technical expertise, became the symbol of France itself.

Not everyone who hated the tower experienced a change of heart. Guy de Maupassant, the novelist best known for *The Necklace*, was said to eat regularly at a restaurant on the tower's second floor. His reason: It was the only place in Paris where he was sure he wouldn't see the tower. (Even some of the characters in his novels hated the tower.)

TOWER FACTS

- Every seven years, the Eiffel Tower receives a fresh coat of more than 300 tons of reddish-green paint. Why reddish-green? Because, tower officials say, it is the color that clashes least with the blue sky over Paris, and the green landscape of the Champ de Mars below.

- The positions of the Eiffel Tower's four "feet" correspond to the "cardinal" points of a compass: they point exactly north, south, west, and east.

- In 1925 the City of Paris wanted to decorate the tower with electric lights as part of an arts exposition being held nearby, but the cost, estimated at $500,000, was too high. When automaker Andre Citroën learned of the project, he offered to pay for it himself . . . in exchange for the right to put his company name and corporate symbol in lights as well. The City agreed. "The Eiffel Tower," Blake Ehrlich writes in *Paris on the Seine*, "became the world's largest electric sign, its outlines traced in lights." The lights were so popular that the tower remained lit with various designs until 1937.

- Sad fact: The Eiffel Tower is the most popular landmark for suicides in France. In an average year, four people commit suicide by jumping off the tower or, occasionally, by hanging themselves from its wrought iron beams. The first person killed in a jump from the tower, in 1911, was not an intentional suicide—the man was a tailor named Teichelt who had sewn himself a "spring-loaded bat-wing cape" that he thought would enable him to fly. It didn't.

America's favorite vegetable: broccoli. America's least favorite veggie: Brussels sprouts.

THE FIRST CENTERFOLD

*Whether you approve of the magazine or not, Playboy represents
a significant part of American culture. One of its trademarks
is the centerfold. Here's the tale of the first one.*

THE BARE FACTS

In the late 1940s Marilyn Monroe was still an unknown
actress, struggling to pay rent. One day in 1948 she borrowed a car to get to an audition, but had an accident on the
way. As bystanders gathered, she announced she was late for an
appointment and had no money for a cab. Tom Kelley, a photographer, gave her $5 and his business card.

A year later when Marilyn needed money, she went to Kelley's
studio to ask if he had any work for her. He did—he was doing a
photo shoot for a poster advertising Pabst Blue Ribbon Beer and
his model had failed to show up. Marilyn happily stepped in and
took the job.

A few weeks later Kelley called Monroe with more work. A
Chicago calendar manufacturer named John Baumgarth had seen
the Pabst poster and wanted a few "tasteful" nude pinup shots.
According to Anthony Spoto in *Marilyn:*

> [She] accepted at once. Two nights later she returned to
> Kelley's studio and signed a release form as "Mona Monroe."

A red velvet drape was spread on the studio floor, and for two
hours Marilyn posed nude, moving easily from one position to
another as the photographer, perched ten feet above her on a
ladder, clicked away.

Baumgarth paid Kelley $500 for all rights to the photos from the
session, and Kelley gave Marilyn $50. They never met again.

PINUP GIRL

Baumgarth did nothing with the photos until 1950, when Marilyn
began to get attention for her role in *The Asphalt Jungle*. He
decided to use her picture on a pinup calendar. It was only meant
to be a giveaway for service stations, tool dealers, contractors, etc.
But in April 1952 *Life* magazine included a tiny reproduction of

the calendar in a cover story they did on Marilyn. As a result, the picture became world-famous. And Marilyn became infamous.

"Marilyn blunted the potential effect on her career," says Spoto, "by giving interviews in which she explained that she had desperately needed money. The public bought it. But the saga of the pinup calendar wasn't over.

PUBLIC EXPOSURE

Just as the furor surrounding Marilyn's pinup shot was dying down, Baumgarth got a visit from a fellow Chicagoan who wanted to use it. According to Russell Miller in *Bunny, the Real Story of Playboy:*

> Because of the risk of prosecution for obscenity, Baumgarth believed there was probably no other use to which the pictures could be put. He was surprised, therefore, when [a young man] showed up at his office, without an appointment, on the morning of June 13, 1953, and asked if he could buy the rights to publish the Monroe nude pictures in a magazine he was planning to launch.

The man was Hugh Hefner; the magazine was *Stag Party* (soon to be renamed *Playboy*). Baumgarth not only sold Hefner the magazine rights, but threw in the color separations as well—which saved the struggling Hefner—who'd barely scraped up enough money for the 48-page first issue—a bundle.

Hefner knew his magazine was finally on its way. Monroe—featured that year in *How to Marry a Millionaire*—was now a star. And Hefner could announce that she would be his first "centerfold." In December 1953, the premiere issue of *Playboy* hit the stands, with Marilyn beckoning from the front cover. Due in part to the famous pinup, *Playboy* was an instant success. Ironically, this exposure made the photos even more famous . . . and more valuable. Spoto concludes:

> More than any other portraits of a nude woman in the history of photography, those of Marilyn Monroe taken in 1949 became virtual icons, everywhere recognizable, ever in demand. Landmarks in the union of art with commerce, the photographs have appeared in calendars, playing cards, keychains, pens, clothing, accessories, linens and household items; for decades, entrepreneurs have become wealthy by claiming or purchasing rights to their dissemination.

Q: What part of your body has the most sweat glands? A: Your feet.

FAMOUS FOR 15 MINUTES

Here's another installment of our feature based on Andy Warhol's comment that "in the future, everyone will be famous for 15 minutes."

THE STAR: Shawn Christopher Ryan, 7-year-old resident of Castro Valley, California

THE HEADLINE: *Second-Grader Smells Smoke, Saves Sixteen*

WHAT HAPPENED: At 4 a.m. on February 9, 1984, Shawn awoke and smelled smoke. He ran into his mother's room, saw that her mattress had caught fire (she'd fallen asleep smoking), and woke her up. He helped her escape, then ran back into the apartment building and knocked on every door, waking up and saving all 16 neighbors. For a few weeks, he was a national hero. He was honored at the state capitol by the governor of California, received a commendation from President Reagan, and was lauded on the floor of the U.S. House of Representatives.

AFTERMATH: Ryan wasn't in the news again until 1995, 11 years later. Ironically, it was because he had pled guilty to the murder of two acquaintances (alleged drug dealers) while they were all high on methamphetamine. "I can't explain it," he said. "I'm not the kind of person to take a life, not for any reason." He was sentenced to 32 years in prison.

THE STAR: Diane King, a 33-year-old night-shift manager at a Portland, Oregon, Taco Bell

THE HEADLINE: *Good Samaritan Gets Heave-ho from Taco Bell*

WHAT HAPPENED: On August, 16, 1995, a fight broke out in a Taco Bell parking lot, leaving one teenager dead and one lying motionless in the street. King, a former nurse's aide, rushed to help. She left another employee in charge of the restaurant, even though she knew it was against company policy. Later, she explained, "I was worried he might die out there." When the police arrived, she went back to work. A few weeks later, she was fired. Newspapers reported the story as an example of both corpo-

---

The largest country in Africa is the Sudan.

rate insensitivity and a screwed-up society that discourages good samaritans.

AFTERMATH: Hundreds of people offered King jobs and money. *People* magazine ran a story on the incident. Oprah Winfrey flew King to Chicago for a show titled "Would You Help a Stranger in Distress?" Finally, Taco Bell—which had tried to reinstate King without admitting it had done anything wrong (she refused)—ran a full-page apology in the Portland *Oregonian*. "Sometimes big corporations make mistakes," it said. "In this case, we did, and we've learned from it." King ignored them and took a job at a convenience store. She also filed a $149,500 suit against Taco Bell for "shock, outrage, and emotional distress." No word on the outcome.

THE STAR: Nicholas Daniloff, Moscow bureau chief for *U.S. News and World Report*
THE HEADLINE: *U.S. Reporter Held Hostage by Soviets*
WHAT HAPPENED: In 1986 Gennadi Zakharov, a member of the Soviet Union's mission to the United Nations, was arrested in New York for spying. A few weeks later, the Soviets retaliated, arresting Daniloff in Moscow and charging *him* with espionage—with a possible death penalty. His arrest was front-page news. President Reagan and Secretary of State Schultz called it "an outrage," but swore they'd never trade a spy (Zakharov) for a hostage (Daniloff). The matter was so serious that it jeopardized the upcoming Summit meeting in Iceland between Reagan and Gorbachev. The United States even announced it was expelling 25 members of the Soviet delegation to the U.N. because they worked for the KGB.

Some fancy maneuvering followed. Daniloff was released. The United States waited awhile (so it didn't seem like there was any connection) then released Zakharov in exchange for a Russian dissident and allowed some of the expelled U.N. workers to stay. Daniloff was welcomed home . . . but a *day* after his release, he was already old news. The Reagan administration changed the subject. Their new focus—it was to avoid scrutiny of the deal they'd made, political pundits suggested—was details of the Summit meeting.

AFTERMATH: Daniloff surfaced again in 1988 when he toured the country promoting his autobiography, *Two Lives, One Russia* (published on the second anniversary of his imprisonment). He became a professor at Northeastern University in Boston and a respected expert on Russia.

Message for Uncle Giant: An elephant grows six sets of teeth in its lifetime.

THE STAR: Lucy De Barbin, Dallas clothes designer who claimed to be Elvis's lover and mother of his child
THE HEADLINE: *Dallas Designer's Daughter Royal Descendant?*
WHAT HAPPENED: In 1987 De Barbin revealed her secret 24-year affair with Elvis in a book entitled *Are You Lonesome Tonight?: The Untold True Story of Elvis Presley's One True Love—and the Child He Never Knew.* She said they kept their involvement a secret so it wouldn't mess up his career. Later she kept it quiet to protect Lisa Marie and the daughter she had with Elvis, Desir'ee. "I was so afraid of what was going to happen [if the secret got out]," she told a reporter. "I thought if one person found out, everybody would know." She didn't even tell Elvis they had a child, she said, although she hinted at it in a phone conversation just before the King's death: "I just said things like, 'I have a wonderful secret to tell you' and 'Her name is Desir'ee,' things like that. And he said, 'I hope what I'm thinking is true.'" De Barbin's publisher, Random House, believed her. And several experts confirmed that a poem the King had reportedly written for De Barbin was in his handwriting. But neither the public nor the Presley estate bought the story.
AFTERMATH: De Barbin never produced blood samples to prove that her daughter was Elvis's. Apparently, she offered no real evidence that they'd been lovers. The Presley estate claimed that because the book was not a success (it actually was), they didn't need to bother suing De Barbin.

THE STAR: Matthias Jung, a German tourist in Dubrovnik, Croatia
THE HEADLINE: *Brazen Tourist Has Dubrovnik All to Himself*
WHAT HAPPENED: Dubrovnik, Croatia, was one of the world's loveliest towns and a major tourist resort. But for seven months, from fall 1991 to spring 1992, the Serbs bombarded it with mortar shells. Tourism fell off, then disappeared. In August 1995 tourists warily started returning—only to be greeted with more shelling. They all fled . . . except one—Jung, a 32-year-old shopkeeper from Hanover. He wasn't a thrill-seeker; he just wanted peace and quiet for his vacation.
AFTERMATH: After a while, things got so quiet that Jung admitted he was bored and went north.

Biggest French-speaking city: Paris. Second-biggest: Montreal.

TONIGHT SHOW
PART VI:
HE-E-ERE'S JOHNNY!

After 30 years on the tube Johnny Carson became synonymous with The Tonight Show. Here's how he got the job. (Part V is on page 681.)

RISING STAR

Johnny Carson had been working his way up the TV ladder for a decade. His first show was *Carson's Cellar*, a comedy-variety program he created in 1951 for L.A.'s CBS affiliate. It only had a $25/week budget, so he couldn't pay guests for appearances. Much of the time, he had to fake it.

One afternoon he had a member of the studio crew run quickly past the camera. "That was Red Skelton," Carson joked. "Too bad he didn't have time to stay and say a few words!" Skelton heard about the joke and was flattered. He made several appearances on the show . . . then hired Carson as a writer for *his* TV program.

OPENING DOORS

Carson left *Carson's Cellar* in May 1954 to host a network game show called *Earn Your Vacation*. But he continued to write jokes for Skelton on the side. Then, on August 18, 1954, while rehearsing a stunt for his show, Skelton threw himself into a prop door that was supposed to open on impact. It didn't—Skelton was knocked cold with less than 90 minutes to go before airtime.

A few minutes later, Carson got a call from the show's producers, who were searching frantically for a replacement host. Carson agreed to fill in . . . and so impressed CBS with his performance that the network gave him his own primetime show: *The Johnny Carson Show*.

It was Carson's first big break . . . and his first big flop. Years later, Carson lamented: "They told me, 'We've got to make the show *important*' . . . How were they going to do that? With chorus girls. They were going to make me into Jackie Gleason! I'd come rushing on in a shower of balloons, with chorus girls yipping, 'Here

---

There are 602 rooms in Buckingham Palace.

comes the *star* of the show, *Johnny Carson!*' . . . That was my first big lesson. If you don't keep control, you're going to bomb out, and there's nobody to blame but yourself."

BUILDING TRUST

Carson's next job was hosting a game show called *Do You Trust Your Wife?* The program was failing: the host, ventriloquist Edgar Bergen, had just been let go, and ABC was only renewing the contract month to month. Carson turned it around by dumping the husband-and-wife format and renaming it *Who Do You Trust?* so anyone could play.

Soon after, the show's announcer left. Word spread that Carson was looking for a replacement, and Chuck Reeves, producer of Dick Clark's *American Bandstand*, decided to help. He'd been at a party emceed by Clark's next-door neighbor, a radio announcer named Ed McMahon. He liked McMahon's style . . . so he got McMahon an audition for *Who Do You Trust?*

SECOND BANANA

McMahon went to New York and talked on camera with Carson for a couple of minutes. Then he went home. Weeks went by, and he heard nothing. So, convinced he hadn't gotten the job, McMahon made plans to take a trip across the Atlantic.

As McMahon recalled in his autobiography, the day before he was scheduled to leave, he got a call from the show asking him to come back to New York. He cancelled the trip and went to meet with Carson's producer, Art Stark. They talked for a few hours, but he still didn't get a job offer. Finally, Stark asked McMahon if he was going to move to New York.

"I don't think so," McMahon replied.

"I thought maybe you'd want to."

"Why?"

"Well, I thought it might be tough for you, doing the show."

"What show?"

"Our show. You start Monday."

"*Next* Monday?"

"For Chrissake, didn't anybody tell you?"

And that's how Ed became the world's most famous second banana.

Number of ice cubes the average American puts in a glass: 3.2.

CANNED LAUGHTER

As on Groucho Marx's *You Bet Your Life*, the jokes in *Who Do You Trust?* were scripted in advance. It was the best-kept secret of the show: only Carson's copy of the script contained the jokes. The television audience—ABC's censors—were kept completely in the dark, which made for racier ad-libbing. With Carson at the helm, *Who Do You Trust?* became one of the surprise hits of daytime television. Meanwhile, Carson kept his talk-show skills fresh by guest hosting for Garry Moore, Dinah Shore . . . and Jack Paar.

HEEERE'S JOHNNY!

Carson guest-hosted *The Tonight Show* as early as 1958, but doubted whether he could ever fill Paar's shoes as permanent host. So when Paar announced in late 1961 that he was getting out, Carson wasn't sure he wanted to give up a safe, successful network quiz show to take a chance on *The Tonight Show*. "How could I follow Jack Paar? I just wasn't sure I could cut it," he wrote years later.

In the end, of course, Carson decided to take the chance. He and McMahon signed on as the host and announcer of *The Tonight Show*. On October 1, 1962, Carson made his debut. The deck was stacked wildly in his favor that first night—he was introduced by Groucho Marx and had Mel Brooks, Tony Bennett, Joan Crawford, and Rudy Vallee as his guests.

Overall, the reviews were positive. "Mr. Carson's style is his own," Jack Gould wrote in the *New York Times*. "He has the proverbial engaging smile and the quick mind essential to sustaining and seasoning a marathon of banter."

PAAR FOR THE COURSE

For some viewers, however, Carson was a big letdown. "America can now go back to bed," Robert Kennedy joked to Jack Paar a few days later.

Even the NBC pages were skeptical. "After that first night," says Kenneth Work, a history professor who was an NBC page in 1962, "the pages went down to the NBC coffee shop and all of them were convinced Johnny wouldn't make it. After working with Paar all those years, we were concerned he didn't have the excitement and outspokenness Paar had. I didn't think he'd last six months."

More to come! See Part VII on page 719 after these messages.

According to research, you'll blow your nose about 250 times this year.

MYTH-SPOKEN

Everyone knows that Captain Kirk said, "Beam me up, Scotty" in every episode of Star Trek *and that Bogart said, "Play it again, Sam" in* Casablanca. *But everyone's wrong. Here are a few common misquotes.*

Line: "Beam me up, Scotty."
Supposedly Said By: Captain Kirk
Actually: That line was never spoken on *Star Trek.* Not once. What Kirk usually said was, "Beam us up, Mr. Scott," or "Enterprise, beam us up." According to Trekkies, he came pretty close just once. In the fourth episode, he said, "Scotty, beam me up."

Line: "Don't fire till you see the whites of their eyes."
Supposedly Said By: Colonel William Prescott to American soldiers at the Battle of Bunker Hill, as they lay in wait for the British
Actually: Sounds like another American myth. There's no record of Prescott ever saying it, but there are records of both Prince Charles of Prussia (in 1745) and Frederick the Great (in 1757) using the command.

Line: "You dirty rat."
Supposedly Said By: James Cagney in one of his movies
Actually: Every Cagney impressionist says it, but Cagney never did. He made over 70 movies but never spoke this line in any of them.

Line: "Nice guys finish last."
Supposedly Said By: Leo Durocher in 1946, when he was manager of the Brooklyn Dodgers
Actually: While being interviewed, he waved toward the Giants' dugout and said, "The nice guys are all over there. In seventh place." When the article came out, reporters had changed his statement to "The nice guys are all over there in last place." As it was repeated, it was shortened to "Nice guys finish last." Durocher protested that he'd never made the remark but couldn't shake it. Finally he gave in, and eventually used it as the title of his autobiography.

In 1915 the average income for an American family was $687 a year.

Line: "Gerry Ford is so dumb he can't walk and chew gum at the same time."
Supposedly Said By: President Lyndon Johnson
Actually: This remark was cleaned up for the public—what Johnson really said was, "Gerry Ford is so dumb he can't fart and chew gum at the same time."

Line: "How I wish I had not expressed my theory of evolution as I have done."
Supposedly Said By: Charles Darwin, on his deathbed
Actually: The Christian evangelist, Jimmy Swaggart, announced in a speech in 1985 that Darwin had spoken the words as he lay dying, and asked that the Bible be read to him. But it was an old lie started shortly after Darwin's death by a Christian fanatic who was speaking to seminary students. Darwin's daughter and son both deny that their father ever had any change of heart about his scientific theory. According to his son, his last words were, "I am not the least afraid to die."

Line: "I rob banks because that's where the money is."
Supposedly Said By: Infamous bank robber Willie Sutton
Actually: According to Sutton, it was a reporter who thought up this statement and printed it. "I can't even remember when I first read it," Sutton once remarked. "It just seemed to appear one day, and then it was everywhere."

Line: "Play it again, Sam."
Supposedly Said By: Humphrey Bogart, in the classic film *Casablanca*
Actually: This may be the most famous movie line ever, but it wasn't in the movie. Ingrid Bergman said, "Play it, Sam. Play 'As Time Goes By.'" And Bogart said, "If she can stand it, I can. Play it!" But the only person who ever used "Play it again, Sam" was Woody Allen—who jokingly called his theatrical homage to Bogart *Play It Again, Sam* because he knew it was a misquote.

Line: "Elementary, my dear Watson."
Supposedly Said By: Sherlock Holmes, in Arthur Conan Doyle's books
Actually: Holmes never said it in any of the stories. It was a movie standard, however, beginning in 1929 with *The Return of Sherlock Holmes*.

Q: **What is the most common disease in the world? A: Tooth decay.**

THE CURSE OF THE HOPE DIAMOND

The Hope Diamond is probably the most famous jewel in the Western world, and it carries with it one of the most famous curses. How much of it is legend, and how much of it is fact? Even historians can't agree.

BACKGROUND

In 1668 a French diamond merchant named Jean-Baptiste Tavernier returned from India with a magnificent 112.5-carat blue diamond. No one knew exactly where he'd found it . . . but rumors spread that it was stolen from the eye of a sacred Indian idol—and people said it was cursed.

Nonetheless, King Louis XIV bought the Great Blue and added it to his crown jewels. Four years later, he had it re-cut into the shape of a heart (which reduced it to 67.5 carats).

In 1774 the diamond was inherited by Louis XVI. His wife, Marie Antoinette, apparently wore it; she was also said to have loaned it on one occasion to the Princesse de Lamballe.

When the French Revolution broke out, the Princesse de Lamballe was murdered by a mob and her head paraded under the window where Louis the XVI and his family awaited execution.Marie Antoinette herself was executed in October 1793.

—*The Book of Curses,* by Gordon Stuart

THE HOPE DIAMOND

In 1792, in the midst of the French Revolution, the Great Blue diamond was stolen. It was never seen whole again.

Thirty years later it emerged in Holland, owned now by an Amsterdam lapidary named Fals. His son stole the diamond and left Fals to die in poverty. After giving it to a Frenchman named Beaulieu, Fal's son killed himself. Beaulieu brought it to London, where he died mysteriously.

—*The Book of Curses*

In 1830 an oval-shaped blue diamond weighing 44.5 carats turned up in a London auction house. Experts recognized it as a piece of the Great Blue, re-cut to conceal its identity.

A drop of rain can fall as fast as 22 mph.

A wealthy banker named Henry Philip Hope bought the jewel for about $90,000, and it became known as the Hope Diamond.

WAS IT CURSED?

Hope was warned about the gem's "sinister influence," but owning it didn't seem to have any effect on his life. He died peacefully.

However, in the early 1900s terrible things began happening again. Lord Francis Hope, a distant relative who'd inherited it, went bankrupt. Then his marriage fell apart. "His wife prophesied," says Colin Wilson in *Unsolved Mysteries*, "that it would bring bad luck to all who owned it, and she died in poverty."

She seemed to know what she was talking about. According to Colin Wilson, over the next few years:

- Lord Francis sold it to a French jewel dealer named Jacques Colot. Francis ultimately went insane and committed suicide.

- Colot sold it to a Russian prince. He lent it to his mistress, a dancer at the Folies Bergere. The first night she wore it, he shot her from his box in the theater. The prince was reportedly stabbed by Russian revolutionaries.

- A Greek jewel dealer named Simon Manthadides bought it. He later fell (or was pushed) over a precipice.

- A Turkish sultan named Abdul Hamid bought it in 1908. He was forced into exile the following year and went insane.

TEMPTING FATE?

One wonders why anyone would want the diamond at this point. But French jeweler Jacques Cartier took possession. He quickly resold it to Edward McClean (owner of the *Washington Post*) and his wife, Evalyn. A fascinated public watched to see if the "curse" would affect them. Did it?

According to some accounts, McLean's mother and two servants in his household died soon after he purchased the jewel.

After her mother-in-law's death, Evalyn McLean had a priest bless the gem. In her autobiography she writes about the experience: "Just as he blessed it—without any wind or rain—this tree right across the street was struck by lightning. My maid Maggie fainted dead away. The old fellow was scared to death and my knees were shaking. By the time we got home the sun was out, bright as anything."

—Vanity Fair magazine

Q: What area of your body has the most bacteria? A: Between your toes.

Over the next 30 years, Evalyn McLean's family was decimated. Her father soon became an alcoholic and died. Her father-in-law went insane. The McLeans' beloved 10-year-old son, Vinson, was hit and killed by a car in front of their house. Their marriage broke up and Edward McLean went insane; he died in a mental institution. McLean's daughter Emily—who had worn the Hope Diamond at her wedding—committed suicide.

AFTERMATH

Through all the tragedy and even her own gradual financial ruin, Evalyn McLean scoffed at the "curse." She continued to wear the Hope Diamond until her death in 1947. Two years later, her children sold it to the famous diamond dealer Harry Winston, to pay estate taxes. He kept it (with no apparent ill effect) until 1958, then decided to give it away. He put it in a box with $2.44 in postage, paid $155 for $1 million insurance, and sent it to the Smithsonian Institution via U.S. mail. "Letters of protest poured in to the museum," writes Gary Cohen in *Vanity Fair*. "Some reasoned that the curse would be transferred to its new owners—the American people."

> Within a year, James Todd, the mailman who had delivered the gem, had one of his legs crushed by a truck, injured his head in a car crash, and lost his wife and dog. Then his house burned down. When asked if he blamed his ill fortune on the diamond, he said, "I don't believe any of that stuff."
>
> —*Vanity Fair* magazine

Today, the diamond is owned by the U.S. government. And we all know what kind of luck the United States has had since 1959.

* * *

WHAT ABOUT LIZ?

It's widely believed that Elizabeth Taylor once owned the Hope. Not true. She owns a larger diamond, often compared to the Hope, but now known as the Burton Diamond.

Did you know the kernel inside a peach pit is poison?

READ ALL ABOUT IT!

We've all heard the expression "Don't believe everything you hear."
Here are a few more reasons not to believe everything you read, either.
Take a look at these newspaper hoaxes, for example:

BRITISH SCIENTIST FINDS LIFE ON THE MOON!
(New York Sun, 1835)
The Story: In 1835 the *Sun* reprinted a series of articles
from the Edinburgh Journal of Science, based on reports sent in by
Sir John Herschel, a respected astronomer. He was at the Cape of
Good Hope at the time, trying out a powerful new telescope.

In the first three installments, Herschel wrote that with his
super-telescope, he could see amazing things on the moon: lakes,
fields of poppies, 38 species of forest trees, herds of buffalo with
heavy eyelids, bears with horns, two-footed beavers, etc.

In the fourth installment (August 28, 1835), he made the
biggest revelation of all: he had seen furry, bat-winged people on
the lunar surface. He wrote:

> They averaged four feet in height, were covered, except in the
> face, with short and glossy copper-colored hair, and had wings
> composed of a thin membrane, without hair, lying snugly upon
> their backs from the top of their shoulders to the calves of the
> legs.

He said their faces looked like baboons' and officially named them
"Verspertilio-homo," or "bat-man."
Reaction: People were lined up at newsstands, waiting for the next
issue. Rival newspapers claimed to have access to the original
Edinburgh Journal articles and began reprinting the series. By the
fourth installment, the *Sun*'s publisher announced his paper had
the largest circulation in the world—about 20,000. A book about
the moon discoveries sold more than 60,000 copies. A committee
of scientists from Yale University arrived at the offices of the *Sun*
to inspect the source writings by Herschel (they were given the
runaround until they gave up). One group of society ladies even
began raising money to send Christian missionaries there.
The Truth: There was no *Edinburgh Journal of Science* . . . and the
Edinburgh Philosophical Journal (which is what they meant to quote)

had gone out of business two years earlier. The whole thing was concocted by a young reporter named Richard Adams Locke, who said later that he'd written it as a "satire on absurd scientific speculations that had gotten out of hand." When the *Sun's* editors realized how out of control their scheme had gotten, they admitted it was a fake . . . and scolded other newspapers for copying the story without giving them credit.

CIVIL WAR WOES: LINCOLN DRAFTS 400,000 MEN!

(*Brooklyn Eagle*, May 18, 1864)

The Story: On the morning of May 18th, two New York newspapers, the *World* and the *Journal of Commerce*, reprinted an Associated Press dispatch in which President Abraham Lincoln, lamenting recent Union setbacks in the Civil War, called for a national day of "fasting, humiliation, and prayer," and announced the drafting of 400,000 additional troops to fight in the war.

Reaction: Wall Street was rocked by the pessimistic proclamation: stock prices plummeted, and gold prices soared as panicked investors looked for safe places to put their money. According to one Lincoln confidant, the story "angered Lincoln more than almost any other occurrence of the war period."

The Truth: The story was planted by Joseph Howard, the city editor of the *Brooklyn Eagle*, who hoped to get rich by buying gold cheap before the story broke and selling it at inflated prices afterward. Howard wrote the fake AP report with an accomplice, then paid copy boys to deliver it to every newspaper in New York. Only two papers, the *World* and the *Journal of Commerce*, printed it without bothering to check if it was true. Howard and his accomplice were arrested two days after the story broke; they spent three months interned at an Army fort without trial before Lincoln personally ordered their release.

The Hidden Truth: As Carl Sifakis writes in *Hoaxes and Scams,*

At the very time the phony proclamation was released, Lincoln had a real one on his desk, calling for the drafting of 300,000 men. When the president saw the impact of the false proclamation on the public and the financial markets, he delayed the real call up for 60 days until the situation cooled.

It feels like thread, but your hair is actually as strong as aluminum.

BROADWAY OBSESSION

What does it take to have a hit on Broadway? Well, judging from this story, it doesn't hurt to be at least a little crazy.

Obsession: Movie producer Ray Stark married the daughter of a former 1930s vaudeville star. As he learned more about his mother-in-law's life, he decided it had all the elements of a great film: determination (she'd become a star despite her homely appearance), romance (she fell in love with a handsome guy), tragedy (he was a gambler), and so on.

He made several unsuccessful attempts to get a film deal while the woman was still alive. No dice. When she died in 1951, he was so committed to the project that he bought the rights to her autobiography and convinced the publisher to burn all copies of the book except his . . . so no one else could make the film. Stark spent nine years working on the script, but still couldn't sell it. Finally in 1960, he gave up on Hollywood and took it to Broadway. If he couldn't make a movie, he'd make a musical.

What Happened: People were more receptive to the story in New York. Stark got some top talent working on it—producer David Merrick, director Jerome Robbins, lyricist Jule Styne, and others. Their first task was finding a leading lady. Front-runners were veterans like Mary Martin, Carol Burnett, and Eydie Gorme. But when Robbins and Styne went to a New York nightclub and saw a 21-year-old singer named Barbra Streisand, they wanted her for the part. Stark wanted a more glamorous star (ironically, since his mother-in-law, Fanny Brice, wasn't glamorous). But Robbins won out and Streisand got the part. Merrick ultimately dropped out of the project—but before he did, he convinced Stark to change the name of the play from *My Man* to *Funny Girl*.

Epilogue: Stark was proved right when his dream of a movie version finally came true in 1968. It was Streisand's film debut, and a huge hit; she won an Oscar for Best Actress.

Vital stat: The world's biggest chicken-eaters, per capita, are the Saudi Arabians.

THE RESURRECTION OF ELVIS, PART II

Here's what the Presley estate did to preserve Elvis's memory . . . and make a fortune from it in the process. Continued from Part I, page 581.

ENTER PRISCILLA

The effort to keep Elvis's estate out of bankruptcy was exhausting and probably contributed to his father Vernon Presley's death from heart disease in June 1979.

In his will, Vernon named three co-executors to take over his responsibilities: Elvis's accountant Joseph Hanks, the National Bank of Commerce, and Priscilla Presley—Elvis's ex-wife and the mother of his daughter, Lisa Marie. Priscilla had no business experience and had known nothing about the King's financial affairs during the marriage . . . but to everyone's surprise, she and her advisors took a leading role in rescuing the Presley estate for Lisa Marie.

FORCED INTO ACTION

With the bulk of Elvis's fortune gone forever, Priscilla was forced to make the best of what remained, namely: 1) Graceland, and 2) Elvis's name and likeness.

She immediately put both to work for the estate. First she opened Graceland to the public, charging $5 a head to the hundreds of thousands who visited each year. Then she took over the Elvis merchandising operations. Her strategy was simple but brilliant. "Since . . . the estate would have to rely on Elvis's memory to generate revenue," writes Sean O'Neal in *Elvis, Inc.*, "Elvis would be transformed into a symbol, a character that could be licensed to merchandisers. The estate would turn Elvis Presley into its own version of Mickey Mouse."

The problem with this idea was that, during the last eight years of his life, Elvis's image was not very Disneyesque. His weight had ballooned and he had been addicted to prescription medication. By the time of his death, Elvis had become a grotesque caricature of the performer he once was. This Elvis would never do as the symbol of the new empire.

Q: Who stowed away on the Apollo XII flight? A: Cockroaches.

Priscilla's solution to this problem was also simple and brilliant: she would act as though the 1977 Elvis never existed. Only the young Elvis, the King in his prime, would be acknowledged. It was this Elvis that would adorn the T-shirts, plates, shot glasses, billboards, and promotional literature of Priscilla's new empire. In her sanitized version of his life, he died after his 1968 *Comeback Special,* an idol in his prime, like James Dean.

COPYCATS

The only problem with this approach was that it had no teeth. After the King's death, hundreds of companies had come out with Elvis posters, T-shirts, videos, calendars, velvet paintings, whiskey decanters, and just about anything else imaginable. The knockoffs were cheap and tacky; even worse, they competed against "official" Elvis memorabilia licensed by the Presley estate.

Obviously, without control of the Elvis image, Priscilla's strategy would never work . . . and Lisa Marie would inherit nothing. So the estate was forced to fight for control of Elvis in court.

The heirs to Bela Lugosi and Laurel and Hardy had put up strong fights, but those battles were nothing compared to the efforts of the Presley clan. They fought lawsuit after lawsuit, in state after state. They put up millions of dollars. But they still couldn't get the issue resolved.

The outcome in every state was different: In New York, for example, the estate won—Presley's name and likeness were considered their exclusive property; but in California and Tennessee, Presley's likeness was judged to be public domain. The upshot: Merchandisers who were chased out of one state could set up business in another. Then the Presley estate would have to start all over again and fight them there, too.

THE ELVIS LOBBY

As the legal battles continued, Priscilla and Co. adopted a new tactic. They began lobbying the Tennessee state legislature to create a "Personal Rights Protection Act." This act was finally passed in 1984, and though it only officially applied in the state of Tennessee, its passage was quickly felt all over the country. Reason: In the American legal system, the laws of the state in which a person dies are the ones that apply in federal court. If someone in Missouri began selling an unlicensed Elvis poster, the Presley estate

There is one Moscow in Russia. There are at least 6 in the U.S.

could now go into Missouri federal court and force the person to comply with Tennessee law. For the first time, the Presley estate had teeth all over the country.

Not long after the Tennessee law passed, California enacted a similar law, the Celebrity Rights Act, thanks in large part to a lawsuit filed by the heirs of comedian W.C. Fields (they had been trying to block a centerfold-style poster of Field's head superimposed over another naked fat man's body).

Several other states, including Virginia, Florida, Utah, and Kentucky, passed their own versions of the law. And as more and more states followed, courts began recognizing that control of a celebrity's name and likeness were as "inheritable" as any other piece of property.

ELVIS PRESLEY ENTERPRISES

These laws changed the face of celebrity merchandising in America. Suddenly, officially licensed products featuring icons such as Marilyn Monroe and James Dean started popping up. And in Memphis, Elvis Presley Enterprises, the merchandising arm of the estate run jointly by Priscilla and Jack Soden, became the "Elvis police." They controlled every aspect of the Elvis image, from T-shirts to TV documentaries to random snapshots that had been taken by private photographers.

Priscilla's original strategy was implemented—and today there are no fat Elvis photos floating around, ruining the King's memory. Licensees only use "approved" pictures of the early Elvis; if they don't have one, they can pick from the estate's library of several thousand acceptable photos. And woe to anyone who tries to use Elvis's name or likeness—no matter how innocent the motivation—without the consent of Presley Enterprises. Charities, cities, artists, and even school teachers have received lawyers' letters.

The result of this effort has been impressive. In 1981 the Presley estate was on the verge of bankruptcy. By the 20th anniversary of Elvis's death, in 1997, it was worth nearly $200 million. And it just keeps growing.

Venice, Italy, is built in a lagoon, on top of 118 different islands.

THEY WENT THATAWAY

More morbidly fascinating details of the death-styles of the rich and famous.

CATHERINE THE GREAT
Claim to Fame: Empress of Russia, 1762–1796
How She Died: Like Elvis—from a stroke, suffered while going to the bathroom
Postmortem: There are probably more rumors about Catherine's death than that of any monarch in history (except "The King": Elvis). Most of them relate to her reputedly unusual sexual appetite. For some reason, many people believe a horse was being lowered onto her when the cable holding the beast aloft snapped, crushing her. That's 100% myth (perhaps invented by the French, Russia's enemies at the time).

    The Truth: Two weeks after suffering a mild stroke at the age of 67, Catherine appeared to be making a strong recovery. On November 5 she began her day with her usual routine: she rose at 8:00 a.m., drank several cups of coffee, then went to spend 10 minutes in the bathroom. This morning, however, she didn't come out. When her footman Zotov finally looked in on her, he found her sprawled on the floor, bleeding and barely alive. She died the next day.

GEORGE EASTMAN

Claim to Fame: Founder of Eastman Kodak and father of modern photography
How He Died: Suicide
Postmortem: In 1932 the 78-year-old Eastman was tired and ill. On March 14 he updated his will; later in the day, he asked his doctor and his nurses to leave the room, telling them he wanted to write a note. It turned out to be a suicide note. "As methodically as he had lived his 71 years [sic]," the *New York Times* reported the following morning, "he penned a brief note, carefully put out his cigarette, placed the cap back on his fountain pen and removed his glasses before firing a shot through his heart."

The Sahara Desert is larger than the entire United States.

ISADORA DUNCAN

Claim to Fame: One of the world's most famous modern dancers
How She Died: From a broken neck
Postmortem: On September 14, 1927, Duncan climbed into the passenger seat of a Bugatti race car wearing a long red silk scarf. The scarf was a little too long: when the car started off, the tail end wrapped around the wheel and yanked Duncan out of the car, snapping her neck and dragging her for several yards before the driver realized what had happened. It was too late. Final irony: A day before she died, Duncan had told an *Associated Press* reporter, "Now I'm frightened that some quick accident may happen."

MARGARET MITCHELL

Claim to Fame: Author of *Gone with the Wind*
How She Died: Run down by an automobile
Postmortem: Mitchell was crossing busy Peachtree Street in downtown Atlanta with her husband. She was halfway across when she saw a speeding motorist bearing down on her. Mitchell had previously said she was certain she would die in a car crash. Perhaps that's why she panicked, darting back across the street and leaving her husband standing there in the middle of the road. She got hit; he didn't. She died in the hospital five days later. The driver who hit her turned out to be a 29-year-old taxi driver with 23 traffic violations on his record.

NELSON ROCKEFELLER

Claim to Fame: Former governor of New York; vice president under Gerald Ford; grandson of John D. Rockefeller, founder of Standard Oil
How He Died: According to official reports, he had a heart attack while sitting at his desk
Postmortem: It was a cover-up. He was actually alone in his townhouse with 25-year-old Megan Marshack, who was on Rockefeller's staff. She had reportedly been working with him on a book about his modern art collection, but as the New York *Daily News* reported, there were no work papers in the house—just food and wine. What really happened? Only two people know for sure . . . and one is dead.

When coffee first arrived in Europe, it was known as "Arabian wine."

THE TONIGHT SHOW
PART VII:
THE CARSON YEARS

How long did Johnny Carson host The Tonight Show?
*Look at it this way: If Jay Leno wants to break the record, he'll
have to stay on the job until 2022. (Part VI appeared on page 703.)*

ROUGH RIDING

Carson's *Tonight Show* got off to a good start in 1962. His ratings were high all over the country—in Chicago, for example, he captured 58% of the viewing audience on the first night. By early 1963 his ratings were even beginning to surpass Paar's.

But Carson wasn't happy with the quality of the program. The interview format was inflexible—if a guest was scheduled for 10 minutes, they stayed on for 10 minutes, even if they ran out of things to say. Some nights were particularly awful. When an interview fell apart, Carson would become so frustrated, he'd yawn into the camera; his eyes would wander as his guests droned on and on.

MAKING CHANGES

In early 1963 the show's producer transferred to another program just as Art Stark, Carson's producer on *Who Do You Trust?* became available. Stark had helped Carson turn the game show into a surprise hit, and Carson hired him to do the same thing with *The Tonight Show.*

Stark immediately went to work on the format. He and Carson agreed that from now on, if an interview ran out of gas they'd go to a commercial as quickly as possible, and the offending guest would slide down the couch and off-camera. When the commercials ended, a new guest or skit would begin the next segment. The flexible scheduling helped the show's pacing, and put a lot of pressure on guests to perform.

Robert Blake, a frequent guest during the Carson years, describes what it was like:

You've got six minutes to do your thing. And you better be good, or they'll go to the commercial after two minutes . . . The producer, all the *federales* are sittin' like six feet away from that couch. And they're right on top of you, man, just watchin' ya. And when they go to break, they get on the phone . . . They whisper in John's ear. John gets on the phone and he talks. And you're sitting there, watching, thinking . . . and then the camera comes back again and John will ask you something else or he'll say, "Our next guest is . . . "

OTHER CHANGES

- Whenever possible, Stark scheduled an attractive woman as the first guest, to appeal to what he felt was a largely male-chauvinist audience . . . and to break up what was otherwise an all-male show.

- He scheduled the biggest stars to run just after the midnight hour, so that viewers would have something to stay up for.

- The third guest would often be a singer or instrumentalist, and the fourth, an author. (When the show was cut from 90 minutes to an hour in 1980, authors disappeared almost completely.)

- And where Paar had abandoned comedy sketches entirely, Carson began putting them back in, borrowing liberally from the comedians of the day. Carnak the Magician was a recreation of Steve Allen's Question Man, Aunt Blabby borrowed heavily from Jonathan Winters, and Art Fern was inspired by Jackie Gleason.

CARSON ON STRIKE

By the mid-1960s the show was on its way to becoming a national institution. Ten million people tuned in every night. Carson was a superstar: when he performed a stand-up comedy routine at the Las Vegas Sahara in 1964, he broke the all-time attendance record.

The program was also making huge money for NBC. It had a smaller audience than most prime-time shows, but because it was produced at a lower cost—and was on five nights a week—it earned more money.

The United States has the most tornadoes in the world—more than 700 a year.

WHERE'S JOHNNY?

Despite his success, Carson was becoming increasingly unhappy with NBC—he didn't feel the network was giving him the star treatment he'd earned. On his second anniversary as host, NBC threw him a party. But instead of renting a swanky nightclub or restaurant for the occasion, they held it in a conference room on the fifth floor, and served cold hors d'oeuvres and drinks in plastic cups. "I've seen smoke come out of a guy's nose before," one person who was at the party recalled, "but I'm telling you this was steam. [Carson] was pissed off."

Another thing that drove Carson crazy was the show's 11:15 p.m. starting time. During the Paar years, most television stations had 15-minute newscasts at 11:00 p.m. But in 1965 many stations expanded to a half-hour, which meant they didn't switch over to *The Tonight Show* until 11:30—after Carson had finished his monologue.

One evening Carson decided he'd had enough. He refused to come onstage until 11:30, leaving Ed McMahon and band leader Skitch Henderson to fill in the first 15 minutes themselves. When he strode out at 11:30, Carson explained that the only people listening at 11:15 were "four Navajos in Gallup, New Mexico, and the Armed Forces Radio on Guam." NBC moved the starting time to 11:30. It was the beginning of a series of confrontations that would last as long as Carson was host.

TAKING CONTROL

The next big showdown came in April 1967, when the American Federation of Television and Radio Artists (AFTRA) struck all three networks. Carson, a union member, participated in the walk-out. The networks responded by playing reruns, with little protest from AFTRA members . . . but when NBC played a *Tonight Show* rerun, Carson accused NBC of violating—and thereby voiding—his contract. He refused to go back to work even after the strike ended. "I know of no business except the broadcasting industry in which a performer becomes a scab to himself and his union because of videotape," Carson said at the time. Like Paar before him, he went to Florida for the duration of the fight.

WHO DO YOU TRUST?

Cynics suggested that Carson, who was making an estimated $700,000 a year, was really using the strike to get more money out of NBC. And while Carson admitted that money was an issue, what he really wanted was greater control over his show—and greater independence from NBC.

He got it. Americans were already hooked on *Tonight*, and NBC was hooked on the estimated $25 million a year the show was bringing in. Besides, after years of ceding the late-night audience to NBC, ABC had launched *The Joey Bishop Show* opposite Carson. Bishop, a nightclub comic, had a style similar to Jack Paar's, and ABC hoped that he would enjoy similar success.

If NBC lost Carson now, his audience might leave, too. NBC couldn't afford to take the chance, so they agreed to Carson's demands for greater control and renegotiated his salary. Carson returned on April 24, 1967, one week after *The Joey Bishop Show* made its debut. Bishop, whose ratings were only half those of *The Tonight Show* even on his best nights, limped along until December 1969.

LATE NIGHT FIGHTS

The Joey Bishop Show was one of the first attempts to steal Carson's crown as King of the Night, but it wasn't the last. Here are some other also-rans of the 1960s and 1970s:

- **The Les Crane Show** (1964–1965). Crane's show bore more similarity to a tabloid talk show than it did to *The Tonight Show*: Crane and his guests tackled the controversial topics of the day, including homosexuality and adultery. He was fired four months into the show, rehired, then fired a final time on November 12, 1965.

- **The Las Vegas Show** (1967). In 1967 a consortium of independent TV stations calling itself the United Network made a stab at becoming America's fourth television network. *The Las Vegas Show*, featuring top casino acts, went on the air on May 1, 1967 . . . and went off the air on May 31, when the United Network ran out of money.

- **Merv Griffin** (1969–1972). Griffin—Carson's original rival for the *Tonight Show* gig—had his own syndicated evening show when CBS came to him about going up against Carson. Griffin didn't want the job—so he demanded double the salary that Carson was rumored to be getting, thinking that CBS would refuse. They didn't. According to Griffin, they agreed to pay him $80,000 a week. "Suddenly I felt sick," Griffin recalls but he

---

Every second, your senses send about 100 million different messages to your brain.

agreed to do the show. Griffin's ratings were consistently higher than Joey Bishop's, but remained far behind Carson's.

- **Dick Cavett** (1969–1974). When Joey Bishop got the axe in 1969, Dick Cavett, a former writer for Jack Paar, signed on to replace him. Promoted as "the intellectual Carson," Cavett won strong critical praise, but low ratings.
- **Jack Paar Tonite** (1973). Paar is said to have envied Carson's celebrity as it grew. So when ABC scaled Cavett's show back from four weeks a month to one in 1973, Paar agreed to take one of the weeks for himself. Paar, however, had lost touch with his audience. Ronald Smith writes in *The Fight for Tonight*:

Paar looked like a refugee from another era with his bowties and wet-look toupee. Viewers didn't understand why he was being a cornball and showing his home movies. He embarrassed himself with his tirades against rock music and long hair . . . His sidekick was Peggy Cass, and together they looked like someone's parents video-taping an evening with dull friends.

Paar's ratings were terrible—worse than Cavett's—so in the Fall of 1973, he announced that he wasn't renewing his contract. "I guess the next event in my life will be my death," he lamented.

KING OF THE NIGHT
Once again, Carson was the unchallenged king of late-night television. His next serious challenger would not emerge for a decade.

Still more to come? Maybe. Turn to page 742 to find out.

Still more to come? Maybe. Turn to page 742 to find out.

* * *

LOST TRADEMARKS
These generic terms were once registered trademarks.

Cellophane: Invented by a Swiss chemist around 1900 and sold to DuPont in 1915. It was declared a generic term by a N.Y. court in 1941, because no other word could adequately describe it.

Dry ice: Once registered by the Dry Ice Corp. to describe "solidified carbon dioxide."

Escalator: Otis Elevator Co. had this trademark.

Linoleum: Originally a trademark of the Armstrong Cork Co.

Did you know that a pig has 44 teeth?

LIFE'S AN ITCH

Uncle John has been itching to write about this subject for a long time. He bets you can't read to the end of this chapter without scratching at least once . . .

ITCH, ITCH, ITCH

"The itch," says Jeffrey Bernhard, of the Massachusetts Medical Center, "is one of, if not the, most mysterious of all 'cutaneous intrusions.'" No one knows exactly why we itch, or how it works.

- Some scientists speculate that its function is to remove parasites and other foreign objects from the skin. Or it may serve as an "early warning system" for the body's borders. Sometimes itching is a warning of a serious disease.

- Itching has a lot in common with pain—they even travel through the same kind of nerve cells (neurons). In fact, scientists once thought itching was a kind of pain. Now they're pretty sure itching and pain are two entirely separate functions.

- Health experts divide itches into two different categories: *sensory itches* and *allergic itches*. They also say that scratching almost always makes itches worse.

SENSORY ITCHES

- These are caused when special nerve endings in your skin called *Merkel's discs* (but referred to by doctors as "itch nerves") detect pressure on your skin. They immediately send nerve signals to the spinal cord . . . which sends them on to the brain.

- Your brain checks out the signals: if they're caused by something your body's used to—like clothes you wear all the time—it files the signals away in your subconscious. You don't even notice they're there.

- But if the stimulus is new and unfamiliar—say you're wearing a new hat, or you have several days of new beard growth—your brain sends out a "foreign irritant" alert and makes you aware something's there. How? By making you itch—trying to get you to brush the irritant away.

- At the same time, your brain is sending signals to the muscles

---

What is the oldest letter in the alphabet? O. It's more than 3,000 years old.

in your hands and arms to start scratching. That's why you scratch even when you sleep.

- Fortunately, your brain adapts to new sensations fairly quickly. So if the irritant hangs around for a while, the brain will calm down and start rerouting signals to your subconscious. The irritant is still there, but the itch goes away.

ALLERGIC ITCHINGS

- *Allergic* itching is what happens when a foreign body, such as medication or venom from an insect bite, irritates your immune system. The immune system responds by releasing *histamine*, the chemical that is the body's main response to allergies. Histamine is the stuff that gives you rashes.

- Histamine does several things to the nearby cells that makes it easier for them to fight off the allergen—it causes the blood vessels to dilate; it makes it easier for fluids to pass through the affected skin cells; and it stimulates nearby nerve endings.

- In most cases, your body will get rid of the histamine naturally in 18 to 24 hours; antihistamine medications can do the same job in a couple of hours, but serious allergies can take much longer.

WEIRD ITCHES

Of course, there are always itches that break the rules—inexplicable itches with no identifiable cause. Four, that Scott LaFee, in the *San Diego Union-Tribune*, has picked as the most interesting:

Mitempfindungen: "Otherwise known as a referred itch, occurs more or less in one spot when another spot is scratched."

Aquagenic pruritus: "Itching provoked by contact with water."

Atmknesis: Itching caused by, or apparently caused by, exposure to air while undressing."

Pruritus prohibitus: "An itch that can't be scratched because your hands are full, because you can't reach it, because it would be unseemly or embarrassing to do so. Most famous case involved Huckleberry Finn."

SCRATCH FEVER

- Why do itches get worse when you scratch them? Because when you scratch, you irritate a *second* set of nerve endings—

Take a guess, Jesse—how many times do you breathe in a year? About 10 million.

the ones that transmit pain. So even if you get rid of the original irritant, you've created a whole new one—*you*.

- Scratching also temporarily thickens your skin. "It sets up what I call a hot spot," says Dr. Nia Terezakis, a New Orleans dermatologist. "Scratching thickens the skin, and when skin gets thicker, it itches more. You've got a nervous itch going. You stimulate the nerves to fire more and more."

- With allergic rashes, the problem is even worse. On top of irritating the nerve endings and thickening your skin, you also spread the histamine into unaffected cells—which makes the rash bigger.

SCRATCH FACTS

- Do you itch when you come in from the cold? That's because cold weather "numbs" your nerve endings . . . which makes them transmit signals more slowly. But when you get back into a warm environment, your nerve endings spring back into action and flood the brain with itch signals. Your brain makes you feel itchy until it adjusts to the warmth.

- Wool is itchier than most fabrics because it stimulates two types of nerve endings at once: the pressure of the wool against your skin activates the itch nerves, and the individual fibers tickle the nerve endings that are wrapped around your hair shafts.

- No one knows why people itch so strongly at the base of the shoulder blades, the very place that's impossible to reach and scratch. "It's an intense itching that drives people crazy," says Dr. David R. Harris, a Stanford University dermatologist. "And no one knows why this occurs. We think it might be a peculiar reaction to the nerve fibers, but we don't know for sure."

ITCHY INFO

- Chicken pox gets its name from the itch, not chickens. The ailment was originally called "gican pox" in Old English, which meant "itchy pox."

- It takes about three minutes from the time a mosquito bites you for the bite to begin itching.

- Everyone itches at least once a day. Even thinking about itching can make you itch.

Q: What do you do every 2 to 10 seconds? A: Blink.

YOU CALL THAT ART?

Here are some more great art fakes.

D. S. WINDLE

Background: In 1936 Windle entered a painting called *Abstract Painting of Woman* in the International Surrealist Exhibition taking place in London. The work was one of the most talked-about and admired paintings of the show.

The Truth: D. S. Windle ("De Swindle") was actually B. Howitt-Lodge, a portrait painter who hated surrealist art. He created his painting out of "a phantasmagoria of paint blobs, variegated beads, a cigarette stub, Christmas tinsel, pieces of hair, and a sponge." Howitt-Lodge chose the materials, he later admitted, because he wanted to create "the worst possible mess" and enter it in "one of the most warped and disgusting shows I've ever seen."

What Happened: Modernists were unmoved by his confession— they accepted Howitt-Lodge's work as genuine surrealist art, even if he didn't. "He may think it's a hoax," one fan told reporters, "but he's an artist and unconsciously he may be a surrealist. Aren't we all?"

ALCEO DOSSENA

Background: In 1922 the Boston Museum of Fine Arts paid $100,000 for the marble tomb of a wealthy Italian woman named Maria Caterina Savelli, who died in 1430. The tomb was suppos-edly carved by a famous Florentine sculptor named Mino da Fie-Savelli, and was so impressive that the museum set the exhibit up right at the building's entrance.

The Truth: As Kathryn Lindskoog writes in *Fakes, Frauds & Other Malarkey*, "No one seemed to notice that the Mino Tomb was dated one year after its sculptor was born, and that the brief Latin inscription on the tomb, which was naively copied from a book about the Savelli family, said, 'At last the above-mentioned Maria Caterina Savelli died.'"

What Happened: No one realized it was a fake until 1928, when an obscure Italian sculptor named Alceo Dossena sued art dealer

There's only one continent that has never seen a war: Antarctica

Alfredo Fasoli for $66,000, claiming that without his knowledge, Fasoli had been selling his copies of Renaissance art as the genuine article.

The Boston Museum of Fine Arts refused to accept that the Mino Tomb was fake . . . until Dossena produced photographs of the work in progress, as well as a toe that had broken off a figure carved in the tomb.

Museums all over the world scoured their collections looking for Dossena's fakes—hundreds were found. The Cleveland Museum of Art was particularly hard hit—after finding modern nails deep inside a "13th-century" Madonna and Child, it replaced the piece with a marble statue of Athena that cost $120,000. That statue also turned out to be a Dossena fake. For what it's worth, not everyone suffered from the scandal: Alceo Dossena flourished. People became so interested in his work that he was able to launch a career as a legitimate artist.

THOMAS KEATING

Background: In 1976 thirteen paintings by Samuel Palmer, a famous English artist, inexplicably came on the market at the same time.

The Truth: When the *London Times* challenged their authenticity, an English painter named Thomas Keating wrote in to confess that he had forged the paintings—as well as 2,500 other paintings during his illicit 20-year career, including works attributed to Rembrandt, Degas, Goya, Toulouse-Lautrec, Monet, Van Gogh, and others. Keating claimed he left a clue in every painting that proved it wasn't authentic—sometimes he used modern materials; other times he painted "this is a fake" on the canvas using lead-based paint, which would show up on X-rays. But he was never caught.

What Happened: Keating was in such poor health when he confessed that he was never put on trial. He became a cult hero in England for fooling art experts for so long, and his own paintings soared in value. One which he called *Monet and his Family in their Houseboat*, sold at an auction for $32,000. By the time of his death in 1983, his work was so popular that other forgers were cashing in by copying his work.

Niagara Falls was created by a glacier.

THE SWORD OF DAMOCLES

Here's another tale from Myths and Legends of the Ages.

There was once a rich and powerful king in Greece named Dionysius. A clever, ruthless man, Dionysius had fought his way to the throne. In gaining the crown, he'd made many powerful and bitter enemies. Yet there were many who envied Dionysius and wished they were in his place.

Among the king's courtiers was a man called Damocles. Damocles was constantly praising Dionysius and saying, "Oh great king, you are indeed blessed of the gods. Everything you could wish for is yours. How happy you must be!"

One day, when Damocles was speaking in his flattering way, Dionysius said, "Well now, Damocles, what are you saying? Would you like to be king in my place?"

Damocles was frightened. He didn't want the king to think he was plotting to seize the throne. Quickly he replied, "Oh no, great king. I was only thinking how wonderful it would be to enjoy your riches for even one day."

"It shall be as you desire," said King Dionysius. "For one day, you shall enjoy the position and power and luxury of a king. You shall know exactly what it feels like to be in my place."

The next day the astonished Damocles was led into the king's chamber. He was dressed in royal robes and told that he could do whatever he wished.

Suddenly, as he leaned back among his silken cushions, he gasped with horror. Just above his head was an enormous sword hanging by a slender thread! If the thread broke, the sword would instantly fall and kill him. He sat, pale and trembling. Pointing to the sword in terror, he whispered, "That sword! That sword! Why is that sword hanging above me? Hanging by so slender a thread?"

Until 1867 Alaska was known as Russian America.

"I promised you," answered Dionysius, "that you should know exactly how it feels to live like a king, and now you know! Did you expect that you might enjoy all of a king's riches for nothing? Do you not know that I always live with a sword hanging over my head? I must be on my guard every moment lest I be slain."

Then Damocles answered, "Oh king, take back your wealth and your power! I would not have it for another moment. I would rather be a poor peasant living in a mountain hut than live in fear and trembling all the days of my life!"

Never again did Damocles envy the king.

* * *

READ ALL ABOUT IT!

Here's another newspaper hoax.

Nuclear War: It's Hell!
(The *San Francisco Chronicle*, 1960)
The Story: In 1960 the *San Francisco Chronicle* posed this question: If there were a nuclear war, "could an average city dweller exist in the wilderness tomorrow with little more than his bare hands?" The paper answered its own question by assigning outdoor columnist Harvey Boyd, his wife and their three children to spend the next six weeks living in a mountain wilderness area near San Francisco. The *Chronicle* called the series "The Last Man on Earth."

Reaction: In his articles, Boyd described the experiences as "the most brutish, hellish, most miserable days of our lives." But after several days of struggle, his son learned to capture frogs and Boyd himself learned how to trap a deer. After ten days, Boyd reported, he was feeling "ahead of the game at last."

The Truth: Editors at the rival *San Francisco Examiner* decided to check up on The Last Man on Earth . . . and found a campsite filled with modern conveniences and store-bought foods, including "matches, canned spaghetti, fresh eggs, watermelon, and the current *Reader's Digest*." The only thing missing: the Boyds themselves. The Last Man on Earth and his family had already gone home.

Aristotle called the wind "the dry sighs of the breathing Earth."

WHAT HAPPENED AT ROSWELL? PART II

The "Incident at Roswell" is probably the biggest UFO story in history. Was it a military balloon . . . or an alien spacecraft? You be the judge, as the story continues. (Part I starts on Page 643.)

DÉJÀ VU

The Roswell story would probably have stayed dead if Stanton T. Friedman, a nuclear physicist, hadn't lost his job during the 1970s. UFOs were Friedman's hobby . . . until he got laid off; then it became his career. "In the 1970s, when the bottom fell out of the nuclear physics business," he explains, "I went full time as a lecturer." His favorite topic: "Flying Saucers ARE Real," a talk that he gave at more than 600 different college campuses and other venues around the country.

In his years on the lecture circuit, Friedman developed a nationwide reputation as a UFO expert, and people who'd seen UFOs began seeking him out. In 1978 he made contact with Jesse Marcel, the Army Intelligence Officer (now retired) who'd retrieved the wreckage from Mac Brazel's ranch 31 years earlier.

At Friedman's urging, Marcel gave an interview to the *National Enquirer*. "I'd never seen anything like it," Marcel told the supermarket tabloid, "I didn't know what we were picking up. I still believe it was nothing that came from Earth. It came *to* Earth, but not *from* Earth."

BACK IN THE HEADLINES

The *Enquirer* interview couldn't have come at a more opportune time: it was 1979, and Steven Spielberg's film *Close Encounters of the Third Kind*, which had premiered several months earlier, had stoked the public's appetite for UFO stories. After lying dormant for more than 30 years, the Roswell story blew wide open all over again.

From there the story just kept growing. Dozens of new "witnesses" to the Roswell UFO began seeking out Friedman at his public appearances to tell him their stories. Soon, the Roswell "cover up" included humanoid alien beings. "Over the years," Joe Nickell writes in the *Skeptical Enquirer*, "numerous rumors, urban legends, and outright hoaxes have claimed that saucer wreckage and the remains of its humanoid occupants were stored at a secret facility—the (nonexistent) 'Hangar 18' at Wright Patterson Air Force Base. People swear that the small corpses were autopsied at that or another site."

- For the record, neither Mac Brazel nor Jesse Marcel ever claimed to have seen aliens among the wreckage. No one went public with those claims until more than 30 years after the fact.

WHY BELIEVE IN ROSWELL?

- Why are UFO conspiracy theories so popular? Anthropologists who study the "Roswell Myth" point to two psychological factors that help it endure:

1) It appeals to a cynical public that lived through the Kennedy assassination, Watergate, Vietnam, and other government crises, and who believe in the government's proclivity for covering things up. As *Time* magazine reported on the 50th anniversary of the Roswell incident,

A state of mind develops which easily believes in cover-up. The fact that the military is known for 'covert' activities with foreign governments having to do with weapons which could wipe out humanity makes the idea of secret interactions with aliens seem possible. Once this state of mind is in place, anything which might prove the crash was terrestrial becomes a lie.

2) UFO theories project a sense of order onto the chaos of the universe . . . and they can even serve as an ego boost to true-believers, because they suggest that we are interesting enough that aliens with vastly superior intelligence actually bother to visit us. Believing in aliens, the argument goes, is much more satisfying than believing that aliens are out there but would never want to visit us.

WAS THERE A CONSPIRACY?

So is our government hiding evidence of an alien crash-landing on earth? In 1993 Congressman Steven Schiff of New Mexico asked the U.S. Government's General Accounting Office to look into whether the U.S. government had ever been involved in a space-alien cover-up, either in Roswell, New Mexico, or anyplace else. The

In about 250 B.C. Archimedes invented the screw.

GAO spent 18 months searching government archives dating back to the 1940s, including even the highly classified minutes of the National Security Council. Their research prompted the U.S. Air Force to launch its own investigation. It released its findings in September 1994; the GAO's report followed in November 1995; then a second Air Force report was released in 1997.

PROJECT MOGUL

All three reports arrived at the same conclusion: what the conspiracy theorists believe were UFO crashes were actually top secret research programs run by the U.S. military during the Cold War.

Take Roswell: According to the reports, the object that crashed on Mac Brazel's farm *was* a balloon, but no ordinary weather balloon—it was part of Project Mogul, a defense program as top secret as the Manhattan Project itself. Unlike the Manhattan Project, however, Project Mogul wasn't geared toward *creating* nuclear weapons, it was geared toward *detecting* them if the Soviets exploded them.

In the late 1940s the U.S. had neither spy satellites nor high-altitude spy planes that it could send over the Soviet Union to see if Stalin's crash program to build nuclear weapons was succeeding. Instead, government scientists figured, "trains" of weather balloons fitted with special sensing equipment, if launched high enough into the atmosphere, might be able to detect the shock waves given off by nuclear explosions thousands of miles away.

Up, Up, and Away

Project Mogul was just such a program, the reports explained, and the object that crashed on Mac Brazel's field in 1947 was "Flight R-4," a Mogul balloon train that had been launched from Alamogordo Army Air Field—near the Roswell Base—in June 1947. The train of 20 balloons was tracked to within 17 miles of Mac Brazel's ranch; shortly afterward, radar contact was lost and the balloons were never recovered . . . at least not by the folks at Alamogordo. The Roswell intelligence officers who recovered the wreckage didn't have high enough security clearance to know about Project Mogul, and thus they didn't know to inform Alamogordo of the discovery.

On the whole, the program was successful—Project Mogul apparently did detect the first Soviet nuclear blasts. Even so, the

The filaments for the first electric lamp were made of bamboo.

project was discontinued when scientists discovered that such blasts could also be detected on the ground, making the balloon-borne sensors unnecessary. The project was discontinued in the early 1950s.

OTHER PROJECTS
The Air Force's 1997 report suggested that a number of other military projects that took place in the 1940s and 1950s became part of the Roswell myth:

- In the 1950s the Air Force launched balloons as high as 19 miles into the atmosphere and dropped human dummies to test parachutes for pilots of the X-15 rocket plane and the U-2 spy plane. The dummies, the Air Force says, were sometimes mistaken for aliens . . . and because it didn't want the real purpose of the tests to be revealed, it did not debunk the alien theories.

- Some balloons also dropped mock interplanetary probes, which looked like flying saucers.

- In one 1959 balloon crash, a serviceman crashed a test balloon 10 miles northwest of Roswell and suffered an injury that caused his head to swell considerably. The man, Captain Dan D. Fulgham, was transferred to Wright Patterson in Ohio for treatment. The incident, the Air Force says, helped inspire the notion that aliens have large heads and that aliens or alien corpses are being held at Wright Patterson for study.

NEVER SURRENDER
Do the GAO and Air Force reports satisfy people who previously believed the object was a UFO? Not a chance. "It's a bunch of pap," says Walter G. Haut, who worked at the Roswell base and after World War II distributed the famous "flying saucer" news release in 1947, and is now president of the International UFO Museum and Research Center in Roswell. "All they've done is given us a different kind of balloon. Then it was weather, and now it's Mogul. Basically, I don't think anything has changed. Excuse my cynicism, but let's quit playing games."

GROUCHO MARX, ATTORNEY AT LAW

Here's the next installment of the radio adventures of Groucho and Chico Marx, from Five Star Theater *(which aired in 1933).*

MRS. BRITTENHOUSE: Is this a detective agency?

GROUCHO: A *detective* agency? Madam, if there's anything in it for me, this is Scotland Yard.

MRS. BRITTENHOUSE: This man told me he was taking me to a detective bureau.

CHICO: You're cuckoo, I did not. You stop me in the hall. You say you want a detective. I say, you go see Flywheel. You say alright. Well, here's Flywheel.

MRS. BRITTENHOUSE: Sir, are you or aren't you a detective? My time is money.

GROUCHO: Your time is money? I wonder if you could lend me ten minutes for lunch, or maybe a half an hour for the rent?

MRS. BRITTENHOUSE: For the last time, are you a detective?

GROUCHO: Madam, for the first time I am a detective.

MRS. BRITTENHOUSE: Well, you don't look much like a detective to me.

GROUCHO: That's the beauty of it. See? I had you fooled already.

MRS. BRITTENHOUSE: Is this man who brought me in a detective too?

CHICO: Sure, I'm a detective. I prove it. Lady, you lose anything today?

MRS. BRITTENHOUSE: Why, I don't think so. Heavens! My handbag has disappeared.

CHICO: Here it is.

MRS. BRITTENHOUSE: Where did you find it?

CHICO: Right here in my pocket.

GROUCHO: Isn't he marvelous, madam? He has the nose of a bloodhound, and his other features aren't so good either.

Number of times Abraham Lincoln actually slept in the Lincoln Bedroom: 0

MRS. BRITTENHOUSE: Well, you're just the man I'm looking for.

CHICO: You're looking for us? Hey, are you a detective?

MRS. BRITTENHOUSE: No, no. You misunderstand me. You see, my daughter is getting married this afternoon.

GROUCHO: Oh, your daughter's getting married? I love those old-fashioned girls.

MRS. BRITTENHOUSE: We're having a big wedding reception, and I want you two men to come out this afternoon and keep an eye on the wedding presents. They're very valuable, and I want to be sure that nothing is stolen.

CHICO: How much you pay us? You know it's very hard work not to steal anything.

MRS. BRITTENHOUSE: I think fifty dollars would be adequate. But you understand, of course, that you're not to mingle with the guests.

GROUCHO: Well, if we don't have to mingle with the guests we'll do it for forty dollars.

MRS. BRITTENHOUSE: Dear, dear, I must hurry. My daughter can't get married unless I get her trousseau.

CHICO: Trousseau? You mean Robinson Trousseau?

GROUCHO: Your daughter's marrying Robinson Crusoe today? Monday? Wouldn't she be better off if she'd marry the man Friday?

MRS. BRITTENHOUSE: Well, I must hurry along now. Goodbye, gentlemen. I'll be looking for you this afternoon.

GROUCHO: Well, why look for us this afternoon when we're here right now?

(*Later, at the Brittenhouse mansion.*)

MRS. BRITTENHOUSE: Hello, Mr. Flywheel. Hives, our butler, will take care of you. Oh, dear, I'm always so nervous at weddings. I'm really not myself today.

GROUCHO: You're not yourself, eh? Well, whoever you are, you're no bargain.

HIVES: Now, on these two tables here, gentlemen, are the presents. Please watch them very carefully. (*Receding.*) I'll have to leave you now.

(*Tap at the window.*)

Food for thought: What country has the lowest birthrate in the world? The Vatican.

GROUCHO: I think there's somebody at the window. You'd better let him in.

CHICO: Hey, boss. He's a great big guy and he looks very tough.

(*Tap again.*)

CHICO: Hey, who are you?

MAN: Never mind who I am. Who are you guys?

CHICO: We're a coupla detectives.

MAN: Oh, you're a coupla detectives. Ha, ha, ha! That's a hot one!

GROUCHO: Well, I've heard better ones than that, but it's fairly good.

MAN: Hey, what are you guys supposed to do here?

CHICO: I watch da presents. Flywheel, he watch me, but we got no one to watcha Flywheel.

MAN: Well, you can clear outta here. I'll do the whole ting for you.

GROUCHO: Ravelli, that fellow certainly is a prince. I'm getting out of here before he changes his mind.

(*Opens and closes door. Footsteps.*)

MRS. BRITTENHOUSE: Why, Mr. Flywheel, I thought you were supposed to stay in that room with the presents!

GROUCHO: Madam, I couldn't stand being alone in that room. I just had to have another look at you. And now that I've had that look, I can hardly wait to get back to the presents.

MRS. BRITTENHOUSE: Why, Mr. Flywheel!

GROUCHO: Don't call me Mr. Flywheel, just call me Sugar.

MRS. BRITTENHOUSE: Oh, Mr. Flywheel, I simply love the things you say.

GROUCHO: Oh, Mrs. Brittenhouse—I know you'll think me a sentimental old softie, but would you give me a lock of your hair?

MRS. BRITTENHOUSE (*Coyly*): Why, Mr. Flywheel!

GROUCHO: I'm letting you off easy—I was going to ask you for the whole wig.

Teddy Roosevelt had 24 pets in the White House, including 1 bear.

MRS. BRITTENHOUSE: Well, we'll discuss that later. It's too bad you can't join us now for refreshments, but maybe some evening you'd like to have me for dinner.

GROUCHO: Have you for dinner? Well, if there's nothing better to eat, I wouldn't mind, but personally, I'd prefer a can of salmon.

HIVES: Mrs. Brittenhouse! Mrs. Brittenhouse!

GROUCHO: Is there no privacy here?

MRS. BRITTENHOUSE: Why Hives, what's the matter?

HIVES: The presents! The presents!

MRS. BRITTENHOUSE: What about the presents?

HIVES: They're gone. We've been robbed!

GROUCHO: Robbed? Where's Ravelli? Quick, find Ravelli!

CHICO: Here I am, boss. How you makin' out?

GROUCHO: Listen, Ravelli. I thought I told you to watch the presents.

CHICO: That's just what I was doing.

GROUCHO: There you are, Mrs. Brittenhouse. You have nothing to worry about.

HIVES: But, madam, the presents are gone.

CHICO: Boss, I watch them just like a bloodhound. You remember that big fellow? He came in da room . . . well, I watch him . . .

ALL: Yes . . .

CHICO: He walked over and picked up da presents and I watch him . . .

ALL: Yes . . .

CHICO: He took them out da window! He put them on a truck and I watch him . . .

ALL: Yes . . .

CHICO: But when da truck drives away . . . then I cannot watch no more.

GROUCHO: You're a genius. And now, Mrs. Brittenhouse, how about our fifty dollars?

Only 2% of women think they should keep their last name when they marry.

LET THERE BE LITE, PART II

First Lite Beer was a hit . . . then Light Beer . . . and then,
Light Food. Finally, it turned into the most comprehensive
labeling law in U.S. history. Here's the rest of this
unlikely story. (Continued from page 676.)

EATING LIGHT

By the late 1980s the term "lite" had spread from beer to every kind of food imaginable. Consumers could buy "light" oil, cheese, salad dressing, ice cream, whiskey, pudding, crackers, hot dogs, even cat food (Tender Vittles Lite). In fact, by 1991 there were an estimated 10,000 "light" products on supermarket shelves.

"Next to foods that can be microwaved," reported a manager of the U.S.'s largest supermarket chain in 1989, "light foods are the fastest-growing segment in our stores. If two comparable products are on the shelf next to each other, the one that says 'Light' will probably sell better."

What was behind the lite boom? Polls showed that although most Americans weren't inclined to radically alter diets or start exercising more, they still wanted to make some kind of "healthy" change. "Lite" food filled the bill perfectly. Everyone knew that "light" or "lite" on a package meant it was better for you. So by eating *lite*, people eat *right*—and still enjoy the same food they always had. It was a way to "have it all."

"Everyone wants to indulge," commented a food industry newsletter in 1990. "This way, you can indulge and not be so bad."

THE HEAVY TRUTH

But to a large extent, lite food was a hoax. It didn't have to be better for you, because legally, *lite* and *light* didn't mean anything at all. The terms could be applied to any product for almost any reason.

A "light" margarine might be lighter in color . . . or sold in a smaller package (which would make it lighter in *weight*). A "light" pudding might be lower in calories . . . or *higher* in calories, with a "lighter" texture. As the customer relations manager of Kroger

---

Rather than sell the first story he wrote, Charles Dickens traded it for a bag of marbles.

supermarkets tactfully put it: "It's kind of confusing for customers. When they pick up something that says 'light,' it may not be at all what they expect." For example: According to published reports, on a shopping trip in 1990–91 you could buy . . .

- **Klondike Lite Frozen Dessert Bars.** Cutting down on fat? These babies had seven grams of fat per serving—more than triple the FDA's recommendations for low-fat claims.
- **Bertolli Mild & Light Olive Oil.** Light in color, but no change in calories.
- **Lipton's Lite Cup-a-Soup Chicken Soup.** Had exactly the same amount of calories as their regular chicken Cup-a-Soup.
- **Fleur-de-Lait "Ultra-Light" cheese spreads.** "Ultra-light" referred to the consistency of these whipped cheeses. Actually a high-fat item.
- **Sara Lee Light Classics cheesecake.** Had *more* fat and calories than its regular products. This product was so misleading that the attorneys general of nine states *sued* the company over it.

Not satisfied yet? You could always choose "Pillsbury Lovin' Lites" cake mixes and frosting, "Hostess Light Cupcakes," or "Spam Lite" (fat was reduced from 16 grams per serving to 12). It seemed like there was no end in sight to the fad.

But there was.

THE LITE AT THE END OF THE TUNNEL

In 1986 Jim Cooper, a bachelor congressman from Tennessee, arrived in Washington determined to stay in shape. He bought "light" food as part of his routine. When he got married a few years later, his wife suggested he read the fine print on the labels, to see what he'd *really* been eating. He was shocked, and began introducing legislation to regulate the use of terms like "lite" and "low-fat."

Gradually, the idea grained acceptance. The FDA, revitalized under President Bush, worked with Congress to develop a label law that would make it easy for consumers to see what they were getting. In 1993, after plenty of compromising, they came up with a set of rules that regulated nutrition claims, required nutritional labeling (at the time 40% of all packaged foods provided no nutritional info at all), and gave specific definitions to words that

Consumer Reports called "overused and underdefined"—such as "reduced," "low-cholesterol," "low-fat" . . . and of course, "lite" and "light."

As a result, we can now compare apples with apples . . . or low-fat salad dressing with low-fat salad dressing. And we know what it means when a label says "lite."

Here are some of the rules to remember the next time you go shopping:

Low-fat: Contains three grams of fat or less per serving.

Low-cholesterol: One gram or less per serving. Plus, gets no more than 15% of its calories from saturated fat.

High fiber: Contains at least 20% of the required daily fiber—i.e., 5 grams.

Reduced or Less: Contains 25% less fat, sodium, cholesterol, or calories than the regular food.

More: Contains 10% more protein, minerals, fiber, etc. than the regular food.

Free: "Applies to foods that have none of the substance cited, or a nutritionally insignificant amount."

Light or Lite: Contains 1/3 fewer calories, and at least 40 fewer calories . . . or contains 50% of the fat in the regular product. If "light" describes a color or texture, it has to be specifically stated that way on the label—for example, "Light in Texture."

SKIRTING THE ISSUE
Labeling laws are important. But they don't keep food manufacturers from trying to pull a fast one. Case in point: When products calling themselves "light" failed to qualify for the term under the 1993 guidelines, the manufacturers tried to fake it. "They're turning to other words they hope sound almost as good," warned *Consumer Reports*. So Pringles "Light Chips" became Pringles "Right Chips;" Kraft "Deliciously Light" Dressing became "Deliciously Right" Dressing; and so on. "In the end," said one consumer advocate," the only protection you have is your own common sense."

Pound for pound, spiders, flies, and grasshoppers contain more protein than beef does.

THE TONIGHT SHOW, PART VIII: SPECIAL GUEST HOST PROFESSOR PEAR

*There's been a slight change in programming.
Uncle John was lucky enough to be able to recruit as a special guest
the illustrious Professor Pear, who'll fill you in on all the wonderful
things you can do with pears. And so, without further ado,
heeeeere's . . . Professor Pear.*

Thank you, Uncle John. It's great to be here.
"The pear must be approached with discretion and reverence;
it withholds its secrets from the merely hungry." This observation, attributed to Paul Bunyard, is testimony that pears are one of
the more mysterious of the fruits we commonly encounter. Unlike
an apple, which is ready to eat from the day it is picked, a pear must
go through a series of changes before it can deliver its full splendor.
It would seem that the pear was not made for humans to easily
enjoy; it must be manipulated in order to present us the flavor, texture, and juiciness that we consider attributes of high quality.

For one thing, pears do not ripen on the tree to our liking. If
allowed to tree-ripen, pears typically ripen from the inside out, so
that the center is mushy by the time the outside flesh is ready. In
addition, the texture of tree-ripened pears is often more gritty than
that of pears picked before they are ripe. So the frequently heard
notion that pears are picked when they are still hard and green as a
convenience for enduring the long truck ride to market misses the
point. Pears are harvested when they are "mature," which in pear
language means when they have reached the point where, after
picking, they will ripen to good quality, sometimes with a little
help, but definitely *off* the tree.

Now the next step after harvesting mature pears is to cool them
down. Commercial storages cool them way down, to around 30°F
(like drunks sleeping in the snow, they don't freeze at 32°F because

---

A wolf's howl can be heard as far as seven miles away. A bullfrog's croak: one mile.

they have so much dissolved material in their juice—in the case of pears, it's sugar). The colder they are, the longer they'll stay in good condition. One unique quality of pears is that they need to be cooled in order to ripen properly. In the case of Bartlett pears, that cooling need last only a day or two, which evens out the ripening within each fruit and synchronizes the ripening of all the fruit in a box. "Winter pears" such as Anjou, Bosc, and Comice, must be cooled for two to six weeks to get the same effect. If one of these pears is picked "mature" and allowed to sit on the kitchen shelf, it will sit and sit and eventually decompose—without ever "ripening."

Ripening a pear must be a closely watched process, since there is a relatively narrow window between "too hard" and "too soft" where the glory of the perfect pear texture lies. The best quality is experienced when the pears are ripened by leaving them at 65°F–75°F. The amount of time varies from about five days for a typical Bartlett, to six or seven days for Bosc or Comice, to anywhere from seven to ten days for Anjou. As ripening begins, pears, like many fruits, begin to produce "the ripening hormone," ethylene gas, inside the fruit. This speeds the ripening along. In fact, the whole pear-ripening process can be kick-started by putting freshly bought or picked pears in a bag with a ripe banana or apple, both of which give off copious quantities of ethylene gas. The bag keeps the apple or banana ethylene around the pears, which soak it up and quickly begin producing their own.

Determining when a pear is ripe depends somewhat on the eater's preference, but here is a time-honored method: Hold the pear gently but firmly in the palm of your hand, as a baseball pitcher might hold the ball while studying the signs from the catcher. Apply the thumb of the same hand to the pear flesh just below the point where the stem joins the fruit. When the flesh beneath the spot yields evenly to gentle pressure from the thumb, it is ready to eat. If you have to push more than slightly, it's not ready yet. After years of study, scientists have found that a really juicy pear is best eaten while naked, in the bathtub, so that you needn't be concerned about the abundant juice streaming down your chin.

Thank you, Professor Pear.

For the conclusion of the Tonight Show story, see page 428.

THE FIGHT FOR SAFE MILK, PART II

On page 634 we told you about the battle to end the sale of adulterated milk. Part II is the story of the fight to pasteurize the U.S. milk supply. An instructive tale. In spite of proof that pasteurization could save lives, Americans resisted it because it was a new idea . . . and because it "cost too much."

SOLID PROGRESS

During the latter part of the 19th century, improvements were made in the quality of the milk sold in the United States.

Bottles: In 1884, for example, Dr. Henry G. Thatcher patented the first practical glass milk bottle with a sealable top. He got the idea while standing in line in the street for his own milk a year earlier. When the little girl ahead of him dropped her filthy rag doll into the milk dealer's open milk can, the dealer just shook the doll off, handed it back to the girl, then ladled Thatcher's milk as though nothing had happened.

Thatcher's bottle wasn't a solution to all of raw milk's problems, but at least it kept impurities out of milk after it left the dairy. Many dairies hated the bottles because they were expensive and broke relatively easily, but they caught on with the public and were soon in use all over the country.

The Lactometer: In the early 1890s New York State began regulating the content of milk using a lactometer, a newly invented device that could measure the amount of milk solids in milk. For the first time, it was possible to compare pure milk with a test sample of a dairy's milk to see if it had been watered down or adulterated. If the milk tested didn't contain the same amount of milk solid as pure milk, the milk dealer could be fined or penalized.

BATTLING BACTERIA

But by far, the most important breakthroughs were scientific. The 1880s and 1890s were a period of great advancement in

If you don't remove an avocado's pit, it won't turn black, even when you peel it.

the understanding of bacteria and its role in causing disease.

In 1882, for example, a German scientist named Robert Koch discovered that bovine tuberculosis, a form of tuberculosis found in cattle, could be spread to humans through diseased milk. This form of tuberculosis attacked the glands, intestines, and bones, frequently killing the afflicted or leaving them deformed for life.

"Children seemed to be especially susceptible to bovine tuberculosis," James Cross Gilbin writes in *Milk: The Fight for Purity*. "[Victims] often spent years strapped into spinal frames . . . designed to prevent deformity while the body slowly overcame the infection.'

Researchers discovered other diseases could be spread by milk as well. They found that if a cow's udders weren't cleaned before milking, bacteria from manure (or anything else on the udders) could fall into the milk. And if the person milking the cow was sick, their germs could infect the milk, too. There seemed to be no limit to the number of ways that milk could be infected with disease.

PASTEURIZATION

As it turns out, the solution to this problem had already been found. In the 1860s French chemist Louis Pasteur invented the process of pasteurization, which uses heat to kill bacteria that cause liquids like milk and beer to spoil. But because his ideas were revolutionary, they spread slowly. The idea of pasteurizing milk didn't arrive in the United States until the 1880s—and even then, it took more than 30 years to find wide acceptance! That acceptance came largely through the work of one man.

MILK MAN

In the 1890s Nathan Straus, co-owner of Macy's department store in New York, was already building a reputation as a philanthropist. In the winter of 1892 he distributed 1.5 million buckets of coal to impoverished New Yorkers so they could heat their homes. The following year, he organized a series of shelters that provided beds and breakfasts to the city's homeless population. In 1893 he tackled the problem of unsafe milk.

Straus had been reading up on Pasteur's work and the theoretical benefits of pasteurization. He knew that nearly 10% of all children born in New York City died by the age of five—and despite all the recent improvements in milk quality, he still suspected that milk was to blame for many of the deaths. His reasoning was

---

In the 1800s you could buy ketchup flavored with lobster, walnuts, or oysters.

simple: Milk spoiled quicker in the heat of summer, and the city's childhood mortality rate increased at the same time. He figured there had to be a connection between the two.

MILK BAR

In June 1893 Straus set up a milk-processing station in a neighborhood on East Third Street. The station pasteurized milk on the spot, then provided it at affordable prices to local families. The station also offered free medical exams for children and free hygiene advice for their mothers. Mothers who couldn't afford 2¢ for a pint or 4¢ for a quart of milk (less than the price of unpasteurized milk) could get coupons for free milk from local doctors and charities.

By the turn of the century, Straus had twelve milk stations in different parts of the city, distributing hundreds of thousands of bottles of pasteurized milk every year. He also had several milk stands where people could taste pasteurized milk for a penny a glass, to see for themselves that pasteurization didn't hurt the taste.

THE ORPHAN TEST

The final proof of the benefits of pasteurized milk came when Straus began providing milk to an orphanage that had seen death rates as high as 42% from tuberculosis and other milk-borne diseases. The orphanage was located on Randall's Island in the East River. All the milk it used was provided by a single herd of cows kept on the island, so it was easy to control the milk the orphans drank.

Straus started pasteurizing the orphanage's milk in 1898. Within a year, the mortality rate dropped to 28%, and continued downward in the years that followed.

AN UPHILL FIGHT

By the turn of the century, pasteurized milk stations like Straus's had been set up in Boston, Philadelphia, Chicago, and other major cities. The programs were voluntary and were run by charities. Although philanthropists were getting into the pasteurized milk business, the dairy industry was staying out of it. Citing the added cost of pasteurization, they refused to pasteurize their own milk, and blocked efforts to require it by law.

Another huge barrier was public resistance: most people were used to "pure" raw milk, and didn't understand science well enough to insist on pasteurization. The few dairies that had begun pasteur-

The Hundred Years' War lasted 116 years.

izing milk to increase shelf life and prevent spoiling did so mostly in secret, out of fear of losing sales to raw milk dairies.

Straus was instrumental in getting New York to create the post of inspector of dairy farms, making it one of the first cities in the nation to inspect the quality of milk at the source. In 1907 Straus tried to help pass a city ordinance requiring the pasteurization of all milk sold in New York. Many milk distributors, doctors, and even the city's Health Department opposed him, arguing that the health benefits of "clean raw milk" outweighed the risks. The ordinance failed.

PRESIDENTIAL SEAL OF APPROVAL

In 1907 the reform-minded president Teddy Roosevelt ordered his Public Health Service to look into the pros and cons of pasteurized milk. In 1908 the Service issued its report: pasteurization, they found, did not affect the taste, quality, nutrition, or digestibility of milk, but it did "prevent much sickness and save many lives."

Compulsory pasteurization was still many years away, though. A second attempt to require pasteurization of New York City's milk supply was defeated in 1909, and a similar ordinance that had passed in Chicago in 1908 was repealed in 1910 after the courts ruled the measure interfered with free trade.

Finally, in 1911, the National Commission on Milk Standards issued a report arguing that "in the case of all milk not either certified or inspected, pasteurization should be compulsory." The American Medical Association followed with similar advice a few months later. These reports and others like them ignited a groundswell of public support for compulsory pasteurization. In 1912 Chicago passed a second pasteurization ordinance; this one stuck. New York passed a similar ordinance, but milk distributors succeeded in delaying and then watering down the law.

THE FINAL STRAW

In 1913 a typhoid fever epidemic struck New York claiming thousands of victims. But now there was proof that typhoid fever was carried by milk, and that it could be killed through pasteurization. New York City finally stopped dragging its feet. By the end of 1914, 95 percent of the city's milk supply was pasteurized. By 1917 nearly all of the 50 largest cities in the nation required pasteurization; the rest of the country would follow over the next several years.

Panama hats are made in Ecuador.

The impact of pasteurized milk on public health was nothing short of astounding. In 1885 the infant mortality rate in New York City was 273 per 1,000 live births—more than 27%. By 1915 the infant mortality rate was 94 per 1,000, a drop of two-thirds.

PASTEURIZATION TODAY

Today the most popular method of pasteurization is called "flash pasteurization" or "high-temperature, short-time" pasteurization (HTST). Raw milk is heated to 161° Fahrenheit and kept at that temperature for only 15 seconds, and then immediately cooled to 50° Fahrenheit.

Products like half-and-half and whipping cream, which are expected to remain refrigerated for longer periods of time, are processed by "ultra-high temperature" pasteurization at 280° Fahrenheit for two seconds.

* * *

BY RITA RUDNER'S THOUGHTS ON LIFE

"I want to have children while my parents are still young enough to take care of them."

"I'm going home next week. It's a kind of family emergency—my family is coming here."

"My mother used to tell me she had natural childbirth. I recently found out it was her version of natural childbirth—she took off her makeup."

"When I meet a man, I ask myself: 'Is this the man I want my children to spend their weekends with?'"

"My boyfriend and I broke up. He wanted to get married, and I didn't want him to."

"In Hollywood, a marriage is successful if it outlasts milk."

"Before I met my husband, I'd never fallen in love . . . though I'd stepped in it a few times."

"My cousin married a man for money. She wasn't real subtle about it. Instead of calling him her fiancé, she kept calling him her financee."

A camel's hair brush is made of squirrel's hair.

ANSWERS

JEFF'S BRAINTEASERS (page 140)

1. One train entered the tunnel at 7 a.m., the other entered at 7 p.m.

2. Start both hourglasses. When the 4-minute glass runs out, turn it over (4 minutes have elapsed). When the 7-minute glass runs out, turn it over (7 minutes have elapsed). When the 4-minute glass runs out this time (8 minutes have now elapsed), the 7-minute glass has been running for 1 minute. Turn it over once again. When it stops, 9 minutes have elapsed.

3. Nine o'clock. Since there are 12 hours between the two times, and half of that time is six, then the halfway mark would have to be 7 o'clock. If it were 7 o'clock, two hours ago, the time would now be 9 o'clock.

4. The other end of the rope isn't tied to anything.

5. Just push the cork into the bottle and shake the coin out.

6. An ear of corn.

7. Throw the ball straight up.

8. They're female boxers.

9. The dates are 1990 B.C. and 1995 B.C.

10. His parachute didn't open.

11. An Infiniti.

12. The tape recording ends with him killing himself. If he'd committed suicide, the tape wouldn't be rewound to the beginning of his statement.

13. She's playing baseball.

14. Captain Russo is bald.

15. He's playing Monopoly. The man with the "car" token has landed on a property that has a "hotel." Since he cannot afford the

rent, he declares "bankruptcy."

* * *

Random Fact: Henry Kissinger's favorite breakfast: "a serving of egg whites, dyed yellow to make them look like yolks."

THE RIDDLER (page 275)

1. An echo.

2. Holes.

3. Mount Everest.

4. Envelope.

5. A ton.

6. A priest.

7. Only one...the last one.

8. Zero...Noah took animals

on the ark, not Moses.

9. Only once. After the first calculation, you will be subtracting 5 from 20, then 5 from 15, and so on.

10. A secret.

11. You can't take a picture with a wooden leg....You need a camera!

12. Darkness.

13. Footsteps.

14. A coffin.

15. An umbrella.

16. Suicide.

17. The year 1961. It reads the same upside down. Won't happen again until the year 6009.

18. The letter "V."

19. "Are you asleep?"

20. A promise.

IT'S THE LAW . . . OR IS IT? (page 662), according to the book *Legal Briefs*.

1. b. Nice try, Bill, but no dice. A number of debts can't be discharged by bankruptcy, including alimony, child support, certain tax fines and claims, most student loans, court fines and penalties, and court-ordered restitution.

   Another note: If Bill goes on a spending spree right before he declares bankruptcy (within 40 days), he's stuck with those debts, too, if

* The purchase totals more than $500
* It was payable to a single creditor
* The money was spent on luxury goods or services

2. c. At last count, 31 states say "No" to marriages between first cousins. But Tom and Sue can still get married in Alabama, California, Colorado, Connecticut, Delaware, Florida, Georgia, and a bunch more.

Note: Cancel your tuxedo rental and send the caterers home if the proposed marriage is between a brother and sister, a parent and child, an aunt and nephew, or an uncle and niece. No state allows these marriages.

3. b. Traffic signs and theft/damage disclaimer signs aren't always enforceable on private property. Police can't give you a court-enforceable ticket for exceeding a private speed limit or making a privately prohibited turn onto a public highway. Courts have ruled that a person violating this type of sign is only "negligent."

   F.Y.I: Police can't issue citations for accidents or other traffic violations on private property, either.

Another bit of interesting info: Signs on private property (like shopping centers) that claim to waive responsibility for theft and damage to your vehicle or possessions while you're doing business there may not be valid. A court has to base its decision on what they see as the property owner's "duty" to provide a reasonably safe environment for people and their possessions.

4. c. Depending on your history, they could have you arrested. Writing a bad check is considered a theft ranging from a misdemeanor to a second-degree felony. The penalty depends on the amount of the check and the legal history of the person who bounced it. In any event, most state laws limit the amount a store can charge you for a bounced check. Usually the fee has to be reasonable, and it has to be agreed to in writing.

5. a. If a bank card is lost or stolen, the owner's liability depends on how quickly the loss is reported to the company that issued the card. If it's within 2 working days, liability is only for the first $50. If it's within sixty days, liability is up to $500. If the loss isn't reported within 60 days of the owner's last financial statement, the owner is responsible for all charges—even if they total more than $500.

6. a. or c. Although a patent provides exclusive rights for 17 years, it may take time . . . and while you're waiting, companies can infringe on it.

Plus, sometimes it's smarter to keep it secret. A good secret can last forever. Had Coca-Cola's formula been patented, for example, it would have expired years ago and everyone could be using it now. By keeping the recipe a secret, Coca-Cola has been able to enjoy its exclusivity for many more years. Bear in mind, however, that keeping a secret can be pretty difficult.

7. b. Only a handful of states honor oral wills. These include California, Illinois, Kentucky, New York, and Ohio. They have strict procedures that must be followed, including having witnesses who are not beneficiaries and putting the words in writing within a certain period of time after the verbal bequest is made.